Praise for *The L*

"It is a tribute to the judgment, research, ~~intelligence, and elegant prose of~~ Marilyn Nissenson that although I disagree with some of her political assumptions, I find her portrait of Dorothy Schiff accurate, nuanced, compelling, and a pleasure to read. Hello, Dolly!"

—Victor Navasky, publisher emeritus, *The Nation*

"More than a biography of Dorothy Schiff, Marilyn Nissenson's *The Lady Upstairs* is a mirror of the rise and fall of American liberalism and a history of the *New York Post.* Nissenson covers politics, newspaper feuds, McCarthyism, race issues, and the social gossip of the times—for the life of Dorothy Schiff and the life of the newspaper are as closely intertwined as the strands of silk Dolly used for her needlepoint."

—*San Antonio Express-News*

"In this exhaustive, detailed biography, Marilyn Nissenson paints a portrait of a dynamic yet oddly simpleminded figure, and in doing so has also succeeded in shining a spotlight on a vanished era in American political and social life."

—*The Washington Times*

"For those too old to remember very clearly, or too young to imagine it, Marilyn Nissenson's *The Lady Upstairs* details just how different the *Post* back in 1960 was from the paper produced under that name today. . . . This is a complex story about a complex woman, in a complex period of political and publishing history."

—*The East Hampton Star*

"All these eccentric tidbits are included in *The Lady Upstairs,* a scrupulously researched book that fairly spills with archival material and personal testimony. . . . The tales of old-school journalism . . . still fill media people with longing."

—Jennifer Senior, *The New York Times Book Review*

"Nissenson . . . coaxes out the contradictions of pioneering newspaper woman Dolly Schiff. . . . Schiff's character brims with spunk and surprise along the way."

—*Publishers Weekly*

"If one measure of a newspaper is the list of enemies it honorably makes, Ms. Schiff's *Post* stood tall for its times. Senator McCarthy, gossip king Walter Winchell, New York mega-builder Robert Moses, FBI director J. Edgar Hoover, political boss Carmine De Sapio, even Roman Catholic Cardinal Francis Spellman—all felt the sting of the *Post*'s news coverage and commentary."

—Peter R. Kann, *The Wall Street Journal*

"Dorothy Schiff was once called 'the only publisher in New York with balls'— an ultimate compliment for a powerful female—but she was also one hell of a woman, as this admirable portrait so vividly illustrates. The author has done a masterful job of intertwining the life of the intrepid Dolly and the frenetic world of New York City newspapers in the last century. I was hooked from page one."

—Marion Mead, author of *Dorothy Parker: What Fresh Hell Is This?* and *The Unruly Life of Woody Allen*

THE LADY UPSTAIRS

DOROTHY SCHIFF

AND THE *New York Post*

Marilyn Nissenson

ST. MARTIN'S GRIFFIN
New York

www.stmartins.com

Nissenson, Marilyn.
  The lady upstairs : Dorothy Schiff and the New York post / Marilyn Nissenson.—1st St. Martin's Griffin ed.
     p. cm.
   ISBN-13: 978-0-312-31311-1
   ISBN-10: 0-312-31311-X
   1. Schiff, Dorothy, 1903–1989. 2. New York post (New York, N.Y. : 1949).
3. Journalists—United States—Biography. 4. Publishers and publishing—United States.
I. Title.

  PN4874.S33 N47 2007
  070.5'092—dc22

                                                                    20060411123

First St. Martin's Griffin Edition: December 2008

10 9 8 7 6 5 4 3 2 1

For Hugh, Kore, Kate, and Alan

Contents

Introduction

For nearly forty years—from 1939 until 1976—Dorothy Schiff owned the *New York Post,* the oldest continuously published daily newspaper in the United States. During her tenure, the *Post* was an important voice of American liberalism and at the same time a chatty, parochial New York tabloid. Dorothy was a very visible presence in the local and national Democratic parties as well as on the New York social scene.

She was born into a world of wealth and privilege. Her grandfather, Jacob Schiff, a leader of the German-Jewish community in New York, built the investment banking firm of Kuhn, Loeb, at which her father, Mortimer Schiff, became, in his turn, a senior partner. Dolly, as she was frequently called, always said that she took a distant second place in her parents' eyes to her younger brother, John, who was destined from birth to become the head of Kuhn, Loeb.

Over the years, Dolly told a story of feeling left out when the men and women at a dinner party separated after the meal. "The women," she told one interviewer, "went to the drawing room and talked about clothes, food, babies' diets, and housekeeping. The men went to the smoking room, where I was always sure they were talking about world-shaking matters. I was dying to get in that room."

Her chance came in the turbulent 1930s. Disturbed by the political and economic implications of the Depression, she turned her back on social frivolities to become active in Democratic politics. In 1939, she acquired the *New York Post,* one of the few papers in America that supported Franklin Delano Roosevelt and the New Deal. For several years, her husband, George Backer, supervised the paper while she signed the checks. The *Post* consumed a great deal of Dorothy's money, and her patience ran out just before her assets did. In 1942, she replaced Backer as president and publisher and soon began actively managing the paper herself.

Women executives in any field were a rarity in mid-twentieth-century America. Career-minded women found their best opportunities in the service professions. Those few who were active in the commercial world had usually inherited the business. In most cases, they did not hold corporate office but gave executive authority to their husbands or sons and moved behind the scenes in the more traditional helpmate role.

This pattern held true among the handful of women who had prominent roles at major American newspapers in the years during and after World War II. Iphigene Sulzberger inherited *The New York Times* from her father, but she had no official position at the paper. Katharine Graham, who inherited *The Washington Post* from her father, took charge of the paper only after her husband's death. Alicia Patterson, blocked by her father from assuming what she considered her rightful place at the helm of the New York *Daily News,* founded and edited *Newsday,* but she was dependent on her husband's financial backing and often thwarted by his opposition to her political views. Only Dorothy Schiff acquired, owned, and operated her paper without other shareholders or family members.

Dorothy came to political life during the thirties and forties. The beliefs of her generation were formed by the Depression, World War II, and the Cold War. The *Post*'s editorial position articulated the liberal interpretation of those events: it championed American liberalism during the period when liberalism mattered. Liberalism assumed that human nature was perfectible, that underdogs could rise to positions of equality with those who had been given initial advantages, and that rational discourse could lead to the solution of most problems.

Dorothy hired liberal editorial writers like James Wechsler and Max Lerner. She fostered the careers of great reporters like Murray Kempton and Pete Hamill. Under her guidance, the *Post* broke the story of Richard Nixon's slush fund. It helped bring down such icons of the day as Joseph McCarthy,

Walter Winchell, and Robert Moses. It endorsed the civil rights movement and opposed the Vietnam War.

At mid-century, New York supported seven daily newspapers. Dorothy Schiff was patronized by the other publishers—all of them male—but she frequently outsmarted them, notably during the fractious strike/lockout that shut down the papers between November 1962 and March 1963. By the end of the sixties, the *Post* was one of just three survivors and the only afternoon paper in town.

Dorothy kept a close eye on the bottom line and courted advertisers. For several decades, she saw to it that the paper operated in the black. In 1968, she told a reporter, "I *like* to make money. If a newspaper isn't self-supporting, it's like being a kept woman. It's good for office morale to make money—it gives the people who work for you a sense of security. They know the owner isn't likely to sell out or fold up."

In the late 1960s, newspaper readers turned increasingly to television for news and entertainment. Circulation began dropping across the country, particularly for afternoon papers. Bucking the trend in the short run, the *Post* continued to make a profit into the early 1970s. But in 1976, the paper was projecting its first negative balance sheet in decades. The liberal optimism that characterized its editorial point of view also began to flag. Profound social discontent fostered by racial tensions and the war in Vietnam posed conundrums to which liberals like Dorothy and her editors had no easy answers.

In 1976, Dorothy Schiff was seventy-three years old, and none of her three children—although they worked for her at times—was interested in succeeding her. An unlikely savior appeared in the person of a young, ambitious Australian press baron Rupert Murdoch, who was seeking a presence in the largest media market in America. Murdoch bought the *New York Post* and soon flipped the paper's editorial slant one hundred and eighty degrees, thereby silencing a distinctive New York voice.

The intertwined story of Dorothy Schiff and the *New York Post* is an aperture through which to view some of the major social and political developments of American life in the twentieth century: the evolving status of women, the transformation of American Jewry from a largely working-class immigrant community to one with political power and mainstream social status, the impact of the Cold War on domestic politics, the ascendancy and decline of postwar American liberalism.

While these events provide an illuminating background, Dorothy's personal story is compelling in its own right. Her private life could have been a staple of the *Post*'s society gossip columns. Endlessly flirtatious, she married four times and had extramarital romances with, among others, Franklin Roosevelt and Max Beaverbrook. She was a friend of politicians as varied as Roosevelt, Adlai Stevenson, the Kennedys, Lyndon Johnson, and Nelson Rockefeller. She used her charm and her social connections in the service of her paper, which became the center of her life.

Dorothy filled scrapbooks with newspaper clippings and other memorabilia from the time she was in her twenties. Starting in her earliest years at the *Post,* she saw to it that vital interoffice correspondence was preserved in her files. Throughout her career, she dictated "memos to file," in which she commented on current and past events and on conversations she had with important political figures. Sometimes she revisited these memos to add further reflections or to make sure her point of view about the subject was clear. Proud of her place in New York City and its political history, she directed in her will that these papers be placed in a public repository.

Though most of Dorothy's friends and colleagues found her laudable, a significant minority tell unflattering stories. She could appear compassionate or aloof, generous or parsimonious, prescient or obtuse. Some people recall her foibles with amusement, some with barely suppressed rancor. Some unflattering recollections may have been colored by envy, resentment of a boss, resentment of a woman boss, or miscommunication. Those who knew her best say that she was shy and often ill at ease in the company of people she didn't know well, which accounts for some, but not all, of the negative perceptions.

Dorothy was separated by privilege and personality from the lifestyle of the majority of her readers, yet she was often quite sensitive to their tastes. She understood that a successful tabloid must indulge its readers' delight in celebrity gossip, while honoring their intelligence with serious reportage and penetrating analysis of political and cultural news. From her penthouse office, she approved and commented on every major story and every minor column that appeared in the *Post.* A quintessential New Yorker, Dorothy Schiff, who could be feisty or decorous as circumstances demanded, was the most dynamic newspaper publisher of her day.

I

THE APPRENTICESHIP

ONE

"The Background"

At the beginning of the twentieth century, New York City had established itself as the center of American society and culture. Its community leaders reflected the varied constituencies that gave the city its vitality and provided rich material for novelists like Henry James and Edith Wharton. The hegemony of the so-called knickerbocracy—the Dutch and English merchant and landowning families who traced their genealogies back to colonial days—was being challenged by nouveau riche industrialists and speculators, and by a close-knit circle of German-Jewish banking families whose wealth matched that of the new tycoons but whose manners more often mimicked those of the old landed elite. As one chronicler of this transition wrote, "These German-Jewish families were more than a collective American success story . . . they were also the closest thing to Aristocracy—Aristocracy in the best sense—that the city, and perhaps the country, had seen."

Dorothy Schiff was born in 1903 into the very apex of this aristocracy. Her parents were the prominent socialites Mortimer and Adele Neustadt Schiff, and her grandfather was the renowned banker and philanthropist Jacob Henry Schiff. The name Schiff was a benefit and a burden in Dorothy's early life. After the third of her four marriages, she resumed using the name, and she strove for the rest of her life to add her achievements to those which had already contributed to the family reputation and to solidify her standing in the family pantheon.

Dorothy's Schiff ancestors had lived for several hundred years in Frankfurt, Germany, where their prosperity and prestige were surpassed only by that of the Rothschilds. Although one of the family's vanities was that its lineage could be traced back to King David, the first Schiff to have an influence on Dorothy's life was Jacob, born in Frankfurt in 1847, the second son of Moses Schiff, a successful stockbroker. Jacob's forebears included prominent rabbis as well as moneylenders; he was sent to a school that combined traditional Jewish education with secular studies. Although Jacob remained respectful of Jewish learning all his life, he was not a scholar. At fourteen he went to work in a banking house owned by a brother-in-law and began dreaming almost immediately of wider horizons.

Despite his father's misgivings, Jacob left for New York when he was eighteen, with $500 in his pocket and his passage paid for by his older brother. He found work at several German-Jewish brokerages and briefly ran his own firm before he returned to Germany in 1873.

The following year, Abraham Kuhn, who had known Jacob in New York, urged him to try again in the States. Kuhn and his brother-in-law Solomon Loeb had been successful merchants and bankers in the Midwest before moving to New York to enjoy their retirement in the big city. But unwilling to miss out on America's post–Civil War economic boom, they started a new stock brokerage house in 1867. Schiff returned to New York and joined Kuhn, Loeb & Co. in January 1875. In May of that year he solidified his connection to the founders by marrying Loeb's daughter, Therese, whom he had met before traveling back to Germany.

Kuhn retired soon after Schiff's arrival, and Solomon Loeb's sons had no interest in commerce. When Loeb retired in 1885, thirty-eight-year-old Jacob became the head of the firm. Schiff was an aggressive and imaginative businessman. He understood the opportunities presented by the westward expansion and the industrialization of the United States. He arranged the primary financing for the major transcontinental railroads and backed the Guggenheim family in their mining ventures.*

---

*In the early 1890s, Schiff acquired $25,000 worth of bonds in the floundering *New York Times,* as did his fellow financiers August Belmont and J. P. Morgan. The survival of a conservative Democratic pa-

Schiff sat on the boards of several of the railroads he helped to create. He served as a director of such major financial institutions as the Western Union Telegraph Co., the National City Bank of New York, and the Equitable Life Assurance Society. By the late 1890s, he was understood to be the second most powerful man on Wall Street after J. P. Morgan.

Schiff was always deferential to Morgan, who barely concealed his dislike of his rival. By the standards of the day, Morgan was not unduly anti-Semitic, but he is said to have repeatedly referred to Schiff as "that foreigner." The two men worked together frequently because they needed each other's contacts in the international financial markets. Schiff's connections to the Rothschilds and the Warburgs as well as his friendship with Ernest Cassel, a native of Cologne who had become the leading merchant banker in London, helped him make Kuhn, Loeb a major force in the sale of American securities abroad and the underwriting of European investments in the United States.*

Schiff's influence extended to international politics: he led the American-British consortium that loaned the Japanese government money to finance Japan's successful war effort against Russia in 1904–1905. His active hostility to the tsar's government because of the persecution of Russian Jews made him particularly eager to help one of its adversaries. During the peace negotiations at Portsmouth, New Hampshire, in 1905, Schiff emphasized to Count Serge Witte, the chief Russian negotiator, that he would not underwrite loans to help Russian economic recovery unless laws protecting the Jews were enacted. Widespread pogroms the following year reinforced his conviction that the Russians did not deserve his support.

---

per, which opposed the free-silver policies of William Jennings Bryan, was especially important to hard-currency financiers, whether Republican or Democrat.

After an October 1951 article in *Editor & Publisher* reported this piece of history, Dorothy asked her brother, John, if he knew what had happened to the *Times* stock. The answer is that sometime after Adolph Ochs bought the paper in 1896, he bought back bonds from Morgan and others. Schiff converted his investment into shares of stock and endorsed them over to Ochs as a gift. Schiff and other prominent New York Jews believed that having a Jewish owner of the paper would be of value to them in the long run.

*In 1882, Cassel commissioned Augustus Saint-Gaudens to sculpt a bronze relief of Jacob's children, which was completed in the summer of 1885. Schiff later commissioned the sculptor to supervise the creation of a marble copy of the original to be donated to the Metropolitan Museum of Art in New York. The copy, which was executed in 1906–1907, is on exhibit today in the Engelhard Court of the museum. In keeping with Schiff's desire for privacy, the names of his children do not appear on the marble version.

Schiff never vacillated in his opposition to the Romanov regime. He refused to allow Kuhn, Loeb to underwrite loans to the Allies during World War I, although several of the firm's principals including Otto Kahn and Schiff's son, Morti, participated privately. Schiff senior would not give money to the tsar's government even when it was England's ally. He relented after the October Revolution, bought Allied bonds, and made large loans to Kerensky's government.

In the last decades of his life, Jacob Schiff was a public figure. He was the subject of admiring coverage in the financial press and in the popular papers of the day, which brought news of America's emerging aristocracy to a generally worshipful public. Jacob lived lavishly, educated his children at the best schools, and traveled in style to Europe or to vacation homes in New Jersey and Maine. But Schiff was not a flamboyant subject for the sensationalist press; he kept no mistresses, he owned no racehorses, he sailed no yachts. Although his manner of living was baronial, his behavior was circumspect, and he received praise as much for his decorum as for his financial skills.

The Schiffs had two children, Frieda and Mortimer, born in the first years of their marriage, and Jacob was extremely involved in their lives. He was quite protective of Frieda: she was never sent out without a chaperone, and, even if she had been interested in attending college, Jacob would not have permitted it.

At the age of eighteen, during a summer vacation in Switzerland, Frieda met and fell in love with young Felix Warburg of the Hamburg banking family. Jacob was not prepared for the prospect of his daughter having an independent life. He returned to New York with a compliant Frieda in tow. When Felix asked for permission to write to Frieda, Jacob insisted that Felix write to him, he would convey the message to Frieda, and she would respond to Felix's mother. Finally, the young people got Ernest Cassel to intervene. Cassel reminded his friend that Felix was an appropriate match, and Schiff relented. But even after Frieda and Felix married in March 1895, Jacob had trouble giving up control over his daughter's life. He sent a family maid along to keep an eye on the newlyweds during their honeymoon. When they returned, he had furnished and staffed the house they were to live in.

By all accounts, Frieda tolerated her father's meddlesome impulses. But Jacob's intrusion into his son's life had more troublesome results. Mortimer Schiff was born on June 5, 1877, fifteen months after his sister. Schiff's high expectations for his only son were probably impossible to live up to, although Morti gave it a good try. Frieda remembered that there was tension between father and son almost from the start: "As a youngster, my brother was always being punished for various misdemeanors. Though my father adored him, they seemed to clash all the time, and Morti was often sent from the table, denied dessert for a week, or otherwise made to do penance."

Morti had a temper, "and his outbursts were often the cause of his clashes with our father," Frieda wrote. "But Morti had a sweet disposition and was the kindest boy, and man, in the world. I think if he had been brought up according to modern methods, which seek to find the reasons for children's behavior and to prevent conflicts, his whole life would have been a happier one. He was born with all the desired attributes—good looks, good health, varied talents, exquisite taste."

Morti was an excellent student at Dr. Sachs's Collegiate Institute, which was the favored preparatory school for sons of the New York German-Jewish aristocracy. The same unruliness that he revealed at home sometimes led to his being marked down in deportment. Frieda recalled, "Whenever Morti's little grey report book showed a lapse in this respect, they had a seance in the bathroom. After the spanking, my father would say: 'My son doesn't have to lead in his studies, but that my son shouldn't know how to behave, that's unpardonable.' I well recall my brother standing at the foot of the stairs, saying: 'I can't sit down. I can't sit down.'"

Jacob Schiff was said to be a penny-pinching manager at Kuhn, Loeb: employees and family members joked about his propensity to save string and to turn out the lights each time he left the office. He wanted his children to be frugal. When Frieda was nine and Morti was eight, they spent much of the year in Europe. They each received an allowance of fifty pfennigs a week. After they returned to New York, their father figured that the American equivalent was twelve and a half cents, so one week they were given twelve cents and the next week thirteen. They were expected to set aside 10 percent for their favorite charity. Increases were allotted grudgingly. By the time Frieda was eighteen and Morti was a senior in high school, they each received a dollar.

When Morti graduated top of his class from Dr. Sachs's at age sixteen, he wanted very much to go to Harvard, but his father announced that it was too big and the rich students there would encourage Morti to be extravagant. Jacob decided that his son would attend Amherst; Morti had no choice but to comply.

He was not happy at Amherst and dropped out after two years. He took a job for several months on a road gang of the Great Northern Railroad in Duluth, after which he was sent to Hamburg and London to learn the banking business. When reports came back to Jacob that Morti was doing well, he made light of them, saying that his son's mentors were just trying to ingratiate themselves with him.

In London, Ernest Cassel took Morti under his wing. The young man became something of a dandy. He once showed up at a reception in London wearing a dove gray suit and a yellow hat. Jacob was also there. In front of the other guests, he berated his son for looking foolish and sent him home to change. Cassel later told Frieda, "I rather encouraged [Morti's] spending money, because I believe a man must learn how to spend gracefully but not showily. Your father, you know, didn't usually hold with many of my ideas."

After almost two years in Europe, Morti came home. He moved in with his parents and began working at Kuhn, Loeb, where he was made a partner in December 1899.* Morti was one of the most eligible bachelors in New York, and although there's no reason to think that he was particularly eager to give up the showgirls and young married women with whom he chose to spend time, he was a dutiful son. He soon became engaged to Adele Neustadt, the daughter of close friends of his parents. The two families were very pleased; subsequent generations assume it was essentially an arranged match. Adele appears to have been somewhat reluctant, and Morti's attitude was enigmatic. Nonetheless, they were married on April 30, 1900.

Jacob's wife, Therese, had wanted to move from their home at 932 Fifth Avenue. While Adele and Morti were on their extended honeymoon, the elder Schiff's built a house just up the street at 965 Fifth. They gave 932 to Morti and Adele as a wedding present. Saying thank you, Morti could not resist adding, "It's wonderful to be the master of the house where you had so many spankings."

Dorothy was born at 932 Fifth Avenue on March 11, 1903. When her brother, John, arrived in September 1904, Grandfather Jacob, who had taken

---

*The man who would be the most dynamic Kuhn, Loeb partner in the post–Jacob Schiff generation was Otto Kahn, who married the daughter of Abraham Wolff, himself a partner, in 1896. At the time, Schiff wrote to Cassel, "I probably must follow Wolff's wishes and agree that his son-in-law, Mr. Kahn, shall enter into our firm, unpleasant as it may be to me."

Why unpleasant? Schiff didn't say. Perhaps, anticipating the day when Morti—then nineteen—would enter the firm, he foresaw that Kahn would be the more aggressive and successful financier. It's one thing to criticize your son to his face and behind his back; it's another thing to put in place a circumstance that will prove you right.

perfunctory note of Dorothy's birth, wrote to friends about his pleasure that the family name would now be continued. Although four of Frieda and Felix's children were boys, they were Warburgs—which was not the same.

Dorothy and John, like most children of their social class, were raised primarily by servants. Although Morti may have been an amiable and benign father, Adele was by all accounts distant and cool. Dorothy's earliest memory was of her mother's insensitivity. She had been put to bed for an afternoon nap but wasn't sleeping when her mother dropped by the nursery with some friends. Dorothy was very proud of the fact that she had already been toilet trained and was not a bed wetter, but there were some drops of water on her sheet—perhaps they were tears. In the event, her mother said, "Look what she's done," and all the women laughed. Dorothy carried the memory of her humiliation throughout her life.

Dorothy loved John; her brother was her ally and often her only companion. He was a sickly boy, vulnerable to bronchial infections, and her parents were terrified that this precious male heir might not survive. Normally the children shared a bedroom in the nursery, but when Dorothy had a cold, she slept on a cot in the playroom, so John was not at risk.

When Dorothy was in her late forties, several people who knew her well told a reporter that she was always aware as a child that her parents lavished most of their attention on John and that this contributed to a lifelong diffidence on her part. Asked if it were so, Dorothy said she wasn't sure it had made her shy or uneasy, but that she "was very conscious that, although the older, I was just a girl, and that there was something very special in a boy."

Grandfather Schiff insisted that his offspring appear at his house every Friday night for a formal Sabbath dinner. Frieda's family treasured the ceremony. "He followed the ancient custom of blessing his children each Friday night . . . and my children remember the Friday evening at their grandparents' house when they held hands in a circle with other members of the family during the blessing, and sat around in a circle afterward to listen to a short traditional service in German which he read." Neither Dolly nor John, on the other hand, though they attended the Friday dinners intermittently into their teens, preserved the same warm memories of those events. Dolly's memories of the exclusion of women from the important all-male postdinner conversations began in Grandpa Schiff's house. Adele and Morti begged off whenever they could. Adele made fun of her in-laws and of their old-fashioned Germanic ways, and Morti was glad to avoid his father's critical eye.

Jacob never let up on his son. Dorothy recalled that one Sunday while dining with her parents, she knocked over a glass of water and was sent from the table. She was told later that even when Morti was a grown man and father of his own children, Jacob had banished him for a similar incident.

Small wonder that Morti and Adele turned their backs on Sea Bright, New Jersey, where the elder Schiffs and the Warburgs spent weekends. Instead, they established themselves at Oyster Bay, on Long Island, where Morti joined Piping Rock, a posh golf club, and put together a racing stable. When Dorothy and John were old enough, they were taken to Palm Beach every winter and to Europe every summer. Morti and Adele were avid members of what Frieda dismissively referred to as "the international set." Morti kept horses in Long Island and Paris. He lived in fear that Jacob would discover this expensive hobby, but fortunately the old man never read the sports pages of the newspapers, and no one told him of Morti's indulgence.

The children grew up amid luxe, though often stultifying, surroundings. Grandfather Jacob's homes were furnished in the approved Biedermeier style. He collected books of Jewish interest, Oriental jades, and crystals. Morti was more acquisitive, and he was thought to have good taste in art. He eventually bought property adjacent to his Fifth Avenue home in which he stored his considerable collections of eighteenth-century French illustrated books, Italian majolica, Oriental rugs, European furniture, and paintings. Northwood, Morti and Adele's Oyster Bay estate, was a gloomy, drafty mansion in the then-fashionable Tudor style, set on a thousand acres, complete with indoor and outdoor swimming pools, stately gardens, riding paddock and trails, and a uniformed staff largely imported from England.

Schiff money set them apart, even by the standards of their class. Dorothy recalled that she never traveled in a public vehicle, not even a taxi, until she was married. "Not counting ocean liners, that is. On trains in this country, we had a private car, because my father was a director of a railroad."

Dorothy and John's lives were privileged but isolated. They had few friends their own age. Dolly was educated at home until she was ten. "Endless teachers came in," Dorothy told a reporter, "for piano, carpentry, French, German, and what-not—some of whom I shared with my five Warburg first cousins." Adele said she kept her children from attending school because she feared exposing them to common childhood ailments. For a time, Dorothy shared her mother's anxiety. She remembered being "terrified of the ragamuffins who came to the house at Halloween." She also sometimes wondered if she had been adopted.

On Saturdays a different kind of teacher appeared, Dorothy wrote years later. "She gave us what we called 'Bible lessons.' The wonderful Old Testament stories, so full of human interest, I loved. And I would gaze fascinated at the often terrifying pictures by Gustav Doré this teacher showed us to illustrate the stories.

"I thought about God a lot and every day resolved to follow his and my mother's commandments to be a good girl."

Morti and Adele's home in the city had a regular staff of thirteen, including a butler, two footmen, and day and night governesses. Every day of the children's lives was highly structured. After breakfast, Dolly and John paid a brief visit to each of their parents. Then came lessons, following which their governesses took them to play in Central Park every afternoon, no matter how blustery the weather. They ate dinner with staff members in the breakfast room, then quickly said good night before their parents went out for the evening.

Soon after the children went to bed, the night nurse checked to see if they were asleep. One woman, who came to work when Dorothy was ten, took particular pleasure in tormenting the girl. If she found her still awake, she would spank her for not sleeping. If Dorothy feigned sleep, the nurse would spank her for the deception. The abuse continued for months until a woman in the next cabin on an ocean liner en route to Europe heard the sounds of the beating through the cabin walls and told Dorothy's mother. Dorothy had never complained, because the nurse had threatened to kill her if she did. After they returned home, Adele fired the woman, who later went mad and had to be institutionalized.

Far different was Dolly's relationship with their proper French governess, Lucette Henneguy, whom she and John called Mademoiselle. Mademoiselle lived with the Schiffs for seven years. She was a loving companion and guide for Dorothy. She encouraged the girl's interest in reading, corrected her French pronunciation, and most important, supplied some of the warmth and affection that her mother failed to offer. After Mademoiselle retired to live in France, Dorothy kept in touch. She sent gifts and cash from time to time and worried about Mademoiselle's safety during the Second World War. When Dorothy learned in September 1950 that Mademoiselle had died, she told John she felt "awfully sad."

At ten, Dorothy was sent to the Brearley School for girls, which her cousin Carola Warburg already attended. Dorothy made one friend—her classmate Ellin Mackay. Like Dorothy, Ellin came from a family of great wealth. Her grandfather had discovered the Comstock lode, and her father was head of the American Post and Telegraph Company. The Mackays' country estate in Roslyn, New York, rivaled the Schiff establishment in Oyster Bay in scale and ostentation. The Mackays were Catholic—a biographical detail that was perhaps even more esoteric at their social level than being Jewish. The two outsiders bonded for life.

Dorothy felt she stood out at Brearley, and not in a good way. Her clothes were different because of Adele's Parisian pretensions. Aside from Ellin Mackay, several Whitneys and an Astor heiress, most of her classmates came from upper-middle-class families. They lived in brownstones with one or two in help. They even ate differently—and better, Dorothy thought enviously. They took most meals with their parents, which meant a more varied menu. She also noted that in these homes, cocoa for the children was made with milk, not water.

Classmates from Brearley were often included in the weekend outings to Oyster Bay, but they were not necessarily girls Dorothy would have chosen. Her parents demanded that she invite only those girls who didn't have country homes of their own, providing a little lesson in noblesse oblige. In the country, there were mandatory riding and tennis lessons, which Dorothy disliked, as well as swimming and bicycling, which she preferred. What she really wanted to do was sit in the library and read her father's leather-bound copies of the classics. She once called Oyster Bay "the graveyard of my childhood."

Nothing Dorothy did brought her closer to Adele either physically or emotionally. "I think she thought I was rather hopeless," Dorothy recalled. "She couldn't be touched by me, always saying she bruised and it might cause cancer in the breast department."

Morti was probably fonder of his children, but a lifetime of submission to his father prepared him to be cowed by his wife. Dorothy believed that her father cared about her, but, she said, "If he said anything complimentary, she always ordered him not to spoil me. Naturally he obeyed; he was afraid of her."

Reflecting on her childhood, Dorothy often said the overwhelming feeling she had was that there was no joy. There were momentary pleasures, but they were undercut by a gnawing fear that she didn't measure up. Being a girl was bad enough, and Adele made matters worse by implying that Dorothy lacked the grace and charm that members of her sex could use to make their own way in the world. Eventually she developed that grace and charm, which she could deploy to great effect, but the sense that she was somehow not quite up to the task was never completely effaced.

With time and psychotherapy, Dorothy came to be somewhat forgiving. She believed that Adele's parents had pushed her to marry because of Morti's family's wealth and prestige, and that after the birth of John—the requisite son and heir—Adele and Morti, though still living under the same roof and appearing together socially in New York or Oyster Bay, no longer lived as husband and wife.

The distance between them was more obvious in Paris, where Adele acquired a town house and titled friends, while Morti lived at the Ritz and followed the races. When the children were still young, their mother began a long friendship with a man named Sidney Smith, a real estate broker who had helped Morti put together their property in Oyster Bay. One of Dorothy's governesses suggested to the girl that her mother and Smith were lovers. At the time Dorothy denied it, but later she believed it was probably so. And, she said, her father eventually found "other interests" as well.

If Dorothy's home life was painful, school was no better. During her last years at Brearley, Carl Van Doren was the headmaster and taught upper-school English. Later he told her he remembered her resisting all his attempts to teach her anything. When her own daughter was finishing Brearley, Dorothy wrote, "I suppose while there, I learned the usual school subjects, but chiefly I remember learning how to knit socks, helmets, sweaters, and wristlets in grey or khaki wool for 'our boys.'" (This was part of the civilian effort to support American troops serving in Europe during the First World War). "We knitted through lectures, concerts and at home in bed after the lights were out, and we were all satisfied that thus we were doing our share to 'Save the World for Democracy.'"

Dorothy graduated at seventeen, and although she wasn't particularly interested in going to college, it offered an escape route. A teacher suggested Bryn Mawr, an idea that Dorothy latched on to and her mother deplored. Adele said Dolly would become a bluestocking and ruin her chances for a good marriage—maybe for any marriage.

They compromised. She could attend Bryn Mawr for one year, then return home to make her debut, a decision that became moot when Dorothy managed to fail every one of her courses and was asked to leave. Although she was evidently unable to overcome the resistance to academic work that characterized her Brearley days, Dorothy always looked back at college with pleasure. Mary Hall Howland, Dorothy's granddaughter, says, "Goggi [the nickname by which she was known to all her grandchildren] would tell me these stories of drinking hot chocolate with the girls and people in her room talking about things. She was never happier."

Weeks into Dorothy's collegiate career, Jacob Schiff died at the age of seventy-three. She came home for the funeral, which was held September 28, 1920, at Temple Emanu-El, the congregation of choice for New York's Reform German Jews. Emanu-El was then located on Fifth Avenue at Forty-first Street. Thousands of people showed up to show their respect, and many followed the cortege all the way to the Salem Fields cemetery in Brooklyn. Schiff was a hero to Jews and gentiles alike, who had profited from his generosity and admired his many philanthropies, his patrician demeanor, and his ability to amass great wealth.

Although Jacob was a persistent presence in Dorothy's childhood, he exerted a more lasting impact on her after his death. She would eventually inherit a portion of his wealth. That bequest and his sense of social responsibility would be among the defining elements in her life. But in 1920, the impact of this legacy on seventeen-year-old Dolly was not so visible. It would take more than two decades for her to come into her inheritance in every respect.

Jacob Schiff's estate was estimated at $50 million (approximately $350 million in 2007 dollars). His will mandated that about $1.5 million be given to specified charities and the remainder be divided equally between his two children. Arthur Brisbane, the admiring editor of the New York *Journal,* hoping to deflect potential anti-Semitic envy of rich Jewish bankers, pointed out that Henry Ford earned more money in a single year than Schiff left behind after a lifetime. It was a gracious gesture but a somewhat specious argument since Schiff had provided separately for his widow and had given away a great deal of money while he was still alive.

Jacob Schiff's religious practices were sincere though increasingly eclectic. However, one religious tenet that he observed faithfully was the obligation to give to charity. He gave spontaneously, and sometimes anonymously, when he heard a story of an individual in distress. Many years after Jacob's death, a lawyer who worked for Dorothy told the following story: During labor negotiations between the typographers' local and the *Post* in the 1970s, one of the union people told the lawyer that his mother always insisted that he be nice to Mrs. Schiff. When the union member was a child, his father had moved the family from the Lower East Side to Colorado in what proved to be a vain attempt to find relief from his tuberculosis. After the man died, his widow wrote to a Jewish charitable agency in New York for help. The agency's response was to offer her children places in an orphanage. The mother was disconsolate. When Jacob Schiff heard the story, he sent money to resettle her intact family back east.

Most of Schiff's gifts were to institutions. He was an early and generous supporter of Lillian Wald's Henry Street Settlement and its offshoot, the Visiting Nurse Service. After serving on the board of Mount Sinai Hospital in Manhattan, he became one of the most prominent and magnanimous founders of the Montefiore Home and Hospital in the Bronx, of which he was president from 1885 until his death.

Schiff helped establish the Jewish Department of the New York Public Library and the Semitic Museum at Harvard. He was a major contributor to Barnard, Columbia, Cornell, and Johns Hopkins among other academic institutions. He was instrumental in the foundation of the Jewish Publication Society, through which he also arranged for the Library of Jewish Classics— translations of a series of Jewish medieval texts and tales. (He may have been inspired by his wife's half brother James Loeb, who was the guiding spirit behind Harvard University's Loeb Classics.) Jacob Schiff started a tradition continued by his son, Morti, of buying great European collections of Judaica and donating them to libraries in the States.*

Many of Schiff's favorite charities were Jewish, but not all. He was a longtime board member of the American Red Cross, for example, because it served clients of all faiths. He always insisted that the Jewish institutions he contributed to be similarly available to all comers. Jacob repeatedly referred

---

*Schiff always tried to be sensitive in his charitable dealings. In 1896, a dealer in Berlin informed Schiff that the renowned Jewish scholar and bibliophile Moritz Steinschneider was in bad financial shape and suggested that Schiff purchase Steinschneider's library for $10,000. Schiff sent the money immediately

to Judaism as a religion rather than to Jews as a race. As a member of the international Jewish banking fraternity, he did not like it when Jews were accused of cosmopolitanism. Sensitive to the issue of separatism, he was an ardent American patriot and urged all the Jewish newcomers to this country to become active and loyal citizens.

Schiff did give to organizations that served only Jews if they were religious in nature. He was the leading financial backer of the Jewish Theological Seminary, a training school for Conservative rabbis and a focal point for American Jewish scholarship. He also helped establish Jewish community centers and schools in New York neighborhoods where poor immigrant Jews were beginning to settle in great numbers.

Jacob Schiff's death epitomized the passing of an extraordinary generation of German-Jewish New Yorkers. Despite their small number, they had helped change the character of their adopted city through their support of the city's leading philanthropic and cultural institutions. Although the importance of the Jewish community in New York continued to grow, its makeup, financial resources, and social goals were about to change radically.

Between 1880 and 1914, approximately two and a half million Jews from Eastern Europe immigrated to America. At the outset of World War I, when immigration virtually ceased, the total Jewish population of the country was slightly more than three and a half million—just over 3 percent of the nation as a whole. In New York, however, the Jewish presence was significant.

Jacob Schiff had from the first recognized his connections to and responsibility for the Eastern European migrants pouring into the city's slums, no matter how alien in style, language, and religious practice they seemed to many of his German-Jewish peers. One reason he was so lionized by the poor at his death was that he had been so visible among them during his life. Schiff not only supported the Henry Street Settlement, he walked the neighborhoods it served and talked with its clients. He was appalled by the living conditions he witnessed and was horrified to learn that many of the young immigrants, unable to find legitimate work, turned to crime. Rather than distance himself from their degradation or worry that it would have a negative effect on the

---

but said that Steinschneider should keep the books until his death. Not for another ten years did Jacob come into possession of the collection, which he promptly donated to a Jewish institution.

reputation of the established Jewish community, Jacob Schiff plunged in to make conditions better.

Schiff, like his friend Lillian Wald, was very positive about the immigrants' potential. He believed that the mostly Orthodox newcomers—many of them barely literate even in Hebrew—could be educated and secularized. With skills and jobs they would move beyond the ghetto into the cultural mainstream. Assimilation was Schiff's goal. Having made his own way into American society, he assumed that the doors were open for everyone. Schiff never argued for complete secularization, which he feared would lead to socialism and anarchy. He believed that religion gave moral fiber and stability to the community but that religious practice should accommodate itself to the society around it and should keep up with the times. High on Schiff's agenda for the new Jewish Theological Seminary was the training of modern-thinking rabbis to serve the Eastern European Jews and wean them from their Orthodoxy.

Although Jacob Schiff may not have anticipated all of the implications of assimilation, he was alert to some of them. In 1917, he wrote to a rabbi from Cincinnati, in a pessimistic mood, "Look at our Synagogues and Temples; they are becoming empty more and more! My children and your children and almost everybody else's children may have some interest yet in our religion, because of the example of their parents, but look at the third generation, with how little attachment for our religion they grow up, because their parents are even more indifferent than their parents' parents may have been in the religious education of their children." The following year, when Jimmy Warburg, a nephew by marriage, married a Protestant woman, Schiff wired him, "I wish you joy to your happiness but cannot refrain from telling you that I am deeply disturbed by your action in marrying out of the faith in view of its probable effect upon my own progeny."*

Schiff was proud of his religion, and he had suffered very little from anti-Semitism in Germany or the United States. What men like Morgan may have said of him behind his back was more than compensated for by the respect and friendship of other businessmen like James Stillman of the National City

---

*In fact, all of Jacob's grandchildren except for Frieda's oldest child did marry out of their faith at some point. Several biographers report that Schiff included in his will the threat that any grandchild marrying a non-Jew would forfeit all claims against Schiff's estate, but this is not true.

Bank, community leaders like Bishop Henry Potter, dean of New York's Cathedral of St. John the Divine, and intellectuals like Charles W. Eliot, the president of Harvard. Eliot was Schiff's summer neighbor in Maine and a frequent correspondent. A true liberal, Eliot encouraged Jewish enrollment at Harvard. He was dismayed by the reports of continuing anti-Semitism in Eastern Europe, and he became a political Zionist, trying vainly to convince Schiff of the importance of a Jewish state.

Although anti-Jewish feeling was actually on the rise in America during the last decades of Jacob Schiff's life, he appeared impervious to it. For his son, Morti, things would be quite different. Morti had been confirmed at Temple Emanu-El—Reform Jews at that time eschewed the traditional bar mitzvah ceremony—but his Jewish education was spotty at best. Ungrounded in his heritage, embarrassed by it, and perhaps frightened by anti-Semitism, Morti never attempted to deny his religion, but he was never proudly assertive about his Jewishness, as his father had been.

Increasing anti-Semitism in America in the late nineteenth and early twentieth centuries came from various sources. One stimulant was the sheer number of Jewish immigrants, particularly in major port cities. Most were Eastern European; many were Orthodox. Their distinctive clothing and personal style seemed alien and unattractive even to their more Americanized coreligionists. After the end of the First World War, a wave of nativism and isolationism swept the country. The Ku Klux Klan spread beyond its Southern roots. In the past, the Irish and the Germans had been the victims of anti-immigrant prejudices; now it was the turn of newcomers from southern Europe and Jews. *The Protocols of the Elders of Zion,* an anti-Semitic screed written by the tsar's secret police, was widely distributed and believed, as was the persistent calumny—revived by Pat Robertson in the 1970s—that Jacob Schiff had financed the Russian Revolution. Henry Ford's anti-Semitic newspaper, the *Dearborn Independent,* gave credence to the most scurrilous of these allegations.

The postwar fear of Bolshevism and anarchism was so profound it became public policy. The United States government deported thousands of so-called undesirable aliens with the enthusiastic approval of large segments of the population. Disproportionate numbers of the deportees, and of the larger pool of anarchists and Communists in America and abroad, were Jews.

Anti-Semitism spread into realms where it had never before been the norm. Hotels at elegant resorts refused to accept Jewish guests. Clubs, like

New York's Union League, that had had Jewish founders rejected their sons. Other Jews trying to get into fashionable clubs often canvassed quietly to assess their chances. When it became clear they weren't welcome, they withdrew their attempts rather than be rejected. Eliot's successor at Harvard, A. Lawrence Lowell, who imposed quotas on the number of Jewish students admitted to the university, personified the new allegedly genteel anti-Semitism. He argued that if too many Jews were admitted, even if they deserved to be, their numbers would drive Christians away.

Many German Jews of Jacob Schiff's generation and of Morti's as well took on the attitudes of Christian society toward the so-called downtown Jews. German Jews who couldn't get into Christian clubs practiced their own discrimination: their strongholds—the Century Country Club in Westchester and the Harmonie in New York City—accepted few Jews from Russian, Polish, or Hungarian backgrounds. As Stephen Birmingham wrote in "*Our Crowd*" about New York's reigning German-Jewish families,

> A certain ambivalent attitude began to reveal itself among upper-class Jews toward their religious heritage. At times it was possible to believe that they were Jews in one breath and non-Jews in the next—that whether to be Jewish or not was rather like selecting the right fork for the right course at dinner. Even those who had converted felt it wrong, really, to deny that they were Jewish, leaving the impression that they regarded Jewishness as a racial as well as a religious matter. At the same time, they did not believe in "making a point" of being Jewish, regarding it as a "personal" thing, implying that Jewishness is purely a religious affair after all.

Frieda and Felix Warburg remained religiously and culturally Jewish. Their charities were primarily Jewish ones; their family home eventually became the Jewish Museum. Their children were given the basics of a Jewish education and were confirmed at Temple Emanu-El. Morti put his children through a kind of confirmation ceremony at Northwood performed by a rabbi specially imported for the occasion, presumably to placate Jacob Schiff. Although Morti and Adele never converted to Christianity, they used their money to buy their way into a world that allowed them—almost—to ignore their origins and to indulge in the fantasy that others ignored them also.

Lewis Strauss recalled that soon after he went to work at Kuhn, Loeb, his nominal boss Morti was invited to a party for some Japanese bankers given by Thomas Lamont at the University Club. Morti could not attend, so he passed the invitation on to Strauss, who had also worked on deals with the Japanese. Strauss turned it down, because no Jews were admitted as members of the club, although Morti played poker there every week. When Morti found out what Strauss had done, he lost his temper and accused Strauss of being very rude. Jacob, passing by, asked what was going on. Morti explained. "The old man, in my presence, proceeded to give him a dressing down such as I had never heard," Strauss wrote. Jacob said that he was horrified that a young member of the firm had a firmer sense of right and wrong than his own son. Morti apologized to Strauss. There's no evidence that he gave up his poker game.

Neither Dorothy nor John had any formal instruction in the tenets or practices of Judaism, and their Jewish heritage was acknowledged as infrequently as possible. Adele would have liked to celebrate Christmas, but Morti was afraid his father would find out. As it was, Grandfather Schiff stopped by every night of Hanukkah to make sure that candles were lit and blessings pronounced. Adele thought that Hanukkah presents were déclassé, so she and Morti gave their seasonal gifts on New Year's Day. The children frequently attended services at St. Bartholomew's Episcopal Church in New York, and Dorothy remembered being taken from time to time to Roman Catholic churches by her governess. She claimed that the first time she set foot in a synagogue was for her grandfather's funeral. A granddaughter of Frieda says, "Dolly's parents didn't want to be Jewish. They were acting out some kind of illusion they had. And I think it must have been awfully hard and very confusing for both John and Dolly."

Over the years, Dorothy told different stories about coming to be aware of what was called in her family circle "the background." She once said that she found out that she was different from the other girls at Brearley when a classmate told her she couldn't invite someone of "the background" to a party. Another time she said she first learned she was Jewish and what it implied during a summer visit to the Adirondacks. She was friendly with two Canadian girls until one of them told her they were not allowed to play together anymore because Dorothy was Jewish. Dorothy remembered that her French governess comforted her and used the word "Israelite," which sounded less harsh. Her brother, John, once said that as a boy he was not aware that the family was Jewish. "What did he think those sessions with the rabbi at Oyster Bay were about?" Dorothy wondered.

Morti and Adele's ambivalence about their heritage marked their children. John married into New York's WASP establishment and raised his children as Episcopalians. Dorothy married two non-Jews and two men who were very self-consciously Jewish. Like her grandfather, she could never make up her mind whether Judaism was a race or a religion; unlike him, she considered herself a staunch nonbeliever.

Society Girl

Dorothy once said, "I was ambitious as a child. I wanted to be like the people whose statues were in Central Park." At eighteen she had no idea of what she might do to achieve recognition. Only a handful of tenacious girls forced their way into medical school or prepared for other professions. Teaching or nursing were possible premarriage options for middle-class girls but not for a Schiff. Attending college was seen primarily as a means to meet an appropriate young man. While at Bryn Mawr, Dorothy was fascinated by a visiting lecturer who worked with Indians in Labrador. She contemplated volunteering at his mission the summer after her freshman year, but Adele was predictably horrified, and that was the end of that.

Adele wanted Dorothy to make a proper debut and then an advantageous marriage—even though she always implied that her daughter's prospects were limited because, Adele believed, Dorothy was unattractive and awkward. Not everyone agreed. Soon after Dorothy's "season" began in November 1921, she was one of the debs who served at the annual Horse Show tearoom. The society columnist of *The New York Times* covering the event commented that the current "crop of buds is one of the best-looking in years" and cited Dorothy as a notable beauty. She was developing into a good-looking young woman—dark-haired, fair-skinned, blue-eyed, slim, of medium height, proud of her shapely legs.

The season was a whirl of private dinners, luncheons, tea dances, formal balls, and amateur theatricals. One of the grandest events was given in honor of Dorothy's Brearley friend Ellin Mackay, whose father hosted more than seven hundred guests at an elaborate ball at the Ritz-Carlton.

Dorothy's official presentation to society took place a few weeks later at a party given by her parents in their home. Lewis Strauss, the young associate at Kuhn, Loeb, was shocked to find that he was among the few Jews invited. Several other well-born German-Jewish girls made modest debuts the same season, but they were not intimates of Dolly nor were their families close to her parents. Adele insisted that her daughter avoid any parties given by the Jewish families and attend only those honoring the Christian debs.

The Mortimer Schiffs had been listed in the *Social Register* since 1904, and few doors were closed to them in New York, although there were subtle slights. The Junior League—a social organization that excluded Jews—ran the Junior Assemblies, which were the most prestigious balls, and league members vetted the prospective debutantes before issuing invitations. Dorothy found the process humiliating. It was unthinkable that she would be totally ignored, but she was asked to attend only one of the three Junior Assemblies. Her family chose to believe she was rejected for the other two because of an odd scandal that had touched their household some years previously. In 1907, Foulke Brandt, one of the Schiffs' footmen, had sent an incoherent love letter to Adele. Morti promptly fired him, whereupon Brandt broke into the Schiff home and attacked Morti with a hammer. Brandt, who proved to have a history of petty crime and mental illness, was convicted of assault. The Hearst press kept the case alive by implying that Adele was romantically involved with the footman, even though there was no evidence to substantiate that claim, and she was not the kind of woman who was likely to have an affair with the hired help. The Schiffs found the scandal a more acceptable explanation of the slight than the problem of "the background." In fact, although a few Jewish girls were grudgingly included in the top parties, they were made to feel that they were there on sufferance.

Looking back on her debutante year, Dorothy disparaged the values it represented, and she commented with some satisfaction that most of the glamorous girls of the day had not made much of their lives. Although she claimed to have had more serious aspirations, it was not apparent at the time that she would eventually choose a different path through life from that of her fellow socialites.

She was restless. She took typing and shorthand classes at the YWCA and courses in accounting and psychology from a correspondence school in Scranton, Pennsylvania. She asked her father for a job at Kuhn, Loeb—even as a secretary—but he said no. So she fell back on the conventional route to adult status: finding a husband.

Early in her debut season, Dorothy met Richard B. W. Hall at a dance at the Plaza Hotel. Dick Hall was six years older than she and had served as a lieutenant in the navy on Vincent Astor's yacht, which was converted for military service during the First World War. Dick seemed more mature than the other boys she knew. He came from a family with acceptable credentials but not enough money. Dorothy was aware that he was a bit of a social climber, but, she recalled, "He was the best-looking man at parties, and since I wanted to be independent—have my own little nest and a lot of children—I went after him."

Timothy Seldes, Dick's nephew, who remained close to Dorothy all her life, says, "Dick was very handsome. And he was quintessentially WASPy. He came from a fine, though impoverished, WASPy social family. So there was something in it for each of them. He got access to her money, and she got his name. In that respect it made sense from both their sides."

Dorothy's parents were not pleased. Morti was afraid of what his family would say about Hall's not being Jewish. Adele thought he wasn't much of a catch. A little detective work revealed that Hall had run up debts around New York and didn't have the means to pay them off. He made anti-Semitic comments about Jews in general and Dorothy in particular. Nonetheless, after several fruitless attempts by her parents to break up the romance, Dorothy and Dick were married at Northwood on October 17, 1923.

Morti and Adele staged an elaborate party for more than two hundred guests. Dorothy's maid of honor was Dick's sister Alice Hall, who was to marry critic Gilbert Seldes the following year. Among the ushers were John Schiff and Sidney Smith, the Schiff family friend who was Adele's reputed lover. The ceremony was performed by the Right Reverend Herbert Shipman, the Episcopal suffragan bishop of New York, assisted by the Reverend George Talmage of the local Oyster Bay parish. Shipman had been the rector of the Church of the Heavenly Rest, which the Halls attended, and he confirmed Dorothy as an Episcopalian after some instruction. Morti and Adele were not troubled by these circumstances, but Dolly once said, "I don't know what would have happened if Grandpa Schiff had still been alive."

The marriage was probably doomed from the start. Years later, Dorothy told a friend that it was apparent to her by the time she married Dick that he was a third-rate—not even second-rate—guy. But, she said, it was the best she could do. She needed to get away from her parents, and for that she needed to be married. She described her wedding night at the St. Regis Hotel as less than blissful. Dick was the first man she'd ever slept with. He was very uncaring, which could have put her off sex for the rest of her life. But, she told her friend, "Luckily, it didn't!"

The honeymoon was no better. They drove to Montreal in her Willys roadster. When Dorothy got sick from drinking too much, Dick moved out of their room and into another hotel. Not surprisingly, they came home early.

That pretty much set the tone for the marriage. They squabbled over major issues and minor misunderstandings. Hall told friends that Dorothy's being Jewish kept him out of the best clubs and that Morti Schiff wouldn't let him work at Kuhn, Loeb because jobs there were reserved for Jews.* Dick soon got a job at another brokerage house, but his salary was low. He and Dolly were not predisposed to economizing. They barely made ends meet on a generous monthly allowance supplied by Morti.

For a time, the Halls continued the social life that had marked their courtship. Dorothy told an interviewer, "We did what most young couples did in the Flapper Age. We went to speakeasies, danced, entertained, went nightclubbing, and had fun. Dick Hall introduced me to a new sort of life. One that was in character with the twenties and the spirit of the prohibition era." Dick gambled at bridge and backgammon. Sometimes they played cards with Aunt Frieda and Dorothy's Warburg cousins, although that side of the clan was basically opposed to the marriage.

The young couple had two children within two years: Mortimer Wadhams Hall was born in July 1924, nine months after the wedding, and Adele Therese followed thirteen months later. Grandmother Adele was heard to say that Dorothy was "having litters like a bitch." Artificial methods of birth control were illegal at the time, but Dorothy read about diaphragms in a book

---

*Although Morti's rejection of Dick Hall probably had more to do with his assessment of the young man's character than his ethnicity, the firm was remarkably inbred. Until 1912, every partner was related by descent or marriage to one of the founders. However, Dick's claim was undermined by the fact that several nonfamily members and non-Jews were brought into the firm in the early '20s, and a few made partner later in the decade.

smuggled from Europe. After her daughter's birth, she tracked down such a device in a Madison Avenue drugstore.

Dorothy was determined to be a better mother to her children than Adele had been to her, but the model for motherhood that she shared with women of her class and time was far from hands-on. Nurses and nannies spent much more time with children than parents did. In 1931, Dorothy hired a Swiss governess, Ida Laissue, who stayed for six years teaching the children French and handicrafts as well as supervising their daily lives. Morti remembered being brought in to see his mother at teatime. Neither of the Hall children remembers many intimate moments with her when they were youngsters.

Dolly was proud of the fact that she took young Morti and Adele with her when she traveled. Many of her friends went off for extended vacations and didn't see their children for weeks. She pulled Morti out of St. Bernard's and Adele out of Dalton for the winter season in Palm Beach, where they were briefly enrolled in a local school. In March 1932, Morti and Adele entered the children's swimming and diving competition at the Sea Spray Beach Club, and Morti won a silver cup in boxing.

Parenthood had almost no impact on Dick Hall's social life; he was out on the town most evenings with bachelor friends. Dorothy seldom accompanied him. Often she stayed home reading—a habit so outlandish in her set that her girlfriends teased her about it.

She did find ways to lead a social life of her own. She was beginning to define her own style. Unlike her mother, she dressed well, but not ostentatiously, and wore little jewelry. She was flirtatious. When she entered a room, she identified the most appealing man present and set to work to charm him. She told a story well, and she liked to use slightly shocking language when it suited her purposes. She could also be a rapt listener. Although—or maybe because—her parents had given her little sense of her appealing qualities, she sought and enjoyed the attention and compliments of suitors. Prohibition encouraged a disrespect for the law and the erosion of social proprieties. Being married was often a convenient cover for conduct that would have been unacceptable for a woman otherwise. Philandering or just pretending, Dorothy seemed to relish the chase at least as much as the catch.

Dorothy and the children spent weeks at a time with her parents in Oyster Bay or Palm Beach. Often she hung out with a crowd of married older men who came to Palm Beach to play golf and play around. One of the few who didn't make a pass was a Boston Irishman named Joseph Kennedy. He didn't drink, and he was more serious than the others. Dorothy liked his company, and they remained lifelong friends.

She frequently went to Europe for part of the summer. There, the cast of characters changed slightly. Dorothy's suitors included a succession of Spanish and French aristocrats. In the summer of 1928, she had a brief flirtation with Averell Harriman, whom she had known for years. She and the children were visiting her mother in Paris, and Harriman and his first wife were also there, separately, getting a discreet divorce. Averell was already involved with Marie Norton, the recent ex-wife of Sonny Whitney, but when he ran into Dolly, a spark ignited between them. They had dinner, then agreed to spend the next day together. During the afternoon, Dorothy rather thoughtlessly left the tennis match they were watching to go with a mutual friend to see how her father's horses were doing at Longchamps. When she returned, Harriman was miffed and begged off dinner. In case she missed the point, he had a dead orchid delivered to her. Harriman soon married Marie Norton, who remained his wife until her death in 1970. Averell and Dorothy resumed a cordial though somewhat distant friendship, which would turn prickly at times.

Even when Dick and Dorothy were both in New York, they went their separate ways. He continued to see other women, while drinking more and more heavily. In July 1930, Dorothy began a romance with a dashing Russian emigré, Serge Obolensky, who was at the time separated from one of her Brearley classmates. Their affair lasted ten months; their friendship endured for nearly fifty years.*

At one point Dorothy mentioned to her father that she was thinking about ending her marriage. He said she'd made her bed and she must lie in it. If she got a divorce, he would cut off her allowance. She didn't seem to hold his opinion against him and agreed to spend the month of June 1931 at Northwood, serving as his hostess while Adele was in Paris. One night when there were no guests, father and daughter sat down for a long, unprecedented, intimate conversation. Morti may have been more reflective than usual because it was the eve of his fifty-fourth birthday. He talked about what

---

*For years, Dorothy and Serge corresponded and exchanged gifts. In the sixties and seventies, he sent her violets every Christmas, and Dorothy made a generous annual contribution to his Tolstoy Foundation for needy fellow emigrés. She was a regular guest at dinners he hosted at New York restaurants. Once, between marriages, he proposed. She was tempted, then thought better of it. She pointed out that he probably wouldn't like sharing her with the *New York Post*.

he perceived as his failures as a businessman, a husband, and a good Jew. About how he adored his mother, who was still living. And above all about his inability to measure up to his father's reputation. Dolly felt that he had never been so open, or so depressed.

Early the next morning she was awakened by the butler, who'd been knocking vainly on her father's door. Together they found Morti dead of an apparent heart attack, sitting in an armchair wearing a silk brocade dressing gown. The funeral, which was delayed till Adele could return from Paris, was conducted at Northwood by a rabbi from Temple Emanu-El. Adele, following the same imperative that had led her and Morti to Long Island in their lifetimes, ensured that they would remain there, separated from Morti's family even in death. Morti was buried in a plot she had chosen for them at the Cold Spring Harbor Memorial cemetery, which was owned by the local Episcopal church, rather than in the family mausoleum at Salem Fields in Brooklyn.

Morti was never as devoted to Kuhn, Loeb as Jacob had been. Although he was dutiful in his professional responsibilities and brought in young hotshots like Lewis Strauss, the firm did not dominate Wall Street during his stewardship. His most astute move may have been to minimize the potential disaster that could have resulted from the Great Depression. As the Wall Street boom of the late 1920s became more and more frenzied, Uncle Paul Warburg, who was married to Morti's mother's half sister, became more and more worried. Early in 1929, he convinced Morti to sell a considerable amount of the stock in his personal portfolio and also, over the objections of partner Otto Kahn, to move large sums of Kuhn, Loeb capital from margin-held stocks to municipal bonds. Although Morti still lost about half his personal fortune in the crash, both he and the firm came out of it in better shape than many others.

Morti Schiff's estate was worth approximately $30 million, according to a front-page article in the June 14, 1931, *New York Times*. His will stipulated that $1 million be given to specific charities, including his father's beloved Henry Street Settlement. John received a bequest of $1 million in cash. Dorothy was given $750,000 (almost $8 million in 2007 dollars), and Dick Hall got $250,000. Dorothy and John were each to receive in trust one-fifth shares in the residual estate. Widow Adele was left 932 Fifth and the adjacent house in which Morti had kept his collections, all the couple's personal effects, a big garage in Manhattan, the use of Northwood for the rest of her life, and three-fifths of the residual estate. A year earlier Morti had given John the money to buy a partnership in Kuhn, Loeb—a presumably lucrative career opportunity that was denied his sister.

Before Dorothy had time to grasp the implications of her new financial status, she accepted an invitation to go to Paris with her mother. At the last minute, Adele delayed her trip because of ill health, but Dorothy and the children sailed anyway. The first night out, Dorothy noticed an odd-looking Englishman across the first-class dining room. He noticed her, too, and dispatched his dinner companion to invite her to join him for coffee. The emissary was a gossip columnist for the London *Daily Express,* and his traveling partner and boss was the mercurial British press lord, Max Beaverbrook. Dorothy shared Beaverbrook's table and his cabin for the rest of the trip.

Beaverbrook was born Max Aitken, the son of a Presbyterian minister in eastern Canada. By his mid-twenties, he had made a fortune in the financial markets, put together a trust that dominated the country's cement industry, owned or controlled several Canadian publications, and was ready to assert his interest in journalism and politics on a bigger stage. Early in 1910, he traveled to London in search of financing for further deals in Canada and to seek out his fellow Canadian, Bonar Law, the Conservative prime minister of England. Max was interested in standing as a Conservative candidate for the House of Commons. His money and his ability to find friends in high places gave him the chance in late 1910 to contest a seat just outside Manchester. His money, which he spent liberally on modern methods of campaigning, and his quick-study mastery of the issues helped him win.

The restless new MP was not content with a political career alone. In 1911 he bought the *Globe,* a struggling but respectable London evening paper, and was eyeing other acquisitions in England. He had already made a substantial loan to the editor of the *Daily Express* to keep it alive and ensure its continuing support for the Conservative party. Between 1912 and 1915, Aitken quietly bought up shares in the *Express,* so that by 1916 he was effectively the sole owner. After World War I, he launched the *Sunday Express,* and in 1923 he acquired the *Evening Standard.* By the time he met Dorothy, he had put together the second largest chain of newspapers in Great Britain. As sharp a journalist as he was a businessman, he limited his holdings so that he could exercise direct editorial as well as financial control over them. In time, the success of the mass-circulation *Daily Express* and its Sunday counterpart earned him yet another fortune.

Max was elevated to the peerage as Lord Beaverbrook in 1916. He was a member of the cabinet during the First World War. His rapid rise was resented by many English politicians, but it was hard to challenge his effectiveness.

Beaverbrook was as ambitious for advancement in his private life as he was in his career. In 1906, while still in Canada, the twenty-six-year-old entrepreneur had married beautiful eighteen-year-old Gladys Drury, whose father was the military commander of the Halifax garrison, making her social status slightly higher than her husband's. During the next six years, Max and Gladys had three children.

When they moved to England permanently in 1911, Max installed his growing family in a Victorian country house in Surrey, about an hour south of London. Max stayed in town at the Savoy or the Hyde Park Hotel, where Gladys joined him infrequently. In 1920, he bought a house in out-of-the-way Fulham, which he used for dinners, meetings, and assignations. Eventually he moved on to a mansion, Stornoway House, in fashionable St. James's. He took up with the crowd of "bright young things" whom Evelyn Waugh satirized in *Vile Bodies* and also formed lifelong friendships with the Churchills and the Mountbattens.

Max, despite his unprepossessing appearance, was successful with women. Lady Diana Cooper once described him as a "strange attractive gnome with an odour of genius about him." He seemed to take special pleasure in seducing socialites, especially married ones. He helped out his new friends with impromptu loans and sometimes also invested their own money for them, although behind his back they gossiped about his overt and thus, to them, unseemly interest in wealth and power.

Everyone in the intersecting worlds of international society, the arts, and politics was eager to come to Beaverbrook's parties at Stornoway House or to be invited for a country weekend in Surrey. Among other things, his guests were often seeking his papers' support for various projects and interests.

In 1925, Beaverbrook began a liaison with Jean Norton, a twenty-seven-year-old mother of two whose husband was an English associate of Kuhn, Loeb. The Nortons lived in a world of rampant infidelity but one in which the social proprieties were always observed. Richard Norton, who had his own peccadilloes, was often included in the weekend parties. Max's daughter Jane was old enough to observe that her father's relationship to Jean Norton, unlike many of his flings, was a real love affair. Perhaps that's why his wife was more upset than usual. In any event, she began to drink and to suffer from depression. At least that's what everyone assumed. She worsened steadily and died suddenly in December 1927, at the age of thirty-nine. In fact, Gladys's problem turned out not to be just psychological. An autopsy revealed that an undiagnosed brain tumor was the probable cause of death.

After several months of mourning, Max resumed his affair with Jean Norton in 1928. They would be together off and on for another seventeen years. Other young beauties continued to catch Max's eye. They usually stayed friends after the affair broke up, and he often gave them generous gifts of cash or jewelry on their birthdays.

Beaverbrook's friends frequently commented on his short attention span and his vulnerability to boredom. In the spring of 1931, he was unusually restless. He had left Parliament but was looking for a way to be politically active again. Several causes and candidates he supported had suffered inglorious defeats. On the outs with Stanley Baldwin, the head of the Conservative party, Beaverbrook was flirting with Ramsay MacDonald and Labour. In June he left for his annual trip to Canada and the States. He hoped Jean Norton would join him, but she had other plans.

On his return voyage, Beaverbrook spotted Dorothy Schiff Hall. In some ways, Dorothy was typical of Max's usual conquests—she was young, sexy, something of a trophy. In other respects she was quite dissimilar. She was not a London beauty, she could be serious as well as flighty, and as the heiress to a considerable American fortune, she did not need his money or his social cachet. On Dorothy's part, after a few years of unsatisfying flirtations and flings, the attraction of a man like Max was precisely his difference from her recent suitors.

Perhaps the fact that Beaverbrook was about the same age as Dorothy's recently deceased father played some part in her seduction; perhaps his prominence and influence in the world of politics and finance brought to mind Jacob Schiff. She certainly wasn't drawn to Max because of his looks. Dorothy noted that he was short, with a head that seemed too big for his body, and he dressed rather shabbily. But she had never met anyone as dynamic, purposeful, and possessive of her as Beaverbrook proved to be.

Max wanted Dorothy to come with him to London, but she and the children were headed for Paris, so he followed her there. In pursuit of something he wanted, Max had extraordinary persuasive powers. Even Adele, while warning Dorothy that he had a reputation as a cad and a conniver, was charmed. After wooing Dorothy with champagne suppers in his suite at the

Ritz, Max begged her to join him in London. At one point he sent her some newspaper clippings attesting to his importance on the current British political scene with the note: "The peacock spreading his tail feathers, hoping to attract the attention of the proud hen."

Who could resist? She moved into Stornoway House (the children and Mademoiselle were installed in a nearby hotel) and was immediately swept up in a world of politics and a general level of intellectual discourse to which she had never before been exposed. She met Churchill and H. G. Wells, Lord Rothschild, and a young MP named Leslie Hore-Belisha, who, blind to the relationship between Max and Dorothy, decided he wanted to marry her. The talk at Max's dinners ranged from the upcoming general election to history and literature. Years later, Dorothy told her daughter Adele that after having a conversation with Max or hearing something mentioned at the table, she would hurry to the library to fill in the gaps in her knowledge. Then she would say, "You brought up something very interesting last night, and I'd like to discuss it with you."

Dorothy always said that she learned more from Max and his friends about politics and the life of the mind than about the newspaper business. But he spoke to her about that, too. He assumed that the first imperative of a newspaper, like that of any business, was to make a profit, but that making money should not be an end in itself. He believed that newspaper owners should have strong political views and should use their presses to advance them. In Max's case, his prickly personality made him as much a liability as an asset to his party. Although he would serve in Churchill's cabinet from 1940 to 1945, his greater power was exercised behind the scenes.

All this was heady stuff for twenty-eight-year-old Dorothy Schiff Hall. "I was so green I knew nothing. Beaverbrook taught me a lot," she told a reporter years later. "It was the summer of my life!" But like many a summer romance, it would not last. Dorothy needed to return to New York for the beginning of the children's school year. Max, trying to keep her in London, discussed marriage but never actually proposed. She held to her plan. Petulant about not getting his way, he refused to see her off.

Nevertheless, a barrage of telegrams reached her on the boat home. Oct. 4, 1931: "Situation [political events] changing daily and only my love for you is constant." Oct. 6, 1931: "My one and only love. Confusion still reigns in politics and you always reign in my heart." But just about the time Max posted these cables, Jean Norton, who'd been temporarily exiled to Paris, moved back into Stornoway House.

When Max arrived in New York in November, he made it clear that his romance with Dorothy was over. He offered to fix her up with Leslie Hore-Belisha, who had admired her in London. Having assumed she and Max would pick up where they left off, Dorothy was stunned. She soon realized that they would never have had a permanent relationship, but she also discovered that she could no longer be satisfied with the way she'd been living before they met. It was only a three-month fling, after all, but Max's impact on her would persist long after their brief affair was over.

Dorothy had always been tantalized by the life of the mind and the exercise of power, but in keeping with her upbringing, she'd suppressed her fascination and discounted her ability to participate. She was flattered that Max took her seriously and captivated by everything he had exposed her to: the excitement of politics, the importance of history, and the stimulation of people with first-rate minds.

She was not utterly transformed. She remained more interested in people than policy. She did not turn her back on her friends from café society; she continued to be intrigued by gossip. She was developing a style that to some people seemed poised and full of aplomb—imperious, even—but her manner masked the doubts about her self-worth that remained the legacy of her childhood.

However, the affair with Max convinced Dorothy that she could hold her own in serious company. She became avid for new information and ideas. She began a lifelong habit of reading ancient philosophers, contemporary historians, and, occasionally, a light novel. She made notes in the margin, dutifully kept a list of everything she read, and confided to her diary what she thought of each book.

Dorothy's daughter Adele says, "My mother was a developing human being, wasn't she? Because if you look back, she was a renegade from the beginning. Clearly how her parents lived was not how she was going to live. She had none of the materialism. She really didn't give a hot damn about clothes or jewelry. Mother always looked wonderful, but my grandmother was—well, I've seen the jewelry. She had the sapphires to go with the blue dress. And houses all over the world, and that kind of thing. And my mother was having none of it. It was the life of the mind that really defined her. She was searching for how to find it at first. That's why she was such a blotter with people like Max Beaverbrook, for instance."

Dorothy may have wanted to find or create a milieu in New York where she could pursue her newfound interests, but first there were family matters to attend to. She had barely settled back into her New York apartment and begun to contemplate how to ease Dick Hall out of her life when her mother complained again about not feeling well. Exploratory surgery revealed that she had uterine cancer. The tumor was removed. The prognosis, which was kept from Adele, was not good. Dorothy was in charge of her care. They spent the winter in Palm Beach, returned to New York in the spring for Adele to have another operation, then settled into Northwood to await the end.

The enforced mother-daughter closeness of those months did not resolve the tensions of a lifetime. Adele, who was probably aware of her imminent death though everyone around her denied it, was as remote as ever. Dorothy's ambivalent feelings about her mother were made more problematic by her guilt at keeping the secret. Adele's pain worsened, but the doctor refused Dorothy's request that he end the agony with an overdose of painkiller. Finally, on July 6, 1932, just before her fifty-second birthday, Adele died. The nurse told Dorothy she could kiss the corpse, but mother and daughter had seldom kissed while Adele was alive, and Dorothy had no intention of doing so after her death.

Dorothy barely mourned. Within weeks, she set off for Reno to get her divorce. Morti's bequest would enable Dick to set himself up in the style to which he had become accustomed. He continued his hard partying. He was not an attentive parent. Family lore has it that Richard Hall found it hard to warm to his children because he considered them Jewish.

His mother and his sister Marian took up the slack. Grandmother Hall, who was more forceful than affectionate, enrolled young Morti and Adele in Sunday school at the Church of the Heavenly Rest, and Marian provided the affection and the fun. Adele remembers that on the rare occasions her father and mother crossed paths, they managed to be quite civil to each other.

For a decade or so, Dick worked as a stockbroker and maintained his social status. In 1939, he married Mrs. Cheseborough Lewis Tullis, another socially prominent heiress. It was downhill from there. He married three more times, sank further into alcoholism, went through his money, and took a series of modest jobs. He ended up destitute and ill and was supported by his children until his death in 1959.

Morti Schiff's will specified that upon his wife's death his children would receive the bulk of his estate, but not in equal portions. John inherited the New York City real estate except for a small garage that went to Dolly, the house in Paris, the house in Oyster Bay plus two-thirds of the acreage of that estate, and all the furnishings and collections. Dolly got a bit over three hundred and fifty acres of the Northwood land but no part of the house. Adele's share of the residual estate was to be divided, with John getting two-thirds and Dolly one-third. The money in Adele's own modest estate was divided equally between her children, and Dolly received her personal effects and jewelry. When both her parents' wills were probated and all the funds transferred, Dorothy found herself in possession of just under $10 million (nearly $120 million in 2007 dollars) in securities plus considerable real estate holdings. Although it paled beside John's inheritance, it was a sizable fortune in the early years of the Depression.

Dolly was financially independent but not quite on her own. Even before her divorce from Dick Hall was granted in September 1932, she had found a candidate to replace him. She'd met George Backer during the months she was tending her dying mother at Northwood. He was a friend of their friend and neighbor, Herbert Bayard Swope, the former editor of the New York World. The Swopes had a lavish estate in Great Neck where they entertained a crowd of sophisticated New Yorkers, including the Gershwin brothers, Harpo Marx, Alexander Woollcott, and Harold Ross. George Backer was such a frequent weekend guest that he kept clothes there.

In 1932, George was a thirty-year-old man-about-town. George Backer Sr. was a Russian immigrant who had become a wealthy builder with substantial real estate holdings in midtown Manhattan. He had died a decade earlier after a breakdown evidently brought on by allegations of corrupt dealings during the previous year with Tammany Hall, the New York County Democratic organization. Young George left the University of Pennsylvania when his father died. He worked briefly at the New York Globe, even more briefly for the family business, and became a member of the Democratic County Committee. Clubhouse politics, however, was not to be his milieu any more than real estate was, and a sustained interest in any career was not apparent.

The Backers were an elegant and cultured family who moved within one generation into the upper middle class. George and his siblings were regulars at the theater, the philharmonic, and the Metropolitan Opera. One brother became a prominent lawyer with Tammany connections; another, having wanted to be an architect, reluctantly ran the family real estate management business. George took no active part in the company, but he lived on income derived from it. Affable, attractive, and well educated, he had ingratiated himself with the Swopes and their friends, although his accomplishments had not matched theirs. He had produced several Broadway plays that had modest runs, and he aspired to be a playwright.

George and Dorothy were immediately drawn to each other. He was of medium height, very good-looking, with wavy, dark hair, a soothing voice, and elegant manners. He was considerate and consoling during the months while her mother was dying, and his disapproval of Max helped Dorothy put that relationship in perspective. He was charmed by her earnest search for intellectual improvement and often suggested books she should read. She enjoyed the company of his theatrical and literary friends, although occasionally she reminded herself that they were not as interesting as the crowd Max assembled at Stornoway House. Just as Dorothy would later characterize Dick Hall as an appropriate husband for the hedonistic twenties, she would say that George Backer was an appropriate choice for the liberal, socially committed thirties.

In later years, both Dorothy and George implied that although they certainly had become a couple, it wasn't clear to either of them that they were passionately in love. During their courtship, for example, Dorothy had a brief fling with a man she met while in Nevada getting her divorce from Dick. Nonetheless, she and George were married in the chapel of the New York City Municipal Building by City Clerk Michael J. Cruise on October 21, 1932. The marriage was announced the following week by her brother, John. *The New York Times* said it would surprise many of their friends since no formal announcement had been made of an engagement.

Dorothy's family was initially not much happier with her second husband than they had been with her first. The Warburgs, who were relieved to see her marry a Jew, were put off by the fact that George's family was of Eastern European origin. John, who was genuinely protective of his sister but was becoming a bit stuffy, feared that George was a bounder like Dick, just less of a social-climbing one. George's engaging personality soon won the family over.

After living briefly with John Schiff at 932 Fifth, the newlyweds moved to the Carlyle Hotel, then settled into a large apartment at 944 Fifth Avenue. They also decided to build a house on Dolly's share of the property at Northwood. Dick Hall's sister Marian, who was the decorator, named the neocolonial mansion Old Fields. What Dolly had first envisioned as a simple country getaway turned out to be a grand estate costing nearly a million dollars. The main floor had a large entrance hall, a living room, a library, a dining room and dining porch, two lavatories, and one bedroom with attached bath. On the second floor there were two master bedroom suites, plus two other bedrooms each with its own bath. The children had a separate wing, in which there were three bedrooms with baths and a large playroom. There were also seven bedrooms for the help and a servants' hall, a six-car garage with a two-bedroom apartment for the chauffeur above it, plus a swimming pool and attached pool house.

Dolly was mortified by the scale of Old Fields, although she had approved all the expenditures. Too unsure of herself to say no, she was resentful that no one else—not Marian Hall, not George, not the men who wrote the checks at Kuhn, Loeb—had put a stop to the increasing scale of the place and the mounting costs.

Soon after Old Fields was finished, a happier event took place—the birth of the Backers' daughter Sarah-Ann in June 1934. Dorothy was thrilled by the baby. But she had moved through the emotionally charged events of the past few years in something of an unnatural calm, and suddenly everything came crashing down in the form of postpartum depression. By the end of the summer, she could barely get out of bed.

A friend of George's suggested that she consult Dr. Harry Stack Sullivan. Sullivan, a forty-two-year-old American-trained psychoanalyst, was beginning to make a reputation for himself as one of the foremost theorists of the post-Freudian generation of therapists. Sullivan's particular contribution was his belief that, though much of what Freud taught about the origin of neuroses in the patient's childhood was valid, more attention should be paid to the person's interactions with other people in adulthood. As one of the founders of the interpersonal school of psychoanalysis, he taught that the doctor must enter into an active therapeutic relationship with the patient so that both could examine the ways the patient created inappropriate interpersonal behavior patterns. He believed that emotional health could be achieved by making patients aware of these dysfunctional mechanisms. Sullivan was a socialist who often took on wealthy private patients to subsidize his clinic patients and his research.

They began a five-day-a-week, $15-an-hour analysis. Dorothy finally had someone who would listen at length to her concerns, which ranged from not knowing how to cope with the servants needed to run Old Fields, to her fear of leaving the house while feeling trapped in it at the same time, and to her terror that she might be going mad. The fact that she did not seem to discuss these matters with George might have been something else to talk about with the doctor.

She began to feel better almost immediately. Although at times she considered Sullivan somewhat patronizing about a rich girl's problems, she stayed in treatment for more than two years. She also contributed funds to support his research. To be in therapy in those years was thought to be a bit daring and therefore quite fashionable in Dorothy's world. Later, she grew critical of Sullivan but remained respectful of psychoanalysis in general.

When Dorothy was well enough to go out, the Backers resumed a busy social and cultural life. In winter, they dined and danced at the Rainbow Room on top of the newly built Rockefeller Center or at the Central Park Casino. In summer, they dressed for costume balls and formal dinners at the homes of their Long Island neighbors, the Paysons and the Whitneys. For Dolly, the cultural side was somewhat new. They attended opening nights on Broadway and galas at the Metropolitan Opera. They had a box at the Philharmonic.

George tried to revive his theatrical career. *Honeymoon,* a play he wrote with his friend Samuel Chotzinoff, opened in New York in December 1932. Chotzinoff was a distinguished music critic and classical record producer, but he was no more of a playwright than was Backer. *Honeymoon* received respectful but unenthusiastic reviews; a modest investment from Dorothy helped keep it alive for seventy-six performances.

George did not lose his fascination with the theater. In 1935, he encouraged Dolly to invest $5,000 in a new drama, *Dead End,* written by his friend Sidney Kingsley. The play, which was later made into a movie with Humphrey Bogart, returned a big profit to its investors. Dolly took a stake in productions of the Playwrights' Company, a cooperative founded in 1938 by dramatists Maxwell Anderson, S. N. Behrman, Sidney Howard, Elmer Rice, and Robert E. Sherwood. The company owned 50 percent of the rights to plays by the five writers.

The project started auspiciously with Sherwood's play *Abe Lincoln in Illinois*. Starring Raymond Massey, it opened in October 1938 to rave reviews, won the Pulitzer Prize for drama, and was made into a film. Dolly put up $10,000 and netted about ten times that much. Not everything the company produced was financially successful. Dolly's first ventures were among her most lucrative, but overall she more than broke even. The quality of the work the company sponsored was high, and she got a lot of pleasure from the association.

The thirties were arguably the most dazzling time in the history of New York theater. Musicals by Rodgers and Hart, the Gershwins, Irving Berlin, Cole Porter, and Kurt Weill debuted virtually every season, as did plays produced by the Playwrights' Company, dramas and comedies by George S. Kaufman and Moss Hart, and revues starring Bert Lahr, the Marx Brothers, Bea Lillie, and Bobby Clark. The Backers were insiders in this glamorous world.

The opening night parties, the suppers at Sardi's, the country weekends in Great Neck or Bucks County took place against the background of the lingering and debilitating economic crisis that caused so much suffering for so many other Americans. The Backers had no real financial woes, although Dolly was perpetually upset at her inability to control her household expenses. She fretted over the size of her staff, particularly at Old Fields, and scrutinized bills from food and liquor vendors, urging her cooks to economize whenever possible. She disconnected her city apartment phone each summer when the family moved to Long Island.

No matter how sheltered the Backers were by personal wealth, it was impossible for them to be unaffected by the distress surrounding them. By the mid-thirties, all but the most hidebound American conservatives had come to believe something must be done to mitigate the hardships caused by the persistence of the Depression. Debate raged about how to change the social and financial structures that had enabled the economy to collapse and made efforts to remedy that collapse so difficult. Socialists and Communists argued that the fault lay in capitalism itself and that nothing less than its elimination would do the job. Most Americans believed that this suggested cure, whether it took place by evolution or by revolution, was much worse than the disease.

Liberal Democrats accepted much of the Socialist critique of capitalism, but they hoped to modify rather than replace the system in order to preserve democracy and its institutions. Such liberals took the view that the government should pass laws and create federal agencies to curb the unbridled ability of business to do as it pleased; they believed that labor unions should be supported as a countervailing power to the bosses; they argued that vast public works projects would give people jobs, a sense of worth, and spending money in their pockets; and they encouraged intellectuals and other citizens who had long viewed politics as a dirty business to contribute their talents to the cause of good government.

George Backer was already a supporter of President Franklin Roosevelt, although he had nothing good to say about the Tammany-driven New York City Democratic party. The Schiffs were hereditary Republicans; John was particularly conservative in his views. Aunt Frieda Warburg had caused a considerable fuss in the family in 1932 when she announced that she voted for FDR. Dolly, influenced by George and his friends, but also by her own sense of fairness, moved closer and closer to the same heresy.

"I never thought much about public affairs until my mother died," she told a reporter. "My first vote was cast for Calvin Coolidge in 1924. But there was so much talk everywhere about the economic conditions and . . . I heard a great deal about the New Deal and its social policy. It sounded very good to me, instead of awful, as the Republicans thought it was."

Dorothy's first gestures of social activism had been in traditional Schiff family stewardships: she sat on the boards of Mount Sinai Hospital and the Henry Street Settlement. Early in 1932, she was invited to lunch with Eleanor Roosevelt and some other women who were organizing a club to aid unemployed women. In 1935, she joined the board of the Women's Trade Union League, a favorite cause of Mrs. Roosevelt, whom Dorothy particularly admired. Within two years she was running a benefit of the Ballets Russes at the Metropolitan Opera House for the league. In her capacity as chairman of the league's legislative committee, she tried to drum up support for a bill to limit domestic servants to a working week of sixty hours and to get them workmen's compensation.* For the remainder of the decade, she saw Mrs. Roose-

---

*"As a volunteer," Dorothy wrote later, "I always felt very conscious of my lack of professional training. . . . I actually envied the paid, trained personnel whom you could count on to be available from 9 to 5 every day, who weren't subject to sudden, unannounced absences due to illness in the family, trips

velt frequently at teas and dinners benefiting charitable organizations whose aims they both supported.

In the summer of 1936, she went to work for FDR's reelection campaign and changed her party registration. Her assignment was to run the radio campaign of the women's division of the New York State Democratic party. Her main responsibility was administrative, making sure that announcements of political broadcasts were sent to all the county committees in the state. She shared an office with Anna Boettiger, the president's daughter. The job and her league work gave her the opportunity to move closer into the Roosevelt family orbit.

Dorothy had first come under FDR's spell at his 1933 inauguration when she and George had sat in the freezing cold to hear him tell the world that the only thing Americans had to fear was fear itself. She was thrilled to hear him speak at the 1936 Democratic Convention in Philadelphia about America's rendezvous with destiny. The day following the convention, she joined a group of other Democratic women on a celebratory pilgrimage to Roosevelt's home at Hyde Park, New York. Years later she wrote about it. "I was asked if I would like to go on a special Presidential train to Hyde Park. Of course I said, 'yes.' I remember being given an upper berth in one of the cars and not being able to sleep all night because of anticipatory excitement."

The next day the president was seated in his open touring car in front of the Summer White House. "His daughter Anna, with whom I had been working, took me firmly by the hand—I was shy—and pulled me up to the side of her father's car and introduced me. The president shook hands with me warmly with a broad grin and said: 'I've been hearing about you, Dorothy, and I'm so glad you're with us. I knew your father well.'

"I answered—nothing! In spite of the President's genial greeting I was so overawed that something happened to me that I have never experienced before or since—my tongue literally clove to the roof of my mouth. I told one of the women about this afterward. She advised me not to worry about having made a fool of myself. She said most party workers when introduced to the President erred in the other direction, burdening him with a long stream of petty complaints."

---

to Florida, California or Europe. I even seriously considered going to the New York School of Social Work myself, but a college degree (which I lacked) was an entrance requirement."

Charmed, Roosevelt saw to it that Dolly returned frequently to Hyde Park. She was flattered to be asked by the president of the United States, an astonishingly dynamic man. In some ways he reminded her of Max Beaverbrook. Looking back, she said that Roosevelt, like Max, enjoyed the fact that she didn't want anything from him. She was also attractive, chic, and capable of being coquettish—unlike many of the women in Eleanor's circle.

"There was a class thing too," Dorothy said later. "He was a snob . . . and he liked women who were well bred and brought up. I was a rich kid of the right kind—not the robber baron type—and had been to the right schools. As to being Jewish, C. P. Snow wrote that once you reach a certain financial level, people don't think of you as anything but very rich."

She was invited to Hyde Park every month or so. She often stayed overnight in Val-Kill, Eleanor's cottage, with Eleanor and her friends. The president would come by Val-Kill in his car and honk for her, which embarrassed her. Often they had lunch together with his mother at her house. Dorothy sensed that the senior Mrs. Roosevelt approved of her presence, at least in part because the old lady loathed Eleanor.

All this made Dorothy uncomfortable around Eleanor, whom she certainly didn't want to hurt. Although her invitations were proffered through the president's appointments secretary, she would call Eleanor's social secretary to accept, in order to reinforce the perception that nothing covert was going on.

Dorothy soon found that life was rather boring at Hyde Park. There wasn't much to do. Sports were out of the question because of the president's paralysis. He could swim—it was good therapy—and she was expected to join him at the pool.

"The President loved to tease and joke," she wrote later. "He was quick to see and laugh at the ridiculous and the pretentious in people. He was the opposite of 'stuffy.' He always wanted to know what was going on in the neighborhood and among people he knew—even the smallest items amused him. I used to save up everything I had heard between visits for his delectation. I had been warned not to discuss the war or politics with him when he was at Hyde Park, because he was supposed to be resting."

It was harder for Dorothy to keep the world at bay. She was genuinely moved by the human suffering caused by the Depression but sometimes believed that FDR was chiefly interested in the effect that devastating economic conditions had on politics.

In the summer of 1937, FDR told her that he wanted her to help him buy a farm abutting his land. He couldn't afford the whole thing; would she be willing to buy half? Reluctant to commit herself, Dorothy asked what she would do with it, and the president suggested having his cousin Henry Toombs, the architect who designed much of the southern White House at Warm Springs, Georgia, design a house for her.

The subject did not come up again, so she was startled some months later when he wrote to say that his lawyer had closed the deal and would she please send him a check for $9,000 for her half of the farm. It was hard for anyone to say no to him, she thought, partly because he was spoiled and partly because of his paralysis. Reluctantly, she sent off her check and was relieved to learn later that the land assigned her was too boggy to allow a house to be built.

Eventually FDR traded her some acreage on the high ground. His daughter, Anna Boettiger, and others pressured her to build. Feeling coerced, she arranged for the construction of a red clapboard cottage with two bedrooms, one bath, and a few public rooms. She called it the Red House. The president claimed to have played a big part in its design. One day a guest at Hyde Park asked Dorothy about her much grander house on Long Island—was it in the style of Louis XIV or XV? FDR jumped in, asking what was the style of her house in Hyde Park, and Dorothy answered, "Franklin the First."

Because she, George, and the children spent their summers on Long Island, Dorothy barely used the cottage, loaning it instead to friends in FDR's circle. By the time the Red House was ready, the intensity of the friendship had cooled. Dolly was beginning to look at the president more realistically. He repeated his stories endlessly, and they weren't that interesting the first time. Aside from naval warfare, which bored her, she felt he was not well informed about history or ideas or the wide range of subjects Max had whetted her interest in.

They remained friends. Dorothy teased him about his flirting with Princess Marta of Norway, who was spending the war years in safety in America. She had no direct knowledge about his continuing affair with Lucy Mercer, which was kept hidden because Lucy was a married woman. She continued to be on call for the occasional weekend or holiday at Hyde Park. She was among the gang of regulars who waited there to learn the results of FDR's third presidential race in November 1940. But she often felt uneasy. She was fond of Roosevelt and flattered by his attention, but she was not in love with him and had never been.

When Dorothy reminisced about her relationship with the president, she was often coy about whether or not it was a sexual one. She was never fastidious about honoring her marriage vows, and George Backer was apparently no obstacle. She recalled years later that her husband, who worshipped FDR, had actually encouraged her to reciprocate the president's attention. "George saw it all in a sort of *droit du seigneur* way, his wife being tapped by the lord of the manor. He was proud of it, and it gave him tremendous prestige with his friends."

Long after the fact, Dorothy continued to take pleasure in the intrigue surrounding herself and FDR. She sometimes used the hint of an old romance to interest a new friend. A man who met her in her later years recalls that when he asked, "Well, did you sleep with him?" She smiled and said, "What do you think?" Or she would say, "I was on the edge of the ledge!" The friend knew that she loved being questioned more than she cared about the veracity of her answer. "You will never know if there was any sexual intimacy between them," he says. "She would say, 'What do you think?' and that's how she wanted it left. It's whatever you think."

James Roosevelt, who was his father's aide in the 1940s, helping him hide the severity of his handicap from the American public, wrote in his memoirs that he believed it would have been very difficult for FDR to manage a sexual affair. In the early 1980s, Dorothy told Ted Morgan, then working on a biography of Roosevelt, that when she visited the president in Warm Springs in 1938, she asked Leroy W. Hubbard, the president's doctor, if Roosevelt could be sexually active. "I had wondered if the President was still potent and the doctor said, 'Don't forget, only his legs are paralyzed.' "

"How does he do it?" Dorothy asked.

"The French way," Hubbard said.

Her question implied that she had no direct knowledge of Roosevelt's prowess. She also told Morgan, "The relationship was not sexual. Although if he had said let's go to bed, I probably would have." In her conversation with Morgan, Dorothy had no flirtatious intent but was presumably trying to set the record straight. It's as close as one will ever come to the truth.

Even when Dorothy ceased to be an intimate of FDR, she remained active in the Democratic political arena. It would have been hard to be exclusively frivolous in the late thirties. Despite various ameliorative programs of the

New Deal, the hardships of the Depression persisted. Ideological rifts widened between New Dealers and their opponents. The Backers straddled the divide, living, as it were, as Republicans during the glittering social whirl at night and as Democrats during the working day.

In 1937, Dorothy was chosen by New York City Mayor Fiorello La Guardia to serve as a member of the Board of Child Welfare, a seven-year unpaid job. That same year she became the executive secretary of the New York Committee for Ratification of the Child Labor Amendment. She was also involved in local Democratic politics in Oyster Bay, where she lost to Robert Moses in an election for delegate to the 1938 New York State Constitutional Convention.

George Backer's political activities were local and international. In October 1937, he put himself forward as a candidate of the American Labor party (ALP) to represent New York City's Seventeenth Congressional District in a special election following the death of the Democratic incumbent. The ALP had been founded the year before by New York labor leaders David Dubinsky of the International Ladies' Garment Workers' Union and Alex Rose of the Milliners Union to give their left-wing members a way to support FDR's reelection campaign without having to vote for him on the Democratic line.

Backer hoped a significant ALP turnout would help him defeat advertising magnate Bruce Barton, who was running on the Republican-Fusion ticket, and Stanley Osserman, the Tammany-backed Democratic candidate. George campaigned hard, and his theatrical friends endorsed him, but the outcome wasn't even close. Barton, with Mayor La Guardia's backing, got 34,618 votes; Osserman got 21,845. The ALP was strong in the working-class neighborhoods of the city but not in the affluent Upper East Side Seventeenth CD, where George managed to collect only 9,647 votes.

He accepted the ALP nomination again in the regular election in November 1938, but he must have realized the hopelessness of his chances. He barely bothered to campaign and got fewer votes than before. Weeks after the election, the ALP rewarded him with an appointment to a party-controlled seat on the City Council.

George was even more active in the other political world in which he had interests—the Jewish community. He was one of the relatively few Jews in his milieu to have taken seriously the dreadful threat posed to European Jews by Hitler's assuming the chancellorship of Germany in 1932. After he traveled to Poland and Germany in 1933 to see for himself the conditions under

which Jews were living, he and several other American Jewish leaders, notably Felix Warburg, tried in vain to pressure the British and American governments to open up immigration opportunities for these imperiled Jews.
George took on the presidency of the Jewish Telegraphic Agency (JTA), a
news service that reported on Jewish affairs around the world. He was also
active in ORT, an organization that provided education and vocational training for Jews in Europe and the States.

The Backer family maintained a strong cultural identification with the
Jewish people, although in a secular context. A niece of George's has no
memory of her uncles or cousins ever attending synagogue. They all had
Christmas trees. Friday night dinners at Grandmother Backer's house were
social occasions with no religious ceremonies to acknowledge the Sabbath.
What the Backers had was a "strong cultural consciousness," she says. "An
historical consciousness. They worried about the fate of European Jews.
They were very strong Zionists. There were gatherings in our apartment of
people trying to put together support for Jewish settlement in Palestine. And
I think that supplanted in the Backer family life whatever religion there
might have been earlier."

At the 1937 national meeting of the Council of Jewish Federation and
Welfare Funds, George, as head of the JTA, articulated the case for secular
Judaism, and he addressed the growing divergence between Jewish identity
and American identity. Much in the spirit of Jacob Schiff, George argued for
assimilation, saying that as a liberal he believed that Jews, even if they were
religiously observant, must reduce their support for institutions that challenged the American pluralist, democratic experience. He was rebutted by a
rabbi who argued for cultural separatism within the democracy, which was
the more popular view.

Backer agreed to serve as chairman of the Palestine Pavilion at the 1939
World's Fair. The dedication of the pavilion on May 29 attracted fifty thousand visitors, contributing to the largest single-day attendance at the fair
since it had opened six weeks earlier. Albert Einstein gave the opening address; Chaim Weizmann, the head of the Jewish Agency, spoke by live broadcast from Paris. The pavilion, which celebrated ancient and current Jewish
communities in Palestine, provided a major public relations opportunity for
Backer and his colleagues to bring the world's attention to the plight of European Jews. It was a direct rebuke to the British, who were limiting Jewish immigration to the Holy Land.

When Dorothy was asked later what George did during the thirties, she cited his domestic political activities but ignored his involvement with the Jewish community. She and George shared a domestic political agenda, but George's forthright advocacy of the needs of European Jews may have made her uneasy. A rabbi she consulted before she married George assured her that, her confirmation by Bishop Shipman notwithstanding, she could consider herself Jewish because she was born a Jew. Dorothy was eager to disavow her temporary conversion to Christianity, but she was not as secure in her identification with Jews as George was. She shared his and Grandfather Schiff's belief that it was possible to separate Jewish cultural life from the practice of the religion, but she was uneasy about embracing the culture. Her Jewish heritage was problematic, because Morti and Adele had done their best to obliterate the legacy of the generations that preceded them.

George's concerns about the fate of European Jewry were well-grounded. Throughout the spring and summer of 1939, Dolly wrote in her diary about theater parties, concerts at Lewisohn Stadium, weekends on Long Island and at Hyde Park. Interspersed among them, however, were signs of the gathering storm. Visiting Europeans told stories of aggressive actions taken by the government in Berlin and confusion in the capitals of the democracies. The Backers and their friends spent hours listening to radio reports that they expected and feared.

In late August, Dorothy wrote that the non-aggression pact between Russia and Germany startled everyone, "but in particular the American Communists." A few days later, she reported George's spin on the Nazi-Soviet pact: "He thinks Hitler is through, he'll have to give up, will be the laughing stock of Europe."

The Backers spent the decisive weekend of September 1–3 at Old Fields obsessed by broadcast reports of Europe going to war. Two weeks later they heard with dismay a speech by Charles Lindbergh urging that the United States remain neutral in Europe's conflict. War took over as the primary topic at their dinner parties. After Germany's lightning assault through the Low Countries and the invasion of France, the combatants were bogged down in what came to be called the Phony War. It was unclear to Americans what was actually happening in Europe and what American policy should be.

By December, reality began to sink in. Newsreel footage arrived from the war front in Finland and from occupied Holland. At Aunt Frieda's, George and Dorothy heard a firsthand account of the Nazi treatment of German Jews from Felix's brother Max Warburg, who had fled from Hamburg.

George and Felix were trying to convince the British and American governments to open doors for other refugees. Dorothy continued her good works. But the Backers were increasingly busy addressing problems generated by an acquisition they had made earlier in the year. They had agreed—almost on a whim—to take over ownership and management of the *New York Post,* an old and respected daily paper that was now floundering. The *Post* was in much worse shape than they had initially understood, and its fiscal situation increasingly vied with events in faraway Europe for their attention.

THREE

Acquiring the *Post*

The *New York Post* is one of America's oldest institutions, dating back to the earliest years of the republic. In 1801, Alexander Hamilton and several fellow Federalists jointly put up $10,000 to establish a newspaper in which they could criticize the policies of President Thomas Jefferson. Hamilton wrote frequently for the paper, supporting a strong central government and endorsing fiscally conservative policies that appealed to New York's business community.

Hamilton died three years later, but his paper, which came to be called the *New York Evening Post* soon after its founding, survived and flourished through the nineteenth century under the leadership of a series of owners and editors whose socially progressive political views helped shape an America that Hamilton would hardly have recognized.

First among these influential editors was William Cullen Bryant, who was also the majority shareholder in the Post Company for nearly fifty years. Bryant, better known in his lifetime as a poet, became one of Lincoln's early backers, helped found the Republican party, and was probably the most respected newspaperman of the day. After Bryant's death, his family sold the paper to Henry Villard, a German immigrant who made his reputation as a reporter covering the Civil War and then earned a fortune as an investor. Villard installed Carl Schurz and then Edwin Godkin, whose magazine *The Na-*

tion he also purchased, as editors of the paper. Godkin was a passionate and powerful editorialist who often forcefully stated his liberal views. Theodore Roosevelt, having felt the sting of Godkin's criticism, once said, "I can never take the *Evening Post* after a hearty meal."

Oswald Garrison Villard inherited both journals at his father's death in 1903. Oswald Villard and his mother, who were ardent advocates of Negro rights, were among the founders of the NAACP. Oswald was also a pacifist, whose unwavering opposition to the First World War was unpopular with the *Post*'s readers and advertisers. Falling revenues led him to sell the *Post,* but not *The Nation,* in 1918 to Thomas Lamont, a partner at J. P. Morgan, for about $1 million.

Under Lamont, the paper continued to falter. Its equipment was outmoded and its staff dispirited. In 1922, faced with mounting losses, the banker refused an offer from Frank Munsey, publisher of the New York *Evening Sun,* who would have paid $1,750,000 for the *Post*'s features and its Associated Press franchise but intended to shut the paper down. Lamont opted to keep the *Post* alive by selling it for a little less money to a syndicate of thirty-four investors organized by the paper's editor, Edwin Gay, an economic historian who had founded the Harvard Business School before trying his hand at journalism. Gay's backers included financier Paul Warburg and Marshall Field III, a wealthy young investor from Chicago. Franklin D. Roosevelt was a token member of the syndicate, owning about 1 percent of the stock.

Within a year, the new owners had had enough. Trying to preserve some of his investment, Lamont arranged to sell the *Post* to Cyrus H. K. Curtis, who folded it into his family-controlled holding company, Curtis-Martin, which also owned *The Saturday Evening Post, Ladies' Home Journal,* the Philadelphia *Public Ledger,* and *The Philadelphia Inquirer.* Curtis promptly shifted the *Post*'s political orientation from left to right. In 1927, he moved it into a new building at 75 West Street and installed up-to-date printing equipment. President Calvin Coolidge, Curtis's political hero, was on hand to start the first press run at the new plant.

Modernization, unfortunately, had no positive effect on the paper's finances. When Curtis died in June 1933, his heirs were virtually unanimous in wanting to close down the *Post,* which was losing more than $1 million a year. The dissenter was Curtis Bok, a judge on the Pennsylvania Supreme Court, who, unlike most of his Curtis and Martin cousins, had become a convert to the New Deal. Bok thought that it would be a tragedy for the family to kill off a paper with such a distinguished pedigree and came up with a plan to prevent that from happening.

Bok was a friend of Democratic National Committeeman J. David Stern, owner of the *Philadelphia Record* and the *Camden* (NJ) *Courier-Post*. He urged Stern to take over the paper and the valuable building in which it was housed for no cash and to turn it into one of the few major newspapers that would support the Democratic party. Stern examined the books, determined that the Curtin-Martin interests had probably lost over $10 million in the decade they had owned the *Post,* and estimated that it would cost him at least $3 million just to keep it afloat. Stern was sensitive to the fact that his papers were among only a handful of metropolitan dailies—including the *St. Louis Post-Dispatch* and the *Louisville Courier-Journal*—that supported the New Deal. The *New York Post* would add a highly visible voice to that meager list. In his memoirs, Stern claimed that FDR called him personally, begging him to save the paper.

Politics and sentiment won out. In December 1933, Stern acquired the paper from the Curtis trust. No cash changed hands, but he assumed responsibility for $1.5 million owed to the existing creditors, even though it would be subordinated to the $1 million of first preferred stock that represented the working capital he needed to raise. Stern put together loans for that stock with the help of some of those same creditors.

"Then began the hardest six years of my life," Stern wrote. To make the paper livelier he eliminated the word "Evening" from the masthead and changed the format from a tabloid back to a broadsheet, which facilitated the reproduction of features and comics from his Philadelphia and Camden papers. The financial coverage in the *Post* had been one of its strengths but also one of its greatest burdens; reproducing the stock tables and commodity reports and maintaining a large reportorial staff were very expensive. Recognizing that the move would cause some readers to drop away, Stern nonetheless scaled back the size of the financial section, and circulation fell in early 1934 to a barely credible fifty thousand copies a day.

Stern was not a novice in the newspaper business. He'd successfully built circulation at his other papers through book promotions. Readers clipped coupons from the paper to claim free unabridged dictionaries or inexpensive complete editions of Shakespeare, Dickens, and other authors whose works were out of copyright. Standard editions were given away practically

at cost, but many readers opted for deluxe editions, which could be re-
deemed for one hundred coupons. Stern and his colleagues figured that if
someone bought the paper for three months, that reader was probably
hooked.

The strategy that worked at Stern's other papers was equally successful at
the *Post*. By the end of 1934, circulation had risen to an average of one hundred thousand copies a day. Within two more years, it doubled again. Losses
were down from $25,000 per week to a manageable $25,000 per month.
Then, just as Stern felt he could relax, he was attacked on his home turf. The
Annenberg family, who had just bought *The Philadelphia Inquirer* from
Curtis-Martin, challenged Stern's *Philadelphia Record* to a circulation and
distribution battle, trying to drive it out of business. The campaign was unsuccessful, but it wiped out the *Record*'s profits, profits Stern had been using
to cover the *New York Post*'s deficits.

By early 1938, the national economy settled back to Depression levels,
advertising revenues were down, and Stern's right-hand man, who had been
responsible for the endlessly inventive promotions, died suddenly. Soon *Post*
losses were back up to $75,000 a month.

Unionized *Post* employees were asked to accept a 10 percent pay cut.
Executives' salaries were trimmed between 15 and 25 percent. Stern was
desperate. The *Post* represented his only money-losing venture in more than
a quarter century in the newspaper business. In the six years Stern owned
the paper, he and his associates had sunk $4.5 million in it. They had no
chance to recoup their losses, but at least they could unburden themselves
of $1.5 million in current obligations and avoid having to pay out several
million dollars of severance pay they would be liable for if they shut the paper down.

Stern knew George Backer from their involvement in Democratic politics. Stern conceived of the idea of transferring to George and Dorothy his
interest in—and his headaches from—the *Post*. Early in 1939, he arranged a
series of meetings with George in which he proposed that the Backers take
over the paper on basically the same terms as he had acquired it: no cash
would change hands, but Dorothy would assume the paper's $1.5 million
worth of current obligations. For all practical purposes, the obligation to pay
another $1.5 million originally owed to holders of the second preferred stock
would be written off. In his book, Stern said he estimated that Dolly would

have to come up with another million for working capital and that it would take an additional $2.5 million investment, or close to $5 million in all, before the paper might see a profit.

In conversations with Stern, Backer got the impression—or wanted to get the impression—that the paper might lose $100,000 a year for the first year or so, but that it would soon be in the black. It seemed a gamble worth taking. Owning the *Post* would make the Backers major supporters of the Democratic party, and running it would give George something to do.

Edward Greenbaum, the senior partner of the Backers' law firm, Greenbaum, Wolff & Ernst, sent George a memo spelling out serious reservations that he and Dorothy's accountant had about the deal. "We think you need some kind of warranty from Stern," Greenbaum wrote, "that things are as he represents them. Even though we know how much you want to go ahead, we feel we must say these things."

He attached an analysis of the *Post* by a veteran of the newspaper business, who doubted that the losses could be held to the $100,000 per year level that Stern had implied. The newspaperman felt that the paper's circulation gains had been illusory, that the promotions designed to attract readers were expensive, and that the new audience did not stick with the paper after they had acquired their premium books. Greenbaum's consultant believed the *Post* was "a hopeless mess and that putting money into it is like kissing the money goodbye. He says he knows of few ways to lose money faster."

Dorothy's brother, John, and his partners at Kuhn, Loeb were also dubious. Adding to their wariness about the investment, these conservative Republican bankers found the *Post*'s political stance distasteful. It was bad enough that Dorothy was an avid fan of the New Deal, but, Stern speculated, the idea that "the estate of their founder, Jacob H. Schiff, might be used to finance a liberal (they called it 'radical') newspaper was unthinkable." On the other hand, John's opposition, which Dorothy would have heeded consciously, may have been just the unconscious goad she needed to take the risk.

Worried that the forces opposing his distress sale were winning the battle for Dorothy's mind—and dollars—Stern brought in his wife to convince Dorothy that owning a newspaper was not just an investment. Jill Stern argued that "it was an opportunity for self-expression, a chance to become a personality, a force in the community, state, and national affairs." There was also the responsibility for a thousand employees who would be thrown out of work if the paper folded. This joint appeal to their egos and their consciences was a pitch the Backers could not resist.*

Dorothy was always adamant that she didn't lay out any money to acquire the *Post*. In 1950, she told a reporter, "The truth is I didn't really buy the *Post*. It was given to me, not sold to me, on the condition that I'd meet the deficits, pay all the debts, and assume full responsibility for future obligations. There was a little minority stock outstanding which I didn't acquire at that time, but it didn't amount to much. Later I purchased that too."

Though her argument was technically accurate, it was disingenuous. She had committed herself to a major investment, even if she paid none of it up front. She had agreed to assume the current debt of the *Post* and to provide enough cash to meet the paper's anticipated operating deficit in the coming months.

The details of the deal were still being worked out when the Backers took effective control on June 1, 1939. Many of the local papers announced that George Backer had acquired the *New York Post,* and the couple's behavior gave the impression that this was so. George moved into the publisher's office at 75 West Street[†] and took over the daily administration of the paper. Dorothy signed the checks, put her signature to various legal documents, and then went back home.

George soon told *Editor & Publisher* that he was working a ten-hour day, mostly on editorial policy. He was not actively seeking new advertisers, al-

---

*In 1973, Gail Sheehy wrote a profile of Dorothy for *New York* magazine, in which she speculated that Dorothy bought the paper not only to please George Backer and the leaders of the Democratic party but also to reconnect with the excitement of her time with Beaverbrook. Supporting this view is a letter Dolly wrote to Max in 1956 asking a favor and reminding him that the strong impression he made when they first met had implicitly changed her life.

It took Dorothy the remainder of the 1930s to create a world for herself that in any way approximated what she had been exposed to during her months with Max. Even in 1939, she wasn't ready to assume the management of the paper herself, but in later years she could see the connection.

†The building itself was acquired by the Metropolitan Life Insurance Company in exchange for the cancellation of back rent and operating expenses that had accrued and not been paid under the Stern regime. Met Life remained the *Post*'s landlord for almost a decade until the building was sold to a New York real estate operator.

though some personal contacts with the Bloomingdale family suggested to him that he might land the store's lucrative account. Dorothy had no spelled-out role. She had mentioned to an interviewer when they acquired the paper that she might like to write a women's column. When *Editor & Publisher* asked George about that, he was dismissive. "She'll have to submit her material the same as every one else would."

Most of her days in late 1939 passed much as they had before the *Post* was acquired. She continued her committee work; she went to a Picasso exhibit, which she thought was "nauseating," and to the opening of the movie *Gone with the Wind,* which she found less exciting than the book. She was reading *The Grapes of Wrath,* Carl Van Doren's biography of Benjamin Franklin, and Will Durant's *The Life of Greece.* The Durant book fascinated her; she went to the Metropolitan Museum to look at the collection of Minoan artifacts and had her dressmaker run up an evening dress in the Cretan style.

Her children were becoming more independent. Fifteen-year-old Morti had just transferred from the Brooks School in Massachusetts to Oxford Academy in Pleasantville, New Jersey. He looked forward to studying aeronautical engineering in college. Fourteen-year-old Adele was a ninth grader at Brearley, where five-year-old Sarah-Ann had just started first grade.

Dolly found time for the occasional lunch with Ellin Mackay and a few new acquaintances, like actress Kitty Carlisle, whom she'd met through George. Carlisle was aware that Dorothy had a rather narrow circle of friends. "I knew she was very picky about her friends," she says. "I knew she was very selective, and therefore I was very proud of her friendship. Looking back I suspect she was shy, but I didn't put it down to shyness then; I put it down to being imperious. She expected people to come to her."

Carlisle says, "Mainly I knew her in the daytime, not so much at dinner parties. We'd have lunch, either at a nice restaurant in the neighborhood, or at her apartment, and we'd talk. We had good gossips. Dolly was fairly kind in her judgments of people. She wasn't mean or scornful. She was very understanding of people's foibles and peculiarities." The two women loved to do needlework. "That was a big part of our friendship. We didn't share patterns, but I saw her work. And I brought her my work once in a while, and she approved."

———

Dorothy's financial interests began to outweigh her social ones. She was a director of the Post Corporation, and she began gradually to address the implications of what that meant. In October 1939, she wrote in her diary: "Lunch at Post with George. Afternoon studied finances of Post. (Awful)." A few days later she was going over payroll figures with the paper's accountant. While she and George grew increasingly discouraged about the financial viability of their acquisition, President Roosevelt became something of a cheerleader. During a visit Dorothy made to Hyde Park in the fall, FDR was particularly interested in schemes to add advertisers. He told her he thought businesses that didn't take out ads in the paper were fair game for editorial criticism.

The task facing the new owners was daunting. The *Post*'s average daily circulation of about 250,000 lagged behind afternoon rivals like the *Sun* at about 300,000 copies, the *World-Telegram* at 425,000, and the *Journal-American* at nearly 625,000. The least widely read morning paper, the *Herald Tribune,* sold 400,000 copies, the *Times* sold over 500,000 copies, the *Mirror* about 800,000, and the *Daily News* had the largest circulation in the country at 1,800,000 copies.

The *Post*'s greatest asset was its excellent editorial staff. Although Henry T. Saylor, who had been editing the *Post* as well as Stern's other papers, returned to Philadelphia in July, he left behind veteran journalists Walter Lister, Harry Nason, and Ted Thackrey to run the newsroom. Twenty-six-year-old I. F. Stone had come up from Philadelphia to write editorials. The *Post* also featured the established columnist Franklin P. Adams, as well as the young stars Samuel Grafton commenting on politics, Leonard Lyons keeping tabs on New York nightlife, and Sylvia Porter covering finance. Showbusiness coverage was strong with columns by Earl Wilson and Richard Manson in New York and Sidney Skolsky's syndicated column from Hollywood. Archer Winsten and Irene Thirer reviewed movies, and John Mason Brown was one of the theater critics. Milton Gross and Art Buck were among the notable names on the sports staff.

Whatever the quality of their product, the Backers could do nothing to stanch the money drain. In June, Dorothy had made a $350,000 advance— secured by a note that was to be paid back at 4 percent—just to cover the paper's outstanding current liabilities, and she had also put up $150,000 in unsecured funds to meet payroll. Without telling her, George rescinded the pay cuts imposed by Stern, which was only one reason why the *Post* was soon losing about $30,000 a month. By the year's end, Dolly had to come up with another $500,000 to keep the paper alive.

Although her net worth was at least $10 million, well over half of that was illiquid or held in trust. Dorothy was a wealthy woman but not one who could withstand significant losses indefinitely. Yet that was what she was facing. The *Post* lost more money in 1939 than it had in 1938, and the projections for 1940 were calamitous. Her financial and legal advisers told Dorothy that she should be prepared either to put in another chunk of cash or to pull out altogether. Lawyer Greenbaum sent a year-end memo to George, with a copy to Dorothy, summarizing the situation:

> Last spring you took over the management of the paper with the honest belief and expectation that an investment of $500,000 of new money would see the paper through for about eighteen months. That expectation has proved wholly unfounded. In the early fall, when you realized this, you took steps to secure new financing. You were successful to the extent of getting Dolly to agree to invest $500,000 additional capital.
>
> Dolly's willingness to invest this additional money was based upon the expectation that this would see the paper through 1940. It does not look now as if it will be possible to have that expectation fulfilled. . . . This situation brings up the question—for what purpose is Dolly investing her money? Surely not merely to keep the paper going for a few months more. It is not fair to expect her to put in money for this purpose.
>
> Within a few months you will be faced with the necessity of getting additional capital or closing the paper. Closing the paper would, of course, be a tremendous disappointment to you personally. However, even more important to you and Dolly would be the blow that would result to all those employees who would lose their jobs and, bitterest of all, would be the collapse of the oldest paper in the United States and the only liberal paper in New York.

Greenbaum had no recommendations to make, except to warn that ignoring the facts was not a good option.

Finding another buyer didn't seem realistic. Shutting the paper down was the emotionally distressing but fiscally prudent possibility. Against that, however, was Dorothy and George's inchoate but real commitment to show their critics that they had been right to keep the paper alive. They worried, too, about putting people out of work without severance pay if bankruptcy were the ultimate disposition, and they wanted to further the interests of the Democratic party.

The Backers turned to a group of trusted colleagues for help. They created an executive committee that met weekly to advise on editorial and business matters. Members included their friend Thomas Finletter, whom they had chosen as the paper's legal counsel and corporate secretary, and David Rosenblum, a young accountant, whom they installed as treasurer and general manager. One early committee decision was to approve the hiring of stage and industrial designer Norman Bel Geddes, a friend from George's theatrical days, to suggest changes in layout and typography.

More commonly, the minutes of the committee reflect high-minded suggestions for the editorial staff: the editors should strive to "eliminate bias in selection, placement in paper, and reporting of news." They should "run special series only when the issue is of real importance and can be promoted," and they should "select pictures with great discrimination." Also recorded in the minutes was a list of young Morti Hall's "favorite Post funnies in order," starting with "Superman" and "Scorchy Smith." It was no way to run a paper, but neither the Backers nor their closest advisers appeared to realize that. Their lack of journalistic knowhow—indeed, their lack of almost any organizational savvy—was telling. David Stern had been invited to join the committee, but he declined, saying that in his experience such groups were usually a waste of time.

During the early months of 1940, Dorothy began showing up at the newspaper more frequently, trying to get a feel for the nature of the property in which she had so much invested. Taking the advice of her friend Joseph Medill Patterson, the owner of the *Daily News,* she visited each department to get a sense of how it worked. She said later that she had gained some understanding of everything but the composing room, which baffled her. She was impressed by the practical expertise of Ted Thackrey, the features editor of the paper.

In April, Thackrey offered some very specific pragmatic advice in the form of a twenty-four-page memo. He said the paper needed a more efficient chain of command, beginning with an executive editor who would have full authority over all the editorial content of the paper except the editorial page and would be responsible only to the publisher. He also advocated clearing up the cluttered format and running fewer and shorter stories, concentrating on crucial news and stories of local interest.

Thackrey reviewed the organization and personnel of every editorial department. The paper had excellent sports writers, but they needed a strong editor. The financial department, which Stern had gutted, needed to be revamped, and Thackrey proposed that Sylvia Porter be made its editor. The entertainment sections were fine, and they should be put in the hands of Dick Manson, who was currently writing a nightclub column but had real management skills. Coverage of Washington news needed more reporters, fewer columnists.

Thackrey offered opinions about advertising. Unexpectedly for a newsman, he believed that ads should be dispersed throughout the news pages, even in the sports section. "Some of the best of this country's newspapers open up these pages for advertising sale and are not suspect by the readers for so doing. But they are, of course, keenly interested in keeping really independent by being economically self-sustaining where that is *honestly* possible. I assume, and trust, that the *New York Post* holds the same view. . . . I sincerely believe that to continue on our present course, if it is a course, is economic suicide."

Even though Dorothy and George didn't act decisively on many of Thackrey's suggestions (for one thing, David Rosenblum pointed out, there were no budgetary constraints in the memo), they endorsed his energy and newsroom savvy. On May 2, 1940, George announced Thackrey's appointment to the newly created job of executive editor, which allowed George to pay less attention to the details of daily management.

Meanwhile, nothing stopped the financial hemorrhage. Circulation dropped. Bloomingdale's did become a regular advertiser, but net advertising linage lagged behind projections. Dorothy completed her buyout of David Stern and his coinvestors, who collectively wrote off $3.5 million in losses. By the end of 1940, Dorothy had put $2 million into the paper, in exchange for which she held a portfolio of potentially worthless bonds and virtually all of the stock in the Post Corporation.

Dorothy tried to economize by selling Old Fields. As the Depression lengthened, there were few potential buyers for such a white elephant. Dorothy was so eager to be rid of the house, which burdened her budget and her conscience, that she was willing to accept the first solid offer that was presented to her. Consuelo Vanderbilt, formerly the duchess of Marlborough and now the wife of French aviator Jacques Balsan, bought 128 of the 350-odd acres Dorothy had inherited, plus the house, which had cost nearly $1 million to build and furnish, for $150,000.* Because George and the children enjoyed spending their summers on Long Island, the Backers rented a house at Sands Point for several seasons, and eventually Dolly bought it.

Dorothy spent more time at the paper. She got into the habit of meeting periodically with Ted Thackrey. She was not willing to undertake the total overhaul of the paper that he had advocated, but his suggestions for smaller changes appealed to her. Thackrey wanted, as she did, to expand the women's pages and to add columnists. Gradually, she came to believe that George was a stumbling block. She thought he had little interest in making the paper more attractive to general readers. Nor was he absorbed by the business side of things. He had no zest for attracting advertisers. And, as a devout liberal, he was uneasy in an adversarial role vis-à-vis the unions. He was a "gentle soul," not a "hard-hitting, city-room type of editor."

On April 25, 1941, the corporation was reorganized again. The name Dorothy Schiff Backer appeared for the first time on the masthead of the *Post* as vice president. Tom Finletter was gone, and David Rosenblum took over as treasurer. Three months later Rosenblum was out, and Dorothy became vice president and treasurer. Only now was Dorothy finally authorized to sign checks on the corporation's behalf—even though the money paid out had always been directly or indirectly hers. She always said that she was vice president and treasurer of the *Post* from the time she purchased it in June 1939, overlooking the fact that it had taken nearly two years for her to acquire those offices. She must not have enjoyed remembering that she had allowed herself to be considered ephemeral for so long.

Relinquishing the pretense that he was still vital to the everyday workings of the paper, George left for Europe in May to see the war firsthand. The news in the spring of 1941 was not good. The Germans had driven the British out of Greece, and the Greek king had abdicated. Rommel's forces,

---

*In 1954, the property was sold to a group of developers who turned it into the Pine Hollow Country Club.

rolling across North Africa, were besieging the British troops defending To-bruk. A German invasion of England was expected imminently. Charles Lindbergh speaking at an America First rally in New York in April said that the invasion would be successful and that there was nothing the United States could, or should, do to prevent it.

George, of course, was of a different political persuasion. He told the BBC on May 26 that he believed America would soon enter the war. He returned home on June 24 with a bomb fragment from the blitz, which he hoped would help publicize England's dire condition and America's responsibility to come to the aid of the beleaguered Allies. George went back to the paper, but the balance of power there had changed for good. Ted Thackrey was in charge. George seems not to have complained. He might even have been re-lieved to be released from his responsibility, but his health began to suffer.

Things came to a head at the end of 1941 when the Japanese attacked Pearl Harbor. George stayed home to write his editorial, and Dolly spent the night at the paper, working beside Ted, enjoying the excitement of getting out extra editions as the news developed. Almost immediately, America de-clared war—a policy the *Post* had long supported—but the international sit-uation remained grim. The Japanese began driving the Americans out of the Philippines and pushing the British from Southeast Asia; they had their sights set on the domination of the South Pacific, and there was reason to fear they would invade Australia and attack the West Coast of the United States.

George felt honor bound to enlist in the army even though he was thirty-nine. At his induction exam, the doctors discovered that he had tuberculosis. He would need to spend the next months at a sanatorium at Saranac, New York. He suggested that his forced absence might make this a good time to close down the *Post,* writing it off as a financial and personal loss.

This was neither a peevish nor a frivolous suggestion. The paper ran an operating deficit of nearly $1 million for 1941. There had been some im-provements in management and production, but circulation was down, and advertising revenues were only marginally better than they had been in 1940. There was just not enough income coming in, and once again Dorothy had been required to underwrite the losses from her dwindling personal reserve.

But she was determined to keep going. She told George she would take up his role at the paper. He was outraged. A working wife was not what he had envisioned. Off went George for his cure. Off went thirty-eight-year-old Dolly to start a new life.

She and Ted set about revamping the *Post*. Theodore Olin Thackrey was forty-one, a self-made newspaperman with flashy credentials. He'd begun as a copyboy in his hometown of Kansas City; he had served in the Canadian Air Force and the RAF in the First World War. He was an editor of the Cleveland *Press* in his early thirties and then worked his way up through the Scripps-Howard chain. A stint in Shanghai to create an English-language newspaper ended when the Japanese invaded in 1936. After returning to the States, he found a job at David Stern's *Post*.

On March 28, 1942, Mrs. George Backer, described in press releases as the acting publisher of the paper, announced that her husband was resigning as of April 4 because of ill health. In an interview with *The New York Times*, she repeated her claim that she had been vice president and treasurer since June 1939 and also pointed out that she had been acting publisher during George's trip to Europe in 1941. The revised masthead now read Dorothy Schiff Backer, President & Publisher; Theodore O. Thackrey, Editor & Assistant Publisher; Wendell Wesley Garver (not destined to last long), Business Manager; and Paul Tierney (who had been a very effective foreign news editor), Managing Editor.

Ted's ideas began to change the *Post*. First he converted the paper from a broadsheet back to a tabloid. The front page had no text; just headlines and promotional banners for articles inside the paper. The first tabloid edition announced "Japs Crack Bandoeng Line (story on p. 2)" and "3 Die in West 16th Blaze (story on p. 3)"—a typical blend of serious international news and a local interest story. Simultaneous with the introduction of the new format, Thackrey raised the price of the *Post* to five cents, which, to everyone's relief, did not harm circulation.

Dorothy was at the paper five days a week. She told the *Times:* "This is a tremendous change for me. It means a complete reorganization of my life. I will live and sleep with this job." She had been cutting back on her community involvement for some time. She resigned from all her boards and committees except for the Henry Street Settlement. She established a policy, to which she adhered for the rest of her professional life, of rejecting all outside board memberships.

The reporter noted that "Mrs. Backer . . . looks younger than her 39 years and wears really feminine clothes, with lace on her collar." Dorothy said that she thought she would be a good publisher because she had average taste. "I like what most people like. I enjoy the play every one raves about, and I like the book every one is reading." She said that she did not expect the editorial policy of the paper to change. She and George had consulted on and agreed upon everything, and she expected to continue on the same, evenhanded, liberal Democratic course.

Dorothy was the first woman publisher of a major New York newspaper.* She attended a meeting of women publishers in New York in the spring of 1942. It was a small group. The main item on the agenda was how to find more women reporters. There were greater opportunities than usual now that men were leaving for war. Dorothy told the *Times* that she did not consider herself a feminist but was delighted when "a girl gets a job on a paper." She said she believed in equal opportunity, not favoritism. Like most of the women at the meeting, she had not worked her way up from the bottom.

In late May, George returned from Saranac. Though he had no illusions that there was a place for him at the paper, he assumed he would resume his place in Dorothy's life. However, she and Ted had been working together every day, and it was probably inevitable that they would soon spend their evenings together as well. An occasional dalliance was hardly fatal to marriages in their circle, and George had already signaled his passive acquiescence during Dolly's Roosevelt adventure. But Dolly had moved on emotionally. The Backers' marriage was over. In a few months, she would leave their apartment for a suite in the Pierre Hotel, and they would divorce the following year.

Dolly was not much given to reflection, but she sometimes told close friends that George was the only husband she had ever really loved. On the eve of their daughter, Sarah-Ann's, marriage in 1959, she told Sarah-Ann that the relationship with George was the best she'd ever had and that she'd probably been wrong not to stick it out.

According to Sarah-Ann, George was equally gracious. "He never had a bad word to say about my mother to me. He thought that she was a lady. And he thought that he was more theoretical, more of a thinker and a dreamer, whereas she was more practical. She was the one who got things done."

George did things at his own pace. When it was clear he did not have

---

*Helen Rogers Reid, though long active in the management of the *New York Herald Tribune,* would become head of the paper only when her husband Ogden Mills Reid died in 1947.

even a nominal job at the *Post,* he went to Washington to work as the director of propaganda at the Office of War Information. He married again in 1946 and moved into an apartment in a building his family owned on East Sixty-fourth Street. During the 1950s and early '60s, he became a key political aide to Averell Harriman, after which Backer returned to his earlier vocation. His novel *Appearance of a Man* was published in 1966. He told an interviewer from *The New York Times* that the hero was based loosely on James Forrestal,* with some similarities to Benjamin Disraeli. Backer said that he wanted to write about a man who is defined by the exercise of power. A man, in short, who was almost the polar opposite of himself.

George's friends and family members describe him in warm but mildly disdainful terms. He had "elegant manners," he was "the perfect dinner companion," "a bit effete," "a very nice man." To disparage him as a lightweight, however, is to overlook his intelligence and influence on Dorothy. Arthur Schlesinger Jr. says, "George Backer did have the air of a dilettante about him, but in fact I think he was a very shrewd man. Dolly learned a great deal from George. He played an important role in her political education."

Julius C. C. Edelstein, a longtime New York political insider and an old friend of George, says, "I remember going to their house, when he was still married to Dolly, and there were all sorts of political big wheels there that dazzled me. George Backer brought her into politics and into the newspaper business. He made the two decisive things in her life happen."

In 1942, Dolly Schiff was the acknowledged owner of one of New York's eight major daily papers[†]—a position of potential importance. Although she had been raised to understand that the men in her family would wield power, she finally had the means to do it herself. Still uncertain how to proceed, she turned reflexively to a man to point the way. Max had awakened her interest in the wider world; George provided the opportunity for her to play a part in it. Now she chose Ted Thackrey to show her the ropes.

Ted had already made the *Post* a better paper. What Dolly needed at this

---

*Forrestal, a prominent investment banker and political insider, became the nation's first secretary of defense in 1947. He committed suicide in 1949 after losing a political battle with the chiefs of the uniformed services.

[†]In the late 1920s, there had been ten major dailies. The Pulitzer brothers closed the *World* in 1931, then sold the name to the Scripps-Howard chain, which added it to their afternoon *Telegram.* The Hearst organization folded one of its morning papers, the *American,* into its afternoon *Journal* in 1937.

point was expertise in making it pay. Under Ted's stewardship, circulation was on the rise, but operations continued at a deficit. Dolly's fortune was repeatedly called on to keep the enterprise alive. Her account managers at Kuhn, Loeb sold off securities on a regular basis to fund transfers to the *Post,* some of which—as in the past—were backed by promissory notes and some of which were outright grants. By the end of 1942, she had put another $500,000 into the paper, meaning that she was out of pocket nearly $3.5 million, or approximately one-third of her net worth.

Leon Cook, a respected accountant, had been comptroller of the company since 1940. Ted asked him to examine the finances of every department of the paper. Together they imposed spending controls on overtime and purchasing and began coordinating financial planning. Management and production costs dropped noticeably. At the same time, advertising revenues perked up a bit.* Ted's innovations in format and additional columnists must also have added to the steady improvement in circulation. Dorothy needed to advance the paper less than $200,000 in the course of the year, peanuts compared to her previous subsidies.

Dolly was pleased with what Ted was accomplishing at the paper and impressed by his take-charge style in private life. Ted, unlike George, was not amused by the fact that she'd had a dalliance with Roosevelt. He told her that even though she no longer spent much time at Hyde Park, most people believed she had been sexually involved with the president. Ted asked if she wanted to go through life known best for having been the president's mistress. Brought up short, she told him, "Of course not. I'm better than that."

Ted's gruff, no-nonsense manner and his common-man style and background distinguished him from the men to whom Dolly had previously been attracted. She knew he was not really her type, but she was dependent on him at the paper, and she wasn't comfortable being on her own after hours. She seems never to have been bothered by the impropriety of having an affair while she was legally married, but she found it hard to live with someone without marrying him if she was free to do so. As had been the case with Dick Hall and George Backer, she had serious reservations about Ted's potential as a husband. Even so, a week after coming back from her six-week

---

*During the war, newsprint was rationed, in part to prevent papers that owned their own mills from having an unfair advantage. Readers, avid for war news, pushed circulation figures higher. The *Post,* like many other papers, could have sold more ads if it had been able to acquire more paper stock.

stay at the Tumbling D-W Dude Ranch outside of Reno with a Nevada divorce from George in hand, she married Ted, who had recently divorced his second wife.

Judge Samuel Rosenman, Dolly's friend and FDR's adviser, performed the ceremony at the *Post* on July 19, 1943. Her nineteen-year-old son, Morti Hall, was Ted's best man. The entire staff of the paper was invited to the reception. Reporters, editors, men from the composing room, and secretaries from the purchasing department mingled in Dolly's penthouse office with uptown guests like Wendell Willkie, Elsa Maxwell, and Ellin Mackay Berlin (who had married Irving Berlin in 1926). The democratic touch was probably Ted's idea.

FOUR

Media Adventures

In the first years of their marriage, Dolly and Ted Thackrey seemed a good team. They settled into an intimate routine, going off to their side-by-side offices at the paper every morning and continuing their working conversations at home. Dolly gave Ted a generous salary of $35,000, out of which he paid his personal expenses and the rent on their new apartment at 133 East Sixty-fourth Street, a building owned by the Backer Management Company.

The apartment was one of two spacious penthouses atop the building at the corner of Lexington Avenue. A terrace, from which dinner guests could watch the sun setting over Park Avenue, surrounded the upper floor, which included a formal entrance hall dominated by an enormous gilded chandelier ornamented with china flowers and birds, a living room with a working fireplace, dining room, kitchen, and serving pantry. On the lower floor were a master suite, three smaller bedrooms, a room for live-in help, and a laundry.

Dorothy liked classic furniture in the English or French style. She preferred comfort to provenance. Her granddaughter Mary Hall Howland remembers that there was "nothing you couldn't sit in or touch." Some Meissen birds and a few other china pieces that had belonged to Frieda Schiff were on display in the dining room. Staffordshire figurines, also from the Schiff home, adorned the living room.

Dorothy's two daughters were part of the Schiff-Thackrey household;

Morti Hall was not. Morti had worked as an office boy at the *Post* during school vacations. After graduating from prep school and briefly attending Carnegie Tech, he became a desk assistant in the drama department of the paper. Morti was drafted into the army in December 1942, but because of impaired vision in his right eye—the result of a childhood accident—he was assigned to limited duty and never sent overseas. Dorothy had told a reporter a few years previously that her two older children were very interested in careers at the *Post;* Morti's ambitions would have to be on hold until the war was over.

Adele attended college briefly before returning to New York and joining the *Post* editorial staff in 1943. "I had worked there in the summer as a schoolgirl. I was a clerk in the library—the morgue," she says. "Then I went to Wellesley. I stayed one semester, got good grades, and then I left. I'd been offered a modeling job, which I thought was just wonderful and mother thought was absolutely terrible. In fact, she forbade it. My choice was either to go back to school or work at the paper. So I went to work, running errands for the editors."

Adele was old enough to have her own life, but Sarah-Ann was just nine when her mother married Ted. She remembers him as a genial but somewhat detached stepfather. She remembers too that most of the conversations around the dinner table had to do with politics and the *Post.*

Partly because it was wartime and partly because the Thackreys were so absorbed in their work, they led relatively quiet lives. Dorothy's regular attendance at the Philharmonic and her involvement as an intimate member of the theatrical social set was a thing of the past. "Moss Hart and Sam Behrman and all of those people, they were my father's friends," says Sarah-Ann. "Mother knew them through him, and I think she saw them not at all afterwards. She had made a huge effort when she and my father were together. And when they were divorced, she said, 'Nobody invited me anyplace. They only liked him.'"

Soon after Ted took on a more active role at the *Post,* he began suggesting that Dorothy consider adding to her media holdings. Thackrey's ideas for revitalizing the *Post* seemed to be paying off. The net operating deficit for the paper in 1942 was only $155,000, although other corporate expenses required an infusion of another half million dollars of working capital. Encouraging projections for 1943 would presumably relieve the pressure on Dorothy's personal assets or free them up for other uses. Not long after Dorothy and Ted were married in July 1943, they went on a shopping spree, deputizing Morris Ernst, a partner in Dolly's law firm, to help them find available properties.

By the beginning of 1944, farsighted entrepreneurs were positioning themselves to take advantage of anticipated financial opportunities in postwar America. Forecasts of pent-up demand for consumer products suggested that advertising and media properties would be growth industries. The owners of the Hearst, Scripps-Howard, and Gannett newspaper groups, as well as those of the Cleveland *Plain Dealer,* the *Los Angeles Times,* and other urban papers were buying up local radio stations and forming small chains. Eugene Meyer, the owner of *The Washington Post,* wanted to acquire a network-affiliated radio station in DC, but there was none to be had. Reasoning that anything was better than nothing, he settled for WINX, a tiny station with a 250-watt signal that he planned to strengthen after the war. In 1945, the New York Times Corporation bought the nation's first classical music station, WQXR, and its FM affiliate.

In February 1944, Ernst told the Thackreys that Marshall Field III, the Chicago department store heir and newspaper owner, was said to have bid $2 million for WNEW, a major New York radio station, and the New York *Daily News* had offered to top that. Knowing that the Thackreys could not afford to compete at that level, Ernst reported that WLIB, a small station in Brooklyn, could probably be bought for $300,000.

WLIB, which had been on the air since 1941, was aimed at an audience of working- and middle-class Jews in Brooklyn, many of whom were also readers of the *Post.* Merchants who wanted to reach these households with print advertising could be approached to buy airtime as well. Of course, there were problems: the station was licensed to broadcast only during daytime hours, and it operated on only one thousand watts. After the end of the war, Ernst estimated, the signal could probably be built up to fifty thousand watts with an investment of an additional $100,000. Despite the drawbacks, the station was attractive to the Thackreys, and the price seemed right. No one stopped to think that you tend to get what you pay for.

Negotiations moved fast. Contracts for Dorothy to purchase all of the assets of WLIB outright for $250,000 were signed by midsummer; FCC approval was announced on September 28, 1944, and virtually the next day, a check for $250,000 drawn on Dorothy's personal account at Kuhn, Loeb was in the mail.

For a time, the Thackreys were delighted with their new acquisition. They applied for FCC licenses to establish affiliated FM and television stations, they acquired two small parcels of land in Fort Lee, New Jersey, on which to build transmitters, and they placed an order for some television equipment. They transferred the offices of WLIB to West Thirtieth Street in Manhattan and built a new studio there as well. Dorothy's capital investment was growing.

There was no return on that investment, however. Operating losses in 1945 were much higher than estimated. Increases in salaries and costs associated with the move to Manhattan were the biggest items on the expense side, while no significant gains were made in advertising sales to offset them. Dorothy had to make a number of loans to underwrite the operating deficits.

Undaunted, the Thackreys were looking to add more properties to their nascent media empire. Ted, more knowledgeable about the world of print, was particularly interested in finding newspaper deals. An intriguing possibility was the *Chicago Daily News,* a respected afternoon paper. Colonel Frank Knox, the publisher and primary owner, was a moderate Republican who had been Alf Landon's vice presidential running mate in 1936, and was serving as Franklin Roosevelt's secretary of the navy when he died in April 1944. Soon thereafter, Knox's widow, Annie, put the paper on the market; the Thackreys offered $15 each for Mrs. Knox's shares, for a total of almost $2.25 million.

Adlai Stevenson, Knox's assistant secretary, who was already looking ahead to a postwar career in Illinois politics, led a competing syndicate of Chicago businessmen. Stevenson consulted his friend John Cowles, owner of the Minneapolis *Star-Tribune* and other properties, who advised him that the *Daily News* was probably worth about $1.5 million, and that to pay more than $2 million would be a mistake. Stevenson's final offer to Mrs. Knox was $13 a share, nearly $300,000 less than that made by the Thackreys. Marshall Field, who had founded the liberal Democratic *Chicago Sun* in 1941, offered to loan Stevenson whatever money he needed to make the deal, but Stevenson would accept only limited support from Field. He may have questioned the wisdom of allowing a competitor, even an indirect one, too much influence.

It looked for a time as if the Thackreys' offer would carry the day, but

Mrs. Knox was put off by their reputation as liberals. She was torn between taking the highest bid or going with the buyer whose politics were slightly more congenial. For a time, the competing groups considered combining forces. In the course of these negotiations, Dorothy met Adlai Stevenson for the first time.

Soon Mrs. Knox found a convenient solution to her dilemma—Republicans who were willing to match the Thackrey bid. John and James Knight, brothers and co-owners of the Akron *Beacon-Journal,* were buying newspaper properties across the country that they would consolidate into the Knight newspaper chain.* Stevenson, who said later that he always regretted not acquiring the paper, instead ran a successful campaign for governor of Illinois in 1948, thus making him a political figure of national potential.

The Thackreys turned their attention to San Francisco. Their friend and West Coast lawyer Bartley Crum informed them in December 1944 that the independent Republican *San Francisco Chronicle,* which was owned by the De Young family, seemed to be on the market. After meeting with George Cameron, the husband of one of the De Young heirs and the principal player on the sellers' side, the Thackreys authorized Crum to offer $3 million for the paper plus a fee to be determined by an appraiser for the real property and assets.

Cameron, who was still seeking other solutions, never responded. In March 1945, Crum told Thackrey that Marshall Field was also courting the *Chronicle* owners. Nothing came of his offer either, and the De Young heirs did not sell the paper for another half century.

Bartley Crum did not let up in his determination to find the Thackreys media properties on the West Coast. Crum was an interesting character in his own right. An ambitious young San Francisco lawyer, he'd made a name for himself and had probably gotten a taste for the power of the media when he represented the Hearst organization. Crum, a registered Republican, had been a close adviser to Wendell Willkie in his 1940 presidential campaign and worked hard in a vain effort to get Willkie the 1944 nomination. But Crum was not a typical Republican: he was a friend and supporter of Harry Bridges, the left-wing longshoremen's union leader on the West Coast; he

*The Knights sold the *Chicago Daily News* in 1959 to Field Enterprises, which kept it alive despite dwindling readership until 1978.

had helped raise money for the Spanish loyalists and supported many left-leaning causes during the Second World War.

By 1945, Crum's political star was no longer on the rise. Willkie was dead, and Crum's left-wing inclinations made him an outsider in the state and national Republican parties. He had lost the Hearst organization as a client, and he was drinking heavily. Crum may have seen the Thackreys as his ticket to a new career.

Crum and Thackrey had been talking since the beginning of 1945 about the possibility of the *Post*'s publishing a West Coast edition during the upcoming Conference on International Organization, which would mark the formal founding of the United Nations. Ted's typically ambitious first plan was to publish twenty-five thousand copies of a weekly special edition that would provide news summaries for the ten thousand international leaders who would be passing through. Ultimately he settled for a more realistic sixteen-page Conference Edition of the *New York Post,* which was composed of the regular *Post* columns plus news summaries.

The Thackreys were pleased with the critical response to their West Coast debut. Ted continued to think that because none of the established San Francisco dailies were first-rate, there should be some way to break into that market. Bartley Crum agreed. In July 1945, he proposed that the Thackreys buy the *Berkeley Gazette.* He pointed out that the population of the East Bay area—a mix of university intellectuals and a growing working class—was similar to the readership of the *Post.* Ted and Dolly, however, were more interested in two California radio stations that Crum was also advocating that they purchase.

Crum was on the board of directors of KYA, a small radio station operating in Palo Alto. Don Fedderson, the general manager of KYA, had a solid background in California broadcasting and ambitious plans for the station, which included moving the signal to San Francisco, a much bigger market. To do so required an infusion of cash, which Bartley Crum assumed Dolly had plenty of.

The deal went through quickly. In May 1945, Dolly agreed to buy the Palo Alto Radio Station Inc. for nearly $450,000. The FCC approved the transaction in October, and the first part of the Thackreys' proposed West Coast mini-network was in their hands.

They then turned their attention to Southern California and to KMTR—one of the oldest radio stations in the state. KMTR had been founded in 1924 by K. M. Turner (hence the call letters) to encourage demand for the radio sets he sold in his appliance shop in Los Angeles. Turner operated the station for some years out of his living room. He sold KMTR in 1932 to a man named Victor Dalton, whose widow, Gloria, was now looking for a buyer. In October 1945, with Crum once again handling the arrangements, Dorothy contracted to pay just under $300,000 for the KMTR Radio Corporation, which included ownership of the building at 1000 Cahuenga Boulevard, where the station's studios and offices were located. She and Ted renamed the station KLAC to underscore the fact that major changes were under way.

Don Fedderson, who continued to manage KYA, took over KLAC as well. Fedderson immediately shook up the broadcast schedule. *Billboard* reported on March 16, 1946, "The way that KLAC (nee KMTR) took to the air this week after two weeks of re-programing has the town convinced that Ted and Dorothy Thackrey, publishers of *The N.Y. Post* and new owners of the station . . . aren't holding onto the purse strings when it comes to buying programs and talent."

By the fall of 1946, Fedderson was able to report that KLAC was running a net profit of about $12,000 a month and that plans for the next round of expansion were under way. Applications had been filed with the FCC for television stations to be affiliated with both KYA and KLAC (a similar application for their proposed creation of WLIB-TV in Brooklyn was also pending). In one of the prepared statements that accompanied the application forms, Dorothy said, "It is because of my passionate belief in the democratic system of government, which has reached its highest point of development in this country, together with the system of free enterprise, that I am wholly devoting my time as well as my capital in efforts to improve the quality and quantity of public information, using the best means available."

It was a formulaic text, drafted by her lawyers, that happened also to be true. Her commitment—and Ted's—to liberal journalism was sincere and unwavering. But although KYA was almost breaking even and KLAC was doing well, Dorothy's other investments were not. The *Post* was losing money. WLIB was losing money. She was underwriting the losses as well as paying the bills for all the expenses related to the purchases and the FCC applications from her personal account at Kuhn, Loeb. The tab was mounting. Her outlays for the broadcasting properties alone now approached $1,500,000. It was probably fortunate that the expansive offers Ted made for the Chicago and San Francisco papers had not been accepted.

The Thackreys never set up a formal group of consultants, nor did they create an appropriate corporate structure to deal with their media expansion. The business managers of the *New York Post,* Leon Cook and Marvin Berger, were responsible for supervising the financial operations of WLIB. Cook and Berger, like Ted, may have been knowledgeable about the New York publishing world, but they knew nothing about broadcasting and lacked expertise outside the city.

Bart Crum, their point man on the California deals, was not giving them unbiased advice; he was cheerleading for the deals to be made. Whether he, the Thackreys, or their New York lawyers and advisers understood how to evaluate a property for its growth potential is not clear. Due diligence was casual at best. No one appears to have made serious market projections or analyses of the strength of the competition. Nor had they thought rigorously about the problems inherent in absentee ownership. Yet Ted's ever-ambitious plans for expansion continued without restraint, and Dolly was either too beguiled by his vision or too cowed by his determination to apply that restraint.

In early 1944, with an Allied victory becoming more plausible, Ted had begun to think about establishing a foreign news service to compete with *The New York Times* and the *Chicago Tribune.* By spring, he was in serious discussions with Paul Scott Mowrer about how to get started.

Mowrer, a Pulitzer Prize–winning foreign correspondent, was then serving as the executive editor of the *Chicago Daily News.* Ted had been impressed with him when he and Dolly were making their abortive bid to buy that paper. Mowrer and his wife, Hadley, (whose first husband was Ernest Hemingway) had lived in France before the war. He was restive working for the new owner of his paper and wanted to get back to Europe as soon as possible.

By November of 1944, Mowrer had quit his job and was negotiating with Thackrey the terms under which he would move to Paris. They agreed that he would report for the *New York Post* and WLIB on long-range developments in Europe, as well as lay the groundwork for a number of bureaus for the proposed foreign news service. He was also to look into the possibility of setting up a new paper to be called the *Paris Post.* The European edition of the long-established *New York Herald Tribune,* which had suspended publication in June 1940, resumed operations in December 1944. No one knew if there was a market for a competitor.

Mowrer moved to Paris in March 1945. Although he filed several pieces from France and Germany and talked with various old Europe hands about the news service, he spent most of his time trying to set up the *Paris Post*. Within weeks he had rented office space, signed contracts for newsprint, arranged for press facilities, and bought a car. His budget was tight. Ted estimated that it would cost about $50,000 to get the news service and the paper up and running. Mowrer hired a few writers, some of whom were still on the payroll of the American military or other government agencies, who would work at piece rates until they were available full time. Hadley would be his office assistant.

On May 16, 1945, he wired Thackrey the exciting news that the *Paris Post* had received an official allotment of paper that would allow it to print about fifty thousand copies a day at a price of three francs. The *Herald Tribune* received a similar deal. The American army agreed to buy an undecided upon number of copies. Mowrer was confident that the paper was economically viable.

The first edition of the *Paris Post* appeared on July 4. Just as the paper seemed to break even, costs of newsprint and staff began to rise. Mowrer was aware that he was adding overhead as he assigned journalists to cover stories in newly liberated parts of Europe, and he worried about the continuing unwillingness of the authorities to devalue the franc, which made the monthly infusions of $10,000 to $15,000 sent him from New York worth less than they would have been in an open economy.

For several months Mowrer seemed more concerned about financial matters than the home office was. He kept asking for help with budgets and currency transactions. Finally, Berger and Cook, the business managers from New York, arrived in October to overhaul the accounting and payroll procedures that Mowrer had created more or less on the fly. They were not happy with what they saw, and they projected significant losses for the months ahead. When they returned to New York, they seemed to be no more successful than Mowrer had been at getting Ted to concentrate on the realities of what was going on.

As of December 1, the *Paris Post* had about $50,000 in outstanding bills with no cash on hand. The projected operating loss of $10,000 per month was running at least twice that. The good news was that advertising revenues and the prestige of the paper were growing. The bad news was that most readers were military personnel who were being sent home, and it was too soon to anticipate a flood of American tourists who could pick up the slack.

Mowrer decided to bring things to a head. In December he wrote Thackrey: "I am sorry to have to write you this letter, but I shall not sleep well until I have had some kind of decision or reassurance from you. You have never questioned in any way anything I have ever asked you for. But that does not allay my worries, or Bob Pell's [his business manager]. The fact is that we are appalled at the losses we have to sustain—of your money." Dolly's, actually.

Thackrey finally woke up. He sent Mowrer a rather brusque cable, restating as if it were breaking news what his editor had been telling him for weeks:

> Your present actual loses [sic] are running approximately ten thousand dollars per week where they should be running a maximum of ten thousand dollars per month but in fact at this point you should be budgeting for a total loss of less than fifty thousand dollars for the year 1946. Stop.
>
> If you will prepare such a budget I will approve it and we will continue financing but if you are unable or unwilling you will force me to come or send a representative armed with full power to reorganize your operation. Stop. Regards Thackrey.

Mowrer seemed relieved to have any direction at all. He wrote New York that he was delighted to have a firm budgetary goal, because he had never previously had any but the loosest guidelines.

An increasingly frustrating transatlantic correspondence followed. Thackrey wanted hard figures. Mowrer warned that it was impossible to make a real budget without knowing at what rate the soon-to-be-devalued franc would be pegged. Mowrer suggested some off-the-books deals for newsprint and personnel that Thackrey became convinced were the equivalent of black market financial transactions.

By early January 1946, further haggling was futile. Mowrer flew to New York, and he and the Thackreys agreed to cease publication, without any prior public notice, on the last day of the month. They arrived at the decision with little rancor on either side. Mowrer returned to Paris to continue work as the head of the French bureau of the *Post* news service. During the remainder of 1946 and throughout 1947, he arranged to send distinguished correspondents to report on conditions in Eastern Europe and the Middle East. Mowrer himself contributed a series of important articles on the Marshall Plan.

The *Paris Post* probably lost somewhere upward of $250,000 in its brief existence—a drop in the bucket compared to what its parent paper was losing during the same period. In 1944, the *New York Post* had shown a modest profit—the first in years—but things turned sour in a hurry. By the end of 1945, with the price of newsprint soaring and circulation and advertising revenues stagnant, the *Post* was losing nearly $100,000 per month.

By the beginning of 1946, Dorothy had invested nearly $5 million in her various newspaper and broadcast properties. That year and the first three quarters of 1947 would be brutal for the New York Post Corporation. Another $1.8 million in loans from Dorothy were necessary to keep it afloat. Some of the debt was occasioned by positive investments in the future—new presses and related equipment for the *Post*—but much of it was to cover the operating deficit of various entities.

By the end of 1947, Dorothy had parted with yet another $2 million, putting her approximately $7 million ($50 million in 2007 dollars), in the hole. She had invested more than half of her assets in her media holdings, including the *Post*. While Kuhn, Loeb continued to refill the corporate coffers from her dwindling personal account, she and Ted remained optimistic that it was only a matter of time until their expansionist efforts paid off.

WLIB required a particular suspension of belief. In mid-1946, the station was losing approximately $20,000 a month. Loans from Dorothy kept it going, loans she could have had little hope of ever seeing repaid. The FCC had not granted the station's request to broadcast longer than during daytime hours, yet many fixed costs such as rent and charges for equipment, for example, were the same as they would have been for round-the-clock operations. To make matters worse, WLIB's ad salesmen were saddled with the highest rates in the metropolitan area relative to the audience delivered.

One of Morris Ernst's partners finally expressed apprehension at the direction in which this was all heading. In the summer of 1946, he wrote Ted that soaring costs of construction had led many applicants for television licenses to drop out. Maybe only the big national radio networks like CBS, NBC, Westinghouse, and Dumont and a few metropolitan newspaper owners would be able to absorb such expenses. "All of this is certainly having the effect of scaring the living daylights out of me when I think of what Dolly may possibly be letting herself in for," the lawyer said, strongly urging the Thackreys to reconsider their plans.

Accordingly, in December 1946, the license applications for FM and television stations in Brooklyn and San Francisco were withdrawn on the grounds that the anticipated costs were much higher than the projected income would warrant. The Los Angeles market was too attractive to abandon, so the application for KLAC-TV was kept alive.

In March 1947, the FCC awarded Channel 13, one of eleven channels allotted to the Los Angeles area, to KMTR Radio Corporation, which by now Dorothy owned outright. The FCC commissioners were known to have liberal political leanings. For once, the *Post*'s editorial policy was probably a factor in Dorothy's favor.

The license for KLAC-TV made her a pioneer in an infant industry. On October 11, 1939, Dorothy had written in her diary, "Saw television for the first time. Image small & rather flickery—programs terrible but could be greatly improved." There was scant improvement in the product in the next few years, but that was about to change.

By the spring of 1947, of the fifty-seven licensed TV stations in the country (there had been nine the previous year), only a handful were actually up and running. WCBW, the CBS station in New York, was on the air less than ten hours a week. In June 1947, there were twenty stations operating in the entire United States; by December, there would be forty-one. At year's end, 864,000 American households had television sets. Of these, more than 40 percent were in the New York metropolitan area. Although an Elmo Roper poll revealed that listening to the radio was still Americans' favorite pastime, the owners of the big radio networks and leading newspaper publishers were betting on the potential of the new broadcast medium and scrambling to compete for licenses.

NBC, CBS, Dumont, and Westinghouse acquired licenses for stations in major cities across the country, and leading newspapers like the *Los Angeles Times,* the *San Francisco Chronicle,* the *Philadelphia Record,* the Cleveland *Plain Dealer,* and others, many of which already owned several radio stations, acquired television licenses in their hometowns.

Southern California was an obvious market in which to invest in the new medium. In the decade from 1940 to 1950, the population of California rose nearly 50 percent, from just under seven million to more than ten million, and growth was expected to continue in the years after midcentury. Jobs were plentiful; industry was growing even faster than the population. Consumer demand led to a boom in the construction and appliance industries, and, as a result of the Cold War, military production never slackened. Although the state was a major agricultural region and actually led the nation in the cash value of its crops, most Californians—new or old—lived in rapidly expanding urban areas, where they found jobs in the shipbuilding, airplane or automotive production, or food-processing and petroleum products industries. Residents of the state had among the highest per capita incomes in the country.

Much of this boom took place in the Los Angeles–Long Beach area. The decentralized, suburbanized sprawl of greater Los Angeles was seen across the country—and around the world—as the paradigmatic city of the future. In this vast market, which included first-time homeowners in tract communities as well as film industry millionaires in the mansions of Beverly Hills, radio was flourishing, and TV looked like a good bet for advertising dollars. Buoyed by the profitable return on their investment in KLAC radio, their only enterprise operating in the black, the Thackreys committed more of Dorothy's assets to its companion television station.

KLAC-TV began broadcasting from its newly completed studio in the property at 1000 Cahuenga Boulevard on September 17, 1948, making it the third station on the air in Los Angeles. The others were locally owned stations backed by big corporations. KFI was part of the Mutual Broadcasting System, and KTLA was a Paramount property. During its first weeks on the air, KLAC-TV was proud to present the UCLA home football games live.

KLAC radio was doing well, but KLAC-TV was a long way from prosperity. On top of the estimated $500,000 investment in studios and equipment necessary to get the station on the air, insufficient advertising revenues led to operating losses of about $30,000 a month.

Even before KLAC-TV went on the air, Dorothy decided to unload her West Coast properties, even if it meant staging a fire sale. Warner Bros., which already owned KFWB, another independent radio station in Los Angeles, agreed in May 1948 to buy KYA and KMTR, the formal entity that operated KLAC and KLAC-TV. In order to gain FCC approval of the sale, Warner Bros. promised that upon receiving its license it would sell either KFWB or KLAC because FCC rules barred ownership of more than one radio station per market.

Warners agreed to pay Dorothy $1,045,000 for the three properties and promised to make an immediate advance of 10 percent of the purchase price, with further payments of up to a total of $500,000 to be made by the end of the year. The deal meant that the money she'd laid out to purchase KYA and KLAC and to set up KLAC-TV would be essentially made good. She would be out of pocket for equipment upgrades and legal fees—a net loss of about $300,000 to show for her three-year adventure as a would-be media mogul on the West Coast.

Had Dorothy stayed the course a bit longer, she might have seen operating profits at all three stations. Don Fedderson was a competent manager, and the California market eventually rewarded the most prescient or persistent pioneers. But Dorothy was playing on an uneven field. KLAC-TV may have been an attractive platform for local advertisers, but the networks could offer national accounts national exposure at more advantageous rates. Independents, even regional chains, were racing to affiliate themselves with the big boys. The Don Lee stations, a powerhouse West Coast regional network of radio and television stations, would soon be sold to the General Tire and Rubber Company, which owned the Mutual Broadcasting System and the RKO movie studio.

Dorothy did not sell her properties after a careful analysis of their potential. Her purchases had been strongly influenced by her admiration for Ted Thackrey. Her willingness to sell reflected her growing disenchantment with him.

FIVE

Ted's Tenure

In 1945, Dolly told an interviewer that aside from attending an occasional political dinner or an unavoidable charity benefit, she and Ted seldom went out in the evening. She enjoyed listening to the radio—particularly dramatized mysteries and political broadcasts—and frequently did needlepoint while she listened. "I used to go night-clubbing," she said, "but I don't care for it any more. I am happier and more lively when I am working."

Although she had dropped almost all of her volunteer obligations, she took on one new activity. She learned how to translate popular texts into Braille, after which she bought a special Braille typewriter on which she produced a number of translations for the Guild for Jewish Blind and the Library of Congress.

She enjoyed cooking when she had the chance. Not in the city where her staff included a cook, a butler, and Sarah-Ann's governess, but on those weekends when she and Ted were able to get away to the country. On these outings, they were often accompanied by Sarah-Ann, with possibly a school friend or a young cousin in tow. Although Ted's daughter, Jane, lived in nearby Westchester County with her mother, she seems never to have been included.

The Thackreys escaped either to Dolly's house at Sands Point on Long Island or to the Red House at Hyde Park, which they found a comfortable retreat now that Roosevelt was dead. Over the years, she had added to the land she'd bought from FDR, bringing her holdings to some 223 acres and her total investment, including the cost of the house itself, to $65,450. The Thackreys tried to turn the property into a paying proposition. They set up an enterprise called Theodoro Farms to operate a dairy and egg business that they hired a local farmer to run. The farm produced income of about $10,000 yearly, but, like so many of the Thackreys' schemes, it failed to break even on an operating basis. Tax advantages and farm subsidies made the project a wash.

Theodoro was the name the Thackreys had devised when they formally reorganized the *Post* corporate structure. The paper had been solely owned by Dolly. In the spring of 1945, she transferred all her capital stock in both the New York Post Corporation and radio station WLIB to the Theodoro Corporation, a newly created entity of which she owned 449 shares and Ted held the remaining single share.* Dorothy Schiff Thackrey was the president and chairman of the board of directors of Theodoro, and Ted was executive vice president. Later Dorothy and Ted founded the Theodoro Advertising Service with the intention of acquiring national accounts for the various media holdings.

Establishing Theodoro made Ted feel he had a stake in their enterprises. It also made good financial sense. Dolly's lawyer explained why: "Based on the assumption that your personal net taxable income for the year 1945 from sources other than the *Post* will be approximately $150,000 ($1.3 million in 2007 dollars), and on Ted's estimate that the New York Post Corporation will show a net profit for the year of approximately $250,000 while WLIB, Inc. shows a net loss for the year of approximately $100,000, there will be substantial tax savings from the reorganization." As the sole owner of the *Post,* Dorothy would have been liable for an estimated $350,800 in taxes for 1945. Under the Theodoro plan, her personal tax would be less than half that. As events developed, 1945 turned out to be disastrous rather than profitable for the paper, so this desirable scenario never materialized, but turning the *Post* from a personal asset back into a corporation made sound financial sense in principle. And later, in practice.

---

*The California broadcasting properties were always held in Dorothy's name; they were never transferred to Theodoro.

Although their West Coast projects might have provided a cautionary tale, the Thackreys were not yet finished with their media acquisitions. In May 1945, Dolly paid almost $2 million for the goodwill and real estate of the *Bronx Home News,* the only daily paper published in New York's northernmost borough. The price was a bit high, but the paper had a circulation of more than one hundred thousand, which added considerably to the *Post*'s base circulation of just over three hundred thousand. Since most of the *Home News* readers signed up annually for home delivery, they were relatively less costly to attract and keep than newsstand purchasers. The subscribers were members of the Bronx's expanding working- and middle-class population, which was attractive to advertisers who were eager to cash in on the anticipated postwar consumer boom. Ted Thackrey was an active overseer of the paper. He changed the format from a broadsheet to a tabloid, which made it easier to share editorial and advertising copy with the *Post.* Although he retained most of the top staff, he cut costs by eliminating duplication of some *Post* and *Home News* departments.

The *Home News* was not placed under the Theodoro umbrella. Dorothy retained sole ownership until the Bronx Home News Publishing Co. was officially merged with the New York Post Corporation in 1948.* Though the paper turned out to be a sound investment in the long run, it was initially another hit on Dolly's personal reserve fund.

The second purchase had intriguing possibilities. In December 1946, the New York Post Corporation bought 80 percent of the outstanding common stock of Jessup & Moore, an old American paper manufacturer, for $758,712. Publishers were becoming aware that if they could control the cost and supply of newsprint—which was, with payroll, one of their biggest expenses—they could run a much more efficient organization. During the period from 1937 to 1957, the New York Times Corporation, for example, showed an average annual profit after taxes of just under 5 percent, and much of that came from the company-owned Spruce Falls paper mill. A decade after the Thackreys bought Jessup & Moore, Phil Graham invested in a Canadian paper mill that would add to the growing success of the Washington Post Company.

At first sight, the purchase of Jessup & Moore looked like a great idea.

*The *Post* continued to publish a separate Bronx edition until 1958, when the printing plant was sold at a slight profit, and the Bronx edition merged into the parent paper.

But once again, the Thackreys seem not to have engaged in anything more than the most rudimentary examination of the financial condition of a company they had their eye on. Jessup & Moore had changed hands many times in the previous decades; its mills were obsolete and not suited for the production of newsprint. The Thackreys would have had to finance a major renovation of the facilities to have them meet the *Post*'s needs. After awarding itself a one-time dividend of $10 a share ($121,440) in 1948, the Post Corporation sold its shares in the paper mill for $225,000, resulting in a net loss of $527,640.

By 1948, the investments Dorothy had made in the *New York Post,* the *Paris Post,* the Pacific *Post,* Jessup & Moore, WLIB, the West Coast radio and television stations, and several other small enthusiasms of Ted's—even when reduced by the proceeds of the pending sale of the California properties to Warner Bros.—totaled about $7 million. About $6 million of that was tied up in the *New York Post,* which at least had the potential to pay her back at some point in the future. The remaining $1 million (about $6.3 million in 2007 dollars) was as good as gone, though the losses were a help to her at tax time.*

Dorothy had come to enjoy the prestige of being head of the *New York Post,* but she was not naturally acquisitive and certainly not a free spender. Although she appeared to acquiesce in all the purchases at the time, she later blamed Ted for railroading her into the buying spree. She contended that she'd cut losses at some of the properties by taking them away from Ted and managing them herself. For his part, Ted began referring to Dolly as a poor little rich girl and an innocent in a world of shrewd operators like himself.

However appreciative Dorothy was of Ted Thackrey's merits as a journalist, she came to realize that he lacked skill as a businessman and to recognize the financial damage she'd incurred by supporting his acquisitions. Finally, in late 1948, she had had enough. She swiftly curtailed her commitments in California. With her cash flow situation eased by Warners' advance payments,

*The apparent loss represented approximately one-tenth of her liquid assets.

During this period, other New York newspapers probably also operated in the red. Although their parent companies did not always break out figures for individual properties, it is likely that the *Journal-American,* the *World-Telegram,* the *Herald Tribune,* and possibly the *Mirror* were losing money. However, they were all owned by large corporations or very wealthy individuals whose deep pockets enabled them to sustain losses at less peril.

Dorothy finally had to address fundamental changes in her professional and personal relationship with Ted.

Financial travails and the accompanying recriminations were among the significant reasons why the Thackreys' five-year-long marriage was failing, but the final straw was ostensibly political. Throughout Ted's career, he had adhered to the newsman's creed of being politically unbiased. He took little interest in the great ideological debates of the 1930s. In the mid-'40s, however, he became increasingly committed to two causes: Zionism and Progressivism.

On the question of Zionism, the *Post* was editorially in favor of expanded Jewish settlement in Palestine. After the revelations of the Nazi atrocities, no New York newspaper was likely to take a different stand. Most American Jews recognized that Europe's surviving Jews needed a place to go and that America was not willing to take them in. (Dorothy did say later that it would have been wonderful for the *Post*'s circulation if the refugees could have come to New York.) Although many of the city's Jewish readers supported the establishment of a Jewish state, many of the city's Jewish leaders were dubious.

This debate had long vexed the American Jewish community. Dorothy's grandfather Jacob had mixed feelings on the subject, as did the Sulzberger family, who owned *The New York Times*. Dorothy's position was also not clear-cut. Zionism raised all the old questions about divided loyalties, about the proper use of Jewish influence in American politics, and about personal identity—questions that Jews who defined themselves primarily as Americans found unpleasant to address and hard to answer.

Just before the end of World War II, Dorothy gave an interview to a German-language Jewish newspaper in New York on the subject of postwar Palestine. She said that American Jews should be united in pressuring the British to permit unlimited settlement there by European refugees. "It is the land where, as my friends tell me, roses bloom in the desert and outstanding achievements have been accomplished. And it is important that the various groups among the American Jews are of one mind in this question, including those who are opposed to Zionism, because they are afraid that their citizenship might be injured by a pro-Palestine attitude. That is, of course, nonsense; every American who is a citizen by birth or naturalization, remains a citizen, regardless of his attitude toward Palestine," she said, revealing her own anxieties.

Ted, on the other hand, had no qualms about the Zionist enterprise. He was quite sympathetic to the Irgun, a faction to the right of the official Zionist leadership of David Ben-Gurion and his Labor party followers. Dolly's natural preference was for the establishment figures Ben-Gurion and Chaim Weizmann, who was a close friend of her Warburg cousins.

The views of Irgun supporters were always welcome in the *Post*. Ted accepted ads from the organization soliciting funds to help Jewish immigration into Palestine. He defended the policy in the face of complaints by other Jewish groups that the funds were really being used to lobby American politicians or to purchase illegal arms for Irgun's paramilitary units in Palestine. Supporters of Ben-Gurion maintained that the Irgun was a terrorist organization. Ted responded that he would never refuse access to the *Post* to "any movement or any group which is willing to fight unequivocally, without regard to the auspices, for the opening up of territory anywhere in the world, into which people who have no national home . . . can be, at the very least, physically accommodated." He deplored the factionalism that hampered the ultimate goal of getting Jewish people to Palestine and making it their homeland.

Although Ted's enthusiasm for the Irgun made Dolly uneasy, her direct opposition to his politics resulted from their disagreements over domestic policy and the emerging issue of the Cold War.

For passionately committed New Deal supporters—a group that included the Thackreys as well as most readers of the *Post*—no one had the stature to replace Franklin Roosevelt in their hearts or in the White House. Harry Truman didn't come close. When FDR dropped Vice President Henry A. Wallace and installed the senator from Missouri as his running mate for his fourth term, liberals regarded Truman, who might succeed the ailing president before the term was over, as a political hack and an inadequate successor to the great man.

Events played out as the liberals feared. Roosevelt died in April 1945. The Russians were determined to hold on to territories in Poland and other parts of Eastern Europe that their army had captured from the Germans. Truman appeared overmatched in his first meeting with Churchill and Stalin at Potsdam that spring. On the home front, he made enemies by clamping down on organized labor during major strikes in 1945 and 1946. The American economy was unstable. Manufacturers were slow to convert to production of items consumers were pining for, and an acute housing shortage faced returning soldiers and their families.

In the 1946 midterm elections, Republicans raised questions about continued turmoil in the economy, about the Russian aggression in Europe, and about possible subversive activities in the United States. The issues struck a chord with the voting population; Republicans captured control of both houses of Congress. Many Democrats said that the country was moving to the right, that it was Truman's fault, and that he should resign.

The question of Communist activity within the United States began to obsess conservatives and liberals alike. The high point of American communism was already past by the mid-1940s, but it was not apparent at the time. Since the end of World War I, many Americans had feared the spread of Marxist ideas, often confusing them with equally reviled anarchist beliefs and activities. Anarchism was associated primarily with European immigrants, who could be deported, whereas the Communist ideology and membership in Marxist organizations attracted many members of some of the nation's longest-established communities, as well as first-generation, hyphenated Americans. For people uneasy about the future, it was hard to know whom to trust.

After the United States recognized the USSR in 1932, American Communists came out in the open. In the 1932 presidential election, the party got 102,785 votes.* The greater threat to those who worried about such things was the covert Communist leadership of ostensibly non-Communist enterprises: the so-called popular front organizations, which proliferated in sympathy with the Loyalist cause during the Spanish Civil War and in support of various victims of injustice at home. Communists and their friends were prominent in the newly organized CIO—the association of industrial unions that was thrown out of the AFL in 1936, partly because of personal rivalries between union leaders and partly because of the Communist issue.

There were also Communist sympathizers within the bureaucracy spawned by the New Deal, notably in the departments of Agriculture, State,

*It was the highest vote the party ever received and is a useful measure of how little support the Communists actually attracted. The Socialist candidate, Norman Thomas, got 884,000. The minuscule total number of voters on the far left was underscored by comparison with the combined 35 million votes of Roosevelt and Hoover.

and the Treasury. Some were merely party members; others turned out to be Soviet spies. As early as 1938, a young Democratic congressman from Texas, Martin Dies Jr., motivated by isolationism, anti-FDR feelings, and personal ambition, chaired the new House Special Committee on Un-American Activities and Propaganda in the United States (HUAC). HUAC looked into Communist influence in the CIO, which was a legitimate target, and uncovered some disturbing evidence. With surreptitious assistance from the FBI, HUAC documented the activities of several American agents of the Soviet Union. On the whole, the Dies committee revealed some valuable information, which was vitiated by its penchant for using the subpoena and the contempt citation to bully those it called to testify.

Nothing the Dies committee or the FBI could do was as destructive to the long-term interests of the American Communist party or Russian spymasters, however, as Soviet policy. The 1936–1937 show trials in Moscow, revelations that Communists had undermined rather than aided the Loyalists during the Spanish Civil War, and the Nazi-Soviet Pact of August 1938 tarnished the popular front's luster and disabused many liberals of sentimental feelings for the USSR. The American party lost half its members and many of its fellow travelers by 1940. Only a small group of dedicated Communists or obdurate sympathizers remained steadfast in their discipline.

After Hitler's attack on Russia in June 1941, the FBI turned its attention to the search for German agents, although it never lost sight of the Communist menace. With the help of informers and, above all, with material culled from intercepted communications between the Russian intelligence services in Moscow and agents in the United States, J. Edgar Hoover and his men kept tabs on Soviet spies in America.

As the collapse of the Axis neared, American liberals began looking ahead to postwar policy. Although they may have had their own quarrels with the new president—they were fearful that Truman was less committed to the ideals of the New Deal than they wished him to be—they were eager to maintain an active role inside the Democratic party. A question that divided them into two camps concerned American policy regarding the USSR. One group on the left wanted to believe that it was possible to do business with the Russians. They thought that, however palpable its flaws, the Soviet experiment represented an honorable alternative to capitalism. They appreciated the great sacrifices the Russian people had made in the war, and they feared that American suspicions of Russian motives were driving the USSR into a more defensive stance.

Other liberals who had toyed earlier with Communist beliefs had learned that it was not possible to reconcile Communist and democratic ideals. Most were suspicious of the long-term goals of the USSR in Europe and favored helping European nations rebuild their economies as a bulwark against Soviet expansion. This group led the struggle against the revival of popular front efforts by Communists and Communist sympathizers who sought to consolidate their hold over CIO unions, veterans' committees, and civil liberties campaigns. They recognized that domestic radicals were a tiny minority who had no hope of overthrowing American democracy, but they feared that the radicals' behavior could elicit repressive measures from the political right.

In late 1946, prominent liberals like Eleanor Roosevelt, Hubert Humphrey, the dynamic young mayor of Minneapolis, theologian Reinhold Niebuhr, labor leader David Dubinsky (who provided most of the start-up funds), and a host of young New Dealers like Joseph Rauh, Jim Loeb, and Arthur Schlesinger Jr. began holding discussions that would lead to the founding of the Americans for Democratic Action (ADA). Although not a founding member, James Wechsler, who was working in the Washington bureau of the *New York Post* at the time, wrote some of the early position papers. Most ADA members were veterans of an organization called the Union for Democratic Action, which had fallen apart over the question of fellow travelers on the left. They believed that, since the Communist threat at home was overstated by the right as a means to attack the Truman administration and Democratic politics in general, it was important to blunt those attacks by preventing any remaining Communist sympathizers from holding positions of importance in the Democratic party. The ADA announced from the start that it rejected "any association with Communism or sympathizers with communism."

Ronald Reagan, soon to become the head of the Screen Actors Guild, was opposed to Communist influences in Hollywood, and he joined the ADA almost immediately. John F. Kennedy, a freshman congressman from Cambridge, Massachusetts, showed interest but never joined. Dorothy Schiff became a dedicated supporter. Anything Eleanor Roosevelt approved of was fine with Dolly.

Former Vice President Henry Wallace was then serving as editor of *The New Republic,* which emerged as a center of anti-ADA Democratic liberal strategists. Wallace and his colleagues at the magazine thought the ADA was much too focused on resisting the Communist threat abroad when they should have been more concerned with countering fascist threats at home. They accused the ADA of warmongering because of its animosity toward the USSR and its support for the emerging Truman policy of confrontation in Europe. Max Lerner, writing in *PM,* accused Mrs. Roosevelt of red-baiting.

The anti-anticommunist left found its most visible politician in Henry Wallace, a respected former government official who'd begun life as a wealthy Iowa farmer. His family ran a well-known farmers' journal, and Henry Wallace had founded one of the most successful seed businesses in America. Wallace left *The New Republic* in 1947 and joined the newly formed Progressive party. Not all of his *New Republic* colleagues were willing to follow him; they worried that, although Wallace denied it, he was the dupe of the Communists in control of the party.

All three parties held their conventions in the summer of 1948 in Philadelphia. The Republicans renominated New York's moderate Governor Thomas Dewey, who had lost to Roosevelt in the 1944 election. At the Democratic convention, Hubert Humphrey made a courageous and passionate speech in favor of including a civil rights plank, drafted by the ADA, in the party platform. The convention adopted the plank, which led to the walkout of Southerners, who chose Senator Strom Thurmond of South Carolina to head their Dixiecrat party. Some ADA members were originally enthusiastic about drafting General Dwight Eisenhower as the Democratic candidate, but when Ike withdrew his name from consideration, they reluctantly turned to Truman. The consensus was that though Truman was the incumbent, he was a long shot to win. Disaffected Democrats on the left—Ted Thackrey among them—moved crosstown to the Progressive party convention and committed themselves to supporting Henry Wallace, who accepted the party's nomination for president.

The disintegration of the Thackrey marriage took place against this background. On August 15, 1948, Ted signed an editorial in the weekend *Post* titled "An Appeal to Reason," explaining why he hoped Wallace would be the next president: "Mr. Wallace's opening campaign speech in Connecticut Thursday night made it quite clear that he is deeply devoted to political freedom, to a system of private profit, to capitalism freed of monopoly, to production for peace, to an economically free world, and to action through the United Nations to bring it into life as a substitute for national economic and military rivalries." Ted discounted rumors that Wallace's party was controlled by Communists and argued that red-baiting was a cheap trick used against him by people pretending to be liberals who weren't really very liberal at all.

"It is possible," Thackrey wrote,

to oppose Mr. Wallace's candidacy on sincere and reasoned grounds: believers in the theory that the boom and bust cycle is inevitable and desirable can make a case; those who prefer sovereignty enforced by military means at home and abroad can find reason enough to deplore his program.

Thus far, however, the outcry against him has been confined to the chant that he is a fool (which his canny business successes alone would tend to belie) or a traitor—a charge as readily sustained against Lincoln or Roosevelt.

It is time for us to emerge from the simulated red fog into the pure air of reason.

In his study of the New York working class since World War II, historian Joshua Freeman writes, "Nowhere was the battling over Communism more intense than in New York City. In much of the country, political radicals acted as gadflies or visionaries; in New York, the Communist left, through its presence in the labor movement, electoral politics, and the cultural apparatus, wielded considerable power. Its strength inspired fear and resentment among conservatives and liberals. Their counterattacks helped make New York an epicenter of anti-communism."

The battle was played out in the pages of the *Post*. Readers of the Sunday, August 22 paper were startled to find a boxed article on page 2 signed by Dorothy S. Thackrey, Co-Publisher and Co-Editor, titled "A Further Appeal to Reason," in which she challenged Ted's basic assumptions about Wallace.

I, a sincere liberal, take issue with Mr. Thackrey's reasoning. First of all I do not believe that the grounds stated above for opposing Mr. Wallace's candidacy are either "sincere" or "reasoned"; in the second place and which is more important, I do believe there ARE grounds on which a sincere and reasoned person can and does oppose his candidacy.

Wallace's own position is not always clear and he, himself, does not always give the impression of being a sincere and reasoned person. For example, in his acceptance speech in Philadelphia, which was televised, broadcast and reported nationally, he avoided any condemnation of Communism, and seemed to be in sympathy with the majority of the delegates, who were always ready to boo United States foreign policy, but who showed no lack of sympathy with the totalitarian government of the U.S.S.R.

However, a few weeks later, in a radio address, at which there was no audience to boo, and which was not made against the background of a national convention, he did say that he didn't "like the limitation of political freedom in Soviet Russia." . . .

This just doesn't make sense to me. How can a man believe so strongly that civil liberties are essential for the progress of his own country, and at the same time believe that the same ideals can be achieved by another country without them?

The article was followed by an editor's note in which Ted promised that his answer to his wife's argument would appear in the following Sunday edition. From then on, the Thackreys issued weekly challenges and rebuttals. On August 29, Ted wrote that since Dorothy controlled the paper, her editorial view would ultimately prevail, but that he would vote for Wallace. He thought Dolly was improperly sidetracked by the issue:

In criticizing Mr. Wallace for his failure to condemn Communism every hour on the hour, my Co-Editor chooses to ignore, for example, that in the radio speech from which she quotes, Mr. Wallace lists Communism among the threats to Democracy, restates his own devotion to progressive capitalism, but chooses to regard monopoly capitalism as the greatest immediate threat to democracy—and I agree with him.

Like so many of Mr. Wallace's opponents, my colleague seems to be infuriated by his refusal to simplify all issues into terms of pro- and anti-Communism. . . . It is true that there are too many Communist Party members on the Progressive Party working committees. But it's because committed liberals haven't fought hard enough to make their presence known.

Back and forth it went. In "Appeal to Reason V" on September 12, 1948, Ted argued that Truman's foreign policy was leading the world to war. Truman asked only two questions: was American policy good for British imperialism and was it bad for the USSR? Ted was enraged that the Western democracies were allowing Germany and Japan to rejoin the community of nations in order to help the West against Russia. The Marshall Plan, which was based on true humanitarian impulses, was being "perverted before our eyes into a weapon for war and for no other purpose." He also wrote,

> I do not pretend to understand the Communist mind, but I do know that ex-
> tension of social legislation and civil liberties and price control are so vital to
> democracy that I shall vote for Mr. Wallace to make it clear that I too cry for
> these things—and if that makes me a fellow traveler, so be it. . . . I am not for
> Russia first, France first, or Bevin first, or Chiang Kai-shek first, or anything
> first except democracy first, last and always. . . .
>
> I say to any liberal who refrains from voting for Mr. Wallace because Com-
> munists are voting for him: what are you afraid of? Are you afraid that more
> housing, more civil liberties, more social legislation at home will somehow cre-
> ate more Communism? That's absurd. Are you afraid that achieving a program
> of constructive cooperation for peace with Russia will make democracy less able
> to compete with Communism—or with Fascism? Again I say don't be absurd.

Dolly was having none of it. Wallace and his supporters, she said, were unwittingly calling for policies that would divide and weaken the free world: "I say that by his words and deeds Mr. Wallace is encouraging and fostering reaction, both on the left and on the right, rather than discouraging it."

She believed that Wallace was naïve at best and dishonest at worst. He blamed the Communist coup in Czechoslovakia on the fact that the American ambassador to Prague had provoked Communist reaction by his support of "rightists" planning a coup. He refused to support the Marshall Plan. As for his alleged concern for minority rights in this country, she pointed out that he had done nothing to aid minority hiring in his departments when he was a cabinet officer.

Dolly did agree with Ted that Truman did not deserve the *Post*'s endorsement. "Mr. Truman seems to me to be an utterly irresponsible public servant, who should under no condition be returned to office." She believed that Truman should have turned down the nomination. He had not been a friend to organized labor, having not pushed for the repeal of the antiunion Taft-Hartley Act. He had tried to keep Humphrey's civil rights amendment off the Democratic party platform. He had not been sufficiently pro-Israel.

On October 17, she wrote, "I cannot vote for candidate Truman because he has proved himself to be one of the weakest, worst informed, most opportunistic Presidents ever to hold the highest office in the land." Unlike Ted, she preferred Dewey to Wallace. "Although well aware of the fact that Mr. Dewey has not defined his program sharply," she wrote in her final message three days before the election, "I feel that a competent and fairly liberal Republican will make a better President than an incompetent and inconsistent Democrat."

She concluded her endorsement by saying that Dewey would be firm in his dealings with the Russians and would treat Israel more fairly than Truman had. Dewey had a good record on civil rights in New York. New York voters should support him and put pressure on him by voting for an even more liberal Senate and House.

To a significant number of people in the *Post* newsroom, the struggle between the coeditors was embarrassing and unseemly. Aside from a small coterie of Wallace supporters whom Ted sheltered, most of the top editors and reporters were anticommunist Democratic regulars. In October, more than a dozen of them, led by city editor Paul Sann and Washington-based James Wechsler, wrote a letter to the editor of the paper endorsing Truman.

All summer long Truman had crisscrossed the country assailing the Republicans for being obstructionists and isolationists. Dewey's campaign was fairly lackluster, and—contrary to expectations—the two breakaway Democratic factions helped Truman more than they hurt him. The Progressives protected him from right-wing charges that he was soft on communism, which reassured Catholic voters, and the Dixiecrat threat brought out frightened black voters in key states like California, Illinois, and Ohio.

Neither Dolly nor Ted had picked the right horse. In the November 2 election, Wallace did well enough in New York to give the state to Dewey, but the president carved out a victory nationally, winning 50 percent of the popular vote, with twenty-five million votes to Dewey's twenty-two million, and taking the electoral college with 303 votes to Dewey's 189. Thurmond's Dixiecrats attracted thirty-nine southern electoral votes and a popular vote of a little over a million. Wallace also collected about 1.1 million votes—half of them in New York—but he came in fourth with no electoral votes.

The Thackreys insisted their political rift was not the symptom of any chasm between them. They told *Editor & Publisher* that the quarrel over the Wallace candidacy was the first they'd had and that it was purely political. Dolly said she thought her arguments were so compelling that she had expected to convert Ted to her point of view. She said, "We always permit our columnists to express their opinion, so why not each other?"

Ted said, "Often business partners, even husbands and wives, disagree on politics. They even vote differently. It just happens that we run a newspaper."

People who knew them well, knew better. Dolly's daughter Sarah-Ann, who was still living at home in 1948, remembers, "They totally differed on the political issue, and the political differences were profound. But there were many things that weren't working. And they were more than political—they were real background differences, real differences in approach to what you needed to do. The political differences were symptoms of a much more fundamental difference, and it all came together at once. . . . Ted was nice to me, but he was definitely not what you would call a suitable man for her. That was not a good marriage."

One of Thackrey's colleagues at the *Post* said that Ted's elevation by marriage turned him from an excellent newsroom manager to an overbearing poseur. "He never traded up to fancier clothes or a more expensive brand of whisky, but suddenly he had an air about him as if he moved in higher circles than we did and deserved to."

Years after they parted, Dolly wrote that she thought that Ted had resented her political connections. One reason he supported Wallace, she believed, was that at the Democratic convention in 1948, she knew many of the party regulars from her days as a Roosevelt supporter and friend, while Ted felt like an outsider. When he showed up at the Progressive party convention, on the other hand, he was welcomed as a significant convert.

Dolly's older daughter, Adele, says that Ted could be fun. He'd been a pilot during the First World War, and he encouraged her interest in learning to fly. Adele says, "I think one of the appealing parts of Ted Thackrey was that he had tremendous enthusiasm for things. And that was infectious. But there was always an air of mystery about him as well. To me. Maybe not to other people. For example, he told me he loved to ski. I did, too. And we were going to ski out in Long Island one day when there was snow, and he put his skis on inside the house, and I thought, this is not a guy who skis. And that suggested . . . I don't want to say he was a liar, but this just didn't make sense."

As the Thackrey breakup played out publicly in the fall of 1948, Ted was thinking about a possible exit strategy. He had talked in July with J. Richardson Dilworth and Joseph Clark, reform Democrats in Philadelphia, about the possibility of their establishing a liberal newspaper to fill the void that would be created if J. David Stern acted on his stated intention of closing the *Record*. Nothing came of this scheme, but Ted kept his ears open.

At this point, the Thackreys' marriage was unsalvageable, but negotiating their breakup would be tricky. Rather than face the issue, Dorothy left for Europe immediately after the election with her friend Alicia Patterson, the editor of *Newsday*. It was too soon after the war for casual sightseeing. Most of their traveling companions on the *Queen Elizabeth* were businessmen or government officials. Milton Eisenhower, Ike's younger brother, was headed for a UNESCO conference in Paris. Dorothy admired Alicia's audacity in asking him whether it was true that the general had had an affair with his wartime driver, Kay Summersby, as Summersby had recently claimed in a memoir. Milton was positive that the rumors were false. Jack Baragwanath, a mining engineer whom both women had known for years as part of the Swope set on Long Island, was also aboard. The threesome took their meals together, and Alicia and Dorothy flirted with their sophisticated and amusing dinner partner.

After landing in Cherbourg, they visited the Normandy invasion beaches, but the American military cemetery was closed because bodies were still being disinterred for reburial back in the States. Signs of wartime devastation were everywhere. At the only available hotel in Barfleur, the women shared a small room. Dorothy thought the other guests unsavory. Alicia put a bottle of whiskey on the dresser for them to share and said she wasn't afraid of anyone. In Paris, John Hohenberg, the *Post* bureau chief, was pressed into service as a driver and interpreter when the women attended several official press conferences given by the foreign ministers of the wartime allies, who were attending United Nations meetings being held there at the time.

At a party at the American embassy, Dorothy and Alicia met General George Marshall, the secretary of state, and his wife, Katherine. Dorothy was pleased to tell Mrs. Marshall that she had translated her memoir, *Together: Annals of an Army Wife,* into Braille earlier that year. Nervous that the secretary would hold it against her that the *Post* had criticized him for not sufficiently supporting the new state of Israel, she asked him what he thought about the role of the press. She was relieved when he said that because all his life he had been surrounded by underlings who were loath to challenge his ideas, commentary in the press sometimes presented him with a valuable, differing point of view.

Before they left New York, the women had received permission from the American military to visit Berlin. The city was still occupied by Allied forces, each of which had its own zone of control. A Russian blockade imposed in

June cut off ground transportation into the city from the rest of western Europe. The only way in or out was on a military transport plane, which Alicia boarded without complaint. Admitting that she was a "sissy," Dorothy chose to forgo Berlin in favor of a visit to Frankfurt, which she could get to by train. Frankfurt was still in ruins. Rubble had barely been cleared from most neighborhoods. The people she met were poor, undernourished, and pessimistic about the future. There was no heat at the Park Hotel, so she slept in her fur coat.

Alicia flew home to the States, but Dolly chose not to push her luck. Killing time before she was due to sail, she returned to Paris for a week of seeing old friends and shopping. There were no decent stockings to be found in the city; she bought a dress and a shawl for herself at Balmain and picked up ties, handbags, and bracelets to give her family. Back at Claridge's in London before taking the *Queen Mary* home, she ran into John Baragwanath again. They began an affair. Baragwanath was married to Neysa McMein, a well-known portrait painter, and Dorothy had no illusions that he was to be the love of her life, but he was an amusing distraction from her troubles with Ted.

Perhaps sensing that he had nothing to lose, Ted committed himself to an increasingly far-left orthodoxy in the weeks that Dorothy was away. She returned in December to find him preparing a year-end editorial that blamed America for most of the world's ills. She considered it a vicious assault on Truman's foreign policy. Enraged, she told Ted he could not print the piece. She asked him to move out of the apartment, and—as if to wash her hands of everything they had shared—she also said she would give the paper to him to run. She then took off for California with Baragwanath.

On January 29, 1949, the following announcement, signed by Dorothy S. Thackrey, appeared in the *Post:*

Ten years ago I was convinced that there was a great need for a militant liberal newspaper in New York City. I still am. At that time I acquired the New York Post, with the hope and determination that I could strengthen it and broaden its influence. Since then I have labored constantly to accomplish that purpose.

The newspaper has steadily grown in prestige, circulation and strength. With the merger of the Bronx Home News, it is now firmly established and my original purpose has been fulfilled.

Accordingly, I have turned over the control and management of the New York Post Home News to T.O. Thackrey, who has contributed so much to its success. Today he becomes its sole publisher and editor. Under him, and with the loyal support of his fellow-workers, the New York Post Home News will be a continuing and growing force for the causes for which it stands.

She was acting on impulse, and that impulse was unrealistic. Ted may have become the sole publisher and editor, but Dolly still owned the paper outright (although technically at one remove, through Theodoro), and she was responsible for its corporate obligations and its debts. Her lawyers made Ted sign an agreement not to change its liberal editorial policies or its pattern of operations.

He hardly had a free hand, although he acted as if he did. Circulation was holding steady at about 365,000 copies daily,* yet the paper was once again facing a financial crisis, which Ted addressed by trying to cut staff. This alienated the Newspaper Guild, whose members threatened a walkout in February that would have shut the paper down. He offered a compromise early-retirement plan, which was theoretically permissible, but he lacked the funds to implement it. Senior editors were as appalled by his lack of managerial skills as they were by his Stalinist politics.

By March, Dolly had returned to New York and returned to her senses. She asked Joseph Lash to analyze the editorial and news columns of the *Post* during the period Ted was in charge. Lash, who'd been a leader of left-wing student organizations in the 1930s, became a close adviser to Eleanor Roosevelt in the forties. As one of the founders of the ADA, he was a friend and political ally of Wechsler, who probably brought him to Dorothy's attention.

On March 10, 1949, Lash sent a letter to her home summarizing his findings: the news coverage in the paper was not notably procommunist, but the editorials—particularly on matters relating to foreign policy—showed a serious bias. Ted was eager to highlight threats to liberal democracy from the right but unwilling to recognize the perils of Soviet policies. His editorials, Lash believed, "fail to recognize, or deliberately ignore, the aggressive, dynamic character of international communism's assault on liberal democracy."

Lash also alerted Dolly to the fact that Ted was to be a featured speaker at an upcoming conference for world peace under the same sponsorship as a

---

*Of its afternoon rivals, the *Sun* and the *World-Telegram* each sold approximately the same number as the *Post,* while the *Journal-American* had a daily circulation of almost 800,000.

meeting the previous summer in Poland at which the participants had issued a proclamation praising the forbearance of the USSR in the face of America's Hitler-like role in postwar politics. "After many painful experiences," Lash wrote, "liberals have to come to realize that cooperation with communists is not possible for liberal ends. It is regrettable that the publisher of this city's outstanding liberal newspaper should help to muddy this issue once again. The net effect will be . . . to diminish the Post's influence in its fight against the grave dangers from the right."

Straightening out Ted's political slant was not the only problem Dolly faced. Her confident assertion in the January announcement that the paper she was turning over to him was in good shape was patently inaccurate. There was barely enough money in the till to meet the weekly payroll. Morale was poor. The Post faced a management and financial emergency that was as acute as any in the past. Once again, Dolly had to decide whether to fold it or underwrite it. If she chose to keep it alive, she had to decide who would run the show.

The outcome was never really in doubt. Within days Ted was out the door, and his name was off the masthead. On April 6, 1949, the Post announced that the directors of the New York Post Corporation "had accepted with deep regret the resignation of T.O. Thackrey as Editor and Publisher. Irreconcilable differences on fundamental questions of policy made a request for his resignation inevitable." Dorothy Schiff Thackrey retrieved her title as president of the corporation and actively took on the job of publisher of the paper. For the moment she retained Paul Tierney as executive editor, and within weeks she promoted Richard Manson from the entertainment section to be her assistant publisher.

The paper, she said, would continue Ted's support for Israel and the United Nations. It would continue to fight for liberal democracy around the world and "oppose with equal rigor all totalitarianism, whether Fascist or Communist." Asked if this implied that Ted was a Communist or a Communist sympathizer, she replied that she was sure he was not.

In the late 1940s, the American press was not yet as self-absorbed as it would later become; "the press" was a relatively minor beat. Nonetheless, the Thackrey imbroglio was too good a story to overlook. The newsweeklies implied that Ted, though perhaps lacking in political savvy, was a sound news-

man (stress on "man") and Dolly was an inconsequential woman who just
happened to control the purse strings. *Time* speculated that if Dolly could
find a buyer with liberal Democratic political views and $10 million in cash,
she would sell in a minute.

Newsweek reported on April 18, 1949, that Ted had been making headway on cutting costs, but Dolly got impatient and booted him out. The same
week's issue of *Time* quoted Ted as pinpointing politics, not finances, as the
source of trouble. He said he'd been given a three-month ultimatum to improve the balance sheet, which he was on the way to doing, but that when "I
was given the choice of supporting the Atlantic Pact or resigning. I resigned."

Dolly was indignant. Then and later she praised his city room skills but
disparaged his business acumen and denied she'd given him an ultimatum of
any sort. In 1950, she told an interviewer that Ted was "a technically perfect
newspaperman. He taught me to listen and learn and to put ideas into practice." But she complained that he always claimed that he'd built circulation
and made the paper profitable. Her interpretation was that circulation
growth had come primarily with the purchase of the *Bronx Home News*. It
was undeniable that the paper was losing money when Ted left. She said that
Ted "always deluded himself as to his success."

Her criticism of him remained most emphatic when she described his
politics: "I would say that he was politically naive. He was taken in by the fellow travelers movement without quite knowing what it was and he found he
had a bear by the tail and didn't know how to let go."

She also challenged Ted's contention that he'd been stabbed in the back
by other men in the newsroom. He sometimes complained that Wechsler and
Sann had conspired against him and gotten Dolly's ear. They had indeed presented her with a plan earlier that winter to run the paper together, which she
rejected, although it may have lodged in her mind. What is undeniable is that
Wechsler's reporting on the presidential race during the summer of 1948
played a part in alerting Dolly to the oversimplifications and duplicities in
Wallace's position, and Sann, who would be much closer to her after Thackrey left, politely but firmly let her know from time to time how unhappy most
of the city room staffers were with Ted's politics.

The subject came up again in 1973 when Gail Sheehy published her article about Dolly in *New York* magazine. Revisiting the brief period when
Dolly turned the paper over to Ted, Sheehy asked if she thought he would

fail. "Yes, I think I knew he would," she answered, citing the fact that his politics alienated advertisers and staff members alike.

When Sheehy's article appeared, Ted wrote a letter disputing Dolly's account. He seemed most wounded by her saying he was destined to fail, and he restated without substantiation that he had reduced the paper's deficit and raised the circulation during his tenure. There was further disagreement about whether Dolly had actually turned the paper over to him or whether the strictures imposed by her lawyers effectively curtailed his freedom to manage effectively. At one point Dolly threatened to sue *New York* if her side of the story did not prevail.

Such contention nearly twenty-five years after the event suggests that both Dolly and Ted had lingering doubts and embarrassments about their behavior. In the interim Dolly had become accustomed to thinking of herself as a competent and decisive executive; she can't have liked to be reminded of the time when she was still vacillating about whether or not to take charge. For Ted the retelling of the episode can only have reminded him of what he had lost and how far he had fallen after he left the *Post*.

In June 1948, Marshall Field III had finally pulled the plug on *PM,* a left-leaning New York daily founded by Ralph Ingersoll that Field and John Whitney, among others, had been underwriting since 1940. Field estimated that in the eight years of *PM's* existence, he had put between $5 million and $6 million into a paper that seemed even more marginal during the postwar era than it was earlier. He announced that he would transfer ownership of the paper to Bartley Crum and Joseph Barnes, a veteran newsman from the *Herald Tribune* and a friend of Crum from the Willkie days. Field took no cash from the new owners, just stock in their venture, and as a final gesture of goodwill he loaned them another $500,000.

Crum and Barnes changed the paper's name to the *New York Star* and tried to move its politics back toward the center, but they were unable to stem its losses. Just before shutting down permanently, Crum tried to work out a partnership with the *Post,* but as Dolly later told Crum's daughter and biographer Patricia Bosworth, "Bart simply could not convince me the *Star* was a good investment."

Within weeks of leaving the *Post,* Ted Thackrey bought the *Star*'s presses and leased some of its space with money he raised from an eighty-two-year-old benefactor, Mrs. Anita McCormick Blaine, the International Harvester

heiress, who did not share the political views of her cousin, Colonel Robert
McCormick, the isolationist, ultraconservative publisher of the *Chicago Tribune*. Ted brought along a few of his cronies from the *Post*, including I. F.
Stone (whom he had just lured back to the paper in January), and signed up
some other holdovers from *PM* and the *Star*.

In his first issue on May 16, 1949, Ted announced that *The Daily Compass*
would be a "liberal crusading newspaper." But its crusades were predictable,
and the paper never attracted enough steady readers to be remotely viable.
Dolly was not inclined to help. In August, she wrote to her assistant from Sun
Valley, Idaho, where she was getting her divorce, asking if it was true that the
Post was making newsprint available to the *Compass*. If so, she wanted the
costs deducted from Ted's severance pay. It turned out that there was no such
transaction, but she was certainly not in a generous mood.*

The debate between Dolly and Ted about the proper attitude a person on
the political left should have toward communism in general and the Soviet
Union in particular may seem remote now, but it shaped much of American
intellectual and political life for nearly thirty years after the end of the war.
Where you stood in the debate affected your attitude toward the Korean
War, McCarthyism, the Cold War, and the struggles for civil liberties and civil
rights. The debate led to the emergence of the New Left in the 1960s and the
generation gap that often separated student rebels from their seniors. The
debate helped define where Dolly and her paper would take their stand during the fifties and sixties, where they would develop the greatest rapport with
their potential readership, and the role they would play in the rise and fall of
American liberalism in the second half of the twentieth century.

---

*The inevitable death of the *Compass* came in November 1952. Ted got a job as the managing editor of
the *Lakeland* (Florida) *Ledger* and then returned to New York to work at a succession of jobs in public
relations and advertising. From 1976 until his death in 1980, he edited the bulletin of a New York civic
organization.

II

TAKING CONTROL

SIX

Transition Time

After having owned the *Post* for a decade, Dorothy, at age forty-six, was fully in charge. Not surprisingly, she had to deal at once with a financial crisis. Newspaper operations in 1948 showed a staggering $665,000 loss, and although some austerity measures had begun to kick in, the paper was still operating in the red in the first half of 1949. Dolly signaled her commitment with another $500,000 investment to meet the paper's current obligations.

She moved quickly to restructure the *Post*'s leadership. She ordered her lawyers to dissolve Theodoro and restore the New York Post Corporation as the official owner of the paper. On May 11, 1949, she consolidated her control, taking the title of editor as well as publisher of the paper and announced, that "to avoid confusion" she would henceforth be known as Dorothy Schiff.*

Her choice of name was an indication of how she saw herself at that point. Certainly she had been influenced by both of her husbands. She had adopted George Backer's liberal politics but rejected his dilettante's approach to journalism; she had learned how to run a daily paper from Ted Thackrey while

---

*More formally, she was Mrs. Dorothy Schiff, a usage she would continue even during her next marriage. It was sufficiently unusual at the time that Geoffrey Hellman, in a 1954 *New Yorker* article about the Schiff and Warburg families, declared her to be a "Don't-give-up-the Schiff Schiff."

rejecting his political views. She was not willing to defer any longer to her mentors, or to give them much credit for their contributions. She erased their names in her new professional identity. Her apprentice years were over. A copy of a portrait of Jacob Schiff hung on the wall facing her desk (the original was at Kuhn, Loeb). His would be her guiding spirit from then on.

The *Post* headlines in late May 1949 were a mix of world news and gossip: Shanghai was captured by the Chinese Communists; the Big Four ministers were meeting in Paris; film star Rita Hayworth was being wooed by playboy Prince Aly Khan; former Navy Secretary James Forrestal committed suicide. Local color was never absent. There was a police corruption scandal in Brooklyn; homeless veterans were squatting in abandoned buildings in the Bronx.

On Friday, May 27, the front page announced "Rita & Aly Married as Nobility Looks On" and "2 Cops Dive in River for 300-Pound Woman." The masthead and a brief article inside the paper revealed that Dolly had assembled a new editorial team. Two weeks earlier she had brought thirty-three-year-old James Wechsler to New York from the Washington bureau to be chief editorial writer; almost immediately she appointed him editor in chief. An ardent anticommunist, Wechsler had joined the *Post*'s Washington bureau in May 1946 when he resigned from *PM* to protest what he perceived as Communist domination of that newspaper's editorial position.

Dolly replaced executive editor Paul Tierney, a close ally of Ted, with thirty-five-year-old Paul Sann. Sann had arrived at the *Post* as a seventeen-year-old high school dropout. Hired as a copyboy, he became consecutively a reporter, rewrite man, night city editor, and assistant city editor. In late 1944, after Thackrey turned down his request to become city editor, Sann left for the *Journal-American,* but within months he was back, first as managing editor of the Bronx edition of the paper and then, since March 1948, as city editor.

When Thackrey was driven out in April, Sann wrote a memo arguing that the paper had gotten too embroiled in political disputes and needed to right the balance between ideology and human interest: "We have abandoned the public. There is no space and no display available, except under extraordinary circumstances (and not always then), for the moving human interest which mirrors the life of the city and nation. We were told that Mr. Thackrey didn't want any overemphasis on 'trivia.' . . . Trivia is the story of the people, the little people, as contrasted with the king-makers and policy-makers whose every utterance, however fleeting, commands the Post's space and display at present."

Dorothy was impressed by Sann's argument. Although she did not take his further suggestion that she let him run the paper, she installed him in a powerful position as Wechsler's right-hand man. Forty-four-year-old Henry Moscow, who'd been at the *Post* for almost a decade as reporter and editor, was named managing editor.

Wechsler was to run the editorial page and shape overall editorial policy, while Sann was in charge of the city room, with Moscow as his deputy. In the years to come, Jimmy would be Dorothy's political guru, replacing George Backer, and Paul would be her nuts-and-bolts guy, replacing Ted Thackrey. The important difference was that now everyone knew who was boss.

With a new editorial team in place, Dorothy turned her attention to the economic condition of her various enterprises. She'd gotten some financial relief earlier in the spring when she'd been able finally to jettison the one remaining lemon among her holdings.

WLIB was always the least likely of all her acquisitions to succeed. Buyers were not clamoring to grab this also-ran among the city's media outlets, but in April 1949, Dorothy's lawyers were in serious negotiations with Morris and Harry Novik, principals in a firm called New Broadcasting. Harry, the moneyman, was a successful merchant from Bridgeport, Connecticut. His brother Morris, the radio man, had run WNYC, New York City's municipal station, under Mayor Fiorello La Guardia in the 1930s and subsequently worked as a consultant in the field. New Broadcasting signed a contract to purchase WLIB in July 1949, and the sale was approved by the FCC in September. The Noviks and their partners agreed to pay Dorothy $150,000, $100,000 less than she had spent for the station three years earlier, and she retained bonds worth nearly $650,000 representing loans she had made to keep the station on the air. She carried them on her balance sheet for years with little hope of ever redeeming them.

It was a galling experience. Dorothy needed someone to blame. She never really apportioned the responsibility between herself and Ted Thackrey for their unproductive media shopping spree. When asked in later years, she deprecated his acquisitiveness but understated her accountability in writing the checks. In the short run, her lawyers took the heat. Disputing a bill, she complained to the senior partner at Greenbaum, Wolff & Ernst that the firm had pressured her to buy WLIB at a price higher than the market rate, and that, while she had continued to pay the firm's substantial fees, she had lost a lot of money as a direct result of this bad advice.*

With WLIB off her books and out of her hair, Dorothy was hoping to be able to devote her full attention to the *Post*. But the FCC delayed that development, refusing to approve the proposed sale to Warner Bros. of her California broadcast properties. The commissioners ruled in July 1949 that because no corporation was permitted to hold more than one operating license for a radio station within a defined geographical area, Warners must sell its existing station in Los Angeles before its application for the licenses of KLAC, KLAC-TV, and KYA could be approved.

Warners' contract with Dolly had run out and so, evidently, had their patience. Warners informed the FCC that they no longer wished to purchase the stations. In a memo outlining Dolly's various avenues of recourse, one of her lawyers conjectured that Warners probably wanted out "because of (1) their discovery that the channel was not as good as it might be, and (2) that the cost of operating the television business proved greater than anticipated at the time the bargain was made."

What should be done to protect Dorothy's interest now? The lawyer suggested that he negotiate a schedule of payments in which she would repay Warner Bros. the money that had already been advanced—which she did over the next five years. Second, he recommended that she take her time before selling the Los Angeles stations, which had some potential, while trying to unload KYA as soon as possible.

Since the goal was to cut losses rather than to charge top dollar, it was relatively easy to find a buyer for the San Francisco station. Early in 1950, J. Elroy McCaw and John Keating, who—separately and together—owned several other radio stations in Hawaii and on the West Coast, bought KYA from Dorothy for just under $200,000, half of what she had paid for it five years earlier, to be paid over a period of several years.

Dorothy and her advisers were willing to listen to offers for KLAC and

---

*Not long after writing this letter, Dorothy transferred her legal business to Poletti, Diamond, Roosevelt, Friedin & Mackay (which became Roosevelt, Friedin and Littauer). Although Franklin Roosevelt Jr. was Dorothy's friend, the lawyer who represented her and the *Post* through most of the 1950s was his partner Jesse Friedin.

KLAC-TV but were not actively marketing them. The radio station proved to be a moneymaker under the guidance of Don Fedderson, and it subsidized KLAC-TV, which, as an independent station, continued to lag behind the network affiliates in the competition for top-rated programs and national advertisers. In 1953, Dolly turned down at least two offers for the television station and then accepted a bid of $1,300,000 from the Copley Press, which owned sixteen daily papers in Illinois and California. The new owners changed the call letters to KCOP-TV and operated the station until 1957, when they sold it for $4 million.

That left only KLAC radio still in Dolly's hands. Her son, Morti Hall, had worked at the station since 1950; he became president, easing out Don Fedderson, in 1953. Dolly sold it to him in 1956. He changed the corporate operating name from KMTR Radio to Hall Broadcasting and sold it seven years later to Metromedia. John Kluge, the head of Metromedia, had just paid the Los Angeles Times-Mirror Corporation $10 million for its independent television station, KTTV-TV, when he acquired KLAC radio from Morti for $4.5 million. Dolly's abortive West Coast media career had cost her more frustration than money, especially since her accountants could take advantage of losses to offset income that came to her from other sources. The one positive effect of the adventure was that it made her son independently wealthy.

Just as Dolly was divesting her broadcasting properties, other families in the newspaper business were expanding in that area. Between 1947 and 1954, for example, Phil Graham, the son-in-law and heir apparent of Eugene Meyer, owner of *The Washington Post,* urged his father-in-law to buy a radio station and a television channel in the District of Columbia and a television station in Florida. In all, Meyer laid out just under $8 million for the properties, which soon turned out to have been a bargain.

In principle, betting on the growth of radio and television broadcasting in the postwar years was a good idea; great fortunes were made by people who made proper investment decisions. Dorothy was a wealthy woman, but her resources were limited compared to those of Marshall Field, Eugene Meyer, or the Hearst Corporation, for example. Because she could not compete for first-rate properties, she was forced to look at secondary ones. Others with a greater knowledge of the broadcasting business, deeper pockets, or better connections to the local community could take such properties and make a go of them. But no one in Dorothy's inner circle knew much, if anything, about the broadcasting business. Don Fedderson in California was a solid broadcasting executive. But as independents, the properties he managed were always at a disadvantage vis-à-vis their bigger competitors.

Dorothy came away from this expensive education having learned two practical lessons—one good, one more problematic. The valuable discovery was that absentee ownership wasn't going to work. If her holdings had been organized as a corporation staffed by responsible corporate officials with sufficient business experience and acumen, they might have prospered. Dolly, who had no taste for empire building and little inclination to work within a multilayered management format, was content thereafter to be a hands-on manager of one property—the *New York Post*.

The problematic result was that she became very wary of spending money. Once or twice over the next two decades she sanctioned significant capital investment, but for the most part she was tight with a buck. She would characterize that as astute management; critics, including members of the newspaper staff, often accused her of compromising the paper's potential through insufficient support.

SEVEN

Finding Her Way

With her distractions minimized, Dorothy focused on what she now saw as her primary task. She was determined that the *New York Post* would have an impact not just on local politics but nationally as well. In the process of reviving her paper, she would solidify her own image. She wanted the *Post,* and by extension Dorothy Schiff, to be taken seriously as an opinion maker and a power broker.

For that to be possible, she needed to make the paper economically viable. Dorothy met frequently with her corporate finance advisers Cook and Berger before she left New York in midsummer 1949 to get her divorce from Ted. She spent the six-week obligatory residency period in Sun Valley, poring over financial reports. She was not surprised by what she saw. The paper's circulation was holding up, which necessitated a continued expense in costly newsprint. Advertising revenues still lagged. The short-term solution, which she told assistant publisher Dick Manson to implement immediately, was to cut costs by reducing the number of pages allotted for editorial use—and to cut staff.

In July, Manson reported on protracted negotiations with the Newspaper Guild. Although minor glitches in the contract prevented a settlement until later in the year, Manson predicted that the paper would get a deal it could live with: a manageable rise in the pay scale and the option to eliminate some redundant positions through attrition.

Back in New York by late summer, Dorothy went into action. She fired general manager Mary McClung, a Thackrey loyalist, and installed her son, Morti Hall, as business manager of the paper.

Morti's past few years had been turbulent. While serving in the army, he had eloped in 1944 with Maryanne Parker, a model. Dolly was disappointed that Morti had chosen to marry when he was not even twenty. "But she bore up well," says her daughter, Adele. "We liked Maryanne a lot. And Mother never excluded her, she just thought they were too young." The family was stunned when Maryanne died of a reaction to anesthesia in a dentist's office a year later.

After Morti's discharge in 1946, he entered the executive training program at Chemical Bank in New York, then moved to Los Angeles where he was employed by the Southern Pacific Railroad. He came east to work for his mother in August 1949, although she would soon send him back to California to help manage her television and radio properties until they could be sold.

Daughter Adele had always seen herself as the adventuresome one. "I always had too much energy—it got me into nothing but trouble," she says. "I learned to fly as a teenager. And I underwrote that enterprise by pumping gas. There's a little field up in Pawling, New York. It was during World War II, and there was no civilian flying within fifty miles of the coast. So I'd get on the train and toot up to Pawling. And I pumped gas in exchange for an hour's flying instruction. Fortunately, my mother was blissfully unaware of what I was doing. She was terribly busy at the paper, so she never really focused on it.

"Although for one of her divorces out west," Adele says, "she needed me to go along, and I did on the condition that I could fly around while we were there." Dorothy was determined not to impose her own biases or anxieties, such as her fear of flying, on her children. "She didn't like the outdoors," says Adele. "She didn't like sports, but she wasn't going to get in the way of anyone who did."

Adele's ambition had been to join the Women's Air Corps. Instead, she married young, just as her brother had. Whatever Dolly's reservations might have been, she was supportive. In December 1944, nineteen-year-old Adele was married in her mother's apartment to Lieutenant Arthur Gray Jr., a decorated member of the Army Air Force. The bride was given in marriage by her uncle, John Schiff. Corporal Mortimer Hall was the best man, and his wife was one of the matrons of honor. Adele's little sister, ten-year-old Sarah-Ann, was a flower girl.

Adele retired from the paper to raise a family. Within six years she and

Arthur had four children. After leaving the service, Arthur went to work at Kuhn, Loeb. Among other responsibilities, he helped find new bidders for his mother-in-law's California broadcast properties in the summer of 1949 after the Warner Bros. deal fell through.

Years later, Adele asked her mother why she hadn't been more vocal in counseling either of her Hall children against the risks of early marriage, based on the failure of her own marriage to their father. That was just the point, Dolly said, she had made mistakes in her own life and didn't feel that she had the right to tell her children what to do.

As part of Dorothy's stepped-up activity at the *Post* in 1949, she set out to increase the paper's advertising base. She consulted Mrs. Ogden Reid, who'd been in charge of advertising at the *Herald Tribune* before becoming publisher. Helen Reid stressed building circulation as a marketing tool and told Dorothy to be forceful with New York merchants who would otherwise try to take advantage of her inexperience and her gender.

Dolly let her salespeople handle the details; she entertained the prospective advertiser at lunch or dinner to clinch the deal. She seldom mentioned rates and guarantees, preferring to make the event a social occasion. Having boned up by reading clippings from the paper's morgue, she talked about her guest's personal interests. If he (it was always he) was enthusiastic about sports, she called in an associate to give her a crash course because she knew nothing about the subject.

Her diligence and charm paid off. By the end of the year, she had added Stern's, Arnold Constable, and Abraham & Straus, among the city's leading fashion and department stores, to *Post* regulars like Macy's, Gimbels, Hearn's, and S. Klein on the Square. As the postwar consumer economy began to grow, she picked up accounts from appliance chains, car dealerships, national cigarette brands, and local supermarkets. Ever flirtatious, she was surely aware of the seductive aspects of attracting and retaining advertisers. Occasionally, the game turned earnest, and she had to elude the romantic advances of a businessman who couldn't believe he was being pursued by a woman for the sake of business.

For the first time since her teens, Dorothy was without a man in her life. John Baragwanath had proved to be charming but superficial. She ended that romance late in 1949. She said later that she was influenced to act by a passage in Plato suggesting that one should not waste time on relationships with those who were not serious enough.

Dorothy was often paradoxical. She was the imperious heiress, given extraordinary advantages by the circumstances of her birth, who also felt herself unloved; the college dropout who spent many evenings reading and annotating the great books yet lived for gossip and insisted that she had the intellectual tastes of the average reader of the *Post;* the traveler who was so terrified of airplanes that she would add weeks to her vacations by taking trains or ocean liners yet begrudged her time away from the office and often second-guessed the decisions her assistants made during her absence; the passive investor who allowed two husbands to saddle her with properties that were misguided choices at worst and challenging ones at best yet figured out how to dispose of what was worthless—including the husbands—and how to revitalize what had potential; the granddaughter of a financial wizard and community leader and daughter of a man who could not live up to this imposing heritage who aimed to emulate the patriarch even if the family encouraged the career aspirations only of its sons.

At her best, the mature Dolly was feisty rather than cowed, personally diffident but professionally forceful. When she felt herself faltering, she reentered psychotherapy, this time with a woman trained in the classic Freudian tradition.* Just to play safe, while professing skepticism, she also consulted astrologers and handwriting analysts.

The struggle for self-creation demanded a great deal of Dolly's energy. Although she was very social, she had few intimate friends. One of her closest confidants at this period seems to have been Dick Manson, whom she named assistant publisher within weeks of Ted Thackrey's departure, made a member of the Board of Directors of the paper in 1950, and appointed general manager in June 1951. They were old friends, having known each other since before she acquired the paper in 1939, even before he went to work there in 1934.

Manson frequently escorted her to the theater, and they exchanged long letters mixing personal and professional news when she was out of town.

---

*Although Dorothy cut short her analysis with this doctor (as she had with Harry Stack Sullivan), she remained fascinated by psychiatric insights. She was friendly for years with Dr. Lawrence Kubie, a fixture of the New York Psychoanalytic Society and fellow liberal. At Kubie's behest, she became a faithful financial supporter of the research program of the Austen Riggs Center, a psychiatric treatment center in Stockbridge, Massachusetts.

Manson was not a romantic interest, and the other men with whom she attended public dinners usually were friends but not potential suitors. She was sometimes lonely, sometimes even depressed. She was becoming increasingly wedded to the *Post,* and it would be the most compelling relationship of her life.

She settled into the penthouse suite at West Street, reached by a private elevator and separated by twelve floors from the rest of the paper. The penthouse had been built and fitted out as a pied-à-terre for the Curtis family. David Stern used the living room occasionally for cocktail parties. Dolly chose the oak-paneled living room for her office and converted the rest of the space for her immediate staff. In contrast to the grubby city room below, her office was comfortably opulent. Four of the eight big windows offered a panoramic view of the Hudson River. She worked at one side of a mammoth partners' desk she had bought in London years before and left the other side conspicuously unoccupied. The portrait of Jacob Schiff on the wall was a kind of guardian angel.

Just when Dolly thought she had imposed stability in the paper's editorial leadership, a clash of personalities disrupted her team. Henry Moscow, the managing editor, a decade older than Sann and Wechsler, resented serving under them.

Sann, particularly, went out of his way to try to mollify Moscow. At one point, he suggested that Dolly include him in a picnic at her summer house in Sands Point to which she had invited the Sann and Wechsler families. Moscow later claimed that the other men repeatedly harassed and second-guessed him and that they criticized him to the boss. Dolly felt, on the contrary, that Wechsler and Sann were "mollycoddling" Moscow rather than trying to sabotage him.

Matters came to a head on November 4, 1949. The evening before, just as Wechsler was leaving the office, he read an insightful piece filed from the United Nations headquarters by *Post* reporter John Hohenberg. Wechsler left a memo requesting that the story get a big play in the next day's paper. In the morning, he was astonished to discover that in place of Hohenberg's copy Moscow had substituted a routine wire service piece on the same subject. Jimmy confronted the managing editor on the floor of the city room. Both men began shouting, and Moscow said he didn't see why he had to ask

Wechsler's permission every time he made a decision. Wechsler reminded him this wasn't just any decision but a clear refusal to follow instructions.

Enraged, Moscow stomped into the office of Morti Hall, the newly installed business manager, to announce that the situation between him and Wechsler had been intolerable for months. The last straw was that "Wechsler had bawled him out in public." He was resigning immediately and wanted Morti to arrange for him to be given his accumulated vacation pay. After failing to calm Moscow down, Morti arranged for the payroll department to cut a check, which Moscow took before leaving the premises. According to Morti, Moscow was "very amiable and said that he was sorry about the whole thing but had made up his mind."

Days later, Moscow realized that his headstrong behavior had cost him nearly $20,000 in severance pay that would have been due him had he been fired. He wrote a conciliatory letter to Dolly saying that although Wechsler and Sann had been persistently rough on him, he would like to continue as managing editor after explaining himself to her personally. On her lawyer's advice, she replied that his decision to resign was irrevocable. Stunned, Moscow tried again: "No, no, you missed the point. I want to talk with you to see if we can get back to basics." She didn't reply.

A few months later, Moscow sued Sann and Wechsler for defamation of character and sued the *Post* for his severance pay. Although his case was dismissed several times, he persisted in refiling appeals. Finally, in January 1952, the *Post* paid him $5,000 in exchange for his agreement not to pursue the matter further.

Moscow was not missed. The incident served mainly to underscore the increasing importance of the working alliances that Dolly was developing with Sann and Wechsler and her trust in their judgment.

The two men were quite different in style and substance. Wechsler came from a middle-class family who lived in Manhattan. His father was a lawyer, as was his older brother. Jimmy graduated from Columbia College in 1935, a precocious twenty-year-old. Before graduation he married Nancy Frankel, a Barnard College student who came from a family much like his.* His senior year he was the editor of the college newspaper, the *Spectator*.

---

*After Barnard, Nancy graduated from Columbia Law School. For many years she was a member of the firm of Greenbaum, Wolff & Ernst, but Dorothy Schiff and the *Post* were no longer clients.

Jimmy was active in campus politics, joining the Young Communist League (YCL) in 1934. Although he served for a few months as a member of the YCL Executive Committee, he was soon disillusioned by reports of the Moscow show trials and of Communist infighting in Spain. After college he and Nancy traveled to the Soviet Union where they saw the abuses of the regime for themselves. Wechsler resigned from the YCL in December 1937 and became thereafter a leading foe of communism at home and abroad.

He went to work at *The Nation,* then jumped to *PM* in 1940, where he stayed, except for several months of military service, until he joined the *Post* in 1946. He became an expert on the American labor movement and the attempted Communist infiltration of various unions. In addition to writing articles about labor and politics for a number of journals, Jimmy found time to produce a biography of union leader John L. Lewis, which was published in 1944.

Wechsler, like many former Communists, could be obsessive in his close reading of statements by political friends and foes to make sure that they met his strict criteria for ideological purity. As a friend and ally of Eleanor Roosevelt and her ADA colleagues, however, he was also willing to acknowledge the realities of the political arena. Above all, he had the energy and instincts of a serious daily newspaperman. A prodigiously hard worker, Jimmy's only outside interests were sports and his family.

He arrived at the *Post* every morning about ten and consulted with Sann and other editors about the first edition of the day, which was about to go to press. He checked in with Dolly, who may already have had several memos deposited on his desk. Depending on the news and whether or not there were management crises, Wechsler might settle down in late morning to shape the editorial page for the next day.

Lunch was either accompanied or followed by a couple of shots of bourbon; his secretary kept a bottle of his favorite brand in her desk. The bourbon led to a nap, after which he wrote his editorials and left instructions for the night editors before heading out early in the evening. If there was a late newsbreak, he could be reached by phone at any hour. If necessary he would write another editorial from home and have a messenger pick up his copy.

Paul Sann, in contrast to Wechsler, was a working-class kid, and he cultivated the tough-guy pose all his life. Born in the Bronx to an immigrant garment worker and his wife, Sann dropped out of high school in 1931 to become a $12-a-week copyboy at the *Post.* He later claimed that his career choice was determined the day he cut class to see *The Front Page* at a Times Square movie house. The hero of this comedy about the city room of a Chicago newspaper was a brash reporter named Hildy Johnson, played by Pat O'Brien. "I wanted to be Hildy Johnson," Paul wrote later.

His parents were irate. "It wasn't a matter of going to college and becoming a doctor or a lawyer, for the family sights were never set that high," he recalled. "My mother was not at all sympathetic about this wild idea of her son becoming a newspaper reporter. I think she thought of that as something the Christians did."

Both men were sports fans. Wechsler was passionately devoted to the New York Yankees and the Columbia University football team. Sann liked the fights and the races. He loved to gamble. For many years he was a client of a man known as Benny the Bookie, who operated on the premises of the *Post*.* Sann was much less obsessed with politics than Wechsler or Dolly, though he shared their point of view. He had, in fact, helped Dolly draft her editorials in the duel with Ted Thackrey. He had a surer sense of the everyday interests of the *Post*'s core audience than Jimmy did. Sann married Birdye Pullman, a girl from his old neighborhood, and they continued to live in the Bronx.

Journalism is an ephemeral craft. The tragedies, scandals, and civic debates that constitute the subject matter of the daily paper are almost always of only passing interest. Few reporters or editorial writers achieve lasting fame. Yet they demonstrate tenacity and zeal, a balance of idealism and cynicism, the ability to make readers understand and care—and do it six days a week. Dorothy Schiff's *Post* attracted and nurtured a notable cluster of extremely

---

*In 1953, two men who worked in the sports department of the paper were accused by the Manhattan District Attorney's Office of supplying some gamblers with basketball scores, which the paper received from a group of bookmakers in Minneapolis in exchange for early racing results. Both men admitted their involvement and were asked to resign, although ultimately the DA did not press charges, and one of the two was eventually reinstated. Sann and Ike Gellis, the sports editor, probably knew nothing about this freelance venture of their employees, but they had approved the unsavory connection with the Minneapolis bookies in the first place.

  Dolly, who ignored the sports department except in a crisis, insisted that the paper stop publishing betting odds immediately. As soon as her attention moved elsewhere, they were reinstated. Bennie the Bookie, who had nothing to do with this particular contretemps, stayed on.

talented reporters and columnists who gave the paper its distinctive tone and earned it a reputation for being serious and idiosyncratic.

Some of the paper's biggest names had been there since before the Schiff-Wechsler-Sann regime took charge. Staying on required that they either share the prevailing liberal philosophy of the editor in chief and the publisher or be apolitical. Wechsler was determined to get rid of anyone he believed harbored Thackrey-like pro-Russian sentiments about the Cold War. His crusade was made easier by the fact that the New York Newspaper Guild local, which had been dominated by Communist party members and followers for years, had recently been taken over by a slate of anticommunists who drove the remaining Reds from its board. Sympathetic to Jimmy's politics, the new union management was willing to help him ease the few remaining political adversaries off the *Post* payroll.

One of the paper's stars during the forties fell out of favor because he was too far to the right. Victor Riesel was a tough-minded, widely syndicated specialist on labor unions. Riesel was born in 1913 into a working-class family; his father was the head of a small garment workers' local. The elder Riesel was beaten up by hoodlums in 1942 and died five years later, in part because of his injuries. Victor reported on conditions in mines and factories for a number of small labor publications during the Depression. In 1941, he joined the *Post* as a reporter and was given his own column two years later. He made his name exposing Communists and criminals in the union movement. His antipathy to these imperfections within organized labor drove him to an increasingly right-wing political stance. Soon after Wechsler's appointment, Riesel moved to Hearst's *Daily Mirror,* where he was much more at home.

Riesel was replaced at the *Post* by a writer who would be one of its defining voices—James Murray Kempton. Born in Baltimore in 1917, Kempton graduated from Johns Hopkins and worked for the ILGWU as an organizer until the *Post* hired him to back up Riesel in 1942. After serving in the air force during the war, Kempton took a job at the *Wilmington* (NC) *Morning Star,* then returned to the *Post* to replace Riesel in 1949.

Kempton, like Wechsler, had joined the Young Communist League as a college student and soon pulled out, having seen for himself the flaws in the Communist position. Though he remained a Socialist for some time, Kempton's true passion was a contrarian determination to look beyond dogma to the vagaries of human nature and to chronicle them with gentleness, erudition, and a dedication to elegant prose that made him one of the most grace-ful stylists in the working press.

Max Lerner came to the *Post* having already established a reputation as a scholar and a journalist. A precocious student, Lerner took his undergradu-ate degree at Yale and his doctorate at the Ph.D. program of what is now the Brookings Institution. Lerner so impressed the Brookings faculty that they granted him his degree on the basis of the papers he wrote during the aca-demic year without requiring that he write a thesis.

Max began a lifelong pattern of moving back and forth between academia and journalism. He taught political science at Sarah Lawrence, Harvard, and Williams, where he was the first Jew appointed to the faculty. While teaching, he wrote articles for the *New York Herald Tribune, The Nation,* and *The New Republic,* in which he frequently attacked the New Deal from the left as be-ing too respectful of property rights. He left teaching briefly in 1936 to be-come editor of *The Nation* and later served as an editorial writer for *PM* and the *New York Star.* Unlike many fellow members of the ADA, Lerner took a long time to recognize that the wartime alliance between the United States and the USSR had degraded into an implacable Cold War rivalry.

Lerner was one of the first people Wechsler hired. His reputation as a pun-dit and a scholar earned him a fee of $250 a week for five columns plus $60.50 for his secretary. Within two years, he was cut back to four columns weekly for the same $250. A further stipulation of Lerner's contract was that he share with the paper any proceeds that resulted from books based on his columns.

Lerner maintained an office at the *Post,* though he used it only intermit-tently. He commuted between New York and Boston, where he was a found-ing member of the social sciences faculty at Brandeis. He consulted frequently with Wechsler and Dolly about editorial policy and was occasionally called on to write editorials when Jimmy went on vacation.

William Shannon was another academic star who moved into journalism, but unlike Lerner, he was eager to leave the university behind. Shannon's ad-viser at Harvard, Arthur Schlesinger Jr., recommended him for a job as Drew Pearson's research assistant. When that assignment ended, Shannon became a freelance writer whose work soon brought him to Wechsler's attention. Jimmy made the twenty-four-year-old Shannon head of the *Post*'s Washing-ton bureau in April 1951. Shannon's training as a historian gave him a deeper understanding of contemporary events than many of his journalistic peers.

A number of first-rate reporters who were already on board in 1949 fit in easily with the new editorial team because they shared political and journalistic sensibilities. Joe Kahn, Bob Spivack, and Oliver Pilat all had outstanding credentials and would continue to break big stories. In some respects, the most remarkable among them was Ted Poston.

Theodore Roosevelt Poston was born on July 4, 1906, in Hopkinsville, Kentucky, the son of the principal of the town's school for Negroes—the term of respect at the time. Ted's older brothers started a paper—the *Contender*—in Hopkinsville and took on young Ted as a copyboy. The brothers moved to Detroit and then to New York. Ted put himself through Tennessee A&I in Nashville working on the railroad. He proudly kept up his membership in A. Philip Randolph's Brotherhood of Sleeping Car Porters for years. After graduating in 1928 with a degree in journalism, Ted left immediately for New York, where his brother Ulysses was a correspondent for the Pittsburgh *Courier* and other Negro papers. Ulysses was still publishing a weekly edition of the *Contender,* which he turned over to Ted.

Ted loved New York. Despite the racism, he enjoyed the freedom of life in Harlem. He became a friend of Langston Hughes and other Harlem intellectuals. Starting in 1931, Ted began writing a column about Negro life in New York for the Pittsburgh *Courier*. He was soon hired by the *Amsterdam News* for $13 a week. He stayed at the paper until 1935, when he was fired for leading an organizing attempt by the fledgling American Newspaper Guild. He then found work with the Federal Writers' Project, which also supported Ralph Ellison and Richard Wright.

In the late thirties, no major New York daily papers employed Negroes except in service positions. Herbert Bayard Swope had hired a Negro reporter on the *World* in the late 1920s, but racism in the city room soon forced the man to quit.

A friend of Poston's and a fellow journalist, Henry Lee Moon, tried to get a job on *The New York Times* in 1936, arguing that New York's growing Negro community deserved to be covered—and by a Negro journalist. *Times* publisher Arthur Hays Sulzberger replied that Moon had made an interesting proposal, but that it "entailed too many difficulties."

Under the leadership of David Stern, the *Post* ran more Harlem news than any of its competitors. Negro papers around the country subscribed to the *Post* and reprinted many of its stories. Stern was also the first publisher to sign a contract with the Newspaper Guild. Knowing this, Poston asked Walter Lister, the city editor, for a job. Lister said if Ted filed an exclusive story that could run on page 1, Lister would buy it at the standard freelance rate of three cents an inch. On his way home, Poston came across a white man being assaulted by a mob in Harlem for trying to serve a summons on Father Divine, a well-known evangelist in the community. He wrote a vivid account and delivered it to Lister. The editor kept his word, and Poston continued to supply him with usable copy.

Lister finally hired Poston as a staff reporter because he cost too much money as a freelancer. Poston was probably the first permanent Negro staff reporter on any paper in the country, and for long periods of time, he remained the only one.* He was shunned by reporters from other papers when he did a stint in the pressroom of the city's police headquarters, but he settled into the city room at the *Post* without incident. He made friends with the many liberal reporters who were his colleagues and became one of the guys who went out for a drink together after work.

In 1940, Secretary of the Interior Harold Ickes asked prominent members of the Negro community to form a Black Cabinet to advise FDR. Among the most active members were Robert Weaver, who would become the first Negro cabinet officer, William Hastie, later to become a federal judge, Poston, and Moon. The group lobbied to get jobs for Negroes in defense industries. When the war came, Ted left the *Post* to act as Negro liaison for the Office of War Information. Just after Hiroshima, Truman met with a group of black journalists, Poston among them. Their complaints were among the reasons that Truman issued an executive order integrating the armed forces.

In the summer of 1945, *The New York Times* expressed an interest in hiring Poston. Ted was willing to be a groundbreaker, but he knew he would be more comfortable back at the *Post,* and its editors would be comfortable with him. They offered him $125 a week to return as a reporter and rewrite man.

Ted's beat was Harlem, but he was assigned many general interest subjects as well. He volunteered to go south to Groveland, Florida, to cover the trial of four Negro boys accused—falsely, it turned out—of raping a white girl. Ted always said that he got on well with white reporters covering civil

---

*T. Thomas Fortune is generally considered to be the first black writer whose byline appeared in the white press. In the early 1900s, Fortune, the editor of a black newspaper in New York, contributed an occasional article to the New York *Sun* and other papers. In the years that followed, other black journalists did freelance work, or contributed pieces that were signed by white men, but no one seems to have broken through to regular employment until Poston.

rights stories. He provided them with access to members of the Negro community, and they respected the fact that he was often at much greater physical peril in the South than they were. Poston's reportage on the Florida trial was a sensational success. He won the Heywood Broun Award from the American Newspaper Guild and the Polk Award (which, *The New York Times* noted, was awarded for the first time to "a Negro reporter"). Wechsler nominated him for the 1949 Pulitzer Prize.

Dorothy Schiff considered Poston one of the stars of the paper. He was among the favored reporters who were summoned for working lunches in the penthouse. Ted was at ease in social situations. Dorothy was grateful that he was not intimidated by her. He often initiated conversation, sometimes greeted her with a kiss. The easy manner that publisher and reporter maintained with each other led some envious staffers to spread a rumor that they were having an affair, but people who knew them best said it was definitely only a professional friendship.

Women's roles on American newspapers were traditionally limited to the fashion and food features. In the late nineteenth and early twentieth centuries, a few intrepid women, notably Margaret Fuller, Dorothy Dix, Ida B. Wells, and Nellie Bly, combined a capacity for self-promotion with reportorial zeal and caught the eye of enterprising editors who emphasized the novelty of their gender while featuring their journalism. Several New York papers assigned women to cover the 1906 trial of Harry Thaw for the murder of architect Stanford White. It was assumed that women were especially talented at human interest stories like prominent murders, divorces, and custody suits, and the role of "sob sister" continues to be a female niche on daily papers to this day. Although Martha Gellhorn, Dorothy Thompson, and Anne O'Hare McCormick made names for themselves as battlefield correspondents during World War II, by and large, general assignment women reporters were uncommon on most American papers.

The *Post,* even before Dorothy Schiff took an active role in its management, had been somewhat more welcoming to women than other New York papers. To a degree this may have been a by-product of prefeminist liberalism. More likely it had to do with economics. As a Guild shop, the paper was forced to offer women the same base salary as men doing comparable work, but as a matter of practice women didn't get the same raises or bonuses. For a paper struggling with the bottom line, every little bit of economizing helped.

During the war, more opportunities opened up. Alice Davidson was one of three women who made up the first all-female rewrite bank in 1942–1943. She had been an assistant farm editor on the *Cedar Rapids Gazette* and was thrilled with her responsibilities in the big city. Davidson married while at the *Post,* something that was impossible at the *Gazette*—"You had to retire if you got married"—and left, somewhat reluctantly, when she had a baby. "I never actually met Dorothy Schiff," she later recalled, "but I rather think she liked having women make good on her paper."

Dorothy would never have suggested to her editors that they go out of their way to hire women. She believed in equal opportunity for men and women, but any thought of affirmative action to make up for the years when women were marginally represented on the staff would have been repugnant to her. However, her very presence made it easier for a promising woman to get her foot in the door. Editors could assume that it wouldn't take any special pleading with the boss to give a woman a chance.* And once hired, women were not condemned to the "women's page" as they were at most other papers. They might be assigned to cover politics, science, or any other story handed out in the city room.

The paper already had one female standout when Dolly took charge. Sylvia Porter was doubly anomalous as a woman who wrote about business, and as a liberal who was respected on Wall Street and Main Street. Sylvia Feldman was born in Patchogue, Long Island, in 1913. Two years after she graduated with a degree in economics from Hunter College, she began a newsletter on the subject of government bonds. She was spotted by the editors at the *Post,* who hired her in 1935. Fearful that a woman writing about finance would not be taken seriously, she called herself S. F. Porter in print.[†] By the time she was given a daily column three years later, she had established

---

*This difference between the *Post* and other New York papers remained true at least into the early sixties. Judy Michaelson, who started at the paper in 1957, says, "A lot of us wouldn't have had our careers without Dolly Schiff." Fresh out of Brooklyn College, Michaelson sent her résumé to most of the papers in the city. "Not hiring women," was the message she got from all but the *Post.* One personnel director called her in for an interview because she'd signed her letter J. Michaelson and was furious when he discovered the deception.

[†]At some point Sylvia changed Feldman to Field; when she married Reed Porter in 1931, she took his last name.

a solid reputation, and her revealed identity became a plus with readers and potential advertisers in the paper.

Fern Marja (who later married and added the surname Eckman to her by-line) became one of the most prominent reporters on the paper and in the city. She was hired as a copy girl just out of college in 1944. The bullying of beginners in the city room was no worse for women than for men, as she recalls it. "Besides," she says, "I had two older brothers, I was used to it." Fern actually waited a shorter time for promotion than some of her male colleagues. "I lasted exactly seven months as a copy girl. I kept handing in pieces for the editor to read, and I think he got tired of reading them so he made me a reporter."

The editor was Paul Sann, who admired Fern's work and entrusted her with some of the top stories in the paper—trials, political campaigns, interviews, and special investigations—as well as the more traditional sob sister assignments. She was drafted to write editorials when the regulars were on vacation or out sick, but she was forced to accept praise and respect rather than adequate pay. As time went on, Fern noticed that a number of men who had been hired after her and who were less prominently featured in the paper were making more money. "I was making the Guild-approved minimum for my level of seniority. I thought I deserved more." But Paul Sann turned down her request for a raise. "I was a woman, my husband had an income, and Sann knew that my parents had some money. So he decided I didn't need the raise." She never asked again.

Like Sylvia Porter and some of the other women at the *Post,* Fern had lunch from time to time with Dolly. "There was a restaurant nearby, and we would go out. Her secretary would call to ask if I could join her. I don't think I ever called her. And we each paid our own way." Sometimes Porter would organize a group lunch for all "the girls" to get together.

These were social, not working, occasions. Fern never mentioned her dissatisfaction with her salary. She steered clear of city room gossip, and she tried not to solicit Dolly's opinions of stories she was working on. "I thought that would be imposing on her. Unless we got to talking about something in the news at the time that I happened to be involved in."

Rose Franzblau was intimidated by Dolly. Rose was the oldest of five sisters who were orphaned during the flu epidemic of 1918. Though she was only a junior at Hunter High School, she was determined to raise the others. She worked through high school, through college, and through her PhD program in psychology at Columbia, somehow managing to keep the family together.

Rose's specialty was what is now called "human resources." She worked for several government agencies helping displaced persons and redundant employees find jobs. She also wrote about interpersonal relations. A friend recommended her to Ted Thackrey, who hired her to write a column for *The Daily Compass*. When that paper closed, Wechsler invited her to join the *Post*. Thackrey had paid her $205 a week for six columns of about a thousand words each. Dolly told Jimmy to pay Franzblau $150 for five shorter pieces.

When Rose was a young girl, she had won an annual prize for the best student in all the New York Hebrew schools that were funded by Jacob Schiff. After the ceremony, the great philanthropist congratulated Rose in person. Franzblau's daughter, Jane Isay, says, "My mother's whole relationship with Dolly was framed by that prize." Upon first meeting Dolly, Rose told her this story; a shrewd psychologist might have guessed that an admiring memory of Grandfather Schiff was just the thing to begin their working relationship on a good note.

Rose's column, "Human Relations," became the basis for several books, and for many years she was the host of a radio show. No matter how successful she became, she never lost sight of the class distinctions that marked her childhood. "Because Dolly was the granddaughter of Jacob Schiff, she represented that great German-Jewish tradition, whereas my mother was the child of immigrants," says Isay. "Dolly once arrived unannounced at our apartment on West End Avenue, and my mother wasn't around, so I invited Dolly in and offered her a cup of tea. I found her to be an extremely agreeable, classy lady. What else could you think? She was totally gracious and lovely. And when my mother came home, it was like, 'Oh my God! She was with Dolly Schiff!'"

What Rose could never have understood was that Dolly felt she had reason to be envious of the immigrant girl. Thinking back on their first meeting, when Rose told her about life in the slums, about neighbors getting together in the evenings to share potato pancakes and sing Hebrew songs, Dolly wrote, "I listened entranced and thought 'Fifth Avenue was never warm and friendly like that.' And I was thrilled that Grandpa Schiff was the bridge that finally brought us together."

———

The *Post* had excellent music, film, and theater reviewers, but the two chroniclers of show business who came to characterize the paper best were columnists, not critics. Earl Wilson and Leonard Lyons recorded New York nightlife at a time when actors, debutantes, politicians, mobsters, and public intellectuals began to cross paths—a time when renown and notoriety became intermingled and the seeds of celebrity-driven news were planted. Wilson and Lyons had somewhat different beats, but the names they dropped were frequently the same, illustrating that, as humorist S. J. Perelman once wrote, "In the aristocracy of success there are no strangers."

Earl Wilson graduated from Ohio State and started out on papers in Columbus and Akron. A college classmate got him a job as a rewrite man at the *New York Post* in 1935. In 1943, the thirty-six-year-old Wilson was 4-F because of a heart condition and was therefore available to take over what was called the amusement column when the incumbent, Richard Manson, went into the army. Manson had used the column to review floor shows and nightclub acts. Wilson added gossip and what passed in its day for scandal. His wife, Rosemary, whom he referred to in the column as the B.W. or Beautiful Wife, usually accompanied him on his rounds. One night Wilson heard her talking with one of the showgirls about falsies. He didn't know what they were. He did a column about the manufacture and sale of falsies and began asking stars if they wore them or not. It was a first for a family newspaper. The *Post*'s editors were fearful that there would be a backlash among regular readers, but the resultant fuss only brought more attention to Wilson's column.

Paul Sann noted that people overlooked what a dogged reporter Wilson was. He broke a lot of show business news and wangled interviews with stars who were being held back by their press agents. Wilson bribed doormen at the big hotels $50 or so to tell him if Grace Kelly, or Judy Garland, or Ava Gardner was in town. He found out from the ladies' room attendant at El Morocco that the duchess of Windsor never tipped.

Sometimes Wilson's irreverence and tenacity paid off in a front-page story: he asked Russian Foreign Minister Vyacheslav Molotov in San Francisco at the founding of the UN how to pronounce "vodka," when that drink was just beginning to appear in American bars. He put Henry Wallace on the spot by asking if he welcomed Communist support for his 1948 presidential bid. Wallace was forced to say yes, with a lot of qualifiers.

By the early 1950s, Wilson's column, "It Happened Last Night," was syndicated in nearly one hundred papers nationwide, which earned him an enviable $75,000 a year, out of which he paid his expenses and the salaries of his two assistants. The *Post* provided an office and a secretary and paid him $150 a week.

While Earl Wilson made no bones about being Everyman, Leonard Lyons aspired to greater heights. Lyons was a Manhattan-born lawyer whose hobby was sending funny stories or anecdotes about celebrities to local columnists. When his items began to be run with some regularity by writers like Walter Winchell, Lyons's wife, Sylvia—who was extremely ambitious— encouraged him to go out on his own. Early in 1934, he submitted sample columns to the *Post* and was hired that May.

Lyons covered some of the same ground as Wilson—the Stork Club, El Morocco, the Latin Quarter—and relied on handouts from the same Broadway press agents. He also cultivated classical musicians, writers, play-wrights, politicians, and other people who were not likely to see their names mentioned in the columns of his competitors. Operating before the age of the computer, Lyons relied on an elaborate file system to fill six columns a week. His resourceful secretaries, first Sylvia Rose and then Anita Summer, developed a card file with typed-up anecdotes about anyone who ever appeared in the column, or might appear at some point. If Lunt and Fontanne were about to open in a new Broadway play, Lyons could fill half a column by claiming to have run into them in such-and-such a restau-rant (which offered the columnist a free dinner in exchange for the plug) and then inserting a story his secretaries had pulled out of the files. If Konrad Adenauer was passing through New York, an anecdote could be plucked from the files. Even if its original (unidentified) source was a three-year-old wire-service account, Lyons would imply that a mutual acquain-tance had shared the story with him or that he had made contact with the German leader himself.

Lyons was the only one of the *Post*'s stable of well-known columnists who was a regular, salaried employee. In the early fifties, he earned a base pay of about $420 a week. The paper also gave him an office and reimbursed some of his expenses. He paid for his secretaries out of his syndication fees. Anita Summer remembers, "Lyons didn't make a fortune from the paper or from the syndication, but he got a tremendous number of perks: free meals, free entertainment, free travel. Press agents would do anything to get a para-graph, a sentence even, in the column. These were the days of payola."

The real payoff, one feels, came when Lyons could report that Harry Tru-

man, Isaac Stern, J. Edgar Hoover, Marc Chagall, or Cary Grant greeted him
as a friend. He worked hard at ingratiating himself. Summer says, "Lyons's
motto was, 'I only say nice things about nice people.' Any piece that came in
that was even mildly risqué or naughty, he wouldn't touch it."

Dorothy Schiff was a faithful reader, which sometimes led to a special
headache for Summer. "Lyons went out at about six o'clock to begin his
rounds. Maybe he'd go to an opening, and then to El Morocco or one of the
other clubs, and he'd get home about two. He'd come into the office about
three the next afternoon, write till about six, and then leave again. I would
type everything up and take it to the composing room. I'd check the column
for typos and mark them up and take the copy back. And inevitably the first
edition would come out with more typos.

"Schiff would go nuts; she couldn't stand it. 'Why so many mistakes in
the column?' And she was right. It should appear the way it's intended to be,
not the way some drunken night shift guy set it." Usually the errors were corrected by the second edition of the paper, but Dolly's impatience did not endear her to Summer.*

Everything about the paper was Dolly's business. In the years of her apprenticeship, she was often seen in the city room or the composing room, or
visiting the accounting or advertising department. Once she settled comfortably into the boss's role, she went downstairs less frequently.

She got to work a little after ten. In the early fifties, before she acquired a
car and driver, she claimed to take the subway to work regularly. Occasionally
seems more like it. Marika Ross, her secretary/assistant, often drove her to
the office, and there were always taxis. When she arrived at West Street, she
did not want to share the common elevator. A frequent complaint of staff
members was that the elevator operators, and later, her chauffeur, shooed
them away when Dolly approached so she could take an empty car on an express run to the fifteenth floor. Her employees might have thought they were
shunned because she thought herself too important to share a ride with
them. In fact, in addition to her nervousness about elevators in general, she

*There was a difference of opinion about culpability. At one point a night editor complained to Sann,
"If only Mr. Lyons could spell names as well as he can drop them!" The copy editors claimed to have
saved Lyons time and again and griped that he never acknowledged their help.

was uneasy about making small talk and was also afraid to reveal that she might not remember their names.

Some employees admired her precisely for her hauteur. Ben Schiff (no relation) wrote for the *Post*'s entertainment section. He recalls, "Dolly was a marvelously elegant lady. She would come down through the city room on the second floor—which was probably the dirtiest city room of any New York paper—and she would drift through in chiffony clothes or well-tailored suits, on the way to Jimmy Wechsler's office. And mostly we remarked on her beautiful shoes and her good legs. But we also knew that she was tenacious about getting the paper the way she wanted it, and she took her job very seriously.

"I always admired her, even though she was a somewhat remote figure," he says. "When she did appear, everybody tried to look busy."

"Remote." "Imperious." "Self-absorbed." Words describing Dolly as aloof or snobbish recur in the memories of many *Post* staffers. She certainly was not gregarious. Nor easily approached. Even her closest friends described her as shy and often unsure of herself. Her airy, little-girl voice betrayed a lack of confidence. In her occasional visits to the newsroom, as Ben Schiff and others recall, she seldom greeted reporters by name, adding to the sense that she felt herself apart from the hoi polloi.

Employees always grouse about the boss. After a while, complaints, based on reality and perception, become formulas. It's unlikely that Dolly was more remote than any other publisher in New York and arguable that she was actually less so. But the staff of the *Post* was small, and there were fewer layers of management between the publisher and a copyboy than at any other paper in town. People in the newsroom and the composing room were very aware that they worked for Dolly Schiff. They expected Dolly Schiff to be aware of them. Some may have envied those few among their colleagues with whom she did occasionally have a social lunch, and they may have resented the fact that those favored were almost always women. There was also an undefinable expectation that a woman boss should be more approachable—more maternal—than a man.

Furthermore, the liberal, even radical, backgrounds of many people working at the paper encouraged informality and a distaste for class distinctions, neither of which was reciprocated by the lady from the penthouse. Dolly was fond of describing herself as someone with a common touch. That was not quite the case. She may have shared the ideals, interests, and concerns of most of her readers and employees, but the cumulative heritage of her childhood—being undervalued by her parents while reaping the benefits of social privilege—almost guaranteed that she would fall back on an austere patrician style when she was ill at ease.

Dolly always justified her alleged remoteness from the city room by arguing for the structure of command from the top down through whatever layers of management were in place. She presumably lost no sleep over what her reporters thought of her.

She arrived at work having read the morning papers and listened to the headlines on the radio. On Monday mornings, she was armed with ideas culled from the Sunday morning political talk shows. She consulted with her top editors two or three times a day by phone on breaking stories and editorial positions. In addition, she issued a steady stream of memos on yellow paper commenting on everything from typos to suggestions for interviews with people in the news and possible questions to ask them. She once said that she was forced to spend too much of her time on money matters, when she would have preferred to focus even more on the editorial content of the paper. She worked till late in the afternoon, barely stopping for lunch at her desk, and frequently went on to dinner with political friends or potential advertisers. Social occasions, to be sure, but the needs of the paper were never far from her mind.

When Dolly lunched alone, she had a sandwich—usually a BLT on rye toast with mayo on the side—and a cup of coffee. When she was joined by a companion, with one of Wechsler's young assistants frequently pressed into waitress service, the menu was still quite austere. "I had at least one editorial conference there," Ed Koch remembers. "It was probably one of the times I was running for Congress. She invited me to her office. And when you're invited by the publisher for lunch at the *Times,* for example, they have a lovely dining room. They have one like that at the *Daily News* even. At the *Post,* Dolly ordered in the driest tuna fish sandwiches I have ever eaten. I could hardly talk. My tongue was clamped to the roof of my mouth. But I'm sure I got their endorsement."

When setting up the meeting with Dolly's guest—whether an important politician, a distinguished foreign visitor, or a staff member summoned for a quiet chat—her secretary was usually instructed to ask the visitor his or her preference in sandwiches. She once made a date months in advance with a local politician whom Dolly wanted to support in the next election. The woman says, "Her office called me in, like, February or March about having an appointment in August and asked what kind of sandwich would I want! I mean, what choice would I make for the dog days of August? I laughed about that for weeks."

It could be no laughing matter, however, if the secretary forgot to ask. Pete Hamill remembers arranging a date sometime in the 1960s for Dolly to meet Meade Esposito, the boss of the Democratic party in Brooklyn. "He came to lunch, and she gave him a meatball sandwich. He was not amused."

What kind of sandwich did she give Pete? "Corned beef. Which isn't even Irish."*

The occasional social gaffe aside, Dolly was doing something right. The business picture began to turn around almost as soon as she took charge. Some of the improvement must have been due to delayed results from Ted Thackrey's cost-cutting efforts in early 1949, but she wasn't going to give him credit. A much greater contribution to the balance sheet was the significant rise in advertising linage, which was Dolly's work.

In 1949, the *Post* ran a net deficit of $86,000, practically nothing compared to the previous years' losses, and for the second half of the year, it actually showed a slight profit. In 1950, for the first time in more than half a century, the *New York Post*—so recently perceived as a charity case—was once again a viable financial operation. Newspaper operations showed a profit of $600,000, and the Post Corporation was able to pay back $250,000 of its indebtedness to its proud owner, Dorothy Schiff. For the next few years, although net profits varied, the paper was always in the black.

Part of the reason for the *Post*'s financial renaissance was the booming postwar economy. After a period of high unemployment just after the war, jobs were becoming plentiful. The Cold War compelled the federal government to continue a high rate of defense spending, and manufacturers invested in new plants and production lines to meet the pent-up need for consumer goods. At midcentury, New York had more manufacturing jobs

---

*A decade later, Hamill's story—which Esposito verified in another context—became part of the standard litany of criticism leveled by young reporters at Dolly for being out of touch. She wrote in the margin of one such attack that the story was a fiction, that she never served anyone a meatball sandwich. It would have been too messy to eat. However, she added, she occasionally offered salami and cheese, which was well received. Her unconscious association between two common types of Italian deli sandwiches may or may not be significant.

than Philadelphia, Detroit, Los Angeles, and Boston combined. Although there was some heavy industry, most people were employed in small or medium-sized enterprises, in fields like garment making, printing and publishing, and food processing. Many others worked in retail stores or on the docks. White-collar jobs were becoming more numerous as well. New York was home to the national headquarters of more major corporations than any other city in the country, and new firms in the expanding service industries, like advertising and public relations, seemed to open every week.

Returning servicemen took advantage of the GI Bill to enroll in colleges and universities, which had to expand their facilities and hire more instructors to meet the demand. These veterans and their new families needed housing and transportation. Young married women who dropped out of the workforce to raise their families wanted homes of their own and furnishings to fill them.

Advertising, which brought the message of manufacturers and their retail agents to potential customers, was placed primarily in the print media. As soon as papers like the *Post* were able to secure sufficient newsprint, they added as many advertising pages as their presses could handle. While holding onto long-term clients among the discount and moderately priced clothing stores, the *Post* picked up advertising from more upscale merchants like Russeks, which was selling Persian lamb coats for $500, and Bond's, which featured two pairs of pants with its $45.75 "pure wool suits" for men.

Local appliance chains plugged Dumont television sets for $280 and Stromberg-Carlson radio–record player consoles for $1.75 down, ninety-one months to pay. Real estate developers in the Bronx offered new rental four-and-one-half-room garden apartments for $120 a month. In Malverne, Long Island, three-bedroom ranch houses cost $11,990, "only $960 down for GIs." Farther out on Long Island, a three-bedroom colonial with a carport fetched $26,000. New York area Buick dealers advertised a four-door sedan available to new commuters for $2,220.38.

Though many *Post* readers were on a tight budget, they had enough disposable income to finance the occasional modest spree. No longer was a winter getaway to warm weather the prerogative of the rich. From October to April, the paper ran pages of advertisements for family-style resorts in Florida and the Carolinas. Owners of hotels and cottages in the Catskill Mountains north of the city promised idyllic weekends and summer rentals.

The *Post*, like its competitors, devoted three or four pages each day to theater, movie, and music reviews, as a lure for entertainment advertising.

Similarly, papers added food service columns—recipes, reports on seasonal bargains, home entertaining suggestions, special sections on holiday foods—to attract weekly supermarket ads.

Postwar New York was a city of newcomers. In 1950, the majority of its eight million people were immigrants and their children. About half the city's residents were Catholic, mostly of Irish or Italian origin; more than a quarter were Jewish. Members of extended families lived in tight-knit neighborhoods in Manhattan, Brooklyn, and the Bronx that were usually quite homogeneous ethnically, religiously, and racially. The north Bronx, Queens, and Staten Island were still underpopulated.

More than a million New Yorkers—nearly one-third of the workforce—were union members. Construction workers, teamsters, and longshoremen were well organized and well paid, but their unions were not notable for their social agenda. The distinctive liberal New York labor organizations were the International Ladies' Garment Workers' Union, with about two hundred thousand members, and the Amalgamated Clothing Workers' Union, for workers in the men's clothing industry, with another seventy-five thousand. The New York needle trade unions reflected and shaped the politics of their members—who were overwhelmingly Jewish or Italian. In addition to securing decent wages and working conditions for their members, these unions were a major force for progressive politics. They were among the leading supporters of the city's unique complex of social services and amenities: subsidized mass transit; subsidized health care; public housing; superb elementary and secondary schools as well as first-rate tuition-free municipal colleges, Hunter, CCNY, Queens College, and Brooklyn College.

Each of the New York daily papers had a core constituency, a core identity. Among the morning papers, the *Times* was the first choice of upper- and middle-class Jews and Protestants who shared its centrist-Democratic point of view. The *Herald Tribune* was the *Times* for Republicans. It was said that the *Tribune* was edited and read by people who knew they were WASPs, while the *Times* was produced and read by people who wished they were. Both papers found most of their audience in Manhattan and some of the long-established affluent enclaves in Brooklyn and Queens.

The other two morning papers, the *News* and the *Mirror,* were mass-market tabloids that appealed to subway riders from the Bronx and Brooklyn as well as non-Jewish working-class Manhattan neighborhoods like Yorkville and Hell's Kitchen. Although readers of the two morning tabs tended to vote Democratic, they were far from liberal. The *Mirror*'s editorial policy attracted a readership that was even more conservative, more Catholic, and more parochial than that of its rival.

The two afternoon broadsheets were somewhat parallel to the morning tabs. The trashy *Journal-American* appealed to virtually the same readers as did its Hearst-owned sister, the *Mirror;* while the Scripps-Howard paper, the *Telegram,** was—like the *News*—a bit more respectable.

All of which made Dorothy Schiff's *New York Post* unique. It appealed to people whose politics were Democratic-left, were likely to be Jewish, and were either members of the working class or intellectuals who sympathized with the proletariat and affected its style. Many *Post* readers picked up a copy of the *Times* in the morning; only a few took the *Tribune* or the tabs. One young boy whose father was faithful to the *Post* begged in vain for the Sunday edition of the *Journal-American,* which carried the cartoon strip "Prince Valiant." His father would not allow a Hearst paper in the house.

To many *Post* readers, the paper was more than a purveyor of news. It was a primer on how to become an American. They knew that Lerner, Lyons, Franzblau, and Sann had come from their world. If those children of the immigrant generation could make their way into the mainstream, so might they.

A woman who grew up in the Bronx says, "To Jews, particularly from the outer boroughs, the *Post* had a message of what it was possible to aspire to. Max Lerner interviewed heads of state; he mixed with leading intellectuals. Leonard Lyons, who we all knew was originally a poor Jewish boy from Brooklyn, got dressed up in a tuxedo every night and went to Broadway openings. He knew presidents and Nobel-winning novelists. This gave us a window into the way life could be, into what was possible for Jews with dreams in America. The *Post* showed us that it could be done."

Another woman, whose family eventually moved from the Lower East Side to Great Neck, says, "The *Post* was very much identified with glamour

*On January 5, 1950, Scripps-Howard announced the purchase of the *New York Sun,* which was incorporated into what became formally the *New York World-Telegram and Sun.* The *Sun,* the second-oldest daily in the city after the *Post,* had been hurting for years; during the late 1940s, it fell to last place in the New York circulation race. However, its disappearance didn't do much to help the *Post;* most *Sun* readers moved on to the *Telegram.*

for Jews. Dolly Schiff who ran 'our paper' was after all a Jewish princess, and not the JAP kind. She was the granddaughter of a man our parents and grandparents remembered with gratitude. Dolly was photographed with leading politicians and intellectuals, she had a cigarette holder that reminded us of our beloved FDR. The *Post* told us what books we should read, which Broadway shows we should see. It was a guide to the world that we wanted to be part of."

In the summer of 1961, Jerry Tallmer, then a cultural critic at *The Village Voice* who would move to the *Post* the following year, contributed an article to *Dissent* titled "The Mama of Us All." Tallmer affectionately recollected his own political allegiance to the *Post,* which developed in the early postwar years. The "throbbing fact" about the paper was "its Jewishness. As it is the green which makes a leaf a leaf, the gray that makes a battleship, it is [Jewishness] which makes the *Post* the *Post*."

Further, Tallmer believed, the *Post* was essentially a woman, "a Jewish woman, a wife, a mama . . . a yenta, a kvetch, a nag, an irremovable conscience, a presence." The paper could be maddening in its endless attention to celebrities, in its unquestioned support of victims and underdogs simply because they were victims and underdogs, and in its reliance on tried-and-true tabloid stories about crime in the subways and adultery in high places. The paper served two different Jewish audiences: the working-class readership based in the Bronx and Brooklyn, and the intellectual community based in Manhattan. "Wechsler and Kempton are up in the clouds. Paul Sann has two feet firmly planted in the ground . . . and it is he who every day makes sure that the rapists are right up there with, and above, the eggheads." And, concluded Tallmer, "He is probably right."

The *Post* was "the good indignant mama of New York City as the *New York Times* is its good gray papa. Papa goes down to the firm and makes the money while mama keeps things hopping in the Daughters of the Negev Anti–Poll Tax and Sane Nuclear Society. Papa keeps us rich, mama keeps us honest. What in God's name would ever become of this city if mama were taken away from us, I do not know."

The 1950s would later be mocked as a vanilla era—the age of "the man in the gray flannel suit," when people practiced "the power of positive thinking" and yearned to live in "ticky-tacky" suburbs, when the "silent generation" was moving through the school system, never questioning authority, never rocking the boat. In fact, it was also a time of widespread economic growth and enormous social mobility. The great majority of Americans worshipped the notion of progress and believed in its inevitability. The children of immigrants emerged from college as protomembers of the middle class. Union members earned enough in wages and overtime to move to the suburbs and enjoy the good life as well.

Cultural self-improvement was an important theme in the popular press. Selections from the Book-of-the-Month-Club arrived every month to acquaint readers with the work of Ernest Hemingway, John Steinbeck, Graham Greene, Thomas Mann, and Pearl Buck. The Columbia Record Club provided staples by Beethoven and Brahms in the new, long-playing 33 1/3 rpm format. New York City's public school system and its free four-year colleges were among the best in the nation. Municipally subsidized institutions like the Lewisohn Stadium summer concerts were free, and the City Center opera and ballet companies offered world-class productions and performers at affordable prices. Museum attendance boomed. *The New York Times* and the *New York Herald Tribune* had long provided their establishment readership with information about the worlds of entertainment and culture. Now the revitalized *New York Post* did the same for its core audience of people who had been on the outside looking in and found in its pages a guide to getting there.

EIGHT

The Fabulous Fifties

On November 12, 1951, the *Post* celebrated the 150th anniversary of its founding. The first page of the paper featured a congratulatory letter from President Harry Truman stressing the role that a free press plays in preserving the nation's freedom. Other well-wishers, whose contributions had been solicited by Dorothy Schiff and Jimmy Wechsler, constituted a secular pantheon for the middle of the twentieth century; they included Charles E. Wilson, the director of Defense Mobilization; David Sarnoff, the president of RCA; Walter Reuther, head of the United Auto Workers; movie mogul Samuel Goldwyn; theologian Reinhold Niebuhr; and psychiatrist Lawrence Kubie.

Henry Steele Commager, the popular historian, contributed an essay about the evolution of goals that Thomas Jefferson had proclaimed in his inaugural address the year the *Post* was founded. Jefferson, Commager wrote, would have been pleased to see that the United States now stretched across the continent and had absorbed more than thirty million immigrants from the Old World. The country had guaranteed their personal liberties, given them the opportunity to provide a good living for their families, and afforded them the chance to participate in the greatest experiment in self-government that the world had ever seen. By ending the institution of slavery and starting to reverse the subsequent disenfranchisement of the Negro community, the

country had even begun to right a heinous wrong that Jefferson and his colleagues had permitted to stain the republic. What remained, Commager believed, was to combat the resurgence of irrationality and suspicion fostered
by the Cold War—a "tyranny over the mind of man," as Jefferson would have
described it—that had lately crept into the national discourse. Commager
was optimistic, as he believed Jefferson would have been, that "people who
have triumphed over the perils of the past, who have shown themselves endlessly ingenious and tolerant, who have remained steadfast in their devotion
to freedom, who have put their faith in education and in free speech and a
free press" would not permit the repudiation of the principles on which their
nation was founded.

Freedom of the press was the theme of a "Message from the Publisher"
that Dorothy Schiff prepared for the celebratory issue. "The Post prides itself
on being a lively independent paper . . . with a long and distinguished tradition," she wrote.

> But our 150th birthday is not just an occasion for remembering the past. It is
> rather, we think, an occasion for dramatizing The Post's established place in
> the community and the nation. We have tried to speak the truth as we see it
> and to grind no axe for any special interest. We do not claim to be infallible,
> but we do believe that our independence has been a major factor in achieving
> the widest audience ever obtained by The Post in its long and memorable his-
> tory. We believe that only by continuing to fulfill that role can we be worthy of
> the freedom which the American press enjoys.

In the September 30, 1951, weekend edition of the *Post,* under the rubric
"Publisher's Notebook," Dorothy explained to her "Dear Readers" that she
had toyed with the idea of writing a column when she first bought the paper
but an editor had discouraged her. However, she wrote, "as the years pass, so
many interesting people and things continue to cross my path that I've decided to risk it. . . . I want to do this to share with like-minded people the excitement and stimulation that keep me burning and active as publisher of a
militantly liberal newspaper, in a world seething with despair and discontent,
but at the same time, in many places, aspiring toward the stars."

This first column reported on a conference about the Israeli economy
sponsored by the State of Israel Bonds. Dorothy explained that she was on
the Board of Governors of the bond drive and had spent seven fascinating

weeks in Israel during the past summer. She hoped her readers shared her hopes for this beleaguered little country and would buy its bonds.

Then she mentioned attending a lunch hosted by the French consul general at the "swanky Knickerbocker Club" for General de Lattre de Tassigny, "who has been doing a remarkable job in Indochina." The general told his audience that the war against the Communists in Southeast Asia was a part of the same war the United Nations was fighting in Korea. "He believes that if this war is lost all of Asia will go Communist and . . . North Africa would also follow suit."

The column appeared regularly in the weekend edition of the paper.* Typically, Dorothy might comment on an item in the news about local politics, make another pitch for Israel, or report on a dinner of Hollywood bigwigs or a gathering of Democratic political leaders. Sometimes she reviewed a play or summarized a book that had caught her fancy. She wrote her own copy in longhand on yellow lined pads. She worked hard on her prose. Occasionally, she ran an idea past Jimmy Wechsler or Paul Sann. If there were any potential legal problems, she checked with Marvin Berger, but she was essentially her own editor.

The Roosevelts figured prominently in Dolly's musings. For *Post* readers, repeated reminders that the publisher was a close friend of the former first family were a plus. On November 15, 1951, Dolly wrote, "I paid my dollar (for the benefit of the National Foundation for Infantile Paralysis) and was admitted to the exhibition and sale of a collection of items belonging to the late President and Mrs. Roosevelt." On display were assorted pieces of china, glass, and about five hundred autographed books. "Collecting these books was quite a hobby of the President's and he spent much time and love on them."

The proceeds of the sale were to go to Eleanor and son Elliott. Mrs. Roosevelt had explained that the family was cutting back on real estate and had no room for these things. Dolly was dismayed. "I hate to be critical of Mrs. Roosevelt, because she has contributed so much to our country, but I must say I was shocked." Some things were junk, she felt, and should have been thrown out, but others should have been given to the grandchildren.

Several months later, Dolly was thinking again about FDR. On January

---

*The name of the column was changed to "Dear Reader" in June 1953.

27, 1952, she wrote that while he may have seemed to some Americans to be radical politically, in her experience he was conservative in his taste. "I remember a little dinner—we usually dressed in the evening—when his charming secretary 'Missy' LeHand, appeared wearing new satin pumps with open toes. These had just become fashionable and were the first ones FDR had seen. He expressed horror at what he termed their hideousness and told Missy he liked mine, which were traditional 'opera' pumps, much better. It was with a slight sense of guilt that a little later I, too, succumbed to the new style, and the President kidded us both for a while, then became resigned."

She concluded that column with her memories of his decline:

The last time I visited him was on Labor Day in 1944. Mrs. Roosevelt had invited about half a dozen grownups and the same number of children for dinner. My youngest daughter, then nine, was among them. First the children were sent into the President's little office for soft drinks (my daughter remembers they discussed sleigh-riding)—then the older people were invited in for cocktails. But FDR's appearance had changed terribly—he was still gay but so thin and ate only baby food for supper—I was heartsick.

On April 12, 1945, I came home from the office earlier than usual because my little daughter was in bed with a cold. She seemed quite happy and as usual was doing her homework with the radio on. I went to my room to rest, but rushed back to my daughter's room when I heard her cry out: "Mother, Mother, come quickly!" "What is it, darling?" I asked with alarm. "Mother, the radio says the President is dead!"

Dorothy not only wrote about politicians, she was becoming one herself. In the early fifties, New York was governed by Democratic officeholders, and Democratic politicians were governed by the party bosses. In Manhattan that meant Tammany Hall. Reform-minded Democrats deplored the control Tammany leaders had over candidates for public office and over nominees for the state and local judicial appointments as well.

One group of reformers started the Lexington Democratic Club in 1949. Dorothy Schiff was among the charter $5-a-year dues-paying members. The club was active in the Ninth Assembly District, on Manhattan's East Side, running roughly from 100th Street to 42nd, between Fifth and Third avenues, and including Central Park South.

"We were having a tough time finding candidates to go up against Tammany," says Russell Hemenway, one of the club's early leaders. "It's always tough to run against the organization, and particularly in those days. There were a lot of technical problems you had to overcome—getting petitions and so on. It's very, very tough to win a primary.

"So we decided we had to find two well-known New Yorkers—people who were well-known in their own right. A young whippersnapper like myself wasn't going to cut it. Mrs. Schiff was one of our choices. We wanted to run her and Lloyd Garrison, the liberal attorney, for state committeeman and committeewoman. Now, these are not major jobs in the party, they're prestigious, but they don't do a heck of a lot. They don't have much say. But they are elective, and it would be a way to cut into Tammany's clout."

Many *Post* editorials and news stories had been favorable to the reformers. "We knew Jimmy Wechsler and Murray Kempton and a lot of the reporters on the *Post,* so it was easy to get a meeting with Mrs. Schiff," Hemenway says. "We all went down to West Street to see her and tell her what she would have to do, and how we wanted her to be our candidate, and we'd give her all the backing she needed. And she was absolutely charmed by the idea."

During March and April 1952, the *Post* covered the reform campaign favorably, while playing down the fact that its publisher was a candidate. The Tammany organization was sufficiently threatened by the upstart candidates that its executive committee circulated a memo discussing whether or not to set up a front organization called Young Democrats in hopes of splitting the reform vote. Schiff and Garrison received the endorsement of both the *Times* and the *Tribune.*

Dorothy reported to her "Dear Readers" from time to time on her visits to other clubhouses and meetings with the electorate. Several years later she told Adlai Stevenson how much she learned by campaigning at the grassroots level. She usually canvassed her district with a young lawyer from the club as her companion. The young lawyer seldom had anything in common with the constituent, often a stay-at-home housewife, whose concerns, Dorothy concluded, had little to do with national politics and more to do with high prices in the local supermarket. Dorothy was not a natural politician. She was not terribly good at small talk. But she was genuinely interested in that housewife—who was a potential *Post* reader, after all.

Dorothy was thrilled to write on April 27 that she and Garrison won. "About twice as many people voted for us as voted for the Tammany candidates." She subsequently discovered that some votes cast for a candidate are really votes against someone else. She learned that she had gotten quite a few votes from clubs dominated by Irish-American Democrats even though their political views differed. They liked the fact that she was said to be for the underdog, and they thought that voting for her and Garrison was better than supporting the Italians who ran Tammany. "In my innocence," she confessed, "I thought that adherence to principle had been the cause of victory. I must admit I was shaken when I heard later that our ticket had been for many merely a choice of the lesser of two evils."

Dorothy served as a state committeewoman for two years and then stepped down, although she remained a member of the Lexington Democrats for the next two decades. She maintained an interest in local politics, but she also enjoyed playing a role at the national level, especially with the status conferred by being the owner and publisher of one of the country's leading liberal Democratic papers.

She and her editors hoped to have an influence on the 1952 presidential election. At the beginning of the year, President Harry Truman had not declared whether he would seek reelection. Senator Estes Kefauver of Tennessee won the New Hampshire primary, with the president coming in second. That solidified Truman's decision not to run, which left the field open. The presumed front-runners were Kefauver, whom Truman was known to dislike, Adlai Stevenson, governor of Illinois, and Averell Harriman.

Kefauver had served ten years in the House of Representatives and made a name for himself soon after his election to the Senate by chairing a high-profile investigation into organized crime. As a senator from a border state, he was more liberal than his Southern colleagues, but he was not considered a party loyalist. Harriman was the first choice of many liberals because of his long involvement in public life and his strong record of anticommunism evidenced during his years as wartime ambassador to the USSR and subsequent work as administrator of the Marshall Plan in Europe. Despite Harriman's admirable history of public service, he was not an ideal candidate because he had never run for office and was a dull speaker who was awkward with the press.

At first, Dolly seems to have favored Harriman, her old friend and one-time suitor. On April 17, she wrote that "it has been interesting to watch him develop from a Long Island polo player into the serious, experienced internationally-minded public servant he now is. Averell is very handsome.

More important, he is a very fine man with great integrity and sincerity and a true liberal, too. Although not as brilliant and witty as Adlai, he has a persistence and selflessness that would make him an excellent Chief Executive."

Stevenson, reputed to be Truman's unannounced choice, was a respected governor but not that well-known outside his home state. Although his most notable successes as governor—prison reform and highway safety—were not ideological, Stevenson was acceptable to liberals because he was an internationalist who had been active in the United Nations, he was a champion of civil liberties at home, and he was a seasoned and agile campaigner. He was not an active candidate, however, and his indecisiveness would come to be seen by opponents as a sign of weakness.

When Truman's preference for Stevenson became clear, Dolly and Jimmy Wechsler, who knew the governor only slightly, traveled to Illinois to talk with him about the American political situation. Jimmy was particularly impressed. Dolly was more ambivalent. Later, she wrote in her column, "Because of my confidence in Adlai's integrity, I feel certain he will shortly do one of two things. He will either withdraw completely from the race and throw the immense weight of his influence into an active campaign to help win the nomination for Harriman, or will announce that he, himself, is available as a candidate."

Stevenson had grown up with Dolly's friend Alicia Patterson, *Newsday*'s founding editor. "They enjoyed each other's sprightly minds," said Stevenson's sister, Buffie Ives. "She was one of the first girls he was in love with." But Stevenson married Ellen Borden, whom he divorced in 1949, just about the time that he and Patterson crossed paths again. Her own marriage was problematic; her husband, Colonel Harry Guggenheim, bankrolled *Newsday* for her but disapproved of her editorial policies. Alicia and Adlai probably became lovers; they were certainly close, politically and personally. In Stevenson's letters to Alicia, this normally reticent man confided his deepest thoughts about politics and life.

The friendship caused Patterson problems during the 1952 presidential campaign. She had been one of the first people to encourage General Dwight D. Eisenhower to run for the presidency. When Truman anointed Stevenson as his preferred heir, Patterson faced a dilemma. Her *Newsday* editorials reflected her plight. Since she felt the country needed a change of party in power, she favored Ike. However, she wrote, "If the nation prefers another Democrat, Stevenson will make a magnificent president."

Patterson tried to help Stevenson in other ways. During the summer of 1952, she arranged a small dinner in New York for him to meet informally with influential publishers. Alicia seated Adlai between Dolly and Clare Booth Luce, the wife of Henry Luce, the president of Time, Inc. According to a *Newsday* reporter who was there, "Dolly got him first. She wouldn't let him go. Clare never got a word in edgewise." Later the reporter saw Mrs. Luce leave in a rage.

Although Dolly wanted Adlai's attention, she was never as devoted to the man or his candidacy as other liberals were. Wechsler, for example, was totally committed. A woman who observed Dolly closely during those years says, "She wanted him to win, but . . . I think there was a kind of femininity about her that really demanded a little bit of playing up to her as a woman. And I don't think Adlai would have done that. I don't think he liked her enough. Whatever it was, there was no spark between them."

Years later, Dolly, in summarizing her thoughts about Stevenson, recalled that Alicia had told her, "with Adlai, sex is not urgent." He had once made a modest move to flirt with Dolly, which she interpreted as more of a gallant gesture than a passionate appeal.

Another woman who knew Adlai well says, "He was not a particularly sexy character. He was not a flirt. She may have wanted him to flirt with her, but that was not his style. Not with anyone." Even around Alicia or other women with whom Stevenson was presumed to be involved, his manner was somewhat aloof.

By the time of the Democratic convention in July 1952, Dolly had chosen to support him. Harriman was politically acceptable to her, but she seemed convinced by this time that Adlai was the better candidate. She and the Wechslers were in Chicago to cheer him on as he captured the nomination on the third ballot. The party bosses decided that nominating Senator John Sparkman from Alabama for vice president would add balance to the ticket.

Two weeks earlier, Eisenhower, who had resigned as head of NATO earlier in the year, had been nominated at the Republican convention. His running mate was California Senator Richard Nixon.

The *Post* threw itself into the fray. The paper serialized an adulatory biography of Stevenson in September. Wechsler, with his boss's approval, contributed several working drafts of speeches for the candidate. William Shannon, who was assigned to cover the Stevenson campaign, and Murray Kempton, who traveled with Ike, filed stories that were unabashedly partisan.

On September 11, for example, Kempton wrote, "The road which Dwight Eisenhower has traveled these past weeks has not gone upward. The image he represented has cheapened and grown coarse. Members of his party are casting him in a mold and it suits him badly. It is the mold of a trimmer." According to Kempton, Ike had begun by saying that Korea was a tragedy of political errors, but that after North Korea attacked, there was nothing to do but fight. Now he was taking the party line that Truman wanted war and encouraged it. He said originally that while it was true that there were scandals in the Democratic administration, it was more important for him to emphasize the good values of the Republican party and not denigrate the Democrats. Now he was on the offensive. "He also has allowed Nixon and McCarthy to run wild and does nothing to rein them in."

Later in September, the *Post* made the news itself by breaking the story of Senator Nixon's slush fund. On Thursday, September 18, a story on page 3 headlined "Secret Rich Men's Trust Fund Keeps Nixon in Style Far Beyond His Salary" revealed that the vice presidential candidate had received $16,000 from a fund set up "exclusively to the financial comfort of Sen. Nixon." The fund had been established in 1950 when Nixon was first elected to the Senate, because he had no private resources and could not make do on a senator's pay of $12,500 and tax-free expense allowance of $2,500. It was administered by Dana Smith, the head of the California Volunteers for Eisenhower, and it existed, according to Smith, "to enable Dick to do a selling job to the American people in behalf of private enterprise and integrity in government."

The paper's editors had been working on the story for several weeks. They had asked Leo Katcher, their West Coast correspondent, to prepare a series of articles on Nixon. He mentioned at the time that there were rumors of "unorthodox political financing." When Katcher had enough material to confront Dana Smith, he expected a denial. To Katcher's amazement, "Like Nixon, Smith apparently felt there was nothing questionable about the ethics of a Senator who allowed men with special interests to take care of his economic needs."

Most papers across the country initially ignored Katcher's scoop. Eisenhower's press secretary, James C. Hagerty, tried to downplay it, saying, "We never comment on a *New York Post* story." The *Daily Mirror,* typically for the Republican press, said, "No matter what diversion is attempted, Democrats must know that corruption is the chief issue of this campaign. The left-wing has raised the Nixon issue to divert attention from corruption in government but it won't work."

The Democrats grabbed the story and ran with it. The front-page headline of the weekend edition of the *Post* crowed "Nixon Uproar Mounts." The Sunday morning radio talk shows all addressed Nixon's plight, and even Republican newspapers were speculating whether Ike should drop him from the ticket. Hoping to save his skin, Nixon announced that he would go on nationwide television to answer his critics.

The now-famous "Checkers" speech was masterly. Nixon began by saying that he was a man whose honesty and integrity had been impugned and that he needed to tell his side of the story. Yes, there was a fund, he willingly admitted, but he had never used any of the money for personal reasons, nor had any of the contributors gotten any special favors in exchange for their generosity. The money had gone to pay for travel when he needed to make a political speech far from Washington or to reprint the speeches that he made. They were speeches with one purpose, he said: "Exposing this administration; the communism in it, the corruption of it."

As a man of no inherited wealth (a dig at Stevenson) Nixon said, he and his wife lived modestly. He acknowledged that he had accepted one gift after his election to the Senate. "A man down in Texas heard Pat on the radio mention the fact that our two youngsters would like to have a dog." The Texan promptly sent them a black and white cocker spaniel. "And our little girl Tricia, the six-year-old, named it Checkers. And you know, the kids, like all kids, love the dog, and I just want to say this right now that regardless of what they say about it, we're gonna keep him."

Nixon ended by asking viewers to let the Republican National Committee know whether they thought he should stay on the ticket or not. The response was overwhelmingly favorable. In truth, Nixon's use of the slush fund, while questionable, was probably not criminal, but it was fair game for his political opponents. Breaking the story reinforced the *Post*'s image as a leader of the liberal Democratic press.

Dolly barely mentioned the fuss in her column. She focused on her role as a Democratic insider. On September 6, she reported on a luncheon at the Waldorf given for Stevenson by Eleanor Roosevelt and others. Among the guests at her table were the New York political boss Jim Farley, whom she liked though they were not political allies, and the actress Tallulah Bankhead, whose father had been a prominent member of the House of Representatives. Tallulah told her fellow guests that "she had never been so thrilled about a man as she was about Stevenson since she had first met John Barrymore more than 20 years ago."

As for the main event, Dolly wrote, "The Governor's speech was light and witty, in spite of his telling three jokes, all of which I had heard before. But most of the audience apparently had not because they roared with laughter. He did however make a serious appeal for participation in politics by nonprofessionals and explained how bad people in government drove out the good."

Later there was a small reception. "I told the Governor how much I had enjoyed his frank speech to the American Legion the day before, but I had been afraid that they would boo him when he told them he would not give in to pressure from them or any other group. . . . Stevenson's campaign manager Wilson Wyatt is a delightful man from Louisville. As a matter of fact all the men around Adlai strike me as being first rate."

She told Stevenson she was reading the biography of him that was being serialized in the *Post*. She said she was particularly impressed by a report about periodic visits the governor made to state prisons in Illinois. "Adlai showed great surprise. 'I can't understand why you think that part is interesting or worth printing.' 'But it is. I know our readers will agree with me,' I insisted. 'I have a flair for these things,' said I, conceitedly."

Dolly accompanied members of the national press on Stevenson's train to a rally in Troy, New York. The next morning there was an old-fashioned whistle-stop ride down the Hudson Valley to Hyde Park, where the candidate and his party had breakfast with Eleanor Roosevelt. "They had scrambled eggs and sausages," Dolly reported. "Adlai enjoyed his so much that he leaned over and speared one that Frank Roosevelt's [Jr.'s] wife had left on her plate, after he asked her permission, of course. Watch your figure, Adlai."

On the Saturday before the election, Dolly reported, "On Tuesday I am going to vote for—guess who? Stevenson, of course." The paper endorsed him as well. Of course.

Throughout the campaign, Wechsler's editorials had supported Stevenson on the issues, arguing for policies favored by most of the paper's readers. The publisher responded more viscerally to the candidates' personalities than she did to their ideological positions. She virtually ignored Eisenhower and Nixon. She reacted to the physical attractiveness of the various Democratic politicos. She savored gossip about their private lives. She was as com-

mitted to the Democratic platform as her editorial staff was, but her willingness to reveal that gut reactions played a part in her decisions validated her
claim that she could speak for the average reader.

To someone who focused on public policy, the 1952 election looked like a
referendum on how Americans wanted to shape the postwar world. There
were international issues: what to do about the fighting in Korea, how to respond to Russian aggression around the globe, how to strengthen compatible
democracies in Europe and Asia. There were domestic issues: how to assess
the threat of Communist agents within the United States, how to balance the
demands of organized labor with those of a traditionally free market, and
what to make of the political scandals involving financial chicanery within
the Truman administration. Postelection analyses revealed that voters, while
cognizant of these concerns, made their decision for more basic reasons. After twenty years of Democrats in the White House, they felt it was time for a
change. And, they liked Ike.

Sixty-four percent of the eligible voters went to the polls, and most of
them voted for the Republican ticket. The popular vote was thirty-four million to twenty-seven million. The electoral college divided 442 to 89. The
Deep South and several border states were still solidly Democratic, but
Stevenson-Sparkman couldn't carry one Northern state. Not Illinois, not
New York, none of the union strongholds like Michigan, Ohio, or Pennsylvania.

The 1952 election was the first to be covered extensively on TV. UNI-
VAC, the mammoth computer at the University of Pennsylvania, predicted
the outcome of the election to Walter Cronkite of CBS at 8:30 eastern time,
although it was eventually revealed that, on the basis of the preelection polls,
the computer was rigged to give an early result.

On November 9, Dolly wrote magnanimously,

Well, Election Day has come and gone. Our wonderful candidate was defeated. General Eisenhower swept this state and most others. I know you are
worried and depressed, as am I. It would be foolish to pretend that the result
has not been a serious setback for the liberal cause. But all is far from lost. Remember, there was a time—in 1948—when the most dedicated liberals, many
of them members of the much maligned ADA, tried to draft "Ike" to be their
standard-bearer. And he was even Harry Truman's first choice this year.

I believe that if President-Elect Eisenhower had accepted the nomination of the Democratic Party, he would have carried every state in the union. A majority of the people believe in him. They know we are in a tough fight against international communism. He has won tough fights for us before—military in character, it is true. Let's hope he can win the war for the minds of men as well.

NINE

Charges and Countercharges

Although their party had been decisively rejected by the voters, liberal Democrats like Dorothy Schiff and her editors were determined to keep the ideals of the New Deal alive. In time, they would press for the continuation of those social and economic programs, but first they were compelled to fend off assaults from Republicans and conservative Democrats who feared that liberal policies had put the nation at risk. The attack on liberalism had been building for some time.

At midcentury, many Americans were convinced that the Soviet Union was on the verge of world domination. The establishment of Soviet puppet governments in eastern Europe, the defeat of Chiang Kai-shek's forces by the Chinese Communists, the announcement that the Russians had exploded an atomic bomb in 1949—all this contributed to the hardening of East-West positions in the Cold War and concerns that the Russians might be gearing up for a series of attacks on the West.

Feeling overwhelmed abroad, Americans reacted by looking for Soviet agents and sympathizers at home. On March 22, 1947, President Truman's Executive Order 9835 established the first loyalty program for federal employees. The House Un-American Activities Committee (HUAC) had been created in 1938 and made a standing committee in 1945. HUAC gained headlines during the late forties by soliciting the testimony of former

Communists—the most sensational of which was the charge by Whittaker Chambers that Alger Hiss was a Communist agent. Hiss had worked at several government posts; he had been one of the American representatives at Yalta; he was a well-connected member of the WASP establishment who became head of the Carnegie Endowment for International Peace in 1949. If Alger Hiss had spied for the Russians, who in Washington could be beyond suspicion?

Republicans, in particular, looked for ways to blame their political opponents for ignoring or even abetting Communist infiltration of American institutions and threatening the American way of life. Richard Nixon and others had just begun using this tactic as a way to further their political careers when Senator Joseph McCarthy, a first-term Republican from Wisconsin, swung into action.

McCarthy, who prior to his senatorial election in 1948 had been an obscure county judge, first came to public attention because of his interest in a group of German soldiers who were charged with the murder of American soldiers at Malmedy during the Battle of the Bulge. Some American critics in and outside the army claimed that the Germans had been mistreated, even tortured, in order to obtain confessions. In April 1949, Democratic Senator Millard Tydings, chairman of the Senate Armed Services Committee, deputized a special subcommittee chaired by Republican Senator Raymond Baldwin to look into the matter.

McCarthy, though not a member, attended the subcommittee hearings, where he first displayed the tactics that would mark the rest of his career. McCarthy read only those accounts that substantiated his belief that the Germans were being railroaded and ignored all other evidence produced at the hearing. He ignored the rules, interrupted and bullied witnesses, and disregarded the sitting senators. When the subcommittee concluded that although there were some procedural irregularities, there was no evidence of torture, and that the army had handled the cases properly, McCarthy launched a scurrilous attack on Senator Baldwin. He had forged his technique; now all he needed was a big enough target.

In late 1949 and early 1950, McCarthy released a barrage of unsubstantiated allegations on the floor of the Senate, where the privilege of office protected him against libel or slander suits, charging that some senior State Department officials were Communist subversives. He accused Secretary of

State Dean Acheson of shielding Alger Hiss* and of being responsible for losing China to the Communists. He said that a Supreme Court justice, whom he did not identify, was being manipulated by a Communist spy.

On February 9, 1950, during a speech in Wheeling, West Virginia, McCarthy claimed to have a list of 205 State Department employees allegedly known to Acheson to be members of the Communist Party of America. Called upon to make the list available to the FBI, he dissembled. Sometimes he denied making the charge; other times he admitted he had done so. Then he began saying that there were fifty-seven card-carrying Communists in the State Department. The excitement these announcements engendered led the senator to make a number of wild accusations in personal appearances across the country and on the floor of the Senate.

The Truman administration and the Democratic leadership of the Senate were alarmed. Senator Tydings chaired a subcommittee of the Foreign Relations Committee that was established to look into McCarthy's claims. During two months of hearings, McCarthy carried on in his familiar fashion, repeating charges, inventing new ones on the spot, while hinting that anyone who oppposed him was doing so in the service of the country's enemies. The Tydings Committee issued a report in July 1950; it excoriated McCarthy, dismissed his various unsubstantiated claims of security risks at the State Department, and said that his statements that Communists were working for government agencies were a "fraud and a hoax perpetrated on the Senate of the United States and the American people."

The New York Times, The Washington Post, and *Collier's* magazine, among other major journals, praised the committee's report as support for their growing criticism of the senator, but their measured editorials did little to soothe those millions of Americans who had just begun to recover from one international conflict and were terrified that they were about to be involved in another.

---

*In 1948, Whittaker Chambers told HUAC that Hiss had passed State Department documents to him in 1938. Hiss, who volunteered to testify in his own defense, denied everything. Later Chambers repeated the charges on *Meet the Press,* and when Hiss threatened to sue for libel, he produced more evidence. Hiss dropped his suit and was tried for perjury, because the statute of limitations on espionage had run out. After one mistrial, he was convicted in January 1950. Acheson, along with Justices Felix Frankfurter and William O. Douglas, and several other prominent Washington figures, defended his character.

The threat seemed to be growing. On June 25, 1950, North Korea, egged on by the Chinese Communists, crossed the demarcation line established at the end of the Second World War and invaded South Korea. McCarthy and others promptly placed the blame for Communist aggression on subversives throughout the government.

Drew Pearson, whose column and radio broadcasts reached a large national audience, was the first major journalist to take the offensive against McCarthy. Pearson reported on scandals that allegedly took place when McCarthy was a young politician in Wisconsin, mocked the flimsiness of his accusations against the Truman administration, and tried to untangle the growing anticommunist mess. In December 1950, McCarthy, who had been a boxer in college, picked a fight with Pearson at a club in Washington, took a swing at him, and then claimed to have kneed him in the groin. More painful to the journalist was the successful campaign the senator and his followers mounted to pressure the Adam Hat Co. to drop its sponsorship of Pearson's radio show and drive it off the air.

McCarthy's power appeared unlimited. In November 1950, he had intervened actively in the Maryland senatorial election, playing an influential role in the defeat of his nemesis, Millard Tydings. When the Senate convened the following year, the Subcommittee on Privileges and Elections—a subcommittee of the Rules Committee—looked into charges linking McCarthy with improprieties during the campaign but decided not to chastise him. Not coincidentally, right-wing Republicans had engineered the appointment of McCarthy to the Rules Committee in the interim between testimony and the report. In midsummer 1951, McCarthy implied that the secretary of defense, and former secretary of state, George Marshall was a Communist dupe, and all too few public figures were willing to defend the man who, perhaps more than any other single individual, had made the Allied victory in World War II and the regeneration of Western Europe possible.

Dorothy Schiff and her editors decided enough was enough. They assigned two top reporters, Oliver Pilat in New York and William Shannon, head of the paper's Washington bureau, to examine McCarthy's career and his tactics. In a September 4 editorial announcing the debut of a seventeen-part series about the senator, James Wechsler wrote,

> The basic fact about Joe McCarthy is that he has been getting away with murder. He has been getting away with it because too many newspapers and too

many politicians have been afraid to fight him. . . . Many men know the scope
of the McCarthy fraud, but too few men—especially in Washington D.C.—
have dared to risk a public argument with him. . . .

President Truman has recently raised his voice in impressive denuncia-
tions of McCarthyism; but his Congressional leaders are too scared to echo
him and the Dept. of Justice frequently seems closer in spirit to McCarthy
than Mr. Truman.

The series was entitled "SMEAR Inc.—The One Man Mob of Joe
McCarthy." Dorothy read every installment before it went to press and had
few amendments to suggest. She hoped to enhance the *Post*'s credentials with
its anti-McCarthy readers, and she had little reason to fear retaliation from
advertisers. No firms that were known to be headed by right-wing businessmen advertised in the paper in any case.

In the first installment, Pilat and Shannon began by ridiculing McCarthy's
alleged expertise in domestic Communist party activity and in Far Eastern
policy. They argued that he had never uncovered a single Communist working
in the State Department or any other branch of government, never discovered
a single spy, never produced a single document to back up his charges against
any individuals, and never had any effect on the indictment, trial, or conviction of anyone for supposed involvement with communism.

In subsequent articles, Pilat and Shannon debunked McCarthy's claims to
have been a military hero, rehashed the improprieties that marked his early political career in Wisconsin, and revived the charge that Communists within the
Wisconsin Progressive party played a vital role in his 1946 defeat of staunchly
anticommunist Senator Robert La Follette. They laid bare McCarthy's history
of tax irregularities and shady finances, suggested that his defense of the Nazis
at Malmedy represented an unsavory pandering to pro-Nazis in the Wisconsin
German-American community, and affirmed the fact that his lists of alleged
Communists in government were completely fraudulent.

Some of their assertions—presented in over-the-top tabloid style—have
been subsequently downplayed by responsible historians, but the majority of
their charges were valid. Thomas C. Reeves, McCarthy's most exhaustive,
and frequently sympathetic, biographer to date, wrote of the *Post* series, "Pilat
and Shannon revealed considerable research into McCarthy's personal history and political career, and they raised some solid questions about his military record, his stock market speculations, his jumbled figures on State

Department Communists, and his direct involvement in the Maryland campaign. The reporters' grasp of detail had to make Joe extremely nervous."

The series ran from September 4 through 23, 1951, and was reprinted and distributed nationally by the big labor unions. Most of the questions raised about McCarthy's conduct could not be rebutted, although Ralph De Toledano, a liberal journalist turned conservative gadfly, said on WJZ-TV, the ABC affiliate in New York, that more than half of the statements in the McCarthy series were lies. Roy Cohn, a young New York lawyer who served as the general counsel to McCarthy's senatorial subcommittee, weighed in with a letter to the editor of the *Post* about the injustice being perpetrated against a valiant American patriot. But while McCarthy's supporters were satisfied to dismiss the series and the related editorial positions as typical of the pinko New York intellectual community, the senator sought revenge.

During a Senate Foreign Relations Committee hearing just a week after the series concluded, McCarthy mentioned the *Post* in passing. He said that editor Wechsler and his wife had been members of the Communist party, and that, although they claimed to have left the party, he doubted they had. Wechsler had never denied that he was a member of the Young Communist League during his senior year in college and for two years after that, until a trip to the Soviet Union and direct exposure to the narrow-mindedness of some American party members transformed him into a leading spokesman of the anticommunist left. Jimmy responded to McCarthy's slur by sending a statement of his anticommunist activity to sympathetic Democrats on the committee who entered it into the record.

In 1953, when McCarthy was at the height of his power, he attacked Wechsler again. As his subcommittee continued its investigation of government organizations, he began zeroing in on the Department of State's propaganda agencies: the Voice of America and the International Information Administration libraries abroad. Roy Cohn and his friend G. David Schine set off on a tour of European cities to investigate allegedly subversive material on the libraries' shelves. Among the examples they uncovered was Wechsler's book about John L. Lewis.

McCarthy pounced. He summoned Wechsler to Washington to defend himself before the subcommittee. Cohn and McCarthy knew that Wechsler had been open about his past, and the book in question was, typically for Wechsler, anticommunist in tone. The object was intimidation. Cohn deputized his friend Leonard Lyons to tell Wechsler that the subcommittee would let him off the hook if the paper would let up on McCarthy. That was a non-starter.

Jimmy was called to testify on April 24, 1953. Dolly accompanied him to Washington to introduce him to her old friend Senator Stuart Symington, who was also a member of the subcommittee. Symington and fellow Democrat Henry Jackson dealt gently with Wechsler, who tried to be a cooperative witness. But McCarthy was not interested in accuracy. He wanted to score points. When Wechsler referred to an anticommunist article that had appeared in the *Post,* the senator cut him off. "I read enough of your stuff, Mr. Wechsler, to find that your paper, as far as I know, always leads the vanguard with the Daily Worker—follows the same line—against anyone who is willing to expose Communists in government."

In response to a question about whether or not the *Post* harbored Communists on its staff, Jimmy said there were none. Were there any in the past? He knew of one. Who was that? "His name is Kempton," Wechsler said, "and he has been for years a vigorous anti-Communist." He said that Joe Lash was also an ardent anticommunist, as were several others whose names Cohn and McCarthy threw at him.

Wechsler concluded his testimony by reminding the senators that he was appearing voluntarily without having been subpoenaed, that everything he had said was already part of the public record, and that he believed the real purpose of calling him was to disparage the editorial policy of the *Post.*

After his appearance, Wechsler was offered a deal: name some other colleagues in the YCL, and we'll leave you alone. Wechsler wanted the full transcript of his April 24 testimony published, and that was also part of the deal. He returned in May and gave the committee a few names of former YCL members who had long since been outed. Cohn complained that he had told them nothing new, which was true.

Before this second session, Wechsler asked Dolly what she thought he should do. "It's between you and your conscience," she replied. Jimmy later told a close friend he had no doubts about her support. Wechsler strained to justify his behavior, but he was always defensive about having cooperated with the committee. The *Post* did not report on the event.

In the mainstream press coverage of Wechsler's ordeal, he, the *Post,* and its publisher came in for a lot of praise. Even on the political right, many acknowledged that McCarthy had nothing on Jimmy and had known it. Eugene

S. Pulliam, the conservative Republican publisher of two Indianapolis papers, *The Star* and *The News,* chaired a committee of editors who issued a statement concluding that McCarthy's attack on Wechsler, and by extension the *Post,* represented "not only a threat to the freedom of the press, but also a peril to American freedom." Arthur Krock in *The New York Times* took a middle position, pointing out that while McCarthy's intent had certainly been to vilify Wechsler and the *Post,* the senator had not actually abridged the paper's freedom to publish articles critical of him. Dorothy Schiff and her editor, Krock said, were hardly blindsided by McCarthy and his right-wing allies, nor likely to be intimidated by them.

Most letters from *Post* readers were positive, and there were no defections by regular advertisers. In fact, one praised Dorothy for the quality of her enemies. William Tobey, vice president in charge of advertising for Abraham & Straus, a major Brooklyn retailer, wrote,

> Dear Mrs. Schiff:
>
> As you know, sales productivity is a major barometer in an advertiser's consideration of a newspaper. And when a paper stands up and fights McCarthy on the all important issue of freedom of the press, and produces sales for its advertisers, as well, the combination is a heart-warming thing, especially to a cynical old advertiser like myself.
>
> I would like, therefore, to applaud you and your editor, James Wechsler, for this courageous battle to uphold the great tradition of a free press, and to offer my best wishes for unequivocal victory.

The most substantial criticism of Wechsler came from the left. In *Scoundrel Time,* her book about the McCarthy era, Lillian Hellman referred to Jimmy as a "cooperative witness." He informed Hellman's publisher that if she did not change the wording in future editions, he would sue for libel. His lawyers proposed the phrase "a responsive but hostile witness." Hellman never agreed to a change, but Wechsler did not pursue it further.

In December 1979, after a lunch with Victor Navasky who was working on *Naming Names,* another account of witnesses before the subcommittee, Dorothy wrote a memo for her files summarizing their conversation. Navasky was not so upset about the names Wechsler revealed, since they were in the public record anyway, but he felt that Jimmy had given implicit credence to McCarthy's vendetta by agreeing to testify at all. Dolly claimed she had not known that Wechsler mentioned as many names as he had. She also noted that she had not known all the details of his YCL past when she hired him. None of this information changed her basic trust and confidence in him. She remained proud that the *Post* had been among the first news sources in the country to go after McCarthy.

Intertwined with the conflicts between the *Post* and Senator McCarthy were parallel confrontations between the paper and Broadway columnist Walter Winchell. It is difficult today to credit how much power Winchell had, but during his heyday, which began in the 1930s, his Sunday night radio and television broadcasts on ABC reached fifty million listeners, and his daily column was carried by more than two thousand newspapers.

Winchell, unlike most show business reporters, included politics in his beat, and he was highly partisan in his coverage. He'd started out as a liberal, a voluble fan of the New Deal and a champion of underdog causes. In the early 1940s, Winchell was a reliable backer of FDR; White House insiders often passed him items that were useful to the administration. Because of their shared political views, Winchell and Dorothy Schiff had several discussions about his moving his home base to the *Post* from the Hearst-owned *Daily Mirror,* but Dorothy was never able to match what Hearst paid Winchell, and he stayed put.

After the war, Winchell's politics began to change. When Roosevelt died, he lost his White House contacts. Disregarded by Harry Truman, he turned against the new president and began to believe that the administration was riddled with Communists. He was a longtime friend of J. Edgar Hoover, who leaked verified as well as unsubstantiated items to the columnist in pursuit of what had become, by the late forties, their mutual goals.

Winchell's fall from power—and the *Post*'s role in his humiliation—began on October 16, 1951. The Negro entertainer Josephine Baker and a group of white friends entered the Stork Club, although they knew that Sherman Billingsley, the owner of the fashionable nightclub, discriminated against blacks. Baker was seated but not served and eventually left the club in a fury. She went public about the insult the next day. Henry Lee Moon, publicist for the NAACP and an old friend of the *Post*'s Ted Poston, complained that Winchell, who'd been in the nightclub during part of the evening, was not properly supportive of her.

According to Neil Gabler, his biographer, "Winchell was incensed at having been dragged into a dispute that wasn't even his own. He was also livid over the implication that he was not a true defender of civil rights. As a Jew, Winchell had experienced discrimination firsthand, and for years, long before most national journalists, he had been an outspoken champion of civil rights."

Walter White, head of the NAACP, wanted Winchell, whom he knew to be a friend of the organization, to chastise Billingsley publicly. Winchell refused to do so. Rather than let the matter drop, Winchell became paranoid on the subject. He went after Baker in his column, accusing her of being— variously—a Communist and a supporter of French fascism. Ted Poston filed a story in the *Post* almost every day about the ensuing charges and counter-charges of the principals in this essentially petty quarrel.

Seeing an opening, many people whom Winchell had offended in the past joined the attack on him. Lyle Stuart, a publicist who sometimes fed items to Winchell, had just started a monthly tabloid called *Exposé*. Stuart's second issue detailed some of the less savory anecdotes about the columnist's career. Winchell tried to get newsdealers to suppress the publication, thereby ensuring that it would sell out.

The *Post,* which had been considering a series about the columnist for some time, decided to move forward. Wechsler and Sann assigned seven top reporters to the project—an enormous commitment for a paper that operated with a very small staff.* Winchell refused to talk to any of them.

The twenty-four-part series began on Monday, January 7, 1952. When Winchell was a liberal, a *Post* editorial explained, the paper had tolerated his excesses because "the air and the newspapers were and still are overpopulated with conservative comment," which Winchell, with his tremendous exposure, tended to balance. But power had corrupted him, and now that he had moved to the right, the editorial concluded, "the venom he is capable of spreading" required a challenge. A series exploring Winchell's biases and misstatements was long overdue.

The thrust of the series was that Winchell felt "compelled on all occasions to remind the world that he is a central figure in the history of the twentieth

---

*Leonard Lyons was not among them. He could have been a valuable contributor because he knew so much about Winchell and his world. But Lyons told Paul Sann that he did not want to be involved, because Winchell had helped him get started in the field and for many years had been his friend.

century," but he was consistently handicapped "by misinformation, lack of knowledge, and capricious judgment." When proved wrong, he never apologized and often repeated his lies. The series covered Winchell's admiration for FDR and the callous way he turned on Truman. One article dealt with Winchell's enduring fascination with organized crime and his friendship with Frank Costello, the head of the New York mob. Another documented his slavish devotion to J. Edgar Hoover and the FBI.

Midway through the run of the series, Dolly devoted a "Dear Reader" column to her feelings about Winchell. She confessed that she read his column in the *Daily Mirror* every morning and was fascinated by the gossip, especially when it was about people she knew. She recalled that she had tried to woo him to the *Post* because she thought it would be great for circulation. She thought he was probably using her as a bidding weapon in his ongoing salary discussions with the Hearst organization, but she didn't hold that against him.

They reopened the subject from time to time. "I was more amused than annoyed at his indecision," she wrote, and admitted that she came to like him. "He's an egomaniac but kind of pathetic." After the Josephine Baker incident, Dolly felt she should not be so forgiving. "One thing that fascinates me about both Winchell and his friend Sherman Billingsley, proprietor of the 'Club,'" she decided, "is the fact that they can dish it out but can't take it."

When word got out that the *Post* was considering a series about the columnist, many mutual friends begged her to suppress it. "Naturally I would never give in to this kind of blackmail," Dolly declared. Some of the friends were vulnerable to being attacked by him, and she was sensitive to their concern. The fact that Winchell had such power, she concluded, was all the more reason the *Post* should look closely into his record.

Winchell claimed not to read the series, and while it was running, he chose not to comment on it. But his closest friends and colleagues said later that he was very upset. His longtime assistant, Herman Klurfeld, told biographer Gabler that prior to the *Post*'s coverage Winchell had seemed like an impregnable wall. "The *Post* series put an almost imperceptible crack in that wall. For years everything he did turned out right. Even if he was wrong, it turned out right. . . . From this point on, even when he was right, it turned out wrong." Three weeks after the series began, Winchell became physically ill and temporarily canceled his column and his broadcast.

The *Post* announced that it would not publish the six remaining articles

162   TAKING CONTROL

until Winchell went back to work. "We believe in the old journalist principle," Wechsler wrote in an editorial, "that a newspaper should not argue
with a man while he isn't in a position to argue back."

Ten weeks later Winchell returned, and the series ran to its conclusion.
"But he was still beleaguered," wrote Gabler, "and few defenders were willing to come to his aid. In the past most of his support had been political, not
personal. But his old liberal friends were understandably wary of him now,
and since most conservatives still didn't trust him either, he was left with the
odd, forgiving right-winger who would welcome him to the cause."

A few weeks after the Winchell series appeared, the *Post* published several articles about the work of Jack Lait and Lee Mortimer, two Hearst writers whose new book, *U.S.A. Confidential,* was the latest in a series—*New
York Confidential* (1948), *Chicago Confidential* (1950), *Washington Confidential* (1951)—that professed to reveal insidious left-wing influences across
America. Lait and Mortimer refused to be interviewed by *Post* reporters, and
just before publication of the articles, they sued the paper, Dorothy Schiff,
James Wechsler, and Murray Kempton, claiming they were libeled in Kempton's review of *USA Confidential.* In a column titled "Ordure au Lait," Murray had referred to the authors of the book as "foul excrement" and claimed
that "their chapter on labor is the first literature in the field to begin with a
flat lie."

The *Journal-American,* Lait and Mortimer's home base, was losing out in
the afternoon paper wars in New York. Eager to strike a blow at one of its rivals, the *Journal* gave the case a great deal of publicity, and its advertising
salesmen allegedly used the issue to suggest that the *Post* was irredeemably
radical. During his pretrial testimony, Wechsler was asked by the plaintiffs'
lawyer to discuss his Communist past, and he acknowledged, as he had many
times before, that he had been a member of the Young Communist League
when he was young. The next day, the *Journal-American* treated his testimony
like breaking news, with a front-page headline: "Post Editor Admits He was
Young Red. Wechsler Ties Bared."

At the time, Jimmy was a regular panelist, along with Alicia Patterson and
Edward Doyle of the *Journal-American,* on a local television show called *Starring the Editors,* which was sponsored by the Grand Union supermarket
chain. Grand Union told the producer of the program that unless he
dropped Wechsler from the panel they would not continue their sponsorship. Patterson and Doyle said they would not appear until Wechsler was re-

instated. Dolly told Jimmy to tell the producer that the *Post* would go public with the story unless Grand Union reconsidered. The sponsor would not discuss the matter. The *Post* ran the story on August 6, 1952. Patterson chipped in with an editorial in *Newsday* criticizing the supermarket chain and corporate cowardice, which led Dolly to describe Alicia in her column as "a very gallant gal."

Wechsler was briefly reinstated; Grand Union did not renew its sponsorship, which was about to run out. No other company picked it up, and the program went off the air. As for the Lait-Mortimer suits, their lawyer admitted to Marvin Berger that they didn't have much of a case. Berger kept postponing Dolly's pretrial examination and delaying every response from the *Post,* and several years later the suits were finally dropped.

Winchell was not about to back down. Still smarting because of the *Post* series about him, he began to go after Wechsler. On September 8, 1952, he purported to reveal for the first time that Wechsler was a former Communist: "Jake Wechsler (the editor of the N.Y. Post) for 3 years was a leader of the Young Communist League. . . . When this 'Ivan' ran his articles 'exposing' me—he prefaced: 'When a man has such a wide audience as Winchell, we believe the people should know his background.' . . . Well, kind Hearts & Gentle People, here's his."

In later columns he referred to the N.Y. Poo and the Posterior; he called it a "pinko-stinko sheet" and the "New York Pravda." On September 22, he told his readers that Dorothy Schiff was having a breakdown. "The disclosures here (of a great number of 'former Communists' directing her former newspaper) are said to have hit her ad department's pocket hard."

He wrote that Wechsler "held important posts in the upper echelons of the Communist apparatus." He referred to Dolly as Dora or Dully and asserted that Dolly and Jimmy had refused to help the FBI or any other government agency collect information about possible subversives in journalism or other areas of public life. And, he concluded, "obviously the Schiff-Wechsler Axis would rather attack the enemies of Communism" than help protect our country against its enemies.

As the 1952 presidential election campaign heated up, Winchell referred to Wechsler in his column as a Communist speechwriter for Stevenson. On his television program he linked Wechsler to the convicted Soviet spies Julius and Ethel Rosenberg. Not only had Jimmy never met the couple, but the paper was unswayed by their cause. The *Post* was about to run a series based on a book by staff reporter Oliver Pilat, which assumed that the Rosenbergs were guilty of espionage and argued that the campaign to defend them was being orchestrated by the Communist party.

The *Post* and Wechsler filed libel suits against Winchell and his employer, the Hearst Corporation. Dolly was eager to sue. Jimmy said he could tolerate Winchell's continuing attack in print or on the radio, because most of the country didn't know, or care, what the fuss was about. On television, with photos juxtaposing his image with those of various Communists, he felt the damage done to his reputation was exponentially greater.

Simon Rifkind, the plaintiffs' lawyer, deposed Winchell in his office. The *Post* team was eager to learn about Winchell's indemnification agreement with the Hearst Corporation and whether it had ever been invoked in previous lawsuits against the columnist. They wanted to establish the possibility that Winchell was seeking revenge for the series about him, to prove that Winchell had actually accused Wechsler of being a Communist at the present time, despite his clear knowledge from published accounts that this was not so, and to show that Winchell had encouraged readers to harass Wechsler, his wife, and Dorothy Schiff, by publishing their home addresses in his column. They also wanted to establish the fact that he had no information to back up his claim that the *Post*'s advertising revenues were negatively affected by his attacks.

These were serious matters, and Rifkind offered to keep the sessions private, but Winchell arrogantly said he had nothing to hide. During several sessions of questioning, he played to the audience of reporters who were present, most of whom thought he appeared to be a blustery buffoon. Their coverage of his testimony was mostly unfavorable. The suits proceeded slowly.

After McCarthy was censured by the Senate in December 1954, he soon disappeared from the public eye. Winchell's decline was more protracted. The columnist, who never stopped praising the senator, was linked in many people's minds with the most egregious aspects of the Red witch hunt and became an embarrassment to many of his previous supporters. The audience for Winchell's broadcasts was slipping, and one major sponsor had already dropped out. In March 1955, ABC outmaneuvered Winchell in contract discussions, forcing him to announce that he would quit at the end of the season.

Simultaneously, the *Post*'s lawyers and those representing the Hearst Corporation worked out an agreement. Wechsler and the paper would drop their suits if Winchell would apologize. If he wouldn't, Hearst would not indemnify him. He was trapped.

Winchell issued what *Time* called "the most abject retraction of his career." Unwilling to apologize directly, however, the columnist arranged for Glenn Neville, his editor at the *Mirror,* to announce that Winchell "never said or meant to say in the *Mirror* or over the air that the *New York Post,* or its publisher, or James A. Wechsler, its editor, are Communists or sympathetic to communism. If anything which Mr. Winchell said was so construed, he regrets and withdraws it." Winchell's weekly broadcast began with a similar text, read by the announcer, and the columnist also agreed to pay the *Post*'s $30,000 legal bill and to drop a countersuit for libel that he had filed against Schiff, Wechsler, and the paper.

Wechsler's subsequent editorial could afford to be magnanimous. "This was not a personal argument, and we derive no vindictive satisfaction from the outcome," he wrote. "The issue, it might be said, was bigger than all of us. It has been fully and clearly resolved by the retraction. . . . We hope the result of his litigation will hearten others who have been the target of unjust attack. As for the Post, we will continue to uphold the proposition that free men need not—and must not—imitate the Communists in fighting to preserve freedom."

The public humiliation of Senator McCarthy and his vocal supporters like Winchell effectively ended the era in which American politics was dominated by the search for subversives in and out of government. For some left-wing anticommunists like James Wechsler, the effort to define the path the nation should take while protecting against the excesses of Communists and aggressive anticommunists alike would remain, nonetheless, the template against which they measured most political struggles. For others, Dorothy Schiff among them, the time had come to allow the anticommunist cause to recede in importance as new concerns came to the fore.

TEN

"I Got Married!"

In the early 1950s, Dorothy Schiff was on something of a roll. Under her direction and that of her handpicked editorial staff, the *Post* was breaking news and making news. Thanks to her efforts, the paper was pulling ahead in the competition for local and national advertising as well. In December 1952, the *Post* proudly announced that it was "New York's Fastest Growing Newspaper." It had gained more than twenty-five thousand daily readers in the previous twelve months. Compared to other afternoon papers, the *Post* ranked first in total retail advertising linage, in clothing store ads, in Herald Square and Brooklyn department store ads, in real estate display ads, and in amusement, hotel, and resort ads.

Dorothy was fearless in pursuit of new advertisers. In January 1952, she mentioned to her friend Robert Weil, the president of Macy's, her inability to sell ads to two leading department stores, B. Altman and Stern's, both of which were run by men who were active supporters of the Catholic archdiocese of New York. Weil suggested that she call Francis Cardinal Spellman, the city's chief Catholic prelate, to ask for his help.

Spellman's secretary told her that His Eminence did not grant interviews. She said that she had met the cardinal at a recent dinner and simply wanted to get to know him better. She was invited for lunch to Spellman's office/

residence—known informally as "the Powerhouse"—which she subsequently described in detail in a memo to Wechsler.

On arrival, she was seated in a formal parlor filled with heavy furniture and decorated with pictures of Spellman. A few minutes later the cardinal arrived, accompanied by Bishop Fulton Sheen, who had arranged several celebrity conversions, including that of Clare Boothe Luce. Dorothy wondered if the churchmen thought she was contemplating conversion. They were eventually joined at lunch by several other priests, whose names she didn't catch. She commented to Wechsler that she felt like "Snow White and the Seven Dwarfs."

Dorothy told the cardinal that she had prepared for the meeting by reading *The Foundling,* a novel he had written. They discussed *The Cardinal* by Henry Morton Robinson, a recent best-selling novel based on Spellman's life. She had also read Paul Blanshard's book *American Freedom and Catholic Power,* an anti-Catholic polemic, which she did not mention.

On the subject of anti-Catholic feeling in the United States, Dorothy said she thought most Americans believed the church had too much power. Spellman replied that Catholics actually had very little power, that few public officials outside of New York were Catholic, and that the prejudice against Catholic candidates was still substantial. She was afraid he was going to call her a bigot and blurted out that her two best friends from childhood were Catholics.

They talked about his abhorrence of communism, and she asked why there were so many Communists in Catholic countries like Italy. He answered that poor ignorant people were likely to fall for Communist rhetoric and that priests in such countries did not deny Mass to parishioners who were also Communist voters. The other priests said that they understood that the poor and those who sympathize with them could be Communists because it is an absolute. Dorothy decided that these priests felt persecuted. "They are still isolated from America. And they seem to have no social or political vision."

There was some talk about how the Western Allies had been duped by Russia at Yalta. Spellman asked her what FDR would make of the international political scene in 1952 if he were to return to earth. She answered that he would think that things were a mess, but that if he'd been around to work with Stalin maybe they could have done better. Everyone agreed that FDR thought he could work with the Russian leader. She said that she understood that, because she had always operated on the premise that "you can usually get something done if you just sit down and talk." The priests laughed and said, "You've certainly proved that today."

After lunch, Spellman led her back to the parlor alone, although she noticed that Sheen lingered outside the door. The cardinal asked if there was anything she wanted to say in private. She said no, that she had called on an impulse because she thought it was not a good idea for there to be distrust between them. She knew they had disagreed in the past and would probably do so again, but thought it was better that they establish some personal contact. Then she mentioned casually that a merchant in New York had pointed out to her that department stores with Catholics in upper management positions didn't seem to advertise in the *Post*. The cardinal said that he couldn't imagine that there was any connection.

Before leaving, Dorothy asked if she could mention the lunch in her column without reporting on it. Spellman said he would prefer not. She sent a thank-you note, to which he responded graciously.

John Cooney, Spellman's biographer, wrote that although the cardinal barely knew Dorothy Schiff, he was wary of her. The *Post* had criticized his periodic attacks on Eleanor Roosevelt, his support for the fascist regime of Generalissimo Francisco Franco in Spain, his handling of various censorship issues, and his demand for the breakdown of church/state barriers. "The gingerly way the rest of the press generally treated the Powerhouse," Cooney wrote, "made the *Post*'s stands appear that much bolder."

Despite Dorothy's effort, the *Post* could not attract advertising from B. Altman and Stern's. However, the paper's overall financial situation continued to improve. In 1951, the corporation had had its first breakthrough year. Newspaper operations showed a net profit of $350,000, and Dolly was able to redeem $200,000 in bonds. Since taking sole command of the paper, she had reduced its outstanding debt to herself by about 20 percent. The paper made money in 1952 and 1953 as well. Since Dolly did not need the income, she used the profits to add to corporate cash reserves and to upgrade pressroom equipment.

Morale in the newsroom was high. A reporter who joined the paper just after the war remembers, "The *Post* was probably the best written of the city papers at that time. We had tremendous pride in what we were doing. The editors gave you great latitude to follow your own story ideas. Most everybody there was naturally comfortable with the politics. You could be apolitical and work there, but you wouldn't have been comfortable if you openly opposed the liberal point of view. And Mrs. Schiff set the tone for that."

Successful as Dorothy was becoming in her professional life, she was at loose ends personally. In her late forties, she had never before gone for so long without a significant man, or two, in her life. She was looking for someone to fill the void.

At a dinner party in the spring of 1951, Dorothy spotted a man who she'd been told was recently separated from his wife. Intrigued, she introduced herself. Since he had no idea who she was, conversation lagged until she mentioned his well-known involvement with the State of Israel. That was the spark. When she said she'd never been there, he invited her to join him on a trip in a few weeks. She accepted, although it wasn't clear if either of them took the exchange seriously.

Rudolf Sonneborn was a fifty-three-year-old manufacturer of petroleum products. He was originally from Baltimore, where the German-Jewish community was much more actively pro-Zionist than its New York counterpart. In 1919, recently graduated from Johns Hopkins, Sonneborn attended the Versailles Conference as the secretary of the American Zionist delegation. Later that year he traveled to Palestine with Chaim Weizmann and other Jewish leaders and then on to Damascus to interview Emir Faisal, the Hashemite leader. He spent nearly a year in the Middle East preparing a report for the Weizmann Commission, a forerunner of the Jewish Agency, the semiofficial organization that would speak for the Jewish community in Palestine during the period of the British mandate. Later, he solidified his reputation as a power in the Jewish community by helping to finance the Israeli War of Independence.

As World War II was coming to an end, it became clear that the British government was resistant to permitting unlimited settlement of European Jewish refugees in Palestine and to the idea of an independent Jewish state. Small groups of Palestinian Jewish soldiers, the nucleus of the Haganah, or defense force, organized armed protection for the illegal landings of boats filled with refugees and attacked British-built bridges and roads leading to surrounding Arab countries. Soon the country was in a state of undeclared war between the British soldiers and the Haganah, a conflict made more complex by the presence of terrorist groups on the Jewish far right that were willing to attack the British directly. The government in London wanted nothing more than to be rid of the whole mess.

In February 1947, Britain asked the United Nations to revoke its mandate and to assume direct responsibility for the Palestinian situation. In November, the General Assembly approved the recommendation of a special commission that the country be partitioned into separate Jewish and Arab states, with Jerusalem having special international status. The Jewish community accepted partition. The Arabs rejected it and prepared to invade the Jewish territories as soon as the British left. The Arabs had a significant advantage in numbers, arms, and strategic positions.

Foreseeing such problems, the leaders of the Jewish community in Palestine had already contacted American Jews like Rudolf Sonneborn for help. In July 1945, Ben-Gurion, who was now head of the Jewish Agency, came to New York for a clandestine meeting with thirteen influential Jewish business leaders at Sonneborn's apartment on East Fifty-seventh Street. The Haganah needed heavy equipment, especially tanks and aircraft. It needed small arms, ammunition, clothing, medicine, and support supplies. To keep a low profile for the program, the funds collected would have to be raised outside the usual Jewish charitable networks like the United Jewish Appeal.

Sonneborn's group was officially called Materials for Palestine and informally referred to as the Sonneborn Institute. The members reported on their efforts at fund-raising and finding suppliers who were willing to sell what was needed without asking too many questions. Sometimes the institute located sympathizers who could arrange warehouse space, set up phony companies, or transfer funds on their own accounts. Rudolf insisted that the program operate whenever possible within American law, and mostly it did.

As supplies, including tank parts, began making their way to Palestine, however, the British prevailed upon the State Department to issue an embargo against the continuance of the trade. Thereafter, although purchases may have been at least technically legal, shipping was definitely not. The group bought eighteen boats, including an old Chesapeake Bay steamer that was renamed the *Exodus*. The boats slipped out of American harbors and made their way across the Atlantic laden with millions of dollars' worth of military supplies, which they delivered to Palestine along with more than seventy-five thousand legal and illegal European immigrants. The efforts of Sonneborn and his group were remarkable, and they were publicly acknowledged after the success of the Israeli War of Independence and the foundation of the state.

Dorothy knew only the barest outline of Rudolf's involvement when she accepted his impromptu invitation. During the next few weeks, they saw a lot of each other and decided that the trip was a good idea. Alicia Patterson and friends of George Backer who were active supporters of Israel vouched for Rudolf's character.

Rudolf, who appeared to the world as a successful businessman and political insider, was seen by his own family as something of a mama's boy. He and his mother exchanged letters every day. He'd had a long affair with the actress Jessie Royce Landis, whom he didn't marry because his mother disapproved of a wife who wasn't Jewish. When he was forty-nine, he got married for the first time to a much younger woman, from whom he separated within two years.

Dorothy and Rudolf sailed for Europe in June 1951 on the *Queen Elizabeth*. They took separate cabins and went dutch throughout their stay abroad. They stopped first in London, where Rudolf introduced Dorothy to leading English Zionists, and she introduced him to Max Beaverbrook and Leslie Hore-Belisha. For twenty years, Max had been the standard against which she measured other men. This time she was in the company of someone who, though not as dynamic as Max, held up well in comparison.

The best way to get from Europe to Israel was to fly, which, as always, terrified Dolly. Because she didn't want to fly home alone, and because Rudolf urged her to stay on, she remained in Israel for nearly two months while he took care of his business.

They met with the leaders of the state—the Ben-Gurions, the Weizmanns, and Golda Meir, who charmed Dolly by cooking dinner. They visited a kibbutz in the Galilee, where Dolly was moved by the hardships the new immigrants faced in building a life. The young pioneers clearing their land so intrigued her that she had a brief fantasy of joining them. Rudolf was not as sentimental; he pointed out that she had no useful skills and reminded her that she liked her creature comforts.

On July 20, King Abdullah of Jordan was assassinated at the Al Aksa Mosque by an agent of a rival Arab faction. There were riots in the Arab sectors of Jerusalem, and, from the supposed safety of their rooms at the King David Hotel in the Israeli quarter, Dolly and Rudolf could hear gunfire almost nightly. She was frightened but determined to stick it out.

Six weeks into the trip, she wrote Dick Manson that she was becoming very devoted to Rudolf and hoped that their relationship would be permanent. A few days later she wrote that she felt as if they were already married. That morning she had even washed Rudolf's socks.

Back in America, the liaison continued. The couple tried to get away on weekends to Twin Hills, Rudolf's country house near Danbury, Connecticut, where Dolly enjoyed puttering in the kitchen. Rudolf was engaging company; he was attractive, he knew interesting people, and Dolly respected his business acumen. His family in Baltimore welcomed her when she joined them for a wedding, a Passover seder, or a Christmas dinner. Though actively identified as Jews, the Sonneborns were ecumenical in their observance of holidays. Rudolf's nieces remember that Dolly fit right in. She seemed to like being part of a family. Even Rudolf's mother approved.

Just as Dolly and Rudolf took separate bedrooms when they traveled, they maintained their separate apartments in New York. The living arrangement suited them, and it was also a metaphor for the parity between them. Dolly did not feel the same need to defer to Rudolf as she had with Max or FDR. She did not feel superior to him, as she had to her three husbands. For the first time in her life, Dolly had found a man whose financial resources and ability to exercise power matched her own. She had found a peer.

Rudolf was persistent in raising the question of their future together, but Dolly was not certain that she wanted an exclusive relationship. She confessed to Manson that while she liked Rudolf's company, she was aware that having a variety of gentleman escorts kept her amused. The failure of her three marriages also rankled.

In August 1953, Rudolf accompanied Dolly on a visit to Los Angeles aboard the Twentieth Century Limited to see Adele and Morti and their children. Morti Hall had married actress Ruth Roman in 1950, and their son Richard was born in 1952. Adele and Arthur Gray's four children—John, Kathleen, Michael, and Wendy—ranged in age from eight to three. Morti seemed to like Rudolf, but Adele had her doubts. "He was very stuffy, a bit grandiose, I thought," Adele says. "I didn't think he was good for her." Dolly did not share her own ambivalence with her daughter, although Adele says it was palpable.

The matter of their marriage had been moot because Rudolf was not free. His wife, Helen, had a history of mental illness. She had had a hysterical pregnancy while they were still together; she suffered from eating disorders that made her weight vacillate wildly. In the summer of 1953, Helen was back in a hospital to which she had been committed several times. Her lawyers made a series of demands for money that Rudolf thought were outrageous. But he was determined to end the uncertainty. By offering a more generous financial settlement than he had previously been willing to consider, he prevailed upon Helen to go to Mexico, accompanied by medical keepers, to get a quick divorce.

Presented with this fait accompli, Dolly acquiesced. She and Rudolf were married on August 18, 1953, in Santa Monica in the chambers of California Superior Court Judge Stanley Mosk. Morti Hall and wife, Ruth, were there. Adele was not invited because of her objections to the match.

At their hotel, Rudolf reregistered them as Mr. and Mrs. Rudolf Sonneborn. As soon as she could, Dolly went down to the desk and amended that: she was still Dorothy Schiff. At checkout, they were presented with a bill for three people. The parsimonious couple were amused, but they quickly informed the hotel of its mistake. No matter what their legal status, they continued to split the cost of the hotel and of their rental car. Dolly had her expenses reimbursed by radio station KLAC, which she still owned and Morti ran.

When they returned to New York in September, Dolly resumed her column:

> In my last letter I told you I was on my way to Los Angeles to spend my vacation with two of my children and all five grandchildren. And I promised to tell you about my adventures in Hollywood upon my return after Labor Day.
>
> When I wrote this I really had not expected to have anything special to report except possibly a meeting with a movie star or two. I *did* meet Danny Kaye and Bob Hope. I *did* spend many delightful hours with my children and their children but something I had not anticipated happened. *I got married!*
>
> In case you missed the item when it was printed on August 19, the name of the (I hope) lucky man is Rudolf G. Sonneborn. Rudolf was born in Baltimore. He is tall, gray-haired and very handsome, with a beautiful speaking voice. More important, he has a wonderfully kind disposition and is well known as a leader in humanitarian causes, especially in the development of the State of Israel. To top it all, although the head of a large oil refining and chemical business and a director of a bank, Rudolf is a liberal Democrat!
>
> My husband, although deeply attached to religious and family tradition, is very modern in his attitude toward careers for women. He reads the New York Post avidly and considers its continuance as the city's only crusading liberal newspaper to be of such vital importance that he is willing to have his

wife retain her maiden name professionally and to continue to devote the major portion of her time to its publication.

Rudolf gave up his apartment. He insisted on paying for some renovations to Dolly's place on Sixty-fourth Street, after which he moved in some of his furniture—much of which had belonged to his grandmother—and put the rest in storage.

Dorothy had employed a succession of married couples who served as live-in butlers and cooks, as well as an occasional lady's maid. In addition, a laundress came once a week. Both Dorothy and Rudolf had drivers. Although Dorothy kept the apartment in her name, she and Rudolf split the cost of the help.

The Sonneborns became fixtures on the New York charitable/social scene. Rudolf was especially in demand at fund-raising dinners for Jewish or Israeli organizations. Dorothy remained loyal to any cause in which Eleanor Roosevelt took an interest. Frequently the *Post* coverage of a formal event in the grand ballroom of the Waldorf-Astoria or the Hotel Pierre included a picture of Dorothy or Rudolf with Chaim Weizmann, Harry Truman, Queen Elizabeth, or other honored guests.

Danbury continued to be a welcome retreat. Sarah-Ann Backer (whom everyone but Dorothy usually called Sally) joined the household frequently. Dorothy's dachshund, Froly, enjoyed a chance to romp in the country with Rudolf's white standard poodle, Tu-tu, who lived there permanently. In January 1954, Dorothy wrote a column about how she had spent the holiday season at Twin Hills:

One of my hobbies is cooking. I tried a variety of dishes such as cheesecake, blintzes, chocolate cream pie, hollandaise, curry and cheese sauces, fried chicken, crab gumbo, muffins and popovers. The cheesecake was quite good though I forgot one of the ingredients. The chocolate pie was a failure. The filling was too soft, and I was quite unhappy about it. However, my husband who is very indulgent, said it was delicious and that he liked it gooey.

The other things turned out well. The first time the hollandaise sauce curdled, so that I was quite nervous every time I made it thereafter. I had exactly the same feeling I have when I face the voting machine on Election Day. Will I do something wrong with one of the little levers, I always worry, and unintentionally help to elect the very candidate against whom I have been campaigning so vigorously?

In late 1953, much tabloid coverage was devoted to an ongoing romantic triangle in which Dominican playboy Porfirio Rubirosa carried on simultaneous affairs with actress Zsa Zsa Gabor and heiress Barbara Hutton. Would Rubirosa dump Gabor, who was still married to actor George Sanders, for a lucrative union with Hutton? Would Hutton succumb to a notorious fortune hunter, who had already married and divorced the phenomenally wealthy daughter of Dominican dictator Rafael Trujillo and Doris Duke, another American heiress?

The *Post,* like every tabloid across America, gave its readers daily updates. Although, as Dorothy reported,

> Some of our more serious-minded readers have written in expressing their disgust at the amount of publicity given to this more sad and sordid than hilarious or romantic affair. Perhaps you think that the story wasn't worth printing. If so I must disagree with you. To me it had almost every element of human interest. My husband, who is quite dignified, was my guinea-pig in this matter. Never, until he met me, had he read a newspaper which gave full coverage to a story such as this.
>
> He saw the morning-after-the-marriage tabloids before I did. The first thing he said to me when I woke up was: "Well, they did it." "Who did what?" I asked. "He and Hutton got married," was the answer. And my theory that stories involving wealth, sex, jealousy are fascinating to everyone was confirmed.

She attributed to Rudolf a sensitivity to popular culture that few who knew him well would have credited.

Dorothy turned to Rudolf for advice about the business side of the paper from time to time, but he never took an active part in day-to-day management. She was not about to share her power, nor did Rudolf show any inclination to get involved on that level, but she found it reassuring to have a husband with considerable financial savvy. Soon after their marriage, they discussed her ongoing concerns about the *Post*'s contracts with its various unions. Rudolf arranged for her to meet Sidney Orenstein, a lawyer who handled labor negotiations for L. Sonneborn & Sons. Orenstein and Dorothy hit it off, and his firm represented the *Post* in labor matters for the next thirty years.

Rudolf looked over the *Post*'s balance sheets and made suggestions about financing and purchasing. He consulted with John Schiff about management decisions at Northwood Finance and Realty Corp., the entity—jointly owned by Dorothy and her brother—that held land on Long Island that they had inherited from their father. Rudolf took an active role in the transfer of ownership of KLAC, the Los Angeles radio station, from Dorothy to her son, Morti.

On the advice of their tax lawyers, Rudolf and Dorothy filed joint income tax returns starting in 1955. Although she remained Mrs. Schiff to the public, in various corporate enterprises she signed herself Dorothy Schiff Sonneborn. She seemed comfortable balancing her two identities.

Soon after her marriage, Dolly lost one of her few intimates at the paper. A two-week strike in November–December 1953 had been stressful for everyone on the paper's management team, but Dick Manson's emotional involvement appears to have exacerbated his already fragile physical condition. Although Dick was only fifty-three, he had suffered for some years from a bad heart and extremely high blood pressure. Soon after the strike was settled, Manson took a medical leave because of ill health. Perhaps he should have retired to take better care of himself, but Dolly's need for his counsel and his own sense of responsibility led him to return to the office in July 1954 before his boss left for Europe with Rudolf.

On August 28, Dolly was boarding the *Andrea Doria* in Genoa to return home when she got the news that Manson had died suddenly of a stroke.

She wrote about her grief in the first "Dear Reader" column to appear after her vacation.

> Dick was . . . a close friend of mine for over 20 years. We had known each other before either of us was connected with the New York Post. . . . He was a gentleman and a gentle man, tho he joined the army when he was over 40 to fight Hitler. He was never discouraged, always fun to be with.
>
> I knew Dick had high blood pressure. During the strike last year he lost 12 pounds and I was worried about him. But his doctor told me later that, sur-

prisingly, he was in better physical condition after that grueling experience
than he had been for a long time. . . .

When I was annoyed or frustrated, Dick, who was not religious, would
say: "You must have faith." Faith in your fellow-man is what he meant. Dick
had that kind of faith in his colleagues. We all felt it and we were strengthened
by it. I hope we shall never forget what we learned from him.

Many people on the *Post* felt that Dolly was partially to blame for Manson's death. Even Jean Gillette, who had recently become Dorothy's principal secretary and seldom criticized her boss, says, "She wasn't very nice to
him. He was sick, and she made him come back to work, and he died. She
was very sad, but I don't think I ever heard her say that she felt responsible."

Murray Kempton wrote to Wechsler at the time, "I think I understand
what the business about Dick means to you because it means something like
the same thing to me. . . . I do not think that I will soon look easily at the
publisher again and I am sure that you can't either."

Dolly grieved for Dick. She sent $5,000 in his memory to the Irwin Ed-
man Fellowship Fund at Columbia University. Presumably Wechsler, who
like Manson was a loyal alum of Columbia College, suggested the charity,
which was named for a well-known philosopher and beloved professor who
had recently died.

In 1958, hearing that Manson's mother was ill and in financial need, Dolly
sent a letter to his sister offering to pay the mother's medical expenses on a
monthly basis. His sister replied that although Mrs. Manson's pride made it
difficult to accept charity, she would do so, because it gave her peace of mind.
The tone of the sister's letter was rather grudging, certainly not effusively
grateful, which suggests that Manson's family shared the view of some of his
colleagues that Dolly's demands had hastened his death.

Rudolf seems to have replaced Manson as Dorothy's business adviser and
confidant. Jean Gillette assumed more and more daily responsibilities at the
Post. Jean became Dorothy's gatekeeper—she was the typist and translator of
the stream of memos through which the publisher communicated with her
employees. Jean was devoted and judicious. She was loyal rather than ambitious. She got along with people. She knew secrets, and she kept them. Eventually Dorothy trusted her enough to make Jean a corporate official as well as
an executive secretary, and she worked for Dorothy for nearly forty years.

III

THE LIBERAL AGENDA

ELEVEN

Party Politics

Stevenson's failure to carry New York State in the 1952 elections had come as a stunning blow to Democrats of all persuasions. Liberals within the party began to think that the root of the problem lay in the local Democratic organizations. They focused their discontent on the old-time political bosses who controlled the party on the local level. The days were long past when party bosses acted as mediators between immigrant groups that otherwise lacked access to jobs and community services and the governing powers willing to supply those services in exchange for support at the polls. Midcentury liberals believed that the views of the voting public were slighted by business-as-usual machine politics. They deplored the corruption of many government officials, whose appointments and candidacies were determined by the bosses, and they felt blocked by arcane procedural rules from playing any part in party governance. The liberals decided to drive the machine from power. In New York, this meant challenging Carmine De Sapio, head of Manhattan's Tammany Hall, as well as the entrenched bosses in Brooklyn and the Bronx.

Dolly Schiff remained active in the anti-Tammany Lexington Democrats. Although she was no longer a state committee member, she stayed on the Executive Committee of the club until 1955 and lent her name to its Advisory Council thereafter.

The *Post* editorials went after the bosses whenever an opportunity arose. Dolly and Jimmy Wechsler were close to the leadership of the Liberal party, which was pushing for Democratic reform. Gus Tyler, who was political director of the International Ladies' Garment Workers' Union, explains, "The Liberal party was part of the Democratic party, but outside of the party. If there was some liberal Republican running for office, or an undesirable Democrat, the Liberal party would go to the Democratic bosses and say, you know if you have a liberal guy, we'll endorse him, and if you don't, we'll run an independent candidate. That was the game.

"But more and more the rank and file began to say, we're really Democrats, so we'll endorse Democrats. So that made the reform of Tammany very important. It made the New York Democratic party more in line with liberal politics, from within."

Most of the time, the Liberal party and the *Post* editorial team worked together. Gus Tyler was the liaison. In the early and mid-1950s, he met regularly with Schiff and Wechsler and pinch-hit as an editorial writer for the *Post* when Jimmy went on vacation. "Dolly was a genuine liberal," Tyler says. "She was a thinking woman. But she may have been more of a liberal than a Liberal. She may have been more of a Democrat at heart. I don't know for sure."

Jesse Simons, who worked briefly as Dolly's in-house labor specialist, was close to Tyler. Simons says, "Dolly aspired to be a spokesman for liberal interests in New York. She was a motivator and a publicizer. To whatever extent the newspaper mobilized thousands to tens of thousands of people, it did its job. Which was her job, too."

Dolly took her liberalism seriously, but she was never an ideologue, and her political decisions could be influenced by personal relations. She was characteristically influenced by personalities in the fight for reform. In February 1953, she wrote,

> Last week I read in the papers that a beef-steak dinner was to be given by the National Democratic Club in honor of the new State Chairman Richard A. Balch. As I dearly love to mingle with politicians and also am very fond of beef-steak dinners, I thought it would be fun to go as a representative of the press. The National Democratic Club is housed in a fascinating old Victorian mansion on Madison Ave. at 37th St. When I came in the front door, I was immediately recognized. The surprise at my presence in the camp of the organization Democrats was obvious. But it was quickly overcome and I was treated

like a queen! That's one trouble I have with political bosses. They are so nice
to me it makes it hard for me to fight them.

She grew more and more fond of Manhattan leader De Sapio. She invited
him and his wife to dinner. She called him "by far the most intelligent Tammany leader I have known" and noted, a propos of his appearance at an annual Liberal party dinner, that, on many issues, his views put him squarely in
the liberal camp. She was not wrong. De Sapio had taken over the leadership
of Tammany in 1949; he was the first Italian after nearly a half century of
Irish pols to run the Manhattan machine. He was receptive to suggestions for
changes in party procedures that were advocated by the reformers. His style
was always courteous and conciliatory; a lifetime in politics had taught him
the advantages of compromise.

At the state and citywide levels, the Democratic machine often produced
adequate candidates—usually in concert with the Liberal party—whom the
Post had little difficulty endorsing. The difference between Liberal and liberal, however, was typified by the choice of Robert Wagner Jr. as the Tammany candidate for mayor in 1953. Wagner's father, the late senator, was a
liberal hero. His son was seen as a dimmer light. Wechsler told Dolly that the
reporters who covered City Hall called Wagner Jr., the sitting president of
the borough of Manhattan, a "bubblehead." The *Post* came out for the Liberal party candidate, Rudolph Halley. But the machine delivered the vote,
and Wagner was elected. Although the *Post* lamented that De Sapio would
control the new mayor's appointments, the Wagner administration did not
repudiate liberal interests. One year into Wagner's term, Dorothy wrote that
she was surprised by how well he seemed to be doing.

In 1954, De Sapio proposed Averell Harriman as the Democratic choice
to challenge U.S. Senator Irving Ives for the governor's office, which was finally being vacated by Thomas Dewey after three terms. Dorothy's former
husband George Backer was Harriman's close political associate. The two
men had known each other since the thirties, when George, Dorothy, and
Averell were part of the Long Island social set. Backer, who had connections
with the reform element in the Democratic party but was also in touch with
De Sapio, may have brokered the deal for Harriman to get Tammany support.

The Liberal party also backed Harriman, and the *Post* soon fell into line.
In September 1954, Dorothy called Harriman "a man of integrity and sincerity." She admitted, "He is not an orator. He cannot read a speech in such a

way as to 'send' an audience. But this is his only liability. I am devoted to Averell."

Ives, a former congressman who did not have to give up his seat in the Senate to run, had never lost an election. Persistently awkward in front of the electorate, Harriman was heard to refer to voters as "stockholders." Alex Rose, who ran the Liberal party, said Averell would have done better had he not campaigned at all. Although the Democrats ran well nationwide, Harriman barely eked out a victory. Nonetheless, he did win, leaving De Sapio—with both governor and mayor beholden to him—with a very strong hand.

After decades of nonelective public service, Harriman loved being governor. He and his wife, Marie, moved into the governor's mansion in Albany and entertained lavishly. Mayor Wagner invited Dolly to social events at Gracie Mansion with some regularity, but the Harrimans did not include her on their guest lists.

De Sapio began encouraging Harriman to think about a serious run for the presidency in 1956. George Backer, though dubious about Averell's chances, agreed to start lining up support. But the De Sapio connection, which New York Democrats barely tolerated within the confines of New York State, was unattractive to the liberal wing of the party when they contemplated national office. Although Harriman was seen by many as slightly more liberal than Adlai Stevenson, Eleanor Roosevelt came out early for Stevenson. Harry Truman favored Harriman but wanted to avoid a nasty fight at the convention.

Dolly fretted in her column that it would be tough for anyone to beat Eisenhower and speculated that perhaps the president's health might keep him from running.* Among the Democratic hopefuls, she favored Stevenson. The Lexington Democrats supported Stevenson for the nomination against the wishes of De Sapio, who wanted to send a solid slate of Harriman delegates to the Democratic convention in Chicago. Although the liberal reformers had not yet moved against De Sapio directly, this assertion of independence was a sign that his control was not as strong as it had once been.

In Chicago, it was clear that Stevenson had the nomination nailed down. He annoyed some party bosses by throwing the choice of his running mate open to the convention. Senator John Kennedy of Massachusetts led on the

---

*In September 1955, Ike suffered a heart attack; in June 1956, he underwent major abdominal surgery for ileitis.

first ballot, but fears about his inexperience, his lack of liberal credentials, and his Catholicism led to an eventual shift among the majority of delegates toward Estes Kefauver, the liberal senator from Tennessee, who had sought the Democratic presidential nomination four years earlier.

The *Post* supported Stevenson, but Dorothy was measured in her enthusiasm. She told Jimmy Wechsler that her daughter Sarah-Ann, now a student at Sarah Lawrence and an ardent member of Students for Democratic Action, was critical of Adlai. Sarah-Ann believed that key issues in the election were civil liberties and civil rights, and that Stevenson was weak on both. In an October column, Dorothy summed up her view of the campaign. She granted that Eisenhower was probably a decent man, but she believed that his adherence to traditional Republican values was detrimental to the nation. Republican foreign policy under Secretary of State John Foster Dulles was a disaster. Domestically, even though the menace of McCarthyism had subsided, she felt the Republicans had handled the anticommunist issue badly and that the assault on civil liberties had lasting consequences. She questioned if Ike was healthy enough to serve a second term, but her endorsement of Stevenson and Kefauver was not precisely passionate.

Eisenhower, the overwhelming favorite, won by a bigger margin than in 1952. Stevenson carried only seven states, of which all except Missouri were from the Old South.

The Democratic party nationally and in New York needed fresh ideas and fresh faces. To the chagrin of liberals and Liberals, the freshest face in New York belonged to a Republican, Nelson Rockefeller, who was back in town after having spent more than fifteen years in Washington, serving most recently as Eisenhower's special assistant for foreign affairs. Neither dour like his grandfather nor diffident like his father, but with his share of their vast fortune at his disposal, Nelson was an attractive, extroverted forty-eight-year-old eager to make his way in politics. New York State Republicans wanted him to run for the Senate in 1956, figuring that an Eisenhower landslide would help them take the seat held by Democrat Herbert Lehman, who was not running for reelection. Nelson was not interested in legislative office. He recommended that the GOP nominate State Attorney General Jacob Javits, a fellow liberal Republican, who was elected.

Rockefeller had his eye on the governorship. He had turned down suggestions that he run against Harriman in 1954, although he would probably have won. In 1956, Harriman named Rockefeller chairman of the bipartisan Temporary Commission on the Constitutional Convention, which enabled him to learn more about political issues and players within the state. By 1958, Nelson was ready. He easily won the Republican nomination and welcomed Representative Kenneth Keating as the party's senatorial nominee. Harriman meanwhile was caught in the middle of a Democratic party squabble for that Senate seat. By the time De Sapio's choice, New York County District Attorney Frank Hogan, emerged as the nominee, Harriman's reputation was tarnished with liberal and swing voters.

Those were the very people whom Rockefeller had to attract to overcome the Democratic advantage in registered voters. Rockefeller accomplished this by accusing Harriman of being controlled by Tammany Hall and by courting the leadership of the Liberal party and the New York unions. He didn't get their endorsement, but they didn't go all out for Harriman either, and word among the rank and file was that Nelson was sympathetic to the ethnic groups to which many of them belonged. The Rockefeller family had ties to the black community that stretched back several generations; Nelson's parents and grandparents had helped establish elite black colleges in the South. He was happy to campaign with Jackie Robinson at his side whenever possible. He had long been interested in Latin America, had worked to stimulate investment there and in Puerto Rico, and he spoke Spanish.

Rockefeller had a good reputation with New York City Jews as well. Like any aspiring New York politician, he was a generous supporter of various Jewish charities. His knish-eating tour of the Lower East Side with ticketmate Louis Lefkowitz made the national news. Rockefeller's policies were liberal, his personality was engaging. His campaign received a boost in mid-October when *The New York Times* endorsed him.

In late October, the *Post* still had not declared its choice, although everyone assumed it would be Harriman. What seemed to clinch the deal was a minor flap concerning Nelson's relationship with Richard Nixon. Rockefeller had gotten along well with Nixon during his Washington days, but he knew that the vice president was anathema to the undecided voters he was trying to attract in New York, and he had pointedly not asked Nixon to campaign on his behalf. Then the press corps forced his hand. If the two men were in the same city at the same time and *didn't* meet, it would look as if Rockefeller was snubbing the number two man in his party and his country. The vice president and the candidate were forced to share a very public breakfast at the Waldorf-Astoria on October 24.

That did it for Jimmy Wechsler. In an October 30 editorial titled "Where the Post Stands," he wrote that, despite Rockefeller's obvious liberal impulses, he was clearly unwilling to repudiate the right wing of his party. The paper, Wechsler concluded, had to endorse Harriman.

Wechsler never made a major editorial decision without consulting his boss, who had been ambivalent about the election all along. She disliked the control De Sapio had over the governor, she resented Harriman's support for a party regular like Frank Hogan rather than her old friend Thomas Finletter as the Democratic senatorial candidate, and she found Rockefeller more compelling personally than Harriman.

In her October 28 column, she wrote, "I first met lovable Nelson Rockefeller in Washington in the New Deal days and immediately was struck by his very attractive personality and amazingly liberal views." She went on to tell of a dinner party she and Rudolf attended at the Rockefeller apartment the previous week. She said she had challenged the candidate about his meeting with Nixon. He said he was humiliated by having to meet with Nixon whom he'd tried to avoid. She took him at his word.

The day after the paper endorsed Harriman, Dolly wrote about the decision in a curiously convoluted and ultimately unconvincing fashion. She described Rockefeller as a "new star on the political horizon, who had served in both Democratic and Republican administrations, who had helped to share the Rockefeller wealth in the most constructive ways possible with people at home and abroad." But his breakfast with Nixon had lowered his stock in her eyes.

She and her fellow liberals had two choices, she wrote. "They could stick to Harriman or they could 'sit on their hands.' Principled intellectuals decided to stay with 'Ave.' Some of them had grievances against him, but they stood on his record." Some people, she thought, would vote against Nelson, because if he won, he would be a tougher opponent than Nixon in the 1960 presidential election.

In her final sentences she seemed to reverse her position once again. "As usual, simpler souls continued to rely on their intuition," she wrote, "and remained switched to the man they instinctively trusted. Perhaps for some reason, they identified him with Roosevelt because, unconsciously, they often called him by that name." A reader might easily have been left wondering exactly whom she was supporting.

At a routine upstate press conference a week before the election, Harriman had accused Rockefeller of being a part of the White House's lack of support for Israel during the 1956 Suez Crisis.* "As far as I know," he said, "Mr. Rockefeller was in the White House when we supported Nasser and the Arab nations. We are committed to Israel, and we must make it plain to the Arab nations that we intend to stand by that commitment."

The remarks were barely noted by the press or by representatives of the organized Jewish community. Having been warned by Drew Pearson that Rockefeller was gaining the respect of Jewish voters, Harriman repeated his accusation on a New York City radio interview show on Friday night, October 31. He specifically criticized Rockefeller for advising Eisenhower to condemn the British-French-Israeli invasion. "There is no doubt in my mind that the big business—the oil interests—have a great deal of influence on the—President Eisenhower's and Dulles' foreign policy has been the oil interests," Harriman said, with his typical lack of fluency. Again, the remarks were hardly considered newsworthy; the next day the *Post* buried his comments in a short article on page 4.

During a weekend in Baltimore visiting the Sonneborn clan, Dolly brooded about the *Post*'s endorsement. Harriman's attack on Rockefeller focused her discontent. She rushed to the office Monday morning and drafted a short paragraph. She insisted Wechsler pull the story already running on page 1—"Heiress Tries Suicide"—and replace it for the day's final edition with the text she'd written:

To Post Readers:
    Gov. Harriman's recent snide insinuation that Nelson Rockefeller is pro-Arab and anti-Israel should not be condoned by any fair-minded person. Rockefeller, far from being anti-Israel, has been a liberal contributor to the

---

*In July 1956, President Gamal Abdel Nasser of Egypt nationalized the Suez Canal, which had been run by an Anglo-French consortium, and at the same time blocked the Straits of Tiran, which was Israel's only access to the Red Sea. After a period of mounting international tension, Israel attacked Egypt's Sinai Peninsula on October 29, and two days later English and French forces seized control of the Canal Zone. Fearing that the hostilities would lead to a major East-West confrontation, President Eisenhower pressured England, France, and Israel into accepting a cease-fire and eventual withdrawal from Egyptian soil.

United Jewish Appeal for 12 years. It is deplorable but true that in political campaigns lower echelons on both sides indulge in vile demagoguery. But when the head of the ticket repeats such libels, he should be punished by the voters. If you agree with me, do not vote for Averell Harriman tomorrow.

Dorothy Schiff
Publisher

Because the blast appeared only in Monday's final edition, it was reprinted in the paper on Election Day morning, and Harriman's name was removed from the list of favored candidates without editorial comment.

Harriman and his advisers were stunned. He had never implied that his opponent was anti-Israel or pro-Arab; he had simply said that as one of Ike's aides, Rockefeller had contributed to the decision to be neutral rather than support the Suez invasion. Rockefeller, of course, sent Dolly his warmest thanks. His campaign had the endorsement reproduced and posted near every polling place on Election Day. It's hard to prove that Dolly's last-minute change of heart influenced a significant number of voters, but while Democrats were making big gains elsewhere around the country, Rockefeller took New York State by more than half a million votes. Nelson's coattails also helped his fellow Republican Kenneth Keating squeak by Frank Hogan for the vacant Senate seat.

Time, which was always eager to poke fun at Dolly and her liberal paper, quoted an anonymous source as saying, "Now she has divorced three husbands and one candidate," and called the last-minute endorsement "one of the zanier episodes in recent journalism."

Three days after the election, Dolly said that after hours of debating with herself about what to do, she had looked up at the portrait of "my forceful, outspoken grandfather, Jacob H. Schiff, hanging opposite my desk. I was sure I knew what he would have done. Time was running out. . . . As the deadline arrived, I stopped the presses and tried to correct what seemed to me to have been a shocking injustice done to a dedicated humanitarian."

In subsequent years, Dolly explained her decision in various ways to various interviewers. While sticking to her guns that the governor's statement about Rockefeller offended her, she also mentioned her worries about Harriman's being controlled by De Sapio and her belief that, by advancing the cause of Rockefeller, she was helping to build a viable alternative to Nixon in his own party.

Muddying the waters, however, was the published record indicating her visceral preference for Rockefeller all along. There's no doubt that, in addition to caring about a candidate's principles, Dolly responded to his personality, and she never denied how appealing she found Nelson. Political pollster Louis Harris says, "My guess is that Nelson sat her down and charmed the pants off of her."

Some observers have argued that the basis of Dolly's antipathy to Harriman can be traced back to their aborted romantic adventure in Paris in 1928, although it seems improbable that she carried a grudge for thirty years. However, despite her long acquaintance with Averell and her support for his gubernatorial race in 1954, she could not help but notice that he seldom went out of his way to win her favor. Harriman's biographer believes that Dolly's anger at this continuing indifference contributed significantly to her last-minute decision, and it is true that there were many times when Dolly and Averell just didn't connect.

In a memo to files that Dolly wrote in March 1958, she recorded an unsatisfying exchange between them. She had invited Charles Abrams to join her, Jimmy Wechsler, and Paul Sann for lunch. Abrams, an old friend and sometime *Post* contributor, was a well-connected Democrat and public housing advocate who had been appointed by Harriman to chair the State Commission Against Discrimination. He had asked to meet on the governor's behalf because Harriman believed that the paper was deliberately ignoring him, on instructions issued by the publisher herself.

Dolly saw things quite differently. She felt Harriman was ignoring her. It was true, she told Charlie, that she and Averell had known each other forever, but she felt she was being ostracized from his inner circle. She was invited only to those events in Albany to which all publishers were invited.

In a follow-up conversation, Abrams said that he had spoken to Harriman, who apologized for causing her distress. Dolly was not really mollified. She told Abrams she believed his visit was politically motivated—that Harriman was trying to mend his fences before the next election. She also told him to tell the governor not to worry, that even if there was a personal chill between them, it would have nothing to do with the paper's ultimate endorsement. "Our policy will not be influenced by a personal or social seduction," she concluded.

Early in October, Harriman held a reception at his home for labor leader George Meany to which Dolly was not invited. She sent a note to Abrams pointing this out. He responded with the lame excuse that had Harriman invited her, she would have been the only woman there, and the governor didn't like events with only one woman.

Later that month, Dolly and Charlie exchanged letters about a Rockefeller speech discussing his commitment to civil rights. Abrams told her he thought Nelson's argument was specious. She replied that she'd looked into it and thought it was pretty solid. In closing, she reiterated that she had not yet made a choice between the two candidates. Charlie said he was happy to hear it. "The rumors have it you're for Rockefeller."

Of course she was. Even if she couldn't bring herself to say so until the last minute. Jimmy Wechsler sent her a memo on Election Day before the results were in. He knew she was as upset about their disagreement as he was, and, although he doubted that there would be any lasting hard feelings between the two of them, he worried that the reputation of the *Post* had been damaged. He knew she had never wanted him to push hard for Harriman, and he thought he had complied. He believed that Harriman's awkward remarks should have elicited only an admonition, not a repudiation. In any case, he wrote, "It seems clear to me now that we should have followed your original impulse, endorsed Rockefeller and given me a brief vacation."

Dolly's decision, which seemed so shocking to observers at the time, was in keeping with the way she usually made political judgments. She trusted her instincts. She had backed Harriman for governor in 1954 against a candidate who was to his right, but in 1958, when Averell was pitted against a man who was as liberal as himself, she chose the candidate whose personality appealed to her more. She prided herself on her being in tune with popular sentiment, and she was right to do so.

Russell Hemenway says, "Dolly's political instincts were pretty good. Sometimes she was a little slow, sometimes she was behind the curve, but she was pretty good. She also liked you to think that she'd done her homework and figured it out. She listened to a lot of people and then made up her own mind. And sometimes she did surprising things like the Harriman-Rockefeller thing. Who expected that? It killed us, just killed us. Of course, we had this candidate who didn't know how to run a campaign. We began by saying, 'Nelson Rockefeller! Who's gonna vote for this rich guy? Most hated family name—most hated family in America.' Turned out to be a fabulous politician." Dolly's instincts were indeed "pretty good."

What was questionable, however, was her timing and her explanations for it. It was hard for her to turn her back on Harriman. But if she preferred Rockefeller—whose political stance was not really so foreign to her ideals—she could have said so in a timely, straightforward fashion.

In the event, Harriman's career as an elected official was over* and un-mourned. He'd been an adequate but unexceptional governor. One of Dolly's stated objections to him was his allegiance to Carmine De Sapio and the regular Democratic machine. Harriman's defeat—however great or small the *Post*'s contribution—was a blow to De Sapio. In time it would lead to the end of Tammany's control over the New York Democratic party.

---

*He was called back to public service by John Kennedy, who acknowledged his strengths in interna-tional diplomacy by naming him undersecretary of state for political affairs.

TWELVE

Protecting the Little Guy

In December 1956, on the heels of Stevenson's second resounding loss to Eisenhower, the *Post* ran a series asking "Where Do Liberals Go From Here?" Reporter Irwin Ross solicited answers from many leading liberals, including Stevenson; Harriman; Hubert Humphrey; Eleanor Roosevelt; Dolly's former lawyer, Thomas Finletter, an ADA-founder and Washington insider; recently defeated vice presidential candidate Estes Kefauver; Roy Wilkins, head of the National Association for the Advancement of Colored People; David Dubinsky; and Reinhold Niebuhr. Most of the people Ross interviewed wanted to ramp up liberal programs from the past; many thought the Democratic party needed to retool and refine New Deal programs like farm subsidies and Social Security, as well as organize a better national program for public housing. On the issue of civil rights, most concentrated on process. They urged a change in congressional rules governing filibusters so that Southern senators and congressmen could not keep civil rights legislation from reaching a vote.

Historian Arthur Schlesinger Jr. was the most forward-looking of the liberal mavens. He saw that there would be a need in the future for some form of national health insurance and for a coordinated plan to reinvigorate the cities. He believed that liberals should promote these causes. Schlesinger told Ross that the late fifties was similar to the Progressive Era at the begin-

ning of the twentieth century. "Then as now there were no life-and-death issues," said Schlesinger, "yet there was a great sense of frustration, of anxiety,
and [Theodore] Roosevelt and [Robert] La Follette fired the country with a
remarkable moral passion. I don't see why that can't happen again."

For over a decade, the *Post* kept its focus on the kind of passion
Schlesinger advocated. Only in the *Post*—with editorials, interviews, articles,
and the multipart series that came to define the paper's unique style and
character—could liberal New Yorkers find reports on abuses of power that
were ignored or condoned by the other papers in town, or critical profiles of
public figures who were used to adulation.

Dorothy Schiff and James Wechsler were particularly interested in promoting the liberal agenda; Paul Sann had a special feeling for the balance between high-minded issues that affect affairs of state and the indignities of
everyday life that matter to the man in the street. The paper's staff was much
smaller than that of any of its rivals; everyone complained about the filthy
conditions in the city room and the restrooms; there were never quite enough
typewriters or telephones or desks to go around. But the esprit de corps was
contagious, and the work produced by the reporters and editors of the paper,
under the ever-watchful eye of the lady upstairs, was a model of what good
urban journalism could be.

The *Post* reported on a full range of national and international news,
much of it culled from the wire services, but it focused on subjects of interest
to *Post* readers. Joe Lash covered the United Nations as well as news from
and concerning Israel. Max Lerner wrote four six-hundred-word articles a
week about Max Lerner and his conversations with leading American politicians and intellectuals about pressing issues of the day. In 1955, Lerner convinced Dolly and Jimmy to send him to India, Thailand, and other South
Asian states to interview heads of state and other worthies. The *Post* syndicated Max's regular column to a small network of about twenty papers. They
tried in vain to recoup the costs of his trip by selling the rights to his overseas
dispatches to a wider audience but had to settle for losing money and gaining
prestige.*

---

*In 1957, Lerner published his major work, *America as a Civilization: Life and Thought in the United
States Today*. This eleven hundred-plus-page celebration of the United States became a surprise best-
seller. In retrospect, Lerner's lack of attention to serious divisions in American society, his understating
of racial tensions, and his Cold War–based belief that American liberal democracy should be trans-

Murray Kempton was becoming one of the paper's significant assets. His coverage of organized labor, civil rights struggles in the North and the South, and government harassment of the beleaguered remainder of the American Communist party made him a favorite of Schiff and Wechsler.

In 1953, Jimmy recommended raising Kempton's weekly salary from $145 to $170, an unheard-of move, which he justified as being "in recognition of the principle that we cherish writers around here." A year later, Schiff and Wechsler discussed making Murray a columnist, and therefore an independent contractor unbound by the Guild pay scale. Unlike columnists Earl Wilson and Sylvia Porter, who had agreed to give up their union-mandated severance vesting in exchange for a larger share of their sizable syndication fees, Kempton was not likely to find a significant market nationally for his nuanced columns supporting civil rights and civil liberties.

It was finally agreed that Murray would write three columns a week for $150, plus another $50 for the occasional fourth. His participation in the paper's severance program was frozen rather than canceled, with the understanding that if he gave up his column and went back on staff within five years he would not lose his credit for prior service. A year later, Dolly recommended that they pay him $250 a week for four columns to give him parity with Lerner. In January 1956, Kempton turned down an offer from the *Journal-American* for twice as much money. It would have been hard for him to operate within the Hearst organization's political framework, and he also recognized that the *Post* had been good to him.

Dolly liked Murray and his work. From time to time, she gave him and his wife tickets to benefits that she was unable to attend. She sent him congratulatory notes on pieces she particularly admired. At the same time, she was alert to his vagaries. She reminded her editors that his columns, in which he frequently chided politicians and labor leaders for ignoring their constituencies as well as their moral obligations, needed to be checked for libel.

The paper's bread-and-butter coverage was the standard stuff of urban tabloids. The day Irwin Ross's series on liberal self-examination began running, the front page announced "Drunken Drivers Face Crackdown," and two well-promoted series—one on airline hostesses, the other on call girls—

---

planted to every corner of the globe seem glib and even fatuous. But Lerner's optimistic, middlebrow chauvinism perfectly suited the times. Dorothy Schiff complained that the *Post* was barely mentioned in the ads and promotional materials touting it.

had just finished their runs. Mixed with the ongoing drama of the Arthur Miller–Marilyn Monroe courtship and the question of whether Eddie Fisher would leave Debbie Reynolds for Liz Taylor were solid stories that reflected the liberalism of the *Post*.

This was not classic nineteenth-century English liberalism but an outgrowth of the New Deal theology that many individuals needed help in their struggle for decent jobs, decent housing, and decent family life, and that it was the job of the government to provide that help. The paper was for the "little guy" against the forces that often exploited him. Hardworking *Post* reporters went after heartless landlords, corrupt city officials, ruthless businessmen, and indifferent bureaucrats who victimized the ordinary citizens of New York. Some stories were assigned by Sann and his assistants, others were brought in by reporters who knew that if they spotted something intriguing on their daily rounds, they would be encouraged to follow it up.

Joe Rabinovich, universally known at the paper as Joe Rab, went to work at the *Post* in late 1955 and became the features editor a few years later. Rab says, "It was a writer's paper, it was more liberal than other papers, and eccentricity was sort of encouraged, or at least not frowned upon. And Mrs. Schiff was a bit ditsy herself, in what I found was a charming way. The atmosphere was conducive for people to find their own way."

Bernie Bard, a reporter who came to the paper during this era, says, "The great thing about working for the *Post,* you weren't there to represent the opinion of the publisher, or the transit workers' union, or the teachers' union, or the tree huggers. You were, to the extent that anyone could be at the time, a free spirit. You could call the shots the way you fucking saw them. Now that may be a romantic view, but it was the way I saw it."

Most of the free spirits who were attracted to the *Post* considered themselves professional journalists who prided themselves on their ability to weigh information and deliver balanced judgments, but they shared the liberal assumptions of their superiors. Bernard Lefkowitz, who went on to a distinguished career as a freelance writer and professor of journalism, remembered rushing to meet a deadline on a story about a strike. Jimmy Wechsler was impatient to turn Lefkowitz's copy over to the desk editors. Lefkowitz wasn't ready; he'd talked to the union, but he still needed to hear from management before he could sign off on the piece.

" 'Forget management. Write the story,' Wechsler told him. 'The *Daily News*'ll take care of management.' "

The *Post* was just the place at which a talented liberal-minded journalist like Mitchel Levitas, for example, could make a mark. Levitas, who was known as Mike, had been an editor of the Brooklyn College daily *Vanguard,* which was shut down by the president of the college who claimed it had a left-wing bias. Levitas was working at the Voice of America when fallout from Senator McCarthy's attacks on that agency forced it to cut back on staff. His father, the publisher of the liberal weekly journal *The New Leader,* asked Wechsler to give Mike a tryout.

Levitas was soon reporting on labor news, federal prosecutions of Communist party members under the Smith Act, and New York area soldiers at Fort Monmouth, New Jersey, who were accused by McCarthy and Cohn of being Communist agents. He even covered a case in which a scam artist was accused of conning Jimmy Wechsler and the editors of *The Washington Post* into thinking he had inside dirt on McCarthy. Though the case was embarrassing, none of the editors who read Mike's copy attempted to suppress or modify his reportage.

"They never interfered," Levitas says. "You knew it was a liberal paper, you were doing crime, politics, you shared a point of view, but they never interfered or imposed."

Levitas broke two big stories in the midfifties. Early in 1956, he was tipped off by a dismayed public health official that Blue Cross–Blue Shield, the nonprofit insurance giant that had been created to make affordable health coverage available to people who were previously uncovered or underinsured, was not operating in the best interests of its clients. In a series of well-documented stories, Levitas revealed that the organization's top executives were paid enormous salaries and given extremely generous expense accounts. Mismanagement was rampant: record keeping was extremely sloppy, and insurance claims were routinely mishandled or underpaid.

In 1957, he followed up this coup by uncovering the scandal of undocumented Puerto Rican workers, many of them were union members, whose unions did nothing to defend them against discrimination. The revelations won Levitas a George Polk Award for Metropolitan Reporting.

Another notable newcomer was William Haddad. Haddad was a Florida-born product of Columbia College and the Columbia school of journalism, who served as a radio engineer in the merchant marine after he left school. He was reassigned from shipboard service to manage the primary campaign for a seamen's union leader who was running for congress in San Francisco.

He moved to the staff of Estes Kefauver during the 1956 Democratic convention. Infatuated by politics and bored by engineering, Haddad, who had known Sarah-Ann Backer when they were both politically active undergraduates, talked his way into a meeting with James Wechsler and a tryout as a cub reporter at the *Post*. He was hired in April 1957, and by July he had his first byline.

One day, Haddad remembers, a disreputable-looking man showed up at the city room with a wild story about burning buildings for a slum landlord. The editors, used to dealing with the occasional nut who promised a scoop, decided to pass this one off on the rookie in their midst: "Oh, the guy who handles that is Haddad!" Haddad decided after listening to the man's semi-intelligible tale that there might be something to it. "If you could get through the nonsense, he claimed he was burning buildings for this guy [Harry] Shapolsky, a slum landlord. So I started digging, and I got into it pretty deep. The DA's office had wired me up. And we got the headline and everything."

For the next three years, barely a month went by in which the *Post* did not run a revelation of graft in the city uncovered by Haddad on his own or in collaboration with his more seasoned colleagues Ted Poston, Joe Kahn, and Stan Opotowsky. Haddad was the lead writer on a series revealing how officials in the city Buildings Department regularly took bribes from contractors to approve shoddy work or to expedite contracts. He uncovered stories about substandard conditions in city housing projects and about eligible black families who were denied access to the projects.

In June 1958, articles by Haddad led to an investigation by the Manhattan district attorney of landlords charging too much rent to welfare recipients, which in turn forced the resignation of the commissioner of housing and buildings. A series later in the year about city abuse of federal funds earmarked for housing development won Haddad a Polk Award. In 1959, he took a job working for a construction company to verify a rumor he'd heard that cement companies were systematically bilking the city by delivering half the cement they billed for.

The origins of the biggest story on which Haddad worked predated his arrival at the paper. In the early spring of 1956, Joe Kahn was walking through his Upper West Side neighborhood when it hit him that a number of buildings in the Manhattantown area, bounded roughly by Ninety-seventh Street, Central Park West, One Hundredth Street, and Amsterdam Avenue, were still standing long after they had been scheduled for demolition as part of a huge urban renewal project.

Kahn's investigation led to a three-part exposé of the four-year-old Manhattantown project. Kahn discovered that nearly two-thirds of the families who had lived in the area designated for redevelopment had been evicted. The sponsors of the new construction were paid to help the displaced families find new housing, yet less than 20 percent of the families had been given any help. Half the buildings in the area had been destroyed, but not one new building had been begun. The city was short perhaps $15 million in lost real estate tax revenues. The developers, on the other hand, had made out very well. They had been able to buy the land at an inflated price because of the government subsidy, they were making a nice profit on the rents from the buildings they had not torn down and from the cleared space that was used as a commercial parking lot, and they were paying themselves large management fees.

Manhattantown was under the jurisdiction of Robert Moses, a public official whose many titles included parks commissioner for New York City, chairman of the Long Island Parks Commission, chairman of the Triborough Bridge and Tunnel Authority, and de facto head of public housing for the city. Moses's spokespeople disparaged Kahn's report on irregularities in Manhattantown as "unwarranted" and blamed the delays on federal red tape.

Moses had served in a variety of capacities in New York State and City since 1914, although he never held elective office. With virtually no constraints on his power, he had redrawn the map of the region. By the end of his career, he had built nearly every major highway and bridge into or around the city. He created more than four hundred miles of parkways and hundreds of city and state parks, including Riverside Park in Manhattan and Jones Beach on Long Island. He made it possible for the Metropolitan Life Insurance Company to build Peter Cooper Village and Stuyvesant Town on Manhattan's East Side and for more than 150,000 units of public housing to be built farther south. He helped the Rockefeller family interests assemble the land on which the United Nations headquarters was constructed. He made Lincoln Center possible.

Moses's biographer Robert A. Caro wrote, "Between 1946 and 1953 . . . no public improvement of any type—not school or sewer, library or pier, hospital or catch basin, was built by any city agency, even those which Robert Moses did not directly control, unless Robert Moses approved its design and location."

Moses was remarkably capable, but he was also ruthless. As Caro pointed out, Moses dispossessed hundreds of thousands of people from their homes, wrecked stable neighborhoods, and reinforced the ghettoization of the city's minority populations. He ignored the law when it stood in his way, and he manipulated government agencies, elected public officials, and the media to suit his purposes. He dispensed contracts to lawyers, insurance agents, and real estate operators without competitive bidding and without oversight. He was vindictive toward anyone who opposed him. Much of his arrogance was based on his confidence in his own abilities and agenda; he also had the unabated support of *The New York Times,* whose primary owner, Iphigene Sulzberger, thought he was a genius.

Dorothy Schiff and Robert Moses had met in the thirties on Long Island. In 1938, Moses defeated her in an election to represent Nassau County at the New York State Constitutional Convention. Their paths crossed from time to time thereafter, and their social relations were always cordial. Dorothy was not as awestruck by Moses as Mrs. Sulzberger was, and the *Post* occasionally questioned the decisions made by the master builder, though not, for years, in a systematic way.

In 1949, Moses, in his role as head of the Mayor's Committee on Slum Clearance, announced that the city would begin four huge urban renewal projects in Manhattan using federal funds available under Title I of the National Housing Act of 1949. From time to time the *Post* carried complaints by residents of Manhattantown about the damage being done to their community by wholesale destruction of housing. In addition, the paper reported that Moses and city officials needlessly displaced thousands of working-class families in the east Bronx in order to build the Cross Bronx Expressway. Opposition to Moses's high-handed schemes was limited, and no one really had a complete picture of what was going on. Mayor Wagner continued to support Moses, as did much of the political establishment and influential construction union officials who saw his projects as a bonanza for their members.

In April 1956, Moses took on the wrong opponents. He wanted to appropriate a small wooded area in Central Park to enlarge the parking lot for Tavern on the Green, a privately owned restaurant within the boundaries of the park. Residents of the Upper West Side, who considered the park sacrosanct, were enraged. Unlike the voiceless working-class victims of Moses's high-handedness in Manhattantown and the east Bronx, the people from this neighborhood had access to the media and were savvy about how to manipulate it. Mothers staged a demonstration to protest the loss of playing areas for their children. Every major paper and television station covered their protest. Even the *Times* joined in the criticism of Moses's plan, perhaps because Mrs. Sulzberger's love of Central Park competed with her admiration for Moses.

Enraged by the bad publicity, Moses sent bulldozers to dig up the park in the middle of the night. It was a major blunder. The press stepped up its attack, casting him as the bully who hit out when he didn't get his way.

Fortunately for the *Post,* Joe Kahn was already on Moses's case. Within a month after the Tavern on the Green debacle, the paper rushed into print the results of Kahn's investigation into the Manhattantown irregularities. Sensing that Moses might be at the heart of a bigger story, the *Post* also ran a six-part series on Moses in June.

Irwin Ross, with the help of Ed Katcher and Joe Kahn, outlined Moses's long career and praised his achievements, but pointed out that most politicians who had worked with him, including Fiorello La Guardia and Franklin Roosevelt, had come to loathe him. They were unable to get rid of him, not only because of the influence of the *Times* but more important because Moses had written the statutes that designed the agencies he controlled, carefully placing them beyond the reach of elected officials. Moses, the *Post* concluded, had no interest in abiding by the rules and had managed to avoid public scrutiny of his projects and their finances for nearly half a century. The paper did not go so far as to accuse Moses of corruption. In fact, a Wechsler editorial criticizing Moses for his behavior in the Tavern on the Green imbroglio admitted that "no scent of scandal has ever invaded any of his numerous and sometimes imaginative public works."

Other reporters picked up the scent. Stimulated particularly by Kahn's work on Manhattantown, Eugene Gleason and Fred J. Cook of the *World-Telegram and Sun* began digging deeper into Moses's operations. For the first time, the stories they filed hinted at financial improprieties. Over the next two years, the *Post* and the *Telegram* kept the heat on but did not deter Moses from pushing forward. Haddad, fresh from his success uncovering ineptitude and corruption in the city Buildings Department, joined Kahn and shared sources and leads with Gleason and Cook.

Haddad says he and Kahn worked particularly well together. "Joe had a very easygoing way. You know in those days a reporter was like a cop. You didn't wait for people to come to you. You went out and interviewed a thousand people to get one. You just did it and did it and did it, until something paid off. And Joe was steady, he was sure, smart as a whip. I had a different personality, but we made a great team."

Finally the other dailies—with the exception of the *Times*—joined in. Haddad says, "We organized all the guys on the different papers around town. Peter Braestrup at the *Tribune*. Woody Klein and Gene Gleason at the *World-Telegram*. Gleason had been on it for a while, and he was terrific. We all did it together." Such cooperation was unusual but not unique. What motivated the reporters to work together was the unprecedented power of their prey. "We were out to get him, and we'd share the story if that was the way to do it," says Haddad. "The *Post* would run the story, and then one of their editors would call them and say, 'Why the hell did the *Post* beat us on that?' And Woody, say, would pretend he knew nothing about it. He'd say, 'I don't know. Let me look.' And that built the pressure. It got momentum."

In May 1959, Haddad and Kahn wangled permission to go to the offices of the Triborough Authority to examine the files of the Slum Clearance Committee. It was the first time in Moses's forty-five years of public office that a reporter had gotten near the files of any of his organizations. Most of the potentially interesting material had been removed by Moses's lackeys, but one overlooked memo indicated that various politicians and their allies had received fees from a consortium of sponsors to deliver influence.

This made it possible for the reporters to trace the ways in which the deals worked. With Moses's approval, his lieutenants would leak news to influential lawyers and politicians in the city about where they were about to purchase land. These insiders would buy it from the current owners, then turn a big profit when they sold it to the Slum Clearance Committee. Other lawyers, real estate agents, and insurance firms connected with them also profited from the transactions.

Stung, Moses and his allies tried to bully the other publishers. Haddad says, "It was hard for them to resist. You know, he would call up and schmooze them, and they all thought he was wonderful. Dolly Schiff was the only publisher who didn't buckle. He called her several times, trying to stop it. We'd have meetings up in her office with Jimmy Wechsler. Never once did she interfere. The only thing you had to do was be absolutely sure you had your facts right. But there was never any of that political pressure. She and Jimmy—they were an incredible team. And Sann, too."

Dolly enjoyed her social connections to prominent public figures like Moses. She didn't go looking for a fight. Her political and journalistic convictions, however, trumped her social aspirations. Thanking a friend who'd commended the *Post* on its willingness to go after people in power, Dolly said she couldn't bear to see people who misused power get away with it. "That's one of the reasons I've been publishing the *Post* for [over fifteen] years," she said.

If there was chicanery in high places, she wanted her newspaper to go after the culprits with no restraints save those of accuracy. "I'd have to tell her the story," says Haddad, "because everything Joe and I did was controversial. She'd have to hear me tell exactly what it was we had. She was not somebody who's just a kind of figurehead. She was hands-on. She was accessible. And she was committed."

Haddad told Robert Caro he was sitting in the city room with Kahn one night, while upstairs in her office, Dolly fielded telephone calls from Moses's personal lawyer—her friend Sam Rosenman*—begging her to call her reporters off the story. Finally, Haddad told Caro, Wechsler came downstairs and said, "Just be sure you're thorough. We're not going to stop anything you write."

"Too often in life you look behind your back," Haddad says, "and the people who are supposed to be there have all disappeared. But at the *Post* when you got into trouble, Jimmy's there all night. Dolly would back it up. Just look at the impact she had on the Moses story. I mean, in a way, she supported all the reporters on the other papers. She became the reason they could do those stories, too.

"She was the right person, in the right place, at the right time," says Haddad. "There was something about her. I don't know much about the rich Jewish world, but I did see the rich gentile world—Jock Whitney† was another Dolly Schiff. His greatest joy was the *Herald Tribune*. These aristocrats, they were special kinds of people."

---

*Rosenman, who'd been legal adviser to Franklin Roosevelt and Harry Truman, had performed the wedding of Dorothy and Ted Thackrey. His law firm, Rosenman & Colin, was involved in many of Moses's deals.

†In 1959, Haddad married John Hay Whitney's stepdaughter, Kate.

By the time Haddad, Kahn, and reporters from other papers finished with Moses, his reputation was considerably tattered. But Moses was too obdurate to resign, and Mayor Wagner couldn't force him to without a major confrontation, which wasn't the mayor's style. More important, if Wagner were to do anything to disrupt the huge construction projects in the pipeline, he would alienate the unions, the banks, the insurance underwriters, and all the other entities that profited from the contracts that Moses's projects promised. The political fallout would have been extremely difficult for Wagner to weather.

Several years later, one more round of scandals about corrupt practices drove Robert Moses from public life. In the muckraking campaign against him, some of the good that he accomplished was overlooked. He built vast housing projects for the working and lower middle classes. Although some of them destabilized vibrant neighborhoods, they also provided the first non-slum housing that thousands of families had ever lived in. Jobs provided for union members on the buildings and roads constructed under his aegis made it possible for thousands of working-class families to improve their lives.

But Moses was a legitimate quarry, whom Kahn, Haddad, and their peers brought to his knees. The *Post* provided a good example of what a crusading newspaper could—and should—do. When Kahn and Haddad won the 1959 George Polk Award for Metropolitan Reporting for their ongoing investigation of the housing scandal, it marked the fourth time in five years that reporters from the paper received this honor.

At the same time as the ongoing Moses exposé, the *Post*—with finite resources—was uncovering examples of civil service inefficiency, malfeasance by union officials, and the indignities that large bureaucracies routinely inflict on their clients. Praising a series by Ted Poston on police corruption, Schiff wrote to Wechsler that it was "terrific. It is going to make us plenty of new enemies!"

Most of the people in the city room, from cynical night editors down to idealistic copyboys two months removed from the editorial staff of their college newspapers, shared a sense of mission. Joe Kahn once said, "Bleeding-heart journalism was what made the *Post*. . . . a poor vulnerable person being subjected to abuse, be it in housing, hospital care, welfare, or whatever, could go to the *Post*. There was no place else to go."

Bernie Bard says, "After the kind of punk papers I'd worked for, coming to the *Post* was a distinct honor. It was a reputable paper, a respectable paper.

If I say it was the favorite of the Bronx liberals, that meant that it was a paper with a heart. When I got the job, my mother was so proud of me that she put a notice in the sisterhood bulletin at the Temple Gates of Prayer. It was like I graduated from Harvard."

Art Pomerantz, a photographer who joined the *Post* in 1952, says, "When I got a job on the *Post,* my folks were very proud—it was like their son became a U.S. senator. It was their paper. It represented everything that they thought was right. And it was the only thing that did so in the city. The *Times* was too highbrow, even though the family was middle class. To them the *Post* was a crusading newspaper. It identified with the underdog. It was the era of Ted Poston, and Wechsler was a hero."

Alan Whitney, who worked on the copy desk during the late fifties, says, "During the fifties and early sixties, we had a five-day week in the union contract, so we always needed extra people for the weekend. We would take them from the other papers. Guys would come down from the *Journal-American,* or the *Herald Tribune,* or the *Times,* sometimes. We called them 'casuals.' And they always said it was the nicest place to work."

Morale in the city room was high. Haddad says, "The *Post* then was like you wish a newspaper would be now. You loved to go to work. I had never had much experience, so I thought that the *Post* was what a newspaper was. It was only later that I found out differently.

"You know, we were all in that terrible pressroom, and we had the old Royal typewriters, and everybody was sitting and yelling. You worked around the clock. At one point, one of the editors wasn't too happy with the stuff I was doing. We were always arguing and whatever. And one night late we brought in the big story, and he said, 'I think I'll stay and help lay it out.' This was a big important layout, and he stayed to do it himself. So you had dedicated guys who worked around the clock. Probably those days on the *Post* were the best days of my life."

THIRTEEN

Civil Rights and Wrongs

*N*ew York Post readers were predisposed by their liberal politics to support the cause of Negro rights. Many applauded the Brooklyn Dodgers for breaking the race barrier in major league baseball. Many worked beside Negro fellow members of the garment workers' unions. Many had read approvingly the dispatches that Ted Poston filed about egregious examples of Southern discriminatory policies.

Most Southern states had statutes on the books that forbade intermarriage, mandated separate access to public accommodations, and kept Negro citizens from voting. In the North, segregation was often as pervasive, but it was enforced by custom rather than law. After World War II—after American Negroes had fought and died to restore freedom from tyranny to millions of citizens of European, Asian, and Pacific Island nations—many were impatient with the constraints of being second-class citizens in their own country.

Harry Truman desegregated the armed forces by presidential fiat in 1948; similarly, Dwight Eisenhower desegregated public facilities in the District of Columbia in 1952 and later authorized the creation of the federal Civil Rights Commission and a Civil Rights Division within the U.S. Justice Department. Other changes came through legislation or legal decisions. In 1947, the U.S. Supreme Court ruled that Negro passengers on interstate routes could not be forced to sit in the back of the bus. The Civil Rights Acts of 1957 and 1960 made it a federal offense to deprive American citizens of their right to vote. Enforcement of the new laws was hampered by resistant police forces and reluctant judiciaries. The pace of change was slow, and Negro leaders, responding to the demands of their constituents, became more assertive.

Officials of the National Association for the Advancement of Colored People began searching for an ideal case with which to challenge state laws that mandated or permitted the segregation of public schools. In the spring of 1951, the NAACP found such a case in Kansas. The federal court that first heard *Brown v. Board of Education of Topeka* in June of that year was sympathetic toward the plaintiffs' arguments but felt bound by legal precedent to deny their claim. Similar lawsuits from South Carolina, Virginia, and Delaware were added to *Brown* when the NAACP appealed the District Court judgment to the United States Supreme Court.

On May 17, 1954, the Supreme Court declared that racial segregation in the nation's public schools was illegal. Though the unanimous decision did not address legal discrimination in other public facilities, nor did it impose a deadline for the desegregation of the schools, it was a remarkable victory for the Negro community and the cause of civil rights.

A year later, in August 1955, a racially motivated murder case rocked the nation. Emmett Till, a fourteen-year-old boy from Chicago visiting relatives in Mississippi, was alleged to have whistled at a white woman in a small grocery store. Hours after midnight on the morning of August 28, two white men kidnapped Emmett from his uncle's home. The boy's body was found in the Tallahatchie River three days later.

Even local whites were offended by the violence of the crime, and the two perpetrators were immediately arrested for kidnapping. At the trial in September, despite an incredibly brave identification of the two men by Emmett's uncle, the defendants were declared not guilty. The resultant furor raised white America's consciousness about the systematic denial of basic rights to Negro Americans.

The pace of Negro challenges to the status quo picked up. On December 1, 1955, Rosa Parks, a seamstress who served as secretary of the local branch of the NAACP, refused to move to the back of a crowded bus in Montgomery, Alabama. Her arrest led Negroes to begin a boycott of Montgomery buses that lasted almost a year. In the course of the boycott, a young minister from Atlanta, Dr. Martin Luther King Jr., was elected head of the Montgomery Improvement Association—the local Negro coordinating committee—and began to attract national attention.

In February 1956, white students at the University of Alabama rioted to protest the federal court-ordered admission of Autherine Lucy as a graduate student at the university's campus in Tuscaloosa. In response to the riots, the university first suspended and then permanently expelled Lucy, who declined to press her case further.

While these events were unfolding in Tuscaloosa, King and other Negro leaders were indicted by a Montgomery grand jury on charges stemming from their advocacy of the bus boycott, which was a criminal offense. King's four-day trial, which began March 19, was covered by all the major Northern newspapers as well as many European and Asian journals. The outcome was never in doubt. As soon as testimony was completed, the judge declared the minister guilty. The trial made King an international celebrity.

In November, King was out on bail but back in the courtroom as a defendant against a charge by the city attorney that the car pools organized by the Negro community during the boycott were illegal and that King's group should reimburse the city for tax revenues lost because of the lack of bus fares. Suddenly word came across the AP ticker that the U.S. Supreme Court had upheld a lower court decision that the laws imposing segregated seating on public buses in Alabama were unconstitutional.

The Court's decision was a major breakthrough that stimulated further demonstrations. Blacks in other Southern cities began to challenge segregation in their own ways. In response, White Citizens' Councils sprang up across the region. In early 1957, a series of mass arrests of demonstrating Negroes, bombings of Negro churches and homes, shootings, and beatings began. King's preaching of nonviolence in the face of these atrocities impressed even his most skeptical fellow citizens. *Time* made the twenty-eight-year-old minister the subject of a sympathetic cover story on February 18, 1957.

Ted Poston and Murray Kempton attended the trial of Emmett Till's murderers in 1955. Kempton, whose column still focused primarily on labor issues, found himself increasingly drawn south by race-based discrimination in South Carolina and Georgia. Poston, meanwhile, kept busy in Alabama. He covered Autherine Lucy's futile attempt to integrate the University of Alabama and commuted between New York and Montgomery during the months of the boycott. He was one of the first reporters to recognize the genius of Martin Luther King Jr.

The *Post* had been interested for some time in expanding its coverage of racial minorities in its own backyard. Schiff and Wechsler frequently discussed how to report on stories that went beyond crime and the occasional community event. Typically, in November 1954, Dolly wrote to her editor that the *Post,* a paper that prided itself on its social conscience, must do more to cover the needs of New York's Negro and Puerto Rican communities— "our city's underdogs." She suggested that Wechsler assign Fern Marja, who was committed to social and racial justice, to augment the work of Ted Poston in covering Harlem.

The catalyst for the kind of reportage Dolly was advocating came from an unlikely source. Grover C. Hall Jr., the editor of the Montgomery *Advertiser,* grew testy at the Northern reporters' coverage of events in his city and claimed that race relations in the North were as bad as they were in the South. In response, the *Post* assigned Poston, assisted by six other reporters and editors, to prepare an eleven-part series, "The Negro in New York," which ran in April 1956.

In his editorial announcing the series, Wechsler admitted that Northerners had no reason to be complacent about race relations, but, he claimed, "the principle of equality is accepted by every responsible public official, no matter how gravely the practice still falls short of the principle in certain realms." He credited the *Post* with being among the leaders in the struggle for equality and promised to continue to fight against whatever abuses were uncovered in the series.

Poston acknowledged that his newspaper had been exceptional in its attention to both good and bad news about race relations in New York. He quoted a colleague who had asked why he needed to do any new research, "What more could the *Post* say on the subject that it hasn't been saying daily over the years? We could probably do the series from our own clips."

The series was one of the more detailed sociopolitical surveys of the Northern civil rights situation that had been compiled to that date. Poston personalized his reportage. He compared 1956 to 1928, when he first came to New York, and to 1945—the end of the war and the beginning of a greater American consciousness of Negro rights.

Poston believed that significant improvement had been made in the enforcement of public accommodation laws, in relations between the Negro community and the New York City police force, in access to decent blue- and white-collar jobs, and in increased Negro political representation at the local level. The picture was murkier when it came to education. Despite the absence of laws requiring school segregation—and notwithstanding the fact that Negro students and other minorities were free to attend competitive high schools if they could pass the entrance tests—most Negro students went to schools that were effectively segregated and usually inferior.

Housing, Poston reported, was the worst headache and a cause of many problems. Local officials conceded that segregation according to neighborhood was getting worse and that Harlem and similar slums in Brooklyn and the Bronx were overcrowded. Even those Negroes with financial means had trouble finding housing in white or mixed neighborhoods, partly because of the prejudices of landlords and partly because of banks' unwillingness to grant them mortgages. Although the concentration of the Negro population into segregated neighborhoods was responsible for the relatively high number of Negroes holding public office, its other effects were punitive. Overcrowding, crime, de facto segregation of schools, and other problems were caused or exacerbated by this core problem.

By the time the series appeared, Poston had returned to the South to report on the tense events in Alabama. Although Grover Hall had originally said he might run the series in the *Advertiser,* he never did. He invited Ted to write a similar series about Montgomery for his paper. Dorothy Schiff and Jimmy Wechsler were worried about Poston's safety, but there were no incidents. Ted told Hall and the other editors of the *Advertiser* that he appreciated how well they treated him, but that they were blind to most of the Negroes in their midst. Back at the *Post,* Ted rewrote his Montgomery material for a series that was published during the summer. He also confided to his friends and colleagues his doubt that true integration would come to pass.

Dorothy herself was not racially intolerant; her prejudices were class-based. She met few Negroes at her social level, but she seems to have been quite color-blind for the era. A curious episode took place in 1953 involving Dorothy, her daughter Sally, and Adam Clayton Powell Jr. Powell was the son of one of the most influential Negro clergymen in America, whose pulpit he had taken over. He was a well-educated, charismatic figure, who was first elected to Congress from a Harlem district in 1945 on the Democratic ticket. In the House, he was an important advocate for Negro causes, but he frequently defied the Truman administration, voting against the Marshall Plan and other programs designed to help keep the Communists out of power in western Europe.

When Dolly was a member of the New York State Democratic Committee in 1952, she joined colleagues who castigated Powell for breaking party discipline. Powell responded to her opposition by letter, explaining that he had voted against appropriations for foreign aid because he believed the American government's first priority should be to end discrimination at home. And, he pointed out, "I do feel that my services to the Democratic Party, which you questioned, at least equal those of yourself, who supported Dewey for President over Truman in 1948!!" Having scored this point, he ended amicably, hoping that they could work out their differences so that "the liberal cause can be strengthened by elimination of a possible present schism."

In her May 11, 1952, "Publisher's Notebook" column, Dolly mentioned the letter, said she looked forward to meeting the congressman, and recounted the following coincidence: "When I came home from the State Committee meeting, my theater-loving 17-year-old daughter, Sarah-Ann, asked me what happened. When I told her, she said with horror: 'You *didn't* vote against Adam Clayton Powell? He sits next to Terry (her girlfriend) and me at all the ANTA* openings. Oh, boy, is he attractive and nice, too. His wife, you know, is the well-known pianist Hazel Scott. They always talk to us and are so friendly.'"

Powell met with Dolly from time to time. In August, he sent her three books, two of which he said were specifically for Sally. In October, he sent a file of press clippings from his congressional record for the current term and asked for her support in his reelection campaign. At the same time he was corresponding with Dolly, rumors spread that forty-four-year-old Powell was courting Sally.

In March 1953, Dolly received a phone call from Hazel Scott saying that she had just heard from a reporter at *Ebony* magazine that the International News Service (INS) had sent out a story that morning that the Powells were getting divorced and that Adam was going to marry Dorothy Schiff. Dorothy was aghast. She was not troubled by a false rumor concerning herself, nor did she assume it would affect her romance with Rudolf Sonneborn, but she

*The American National Theater and Academy was an important nonprofit producer of Broadway plays.

wanted to prevent the story from going any further and spreading gossip about Sally. She told Hazel Scott that she had seen Adam about six times in her life. She asked if the divorce part was true. Hazel replied that she knew that Adam was not always faithful, but they were not getting a divorce.

Dorothy tracked down Powell, who was in Alabama to give a speech. They agreed that the story, however ridiculous in its garbled form, was dangerous to the congressman and Sally. Dolly told Powell he should break off the relationship and he complied.

Days later, Powell wrote to Sally, "My dear Sally, I'm very proud of you—so many ways I cannot write them. You are good and great-hearted and so unaffectedly mature. You are going to keep on growing in many wonderful ways and I will always help not hurt. I am speaking in Alabama and will call you later. My best for you and that beautiful lady who tries to make people think that she is your mother. Adam."

A week later, *Jet* magazine—owned by the same Chicago publishing company as *Ebony*—reported a rumor that Adam Clayton Powell and Hazel Scott were divorcing, and that he had been romantically linked to Dorothy Schiff, an old friend. Dolly pasted the item in her scrapbook without comment.

Throughout the decade, the *Post* ran an occasional story about individual Negroes who suffered from racial insults. Many, though not all, were celebrities. In October 1958, for example, the paper reported that Harry Belafonte and his wife were having trouble trying to rent or buy an apartment in a fashionable neighborhood of Manhattan. The paper did not take on the institutions identified in the Poston series as villains in the de facto segregation of New York. The banks, the administration of the public schools, the residential real estate industry—any of these would have been fair game for exposure by the paper that claimed to challenge abuses of power and to speak for the disadvantaged in the larger community.

Throughout the mid-fifties, *Post* reporters repeatedly uncovered stories of aggrieved citizens who were mistreated by the city's bureaucracies. Sometimes these citizens were Negro, sometimes not, but seldom was the focus on systematic harassment of members of a minority. In general, the tone of the *Post*'s editorial coverage of the Negro community vacillated between hard-hitting and starstruck. Ted Poston's seven-part April 1957 series on Martin

Luther King Jr. was soon followed by a series on Harry Belafonte, who was clearly a favorite of the editors.

Schiff and Wechsler were excited about a twelve-part series on Harlem being prepared by reporter Stan Opotowsky, with the help of Alfred T. Hendricks, a freelance reporter who lived in the community. Opotowsky's articles, which ran in March 1958, featured a former madam turned political donor as well as a middle-class couple living in what was, for Harlem, an upscale housing development. The numbers racket, the Apollo Theater, Negro politicians and ministers, and the lack of up-to-date facilities and textbooks in the neighborhoods schools got equal time.

Dorothy was proud of the series but afraid that the tone was patronizing at best and derogatory at worst, painting too many of the people it profiled as immoral and superstitious. Her concerns presaged the response of leaders of the Negro community. Roy Wilkins of the NAACP complained to Wechsler that it stressed only bad things. Many letter writers pointed out that the series ignored the Harlem Renaissance and the coming generation of Negro artists; some questioned the choice of a madam as representative of the financial oligarchy; others felt that as an institution dedicated to supporting Negro rights, the paper should have stressed only the positive side of the Negro community.

On March 31, Dorothy held a meeting in her office with community leaders who wanted to discuss the series and to propose different coverage in the future. A. Philip Randolph helped put together the group, which included school principals, several ministers, and branch bank managers. Dorothy was impressed with their sincerity, though she felt the paper had nothing to apologize for. She reminded them that the series had stressed how poorly equipped the schools were and how difficult it was to obtain decent housing. After the meeting, she told Wechsler that some of her distinguished guests should be featured in the Closeup section of the weekend magazine in the coming months.

Despite the fracas, the *Post* went ahead with a similar series on Bedford-Stuyvesant in May 1958, and in August, it opened its pages to the so-called Battle of Harlem. Tammany Hall refused to endorse incumbent Congressman Powell on the grounds that he had been insubordinate and instead nominated a party hack named Earl Brown to run against him in a primary. For the benefit of its considerable Negro readership, the *Post* asked both candidates to write a series of letters on the issues at stake, which it ran during the two weeks leading to the election. The paper endorsed neither man, calling the choice between a demagogue and a product of the machine a poor choice that was not in the interest of the voters affected. Despite—or maybe because of—increasing disapproval of Powell's peccadilloes by the white community, he remained a hero to his own constituents. He easily won reelection.

Charles Stone, who was Powell's press secretary in the 1960s, believes that Dorothy never forgave Powell for his involvement with Sally and says that the *Post* never supported him either in his reelection campaigns or in his subsequent struggles with his colleagues in Congress over charges of financial chicanery and misuse of his office. But neither did any other mainstream newspaper, so it's hard to prove that personal intrigue played a role in the *Post*'s positions.

Schiff, Wechsler, and company were more comfortable with stories that appealed to readers of both races without attracting controversy. In July 1958, Ted Poston profiled Kwame Nkrumah, the first president of Ghana, the first independent postcolonial African nation. A few months later, he wrote a history of the NAACP on the occasion of its fiftieth anniversary. In 1959, Paul Sann arranged for the *Post* to hire Jackie Robinson as a columnist. Robinson, who'd retired from baseball in 1957, was a Republican, but he was expected to write primarily about sports, and his status as an authentic New York hero was not affected by partisan politics.

In the course of Bill Haddad's exploration of corruption in the construction industry, he received an odd phone call in November 1959. The anonymous caller asked the newly married Haddad if he would like a wedding present. Before Haddad had a chance to reply, the caller repeated an unsubstantiated rumor that had been floating around town asserting that a well-known real estate developer named Sidney Ungar had paid $11,500 for the remodeling of the apartment of Manhattan Borough President Hulan Jack, a Negro career politician. The proffered wedding present was the name of the contractor who'd done the work.

The contractor, it turned out, was willing to talk because, he said, Ungar had failed to pay for some extras requested by Mrs. Jack. He had the work orders and bills from his suppliers to back up the assertions. After Haddad met with the contractor and his wife, he consulted with Wechsler. Reporter and editor realized they were sitting on a very hot story. Ungar had a proposal to build a $28 million Title I housing project pending before the Board of Estimate, and Jack had ex officio final approval over all such projects proposed in his borough. The *Post* deferred publication in order to alert the office of the district attorney.

Within days, the DA questioned Jack, Ungar, and the contractor, and subpoenaed relevant papers. Ungar made no statements to the press. Jack demanded that Haddad "get the hell out of here" at a press conference in his office. He denied any wrongdoing and remained defiant in the next weeks as the DA charged him with conspiracy to obstruct justice and violations of the City Charter. (Ungar was not charged in the matter.) The *Post* went public with its fantastic scoop and prided itself editorially for having played an important part in exposing corruption.

What Wechsler, Haddad, and Schiff had not foreseen was the reaction of the Negro community. The word around Harlem was that the white establishment was out to get a successful Negro politician and that the *Post* had betrayed Negro trust by participating in a racist plot. Preachers in mainstream Harlem churches and editorial writers in the *Amsterdam News* argued that the borough president was being framed, or—if they conceded that the evidence cited by the *Post* and the DA looked bad—that the charges were not very serious to begin with. In his column on the *Post* sports page, Jackie Robinson said he hoped Hulan Jack, an old friend, could clear himself, but that if Jack were guilty, this was not a racially inspired event. Robinson's was a minority minority view.

Hulan Jack could not give a satisfactory account of his role in the affair. In January 1960, he reluctantly recused himself from the borough presidency pending trial. He was convicted in November and, after an unsuccessful appeal, was given a one-year suspended sentence, which automatically forced him out of office, although he retained his role as Democratic district leader.

The *Post* tried to repair its reputation as the New York paper most supportive of and responsive to the Negro community. Almost immediately after the scandal cooled, the paper ran an adulatory series about A. Philip Randolph, the most revered man in Harlem. The ill will created by the Jack affair seemed more an anomaly than a portent of things to come.

FOURTEEN

Bringing Down the Titans

By the mid-1950s, the top brass at the *Post* and like-minded New York liberals had Carmine De Sapio, Robert Moses, and other perceived menaces to the common good on the ropes. Now it was time to see if they could finish them off.

De Sapio was responsive to liberal concerns. Having been stung by the successful challenges made by the reform Democrats to his organization, the Tammany boss was trying to work with the insurgents, hoping perhaps to vitiate their attacks. His attempts were not successful. In 1957, a group of reform-minded Democratic insurgents founded the Village Independent Democrats (VID) to challenge De Sapio in his own district.

Although De Sapio put down the VID challenge, and the regulars held on to Manhattan as a whole in the 1959 elections, the reformers smelled blood. The year 1961 was the make-or-break year. Reformers and regulars challenged each other in every district in Manhattan. Mayor Robert Wagner, De Sapio's creation, had previously been unwilling to repudiate his mentor. But Wagner was a politician; he could read the omens. He named his own ticket for the upcoming citywide elections without consulting the Democratic bosses. At the start of the campaign the mayor called James Wechsler to sound out whether the *Post* would support him if he organized his campaign around the reform theme. Though not enthusiastic about Wagner, Dorothy Schiff and her editor had no alternative but to support the mayor and his slate.

Wagner led a reform sweep. In Manhattan, insurgent clubs won in fourteen of sixteen districts. De Sapio was defeated in his home district by a three-to-two margin. Having failed also in his bid to stay on as a member of the county committee, he suddenly held no political jobs. Publicly humiliated but ever courtly, De Sapio congratulated the winners and said privately that he'd be back in two years because the reformers were not willing to work hard on day-to-day party issues. However, State Assemblyman Edward Koch, the new head of the VID, was made of tough stuff. He held off De Sapio's comeback bids each of the following three years. After which, even as tenacious a competitor as De Sapio had to admit he was licked.

For better or worse, the reform movement was now the Democratic establishment in Manhattan, and the *New York Post* had played an important supporting role in the transformation.

In October 1958, Dorothy Schiff and Jimmy Wechsler decided that the paper should take on another stock enemy of liberals and liberalism. Reaching beyond New York to the national political scene, they authorized a series about J. Edgar Hoover, the powerful and secretive director of the FBI. Reporters David Gelman and William Dufty were assigned to the story, and other reporters and editors joined them as needed.

The *Post* had long railed against Hoover's unfettered power. Dolly and Jimmy felt that the director operated more like the head of the secret police in a totalitarian state than as a civil servant in a democracy. They believed he ignored civil liberties and favored his conservative political positions over the impartial search for justice. Hoover's admirers feared that the series would be highly biased, if not libelous.

"Almost immediately," Dolly later wrote, "the going got rough. Our men were refused interviews by Director Hoover. His assistants and other members of the FBI were ordered to stay away from representatives of the Post. We interviewed key Congressmen. Later the same men, apparently intimidated, notified us that all comments must be considered off-the-record."

Hoover's friends in Washington and elsewhere challenged the *Post*'s intent before a word had appeared in print. Preston Moore, the national commander of the American Legion, charged in October 1958 that a "smear campaign" was being launched against Hoover and the FBI, and implied that anyone who would do such a thing must have Communist connections. Similar attacks followed from other conservative organizations.

Wechsler's standard letter of response—"We are preparing a factual study of J. Edgar Hoover. . . . We trust Mr. Hoover does not share the view that he, unlike all other government officials, should be immune to objective reporting"—did not deter the director's supporters.

Early in 1959, the official publication of the National Association of Manufacturers, the *NAM News,* weighed in with a long editorial:

> The business world in America has long been proud of the FBI and its Director, J. Edgar Hoover. This agency is one of the most efficient, well-run, and businesslike agencies in the Government. Time after time Mr. Hoover has been a forerunner in adapting new business techniques to the operations of the FBI. . . .
>
> Unfortunately, this efficient business-type organization is today the object of a vicious smear campaign. The purpose is to destroy the effectiveness of the FBI as a bulwark of our internal security. In the forefront, as could be expected, is the Communist Party. . . .
>
> A New York newspaper long noted for its propensity to slant and distort information concerning law enforcement against subversive organizations and individuals also is joining in the attack on Mr. Hoover and the FBI. Under the guise of "objective reporting," this newspaper has announced it will publish a series of articles concerning the FBI and its director. It begins to look as if a concerted campaign is afoot among those who always seem to deplore efforts to deal effectively with subversion and subversives to get J. Edgar Hoover's scalp and curb the activities of the agency he heads.
>
> This has been tried a number of times before with conspicuous lack of success. The effort will fail again if the American people know the truth and are not misled by the sly propaganda of the anti-anti-communists.

Dolly promptly sent off a letter to Stanley C. Hope, a businessman from New Haven, Connecticut, and president of the association. On the advice of her attorney, she claimed that the editorial libeled the *Post*'s reporters and that unless the charges were retracted, she might seek legal remedies. Although no apology was printed, her lawyer prevailed upon her not to sue.

Pressure continued. In April 1959, Dolly received a call from Joe Eckhouse, the head of Gimbels, a major advertiser in the *Post*. Eckhouse had been approached in a New York restaurant by Hoover and Clyde Tolson, his companion and assistant. Hoover told Eckhouse, whom he knew to be a friend of Dolly's, that he was sure the series would be a smear that would damage the FBI in the eyes of the American public. He added that Jimmy Wechsler had carried a grudge against him ever since the FBI had had Jimmy's wife, Nancy, fired from a government job because she was a Communist. This was an old canard that had been effectively refuted in the public record. After Dolly explained this to Eckhouse, Hoover appeared to drop the subject.

Eckhouse volunteered to set up a meeting between Hoover and Schiff. The director ducked, saying that there was a government regulation prohibiting such a meeting, which was absurd, especially since he was concurrently being interviewed for a laudatory profile that was about to appear in the Hearst papers. Dolly and Jimmy assumed that Hoover's concern was not so much for the reputation of the FBI but that the series might provoke speculation about his private life, a subject about which he was sensitive.

Robert Spivack, the White House correspondent of the *Post,* was warned by a confidential source that the FBI was investigating Dorothy and her daughter Sarah-Ann. A few weeks later, Spivack said that he believed he too was being watched and perhaps even wire-tapped. Dolly eventually wrote a two-part introduction to the series, "My Secret Life with J. Edgar Hoover," in which she said that none of the director's attempts to intimidate her succeeded, but he kept trying.

In May she sent Wechsler a memo reporting a phone call she had just received from Leonard Lyons, who said he had run into Si Rifkind* a few nights before. Rifkind told Lyons he'd heard that the *Post* was "planning to

---

*An old friend of Dolly's, Rifkind was a senior partner at the law firm Paul, Weiss, Goldberg, Rifkind, Wharton and Garrison. The firm had begun representing the *Post* and its owner in 1954. Rifkind, who had played a leading role in defusing Walter Winchell's lawsuits against Dolly and the paper, was usually her contact.

write a series about the sex life of J. Edgar Hoover" and that enormous pressure was being brought on the lawyer from unspecified Jewish organizations to get the *Post* to kill the FBI stories. Rifkind told the organizations that he would never dream of asking Dolly to suppress a journalistic effort, but presumably he wanted her to know that Hoover's expected retaliation might be unpleasant for individuals or groups within the Jewish community.

Finally, in October 1959, the twelve-part series ran. Half the articles were about the bureau; the other six focused on the director. The articles charged that Hoover had too much power, because of the lack of legal constraints on his organization and because he was personally unassailable. He was accused of being indiscreet, leaking gossip and confidential information to his journalist friends and trusted allies in the government, who defended and protected him against legitimate oversight. The paper criticized his ultra-conservative political opinions and claimed that his beliefs influenced whom he went after and whom he ignored. And finally, one article hinted that his private life was not what he wanted the world to think it was.

An ambitious promotional effort—ads on city buses, on the radio, and in competing newspapers*—alerted New Yorkers that the *Post* was doing something important. The usual press run was expanded, and circulation manager Roy Newborn was happy to report to publisher Schiff that the paper was selling out.

Despite the length of time and the number of reporters and editors devoted to the project, its content was neither new nor sensational. Most of it was the standard criticism of Hoover and the bureau from his opponents on the left. *Time* magazine believed that Dorothy's accusations that she and her daughter were under surveillance were offered "without a shred of evidence"—which was unfair—and concluded that "the series had produced nothing more damaging than the fact that the director of the FBI, as a boy, sang soprano in the church choir"—which, though arch, had some merit.

Hoover was offended by the series. He called it "scurrilous" and "unjustified," but he was too powerful to be hurt by it. He continued to have the

---

*Ads ran in the *Daily News,* the *Tribune,* and the *World-Telegram.* The *Times* accepted the advertising, then didn't run it the first day it was supposed to appear. The paper was presumably worried about political pressure, although it offered an excuse about not having enough space. Called on this, the *Times* agreed to run the subsequent ads at a reduced rate.

public support of every president under whom he served* because his standing with the public and many members of Congress was so high. He was also said to have compromising files available to blackmail politicians who might have opposed him. The *Post* could congratulate itself on fighting the good fight against a legitimate target, but it could hardly claim to have made headway in a campaign to bring him down.

Another target of reform-minded liberals continued to be Robert Moses. Moses was no longer untouchable. In December 1962, he was outmaneuvered during a quarrel with Nelson Rockefeller over the State Park Commission and forced to resign all of his New York State appointments. But, while criticism of his projects and his personality intensified, he held on to many other posts until his never-assuaged ambition gave his enemies another chance to dislodge him. Moses had long nurtured a dream to create a great park—larger than Central Park—in Flushing Meadows, Queens. His original plan had been to pay for the park with the proceeds from the 1939 World's Fair, which he had arranged to have built on the site, but the fair was a financial flop. So Moses put his scheme on hold until the late fifties, when he persuaded federal and local officials of the desirability of another fair to open in 1964.

In addition to the possibility that such an undertaking would be good for the local construction business and for American industrial prestige in general, the fair offered Mayor Wagner an opportunity to get Moses off his hands. In exchange for an agreement whereby Moses and some of his key aides would resign their appointed city jobs, the mayor committed the city to making substantial loans to the Fair Corporation, of which Moses would be president.

Moses hated to relinquish any power, but the business generated by the fair gave him new financial favors to dole out. Samuel Rosenman's law firm was chosen to represent the fair; Carmine De Sapio was allotted a modest portion of the insurance brokerage.

To make his project successful, Moses needed to attract major exhibitors and build anticipatory excitement among potential visitors. Local businesses

*Hoover was appointed director of the FBI in 1924 by Calvin Coolidge. He continued to serve for forty-eight years, under Herbert Hoover, FDR, Truman, Eisenhower, Kennedy, Johnson, and Nixon.

joined the promotional effort—the fair was the theme of Macy's Thanksgiving Parade in November 1963. New York newspaper publishers, who took seriously their role as hometown boosters, were delighted to lend a hand. The *Times* established a special bureau to cover fair-related news. Other papers printed the press handouts created by Moses's public relations office as if they were hard-breaking news. No paper, the *Post* included, wanted to be accused of undermining a project that promised to enhance New York's reputation, bring millions of visitors from around the world to the city, and enrich local merchants, hotels, theaters, and restaurants.

Reporters, however, had learned to be suspicious of Moses's pronouncements and his motives. Joe Kahn began to snoop around. He recognized that Moses had brought together all his old cronies to run the fair, and Kahn was wise to their tricks.

Kahn told Robert Caro, "I was never assigned to the World's Fair. Nobody in his right mind would assign me to a thing like this—it took too much time. So I was doing it all on my own, at the same time that I was doing my regular assignments."

Kahn checked out foreign governments, state governments, and other announced exhibitors. "I couldn't call Panama, for Christ's sake—the *Post* would have gone out of its mind. So what I did was I called the embassies here. And I wrote to every Governor whose state was supposed to be in." His digging led to the revelation that, although fair officials claimed that every Western European government was sponsoring an official pavilion, none but Franco's Spain was in fact doing so. Nearly half of the American states that Moses said were participating were not, and many other announcements of prospective exhibitors proved to be fictitious. Kahn's revelations appeared in a series titled "Who-Do-You-Have-to-Know Or: How to Do Business with the City," on which he collaborated with Stan Opotowsky. The series revealed lucrative insider deals, like the restaurant franchise Moses awarded to two cronies without competitive bidding.

Kahn then began working with Sidney Zion, a young lawyer turned investigative reporter, to probe further. In early August, Kahn and Zion drafted a five-part series. Forwarding it to Dorothy Schiff for her approval, editor Al Davis described it as "highly unfavorable to the Fair and to Moses." Davis wasn't sure if the material was libelous or if it was the tack the *Post* wanted to take.

Marvin Berger found only a few statements he considered potentially libelous, and they could have been excised. The bigger problem, as Dorothy wrote back to Davis two weeks later, was that some of the material had already been published and much of the rest took a tone that she characterized as antagonistic rather than constructive. She would be very interested, she said, if Kahn and Zion could get more information on the troubling question raised in the articles of whether or not the city had asked for proper guarantees from the Fair Corporation for the repayment of funds. Dorothy volunteered to intercede on her reporters' behalf if they were being stonewalled in their efforts to find this out.

She had less clout than she thought. Sam Rosenman's office refused to answer her calls, and the spokesman for the fair told her, "Your reporters can still attend press conferences. Our information has been regularly distorted by the *Post*. Surely it is no news to you that your editorial policy is anti-Fair."

While the editors were figuring out what to do, the *Post*'s advertising director, Daniel Lionel, had unpleasant news. He reported to Schiff that the fair had placed several big ads announcing a Christmas Gift Package in every New York newspaper except the *Post*. The J. Walter Thompson advertising agency, which was handling the campaign, had originally scheduled the ads for the *Post* as well, but Moses himself canceled them, according to Lionel's sources. "We were sliced off the schedule because of our anti-Moses and anti–World's Fair policies. This has been admitted by every top official of the fair to whom I have spoken in the last hour," Lionel said.

The series by Kahn and Zion never ran. Dorothy and the editors decided it did not contain enough substantiated new material; they were concerned that it made the *Post* seem unnecessarily hostile to the fair, and they might have been sensitive to the question of lost advertising revenues.

At the same time, *Post* editorials kept up the heat by challenging Moses and city officials to release more information about the bidding processes, which they never did. The reporters were still free to dig up what they could. In late November, Joe Kahn thought he had a great scoop about a rigged bid for the construction of the New York State Pavilion. Once again, though, he ended up having to tell Sann that he couldn't get his hands on corroborating material, and that story also never appeared.

Despite failing to land advertising created by the Fair Corporation, the *Post*, like every other New York newspaper, did profit from fair-related ads placed by enterprises that hoped to attract customers among the millions who were expected to attend the exhibitions. The paper ran a thirty-page supplement in November 1963 containing ads from restaurants and hotels, an eighteen-page section in January 1964 featuring stores selling fair-related merchandise, and a fifty-six-page guide to the fairgrounds and various exhibitors, which appeared the week the fair opened in April 1964.

It was soon clear that the fair was going to be a box office flop and a financial fiasco. Moses needed to attract nearly a quarter of a million visitors daily in order to pay back the loans he had received from New York state and city governments, let alone show the profit he counted on to create his grand park after the fair closed. Attendance on opening day was just under fifty thousand. During the first three months of the fair, attendance never once reached the break-even point. Moses had projected earnings of $90 million for the first season, but by November 1964, actual revenues were just a little over one-third of that. Audits revealed that, far from turning a profit, the first season had produced a deficit of nearly $18 million.

When the fair's second, 1965, season opened, the *Post* maintained its critical stance, reporting on pavilions that remained shuttered and criticizing Moses for allowing entertainment that was too close in spirit to the Times Square "girlie" shows. City Hall reporter Oliver Pilat repeatedly asked Mayor Wagner, who always fudged his answer, about the city's passivity in the face of Moses's inability to repay his obligations to the city. Joe Kahn stayed on the trail of bidding irregularities, though he never was able to document them. When a reporter submitted a story about low night attendance at the fair, Dorothy vetoed it, reminding Sann that it was not the paper's role to make things worse.

Sidney Zion left the paper in late 1964 to join *The New York Times*. In January 1965, he made some allegations that were reported in *The Village Voice* and that Zion continues to repeat, with variations, from time to time. Zion claims that the series he and Joe Kahn prepared was killed by Dorothy Schiff and her editors because the *Post* did not want to lose the chance of selling—presumably to the Fair Corporation—an advertising supplement worth $100,000.

When the *Voice* article appeared, Dorothy was furious. It wasn't true that the series had been killed on the eve of publication because of advertising, she maintained, because the Fair Corporation never advertised in the *Post*. But she didn't remember exactly what had happened. She sent out a stream of memos to her staff: Had she even seen the series? Had she ever approved it? Who had initiated it? Should she sue the *Voice* for libel? The editors rushed around to cover themselves from blame. Eventually Jean Gillette found the memos among Sann and Davis and Schiff discussing the flaws in the series and their unwillingness to publish its unsubstantiated claims. Dorothy was dissuaded from suing the *Voice,* and the fuss subsided.

It is not clear if worry about commercial advertisers for the *Post*'s own advertising supplements may have played some small role in the editorial decision. But the paper's persistence in reporting financial irregularities when they could be documented and in demanding a public accounting of the fair finances makes it hard to believe that Dorothy buckled under pressure and backed off.

The fair's second season showed a small profit but not enough to make a dent in the overall deficit. Eventually the Fair Corporation agreed to settle its obligation to the banks for about thirty-three cents on the dollar. New York City's $24 million investment was written off. Moses did hold on to some funds that he used to clean up the fairgrounds and make a park in Flushing Meadows, though it was nothing like the project he'd dreamed of.

In 1968, Moses's fifty-four-year career in public service ended when Nelson Rockefeller forced him to give up chairmanship of the Triborough Authority. Although the *Post* could claim no role in his ultimate downfall, there is no question that the pioneering attacks on Moses by Kahn, Haddad, and their colleagues a decade earlier had been the first to reveal that he was vulnerable.

The *New York Post* in its heyday was a model of what a crusading liberal newspaper could be. Its editorials championed American democracy in the Cold War era while warning that any lessening of civil liberties by would-be demagogues in the defense of that democracy was unacceptable. The paper fought against abuses of power by government or corporations that made it harder for *Post* readers, and by extension all New Yorkers, to exercise their full rights as consumers, wage earners, and citizens.

The *Post* was not perfect. It was not as thorough as it might have been in pursuing corruption in every corner. Although Murray Kempton occasionally chastised local labor leaders for some oversight or other, David Dubinsky, for example, was never subjected to the same editorial scrutiny that Robert Moses was. The *Post* never went after the network of law firms, real estate interests, insurance agencies, and labor unions that profited from

Moses's ventures and that were often led by friends and acquaintances of the publisher.

Nonetheless, no other New York newspapers, most of them with much greater resources, took the crusading role of the press as seriously as did Dorothy Schiff's paper. Years later, Bob Friedman, a longtime night editor, speculated about why the publisher was so willing to do so. "I think one of the remarkable things about Dolly is that she was often petrified with fear about taking unpopular stands in the paper or printing tough stuff about powerful people, yet often did so. . . . I never could figure out whether her readiness to take on Hoover, or Moses . . . or other like matters was courage and conviction, or an ingrained feeling that no one was going to mess around with Jacob Schiff's grand-daughter." It was surely a combination of both, and it brought results.

FIFTEEN

Ethnic Journalism

Well into the 1950s, New York politics was ethnic politics, and it went without saying that ethnic politics was largely Democratic. Even as reform-minded Jews and WASPs drove Tammany Hall out of power in Manhattan, it was business as usual for the Irish and Italian bosses in the Bronx and Brooklyn. It would take another decade for their followers to question their allegiance to the Democratic party and its generally liberal agenda. In the meantime, struggles for power took place within the party and the city as a whole.

On September 7, 1957, fifty thousand people streamed into Yankee Stadium to celebrate the twenty-fifth anniversary of Francis Cardinal Spellman's consecration as a bishop. As head of the Archdiocese of New York since 1939, Spellman had presided over a period of unprecedented prosperity in his see. The Catholic church was the largest and wealthiest religious organization in the city, and Spellman initiated a vigorous construction program of churches, schools, hospitals, and other institutions. After New York City itself, the archdiocese managed the biggest building budget in the metropolitan area.

Although Catholics often thought of themselves as a beleaguered minority, they were a dominant power in the city. There had been an unbroken line of Catholic mayors for more than fifty years, except for Fiorello La Guardia, a Protestant who many mistakenly believed was Catholic because of his name. The Democratic political bosses of Brooklyn, the Bronx, and Manhattan were Catholic. Graduates of Catholic colleges Fordham and St. John's— often the first members of their families to go to college—were moving into leading positions in the professions and on Wall Street.

Spellman, an unprepossessing man physically, exerted a tremendous amount of influence in the city. The most important leader in the American church, he was also the closest American friend and ally of Pope Pius XII.

A few weeks after the celebration in Yankee Stadium, the *Post* ran an eight-part profile of the cardinal, assessing his role in the city. The articles by Irwin Ross outlined Spellman's brilliant job as steward of the church's fortunes, his modest, genial personal style, and his history of openness toward representatives of various racial and religious groups. But a critical tone recurred throughout the series. One article recounted an episode in which Spellman accused Eleanor Roosevelt of anti-Catholic prejudice in a dispute over federal aid to parochial schools in 1949. Having mistakenly taken on an American icon, Spellman had been forced to back down. In another piece, Ross mocked the cardinal's denunciation of Hollywood films for their immorality. Spellman had asked Catholics to stay away from *The Moon Is Blue,* an innocuous comedy in which the dialogue included the words "virgin," "seduce," and "pregnant," and he had recently announced that he was anguished equally by the Communist suppression of the Hungarian rebels and by *Baby Doll,* a somewhat steamy movie written by Tennessee Williams and starring Carroll Baker as an infantile young bride.

The series was not all negative. Ross praised Spellman for his usual practice of avoiding endorsements in local political races, even though the cardinal was thought to collaborate behind the scenes with Democratic bosses in the choice of many candidates and political appointees. However, Ross deplored Spellman's public support of Senator Joseph McCarthy and his activities. Because the church taught that atheistic communism posed a great threat to America and that it must be struck down by whatever methods, Spellman viewed McCarthy's investigations and hearings as properly motivated and properly carried out.

At that time, New York newspapers seldom wrote about the cardinal with anything other than adulation. Irwin Ross remembers that he was careful to be as balanced as possible in his tone and judgments. And he had the full support of his boss.

"Dolly had more courage than most publishers in New York," Ross says. "When she commissioned the series about Cardinal Spellman, about the political figure he was, we treated him neither with reverence nor antagonism. He wouldn't see me, and Mrs. Schiff intervened with a friend of hers who was a big Catholic layman. I was finally given twenty minutes in the cardinal's presence."

Ross recalls that some of the *Post*'s Catholic readers were irate, and some stopped buying the paper for a time. "I was very proud of that series," he says. "And only Dolly would have permitted it. Let me tell you, the *Times* would not have done that."

The Ross profile in 1957 was followed in a few months by a series of articles by Joe Kahn and others that criticized the church's successful efforts to block the distribution of birth control information and devices in municipal hospitals, where the dissemination of such materials was perfectly legal. Kahn's articles put the administration of Mayor Robert Wagner on the spot for refusing to enforce the law, in deference to Spellman's influence.

Lenore Kahn, Joe's widow, remembers that Dolly was resolute in supporting the story. "Joe prepared the story, but the men on the city desk didn't want to take on Cardinal Spellman. Forget the *Times* and *Tribune,* the *Journal,* all those papers—they wouldn't go near it. But Dolly said to him, 'You go ahead. You do this.' She was the one who had the courage and said to the city desk, 'You back him up.' And they carried out this birth control campaign, and then Planned Parenthood came out of the shadows. But the other papers didn't pick it up till later."

The *Post*'s spirited criticism of the city's medical policies appeared soon after it had run an admiring profile of Dr. Morris A. Jacobs, the city's newly appointed hospitals commissioner. Jacobs was the man in charge of administering those policies. The *Post* was always eager to highlight successful Jews in any aspect of public life, and although Jacobs would subsequently be chastised by the paper for his conduct in office, his appointment was an occasion to celebrate.

Jacobs was one of many New York Jews who'd made it into the city's middle and ruling classes. The transition from the prewar Jewish community— foreign born, working-class, and unionized—was startling. By 1955, about half of all New Yorkers with college educations were Jewish, and two-thirds of all the employed Jewish men in the city held occupations that were considered middle-class or professional. About half the teachers in the city school system were Jewish, as were the majority of principals and other supervisors. More than half the members of the city's bar were Jewish, though Jews were still underrepresented at the most prestigious law firms; similarly, more than 50 percent of the doctors were Jewish, but they were still fighting for privileges at the leading hospitals.

While continuing their dominance in the garment trades, Jews flocked to new industries where their way was not blocked by tradition or unofficial quotas. Jews moved into prominence as real estate builders, developers, and owners. Advertising, public relations, radio and television broadcasting, the arts, and arts management attracted a number of Jews as well. The old internal division between German and Eastern European Jews was beginning to erode, as Jews from all backgrounds joined organizations, moved into apartment buildings, and took seats on the boards of cultural institutions that would have barred them before the war and were now more interested in the depth of their financial resources than their family backgrounds.

Jews had always been the core audience of the *Post*—by some estimates nearly 70 percent of the paper's regular readers were Jewish—and their increased affluence and prominence in the larger community were not so subtly chronicled in the paper. The personal profiles, the series based on celebrity biographies, and the special section on the Bronx all frequently featured Jews.

The *Post* had given first-page coverage to events concerning Israel since before the turbulent founding of the state in 1947. The paper paid constant attention to the travails of the young country. Articles about Israel were sometimes the only foreign news reported in the paper for days on end. In the fall of 1956, General Gamal Abdel Nasser's seizure of the Suez Canal and the subsequent invasion of Egypt by France, Britain, and Israel were in the headlines daily. Speeches by Abba Eban, the eloquent Israeli ambassador to the United Nations, were often reprinted in full. Freelance journalists on their way to the Middle East found a ready market at the *Post* for a series of dispatches "from our special correspondent." Every visit to New York by Israeli leaders stimulated news accounts and personal profiles in the paper.

The topics of concern to the readers who solicited advice from Dr. Rose Franzblau were of general interest: how to deal with intrusive in-laws, what to do if a young mother wants to reenter the workforce, how to make sure children study hard, what a wife can do to keep her straying husband at home. A close reading of the letters, however, revealed that the writers were almost surely Jewish. Although the word "kosher" is never mentioned, a distraught mother is incensed that her son's household does not observe food rituals that are "meaningful to her." A sullen wife laments her lack of standing in the family constellation because—unlike his brother, the doctor—her husband, though he makes a good living, is a salesman for a dress manufacturer. One of the most popular features of the Yiddish-language daily, the *Forward* was "Bintel Briefs," a column of advice to newcomers about how to adapt to American life. Rose Franzblau's column was Bintel Briefs updated for the children of those immigrants.

Alan Whitney, who came to the *Post* as a copyreader in the late 1950s, was struck by the parochialism of the paper. "There was a nice little Irish lady named Agnes Murphy, who handled all the so-called women's stuff," Whitney says. "Every once in a while Agnes would run a piece about the prices of food in the stores right at that moment, what's cheap and so forth. The rule was that she could mention pork, but it could never be the first meat that was mentioned."

Agnes Murphy initiated a feature called "At Home With . . ." in which she interviewed celebrities. She asked about their family lives, their hobbies, and their favorite dishes. So many of her interviewees were Jewish that a kosher cookbook could have been compiled from the accompanying recipes for brisket, matzo ball soup, and noodle pudding.

Murphy and Whitney were certainly not the only non-Jews at the *Post*— the majority of pressmen, lithographers, and composing room workers were Italian, for example. But the atmosphere in the city room was heavily colored by the high percentage of Jews who worked there. Joe Rab says, "We had a mixture, of course. Ted Poston, Earl Wilson, some of the city editors. But the Jews were in charge. Let's put it that way."

The person most in charge—Dorothy Schiff—had as compelling an interest in the subject of Jewish identity as any reader or staff member. "But," Rab says, "we had to take a different tone with her. Not Yiddish, certainly not."

"There is a huge gap between Jewish identity and 'Jewish identity,' " says Dolly's son-in-law Wynn Kramarsky. "Dolly was fascinated by all Jewish culture, as long as it didn't come too close. She was one hundred percent Jewish. And two of the men she married were Jewish. But there was nothing, not a single word of Jewish, or Yiddish, that she knew. And even after her years at the *Post,* that part of Jewishness, *haimish* Jewishness, never reached her."

Many nonreligious American Jews questioned how they could continue to be "one hundred percent Jewish" and yet lead secular lives. They debated the strength of the ties between themselves and Orthodox Jews, and the most thoughtful among them asked how much of the distinction that they insisted upon between the two groups was a reflexive response to anti-Semitism in the non-Jewish community that surrounded them.

A member of one of New York's old German-Jewish families says that Dolly Schiff's anxiety about identity was common in her crowd. "You worried if Jewish issues were too prominent. You didn't want to be associated with anything that made Jews look bad, or even just foreign. You were taught never to let your head get above the parapet. Don't forget we grew up in a world where the anti-Semitism was real and painful. We still couldn't live in most of the big Park Avenue or Fifth Avenue buildings—except for the 'Jewish' ones."

Although the barriers were falling and would virtually disappear in the years to come, there were clubs to which Jews were still denied entrance or allowed in only on sufferance, there were elite schools and colleges that operated on rigid quotas, and there was always the subliminal tension of wondering how the other dinner guests described you after you left the room.

Dolly struggled with the admittedly complex interplay between Jewish culture and Jewish religion that has bedeviled Jews since the emancipation of European Jewry in the nineteenth century and became only more complex after the Holocaust. Typically, in April 1954, she reprimanded her editors for illustrating the beginning of Passover with photographs of "the most orthodox foreign-looking gents with long beards." She reminded them that she and most other American Jews were not accurately represented by such stereotypical images. Like many New York Jews, she believed the holiday was primarily an occasional for a family dinner and a brief discussion of Jewish history. The image of an Orthodox Jew, "dressed in strange clothing, absorbed in Hebrew writings," she concluded, had little in common with the editors of the *Post* or most of its readers.

Dolly was clueless about the observance of the religion itself. At one point she agreed to answer a questionnaire from a Hadassah group about her Jewish identity. Her parents were not religious, she wrote in a draft, although Morti Schiff "observed Jewish holidays and fasted on ??" Jean Gillette filled in Yom Kippur.

Dolly sometimes exhibited a tone-deafness on the subject of Israel. On March 13, 1955, she proudly told her Dear Readers about a visit she and

Rudolf had paid to Albert Einstein in Princeton. "My husband, who has known Professor Einstein for a long time, due to a mutual interest in Israel, had made an appointment for us to stop by and 'pay our respects' to the grand old man of physics, who has lived there for 20 years," she wrote.

Einstein's house was unpretentious and underheated, in her view. "Saint-like, simple, gentle" Professor Einstein was sitting in a chair facing a table covered with books and "sheets of white paper covered with tiny, neat symbols." He told Dolly and Rudolf that, at seventy-six, he no longer had the energy to play his violin. He spent a lot of time listening to the radio but disliked popular science programs because they encouraged people to write to him with their half-baked theories. He said he believed there was no place for God in the scientific world. He believed in the probability of other populated universes. He worried about the H-bomb. He admired Gandhi. He loved Franklin Delano Roosevelt.

Dolly concluded her report on the visit by noting, "Standing on the stairs as we were leaving, the disillusioned idealist called to my husband: 'We had great hopes for Israel at first. We thought it might be better than other nations, but it is no better.' "

Einstein's agnostic views barely registered with readers, but his mild criticism of Israel ignited a firestorm. In response to a request by a reporter from the *Jewish Chronicle*—a London publication—to clarify his comments, Einstein claimed, "Miss Schiff has used a private visit she paid me by incorporating (without asking my permission) casual remarks in a tendentious newspaper article. This article does not, by any means, represent my views."

Dolly was stunned. Rudolf, wiser in the ways of insider Jewish politics, realized that although many Jews made similar comments privately, the official Jewish organizations could not allow the published statement to go unchallenged. Dolly drafted a letter to offended readers in which she pointed out that Einstein had never said he was misquoted but had implied simply that his words were taken out of context. She also noted that the professor never wrote her to spell out the ways in which his words were allegedly misused.

She told Jimmy Wechsler that many Israelis and prominent American Jews had told her privately that Einstein had been known to make similar comments in the past, but never in public. Einstein died on April 18, 1955—weeks before he was scheduled to deliver a speech marking the seventh anniversary of Israeli independence. In the worldwide commemoration of his death, his encounter with Dolly was hardly noticed. But it remained a sore spot to her.

Years later she clipped an article by Isaiah Berlin about Einstein and Israel from *The New York Review of Books*. She underlined one passage in which Berlin wrote that Einstein "deplored the shortcomings of Zionist policy toward the Arabs; but he never abandoned his belief in the central principles of Zionism," and another in which he commented that "any decent and sensitive man cannot but feel bad about acts done in the name of his people which seem to him wrong or unwise."

Dolly was fascinated by discussions of ethnic identity. She was always interested to learn which celebrity was Jewish, or which one was not too forthright about a Jewish grandmother. Reporters at the *Post* claim that a mandate came down from the executive office: when there was some doubt about the ethnicity of the subject of an interview or a profile, try to get the mother's maiden name. If there was intermarriage, pin down the details.

Soon after Jerry Tallmer joined the *Post,* he inherited the "At Home With . . ." feature from Agnes Murphy. Dolly was very involved in the selection of subjects. "I was required to submit to Joe Rab, to submit to her, candidates for these things," says Tallmer. "Twenty of them and she would cross out eight and let me do the rest. That was all right. It was a lot of fun."

Dolly signed off on every decision. "Absolutely," Tallmer says. "Like Stalin. Sometimes the reasoning was inexplicable. Sometimes it was too explicable: someone she liked. And she read these things." A high percentage of the candidates Dolly agreed to—or suggested herself—were Jewish. "You could never tell from day to day which line to take," says Tallmer. "Not to overdo the Jewish thing, but at a certain point she would want it mentioned. I spent much of my professional life trying to figure out—Jewish in or out?"

Most of the time, despite the ambivalence of the publisher, the solution was "Jewish in." From 1955 on, the percentage of subjects of profiles, series, or interviews who were Jews was extraordinarily high. Readers of the *Post* got to know Edward G. Robinson, Sid Caesar, Mrs. Sid Caesar, Sandy Koufax, every president of Hadassah and the United Jewish Appeal, Herman Wouk, Saul Bellow, Leonard Bernstein, Jonas Salk, and countless others whose life stories helped reinforce the good news that Jews were making their way into the aristocracy of success.

At the time, few commentators recognized what the *Post* was instinctively demonstrating—that real power in New York was being transferred from the Catholic hierarchy and its political allies to Jewish business and cultural leaders. This transformation would be identified and explained in a 1963 best-seller—*Beyond the Melting Pot,* by Nathan Glazer and Daniel P. Moynihan. The book's genesis owed much to Dorothy Schiff's fascination with ethnicity and its role in the community.

Late in 1956, the *Post* ran a series on Great Neck, an affluent Long Island suburb that had attracted an influx of young families the articles identified as "arrivistes, a new class of people in their first heady exhilaration of money." The series emphasized the conspicuous consumption exhibited by the newcomers. One piece, titled "Shirley in Suburbia," portrayed local wives and mothers with too much time on their hands.

> You see them—whole platoons of them. They shop in the supermarkets, they sit at animated luncheons with their friends, or they drive with well-tailored assurance to an organization meeting in snug afternoon control of their manless matriarchy.
>
> Shirley has one advantage over her less-favored sisters in more modest suburbs. She has more money. That means that in today's market for domestic help, she has the admission price for leisure.

The article featured four such "Shirleys":

> They sat with the poise of professional models, their backs straight, their silken legs gracefully crossed. One turned to the others suddenly and asked, "How many happy women do you know in Great Neck?"
>
> They pondered the question carefully for a moment and shook their heads in melancholy agreement. "None," they said.
>
> They've turned their children over to nannies, their houses to interior decorators and housekeepers. How well their house is decorated has an important place in their social standing. Some have affairs, some with the plumber. But neighbors are also home, and they're very alert.

Only in the last article of the six-part series—in a description of the religious life in Great Neck—was it revealed that most of the people who were profiled were Jewish. The condescending attitude toward upwardly mobile Jews might have been typical of many academic sociologists and popular critics of suburban culture at the time, but it was quite unusual for the *Post.* Dorothy Schiff loved the series. She believed it provided a provocative view of people who had not solved the problem of "purposefulness in life."

Soon after the articles appeared, Dorothy suggested to Wechsler that they be expanded into a book on various Jewish communities in New York. Nothing came of the idea at the time, but she didn't give up. A year later, she wrote Jimmy that she'd been reading *Life Is With People,* a study of the Jews of prewar eastern Europe by sociologists Mark Zborowski and Elizabeth Herzog, that had been published in 1952. The book suggested to her that a study of the Jews of New York that explored their backgrounds, their economic achievements, the range of their religious practices from nonobservance to extreme Orthodoxy, and their evolving social status would make a great series for the *Post.* Nothing came of that suggestion either, but Dolly and Jimmy continued their discussion.

By the summer of 1959, they had agreed that such a project should be increased in scope to include several ethnic groups, and that the paper should probably commission a prominent sociologist to write it or collaborate with the paper's regular reportorial staff in the writing. Wechsler asked his friend Daniel Bell if he would take on the assignment, and Bell, who declined, proposed his friend and colleague Nathan Glazer.

"Dan approached me with this idea for the *Post,*" Glazer recalls. "This was a period when no one thought that large-scale immigration would ever recur in the United States. So the question was—What has happened to the second generation? And that's interesting. I'd be willing to do that."

In a contract signed in February 1960, Glazer agreed to prepare articles on six ethnic or racial groups in New York: Jews, Negroes, Puerto Ricans, Italians, Irish, and another to be decided later. After appearing in the paper, the texts would be published in book form by the M.I.T. Press under the auspices of the Joint Center for Urban Studies of the Massachusetts Institute of Technology and Harvard University. With the Joint, as it was familiarly called, as the intermediary, Glazer would be paid $15,000 in three installments of $5,000 each by the New York Post Foundation. The foundation, which owned a token share of the paper, was a mechanism that allowed Dorothy to make charitable donations in the name of the paper rather than herself. It could also be used on rare occasions like this one to pay more than the going rate for journalism the paper wanted to commission but for which it didn't want to skew the Newspaper Guild pay scale. The first payment to Glazer was made in March 1960, and the second followed in June.

The first three articles were to be submitted by September 1, but Glazer needed more time than he had anticipated to finish the project. Accordingly,

Wechsler held up the third payment. In October, an apologetic Glazer delivered a draft of his articles on Negroes and Puerto Ricans. A month later he finished his chapter on the Jews.

Schiff and Wechsler were not pleased with the results. Dolly thought the draft about the Negroes was "sloppy" and "superficial," and the article on the Puerto Ricans not adequately researched. By the middle of November, it was clear that—if done properly—the project would take too long and cost too much for the *Post* to continue its support. The contract between the Post Foundation and the Joint was canceled. The foundation would receive royalties against the money it had already invested, and the paper retained second serial rights to the book if Glazer went on with the project, which he did.

Beyond the Melting Pot was published in September 1963. The preface stated that "a grant from the New York Post Foundation made possible much of the research and writing" and that "this work was conceived and organized by Nathan Glazer." Glazer wrote the chapters on New York's Puerto Rican, Negro, Jewish, and Italian communities, and he enlisted Moynihan, then a professor at Syracuse, to write the chapter on the Irish. The idea of a sixth group was dropped.

The book was a critical and commercial success.* Freed of what was obviously an unrealistic timetable dictated by the *Post*'s needs, Glazer collected data that offered fresh insights into the urban community. He and Moynihan observed that, contrary to popular rhetoric, the pot, at least in New York, did not melt. Third- and fourth-generation members of ethnic and religious groups may have participated more and more in mainstream culture, but they retained their distinctive identities as well. The authors argued that ethnicity was the key to understanding the complex social, political, and economic life of the city.

Glazer graciously gives Moynihan credit for identifying significant political changes in his substantial contributions to the conclusion of the book. "Pat had written his first article for *Commentary* about politics," says Glazer. "And it was an entirely ethnic story, about how the Jews were coming in and replacing the Irish, and in replacing them, were moving in a very different way than what the Irish moved in. . . . He certainly knew much more about ethnics and politics in New York State and City than I knew. So I said, 'Okay, that's fine.'"

---

*The Post Foundation eventually received royalties of about $3,500 against its paid advance of $10,000 for the project.

Beyond the Melting Pot spotlighted a change in New York that was occurring in cities across the country. The Catholic political hegemony—usually Irish-led—that had dominated urban politics for decades was losing its grip. In New York, the Jews were ousting the Powerhouse from its centrality. In other metropolitan areas, there were other challengers. Moynihan and Glazer identified this transition and substantiated it with sociological data and observations.

"The central issue clearly was Jews moving into Democratic politics," Glazer says today. "They'd always been there, in Tammany, and in organizations in Brooklyn and the Bronx. But those Jews were the kind who were following the Irish pattern of neighborhood politics and working your way up. And then, just around this period, you have a new group coming in."

Glazer remembers a news photo of four or five young Manhattan reform activists who were fighting for the Democratic nomination for a congressional seat on the Upper West Side. "They'd all gone to Harvard or Yale. They all had rich parents in the background. And one of them was going to become the congressman. It was all so different from the world before where you worked your way up. These Jews were individually mobile, and they figured if they were smart and able, why not go for it?"

Jewish readers of the *Post* typified and profited from this transition, whether it was manifested in politics, business, or access to social and cultural leadership. Its editor-publisher had understood what was happening from the start. Her own background had made her familiar with the exercise of power. Her uncanny ability to tap into what was going on in the minds of her readers alerted her to the change that *Beyond the Melting Pot* chronicled and to initiate the project itself.

IV

SUNNY DAYS

SIXTEEN

Alone Again

By the mid-fifties, Dorothy Schiff had reason to be proud of her accomplishments. Although the *Post* was still considered weaker financially than its competitors, politicians and other community leaders were forced to take the paper seriously. Its editorial voice carried weight, and its reporters were respected and honored by their colleagues throughout the city.

The daily operations of the paper were running smoothly. There were few upheavals in personnel at the top levels. Wechsler and Sann divided the editorial responsibilities equitably. Each man had his favorites and cronies, but aside from the normal tensions that arise from working under pressure in close circumstances, they all got along reasonably well.

Leon Cook and Marvin Berger were in charge of the business side, and Rudolf Sonneborn looked over their shoulders. The financial statements were reassuring. Publishing operations showed a profit every year, as did the parent Post Corporation. Because Dorothy was the sole owner of the corporation, her overall personal income tax liability dictated the annual decision about whether profits should be distributed to her as income, transferred to her through a redemption of her outstanding bonds, or retained by the corporation as a reserve fund against the possibility of major capital investment in plant and machinery—which was the usual disposition.

In the winter of 1956–1957, new presses were installed that made possible a change in the length of the paper. The maximum capacity of the old presses was ninety-six pages. While the Monday and Tuesday papers ordinarily ran at forty-eight pages, increased demand from advertisers toward the end of the week or preceding major holidays often pushed the paper to its maximum length. The new presses could print a paper of 104 pages, providing space for eight more lucrative ad pages.

Dolly and her editors decided to capitalize on their increased flexibility by introducing a new format. The regular paper consisted of news, sports, and business sections as well as the advertising pages. The profiles of prominent citizens, regular columns, and series about people and issues in the news that characterized the particular voice and point of view of the *Post* were pulled together in a new eight-page Daily Magazine section.

Dolly was delighted by the string of profitable years but always pessimistic about the future. As the decade proceeded, she noted that many papers in New York and cities around the country were in financial trouble. Suburban papers like Alicia Patterson's *Newsday* were beginning to pull ahead in the competition for advertising dollars, as was television. The Hearst Corporation was reported to be swallowing losses at both the *Daily Mirror* and the *New York Journal-American*. Hoping to repair the damage, Hearst doubled the newsstand price of the *Journal* to ten cents in early 1957. The *Post,* along with the *Telegram,* followed suit. The *Post* introduced its price rise on May 26, 1957, the same day the reorganized paper with the Daily Magazine was rolled out.

Dolly pored over the reports generated by her business department each month. She participated in every important decision concerning union contracts, equipment purchases, and financing. She insisted on approving any expenditure of more than $500. Although she was obsessively attentive, she was not fiscally savvy. She was most comfortable reviewing line items: she scrutinized expense accounts, questioned telephone bills, and worried about whether or not the paper got full value from its $170-a-month rental of the Dow Jones ticker tape. Perhaps her concentration on such minor matters kept her businesspeople on their toes. Without a doubt, it contributed to her in-house reputation as a penny-pincher and a scold.

Dolly's attention to the fine print was evident in her reading of the paper itself. Grammar was always on her mind. She sent repeated reminders to Leonard Lyons about errors in the tenses of verbs. She marked up a column by Murray Kempton in which he used the word "inferred" when he should have written "implied." She asked Wechsler to instruct Max Lerner on the proper use of "fewer" rather than "less."

Every day her administrative assistant, Jean Gillette, sent memos to Sann and Wechsler that reflected the publisher's thoughts about something she'd just seen in the first edition. Commenting on a new promotion in a November 1954 paper, she complained that Wechsler had not sent it upstairs for her approval and reminded him that she insisted on approving any changes in the paper's format, "including indexes."

She had her pet subjects. She told Wechsler that she had become a fan of a cooking show on a local television station presided over by Mr. and Mrs. Charles Bontempi, and she urged him to assign a reporter to write a close-up of the couple. She hoped that their Italian surname would appeal to Italian readers. Similarly, she pushed for an article about Liberace, unaware that he usually identified himself as being of Polish origin. She said she wanted to expand the *Post*'s profile in the Italian community and make it an attractive venue for advertisements of Italian products. Three weeks later, she asked Jimmy what had been done to implement her suggestions. A close-up of the Bontempis ran a few weeks after that.

Mike Levitas says, "She had the reputation of being interfering. As if she owned the paper! There were enough stories in the newsroom about how she drove Paul Sann and Jimmy crazy, and drove reporters mad. And it must have been humiliating. All Paul could do, and Jimmy could do, was tear their hair out and keep their mouths shut when she was . . . you know, why don't we do a story about that?

"Once I was assigned to cover a lunch of some organization at a hotel in midtown," Levitas continues. "I think Dolly Schiff was supposed to get an award. That was not the kind of assignment I normally got, because anybody could have done it, but I guess there was no one else that day, so I was sort of the sacrificial lamb. So I went with a wonderful photographer, Tony Calvacca. Very cheerful and very good. He knew his way around town.

"On the way up he said, 'Let me give you some advice. Stay out of her way. Don't introduce yourself. Just take some notes unobtrusively, and when you're finished, go. If she doesn't know who you are when you came in, or went, that's good. Don't give her any opportunity. . . .'

"So I was like an undercover reporter. I stayed out of her line of sight. I'm sure she didn't know I was there."

Levitas explains his trepidation. "You don't want to give her any excuse to be irritated with you. I didn't want to know her, because I had a job, and I was doing fine. There was nothing to be gained. There was only risk with a woman who was that capricious. To be on her radar meant that you could be shot down or wounded.

"You only heard stories about how idiotic she could be and how intolerable it was, but I don't know what she vetoed or what she inspired," Levitas concludes. "When she was good, she was very, very good, and when she was bad, she was horrid. And what the proportion of good to horrid was, I have no idea."

The ratio may be impossible to calculate, as Levitas, who spent more than twenty years in senior editorial positions at *The New York Times,* suggests. The mistake is to laugh at Dorothy's foibles and lose sight of the fact that she was also a solid newspaperwoman. She had a keen sense of what boosted newsstand sales. On June 8, 1955, she criticized the page-1 headline. "38,000 Out at GM" would not attract potential readers, she told Wechsler; "Dead 'Model Boy' Charged by DA" would. A week later, she pointed out that "Bomb Peron HG" generated little excitement, while "Peron Excommunicated" would have interested Catholic readers.

She never lost sight of the bottom line. In May 1957, she objected to fashion page photographs of two dresses from Franklin Simon, a store that did not advertise in the *Post* and that she thought was "an obnoxious store, anyway." She admitted that nonadvertisers sometimes warranted the paper's attention, but two photographs seemed excessive.

She asked questions her readers might ask. After reading a proposed article about the City Planning Commission, she told Wechsler the piece needed to explain the structure and purpose of the commission. She wanted to know what its annual budget was. She wanted details about a proposed plan for rezoning the city that was on the commission's agenda, wondering if the *Post* should support it.

And she floated story ideas that no other tabloid publisher in the nation would have thought of. Noting that 1956 was the hundredth anniversary of the death of Heinrich Heine, who she said was "considered to be the German Voltaire," she told Jimmy she thought Heine would make a wonderful subject for a feature in the Weekend Magazine.

Even when Dolly was out of town, she kept her hand in. Though she gave Marvin Berger and, eventually, Jean Gillette her proxy to sign off on routine

Dorothy Schiff and Richard Hall at
their 1923 wedding. (Courtesy of Marian Seldes)

On his return from London in June 1941, George Backer shows
Dorothy a fragment of a bomb dropped during the Blitz.

LEFT: Old Fields, the thirty-plus-room country house that Dorothy had built in 1934. Its
size and ostentation dismayed her, and she sold it in 1941. RIGHT: After Dorothy eased
George out of his active role at the *Post*, he continued to serve as an advocate for Jewish
causes, acting as head of American ORT until 1950. (Courtesy of American ORT)

Showing increased responsibility for the paper, Dorothy visits the composing room in March 1945. Ted Thackrey, cigarette in mouth, looks on. (*New York Post* Archive)

Dorothy and Ted Thackrey in the penthouse office suite at 75 West Street. (*New York Post* Archive)

Dorothy and Don Fedderson, second from left, the manager of her West Coast radio and television properties in 1946. (*New York Post* Archive)

Aboard the *Queen Elizabeth* en route to Europe, November 1948. (*New York Post* Archive)

Dorothy and Eleanor Roosevelt work the phones for a UJA
fund-raiser in 1952. (*New York Post* Archive)

Dorothy joins socialites Jane Pickens (left) and Jinx Falkenberg (right)
to plan a charity event. (*New York Post* Archive)

Sarah-Ann Backer, grandson Michael Gray, daughter Adele Gray, and son Morti Hall visit Dorothy at the office. (*New York Post* Archive)

Daughter Sarah-Ann Backer and Dorothy attend an NAACP rally in May 1956. (Sonneborn Papers)

Dorothy and Rudolf Sonneborn at a New York nightclub, 1955. (Sonneborn Papers)

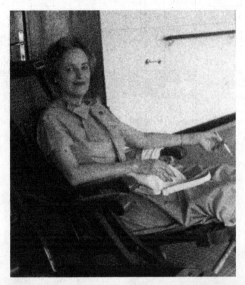

Rudolf enjoyed documenting their travels in snapshots. TOP: Dorothy relaxes on the deck of the *Liberté* en route to Europe, 1957. (Sonneborn Papers) LEFT: Dorothy on the landing pier in Plymouth, England. (Sonneborn Papers) RIGHT: Dorothy devotes some time to her needlepoint on the train to Paris. (Sonneborn Papers)

Dorothy breaks with the other publishers and the *Post* goes back
to press, March 4, 1963. (Associated Press)

Dorothy chats with ex-President Harry Truman and New York State Democratic head James Farley. (*New York Post* Archive)

Dorothy supported Adlai Stevenson in his two failed presidential races, but they were never close friends. (*New York Post* Archive)

Dorothy always had a soft spot for the Kennedys. With Bobby Kennedy and his wife, Ethel, at the 1964 Democratic convention. She favored his doomed candidacy in 1968. (*New York Post* Archive)

Nelson Rockefeller won Dorothy's support in his 1958 race for governor of
New York, and she always enjoyed his company. (*New York Post* Archive)

Dorothy was fascinated, but not won over, by Republican
strategist and eventual secretary of state Henry Kissinger.
(*New York Post* Archive)

A gathering of the clan in the summer of 1967. Morti Hall at left, Sally Kramarsky holding infant at rear center, and Adele Gray in the right rear.

Rupert Murdoch and Dorothy Schiff commemorating his purchase of the *Post* in November 1976. (*New York Post* Archive)

Dorothy escorted to a Lincoln Center gala by her biographer, Jeffrey Potter,
in December 1973. (*New York Post* Archive)

With granddaughter Mary Hall Howland at
Mary's wedding, July 1986. (Photo by Mary Hilliard.
Courtesy of Mary Hall Howland)

matters, she wanted to be informed immediately about any extraordinary event. If she was in the United States, she expected to have the *Post* delivered to her as soon as possible and circulation figures to be forwarded on a timely basis.

The Sonneborns took annual summer trips to Europe, which Rudolf documented in leather-bound scrapbooks filled with photos, hotel bills, restaurant receipts, and entrance cards to gambling casinos and other tourist attractions. In 1954, they sailed to Le Havre on the *Île-de-France*. A chauffeur/guide took them through Normandy to Mont-Saint-Michel, then south to the Loire Valley, where they stopped at a winery in Montrichard and visited the châteaux of Blois, Chambord, and Chenonceau. From there they headed south to Lyon and the Riviera. They stayed at La Reserve in Beaulieu and the Majestic Hotel in Cannes and gambled in Monte Carlo before returning home on the *Andrea Doria*.

Dolly summarized some of the highlights of the trip in her first column after their return: "The *Île-de-France* is noted for its cuisine. You know that I am an amateur cook, so I was very much interested in the menu. . . . The wine waiter is always a problem at first, because we are not accustomed to drinking this beverage with our meals. Although it is not mandatory to order any, one feels like a heel and a hick if one turns it down, so we had a half bottle with every meal (except breakfast, of course)."

Not much had changed in France since Dolly's 1948 trip with Alicia Patterson. Signs of war devastation were everywhere. The French people told her they still hated and feared the Germans, and she sympathized. She believed Germany should not be allowed to rearm or join NATO.

The Sonneborns' 1955 itinerary was similar. After leaving the *Liberté* in Calais, they were driven through Chartres, Tours, and Bordeaux to Biarritz, where they spent a week at the Hôtel de Paris. They spent another week at the Ritz in Paris, went to several museums and a Jacques Fath fashion show, and then returned to New York on the *Nieuw Amsterdam*.

Once again Dorothy issued a report. She began with a reference to her first visit to Biarritz in 1910, when she was seven. "My recollection is of a beautiful spangled pearl-grey dress sent from Paris and displayed on a bed in the Palace hotel. It was for my mother to wear at an informal dinner arranged to entertain King Edward VII by his lady friend." During her next visit in the summer of 1929, "decadent Spanish grandees and American café society danced at parties which lasted till dawn." By implication, her fellow guests in

1955 were less glamorous. They were upper-middle-class Americans who, thanks to the cash in their pockets, were on the grand tour. They lacked titles, but they were the new international set.

After a hiatus in the summer of 1956 because of the political conventions, the Sonneborns resumed their European travels the following year. They sailed to London on the *Liberté,* took a ten-day cruise to Scandinavia on the *Stella Polaris,* then returned home from Le Havre on the *Île-de-France.* Dorothy did not like the Scandinavian cruise. In a letter home, she confessed that she found her shipmates to be "bourgeois" and boring.

Dolly always checked the list of fellow first-class passengers on the transatlantic crossings. She usually found friends: Senator Bill Benton of Connecticut and his family and the Paul Warburgs one year; Mrs. Theodore Roosevelt and Mrs. Wendell Willkie another. The Sonneborns carried formal clothes in their luggage; they were always invited to a dinner at the captain's table.

Their annual routine included at least one trip to Los Angeles to visit Dolly's children and grandchildren. In March 1956, Morti divorced Ruth Roman and married actress Diana Lynn. Their first child, Matthew, was born in 1958; Dolly, Mary, and Daisy would follow over the next six years. In 1958, Adele divorced Arthur Gray and soon married A. Frederic Leopold, an entertainment lawyer who was active in Democratic politics. The Leopold marriage produced two children, Frederic and Tess.

Rudolf's house in Danbury remained a getaway for a day or a week. In June 1956, Dolly told an interviewer that she was happy there. She had time to catch up on her reading, "especially the love stories and the cooking articles" in the women's magazines. She relaxed at her needlepoint, having recently completed twelve dining room chair seats with signs of the zodiac.

Rudolf's niece Deborah Hermann remembers dinners at Sixty-fourth Street with her husband and sons when they visited New York. "Dolly was always nice to me," says Hermann. "Always nice. She would let us be there with the boys. The dining room was quite formal; my boys used to joke about the finger bowls."

The Sonneborns' domestic tranquillity was shattered one evening in May 1959, when Rudolf suddenly went rigid at dinner. He couldn't speak; he couldn't move. An apparent stroke left him comatose. Terrified and panicky, Dorothy called her doctor, who lived nearby.

The doctor and Dorothy's butler, William Neuenhausen, got Rudolf into an ambulance. Dorothy refused to ride along. Years later she said, "I couldn't. . . . I wanted to run away, and I knew I couldn't." She seems to have had no impulse to take care of Rudolf. "He was supposed to look after me—that's what he said he was going to do—and he didn't. Well, he did for a while." Observing him in his changed state, she could only imagine how she would look if she were that sick. "It was all too much," she said. "I didn't want any part of him."

After six weeks in the hospital, Rudolf returned to the apartment, a changed man, permanently impaired. He couldn't write, and for a time he could barely speak. There were round-the-clock nurses and physical therapists. The apartment was rearranged to accommodate his needs. Eventually he regained some strength. He could attend the theater and travel, but his right side remained quite weak, his difficulties in communication continued and he required a wheelchair to get around.

For some months, Rudolf maintained the dream that he would eventually regain mobility. Perhaps Dorothy made some effort to believe so, too. In 1960, they traveled to Los Angeles together for the month of July so that she could attend the Democratic convention and see her family. Rudolf was tended by a full-time nurse. They stayed briefly at the Bel-Air and then moved in with Adele. Rudolf was given the guest bedroom, and Dorothy settled into a small maid's room off the kitchen. She wrote to Jean Gillette that Adele was a "saint" and Adele's children were delightful. Dorothy said she wished she were one of them.

Dorothy spoke often of the lack of mothering she received in her childhood. She was more circumspect about admitting her lingering hunger to have that deficit compensated for in her adulthood. Rudolf's incapacity made her hunger more acute. She had hoped he would take care of her; now she flittingly dreamed that Adele could take over.

The next two summers, Dorothy went to California on her own. In 1962, Rudolf was well enough to take a cruise on the *Queen Mary* with an attendant. Dorothy bought a house just up the street from Adele in Los Angeles, but she stayed in it only once. She began to spend her summer vacations on Long Island, and eventually Adele moved her family into the house her mother had purchased but never really used.

For a few years, Dorothy accompanied Rudolf to Sonneborn family events, but she gradually dropped out. Deborah Hermann thinks that when Dorothy realized that Rudolf's disabilities were permanent, she became impatient with his limitations. "And he was humiliated as well," says Hermann. "Suddenly he went from being someone who could organize and do everything. He had troubles with speech, he was in a wheelchair. He had to give up the presidency of L. Sonneborn & Sons. He gave up his Israeli connections. You know, he had been a hero. There would be invitations from Teddy Kollek and Ben-Gurion saying, you know, where are you? Come visit us. But he couldn't go back as a damaged person."

Adele Sweet believes the marriage was foundering even before Rudolf got sick. She says, "I think the mistake is to think that it lasted until he got sick. I think she got to know him better and better. He was demanding." According to Adele, who admits she was never Rudolf's biggest fan, the stroke only intensified his self-involvement. "After he had his stroke, he needed help from his valet, who would do up his shoelaces. I would have gone nuts under those circumstances, but he didn't mind at all. He liked the idea of having someone do up his shoelaces. He liked being taken care of, and she was not the person to do that. It was intolerable."

Lisa Schiff married Dolly's nephew David in 1963, after relations between Dolly and Rudolf had soured. "The Sonneborn thing ended so poorly," Lisa says. "Dolly was cruel to him. Cruel. Some of the comments she made about him were horrible. The evenings we spent together were horrible. I wanted to shoot myself. They did not get on, and I guess nobody else was really nice to this guy. By that time, they had nothing to say to each other."

In July 1965, Rudolf finally moved out—first to a suite at the Pierre and then to the Regency Hotel. He took his furniture with him. Several years later, Gail Sheehy asked Dolly if she thought a powerful professional woman could sustain a permanent relationship with a man. Dolly replied, "I'd like to have both, but that I haven't been able to do. When I'm away from the *Post,* I don't feel myself. . . . I think weekends and vacations it would be nice to have the other thing (marriage), but then what do you do with the men the rest of the time? They can get in your hair."

After Rudolf left, Dolly hired the fashionable interior designer Renny Saltzman to refurbish her apartment. She employed the equally well-known decorator Carleton Varney for other jobs. Both men respected her taste; they didn't change her rooms so much as refresh them. Over the years, Dolly added to her modest but thoughtfully assembled art collection. In the late 1950s, she acquired two snow scenes by Grandma Moses, one of which was appraised in 1960 at $4,000. In 1959, she bought a Picasso crayon drawing,

Flowers, for $1,400; the following year she bought his drawing of a bullfight for $1,500. Later she added several paintings by lesser-known artists she spotted in the windows of Madison Avenue galleries.

The butler who'd been so attentive to Rudolf, William Neuenhausen, and his wife, Ellie, worked for the Sonneborns until the spring of 1961, when they returned to Germany. After the Neuenhausens gave notice, Dorothy answered a Jobs Wanted ad in *The New York Times* placed by a young couple named Aery and Everette Lawson. Soon they were her live-in butler and cook, and within several years, Everette took over as her chauffeur as well.

The Lawsons became something of a surrogate family. Dorothy began the day chatting with Aery over her breakfast tray about menus and household chores; she often discussed the morning headlines with Everette as he drove her to the office. "When we had different dignitaries in the car, or when we would go to meet them," he says, "she would talk to me all the way into work the next day. 'What did I think about them? Or what they talked about.'

"She would always give us our Sundays and Thursdays, because she knew we had a life, but basically we were at her beck and call twenty-four seven. The only time we had to ourselves was when she went away in the summer. When we first came, she used to go to France with Mr. Sonneborn, but she had her own suite on the boat. I would take her luggage and settle her in her stateroom."

After Rudolf got sick, Dorothy never visited Europe again. She preferred to travel as little as possible. After Adele and Morti moved their families east in the late 1960s, she never even had to go to the West Coast. She took her summer vacation in the Hamptons.

Everette Lawson says, "I'd drive her out to Long Island. Sometimes I'd go out a day early with her things and then come back to pick her up. And we'd do the reverse at the end of the vacation."

Every other year, Dorothy gave Everette money to buy a new car. "We always had a black Cadillac, with white leather top and white upholstery. I don't remember know how we settled on the black and white, but once we had it, she liked it. And no other car was like that. I had to special-order it. So when I used to pull up in the front of the theaters at night, with this white top, it was so distinctive."

Dorothy became deeply involved in the Lawsons' lives and the lives of their children. Almost as soon as she hired the couple, she began supplementing their income with loans, which she sometimes collected and sometimes forgave. Later she gave their children substantial gifts and paid their college tuition. Everette and Aery received their health insurance through a special arrangement with the *Post,* and Dorothy paid medical bills for the children. She helped the Lawsons buy their house in Teaneck, New Jersey. One summer she saw to it that Everette Jr. got a job in the *Post* pressroom. Everette Sr. says, "She got him that job, and he got a union card. In those days you couldn't get into the union unless you were related to someone, and of course that was the way they kept black people out. So all the men used to call him her grandson.

"That was a period of prejudice," Everette says. "When some of the people at the *Post* would see our car drive up, and I would get out and open her door, and lead her to the elevator and then up to her office, there was a lot of things said. And lots of things said to me alone. But she had trained me, you can't let an insult get into you. It wasn't easy in the beginning, but it got better."

Sally Backer lived in her own apartment in New York. Sally was interested in politics, not journalism. After graduating from Sarah Lawrence in 1956, she worked with her father, George, on the Harriman campaign in 1958 and was actively involved with the New York City reform Democratic organization. In the spring of 1959, she met a young fellow reformer named Werner Kramarsky. The couple got engaged in the fall, just before Wynn, as he was called, took a job as a stockbroker with Bache & Co. in Frankfurt, Germany.

Wynn's parents were German Jews who had moved to Holland in 1923 at the first sign of Nazi violence in their native Hamburg. Their son was born in Amsterdam in 1926. Mr. Kramarsky was a successful investor in the Dutch stock exchange and amassed a valuable collection of nineteenth- and twentieth-century European paintings. Dolly told Max Lerner that the senior Kramarskys were Orthodox Jews. Their son was not, although he wanted what she called a "traditional" wedding.

Sally and Wynn were married in Geneva on December 19, 1959. According to the wedding announcement in *The New York Times,* "The bride's mother was unable to attend because of the illness of her husband." It was really her fear of flying that kept her away, according to Sally. When the Kramarskys' first child, Daniel, was born in Paris in 1961, Dolly was eager to see the baby but waited for them to come home later that year before meeting her grandson for the first time.

Dolly's inner circle, never large, was diminished by the death of her dear friend Alicia Patterson. Alicia suffered from colon cancer, which had been treated surgically. In the spring of 1963, she experienced a recurrence of cancerlike symptoms, which proved to be bleeding ulcers. Following several unsuccessful operations, fifty-six-year-old Alicia died within weeks.

Among Dolly's small group of intimates was a woman named Jenny Baerwald, whose family considered Dolly rather dull and wondered at her loyalty. Jenny was a childless widow of limited financial means, who had dinner with Dolly or shopped with her from time to time. From the late forties on, Dolly arranged to have Kuhn, Loeb send Jenny a small monthly stipend from her personal account, which Dolly augmented by occasional checks for $500 or $1,000. Jenny was very grateful. In an undated note thanking Dolly for a check, she wrote, "Since Sigmund's [her husband's] death you are really the only one who cares what happens to me, and who helps in a different way than others, and that means more to me than words can tell you."

Jenny was always Dolly's champion. In May 1964, she despaired of Dolly's domestic situation. "I get so upset about you and mad at Rudolf. You are so lovable & wonderful—you ought to have someone to care for you and spoil you—instead of you doing everything for everybody. Just had to tell you! Love, Jenny."

Jenny was older than Dolly, almost old enough to be her mother—which proved to be the source of their attachment. As a girl, Jenny had been close to Dolly's maternal grandparents and their daughters. There are frequent references to Adele Schiff in Jenny's correspondence: "The older I get, the more I seem to think of your mother & all the old memories, and it means more to me than I can say, that, because of her, you are so dear to me. All my love, Jenny."

And again: "Dolly dear, I cannot let 1961 pass without telling you a few things that are in my heart.

"That I am deeply grateful to be permitted to 'bemother' you a bit—it brings back beautiful memories of your mother. That if I had a daughter I would wish her to be like you in every way. And that because of you—and because I see you often, I have the courage, as I face the troubles of old age—without any children, to carry on.

"And that I love you."

Jenny died in 1965. In her will, she left Dolly a clock and a ring and directed that other pieces of jewelry be passed on to Dolly's daughters. It appears that these items had originally belonged to Adele Schiff. Perhaps, with time, Dolly's ambivalence about her mother had abated. She seems to have been genuinely grateful for Jenny's reminders of the mother whom she had previously so disdained.

Dolly's daily routine was dominated by the needs of the *Post*. She rose early, read and marked up the first edition, which was waiting at her door, and scanned the morning papers. She was driven to the office by ten, stopping en route several times a week for a comb-out at her hairdresser's, where she had a full wash and set every Saturday morning. She shared the hairdresser with Pat Nixon and her daughters, and several members of the Rockefeller family, among others.

Dorothy shopped mostly by appointment. She occasionally used the services of a personal shopper at Bergdorf Goodman. Her favorite store was Evelyn Byrnes, a ground-floor establishment on Park Avenue, where she didn't have to use an elevator. The shop offered elegant, expensive clothing to an elite clientele. Dorothy was not the sort of woman who needed to purchase the latest Paris fashions. She bought a few things each year, and she liked classic designs that flattered her figure without being showy.

She found time for the occasional lunch with old friends like Ellin Berlin. Several evenings a week, she attended benefit dinners organized by political or cultural groups. She showed little interest in opera or other music, although sometimes she still went to the theater. She was always on the lookout for an attractive new man to add to her roster of old friends available for escort duty. She enjoyed an occasional dinner party with pals and entertained from time to time in her apartment. Her style was formal. Everette Lawson announced the guests as they arrived. Aery prepared the food, and, if necessary, additional help was hired to serve dinner and drinks. Dorothy usually invited a mixed group of politicians, business leaders, and members of her family. Guests report that she was a gracious and generous hostess, but she described herself as always nervous about such events.

SEVENTEEN

Changing the Guard

During the late fifties, New York still supported seven daily papers, plus several in nearby suburbs, but only *The New York Times* and *Newsday* on Long Island showed steady circulation growth. While the readership of the *Daily News,* the *Mirror,* and the *Journal-American* held more or less steady, the number of copies sold by the *Tribune,* the *Telegram,* and the *Post* dropped. After the *Post*'s daily circulation peaked at approximately 420,000 copies during the mid-fifties, sales shrank by nearly 25 percent to about 335,000 in 1960.

The *Post* eked out a profit every year through 1957, but by an ever-narrowing margin. Doubling the newsstand price midway through 1957 helped keep the paper in the black that year and the next. 1959 was basically a wash. In 1960, the paper showed a net operating profit of $20,000, but the parent Post Corporation was in the red. 1961 looked as if it would be the same.

In September 1960, the *Post* announced an attractive new promotion, designed to build circulation. To readers who mailed in $1 plus coupons collected from five consecutive daily papers, the paper sent one long-playing record and an instruction manual from an acclaimed foreign-language study program. Four dollars and twenty coupons bought a complete set of four records. The promotion was a big success. By the spring of 1961, more than three hundred thousand records had been sold, and the paper's management anticipated they would show a profit of $25,000 on royalty fees for the year.

They were selling newspapers, too. As many as six thousand a month more during the winter of 1960–1961. Approximately 40 percent of the added readers also bought the *Times*—an attractive demographic for potential advertisers. But the *Post* could not hold their attention. By the spring of 1961, as circulation dropped again, it was clear that most had bought the paper only for the promotion. As soon as they had enough coupons in hand, they had no further interest.

Dorothy studied every weekly report issued by the accounting department and sent off a stream of memos in response: Was last week's decision to pay overtime to pressmen and deliverymen because of breaking news justified? Were the managers alert in raising or lowering daily pressruns because of weather, holidays, or school vacations? Why do readers report that their neighborhood newsstands are sold out when they go to buy the paper? Was the paper paying too much to the truckers? She checked the circulation audits of the competition; she did the math in pencil right on the printed reports—did the *Journal-American* sell more copies, on average, this June than last year? Is the sales trend at the *Mirror* flat or down?

Although Dorothy was unhappy with the *Post*'s financial position, she did not commission a systematic review of the options available to address the situation. Selling more ads was one obvious solution. Dorothy began suggesting editorial projects that might make advertisers happy, and she opened a dialogue with James Wechsler about the importance of advertising in general. She reminded Jimmy that women were particularly receptive to advertising, which they read as carefully as they did the editorial copy. She cited statistics demonstrating that women bought almost everything their families used and wore except for cars and alcohol. Women loved sales, she said, and the only way they could find out about them was through newspaper ads. Dorothy acknowledged that some advertising was misleading, but she believed that on the whole it was accurate and served an important purpose.

Jimmy assured her that he agreed. His only complaint about advertising, he said, was that it dictated the format of a newspaper. He would prefer that the first twenty-four pages be ad-free. The advertising would follow, lumped together, with an index of the stores and services included. Some editorial copy might run on the advertising pages, but it would be soft in content and chosen to support the advertising. Dorothy thought Wechsler's idea would be unpopular with readers and advertisers.

She wanted the editors to come up with special features—series and news coverage—that would give the ad salesmen talking points with new advertisers, who might then become regulars. Series about diets and other health fads, cosmetics, sports, and exercise regimens appeared periodically in the paper. At one point, Jean Gillette wrote Jimmy, "Mrs. Schiff suggests a series on dogs and cats in NY. [It] should be light and not critical. Remember we are soliciting dog and cat advertising to accompany it."

To be clear, Dolly was not suggesting that news coverage should go easy on advertisers or potential advertisers if they needed to be chastened. In the fall of 1957, the paper ran a series on the Arthur Murray dance studios, a small but steady advertiser, that criticized the company for delivering less training than students were led to expect when they signed up. That was followed by a series about Slenderella, a diet chain, that questioned some of its claims for success. Slenderella had bought nearly $10,000 worth of ads in that calendar year, and their continuing to do so was doubtful. Dolly loved the series and said it was exactly the sort of work her editors should assign.

Dolly's corporate officers urged her to increase the *Post*'s sketchy business coverage in hopes of attracting more readers, and therefore potential advertisers, from New York's growing financial services community. Major improvements to the business section would mean beefing up the staff, but Dolly was averse to adding payroll. A simpler solution presented itself— publish stock market tables in the late editions of the paper. This would presumably make the *Post* more attractive to afternoon commuters who either worked on Wall Street or were among the growing number of white-collar Americans who were becoming members of the investor class.

Paul Sann, the executive editor, was enthusiastic about reaching this audience. In the summer of 1959, he sent Dolly a memo speculating about the benefits of adding the stock tables to the *Post*'s late editions. He estimated that it would cost just under $500,000 in syndication fees and labor costs that would be necessary to make sure that the *Post* hit the streets before the *Journal-American* and the *Telegram*. He assumed that twenty to twenty-five thousand new readers would cover the cost. Any gains above that would be gravy.

Wechsler was balky. He believed it would signal a change in the paper's political commitment. As he explained in a letter to Joe Rauh, "I have no principled objection to stock tables, but I fear that the issue lies between those of us here (mostly myself) who regard the Post's liberal identification as its reason for existence and those who would like to make it more congenial to the increasingly conservative . . . middle class of suburbia."

Jimmy had been feeling defensive for some time. He'd been brooding about a comment Dolly had made during one of their many conversations. "You said that our Page One looked too much like a 'cause paper,' " he wrote her in June 1961. "I do not differ with your judgement [about a particular story], but I am disturbed by the suggestion that we should be apologetic about our identification as a crusading paper. I think part of our future rests on exploiting that identification on a national scale."

Wechsler spent time in the wake of Stevenson's two decisive defeats thinking about national politics. He remained a champion of Stevenson, even though he was almost certainly to the left of the former candidate. In 1960, he published *Reflections of an Angry Middle-Aged Editor,* a rather bitter book defending the liberalism of his generation and deploring the seemingly apolitical stance of the young.

He showed his manuscript to Dorothy before publication. She read it carefully and gave him nearly five single-spaced pages of notes and comments. While praising Wechsler's effort, she couldn't help saying that she thought many assertions about the young were "highly debatable." On the whole, she was more sympathetic to the next generation than the book was. She concluded that young people were probably more skeptical than her peers had been and that they would not necessarily "accept 19th Century idealism even when expressed in the felicitous language of Adlai Stevenson."

Presidential politics in 1960 played a part in perpetuating the tension between publisher and editor. The sixty-year-old Stevenson was not eager to run a third time, but he was not quite willing to pack it in, either. The Cambridge crowd led by Arthur Schlesinger Jr. and John Kenneth Galbraith was attracted to young Massachusetts Senator John F. Kennedy. Phil Graham, the publisher of *The Washington Post,* was backing Senator Lyndon Johnson from Texas. Senator Hubert Humphrey of Minnesota was not an official candidate, but he was busy trying to line up supporters, Dorothy Schiff among them.

Dolly was not receptive. She told Humphrey's chief fund-raiser in March 1960 that even though she and Hubert had been friends for years and shared many political views, she thought he was not good at sticking to his principles. Jimmy Wechsler defended Humphrey to her, even though he was still smitten with Stevenson. But Dolly was looking for someone else to back.

She was ambivalent about Jack Kennedy. In a 1956 column, she wrote, "I have just read a provocative book by the fascinating young Senator from Massachusetts, John F. Kennedy. It is called 'Profiles in Courage.' " She mentioned that Joe Kennedy, her old friend but frequent political adversary, had given money to Senator Joseph McCarthy, and Bobby Kennedy had worked for McCarthy. Jack had ducked the vote to censure Joe. "Perhaps Jack Kennedy's book," she wrote, "is the child of his agony concerning McCarthy."

Wechsler's enthusiasm for Stevenson led the *Post* on the eve of the Democratic convention to propose in an editorial that the party nominate Adlai once again for president with Jack Kennedy as his running mate. At the convention in Los Angeles, which Dolly attended, Kennedy was chosen as the presidential candidate on the first ballot.

During several meetings in the months that followed, Dolly began to warm to Jack. He was good-looking, charming, and in some ways he reminded her of FDR. In October, he came to West Street to ask Dolly and Jimmy Wechsler for their editorial support. She told him that it was probably forthcoming but that she and Jimmy were upset by his hawkish remarks about China and were not happy with his choice of Lyndon Johnson as running mate. They talked about Jack's father and what a public liability he was to Jack's campaign. Dolly said that Joe had always been gracious to her, from their early days in Palm Beach to the present, when they had dinner together from time to time. Jack's noncommittal answer when she complimented Jackie, whom Dolly admired but barely knew, convinced her that he had little interest in his wife.

Obviously, the *Post* would endorse Kennedy in the presidential race. Richard Nixon, the Republican candidate, was not a plausible choice for liberal Democrats. Joe Kennedy took Dolly to dinner in December to thank her for the *Post*'s support of Jack, even if it had never really been in doubt. She was touched by how devoted Joe was to his children and remembered that, although he was known to be ruthless in business and in politics, she had always liked him better than his wife, Rose, who she thought was a social climber.

Although Dolly retained some reservations about Jack Kennedy's earlier politics, in the months after his election, she fell more and more under his spell. Wechsler, like many staunch liberals, had given his heart to Stevenson and was less receptive to the new president's charm.

Pete Hamill began working in the summer of 1960 on the night rewrite desk. Hamill also heard talk about how falling circulation was jeopardizing the *Post,* but he thinks that Kennedy's election put pressure on the editorial policy of the paper in another way. "I was only a kid, I had no access to the higher-ups," Pete says, "but I think Dolly understood, whether she could articulate it or not, that Wechsler's vision of how to put out a paper really worked when we were in opposition. If you had a Republican president and a Republican Congress, then Wechsler's liberal vision worked, as a kind of correction to all that. But when you had Jack Kennedy in the White House, there had to be an alteration. You can't use the same stance against somebody whose policies you generally accept, even if they didn't support him in the Democratic primary.

"So," Hamill believes, "in that sense, it wasn't that Wechsler was doing a bad job or anything, it was just that times were changing and the paper had to change with them."

Some interested parties at the paper, having noticed the accumulated tensions in the still close relationship between publisher and editor in chief, found ways to exploit them in their own interest. Without ever attacking Wechsler directly, Paul Sann and some of his allies had been lobbying for a shift in editorial policy away from what they considered too heavy an infusion of politics into daily news coverage. They began to second-guess the stories Jimmy assigned and to mock his propensity for crusading series. Jerry Tallmer says, "Sann and Davis,* and some of their acolytes, they were all liberal, but they were dismissive of Jimmy. He represented knee-jerk left, bleeding-heart politics to them. . . . They were very anti anything that could be construed as liberal, knee-jerk. They had a tough guy attitude, like *The Front Page.*"

Sann and company slowly planted in Dolly's mind the notion that the editorial policy of the paper should be shaken up. They never suggested abandoning its defining liberal politics—she would not have tolerated that—but they implied that readers would respond to news coverage that placed more emphasis on flashier stories. Judy Michaelson, who was Wechsler's assistant before she became a reporter, says, "The conflict was, should we do crusading stories about slumlords or do we do tabloid journalism? And Sann was a true tabloid journalist in the best sense of the word."

Wechsler told his friend Irwin Ross that he knew that Dolly was becom-

---

*Alvin Davis, who had been at the paper since 1942, was promoted from night managing editor to managing editor in August 1960. At the time, he and Sann were close friends as well as colleagues.

ing critical of his editorial judgment. He felt that he was no longer free to follow his own instincts. Although he was certainly aware that Sann disagreed with some of his decisions, he did not indict Paul for politicking against him. Jimmy may not even have understood how threatened his position was. Jesse Simons, who was in charge of labor relations at the *Post,* says, "Wechsler had no time for office politics. He was always reading, thinking, writing. Sann was the mechanic of the paper. He took care of all the crap."

Not every observer saw the conflict as being a high-minded debate about journalistic values. Another reporter who was put off by both men's behavior says, "When Sann and Wechsler began their feud—and once they got Dolly involved with their childish bullshit—it was like a fight between two little bad boys. They would fight and then one of them would go tell her about it; they ratted each other out. These two putzes would run to her and get her involved instead of sitting down and working it out among themselves."

In retrospect, the long-term financial peril of the paper made it probable that Dolly would want to make some significant change and that Sann would win out. The problem was brought to a head by the circulation figures for the summer of 1961. Summer is always the slow time for newspapers. Many readers are on vacation; aside from July Fourth, there are no major holidays to stimulate advertising promotions. Predictably, average daily sales drifted downward: 335,961 in April, 329,467 in May, 318, 572 in June, and then, horribly, 291,771 in July and 290,972 in August. In each of these months, the average circulation was between five thousand to seven thousand copies fewer than it had been the year before.

When Wechsler returned from his vacation in late August, Dolly called each man separately into her office and told him her decision. There was to be a formal division between the news department and the editorial pages. Sann would take sole charge of the city room, and Jimmy would be responsible for the editorials. She told them she had made her judgment strictly on economics and gave neither of them much chance to discuss it. Dolly did not like scenes.

Wechsler had tried to schedule more attention-grabbing stories. Ed Kosner, assistant night editor at the time, remembers being assigned to an exposé on sex in the city high schools. But readership did not rebound. "Jimmy tried all kinds of stuff," says Kosner. "He was a good man, a very serious guy. My sense was that Dolly loved him, and yet it had gotten to the point that the paper was barely viable commercially. And that was the main reason for the shift."

Dolly cared about Jimmy Wechsler. He was her conscience, her confidant, the man who had supported and guided her when she shucked Ted Thackrey and began to run the paper herself. Sally Kramarsky says, "Mother adored Jimmy. She really did love him." Along with Sally's father, George Backer, Jimmy was probably Dolly's most important political mentor.

But Dorothy Schiff cared more about the *Post* than she did for any man. Just as she had jettisoned George Backer in favor of the more tough-minded Ted Thackrey, she moved James Wechsler from center stage in favor of the more tough-minded Paul Sann. On September 5, 1961, the *Post* announced that, beginning on September 18, Wechsler would continue as chief editorial writer and editor of the editorial page, and he would continue to be identified on the masthead as editor. In addition, Jimmy would produce a signed column four days a week for the daily magazine. He would spend some time in Washington, DC, to fill the gap in national political coverage created while William Shannon, head of the Washington bureau, went on sabbatical to write a book. In order to take on this extra work, Dorothy was quoted as saying, "Mr. Wechsler has relinquished his administrative duties in the news department."

This was a rather delicate way of saying he had been kicked upstairs. (Literally, as he was to move from the city room on the second floor to new offices on the fourth floor.)

Dorothy also said that she planned to assume a larger role in the editorial operations of the paper, in association with Paul Sann, who continued as executive editor, and Alvin Davis, who continued as managing editor. Given the parlous condition of the *Post*'s finances, it is no surprise that Dolly did not see fit to reward Sann with a raise beyond his current salary of $33,000 in recognition of his new responsibilities. Nor was Jimmy given a financial consolation prize. Under his two new contracts—one for services as editorial page editor and one for his column—his total remuneration also would be $33,000, what he had earned before.

Wechsler was a good soldier. Two days after the announcement of the shift, he wrote a memo to Dolly summarizing a talk he'd just had with a reporter from *Time*. "I told him that you and I both felt that Shannon's leave of absence left a very big hole in the paper and also dramatized our feeling that the magazine needed something new. I told him that I was very flattered when you suggested that a column by me would be the best answer to the problem, that we had initially discussed my writing out of Washington but agreed that it was important that I continue to run the editorial page but that it would not have been mechanically practical to do so from Washington. . . . I put the whole matter affirmatively, and it will be interesting to see how they manage to fog it up."

Time chose to ignore the story altogether. *Newsweek* was more direct, reporting, "There were rumors around town that Wechsler was kicked upstairs, or demoted, depending on your point of view. The gossip had it that advertisers disliked Wechsler's persistent crusades against such targets as nonunionized hospitals and tenement landlords. There were tales of an inside campaign for Wechsler's removal, waged against a background of shouting matches between Mrs. Schiff and top editorial writers at The Post."

When Dorothy Schiff pasted this item in her scrapbook, she wrote "!" in the margin.

Judy Michaelson says, "The change may have been good for the paper, but, at least at first, it was bad for morale, because you should never be in the position that you think you could be demoted. Because it was a demotion for Jimmy. And that was the problem. He went from being boss to not being boss. And then Sann was never named editor in chief, he was just executive editor, and that rankled Sann. So Jimmy had the editorial page, and he had the stature that Paul didn't have. So they each came away with something, but neither of them was content."

"Dolly did a shrewd thing," says Irwin Ross, "when she gave Jimmy a column. He had great aspirations for that column initially." It probably kept him at the *Post* despite his demotion. "He was forty-five years old," says Ross. "He was presumably very marketable. But what could he have done instead? Go to the *Times,* where he'd have been one of many and probably wouldn't have gotten a column? Gone to *Time,* where he'd also have been one of the crowd and disagreed with the politics to boot?"

Nancy Wechsler, Jimmy's widow, says that although her husband never complained publicly, he was wounded. "Jimmy wasn't thrilled. He was glad to have a column. But no, he wasn't thrilled. And Paul had more power at the paper now than Jimmy did. Jimmy had been the boss. Paul was a very good newspaperman, but he was not political. He was not an intellectual. He was a *Front Page* newspaperman in every way. The talent, the manner. He was a gambler, they lived in the Bronx and never moved. . . . Paul was an anti-intellectual in some sense."

In the city room not that much changed, and yet everything changed.

Sann had always been more concerned with the nuts and bolts of getting out the paper each day, so his activities looked much the same, although his underlying authority was accentuated. Wechsler remained involved with policy issues, but his physical removal from the scene made manifest the degree to which he was shorn of power.

Dorothy seldom second-guessed herself. At least not in public. She was used to summoning and dismissing people—husbands, lovers, and employees. Even so, she recognized that she needed Jimmy Wechsler and owed him some respect. A week after the changes went into effect, she sent him a personal note reminding him how much she valued his judgment and how much she respected him as a journalist. It was as close as she came to acknowledging that she had hurt him.

People began jockeying for position within the new regime. There had always been reporters who were closer to one man than the other. Some loyalties were rewarded, some were punished. Some people tried to sidestep the whole campaign.

Judy Michaelson says, "I was a brand-new reporter, I had barely passed my tryout, and Ed Kosner stopped me one day, and said, 'So who are you loyal to?' Almost like a challenge. What side are you on? And I said like, 'Why do I have to choose?' "

Some reporters felt they could never be part of Sann's team. Bernie Bard had been hired by Wechsler to produce a daily "school" page—a full page of copy covering the New York City public schools—in a vain effort to increase circulation among teachers and other school officials. He was aware that Sann disliked him. "Sann greatly resented Wechsler and resented anybody he viewed as one of Wechsler's boys. So for whatever reason, either because Wechsler hired me, and I admired him, or because I was under the aegis of Wechsler and reported to him, or for some other reason that I don't know about, Sann took a dim view of me. Maybe he took a dim view of education in general, but I was never one of his boys."

The school page proved ineffective, and Bard, who stayed at the paper on the education beat, solved the problem of Sann's animosity by remaining out of sight. He spent most of his time at the Brooklyn headquarters of the Board of Education and came into the city room only on occasion.

Ed Kosner also felt a chill. "I think Paul thought I was like a college punk.

I wasn't one of his guys. He liked the tougher guys." Another reporter says, "I had little respect for Sann. He walked around in his cowboy boots and a cowboy belt. I didn't have any regard for him as a great thinker, or as a committed liberal. Maybe he was a great editor. But I was never one of his guys."

Nora Ephron, who worked at the *Post* in the mid-sixties, says, "The people who made their way there, with some exceptions, were people Sann could feel comfortable with and could, if not control, not be threatened by. Again, with exception, they were not necessarily well educated." But she cautions, wisely, "You have to be very careful not to apply retroactive standards. The *Times* had gentlemen journalists, and they may have had a thing about people being college graduates. But the *Post* and the *News,* none of them did. So what if Paul was not looking for people with breadth of knowledge? Why should he have? That isn't what makes a good newspaperman, or certainly a good tabloid journalist.

"I think the real question was, could you be a good tabloid journalist?" says Ephron. "And not anything else. I think Paul probably was anti-intellectual, but there was no reason then and there is no reason now to equate education with skill. I mean, all this education and graduate school and so on doesn't make people better journalists." But it doesn't make them worse journalists, either, and yet on the whole, Sann was wary of them.

Many top investigative reporters who had been Wechsler favorites were relegated to lesser stories or moved on to other jobs. Irwin Ross, who had written some of the most thoughtful series on politics and political trends at home and abroad, found refuge at the *Reader's Digest.* Within a little over a year, Kosner would leave for *Newsweek.* William Shannon came back to the *Post*'s Washington bureau after his sabbatical but left to join the editorial board of *The New York Times* in 1964. Joe Kahn stayed around but found less support for his stories in the new regime. He began to spend more time drawing and painting.

Bill Haddad took a break from journalism. Even before the shift in leadership at the *Post,* Haddad was caught up in the excitement of Jack Kennedy's call to service. Haddad took a leave of absence to assist Sargent Shriver in founding the Peace Corps. At first he planned to be gone a few months, but in May 1961, he asked Wechsler for an extension of his leave because there was such important work to be done in Washington.

Dolly told Jimmy that she felt Haddad was disloyal. She believed passionately that newspapers played as vital a role in safeguarding American freedoms as the government did. She understood that joining the Kennedy administration was a glamorous option for Haddad, but she thought he was abandoning an equally important career, in which he had just begun to make his mark. If too many young liberal journalists were seduced by Washington, she mused, what would become of papers like the *Post*?

Haddad tried to keep his options open. He visited Paul Sann in September, soon after Sann replaced Wechsler, to say that he would like to come back in several months. He asked Paul if the paper was still committed to the kind of hard-hitting investigations that he and Joe Kahn had done in the past. Sann—who considered Haddad one of Jimmy's boys—answered affirmatively, but his memo recounting the conversation to Dolly belittled Haddad's presumptuous tone.*

For reporters who attracted Sann's attention, it was another matter. They loved his swagger, his Bronx smarts, his tough-guy attitude, and most of all his support for their work. Even when Wechsler was on top, Sann handled most assignments; his was the final editorial word on most stories. Although his prose often mimicked the overripe rhetorical style of his heroes Damon Runyon and Ring Lardner, he was considered by most of his colleagues to be a cleaner, crisper writer than Jimmy. And he enjoyed promoting the careers of the young guys who mirrored his image.

Pete Hamill was the paradigmatic Sann protégé. Pete was the son of a longshoreman from Brooklyn. He'd spent some time in Mexico. Working as a graphic artist, daydreaming about a possible career as a cartoonist, Hamill wrote a letter on impulse to Wechsler, who was impressed enough to give him a tryout as a reporter. Although Pete's politics were as left-liberal as those of anyone on the paper, his real strength as a writer would be his natural feel for the city and its people. He soon caught Sann's eye.

Hamill says, "I loved Sann. He was exactly what I thought a newspaperman should be like. . . . I think he looked at me, and said, 'I can make something out of this dumb Mick.' Because he saw the same thing—that I loved doing it, that I wasn't there to get a parking spot. And I reminded him of himself. I think he had a genius for discovering talent.

"I think Dorothy Schiff trusted him for his tabloid sense. He came off the

*In March 1962, Haddad formally resigned. In the fall of 1963, he returned to New York to work for his father-in-law's paper, the *Herald Tribune*. He has since continued to move back and forth between journalism and public service.

streets of the city, loved the city. He knew the city in a way she never could know the city. She couldn't begin to understand what he knew, so she trusted him. . . . She hired the best guy she could get and let him do it. Within budget constraints, and everything else."

Sann and his assistant, Al Davis, taught Hamill how a newspaper works. "They always needed somebody who could make the pages sparkle," Pete says. "The reporters were basically doing double duty. They were reporters, but they also had to make the story happen. Most papers had the old system—a reporter on the street who'd call in to a rewrite man. So a lot of reporters on those papers couldn't write. There were so many people there it didn't matter."

At the *Post* the staff was small. Everyone had to do double duty. Sann showed the novices how to shape their copy. Years later at Sann's memorial service, Hamill paid tribute to his mentor's technique.

It is 6 in the morning and . . . the windows [are] open to the morning heat. Paul is the executive editor and he sits at his desk and lights a Camel and reaches for the coffee. "Copy boy!" he shouts, and the day's business has begun.

Typewriters are hammering against the deadline through the large dirty room and you can hear the Linotype machines grinding in the composing room. Paul Sann is reading the dupes, the carbon copies of the night's stories, with their familiar toll of mayhem, tragedy and disaster. He is writing the "wood," the large type used on Page One.

Then he looks up. He calls a reporter to the desk. "You can't write that, pal," he says. "This is a blur. Pure rewritese. What color was the dead guy's socks? Where did the bullets hit him? Where are the goddamned details?" . . .

"Keep it short," he would moan, while examining copy. "Give me active verbs. Don't use the same verbs all the time or the copy gets dull. The verbs are the Teamsters; they get the nouns to the market." He'd read some piece of copy and shake his head and peer over his glasses and light another cigarette and say: "What's the point? Why should anyone care? You gotta make us care, boy."

Day in and day out, the paper under Sann's leadership was actually little changed from before. There was a bit less emphasis on international news, although anything having to do with Israel continued to get heavy play. Standard tabloid series on "What Do College Students Think About Sex?" or "Secretaries of the Rich and Famous" appeared with regularity. The breakup of Governor Nelson Rockefeller's marriage and the disappearance of his son Michael in New Guinea held the front page for several days in late 1961. There may have been fewer muckraking attacks on local politicians, but series on "New York City's Traffic Court," "Working Women," and "What's Wrong with Our Hospitals?" or anything to do with the Kennedy family could just as easily have appeared in the Wechsler years.

The first significant action taken under the new regime was the October introduction of the stock market tables in the final editions of the daily paper. Dorothy tried without success to attract the so-called tombstone ads in which brokerage firms announced underwriting deals. Tombstone ads were a very lucrative business for the *Times,* the *Tribune,* and *The Wall Street Journal,* but the *Post* was never considered a player in that league. She pestered her brother, John Schiff, the senior partner at Kuhn, Loeb, to instruct his advertising department to consider the *Post.* She sent John a survey indicating that *Post* readers were as likely to be investors as readers of the *Times* and more likely than readers of the *Tribune* or the *World-Telegram.* He was not convinced.

Early in 1962, the balance sheet began to look better. A new $125,000 Scott press went into service, making it possible to expand the advertising-rich Wednesday and Friday editions to 112 pages because its greater speed enabled advertising pages to be printed in advance and then inserted into the Wednesday and Friday papers. Although the foreign language–record promotion did not lead directly to permanent circulation gains, it did prove a moneymaker for the paper, netting over $50,000 in royalties by the spring of 1962.

Sann made the sports section, which was strong to begin with, even better. Readers followed the competition between Mickey Mantle, who hit a career-high fifty-four homers, and Roger Maris, whose sixty-one home runs broke Babe Ruth's record. The Yankees went on to win the World Series in 1961, as they would the next year. In 1962, the *Post* ran a very successful promotion to welcome New York's new entry in the National League—the hapless but lovable Mets.

The advertising department made a noticeable effort to reach new customers. In mid-January 1962, a twenty-four-page supplement called the "Financial & Business Review" appeared. Filled with ads from financial institutions, it featured articles by Sylvia Porter and others explaining why the national economy was booming and why investments in stocks and bonds were a sensible option for middle-class families. In February, a thirty-two-page "Catering Guide" featured party plans, menus, and information on protocol and etiquette for formal entertaining. Although most of the advertisers proclaimed that they were kosher establishments, a sample wedding invitation welcomed guests to the marriage of Mary Grace Thurman, daughter of Mr. and Mrs. Joseph Thurman, at Trinity Church, Brooklyn.

Cumulatively, something was working. In May 1962, Dorothy Schiff announced proudly that the *Post*'s circulation for April—an average of 342,500 copies sold per day—was the highest it had been since 1958, and that daily and weekend advertising linage had reached a three-year high.

She announced a series of executive appointments at the paper, some of which were consolidations of the big changes made the year before. Dorothy herself assumed the title of editor in chief in addition to her previous designation as publisher. Wechsler would now be identified as editorial page editor rather than editor. She explained to Jimmy that she didn't think it was fair for him to be vulnerable to criticism for the paper's news coverage since he was no longer responsible for it. She did not explain to Sann why she chose the top title for herself rather than giving it to him.

Dorothy's daughter Sarah-Ann Backer Kramarsky joined the paper as special assistant to the publisher for editorial matters. Leon Cook, who had been with the *Post* since 1940, resigned as treasurer and comptroller. He was replaced as treasurer and assistant to the publisher in charge of production and purchasing by Robert Gray, who had been hired in January as mechanical supervisor and had quickly caught the publisher's eye.

The roles Dorothy envisaged for Sally Kramarsky and for Robert Gray were not spelled out. What was crucial was the development of an ever closer mutual dependence between Dorothy and Paul Sann. Theirs was not the same relationship as Dorothy had had with Jimmy Wechsler, which was based on a shared ideology and the sense of playing an important part in the development of postwar American politics. Sann's politics were local; his frame of reference was New York City and its sixth borough—the State of Israel. The city room was his preferred sphere of influence. To maintain his power there, he needed to maintain his good relations with the owner. Paul and Dorothy were already in the habit of conferring daily; now the memos and phone calls increased.

Paul's wife, Birdye, died in November 1961 after a short illness, and he soon moved from their home in the Bronx to an apartment in Greenwich Village. His daughter was married; his son was also on his own. Sann had a series of girlfriends, many of them young employees of the *Post*. His primary extracurricular activity was his gambling, which was more than an idle pastime. His son, Howard, remembers, "When I was young, if my mother didn't get the check from him as soon as he got home, it was gone. He and Ike Gellis, the sports editor—it was terrible. They just didn't stop. Horses, games, anything."

Sann used his vacation time to hit the casinos. He was well-known in Las Vegas and Atlantic City. Hotels frequently offered him free accommodations, a common device for luring regular losers, but he insisted on paying his way.

Most reporters and other colleagues considered Sann a good newspaper writer. He sought recognition of his skill from a wider audience, publishing books—on the Wild West, the twenties, professional basketball, and jazz—that reflected some of his eclectic interests. Dolly paid minimal attention to the books themselves, though she was always slightly testy about them. He had to reassure her that he had written them on his own time, and that if one of his books got a bad review it did not reflect badly on the *Post*. She seems not to have cared about the girls or the gambling.

Dolly and Paul settled into an intimate, bantering style. She felt comfortable with his swaggering, up-from-the-streets manner. Sally Kramarsky once told a friend that her mother said that Sann could use the word "fuck" with charm, although she usually detested hearing other people say it. Staff members sensed a warmth between them that transcended their inevitable spats. From time to time, something she did or said so riled him that he threatened to quit on the spot. Sometimes she took him seriously, sometimes not.

Whatever it was that led to one such blowup in June 1965 is lost to history, but Dolly dutifully made a note to herself that Paul had just called to say he was resigning—even though he had no job prospects and no savings—because she did not respect him as a first-rate editor. Dolly called him back to say that she would not accept the resignation, which mollified him.

Dolly tried to meet Sann's ego needs halfway. After the Newspaper Guild strike in 1965 that shut down all the *Post*'s competitors, she wrote him a note on her letterhead (not the usual yellow memo sheet), admitting that she rarely praised him and thanking him for having worked doubly hard to get out extra editions of the paper during the crisis. She asked him to tell everyone who helped him that she was grateful for their efforts.

Still, Paul sometimes felt unappreciated. At one point, he got huffy because Dolly told him that the circulation of the *Los Angeles Herald Examiner* was a tad higher than that of the *Post,* so the *Post* could not call itself the most successful evening paper in the country. He reminded her that by her own admission she was happy to criticize, not to praise. "The problem," he said, "goes even deeper. . . . Here is a senior editor, and some other editors, with one eye on the news and one eye on the phone and the inter-office mail. You understand, I am not saying that the penthouse is an unnecessary appendage here, nor that your judgment, as the editor-in-chief and owner, should not prevail. Nor that the sub-editors should not be wholly responsive to your wish. I am saying that the inhibitions in this particular kind of regime—for me, at least—have been massively imposing since 1961 and, indeed, more imposing as time unfolds."

She took his complaint seriously. She apologized for not giving praise more often, blaming it on her upbringing. She said that her mother had believed that compliments could weaken a child's character. But, she also said, the problem was solvable. She suggested that rather than "trying to second-guess the ogre in the penthouse," he or his colleagues should call and ask what she thought.

Sann had a special red phone by his bedside that was linked to the phone in Dolly's apartment and to the city desk, so he could be reached—or could reach her—at any time. Most of the time he ran the paper unimpeded by strictures from on high. Sometimes he vetoed an idea one of his editors or reporters proposed by saying, "The lady upstairs won't stand for it," when in fact he'd never bothered to find out if she would or wouldn't.

Dolly's discourse with Sann covered everything in the paper that interested her—the subjects of the weekly personal profiles, for example, or reports on medical breakthroughs. When she became fascinated with something that caught her eye, whether or not Sann's journalistic instincts agreed that it was newsworthy, he dutifully assigned a reporter to look into it. And frequently, it turned out she was right.

She did have her idiosyncracies, which Sann had to honor. Even after the release of the 1964 Surgeon General's Report linking cigarette smoking and the incidence of lung cancer, Dolly, who smoked at least one pack of Kools a day, continued to deny its validity. She frequently toyed with the notion that all cancers were psychosomatic. If the editors allowed a hint that there was a link between smoking and cancer to appear in the paper, they were immediately reprimanded. She sometimes justified herself by saying that she didn't want to offend the cigarette companies that advertised in the paper, but no one was fooled. In general, her internal moral compass, like Sann's, did not permit her to condone bending editorial policy to accommodate financial concerns.

A reporter named George Carpozi, who came to the *Post* in 1965, wrote to Sann praising the paper for its integrity in such situations. "The Post gave me basic training in areas I found totally lacking at the *Journal-American,*" wrote Carpozi. "At the J-A," he went on,

> editorial people were the advertising department's peons. We bowed to the pressures of red-ink figures. If a woman was stabbed in the sixth-floor toy department in Macy's, [the editor] would have us write that the poor creature was shivved on the Herald Square sidewalk. When Bernard Gimbel spoke at the Association of Commerce and Industry on some rattle-brained idea of his, we had to report the speech as the Second Coming. . . .
>
> So, when I came to the Post I found, very quickly, it didn't matter that Alexander's, our biggest advertiser, was in a jam for one thing or another. It was news and was played down the middle as such. And it saw the light of print on the Post's pages regardless of consequences. This then, is what I found about the Post—it had guts.

Although Dolly spent more time conferring with Sann, her involvement with Jimmy Wechsler did not cease. As in the past, they discussed editorials and editorial policy. They might discuss his column. If she disagreed with his viewpoint, she certainly told him, but she never vetoed an idea. Dorothy always believed that although the *Post* had the right to demand accuracy of its columnists, and to edit their copy for that purpose, it had no right to censure individual columns, which were the personal opinion of the writers. If too great a divide opened between the paper and the columnist, the proper recourse was to terminate the contract between them.

Dolly and Jimmy continued to chatter about their friends in liberal Democratic circles. They shared opinions on books and political developments. She included him in lunches with political leaders. On her part there was no change in the expectation of intimacy; whatever he thought, he didn't reveal.

The impact of the 1961 shake-up was undoubtedly momentous personally for all concerned—Dolly, Wechsler, Sann, and individual members of the news staff. In retrospect, the reshuffle probably mattered little to the fortunes of the paper. The *Post* did come back from the financial brink under Sann's guidance, although progress was gradual and never decisive. It would take external events to change the *Post*'s fortunes dramatically.

EIGHTEEN

"The Only Survivor"

With the *Post*'s leadership reshaped and the paper regaining solvency in 1962, Dorothy began to focus on increasing her role in New York's public life. She would succeed, not because of internal changes at the *Post* but as a result of a punishing strike that would shut down every general-interest paper in the city. Further labor strife would continue to weaken her competitors and strengthen her position in the afternoon field.

Although relationships between New York's newspaper owners and their unionized workers were often rancorous in the years following the war, and there were occasionally work stoppages at specific papers, the city's papers were not hit by the kind of paralyzing strikes that forced prolonged shutdowns elsewhere across the country.

This relative stability no doubt made it easier for the *Post* to sustain its editorial support for the surging postwar American labor movement: inveighing against the antiunion Taft-Hartley Act of 1947, applauding the significant gains in wages and benefits that union leaders delivered to their rank and file during years of successful negotiation with the leaders of the nation's industrial giants, supporting the purge of Communists from major union roles, and celebrating the triumphant merger of the AFL-CIO in 1955—which, in retrospect, was the high-water mark of American labor.

The first signs that the *Post* was going to have to give more thought to its relations with organized labor had come in the fall of 1953, when it was struck by one of the nine so-called mechanical, or craft, unions representing pressroom employees and the men who delivered the papers. Along with the Newspaper Guild, which represented reporters, secretaries, and clerks, the craft unions tried to present a consolidated front in their contract negotiations with the publishers.

That fall, the publishers thought they had avoided a strike when they had worked out an industrywide package that offered all union members a raise of $3.75 a week in wages and benefits, but the rank and file of the photoengravers' union refused to ratify the contract. They wanted more money and a reduction in their workweek from thirty-five to thirty-two hours. On November 23, the photoengravers struck the *Post,* the *Journal-American,* and the *Telegram.* Since other union members would not cross the picket lines, the strike shut down the three afternoon papers, which were perceived to be the weakest financially and therefore the most vulnerable to the loss of Christmas advertising and newsstand sales. The next day the *Times,* the *News,* and the *Mirror* halted publication in support of their fellow members of the Publishers Association. A day later, the *Tribune,* which did its photoengraving outside the city, joined the lockout on principle.

The strike was settled on December 8, and the papers resumed publication the next day. It appeared to be a victory for management. They had not budged on their offer of $3.75, and the question of a shorter workweek was deferred to a committee. A blizzard of last-minute holiday ads helped the publishers minimize their anticipated losses. Dorothy Schiff, accustomed to thinking of herself as labor's friend in the otherwise hostile publishers' camp, could not bring herself to view the matter solely as a question of dollars and cents. In her column later that month, Dorothy complained about labor ingratitude.

> The Post was terribly hurt, much more hurt than the other New York newspapers which were struck. These were only hurt in the pocketbook. . . . The Post was hurt in its heart.
>
> The Hearst-McCormick press has often sneered at people like us. They have called us do-gooders, fuzzy-minded liberals, bleeding hearts because of

our championship of the cause of the underdog. During the strike, when labor made no distinction between its friend and its foe, I began to think that these charges might be true.

For years I had been warned and even had concrete evidence of the fact that the labor bosses are utterly ruthless when they are out to do a job. It has been their strategy to pick the newspapers most sympathetic to labor to use as an instrument to set the scale for the entire industry.

They do this because usually these are the weakest papers financially, therefore least able to stand a strike. Why are liberal newspapers apt to be poor? Because many big advertisers are reluctant to help build a medium which they believe has an editorial policy adversely affecting their special interests. . . .

Fuzzy-minded idealist I may have been, or perhaps just a conceited fool. That is immaterial at this stage of the rough game. *I must confess I didn't think they would do it to a nice girl like me.* But they certainly did, as you may have noticed.

The publishers were all at fault, Dorothy granted, for not having seen the strike coming and not having found a way to prevent it. To be better prepared in the future, she turned to her then-new husband Rudolf Sonneborn for advice. He asked Sidney Orenstein, his labor lawyer, to examine the *Post*'s union contracts.

Orenstein says, "I found that in almost every area that counted—in severance pay, vacations, holidays—the *Post* had more onerous conditions in its Guild contract than any other paper. The *Post* had a very liberal orientation, and Jimmy Wechsler was Dorothy's confidant, and I guess they didn't pay much attention to their union negotiations."

Jesse Simons, who was the paper's in-house labor specialist, says that the *Post*'s generosity with the unions preceded the Schiff-Wechsler era. "The best contract the Newspaper Guild had was with the *Post*," says Simons. "They had negotiated it with David Stern. He gave away the store. And it cost the *Post* an enormous amount of money. They were pissing it away. We had a sick pay clause, unlimited coverage, no matter how long you were out. It was very costly if you had one or two of these people, at twenty-five grand a year, say, or two or three of them. We couldn't afford it.

"Our severance pay clauses with the Guild were also very, very onerous," says Simons. "We had no pension plan. Instead, we had the severance plan, and that was okay, but we paid more than anybody else. I think Stern was a very liberal guy and gave these things to the union because he believed they were right. I'm not saying they were wrong. But you're in business, and you have to compare yourself to the other papers. He should have said, 'Look, I'll give you whatever the other guys are getting.'"

At Sonneborn's request, Orenstein prepared a report, which Sonneborn took to Richard Manson, who was assistant publisher at the time. Orenstein says, "Manson said, 'Well, it's the relationship that we have with the unions that counts, not the printed word in the contracts, that's not as important.' And Rudolf said to him, 'How is it that during the strike in 1953, the *Post* was the only paper that wasn't permitted to print a Sunday edition?' Manson had no answer for that. I don't know the details, but somehow the other papers were allowed to print a Sunday edition, and the *Post*—which supposedly had these good relationships—was not. So with that, Rudolf asked me to meet with Mrs. Schiff and help her."

Independent of the biennial industrywide negotiations, Orenstein and Simons tried to level the *Post*'s playing field with the Newspaper Guild. Orenstein says, "Each contract period we attacked a particular section of the contract, and we succeeded to some degree. But it was not easy, believe me." He managed to negotiate a sick leave provision based on years of service, but the paper never achieved complete parity with its competitors.

"The union leadership could not get their membership to agree," says Simons. "Many of the Guild members were liberals. But they did not like Dolly, or they thought her pockets were deep enough. She was the rich lady upstairs. We tried to get them to agree to accept something like the *Daily News* clause, or the *Times* clause, and they'd just laugh." Dolly's supposition that the *Post*'s editorial policy trumped its unionized employees' financial interests was a fantasy.

Strikes were not undertaken lightly by the unions, especially since they frequently ended without any further concessions from management. Walking out meant that workers surrendered income during the holiday season when it was particularly nice to have some money in your pocket. Strike benefits varied from union to union, depending upon how much money the membership had authorized to be set aside from their dues. No matter how generous the benefits were, they seldom replaced a worker's salary.

Similarly, strikes were financially punitive to ownership, even if insurance reimbursed a portion of their losses. The newspaper industry is unique. Publishers cannot build up their inventory in anticipation of a strike, or go back afterward to catch up on unfilled orders. Some savings are achieved. There is no overtime, and newsprint and other materials can be stockpiled. But most fixed costs continue. Nonunion personnel must be paid, as must interest on loans. After publication resumes, advertisers may temporarily increase the amount of linage they buy to welcome back their shoppers, but the temporary hike in ad revenues seldom makes up for that which was lost.

The larger community suffers as well when a strike is prolonged. After a two-week shutdown late in 1958, the *Times* noted that Broadway shows were playing to much smaller audiences, and contributions to the *Times*'s year-end charitable drive, the Times Neediest Cases Fund, were running 25 percent below expectations.

Newspaper readers are usually loyal. During the 1958 strike, many New Yorkers said that although they followed the news on broadcast media, they missed their paper. Some readers, however, slowly switched their primary allegiance to radio or to local and network television. Many commuters began relying on suburban papers that, because they were nonunion shops, never stopped publishing. These were trends that would accelerate during the sixties and seventies.

Management and union leadership knew that negotiations in 1962 were going to be difficult. Since 1950, the publishers had established a pattern of working out details of new contracts with the Newspaper Guild, whose contracts expired on October 31. At the same time, a representative of the publishers was also in unofficial contact with the leaders of the craft unions, whose contracts were up on December 7. The publishers were adamant that every union accept the same package—the agreed-upon dollar amount by which they were willing to raise per capita remuneration for the following two years. Different unions might choose to configure the net amount in different ways—the basic wage hike, vacation time, sick days, for example. The publishers were willing to negotiate any or all of these variables as long as the total cost to them did not exceed the package.

The principle of the package was not at issue in the 1962 negotiations. The role of the Guild at the head of the union pecking order, however, was being challenged by Bertram Powers, the new head of the printers' union. Powers, who had been vice president of New York Local 6 of the International Typographical Union since 1953, became president in 1961.

Powers believed that the needs of the various unions diverged too much for a one-size-fits-all solution. He thought the Guild was too complacent in accepting what the publishers had to offer and that a more vigorous union needed to take the lead. "Different unions had different issues," says Powers. "The lower-scale, less-skilled unions—the drivers, the handlers, the pressmen—were interested in flat wage increases, but the group that I identified with were the engravers, ourselves, and the machinists and electricians. We wanted percentage increases."

Workers in the less-skilled unions drew a lot of overtime, working extra hours to earn extra income. The more skilled union members did not. The typographers' local limited overtime hours to spread the work around. Workers with steady jobs stepped aside for their unemployed union brethren when the call came to work more than forty-six hours a week.

"So our guys lived on scale," says Powers. "It was difficult. We weren't crying, but we weren't doing well. We were falling behind year after year. So I decided that the only way to break the pattern would be for me to hit the street before the Newspaper Guild did. That's what I did in '62."

Critics pointed out at the time that Powers was a bit disingenuous in his explanation; no contract was signed with the Guild until the other union chiefs had agreed in principle to its provisions. His enemies claimed that his was simply a power grab—that Bert wanted to impress his membership with his aggressiveness on their behalf. No one doubted Powers's quick intelligence, his obvious charm, or his deep understanding of the immediate and long-term issues at stake in the newspaper business. What caused controversy were his methods. Walter Thayer, publisher of the *Herald Tribune,* said of Powers during the course of the ensuing negotiations, "He's serious, sincere, dedicated—and wrong."

Powers held several meetings with Amory Bradford, the vice president and general manager of *The New York Times,* during the summer of 1961. Bradford had been chosen by the Publishers Association to head their negotiating committee, although he was known to have an abrasive manner and a short fuse. Bradford, who came from a middle-class Boston family, had adopted patrician affectations that did not sit well with the self-educated Boston Irishman, Bert Powers. Some observers think their efforts to find a common ground for negotiations were fated to fail because Powers, who refused to tell Bradford any specific numbers that he could live with, was not negotiating in good faith.

Sidney Orenstein, Dolly's lawyer, who admired both men, says, "In my view of things, Bert Powers had arranged *not* to settle in order to become top dog among the craft unions. And the proof of it was that at the end of [months of talk], there were something like eighty-six unresolved issues. And anyone that's interested in settling, you get down to a few. It wasn't just a question of the publishers refusing to make any moves. We didn't know what moves were called for, because the union would not discuss it."

After the pay package, the chief unresolved issue was a tiny first step toward what both sides knew would be a big item in the future—automation. Management, particularly at the *Times* and the *Tribune,* wanted to use teletape fed them by the Associated Press to set their stock market tables. They promised not to lay off any of the typographers whose work would not be needed. The union responded by asking for a share of the money that would be saved by automation, but the papers were not ready to accede to this. Both sides were wary of establishing far-reaching precedents.

Despite the bleak prospects, as midnight approached on December 7, Bradford assured the assembled publishers that Powers did not have the guts to call a strike. The class-based animosity between the two men blinded Bradford's judgment. Powers saw things more clearly. He had already explained to the president of his international union that there would probably be a strike and that it might be a long one. In anticipation, he had been building a strike fund of more than $1 million, which would make it possible for his men to stay out a long time if necessary.

The printers struck the *Times,* the *Daily News,* the *Journal-American,* and the *Telegram,* which were presumed to be the best-heeled papers. The other members of the Publishers Association—the managements of the *Post,* the *Mirror,* the *Tribune,* and two Newhouse-owned papers on Long Island—locked out their employees in support. Powers says, "I thought from a public relations standpoint, it would be good if I struck some and the others locked us out, and therefore I wouldn't be solely to blame for the news blackout. But that didn't happen. I was still blamed."

The Christmas season passed. The New Year began. Weeks dragged by, and there was no progress. Dorothy Schiff was worried about how long her paper could continue to sustain losses. She felt that the other publishers were dismissive of her ideas and her concerns. On January 21, Dorothy walked out of yet another meeting. She called Mayor Wagner to say she wanted to discuss the matter with him. He invited her to Gracie Mansion, his official residence, where labor leaders were gathered on a similar mission.

Accompanied by Sidney Orenstein, Dorothy talked with Bert Powers and his colleagues for several hours, ending up over dinner at a nearby German restaurant. The conversation was pleasant. Dorothy got the feeling that Powers was brighter than most of the men on her side and had thought carefully about the larger issues on the table. The evening stayed in her mind.

A few days later, the mayor was having lunch with Theodore Kheel, a New York labor lawyer, whose reputation as a mediator was already well established. Wagner asked him for help. Kheel didn't know much about the newspaper business, but he knew how to get rival parties to work together, and he figured he could make some progress in two or three days.

At that point, the employers' committee consisted of Bradford, whom Kheel soon booted out, to everyone's relief; Walter Thayer, publisher of the *Tribune;* Jack Flynn, publisher of the *News;* and Dorothy Schiff, who had fought her fellow bosses to be included. At first Kheel's presence reenergized the proceedings, but ultimately nothing substantial was achieved.

By the end of February, Dorothy had had enough. The publishers' strike insurance of $11,000 a day had long since expired. On February 6, the printers' international authorized an assessment to be paid by its members across the country. Payments from the collected funds, their own strike reserve, and the New York State unemployment insurance they were now eligible to receive brought the weekly income of the members of Powers's local to $120, not much less than their base pay of $141. Dorothy could not imagine anything that would induce them to give up their fight.

She was annoyed by the patronizing attitude she felt the other publishers and their representatives—all men—exhibited toward her and Orenstein. Although her colleagues had finally appointed her to the executives' committee, they rejected her demand that Orenstein join labor specialists from other papers on a new negotiating committee. Walter Thayer told Dorothy, "There is no rule of the Publishers Association that the *Post* has to be represented on every subcommittee."

To which she replied, "There is no rule that says the *Post* has to be a member of the Publishers Association!" and announced she was leaving.

Dorothy later admitted that her decision had been long in coming. The rejection of her request was just the final blow. The other publishers were furious with her, but she was unmoved. She knew exactly what she wanted to do next. She called Bert Powers to tell him she was going to resume publication.

To her surprise, he said he would not let his members return to work. Dorothy was "flabbergasted." She surmised that he feared advertisers would boycott the *Post* if it seemed to be double-crossing the other papers, and that he wanted to protect her from that eventuality. After some discussion, Powers backed down and agreed that the paper should appear.

The other publishers had asked her as a parting favor to try to find out what Powers's rock-bottom settlement figure would be. She failed, but she didn't really care. She told him that she was willing to pay her union employees at the old rate until a settlement was worked out, which she would go along with.

Powers says, "That was the deal. She would accept the settlement. In fact, if she had had a problem with that, if she had wanted something special—if she'd said, I can't afford X and Y—I would have recommended that we negotiate with her."

The next day, February 28, at a press conference with Bert Powers at her side, Dolly announced that the *Post* would resume publication on March 4. She said, "Bert told me to hold a press conference at the *Post* to announce resumption of publication, so I did. I didn't know how you hold a press conference, but he told me. I'm terribly shy, but he gave me strength to do it."

She was not really that naïve. Lisa Schiff, the wife of Dolly's nephew David, recalls an urgent phone call on the eve of the press conference. "She called me one night. 'Lisa, this is a business call.' 'Okay.' 'Do you have a Banlon dress that's kind of ugly?' I said, 'That's remarkable. I must have a closet full of them! Why are you asking me this? This is insulting, for God sake! May I ask why you need a Banlon dress?'

"She said, 'I have to go on television with Bert Powers. I have to plead why the *Post* cannot afford to continue to take this strike, and why I'm pulling out of the Publishers Association. And I have to look poor and unattractive!'

"I said, 'Thank you for asking me what I have.' She said, 'I didn't mean it that way.' 'Of course you meant it that way! I happen to think my clothing's okay. But I will look in my closet and call you back.' And I called back and said, 'The best I can do is a Pucci that David doesn't like. Will that do?'

" 'No. No,' said Dolly. 'Even at his worst, Pucci always looks expensive. I'll find somebody else. I'll ask somebody on my staff at the paper.'

"I said, 'Dolly, don't you dare. I don't think you should do that.' She said, 'Well, I have to get hold of a dress.'

"I watched the news conference. She had on a rag like you wouldn't believe. God knows where she got it. And she's crying. She'd told me that she was going to cry! David and I were both hysterical. Seeing how Dolly looked. She looked terrible! Terrible!

"Her hair was perfect, though."

The other publishers were outraged. Marian Heiskell, widow of Orvil Dryfoos, the publisher of the *Times,* remembers that "Dolly was a traitor as far as the newspaper people were concerned. Oh, sure. At the time, it had a terrible effect, because if one gave in, it raised the question, were the rest going to cave? It was a traitorous act, and it certainly prolonged the strike. It must have."

Kheel says that while the others were quick to berate her, they were being unfair. "They thought that she was the equivalent on their side of a strike-breaker. They believed she undermined their position." Did she? "No, not really," he admits. "Well, she did a little bit psychologically, because she broke ranks, though she didn't make a deal. If she had made a settlement with Powers to break that package—that would have been very serious. Psychologically that she broke ranks was an irritant to them, but it was not all that important."

In addition to saying she had been insulted by her colleagues, Dolly explained her change of heart as being responsive to the needs of all her employees. Powers thinks this was true. "She really was pro-labor," he says. "And she knew that in the long run, her interests were not the same as the other publishers. They weren't going to protect her. And she was debating going back a long time before she did it. She used to say, 'I know I shouldn't publish, but . . .'"

The *Post* appeared on the newsstands on March 4 with a business-as-usual front-page headline, "Auto License Boost Is Dead," and a reminder that this was the last day to see the *Mona Lisa* at the Metropolitan Museum of Art. On page 3, a brief statement from Dorothy Schiff thanked everyone who had expressed gratitude that the *Post* was resuming publication and hoping that the other papers would soon be able to follow.

In their absence, the *Post* made hay. For the duration of the strike, the paper's print run was six hundred thousand copies daily—nearly twice the pre-strike average. Byron Greenberg, the circulation manager at the time, says, "We made our bones in 1963. We did not have proper production capabilities. So we were running those presses from the time I walked in in the morning until sometime in the evening when I finally notified the press foreman that that's enough."

Advertising sales were brisk. The big department stores like Macy's withheld their ads, declining to support one paper to the potential detriment of the others. Discount stores like EJ Korvette, Alexander's, S. Klein, and other retail merchants, supermarkets, theaters, and restaurants rushed to reestablish rapport with their customers. Every edition of the paper ran the full ninety-six pages, and nearly 60 percent of the content was advertising. Several reporters and advertising salesmen had been working on interim papers that had sprung up during the strike, but all were happy to go back to their regular jobs.*

After Dorothy broke ranks—but not because of it—things began to move fast. Elmer Brown, Powers's boss and friend, was upset by the drain on his members' finances and concerned, too, that the strike was giving his union a bad reputation. He came to New York and, within a week, worked out a deal with Kheel behind Powers's back. The package would be $12.68 a week to be phased in over two years. The common expiration date of all the new contracts would be two years from the date of signing. The union would get its requested thirty-five-hour week, and the New York and American stock exchange tables could be set from teletape, with the formula for dividing the savings to be determined by a labor-management committee. It took Powers a while to swallow his pride, but Brown persuaded him that this contract delivered all the major victories he had sought. Following the lead of Local 6, every union, including the Newspaper Guild, soon ratified the deal. On April 1, after 114 days, the strike/lockout was over.

Not all readers resumed their regular habit. In a survey that had alarming implications for the future of the industry, journalism professor Penn Kimball discovered that, since his previous survey four years earlier, a number of readers had replaced their loyalty to newspapers in general with a reliance on television and radio.†

By the middle of April, Byron Greenberg reported to Dorothy that her competition was suffering. The six city papers that had resumed publication at the beginning of the month saw their combined circulation drop by more than

---

*Most replacement papers, like the *New York Standard,* were thin, cobbled-together sheets that disappeared as soon as the strike was settled. However, *The New York Review of Books,* founded by Jason and Barbara Epstein, Robert Silvers, Elizabeth Hardwick, and Robert Lowell to fill the void left by the absence of the book sections of the *Times* and the *Tribune,* was so popular that it continued publication.

†It was only partly coincidental that the *Post* introduced a new eight-page television section with full listings, articles, and columns as an addition to its regular sixteen-page weekend magazine as of April 15.

five hundred thousand copies daily. The *Post*'s afternoon rivals were badly hit. The *Telegram* had lost about seventy thousand readers, making its circulation roughly the same as the *Post*'s. Things were even worse at the *Journal-American*. Although the Hearst paper still led afternoon sales with just over five hundred thousand daily customers, that represented a drop of about one hundred thousand since the comparable period in 1962. The *Times* and the *Tribune* each retrieved revenue by raising their daily newsstand price from five to ten cents. The *News* held fast at five cents, which forced the *Mirror* to do the same.

In October, the Hearst Corporation closed the *Mirror*. Though the paper still had the second highest circulation in the country after the *News*, it was reported to have lost as much as $2.5 million each year since 1960.

The *Post*'s circulation gradually slipped back to just above prestrike levels, which was something of a victory compared with the competition. Although the other publishers continued to think of her as a traitor, Dolly found herself a new pal in the industry.

Bert Powers says, "When the strike was settled, we continued to be friends. My wife and I spent many hours drinking wine with Dorothy in her penthouse and going to restaurants and so forth.

"Once I was there alone. I lived in Massapequa at the time, and it was a long trip. And she said, 'Why don't you stay here? There's nothing wrong with that.' And I said, 'I know. But I'm not going to.' I said, 'You know, Dorothy, if my wife came home one day and said she had stayed with the publisher, and nothing happened, I don't think I would accept it. And I don't think she would accept it.'

"Dorothy was flirtatious. Yeah, she had a lot of husbands. And I knew that. That doesn't mean she had any ideas. I think she was just being kind. But that never happened."

Friendship aside, Dorothy and Bert Powers remained opponents at the bargaining table. Ted Kheel recalls a typical interchange between them. "Bert is very atypical for a union leader. He's polite. He's stubborn, too, but he will listen, and he doesn't interrupt. He waits till you finish, and then he simply says, 'No.' And he doesn't offer any explanations.

"We were in her apartment on Sixty-fourth Street, and she wanted a concession from him. She would say, 'Bert, we liberals have to stick together.' Then she explained what she wanted and why. And went through all the reasons why she should get a concession. She's talking away, and Bert is listening. And she finishes, and he says, 'No.'

"And she'd start all over again. You know, 'We liberals, Bert,' and so forth. She goes through it again, and she gets to the end, and he says, 'No.' And that was that."

The concession Dorothy wanted had to do with automation—the issue that was swept under the rug during the 1962–1963 negotiations. When the time came to renew the contracts, automation could no longer be ignored. Most papers were already setting stock tables with tape, and the *Times* and the *Daily News* had been bargaining with Local 6 since the summer of 1964 about adding more automated typesetting machines. It was estimated that the *Times* had saved about $70,000 per year and the *Tribune* about $40,000 since the experiment had begun. The union asked that the papers pay a percentage of such savings into a fund for workers who would be displaced.

The atmosphere was so charged that by mid-March 1965, the publishers broke off talks with Powers altogether and turned instead to hammering out a deal with the other unions. On March 31, on the eve of the deadline, they settled on a package of $12 a week in wages and benefits, once again deferred a formula for automation compensation, and agreed to keep publishing without a contract until several disputed items were resolved.

While these issues were being fought over, Dorothy moved ahead with an automation experiment. Without consulting Powers, the *Post* leased a composing room computer—IBM's 1620 Model 10—which could feed six hundred lines of text per hour, three times the rate of an experienced linotype operator. The computer was not the most expensive state-of-the-art machine, but it was adequate for the needs of the cash-conscious *Post*.

The paper had stipulated that the computer was acquired for training purposes only, but on June 22, again without union approval, Dorothy insisted that it be used to set copy for the late morning edition of the paper. When the union typographers refused to cooperate, she fired them. Local 6 shop stewards started to call everyone off the job. Bert Powers happened to be in the composing room on union business at the time.

Powers says, "It was about noontime. I saw her coming along with the top superintendent. And I said, 'Dorothy, you're making a mistake. Wait till the market closes at three o'clock. Then you'll have your plates on the press, and you'll run. People won't be angry buying the *Post* and not getting the final market.' And she said to the guy, 'Is he right?' And he said, 'Yeah.' So they changed the deadline.

"I didn't want to hurt her or the paper unnecessarily. And that was the kind of relationship we had. She was forcing my hand, but at least I could save her some trouble."

The strike lasted one day. When publication was resumed, the new computer sat idle until the lease ran out. Murray Kempton, temporarily working at *Telegram,* said "Mrs. Schiff, as an apostate from the Publishers Assn., seems to have expected more tolerance from Bert Powers, although she really should have known that he wouldn't lower the overtime scale to help St. Francis print the Canticles."

Despite the failed automation experiment, things were definitely looking up. The paper showed a modest profit in 1963; losses from the two-month strike cut into but did not erase all the gains made during the month that the *Post* had virtually the entire New York newspaper audience to itself. In 1964 the corporation showed a modest profit. 1965 was even better. At the end of the year, circulation and advertising revenues were at five-year highs. And true prosperity was just around the corner.

On March 21, 1966, one of the *Post*'s afternoon competitors disappeared. The owners of the *Herald Tribune,* the *Journal-American,* and the *World Telegram* announced a merger. The new corporation would publish two daily papers—the *Herald Tribune* in the morning and an afternoon paper to be called the *World Journal*—as well as a Sunday paper to be known as the *World Journal and Tribune.*

A major concern was what would become of the fifty-seven thousand current employees of the three existing papers. The newspaper unions took the position that their contracts were nullified by the merger, that they would have to negotiate new agreements with the new entity, and that elaborate severance and buyout provisions were high on the agenda. For a time it looked as if new contracts would be agreed upon, but these were false hopes. On August 13, Matt Meyer, the former president and business manager of the *Telegram,* who was head of the new combine, announced that the morning *Herald Tribune* would never appear, though he still had plans for the afternoon and Sunday papers. Finally, on September 12, the *World Journal,* referred to as the Widget, made its debut, followed five days later by its Sunday sibling.

The Wall Street Journal predicted that the new arrival would be a success:

Several ad agency executives stressed that there is a need for an afternoon paper with a broader appeal than the New York *Post.* The *Post,* the only other

general-interest afternoon paper published in Manhattan, appeals largely to
a liberal, predominantly Jewish audience. During the long closedown, the
Post picked up popular columnist Murray Kempton from the defunct *World-
Telegram* but did little to expand its news coverage and diversify its features.
Had it done so, it would have laid the groundwork for permanently keeping
more readers and advertisers than it now will, the reasoning goes.

On the eve of the Widget's appearance, Dorothy asked her lawyers if they
should seek an injunction against it on grounds that it violated antitrust regulations. Morris Abram, the partner at Paul, Weiss who was now her most active legal adviser, suggested that they do nothing. Probably the paper would
fail on its own merits.

Within a week, Abram was proved prescient. The new paper was fatally
flawed. Byron Greenberg reported that the Widget was having trouble getting its Wall Street closing edition out, while the last edition of the *Post* was
clearly identified as having final market figures. Loyal readers of the *Telegram*
and the *Journal-American* did not automatically transfer their affections to
the newcomer. Newsstand owners were already cutting back the number of
Widget copies they were willing to take.

Advertising linage was low to start and, ominously, did not expand much
during the usually lucrative Christmas season. Circulation barely rose above
what the *Journal-American* alone sold in its final days. The corporation was
said to be losing about $700,000 a month. After debating whether or not to
close the Sunday paper, the publishers decided instead to end the whole venture on May 5, 1967. The partners lost $10 million, in addition to their com-
bined liability of $7 million in severance obligations, before they called it
quits.

Dorothy Schiff and her *New York Post* had the afternoon to themselves. Operating its presses at top volume, the paper printed 700,000 copies in house,
plus another 140,000 on presses rented from Generoso Pope, the owner of
the uptown Spanish-language newspaper *El Diario/La Prensa*. Dolly began
thinking immediately of moving into bigger quarters. She told Byron Greenberg to find out from Matt Meyer which plant abandoned by the Widget
might be available.

It was a remarkable turnaround for the paper that had always been considered the weakest competitor in the New York market and a tremendous victory for its owner. Dorothy later told a reporter that the men who created and then killed the Widget had, by their actions, actually saved the *Post*. "But I don't think they saved me on purpose, do you?" she asked.

James Wechsler said that if you had prophesied in 1949, when Dorothy assumed active management of the *Post,* that hers would be the only afternoon paper left in town fifteen years later, you'd have been laughed out of the room.

Max Lerner exulted in his column, "By every rule of newspaper economics the *Post* should have been the one to fall by the wayside, yet today it is the only survivor in the afternoon field, and is going strong." The reason, Lerner said, was that the *Post* had a definite personality and a distinctive point of view. Its reader knew that the paper "cares, whatever his irritations with it can be."

Newsweek, picking up on Lerner's words, said, "Much of the warmth and most of the irritations flow directly from the *Post*'s indefatigable lady boss, Dorothy Schiff. At 64, Dolly Schiff rules the paper by an intensely personal formula of one part journalism, one part pap, and one part whim. 'She's a hopeless amateur,' bemoans one staffer. Yet the amateur has succeeded where well-heeled professionals failed utterly."

John Knight, head of the Knight-Ridder chain, wrote that the *Post* could play much more than its current marginal role "if only the unpredictable lady would supply the money and the imagination to expand its news coverage and make it a newspaper of wider general interest.

"At least," Knight went on, "the *Post* does have an editorial policy, an important element of newspapering which has somehow escaped the attention of its evening competitor, which was edited by committee."

Everyone seemed to agree that the *Post*'s strengths were its editorial stance, the range of interests of its columnists, outstanding sports coverage, a solid if not extensive financial section, and its muckraking reporters. The paper's quirky urban character and the idiosyncratic personality of its owner were praised or pilloried depending on the point of view of the commentator.

Dolly pasted most of the observations in her scrapbooks without comment. She said later that she had terrible panic attacks when she realized the immensity of her victory and the challenge it represented. Her doctor prescribed tranquilizers. But the real antidote for her anxiety was activity and the threat of competition. Her victory was made ever more sweet when the

Daily News and the *Times* dropped their plans to publish afternoon editions. When the *Times* announced it was leaving the field to her, she said simply, "I have great respect for the judgment of *The New York Times* and if they have come to the conclusion to stay out of the afternoon, they are probably right."

Some years later, Dorothy told Gail Sheehy that the fact that the other publishers were often contemptuous of her had worked out in her favor. " 'All the men were team players,' " Sheehy quoted Dolly as saying. "And that's not how she ever thought of herself. 'I think the other publishers, the ones who gave up, would have been furious if I hadn't been a woman. I wonder if they would have left the evening field open to another man.' " Maybe it was better to lose to a woman than a man, especially if you could slyly deride her at the same time.

Her fellow publishers could no longer mock Dorothy for not making money. With the permanent disappearance of direct competition, the *Post*'s circulation during the period between 1966 and 1969 stabilized at about 700,000 copies of the daily paper and about 370,000 on weekends. Advertising revenues soared. The Post Corporation reported retained earnings of approximately $500,000 in 1966, $350,000 in 1967, and nearly $1 million in 1968.

After the demise of the Widget and the subsequent rise in the *Post*'s fortunes, Dorothy did not need to question every dime the paper spent. It remained to be seen how she would adjust to prosperity. Now that she was ruler of the afternoon, how would she manage her kingdom?

NINETEEN

Planning for the Future

Though Dorothy's Schiff's *New York Post* was perceived as only marginally viable until it outlasted its principal rivals in the mid-sixties, the ownership structure and organizational resources of *The Washington Post* and *The New York Times*—two newspapers that would epitomize journalistic distinction and sustained financial growth in the next decades—were not significantly different from that of the *New York Post*. They were both still paternalistic family-owned and operated businesses.

The New York Times Corporation was owned by the descendants of Adolph Ochs and led by men who married into the family. In pursuit of journalistic excellence, the Ochs-Adler-Sulzberger clan frequently ignored the bottom line. The paper maintained an expensive chain of foreign bureaus despite the cost, to ensure worldwide coverage of the news. The paper employed many more editors and reporters than others with a similar circulation. Often the newspaper lost money and was subsidized by the Times-owned paper mill.

Financial planning was rudimentary. The Times Corporation published its first financial report only in 1958 as part of a structural reorganization undertaken to ensure family control into the next generation. Even after the reorganization, the paper was still not a consistent moneymaker. The 114-day strike/lockout of 1962–1963 was punishing—the corporation absorbed nearly $4 million in losses in less than a year. When Arthur Ochs Sulzberger took over as publisher in May 1963, after the death of his brother-in-law Orvil Dryfoos, he doubled the newsstand price of the daily paper and began to impose fiscal controls. He trimmed the bloated management structure and insisted that, for the first time, each department of the paper prepare and live within an annual budget.

The Washington Post was also a family-controlled operation. Eugene Meyer, a successful businessman, had picked up the bankrupt *Post* at auction in 1933. Not until 1954, when Meyer bought the rival *Times-Herald,* did the *Post* begin to make any money. Meyer died in 1959. He left the paper to Katharine and her husband Phil Graham, who turned it into a corporation in which they owned all the stock. Phil had already invested in a new, modern plant, beefed up the news staff, and brought in a seasoned business manager named John Sweeterman to help him with financial decisions. The paper continued to be subsidized by the radio and television stations that Meyer and Graham invested in. In 1961, Graham engineered the purchase of *Newsweek,* which added two more radio stations to the corporate fold and brought with it another savvy manager, Fritz Beebe.

When Phil Graham died in 1963, leaving his widow, Kay, in control of the company, no one expected her to run it. However, Kay bided her time, consulted friends and experts, and retained corporate officers like Sweeterman and Beebe. In November 1965, she made her first dramatic move, dislodging many of Phil's pals in the editorial department and appointing Ben Bradlee managing editor.

Despite this clear signal that Kay Graham was going to make her presence felt, she was still perceived as a figurehead. Few people took a female CEO seriously. She once told a story that mirrored Dorothy Schiff's experiences. She was at a meeting with a group of other publishers—all men—when one announced that he was going to ask each of his colleagues for an opinion on the matter at hand. "I was thinking all the way around the table what I was going to say," Kay said, "and then he skipped me! He ended at my right."

Compared to Dorothy Schiff, Arthur Sulzberger and Katharine Graham were novices at their jobs, but they shared an attitude that Dorothy lacked: a clear sense that leadership of the papers they ran had been handed to them by their families as a sort of public trust, and that one of their primary responsibilities was to maintain the properties so they could be passed on in turn to their heirs.

Dorothy had no such heritage, no family training in stewardship, no instilled sense that publishing the *Post* implied an obligation to the greater community. Almost as soon as she acquired the *Post* in 1939, there were rumors that she was about to unload it. Such rumors persisted throughout the early postwar era. From time to time, Dorothy and Alicia Patterson of *Newsday* discussed merging their papers, but nothing ever came of these conversations. Alicia's husband, Harry Guggenheim, abhorred both women's politics, and he controlled the majority of *Newsday* stock. As late as 1962, Dorothy and Alicia returned to the topic, with the same result.

Occasionally buyers inquired if the *New York Post* was on the market. In 1961, Phil Graham had introduced Dorothy to Steven Smith, who was presumably sniffing around on behalf of his father-in-law, Joseph Kennedy. The Kennedys had heard talk that she was thinking of selling the paper, and they wanted to make sure that whoever bought it would keep it firmly in the Democratic camp. Dorothy authorized Simon Rifkind to say that she would listen to an offer of $15 million. It's not clear how she arrived at that figure.

Phil Graham enlisted Jimmy Wechsler to help move the deal along. Dolly confirmed Jimmy's feelings that while she had never really wanted to give up control of the paper in the past, she had to be mindful of the fact that she was fifty-eight and wouldn't be around forever. She was impressed with Smith, and she thought that maybe a younger publisher might be just what the paper needed. However, she wondered how the *Post* could possibly keep its independence—or the perception of its independence—if it became known that the Kennedy family were investors.

Wechsler suggested an alternate option: a group of Sympathetic Democrats led by Senator Herbert Lehman might buy the paper. Dolly deputized Rifkind to see if this made sense. Curiously, the people who seemed most interested were not the principals but Phil Graham and Wechsler. Perhaps Jimmy, who was beset by signs that Dolly might replace him as editor, thought he could maintain his position by ingratiating himself with new owners. None of the reputed principals—neither the Kennedys nor Dolly nor Lehman and his friends—seemed in a hurry to make a deal. According to one participant in the talks, nobody got so far as to examine financial records, put together any kind of prospectus, or even establish a plausible price range within which to negotiate.

The following year, Sylvia Porter told Dolly that a Washington businessman named David Karr wanted to talk with her about purchasing the paper. *Advertising Age* got wind of the story and added that a rival syndicate headed by Adlai Stevenson was also interested. The asking price was said to be $6 million. Dolly adamantly denied everything, even as Rifkind was holding exploratory talks with Karr.* Once again, Wechsler (who by this time had been moved from center stage and was probably trying to find owners who would allow him to move back) tried to entice Eleanor Roosevelt, Herbert Lehman, and other New York Democratic bigwigs into entering the bidding. Jack Kaplan, head of Welch's, was also said to be interested. Once again, it all came to nothing.

Was Dolly serious about selling? During the early years when finances were precarious, it might have made sense for her to sell. As time passed, the paper became central to her identity, gave her stature in the community, and provided her access to that room where the big boys congregated. The value of that would be difficult to measure in dollars.

In January 1964, the beginning of her second quarter century of ownership, Dorothy told an interviewer, "I like running a newspaper, although I'm getting bogged down in administrative detail. That's the fate of newspaper ownership today. Personal initiative, the pleasure of being with newsmaking people, even the competitive spirit is stifled by all the problems of keeping a paper solvent."

She said she was proud that the *Post* had made money consistently over the past fifteen years and was confident that it would continue to do so. Rumors that she would sell it or shut down were nonsense. "The *New York Post* is very much alive," she said, "and so am I. It keeps me that way."

Although Dolly effectively committed herself to preserving her ownership of the paper, she appears—again unlike the Sulzbergers or the Meyer-Graham family—to have given little sustained thought to questions of corporate structure or what role her family might take in the future. Her two oldest

*It was not clear who the money people behind Karr's bid were, or exactly what Karr was up to. He had first made a name for himself as a legman for Drew Pearson, then got involved in several corporate takeovers. Later Karr appeared as a sometime associate of Aristotle Onassis and Armand Hammer, among others, although his exact role in various deals was always hard to pin down.

children, Adele and Morti, were still living in California. Morti had several business interests, among them a radio station in San Diego. Adele was active in local politics and would eventually serve as the women's chair of the state Democratic party. Sarah-Ann, the child to whom Dolly probably felt closest, had returned to New York from Europe with her husband and infant son. As part of Dolly's general reorganization of the paper in 1962, she had appointed Sally special assistant for editorial matters, but Sally's apprenticeship was not successful.

"I worked at the paper very briefly," Sally says, "but I had no interest. I was really interested in politics. I was never interested in journalism. Not even remotely. I did it for a little while, because she really wanted me to, but no. No. I never wanted it."

The experiment lasted less than a year. "It ended amicably. Mother said, 'I guess this isn't going to work.' And I said, 'No.'

"First of all, I didn't like the field, and secondly, I couldn't work for her. It just was too difficult to separate your relationship as people and family from your relationship at work. She said, 'Well, it's all right.' I said, 'Well, can I go now?' And she said, 'Yes.' We were totally different, and it just never could have worked."

With none of her children as a realistic option to fill the role of deputy and potential successor, Dolly sought help elsewhere. Among the first candidates was Robert Gray, who came to work as mechanical supervisor in January 1962. Gray was an Englishman, a former pilot for British Overseas Airways who'd won a Distinguished Flying Cross with the RAF during the war. He joined *The New York Times* in 1948 and earned several promotions while moving from the engineering department into production management.

Gray immediately made his presence felt at the *Post*. In July 1962, Dorothy sent him a memo praising him for quickly gaining control over production expenses, especially in the composing room, where rigid union rules often prevented the imposition of cost-cutting strategies. Five months after hiring Gray, Dolly appointed him her assistant publisher for production and made him treasurer of the Post Corporation. Many on the staff of the paper assumed her enthusiasm went beyond professional admiration and that the two were having an affair, but Dolly denied it at the time to Sally, and Sally says there's no reason to believe her mother was less than candid. "Look, he was a good-looking guy, and she did a certain amount of flirting with men, always. But no, there was nothing there."

Although Gray was undoubtedly good at his work, he had serious personality deficits, which may have been exacerbated by his rapid advance. He raged at underlings and threatened to fire them for minor offenses. He tried to intercept visitors and messages from editors that were intended for Dolly. After performing valiantly during the week the *Post* went back to press after the strike in March 1963, he was incensed when Dolly ignored his request that he be promoted to executive vice president. His behavior grew more unpredictable. He became more confident and self-aggrandizing. Allegedly, he boasted he would soon "push the Publisher out of the paper and force her to retire."

He began to express opinions about editorial matters. At a routine meeting on October 16, 1963, with the editors and other department heads in Dolly's office, Gray got embroiled in a discussion about the appropriateness of an article in the day's first edition. The others ignored him and tried to move on to other subjects. Still upset as the meeting broke up, he evidently had harsh words with Dolly and then stormed out of the building.

Shaken by the exchange, Dolly called Leonard Arnold, the personnel manager, and told him to see to it that Gray was not allowed back into his office. She also asked Arnold to alert the local police precinct that there might be trouble.

Gray reappeared in midafternoon. The maintenance staff had rigged the elevators so that he could not return to the executive suite but was deposited instead on the fifteenth floor, where Arnold's office was located. Arnold, a city detective, and several physically imposing men from the composing room appeared and persuaded him to leave the building quietly. One employee, who witnessed the scene, remembers that Gray was escorted by Al Amburato, the strong-arm man for the delivery department. The other executives were taking no chances.

That evening, Leonard Arnold was deputized to call Gray, offer him Dolly's thanks for the good job he had done, and tell him that he would be getting an exceptionally generous severance payment of $10,000 on condition that he never show up at West Street again. All the locks in the building were changed. Afraid that Gray might be personally vindictive, Arnold engaged the Pinkerton agency to guard Dolly for a week.

Lisa Schiff, Dolly's niece, remembers having dinner that week with Dolly at a chic restaurant in her Upper East Side neighborhood. "David and I walked into the restaurant, and she was sitting alone. I noticed that there were very strange people standing in the corners of the restaurant, and I said, 'Do you notice those really odd people standing there?'

" 'Oh yes,' Dolly said. 'These are policemen. Somebody threatened to kill me tonight.'

"And she went right on eating, cool as a cucumber. I couldn't believe it. She was going to show her face. She was going to do the usual things that she did. It was so Dolly-like."

In romance and in business, Dolly seldom looked back when she moved on. She continued to keep an eye out for someone with whom she might share the burdens of management. If he was attractive, so much the better. In 1965, Blair Clark appeared to be such a man.

Clark was wealthy and well connected, with an impressive résumé. A former editor of the Harvard *Crimson,* he joined CBS News in 1953 as a foreign correspondent in Paris, while serving also as a stringer for *The New York Times.* He came back to the States as a newscaster for the CBS Radio Network and eventually became vice president and general manager of CBS News in 1961. On losing out for the presidency of the news operation, he left the television business. He helped raise money to found *The New York Review of Books.* In addition, Clark was active in liberal Democratic politics, having worked for various Harriman campaigns.

In 1965, Clark, an attractive man in his midforties, was looking for something to cap his career. Dorothy Schiff, an attractive woman in her early sixties, was looking for someone who might solve her social and professional needs. Russell Hemenway, Dorothy's friend from Lexington Democratic Club days, says, "There was a job on that paper, it was called assistant to the publisher. I could have had the job four times. A lot of people could have had it. Sally had it. Frank Roosevelt Jr. could have had it. It didn't have any power, and it implied serious responsibilities. When she needed an escort, for example. You know, she was alone, and she entertained, and needed to have people around."

Dorothy Schiff and Blair Clark met in the early months of 1965, sized each other up, and decided that working together might be mutually advantageous. On May 24, Clark became the associate publisher of the *Post.* He signed a six-month contract for $35,000 annually, waiving all severance and retirement benefits. He and Dorothy also signed a Declaration of Intent stating that during the six-month trial period they would negotiate an agreement outlining the terms under which he might buy the paper from her. It was contemplated that he would first buy a 25 percent share at a price of not less that $500,000 and have the option to acquire the rest when she was ready to retire and sell. The Declaration of Intent was just that—a statement of mutual wishes without any binding provisions.

Years later, Clark explained what the Declaration of Intent represented to him. He said he began their relationship determined to buy the paper from Dorothy, but he couldn't afford to buy it outright. "I lacked the capital for anything but a grubstake," Clark wrote. "I was worth perhaps two million dollars, not enough to make a ripple in that big metropolitan pond." He acknowledged that the appearance of being a purchaser was important to him. "I should admit that there was a matter of status or dignity—it was better to be able to say that I had an option to buy an interest from the lady publisher rather than just to be her employee.

"From that point a torrent of fantasy flowed," Clark admitted. He came to think that his option to buy represented a done deal. "I saw myself, by then a one-fourth owner of the paper, acting vigorously to protect my investment. I did not shrink from the notion that I would charge mismanagement and, after a legal struggle, gain control of the paper, buying out Mrs. Schiff's interest." In pursuit of his dream, Clark set about trying to find financial backers, estimating that if the paper were worth approximately $15 million— a figure presumably based on rumors about Dolly's discussions with the Kennedy family interests in 1961—he would need nearly $4 million to secure his anticipated quarter share.

In the meantime, Clark plunged into editorial matters. He contributed his political insights to the *Post*'s coverage of the New York mayoral election. He wanted to add reporters, particularly in Washington, because he believed the paper needed more national coverage. He was unable to convince anyone to join the staff full-time because "the kind of people I wanted had understandable doubts about job security on any New York newspaper except the *Times*." Clark was instrumental in signing Joseph Kraft's syndicated Washington column, arguing that Kraft was the rightful heir to Walter Lippmann. He tried, without success, to get rid of Max Lerner, who he believed was becoming increasingly pompous and irrelevant.

Clark was equally active on the business side. He and Byron Greenberg supervised the ill-advised automation trial that led to the one-day Local 6 strike against the *Post* in June 1965. He reviewed the paper's policy of advertising on local radio and television. He wrote memos about how to position the newspaper in an era when television was taking away many longtime local advertisers.

Clark worked closely with Dolly and was the man in charge when she took her vacation in the summer of 1965. As he studied how Dolly operated, he decided that her reputation for being flighty had more to do with her gender than her actual behavior. "Behind the airy manner lay great shrewdness and disciplined habits of work. . . . [Her] penny-pinching cost controls and minimum promotional effort seemed a prudent policy." Clark admired the fact that Dolly had kept the paper going for more than two decades. He also came to believe that she would not be willing to make the changes he thought necessary to ensure its survival in the future.

Although the experiment with Blair Clark was never going to last, there are alternate versions of what specifically brought it to a close. In a note Dolly wrote some years later to Jimmy Wechsler, she said she had agreed to keep Clark on after the original six-month trial because he argued that the Newspaper Guild strike at the *Times* and other papers and the subsequent announcement of the Widget merger distracted him from his original timetable. She told Wechsler she had decided that things weren't working out by March 1966. She gave no reason for her decision, other than to say that Clark hadn't made much of a mark at the paper. And, she added, he never made any hard offer to purchase any *Post* stock as contemplated in the Declaration of Intent, offering as evidence a December 1965 memo reporting that her lawyer Morris Abram was still waiting for a proposal from Clark's representatives.

Clark had a more detailed memory of the breakup. He and Dolly had fallen into the habit of having dinner together once a week or so. One evening, having taken her back to her apartment, where Clark recalled she had more to drink than usual, she made "what I can only call a pass, however ladylike. . . . Even though I had been anticipating, not to say dreading, such a development, I was so appalled and embarrassed at its occurrence," he wrote, "I stammered something about [another] involvement and said I had to go now." He left the apartment knowing that his career at the *Post* was over.

Clark later said he believed that the events of that evening were only a proximate cause of his leaving the paper. Dolly really didn't want him there, and, he decided, she took some pleasure in triumphing over men. He acknowledged that he never forcefully pursued the possibility of buying the paper, never initiated any substantive discussions about process or price, but he also argued that Dolly never intended to sell.

To a few of her colleagues, Dolly gave the impression that she was serious about the deal. Byron Greenberg recalls, "I think that she believed that Blair was in a position to buy the paper. Financially, I mean. I don't know whether she was disappointed or relieved when it didn't happen. But on the surface, it appeared that his buying it was what she had in mind."

Pollster Lou Harris had worked with Clark on Harriman campaigns. "Clark was a rich boy dilettante," says Harris. "He got himself into all kinds of enviable jobs, partly because he knew everybody, and because he was so affable and so rich. But he never accomplished much." Blair and Dolly understood each other, Harris believes. "They were perfect partners. They both loved titillation. He played the game at all sorts of places, and when he walked away, he never seemed to have lost anything. When he walked away from the *Post,* there was no acrimony."

Once again Dolly needed an assistant. She turned to her nephew, Tim Seldes, the son of one of Richard Hall's sisters. Seldes was working at a publishing house in New York. By his own account, he had no specialized skills or prior training for the job. He says, "Because Dolly stayed close to my Aunt Marian, I would see her from time to time. She called me up one day. She always liked to have a number two, although she liked to have them for relatively brief periods of time, which I was aware of. But the thing is that you don't get second chances to be the assistant publisher of a major city newspaper and see what that kind of life is like. So I couldn't possibly have said no."

Seldes's duties were vague. Sometimes it seemed as if Dolly just wanted company. "She could be absolutely charming. She liked to have sandwiches at her desk. And she was a wonderful narrator. She had a wonderful memory and told very funny stories. She had a very nice sense of humor. Life wasn't all grim with Dolly. It could be great, great fun."

At times, Dolly used Tim as a buffer between herself and the editorial staff, although she never delegated real authority. He says, "She was sort of ambivalent about working with other people. I think she thought that her authority would be diluted, because she really ran it very autocratically. And her delegation was really a booby trap, because she didn't want you to be bright, really. She wanted to prove that she was essential."

Having a family connection provided some benefits. Dolly made Tim Seldes a vice president of the Post Corporation, which Blair Clark never was. But his being a relative also eliminated the possibility of a flirtation. In any case, Seldes's tenure was no longer than Clark's. There was no particular blowup that presaged the end. "It was in the cards. And I knew that when I started," he says. "She just fired people in that position. Sally, Blair. I always knew she'd fire me. I stayed nine months or so, and then she did it. She also gave me a year's salary, which wasn't bad!"

Although questions of who might serve as Dorothy Schiff's managerial number two, and ultimately succeed her, were still unanswered in the mid-sixties, the fallout from the failure of the *World-Journal-Telegram* galvanized her to make a significant investment in the *Post*'s future. As soon as it was announced that the Widget had collapsed, Dorothy began serious negotiations to buy one of its printing plants. The South Street home of the *Journal-American* offered the *Post* significantly expanded office space, greater storage areas for newsprint and other bulky supplies, easier access for delivery trucks, and, most important, room for newer, more efficient presses to meet the greater circulation demand.

The purchase of 210 South Street was announced on September 16, 1967. The price was $1,500,000, of which $865,000 was for the land, and the rest was to cover building fixtures, machinery, and equipment. The *Post* would take possession of a six-story building that covered almost a complete city block bounded by South Street, Water Street, Catherine Slip, and Market Slip. Paul Sann went to South Street to see the site for himself. He sent Dorothy a memo of his observations. Sann discovered that the area around the building was desolate. He recommended that a cafeteria be installed because there were no luncheonettes nearby. The subways were several blocks away, as was the only bus, although the transit authority could probably be persuaded to reroute it. There was not much parking.

"All in all, I now understand the asking price," Sann concluded. "I no longer see it as the biggest steal since Brink's." Still, he admitted that the property had great possibilities and was better than anything else available, including—most assuredly—their present quarters on West Street.

The delivery and storage areas at South Street would, of course, be on the ground floor. The pressroom would occupy the second floor; the plant supervisors, as well as the purchasing, advertising, and production departments, would be housed on the third. The city room and columnists' offices would be on the fourth floor along with the composing room. The fifth floor would be sublet to a tenant yet to be determined, and Dorothy's suite plus the offices of her top executives would be installed on the sixth. For the first time, she would have a private dining room and kitchen.

The Hearst Corporation expected to vacate the building by the end of the year, at which time the *Post* would begin extensive renovations and add four-color high-speed presses and other new equipment. Even before the renovations began, Dorothy and Byron Greenberg hoped to produce up to one hundred thousand copies daily on the existing South Street presses to meet demand. The unions announced that this would violate their existing contracts, so the plans had to be modified. The paper continued to operate at full capacity at West Street, on the presses rented at *El Diario,* and, to the degree the union would permit, at South Street.

The provisional budget for renovations came to $6,800,000. In November 1967, the *Post*'s investment account at Kuhn, Loeb held $1,568,000 in government securities and corporate paper. For the first time in Dorothy Schiff's tenure, the Post Corporation would have to look beyond its own reserves and owner's personal resources for financing. John Schiff introduced Dorothy, Byron Greenberg, who was by now business manager of the corporation, and Frank Daniels, the controller, to his colleague Henry Necarsulmer, who would serve as her investment banker and financial adviser. Necarsulmer negotiated for the Chase Manhattan Bank to make available to the *Post* up to $4 million in revolving credit.

The contractor for the renovation of South Street was W. H. Barney Corp. of New York, which specialized in work for the newspaper industry. Renny Saltzman, the interior decorator who had done some work in Dorothy's apartment, was hired as design consultant for the renovation of the lobby and the executive sixth floor. Hearst finally vacated the building in March 1968, and the renovations began in June.

By December it was clear that the budget was unrealistic. The original estimate of less than $7 million was increased to $7.5 million. By June 1969, it had risen to more than $8 million. The building needed a new roof and a new boiler house, neither of which had been foreseen. The structure stood on landfill, so piles had to be driven into the rock bed to support a new truck approach in the newsprint receiving bays. A fee of $57,000 for soil testing needed to be paid before that work could begin. Plumbing costs would eventually run nearly $400,000 above the estimates. On the other hand, the engineers pointed out that canceling the special elevator to the executive floor—to which Dolly reluctantly agreed—would save $100,000. By September 1969, the *Post* had increased its Chase line of credit to $6 million and used nearly $4 million of that.

Dolly was involved in almost every decision. One of the first orders to be placed was for the new presses. Byron Greenberg and the engineers solicited bids from two of the leading manufacturers—Hoe and Goss. Hoe had provided the most recent presses installed at West Street, and Greenberg was inclined to give them the order. Dolly thought the Goss proposal offered a more realistic delivery time and better financing. "She made the judgment to go with Goss," says Greenberg, "and it was the right decision. Because sometime afterward Goss dominated the field, and I think Hoe had a problem. She didn't really know that much about it, but she made the right decision."

The contractors, engineers, and plant supervisors for the *Post* met every week while the work was under way. Dorothy did not attend, but she read the minutes carefully. She took particular interest in the plans for her suite. Decorator Saltzman estimated that it would cost $45,000 even though she planned to retain some prized possessions from West Street, including her desk and Grandpa Schiff's portrait. As the work progressed, the price went up by nearly a third despite some cutbacks in the original plans. Dorothy sent off a stream of queries: Why are the toilets so low? How much would it cost to install venetian blinds in the bathroom? Who will clean the kitchen? Who will staff it?

Press operations were consolidated on South Street in February 1970. The new press lines made it possible to print editions of up to 120 pages, and, because they accepted paper whose trim size was two inches wider than the old West Street machines, the format could be changed to a more pleasing six columns per page rather than five.

The executive offices were ready for Dorothy and her associates a few months later. The cafeteria opened in June; there were also twenty-four-hour vending machines and check-cashing facilities. The *Post* prevailed upon the Transit Authority to reinstate bus service between South Street and the nearest subway station. It also leased a vacant lot under the East River Drive to provide parking space for about one hundred cars, for which it charged employees about sixty cents a day. By the end of the year, the *Post* had completely vacated West Street and sold the remaining years of the lease back to the owners of the building. The final cost of the new facility, including the original purchase, renovations, and fees, came to about $11 million.

Summing up the move, Greenberg wrote Dorothy that it was wonderful to have all operations reunited in one centrally air-conditioned, thermopaned facility. Certainly the working conditions in the new building were an impressive improvement on those they had coped with in the past. It was more efficient as well; Greenberg estimated that with the modern new pressroom, production costs would drop by as much as $1 million annually over the next few years.

Life on South Street, he said, will be nice, but not perfect. "We will still have our problems. Who else in this industry will be faced with publishing 6 editions every day, grinding out 200,000 copies per press, fighting the clock on the Wall Street Closing edition, the traffic everywhere, and the diehards who are still mad that the *Post* succeeded in the wonderful world of P.M. journalism in New York City?"

V

CLOUDS ON THE HORIZON

TWENTY

The Rise of the New Left

The *Post* had survived every effort by its journalistic rivals to put it out of business. What Dorothy Schiff and her lieutenants did not foresee was that the sharpest challenge to the paper's success would arise not from commercial pressures but from political developments in the years to come. From the mid-forties on, the liberal ideology that had guided Dolly's thinking and that of her colleagues was reflected in the paper's coverage and interpretation of events at home and abroad. But as the Cold War dragged on, political problems began to emerge for which doctrinaire solutions seemed neither clear nor viable.

The first liberal tenet to come under scrutiny was the belief that reform would be good for the Democratic party. Dorothy Schiff, though personally fond of boss Carmine De Sapio, had joined Jimmy Wechsler and allies like Eleanor Roosevelt and Herbert Lehman in cheering every step of the demolition of Tammany Hall. With the collapse of Tammany and the discipline it imposed, however, the New York Democratic party lost its traditions, its core identity, and its hold on city and state offices. The first warning had come as early as 1958. The reformers' hostility to De Sapio and all he stood for was probably responsible for the failure of Frank Hogan, Tammany's chosen candidate, to defeat a vulnerable Kenneth Keating in the Senate race that year.

New York Democrats temporarily resolved their parochial difficulties in

1964 to back Robert F. Kennedy in his challenge to the incumbent Keating., After entering the race at the last minute, Bobby was given the Democratic senatorial nomination at the state party convention on September 1. Three days later he came to the offices of the *Post* to seek Dorothy's thoughts about his campaign. As a family friend and loyal Democrat, she was prepared to support his candidacy in any case, but she was flattered to be consulted so prominently.

Bobby reminded her of Jack, but she thought he was neither as good-looking nor as aristocratic in manner. She assumed Jack had acquired the style of the British upper class when his father was ambassador to England. She thought of Bobby as somewhat ruthless, as something of a "young man in a hurry." When she told him to remember that "it wasn't what New York could do for him, but what he could do for New York," he didn't reply.

She arranged for him to meet with some important Jewish leaders in the city and contributed $1,000 to his campaign. Given the reservoir of goodwill toward the Kennedy family, and the Democratic landslide across the country, it is not surprising that Bobby defeated Keating.

Despite Bobby's win, the collapse of the New York Democratic party was imminent. The Democratic reformers included some hard-nosed operators in their ranks, notably Ed Koch, but many were dilettantes. Although the insurgents now controlled the party machinery, they didn't know how to play the game as well as the old-school pols had, and their deficiencies became obvious during the 1965 mayoral race in New York City.

Mayor Robert Wagner, who hoped (in vain) to run for governor in 1966, decided not to seek reelection. This set up a primary fight between two party regulars, President of the City Council Paul Screvane and City Comptroller Abe Beame, which Beame won. Many reform Democrats, who disliked Beame, broke with the party to support John Lindsay, the Republican candidate, who was also running on Alex Rose's Liberal party line.

Lindsay, a well-connected young lawyer, was first elected to Congress from the seventeenth district on Manhattan's East Side in 1958 and won three subsequent terms by ever greater majorities. Dorothy Schiff, a constituent, contributed to each of his campaigns and became a friend of the congressman and his wife, Mary. When Dorothy bought an apartment for Wynn and Sally Kramarsky on their return to New York in 1961, she asked Lindsay to write a letter of recommendation to the board of the building.

Lindsay established himself as a leading Republican liberal by supporting civil rights, immigration, and refugee/asylum reform. His youth and good looks reminded people of the Kennedys, and his mayoral campaign acquired its slogan from Murray Kempton, who dropped his wariness about reformers to say of Lindsay, "He's fresh, and everyone else is tired."

James Wechsler's editorials and columns in the *Post* lacked Kempton's phrasemaking skills but made the same point. A month before the election, Jimmy rebutted Bobby Kennedy and Hubert Humphrey, who both said at a Beame rally that Democrats must support the candidate of their party. Wechsler reminded his readers that in 1941 President Franklin Roosevelt had urged the reelection of Republican-Fusion Mayor Fiorello La Guardia, because, said FDR, he was the better man.

In mid-October, Beame was ahead in the polls. William Buckley, running on the Conservative ticket, attracted about 10 percent of the potential voters; Buckley supporters were right-wing Republicans who understood that Lindsay did not represent their views. On the eve of the election, the *Post* urged readers to vote for Lindsay. "A Beame victory," said the paper, "would mean a return to the ancient era of backroom government. It would impose upon the city an awesome flood of hacks, hangers-on, and influence-peddlers. . . . Beame was unable to rise above the machine men in the campaign. He will be their agent and prisoner in City Hall."

On November 2, this message resonated with a significant number of traditionally Democratic voters. Lindsay captured precincts in Jewish and Italian neighborhoods in the outer boroughs that had been a sure thing for Democratic candidates in the past. On election night, the disgruntled Democratic loser told a *Post* reporter that the paper was responsible for his defeat.

The Republicans took over City Hall for the first time since 1944. Gone were the Democratic "hacks" and "machine men." New York State now had a Republican governor, one Republican senator, and a Republican mayor of its biggest city. Bobby Kennedy's election to the Senate from New York in 1964 was seen as a temporary way station in his march toward the White House. The city and state Democratic parties were in tatters. By supporting reform without foreseeing its costs, the *Post* played a leading role in the debacle. Offended by Tammany corruption, Dorothy Schiff and her reform friends overlooked the practical benefits of deal making and delivering the vote.

Dorothy continued to see the Rockefellers and the Lindsays socially. They were her kind of people, in the way that even Yale-educated Robert Wagner never was. Finally she was chummy with the incumbents of the White House as well. During the Eisenhower years, she had been an insider in a party on the outs. Now that the Democrats were back in power in Washington, Dorothy moved her game to a higher level.

She had run into Jack Kennedy from time to time at political events in New York, and she was pleased when he invited her to the White House in May 1963. She had not been there since she visited Roosevelt in the late thirties. The meeting with Jack was informal. After asking about his parents, Jackie, and the children, Dorothy asked the president what he would do with himself after his second term. When he said he'd enjoy becoming a publisher, she offered him her job at the *Post,* saying that she would be ready to retire by then.

After Jack's assassination, Dorothy, like many Americans, became ever more fascinated by his glamorous widow. When she talked to Bobby before the 1964 senatorial election, she told him she wanted to meet Jackie. Bobby passed on the message, and Jackie invited Dorothy for a drink on Saturday, October 10, 1964. Nervous about the occasion, Dorothy jotted down some notes beforehand. She wanted to tell Jackie that she had known her father, Jack Bouvier, when she was a debutante, and she wanted to offer her the chance to write a column for the *Post.*

Jackie was staying at the Carlyle Hotel until renovations were completed on her new Fifth Avenue apartment. Dorothy found Jackie, who was dressed very simply and wore little makeup, even more beautiful than she had expected. They each had a drink, and Dorothy expressed concern about Joe Kennedy's recent stroke. She told Jackie about her experiences with Rudolf.

Jackie teared up several times when the conversation turned to Jack. She also spoke warmly about Bobby and sought to dispel the public image of him as ruthless. They talked about the *Post,* which Jackie indicated that she read with some regularity. That gave Dorothy her opening to ask Jackie to write a column on any subject she chose. Jackie said she'd already been asked by several magazines and had turned them all down. She had also rejected the kind offer of President Johnson to appoint her ambassador to France or Mexico or anyplace else that she might choose. After an hour, Dorothy decided not to overstay her welcome. They spoke of getting together soon again.

A month later, Jackie invited Dorothy to join her at her new apartment for lunch. Once again, Dorothy noted, Jackie was dressed very simply, this time in a white silk blouse, a dark cotton skirt, and Gucci loafers. The lunch took place a week before the anniversary of Jack's death. Jackie seemed downcast as she reminisced about Jack's courtship of her and about their private moments together. Dorothy observed that Jackie fit the eighteenth-century model of the perfect courtesan, companion to a prime minister or a king. But Jackie made it clear that she wanted only to be a wife, never a mistress.

These two visits were the high points of intimacy between the two women. Dorothy remained fascinated by gossip about Jackie—at a dinner party in 1969 she grilled André Meyer, Jackie's financial adviser, about the details of Jackie's recent marriage to Aristotle Onassis. The two women saw each other infrequently. Each occasionally invited the other to dinner parties. Mostly they crossed paths at public events.

Dorothy's early meetings with Lyndon Johnson suggested she was flattered that he sought her friendship. She invited him to visit the *Post* on October 16, 1963. He shared a sandwich lunch with Joe Lash, James Wechsler, and Dorothy, and toured the city room and composing rooms afterward.

On November 27, less than a week after Johnson became president, he called to thank Dorothy for a series the *Post* had just run about him. In mid-December, she was invited to meet with him at Adlai Stevenson's suite in the Waldorf-Astoria hotel.

Johnson greeted her warmly, then jumped directly into a brief political conversation. He said he was worried about getting his civil rights bill through Congress. As she was leaving, Dolly chatted for a few minutes with Lady Bird Johnson, whom she had previously met only in large gatherings. Dorothy liked her manner. LBJ, on the other hand, she judged unsophisticated and somewhat relentless in making his points.

Johnson was in a wooing mode. In January, he asked her at the last minute to be one of two American representatives at the inauguration of the president of Liberia. She turned him down, saying that she didn't have time to put together an appropriate wardrobe. When pressed, she admitted that she was afraid to fly, at which point Johnson relented, teasing her about the "meager" sandwich she'd served him at the *Post* before he rang off.

They were still in the honeymoon phase the following year, when the president sent Dolly a note thanking her for an editorial Wechsler had written praising his State of the Union address and his proposed domestic legislation, which would advance LBJ's liberal agenda. He invited her to a state dinner given at the White House in August 1964 in honor of U Thant, the secretary-general of the United Nations.

After going through the receiving line, Dorothy chatted with Lady Bird about their mutual interest in needlepoint. Peter, Paul and Mary entertained. "Apparently they are very famous," Dolly told a friend, "but I had not heard of them."

She danced with Lyndon. "He held me close, placing his right cheek against my right cheek. . . . Then the President said, 'You are a lovely dancer, Dorothy.' I looked up at him and said, 'You are a wonderful President, Mr. President!' "

She observed that Johnson was wearing a white dinner jacket. Other men wore dark. "I understand there is a controversy about which is correct. In the top social circles in which I have traveled, white dinner jackets are not considered *comme il faut*."

Nationally, the Democratic party appeared to be immune to troubles. Johnson and running mate Hubert Humphrey trounced Barry Goldwater and William Miller in the presidential election that November, and the Democrats won the largest majority in both houses of Congress that either party commanded at any time during the twentieth century.

Despite the aura of invincibility that surrounded the party, potential challenges to the hegemony of its nearly thirty-year-old liberal amalgam of New Deal– and Cold War–based ideologies were developing at home and abroad. While Americans were mesmerized by the complicated dance of the superpowers advancing toward and retreating from the brink of global annihilation in confrontations over Berlin, Cuba, and the Middle East, a small war in Southeast Asia was about to confront liberals with a vexing set of problems that were not easily resolved within their standard belief system.

The French had been colonial masters of Indochina since the middle of the nineteenth century, but the local population had never given up hopes of independence. During World War II, Japan captured much of Vietnam and its neighbors. On September 2, 1945—the day Japan surrendered to the Allies and formally relinquished its conquests—Vietnamese patriots, led by Ho Chi Minh, who described himself as a Marxist and a nationalist, declared their independence in the northern capital city of Hanoi. When France insisted on regaining control of the southern part of the country, Ho began a war of national liberation.

The Communist takeover of China in 1949, and the assault by Communist North Korea on South Korea in the early fifties, reinforced the belief that the Vietnamese independence movement was part of the unified surge of Communist aggression around the globe. As such, many liberals and conservatives agreed that it must not be allowed to succeed. By 1953, America was paying for 80 percent of the French military effort to defeat Ho but was not getting much for its money. After a humiliating defeat at Dien Bien Phu in May 1954, the French gave up.

At the peace conference in Geneva, Vietnam was divided: Ho controlled the north, and a little-known Catholic nationalist, Ngo Dinh Diem, headed the government in the south. After a two-year cease-fire, there would be a nationwide election in 1956, which everyone expected—with enthusiasm or dread—that Ho would win.

To forestall that possibility, Eisenhower propped up Diem's regime with money and military advisers. The United States also saw to it that the promised election never took place. When Jack Kennedy became president in 1960, he felt he had no option but to continue the Republican policy, increasing the amount of money and military support first to Diem and then to several equally corrupt and unpopular successor governments in Saigon. After Kennedy was assassinated in November 1963, Lyndon Johnson renewed his predecessors' commitment to preventing a Communist victory.

It made little difference to Ho's government that America had replaced France as their Western adversary. They infiltrated more soldiers into the South and attacked American installations. As the war escalated, Washington dropped the pretext that it was only advising South Vietnamese troops. Americans began bombing the North, claiming that U.S. naval vessels had been attacked in the Gulf of Tonkin. In March 1965, 3,500 U.S. Marines landed to protect the air base at Danang. By midsummer, Johnson felt forced to authorize the use of American ground troops for offensive operations in Vietnam. Two hundred thousand troops were committed by the end of the year.

The war had initially been popular in America, but by midsummer 1966, U.S. casualties were mounting. Statements by President Johnson and his colleagues that the war effort was going well were greeted with increasing disbelief. By 1967, nearly a half million Americans were serving in Vietnam, and official reports of their success were contradicted by journalists on the scene.

On April 15, three or four hundred thousand people gathered in New York to express their opposition to the war. In October, antiwar protesters marched on the Pentagon.

Many young men dreaded the prospect of serving in a conflict with which they had no sympathy. Draft resistors refused to register, burned their draft cards, went underground, or, in extreme cases, fled to Canada. College campuses were roiled by dissent, triggered by anger about Vietnam and fueled by general resentment of authority figures.

Todd Gitlin, one of the early leaders of the student movement, is now a prominent sociologist and writer. His history of the sixties combines an activist's view of the events at the time with a scholar's retrospective evaluation. Members of Dorothy Schiff and James Wechsler's generation, Gitlin wrote, believed in government, having grown up with the New Deal, Social Security, and labor-protecting laws. "For them the government was the natural ally of the common people at home and the natural enemy of totalitarianism abroad." They may even have started as Socialists, wanting to throw over the old system, but they had become members of the middle class and wanted only to modify it. The young, by contrast, mistrusted all inherited systems, all perceived wisdom, all authority, except their own.

"The liberal generation half-succeeded and nothing is so unsettling as half a success," Gitlin wrote. Liberalism stood for racial and economic equality "but lacked the means, or the will, or the blood-and-guts desire, to bring it about. The leadership, if not all of the base, also stood for permanent Cold War mobilization, which to many of the next generation seemed much too dangerous." Liberals passed on their concerns to the next generation without, it appeared, offering any solutions.

The war in Vietnam posed a particular set of dilemmas for liberals. They had to decide if Ho's effort to take over the southern part of Vietnam was part of a worldwide Communist plot or a legitimate movement for national unity and independence from Western colonial supremacy. If they supported the anticommunist puppet regimes in Saigon, they were forced to acknowledge that these governments were unpopular and corrupt. If they praised the young for their eagerness to challenge outdated assumptions, they might endanger the consensus that makes democracy work.

The liberal coalition began to splinter. In general, organized labor and working-class Democrats continued to support the war. Many members of the middle class, uneasy about sending their sons to fight, and intellectuals, unless they were staunch Cold Warriors, opposed it. Despite their fears about Communist-led expansion in Southeast Asia, Dorothy Schiff and James Wechsler believed that the American policy in Vietnam was misguided and destructive. The *Post* urged a settlement through international negotiation with all the parties involved and assumed that something much like the Geneva agreements would prevail.

The rupture between generations was explicit during the run-up to an antiwar rally in Washington in April 1965. The organizers invited all antiwar groups, including some old-fashioned procommunist groups, to participate. This elicited an open letter of concern from otherwise sympathetic anticommunist liberals, including James Wechsler, who did not want the cause sullied by association with their old enemies.

About twenty-five thousand people showed up in Washington for what was the largest peace march in America to that date. Furious at being admonished by their liberal elders, the leaders of the event cut their ties with any liberal groups, even those like the League for Industrial Democracy (LID), which had supported them, and turned toward more radical agendas. According to Gitlin, "The unstated background murmur: Liberals had defaulted, even the good ones were helpless, they made lousy allies. Liberals! The very word had become the New Left's curse. The litany crystallized: Atlantic City*-LID-*New York Post*."

The kids of the New Left were unforgiving. They ignored the fact that Lyndon Johnson's administration was responsible for some of the most far-reaching social legislation since the New Deal, including the Civil Rights Act of 1964; Medicare and Medicaid, which provided federally funded health insurance for the elderly and the indigent; the War on Poverty, which included funds for urban renewal and Head Start; and many other programs mandated by the liberal agenda. They focused instead on the administration's greatest failure—its inability to find a solution to the widening conflict in Vietnam. The president could not appear in public without being greeted by demonstrators shouting "Hey, Hey, LBJ, how many kids did you kill today?"

In January 1966, Schiff and Wechsler met with Hubert Humphrey at the Carlyle Hotel in New York. As Johnson's vice president, Humphrey seemed

---

*Site of the 1964 Democratic Convention at which the attempt by a group of Negroes to supplant the all-white official delegation from Mississippi was defeated in the interests of party unity by candidates Johnson and Humphrey and many of their liberal supporters.

genuinely to endorse the administration's policy in Vietnam. He believed in a military solution, maintaining that there was enormous popular support in both North and South Vietnam for the opponents of Ho Chi Minh. He also said that a Communist victory in Vietnam would place neighboring Thailand at risk. Dolly and Jimmy were dismayed.

Later that year, Dolly invited Secretary of State Dean Rusk to meet with her, Wechsler, and Tim Seldes at the *Post*. At a White House dinner some weeks before, Rusk had complained to Sylvia Porter that he was wounded by *Post* editorials asking for his resignation and wanted a chance to explain himself. Dolly told Rusk that she took responsibility for the editorials. She said that she felt the ongoing peace negotiations were stalled and needed to be reenergized. She told Rusk that her experience with labor negotiations suggested that a fresh face was sometimes crucial; she believed the dismissal of Amory Bradford during the endless negotiations in the 1962–1963 newspaper strike enabled her to approach Bert Powers directly and work out a deal. Though this was not exactly what had occurred, it made her point.

Rusk replied with the bureaucrat's classic argument that there were too many unknowns for the negotiations to lead to a sudden conclusion, and that Russia, China, and North Vietnam did not have identical agendas. America had to proceed cautiously, because if she appeared too eager for a settlement, it would be interpreted as a sign of weakness, and the others would concede nothing. Dolly and Jimmy were polite, but they were not impressed. Dolly began to describe herself as a "dove" where Vietnam was concerned.

Being a dove did not mean that she favored the immediate unilateral withdrawal of American troops. Few Americans in positions of power or influence saw any way out of the mess save through international negotiations. Even Wechsler's generally optimistic liberal faith began to flag.

Tensions got worse in 1968. Ho launched the Tet Offensive on the last day of January. Vietcong units threatened Saigon, although eventually they had to pull back. The offensive ended in a stalemate on the battlefield, but it had an enormous impact on American politics. The initial Communist success reinforced the growing perception that Johnson's government was dissembling about the nature of the war effort, and it stimulated increasingly angry college students to demonstrate against the war and whatever else bothered them.

Student protests had been shutting down campuses and capturing headlines since the free speech movement disrupted the University of California at Berkeley in the fall of 1964. The university administration abruptly canceled its long-standing permission for students to distribute pamphlets and other political materials just across the street from the main gates to the campus. Organized student protests forced the administration to reverse its policy. Students in other parts of the country began to act out about their own grievances, which in turn offended many adults who didn't understand what right the kids had to complain.

Many of the post-Berkeley protests were spontaneous affairs, but increasingly the leadership of the demonstrations was in the hands of members of the Students for a Democratic Society (SDS), the group that also coordinated the 1965 antiwar demonstrations in Washington. SDS members and sympathizers dedicated themselves to opposing the power of large impersonal institutions like universities and state and national governments and to restoring that power to "the people." A number of campus confrontations across the country gave at least lip service to this New Left ideology, which also came into play in various centers of urban unrest.

The *New York Post* generally supported student demands for First Amendment protection for their demonstrations, whether the cause was civil rights, concerns about the war in Vietnam, or various local issues. As it became clear that a number of the student leaders were children of members of the Old Left, the paper cautioned against possible Communist influence within an otherwise laudable movement. This was familiar territory for Schiff, Wechsler, and other veterans of the anti–Henry Wallace days.

What was something of a theoretical issue came startlingly close to home in the spring of 1968. On April 24, students at Columbia, irate that the university planned to build a gym in a nearby park and demanding that it no longer accept research funds from the federal Department of Defense, stormed into the offices of college administrators, trashed the space, and held several deans captive for nearly twenty-four hours. The next day students under the leadership of Columbia SDS president Mark Rudd seized control of two more campus buildings.

It got worse. Black students occupying one building forced white students to leave. The university administration suspended classes for two days, which did little to lower the tension. After a weeklong standoff, President Grayson Kirk and his deans allowed the New York City police to drive the students out of the college buildings and arrest several of the most vocal or violent demonstrators.

Opinions at the *Post* were divided. Murray Kempton sympathized with the students. He believed that Columbia was a morally bankrupt institution. Its plans to build a gymnasium on city parkland while limiting access to the facility for the surrounding Harlem community showed that the university had no respect for its neighborhood or for the city in which it stood. He excoriated the faculty for not having the courage to stand up to Kirk's administration, even before this crisis.

Max Lerner disagreed. Even though the administration of the university could have handled the crisis more intelligently, the student rebels were "little Lenins and vest-pocket Castros," who needed to be dealt with harshly. Lerner was relieved that, contrary to what he assumed were the wishes of the SDS leaders, the police action triggered no popular uprising. He concluded that most Americans—even disenfranchised and disgruntled residents of Harlem—were not eager for revolution.

Fern Marja Eckman ignored politics altogether when she interviewed Mark Rudd in early May. She recounted his past as a high school honor student in New Jersey. She spoke on the phone to his mother, with whom she seemed to agree that Mark was a good boy.

Wechsler was dismayed by the events at his beloved alma mater, but he wrote sparingly about it. He did not comment when Columbia College canceled its classes for the rest of the semester, nor during the recurrent demonstrations and mysterious trash fires that occurred on campus from time to time during the next few months. He did interview the current editors of his old paper, *The Spectator,* and commented in his column that while the seizure of the buildings by the SDS was inexcusable, there were real problems at Columbia with which its administration seemed to be totally out of touch. When President Kirk stepped down abruptly in August, Jimmy's editorial said simply that the resignation was good for the university, which needed to make a clean break with the past and reminded readers that many students "were motivated by honest convictions not doctrinaire destructiveness or nihilist exhibitionism."

Even though events at Columbia dominated the *Post*'s headlines when the struggle between rebels and authority figures was most intense, they were in general overshadowed by astonishing developments on the national political scene. The most far-reaching impact of the Tet Offensive was the psychological blow it delivered to the administration of Lyndon Johnson.

After Tet, *New York Post* editorials, which had been hostile to the president and the war effort for some time, were joined by an ever-growing chorus of calls for Johnson to resign. The *Post* took the position that Johnson's departure would make possible a wide-open Democratic primary fight from which an antiwar candidate for the November election would emerge.

Senator Eugene McCarthy of Minnesota had already declared himself to be that candidate, and most Democratic reform clubs in New York immediately endorsed him. Wechsler's columns and editorials enthusiastically praised McCarthy. "Not since Stevenson," Jimmy wrote, "has there been so distinctive a political voice so committed to talking sense to the people." He cast McCarthy as a political reformer and feared that if he were defeated, young people who had been flocking to his support would feel victimized. They would be convinced "that machines, money and muscle are still the decisive weapons in the political arena; and that the solitary man—no matter how boldly he fights and how much ardor he enlists—cannot beat the system." Never mind that Stevenson had lost two times, and that the reform of the machine had led to disaster for New York Democrats—Wechsler's position was consistent with his long-treasured liberal beliefs.

Dolly was more wary. She favored McCarthy but kept her ties open to the Kennedy camp in the event that Bobby were to jump in. She had reservations about the political skills of the people behind McCarthy, among them his campaign manager—her former assistant publisher, Blair Clark. Nonetheless, she and the senator were on a first-name basis by the spring of 1968 when he called to thank her for the fair hearing the paper had given him so far. Eventually she donated $500 to the McCarthy campaign, which was off to a good start. McCarthy nearly defeated Johnson in the season-opening New Hampshire primary, which convinced Kennedy that the president was beatable and encouraged him to join the fray.

Bobby had come to Dolly's apartment in January to discuss his options. He felt that McCarthy did not have enough strength to unseat an incumbent president who had, Bobby believed, more support across the nation than the polls and the demonstrations indicated. Dolly said she would love him to enter the race. The *Post* currently favored McCarthy, but a more complex political situation would be hot news and would sell papers. Kennedy asked for her advice, and she told him to follow his own instincts as she said she always did.

Soon after Bobby decided to run, he invited Dolly to lunch at La Côte Basque to sound her out about getting the *Post*'s endorsement, though he

didn't ask directly. He told her he and his advisers were more and more convinced that McCarthy was a weak contender. She asked him if he was nervous
among crowds, and he replied that everyone seemed very friendly.

Then Lyndon Johnson shook everything up. On March 31, the president
declared that he was ordering an immediate end to the bombing of North
Vietnam* in the hopes that it would lead to a resumption of negotiations between the involved parties, and that "in interest of national unity" he would
not be a candidate for reelection in the fall.

Four days after Johnson's announcement, the nation was stunned by the
assassination of Martin Luther King Jr. in Memphis, Tennessee. Riots broke
out in many American cities; more than forty people were killed, and thousands were injured.

Vice President Humphrey officially joined the race for the Democratic
nomination in late April, but smart money said the winner would be either of
the other two men. Kennedy won the next two primaries in Indiana and Ne-
braska. Wechsler feared that McCarthy would win only those primaries in
states without a strong party apparatus. States with a powerful machine in
place would support Bobby. The thought of Kennedy as his successor would
enrage Johnson, who detested him. The president, Jimmy speculated, would
be forced to throw his support behind Humphrey, who would be the first
choice of few but the compromise choice of many.

Although Kennedy's ascendancy was temporarily stalled when McCarthy
took Oregon, Bobby became the front-runner again on June 4, when he won
South Dakota and California. That evening, after he spoke before cheering
supporters—among them Dolly's granddaughters Kathleen and Wendy
Gray—in a ballroom at the Ambassador Hotel in Los Angeles, Bobby was
murdered by Sirhan B. Sirhan, a disturbed twenty-four-year-old Palestinian
nationalist who had made his way into the crowd surrounding the candidate
as he was leaving the hotel.

———————

*In actuality, the bombing was halted only north of the twentieth parallel, leaving a two-hundred-mile
zone between the North and South that would continue to come under fire. The *Post* editorial, which
approved any cutback in attacks on North Vietnam, called the policy the "unconditional cessation of
most of the bombing."

America in midsummer 1968 felt as if it was spinning out of control. The revived peace talks in Paris were going nowhere. Campus unrest and urban lawlessness threatened to destabilize the country. Events surrounding the two political conventions only reinforced that view.

The Republicans, as the party out of power, met first. Convening in Miami during the first week in August, the GOP chose Richard Nixon over Nelson Rockefeller and Ronald Reagan as its presidential candidate, and Nixon named Governor Spiro Agnew of Maryland as his running mate. The speeches at the Miami Beach Convention Center vied for news coverage with the reports of rioting and looting in Liberty City, Miami's black neighborhood.

The Democrats were scheduled to meet in Chicago from August 26 through 29. Dolly always attended the Democratic conventions. This time she would have a chance to visit with Adele, who was a member of the California delegation. Granddaughters Wendy and Kathleen Gray were working on the floor, but they were hardly aware that their grandmother was at the convention.

For almost a year, opponents of the administration's policies in Vietnam and at home had made plans to converge on Chicago in protest. The organizers of the march on the Pentagon in the fall of 1967 had attracted at least one hundred thousand participants, and they hoped to draw an equivalent crowd to Chicago.

Days before the convention, the *New York Post* featured a profile of Chicago's Mayor Richard Daley. The mayor was confident he could prevent trouble. Six thousand National Guardsmen had been mobilized and were practicing riot-control drills. Special police platoons were prepared to do the same. Daley said, however, that he expected none of these special forces would be necessary because there was more bluff than reality in the protestors' plans.

He couldn't have been more mistaken. Trouble started even before the opening session of the convention. On the night of August 25, several thousand people assembled for a concert in Lincoln Park. Daley had announced a curfew to take effect at eleven o'clock, at which hour the crowd left the park, followed by police, but did not disburse. The police moved in, shoving and clubbing protestors and bystanders alike. Small pitched battles continued through the night, and dozens of people were arrested.

At the convention itself, there was important business to transact. The *Post* story on the 26th was headlined "McCarthy Camp Hopes for a Miracle." After Kennedy's death, Humphrey had lined up most of the party regulars. McCarthy delegates, among them Murray Kempton, who had taken a leave of absence from the paper, were a minority even in the New York State Democratic contingent. By the time of Humphrey's inevitable nomination, which came on the first ballot two days later, and his choice of Senator Edmund Muskie of Maine for vice president, convention business was completely overshadowed by events on the street.

During the day on the 28th, as the delegates rejected a plank in the party platform demanding peace in Vietnam, some six thousand demonstrators, surrounded by tense city police and National Guardsmen, began to march toward the site of the convention although they had not obtained a permit allowing them to do so. In full view of television cameras from around the world, the police waded into the crowd, battering and kicking at will. Paul Sann, who spent the week in Chicago as a reporter on the street rather than on the floor of the convention, narrowly missed being hurt.

The violence continued into the night. At one point Kempton was arrested in a skirmish at the Hilton Hotel. On the morning of the 29th, Gene McCarthy addressed a crowd of about five thousand in Grant Park. Demonstrators trying to make their way to the convention center were turned back by tear gas. In the course of the week, several thousand demonstrators and two hundred policemen were injured. Nearly seven hundred people were arrested, mostly for disturbing the peace.

The convention had ended ignominiously at midnight of the 28th, with everyone's reputation tarnished by the violence. Mayor Daley and his police had become international symbols of intransigent authority. In their columns following the debacle, Max Lerner and James Wechsler agreed that candidate Humphrey had started his campaign off on a bad foot when he failed to come up with a formula whereby he could criticize the Chicago police while expressing respect for law and order.

Several days later, Humphrey tried to explain himself in an interview with Roger Mudd on CBS. The demonstrations were premeditated, said Humphrey (as if that made them a priori bad), and the demonstrators used foul language in public. "Is it any wonder that the police had to take action?" he asked. He regretted the violence. "I certainly don't like to see anybody injured. Goodness me, anybody that sees this sort of thing is sick at heart, and

I was. But I think the blame ought to be put where it belongs. I think we ought to quit pretending that Mr. Daley—Mayor Daley did something that was wrong. He didn't—he didn't condone a thing that was wrong. He tried to protect lives." Dorothy obtained a transcript and marked these passages with disapproval.

She kept up the pressure in the week after the convention. Jimmy Wechsler was on vacation, so she drafted Max Lerner to write a stinging editorial calling for a complete bombing halt and immediate negotiations. Johnson had once told her that *Post* editorials were read in Hanoi and Moscow. Presumably he was accusing her of giving comfort to the enemy, but she saw the issue as one of American patriotism.

Two weeks before the election, Hubert Humphrey called Dorothy directly, asking for the chance to present his point of view in person. *The New York Times* had just endorsed him, and Wechsler was advocating for the *Post* to do the same. Dorothy was resistant. She said that there were many vexing issues in the forthcoming election in addition to Vietnam, about which she disagreed with the vice president's position. She wanted to hear what he had to say about the rise in urban crime, the alienation of blue-collar workers from their traditional liberal affiliations, and the disaffection of young people.

Dorothy and Jimmy Wechsler met with Humphrey and Joe Rauh at the Waldorf-Astoria on October 21. Soon after the meeting began, the candidate said he wanted to cut out the niceties and asked directly for the *Post*'s editorial support. Dorothy couldn't help but think that "HHH would be a quickie in bed." He was always rushing.

Hubert said that it would be possible to gain peace through negotiations as long as the United States kept up the military pressure on the North Vietnamese. He was sure that recent changes in the international situation strengthened America's hand; the Russians had incurred a great deal of ill will when they invaded Czechoslovakia in August to put down a popular Czech reform movement.

Dorothy tried to imply that her endorsement was not a given, but of course it was. The *Post* was never going to give its imprimatur to Richard Nixon, who promised that he had a secret plan to end the war but offered no details.

On November 5, Nixon won with a thin plurality of the popular vote and a wide majority in the electoral college. George Wallace, running on the pro-segregation ticket of the American Independent party, attracted 12 percent of the vote overall but carried only five states in the Deep South. Humphrey, who had been way behind in the polls in early October, closed well, but he could not overcome apathy on the left and defections of former Democrats to Nixon or Wallace on the right. Democratic regulars blamed each other, and the increasingly bitter young blamed everyone over thirty.

The single-minded oppositionalism of the New Left, coupled with growing rage in the black community, affected thousands of unaffiliated young people who registered their sympathy with the antiauthoritarian mood of the day by growing their hair, dressing in tie-dyed clothes, listening to rock and roll, and experimenting with drugs. They also got more involved with politics. In addition to the battle-hardened SDS members who got beat up in Chicago, thousands of less rebellious youth, the "Clean for Gene" kids who had canvassed their neighborhoods and schools to support the McCarthy campaign, were left at the end of the 1968 election with few positive feelings about their country and the liberal establishment which, they believed, was largely responsible for their distress.

This perception that progressive forces in America were being thwarted by the liberal establishment began to spread from the young people into another increasingly vocal and agitated community. Large segments of the nation's black population, who had long chafed at their oppression by the white establishment as a whole, began to complain about what they perceived as ill treatment by their erstwhile allies in the white world—the already beleaguered liberals.

TWENTY-ONE

Blacks vs. Jews

From the start of the civil rights revolution in the South, Dorothy Schiff and her editors determined that the *New York Post,* despite its limited resources, would keep its readers on top of this remarkable development in the nation's history. Until *The New York Times* finally turned its full attention to the story in the late fifties, the *Post* covered the civil rights revolution better than any other major newspaper in the country. Implicit in this commitment was the belief that its readers identified with and supported the struggle of blacks, as they were beginning to call themselves, for dignity and justice.

Black communities in the South slowly achieved many of their goals. Public facilities were desegregated, black children began to attend previously all-white schools and colleges, and black citizens slowly added their names to voter rolls. At the same time, however, the potential for racial strife was spreading north. During the sixties, the minority populations of major Northern cities grew swiftly. In New York, the black population rose from 14 percent in 1960 to over 20 percent in just five years. At first it was assumed that the city's abundant social services and generally liberal outlook would make it possible for the newcomers to be assimilated. After all, this was the paradigmatic city of immigrants in a country of immigrants.

The newcomers were from the rural South. Many were unskilled and un-lettered, and they did not adapt easily to urban living. The city's job market no longer absorbed unskilled workers; unions resisted hiring or training them; the school system was unprepared to cope with the special needs of their children; residential segregation forced them into already overcrowded ghettos. Perhaps it was inevitable that members of this disaffected subculture would begin to act out their frustrations.

On June 18, 1964, thousands of blacks, protesting the killing of a local youth by a policeman, spilled into the streets of Harlem, breaking storefronts, looting, and refusing police demands to disperse. Trouble flared several nights during the following week. Smaller disturbances broke out in Brooklyn.

A disquieting murmur could be heard in the justification by some blacks for these events. Jewish landlords and shopkeepers had been the targets of much of the property destruction, and the rabble-rousers said that they deserved to suffer because of their long-standing exploitation of their tenants and customers. Jewish organizations like the Anti-Defamation League protested, but their protests were, on the whole, disregarded. The incidents received scant attention in the *Post*.

In the next few years, virtually every major city in America endured some form of urban disorder. In August 1965, a riot broke out in Watts, the heart of the black section in Los Angeles. Before it was quelled after a turbulent week of violence, thirty-four people were dead, nearly nine hundred had been injured, city blocks were destroyed by fire, and images of enraged blacks, often in the act of looting local businesses, terrified the rest of the nation.

There were bloody riots in Chicago, Cleveland, and once again in Watts in the summer of 1966. The following year, trouble occurred first in Boston and then in Newark, New Jersey, where twenty-seven people died and hundreds were arrested. Downtown Detroit was virtually destroyed in a week of riots that ended only when President Lyndon Johnson sent in federal troops.

In late July, rioting broke out in East Harlem, a black and Puerto Rican neighborhood, after a policeman killed an allegedly unarmed man. Although sporadic demonstrations and looting took place over several nights, steady rain and the willingness of Mayor John Lindsay to show up in person on the streets of the ghetto urging calm kept the disorder from spreading.

In all, more than one hundred American cities experienced some level of racial violence in the summer of 1967. Eighty-three people were killed, about two thousand seriously injured, and more than twelve thousand arrested.

In response, President Johnson named Governor Otto Kerner of Illinois to head a National Advisory Commission on Civil Disorders. The commission's findings—issued the following year—stated that the United States actually contained two nations, separate and unequal, and blamed most of the urban discord on racial policies designed by the dominant white community that left blacks and other minorities with inadequate housing, schooling, employment, and social services.

Dorothy Schiff had serious reservations about the Kerner report. In a memo to James Wechsler, she worried that the report placed all the blame for the riots on "white racism"; she feared that black extremists would take this as justification for further violent actions. She also criticized the report for not encouraging responsible black leaders to assert themselves within their own communities.

She pointed out that the schools failed to meet the needs of many white children, and that the report, while blaming racism in general for poor education in black schools, did not spell out what role black parents and teachers played. She asked rhetorically about other forms of racial and religious intolerance in America and wondered if the victims of prejudice ever played a part in encouraging the stereotypes that were invoked about them. She concluded, she told Jimmy, that the Kerner report was "not sufficiently profound."

Evidence that New York City was beginning to polarize around the race question had surfaced in 1966 when Mayor Lindsay, responding to repeated claims that the police were brutal to blacks and Puerto Ricans in their custody, proposed to add four civilians to the review board that had traditionally been staffed by three officers from the department. The police, enraged at the suggestion, forced a special election to ratify or disallow Lindsay's initiative.

Lindsay counted on the support of all the constituents of the old liberal coalition—the city's intelligentsia, civic and political leaders of both parties, major Jewish organizations, civil rights groups, and organized labor. But many white voters were scared by the lawlessness in the ghettos. Middle-class and working-class families feared that minority families were about to move into their neighborhoods, imperiling their schools, their property values, and their physical safety. They cared more about law and order than about civil rights.

The civilian review board was rejected in every borough except Manhattan. Seventy-five percent of outer borough voters backed the police. A majority of traditional Democratic party supporters—many of them unionized blue-collar workers, city employees, and people holding clerical or sales jobs—turned their backs on the liberal coalition to vote along racial lines. Nearly 90 percent of the Italian Americans in Canarsie, a Democratic strong- hold in Brooklyn, rejected Lindsay's board. In Jewish neighborhoods in Brooklyn and Queens, the board got less than one-half the vote. Working- and lower-middle-class Jews—many of them loyal readers of the *New York Post*—separated themselves from the liberal gentry in Manhattan. The racial fears that they shared with their mostly Catholic neighbors were stronger than their traditional sense of support for the underdog and concern that prejudice expressed against any group in society would soon be turned against the Jews.

The *Post* supported Lindsay's proposal. Nothing in the paper's subse- quent analysis of the vote suggested that Dorothy Schiff or James Wechsler recognized that a gulf was emerging between the paper's editorial policy and the political sensibilities of its core readers.

The split was impossible to ignore, however, during the ensuing conflict among the Board of Education, the United Federation of Teachers (UFT), and community activists that shut down the city's schools for weeks at a time in 1967 and again in 1968. The bitterness engendered by this tragic struggle would poison New York City politics for years.

The New York City public school system, long thought of as one of the nation's finest, faced a serious crisis posed by significant changes in its stu- dent population. Between 1950 and 1960, the white population of New York dropped by more than eight hundred thousand as middle- and working-class families left for Westchester County, Long Island, and New Jersey. Many of those who stayed sent their children to private or parochial schools, resulting in a 20 percent drop in white enrollment in the public schools. Meanwhile, the children of newly arrived Puerto Ricans and blacks crowded into schools in ghetto neighborhoods. By 1960, there were more minority children than whites enrolled in the schools. In Manhattan, where white enrollment in pri- vate schools was proportionately highest, three out of four public elementary school students were black or of Hispanic descent.

Leaders in the minority communities pointed out that their neighbor- hood schools were on the whole second-class: they were housed in older buildings, they did not get their fair share of resources, they were staffed by fewer veteran teachers, and staff turnover was high. Drawing an analogy to the *Brown v. Board of Education* ruling that no state could maintain two sep- arate school systems, black parents and politicians began demanding that

New York City schoolchildren no longer be segregated by race, even if they acknowledged that such segregation was a de facto result of residential segregation rather than imposed by law. Activist parents in minority communities began to demand some say in how their children's schools were run.

Formal parental involvement was not on the face of it a bad idea. Many supporters—in both racial communities—agreed that encouraging minority parents (who were frequently criticized for not being sufficiently interested in their children's education) to take responsibility for local schools would have a positive influence. Some cynics saw community involvement as a constructive way to engage the energies of minority activists by ceding them part of the system at no sacrifice to anyone outside the ghetto. Ideologues saw it as a manifestation of "power to the people." Conservative whites recognized that minority control of minority schools implied they should be able to maintain control of the schools in their own neighborhoods.

Enthusiasm for community control was not shared by the teachers' union. The UFT, under the energetic leadership of Albert Shanker, was apprehensive that its members' hard-won job rules, including tenure, seniority, and specified grievance procedures, would be disregarded. The Board of Education was also opposed. The board argued that its mandate to run the city's schools could be modified only through legislation. Nonetheless, the board agreed in the spring of 1967 to set up three experimental projects, encompassing some unspecified degree of local control.

One of the three neighborhoods chosen for the experiment was Ocean Hill–Brownsville in Brooklyn, where a group of parents and teachers began to work on plans for the nine-school district. The community group chose Rhody McCoy to be its acting administrator. McCoy had worked in the city schools for eighteen years, rising to the rank of acting principal. He was convinced he had been repeatedly passed over for advancement in favor of less competent whites, who were often Jewish. One of McCoy's first defiant acts was to appoint Herman Ferguson to be principal of IS 55. Ferguson had earned a reputation as a very militant assistant principal in Queens. Despite a request from the Board of Education to cancel the appointment, the community members of the community board voted to affirm it. The teachers on the board abstained. An ominous racial division was becoming apparent.

Simultaneously, the UFT was threatening a citywide strike. As usual in labor negotiations, the chief issue of contention was pay, but teachers also de-

manded changes in their job rules, including a greater ability to discipline kids
who disrupted their classrooms. The UFT, whose membership was more than
90 percent white and more than 50 percent Jewish, was also eager to retain
rules of tenure that had been written to protect teachers from being at the
mercy of arbitrary principals. Many people in the black community accused
the union of using those rules to protect incompetent and racist teachers.

On September 11, 1967, which was to be the first day of school, there was
still no contract. Most teachers went on strike. Many picketed the schools.
The schools tried to make do with parents and other volunteers, plus those
teachers who showed up, in defiance of the union, because of their loyalty to
the students. The demonstration schools tried particularly hard to stay open.
The strike lasted for three bitter weeks and exacerbated previous tensions
among all concerned.

Frank Sinatra's dispute with the owners of a Las Vegas casino dominated
the front page of the *New York Post* the week the teachers went out. The paper barely noticed the strike. When it was finally settled, Wechsler editorialized that although the UFT had long upheld "the principle and practice of
teacher unionism," it had not been acting entirely in good faith in this event.
He castigated the Board of Education and various city and state politicos for
not paying more attention. He said nothing about the community activists.

When school resumed, the problem of Herman Ferguson had not been
settled. Worse, almost all of Ocean Hill–Brownsville's twenty-one assistant
principals claimed they were being harassed by parents and community activists and asked to be transferred to other districts. The governing board
wanted to replace them without reference to the Board of Examiner's list of
eligible candidates. The board also wanted to install its own principals.

At this point the Ford Foundation, which was becoming an active player in
the crisis at the request of Mayor Lindsay, issued a report asking for greater decentralization than had been previously espoused by anyone but the most militant black community activists. The so-called Bundy Report* recommended
that local school districts have the power to hire and fire superintendents and
new teachers, using new streamlined procedures for the recruitment and certi-
fication of new candidates. It also outlined methods of dealing with teachers
whom the local boards deemed not responsive to the needs of the community,

---

*Named for McGeorge Bundy, one of the architects of Kennedy's and Johnson's policy in Vietnam,
who had become president of the Ford Foundation in 1966.

while claiming not to vitiate their tenured rights. The New York Urban Coalition, a self-appointed panel of Manhattan-based do-gooders and business leaders, applauded the report and began to advocate for its implementation.

The UFT was upset. The Bundy Report seemed to endorse an end to the merit system of hiring and job security, and it appeared to imperil long-standing protections for teachers who might be the victims of unjust accusations against them. The local board in Ocean Hill was upset because, in its view, the report did not go far enough in supporting community control. The local board was now asking for total control over budgets, hiring, firing, and choice of teaching materials. The Board of Education pointed out that all of this was illegal but made no attempt to work with the community board toward any compromise.

The following spring, the Ocean Hill board decided to assert its complete independence. It announced the dismissal of thirteen teachers and six supervisors. It also recommended that their replacements be hired without adherence to Board of Education guidelines. McCoy claimed that he had not fired the nineteen people in question; he had just transferred them back to the Board of Education, which was welcome to reassign them.

In response, the UFT pulled all its members out of the Ocean Hill–Brownsville schools, which the Board of Education then closed for the seven remaining weeks of the school year. In a season already poisoned by the murder of Martin Luther King Jr., the forced closing of Columbia College, and increasingly unpleasant racial rhetoric, the shutdown of the Brooklyn schools was one of the low points.

In the next weeks, the state legislature, galvanized at last by the magnitude of the crisis, passed a law enabling the Board of Education to expand, effectively permitting the appointment of more pro-community members, and empowering it to delegate functions to local boards as it saw fit. Local boards appeared to have gotten most of what they wanted, and the UFT went along because it was assured that teachers' rights would be unchanged.

It was not to be. Just before school opened in September 1968, McCoy announced that he would replace all the teachers who had gone out on strike the previous spring. In response, the UFT called its second citywide strike in two years.

McCoy was determined to keep his schools open. He hastily staffed the classrooms with a few UFT defectors and a host of young idealists and opportunists who showed up for work. The UFT called them scabs.

It appeared that the strike would be brief. The Board of Education agreed that the replacement teachers had no standing and that all the teachers who had walked out or been dismissed the previous spring were entitled to resume their jobs in Ocean Hill. But when UFT members showed up on September 11 and 12 to reclaim their classrooms, they were met by angry demonstrators who tried to prevent them from entering the buildings and shouted abuse at them. Shanker pulled everyone back off the job the next day.

Once again the demonstration schools were among the few to stay open. McCoy's new hires did the best they could to maintain some order in their classrooms, while outside their schools, the scene turned increasingly nasty. UFT pickets were assailed by members of the community screaming anti-white and anti-Semitic slogans. At a UFT rally a few days later, Shanker displayed anti-Semitic pamphlets he said were in wide distribution.*

Anti-Semitic blacks asserted that asking their children to attend schools with Jewish teachers and administrators subjected them to a form of "mental genocide." Such outbursts were not condemned by any major city officials, nor were they sufficiently denounced by the mainstream media.

This ugly episode dragged on for two months. Excluding a two-week period in early October when the union members briefly went back to work, the citywide strike lasted until November 17. Finally the Board of Education took over control of the Ocean Hill–Brownsville school district, suspended the community board, and announced that any of the dismissed teachers who wished to have their jobs back could have them.

Throughout the crisis, *The New York Times* framed the issue as one in which the Ocean Hill–Brownsville board, while perhaps naïve in its decisions, was basically protecting its community's legitimate interests against the intransigent white establishment. The *Times* also downplayed the lurid anti-Semitism as just one expression of antiwhite discontent, and it blamed the UFT for widening the dispute and, by implication, for eliciting the anti-Semitic attacks.

At the *New York Post,* matters were more complex, and policy shifted. During the 1967 strike, the paper reflexively sided with the union. Teachers were its natural constituency—they were unionized civil servants, the children of im-

---

*The origin and dissemination of these pamphlets remains a subject of contention. They were almost certainly produced and distributed originally by black militants. However, subsequent allegations that the FBI and/or the UFT itself fanned the flames by reprinting them in greater numbers and adding to their circulation have never been proved or disproved.

migrants, many of them Jewish, many the first in their families to go to college and begin the trek into the middle class. Even before the trouble broke out, Jimmy Wechsler met with several junior high school principals to discuss problems in the schools. They alerted him to the fact that black militant groups were beginning to harass white teachers and staff members and were asking for their replacement without cause. Jimmy reported back to Dorothy Schiff that this was an outrage against everything the teachers and their unions stood for.

Bernie Bard, the *Post*'s education columnist, commenting on the 1967 strike, was sympathetic to the UFT. Obviously there were some slackers among the city's twenty-five thousand teachers, Bard wrote, but most of them worked hard and long hours, even though they earned no overtime. They were paid less than members of the police and fire departments; they deserved the salary increases they were asking for. He barely acknowledged the grievances of the community boards and their backers.

Bard continued to favor the UFT in the fall of 1968 when troubles broke out anew. He castigated the efforts of community activists like McCoy as anti-Semitic and antiunion, and he also lit into the Ford Foundation and other pillars of the liberal establishment for misreading the situation. Dorothy Schiff, who had hitherto paid little attention to the issues, called her reporter in for a meeting.

Bard says, "I got an invitation for a command performance to go up to Dolly and talk with her in her office. The one impression I had was that she was very curious about where I stood and why I stood there. I believed that the Jewish liberals were being suckered by the black militants. At our meeting I had the impression that she was not in the teachers' corner on this issue, although she didn't say so directly to me. But she in no way attempted to talk me out of it or have me change my position or my attitude."

By 1968, Dorothy and Jimmy Wechsler, like many Manhattan liberals who were geographically and psychologically removed from the daily turmoil on the streets of Ocean Hill, had cast their lot with the advocates of community control. Having sent their own children to private schools, they perhaps took for granted a system in which parents' wishes were heeded. And, although such liberals were often unquestioning supporters of unions, their mind-set was attuned to unions of blue-collar workers. They did not know what to make of the teachers, often women, whose demeanor if not their incomes did not fit the image.

While *Post* reporters told the story of what was happening in the streets,

Dolly and Jimmy—perhaps in denial about some of what they were seeing—supported the Ocean Hill community board and condemned the union. Weeks into the strike, Jimmy sent a memo upstairs restating their position: the teachers' strikes were illegal; if the UFT believed that dismissals of its members by McCoy were invalid, they could challenge them in court rather than closing the schools. While deploring some behavior of community activists and presenting the union's arguments (all of which, Jimmy reminded Dolly, the paper had covered at length in its news stories), the *Post* took the position that decentralization was an idea whose time had come and should therefore be encouraged, whatever the temporary setbacks.

On the eve of the reopening of the schools, Wechsler pointed out that the community board had promised to cooperate with a settlement plan put forward by the state Department of Education, even though it disagreed with many of its provisions, whereas the UFT rejected the plan because it did not grant the union all of its demands. "It would be hard to draw a sharper contrast," wrote Wechsler, "between the consistently maturing spirit of compromise displayed by the Ocean Hill board in the recent stages of the crisis and the UFT's distressing retreat into sullen intransigence."

Murray Kempton went even further in his partisanship: "I don't know anyone who has seen one of McCoy's schools and not come away impressed with the deportment of the pupils, the quiet dignity of the corridors, the engagement of the teachers. . . . Yet Shanker has been able to ride on a general public impression that Ocean Hill has no curriculum beyond drills in karate and mass recitations of the speeches of Marcus Garvey." Kempton blamed the mayor and any citizens who did not wholeheartedly support the community school board with contributing to the end of the social compact in New York.

Many *Post* readers were furious, Bernie Bard among them. He admired Murray Kempton as a colleague and as a gentleman, but he thought this was a case where Kempton had gone too far. "I disagreed enough with what he said to write a letter to the editor of the *Post*," says Bard, "and they printed it!"

Many aggrieved readers let the paper know how they stood. Some were thoughtful:

Dear Mrs. Schiff:
What is happening to the Post? I am shocked and upset over Murray Kempton's enclosed column. . . . I cannot understand how you can permit such irresponsible words to appear in your newspaper. What happened to

the Post's liberal stand for peace and understanding? Are you deserting the
"little people" who have depended on you for so long? Please don't.

And what has happened to Murray Kempton? . . . He is serving no cause
except the cause of violence and disruptions. . . . I appeal to you to show the
responsibility that is needed to the people who depend on you.

Sincerely,
Allen Green

Some were more personal and vitriolic:

Dear Dorothy Schiff,

Instead of writing smarmy editorials about how we mustn't get violent on
the Negro–anti-Semitic–anti-teacher question, how about really letting the
public read all the facts . . . instead of Murray Kempton's "Get that middle
class Shanker" version. . . . you never do know where the fire'll be next
time . . . and it will be your fault for slanting the truth. The anti-Semitic
literature passed out on 145 Street is not trivial, precisely because it builds
up to an almost automatic acceptance of anti-Semitism and anti-teacher
unionism as the American way. And your sort of ancient Marxist-based guilt
about Jewish merchants in Harlem is no help either.

Just to remind you . . . to print the whole truth instead of leaning on it so
hard.

Esther Soretsky

Dorothy always insisted on answering mail. In this case, polite and abrasive letters received the same response, signed by her executive secretary:

We have received your communication concerning the UFT strike. We
feel strongly that our major concern should be to find a way to solve the
problem of educating the children. To achieve that goal, it will be necessary
for all elements in our society to work together with dedication and good
will. We shall continue to try to further that objective.

Sincerely,
Jean Gillette

Many letter writers called Dorothy a traitor to her people. Some were sure
her grandfather would be ashamed of her stance.

In general, the letters were indicative of a growing rift within the *Post*'s constituency. As the alliance between blacks and Jewish liberals was fraying, the split between those in the Jewish community who were trying to repair the damage and those who saw it as permanent, and even inevitable, grew ever wider. The United States was a more welcoming home for Jews than Europe had ever been. The assimilationists among them responded to this higher comfort level by merging with the mainstream community. Others clung more strongly to their ethnic and religious ties.

Those Jews who wished to assimilate were free to do so. The barriers that had kept their parents out of leading universities, social clubs, and many industries were dissolving. Jews assumed the leadership of a variety of organizations that would have barred their participation a generation earlier. These were the Jews who believed that the best way to protect their new status was through alliances with other liberals. They were active supporters of civil rights and civil liberties campaigns. Because New Yorkers lived in neighborhoods and sent their children to schools that were often segregated by economic level at least as much as by ethnic or racial differences, Jewish assimilationists spent much of their time isolated from some of the more fractious aspects of city life. When anti-Semitism intruded, whether in a private conversation or on the streets of Ocean Hill–Brownsville, they tended to explain it away as a last vestige of ignorance or as an unfortunate expression of a benighted population that perhaps even had a legitimate grievance. Jews who protested too strongly about such anti-Semitic behavior were, in their view, overreacting and making matters worse.

Such assimilationist Jews, among them Dorothy Schiff and many of her Jewish employees, lost sight of a countervailing trend among Jewish New Yorkers who were less isolated from the social turmoil engulfing the city and the nation. Jews living in Brooklyn and the Bronx were worried about violence on their local streets and the eroding quality of their local schools. Many of them were first-time homeowners who feared that property values in their neighborhood were threatened by the encroachment of nearby ghettos. Having worked hard to get where they were, they were resentful of people who argued that blacks, as an especially put-upon minority, deserved special breaks.

Most of all, Jews from the outer boroughs felt that their status as Jewish Americans was more marginal and imperiled than their Manhattan brethren did. The most extreme among them were drawn to a new organization, the

Jewish Defense League (JDL), which was founded in 1968 by a charismatic young rabbi, Meir Kahane. Kahane played upon vivid memories of the Holocaust, claiming that just as Israel was at risk of annihilation by the surrounding Arab nations, so were American Jews vulnerable to attack by anti-Semites around them. He encouraged his followers to arm themselves in their own defense because the mainstream Jewish organizations, he said, would sell them out to gain favor with the powerful non-Jewish establishment.

Actual membership in the JDL was tiny, but many nervous Jews shared some of Kahane's worries—the sense of betrayal by Jewish leaders was prominent among them. This fear came to the fore during the school crisis. Many working- and middle-class Jews, who identified with the teachers, believed that the elite Manhattan Jews tolerated bad behavior on the part of black community activists and turned their back on the UFT because of class bias that blinded them to the dangers of anti-Semitism and prevented them from defending their fellow Jews.

For someone who prided herself on her ability to empathize with the concerns of her readers, Dorothy Schiff seemed oblivious to this division. James Wechsler shared her blinkered vision. Paul Sann, always less of an ideologue, did not. In the spring of 1969, Sann sent Dolly two articles from *Commentary* that reflected his concerns on the Ocean Hill–Brownsville mess.

The first was "Is American Jewry in Crisis?" by Milton Himmelfarb, who took the position that anti-Semitism was a serious menace to the Jewish community. Himmelfarb believed that mainstream America revealed a latent anti-Semitism in its eagerness to accommodate the most outrageous demands of black militants. He thought that quotas would soon be imposed, limiting the number of Jews in various professions, and that if the Jews attempted to protest such laws, they would find few allies in the general community. Himmelfarb concluded his argument by saying, "In New York our remaining years in the civil service, and above all in the schools, are not many: if policy does not drive us out, terrorism will. (It has started.)"

Dolly told Sann she thought the article was unclear and overwrought. She did not believe that quotas were going to be imposed, she thought the schools would benefit from more black teachers, and she assumed that any Jewish teachers who chose to leave the city system would find jobs in the suburbs.

The second *Commentary* article that Sann brought to Dolly's attention was a more measured piece, "Blacks, Jews & the Intellectuals" by Nathan Glazer, which appeared a month after Himmelfarb's diatribe. Glazer made it clear that not all black leaders were anti-Semitic and that many had taken forthright stands against racism of any kind. Glazer admitted that some Jews might be displaced as shopkeepers, teachers, or civil servants, but he was confident they would find other jobs with the support, if necessary, of Jewish organizations.

Glazer's conclusions that anti-Semitism did not pose a clear and present danger to the American Jewish community and that helping blacks achieve their economic and political goals would go a long way toward resolving tension made sense to Dolly. She remained convinced that Jews who claimed that anti-Semitism motivated their opponents caused a great deal of harm to the Jewish community. She told Sann she believed that Shanker had been wrong to reproduce and distribute the anti-Semitic pamphlets. She also argued that the crisis in the schools was not so much a result of race tension, pitting Jewish teachers against black students and their families, as it was a problem of social class, in which middle-class teachers were hard put to communicate with "lower-class" students and their families.

Nothing could make Dolly understand that the UFT, though its tactics were inappropriate, reflected the genuine worries of its members and of many ethnic communities about the perceived threats posed by militant black leaders. Her son-in-law Wynn Kramarsky, who was a member of the Lindsay administration during the period, says, "She couldn't reach beyond the young, the Manhattan orientation, to see what there was beyond that. When I first met her, I don't think she'd ever been in Brooklyn. It was very complicated. And Jimmy didn't help.

"She couldn't go far enough to the right to be totally antiunion. But she was attracted to populism. You know, populism is such a dangerous concept. It's a perfectly lovely thing to embrace, but . . ." In general, Kramarsky believes that Dolly ducked a forthright editorial position in the Ocean Hill–Brownsville issue because it was hard to find a solution to the problems it raised, and "it was very ugly, and she didn't like ugly."

The solutions were indeed hard to find, but they did exist. The *Post* could have exposed the reluctance of banks to lend to blacks who wanted to buy homes outside the ghetto; it could have gone after real estate agents who encouraged white stampedes from neighborhoods into which minority families began to move; it could have encouraged the police to get tough on street violence; it could have pointed out that the victims of most street crime lived in the ghettos whose residents would have welcomed color-blind police protection; it could have condemned racism whatever its source. The *Post* could have made a greater effort to address the fears—real and imaginary—of its working- and middle-class Democratic readers and educate them about the differences.

All of these editorial positions would have been consistent with liberal ideology. But while Dorothy Schiff, James Wechsler, and Paul Sann had been willing to wrestle with the complexities of postwar anticommunist liberalism and to formulate a coherent response to them, they were unable to face the challenges posed by the politics of the late sixties with that same zeal. Perhaps, like many of their generation, they were tired and lacked the intellectual energy to enter the fray. Perhaps they were not viscerally engaged by the issues or were put off by the spokesmen for them. Perhaps they identified with the political establishment. Whatever influenced them, they failed to grapple meaningfully with the racial and economic conflicts that engulfed their city and their nation.

TWENTY-TWO

The Candy Store

Dorothy Schiff and her editorial and business teams reacted defensively to the new political and economic landscape of the mid- and late 1960s. Accustomed to the role of plucky underdog in the hierarchy of New York newspapers, they did not move boldly in their new position as undisputed winners in the afternoon field.

Freed of competition for afternoon readers, the *Post*'s average daily circulation remained above seven hundred thousand throughout the later part of the decade. Advertising revenues grew as well. In 1967, the paper retained net earnings of nearly $1 million; in 1968, it earned approximately $1.25 million, and in 1969, nearly $1.75 million. Although costs associated with the South Street plant led to the Post Corporation taking on nearly $6 million of debt, Dorothy's equity in the company doubled between 1965 and 1969 to nearly $10 million.

Even so, Dorothy continued to steam unused stamps off return envelopes and to spend hours trying to prevent employees from using company phones for private calls. She once chastised Byron Greenberg for photocopying old memos and attaching them to new memos. This was an unnecessary waste of paper, she complained. Just reference the date of the original and her secretary could find it in the files.

Greenberg says, "She did spend some money in the late sixties. The new plant and equipment, of course. And investment in automation was almost a requirement. But the product itself needed attention. And that was tougher to get approval for. We did things, but Paul Sann and I thought we should have loosened the purse strings a bit more."

The editors, mindful of her obsession and fearful of being second-guessed, turned stinginess into an art. Reporter Roberta Brandes Gratz says, "On certain issues, they anticipated Dolly—they went beyond Dolly—and there were times when they drove us crazy in that way, and you couldn't be sure whether Dolly cared or not."

Gratz invited the subject of an article to her home for dinner rather than entertain in a restaurant, believing the setting would be more comfortable, and not incidentally, the costs would be lower. Her expense account came under special scrutiny, because of the possibility that she had asked to be reimbursed for something that her family may have eaten. "Dolly will want to know who got the extra coffee," an editor told her.

Another reporter remembers being assigned to look into an antipoverty program in Philadelphia. His editor told him to cover the story completely but not to spend the night. Night editors complained about having to rewrite stories without conferring with the reporters who had filed them, because the reporters had gone home for the day and calling them for clarification would make them eligible for overtime.

Overtime was a big deal. Sann was under strict instructions to keep it down. Some reporters accepted time off in lieu of extra cash. They were happy to supplement their incomes working on other projects during their free time. On a paper that was already thinly staffed, however, the benefits to the balance sheet of restricting overtime pay had to be set against the losses in the quality of reportage.

Unusual expenses of any kind were a red flag to the editors. "Here's a story," says Bernie Bard, "that goes back to the Dolly days. Once the principals' union invited the three education journalists—one from the *News,* one from the *Times,* and me from the *Post*—to come down to Nassau to cover their convention. The *Times* and the *News* had policies against free trips. They said to their guys, 'Go down. Cover the convention, and put in your expenses when you get back. We'll pay your way.' "

Johnny Bott, the city editor at the *Post,* never raised the possibility of picking up Bard's tab. He focused on a more picayune matter. "Bott said to me, 'What's the Western Union rate from the Bahamas? What's it going to cost us if you wire in some stories?' So I call up Western Union, and they tell me the overseas press rate is something like eleven cents a word. Bott says, 'Too much. The higher-ups will never buy it.'

"So he said, 'Just go down there, have a good time, take the days off your vacation time, and whatever you do, don't send back any stories!'"

During the convention, the commissioner of the city schools made a speech about a major shift in policy. "Naturally," says Bard, "the News and the Times went to town with this story. It was a big story. But I was under instructions—zippo, not a word. Lay on the beach, Bard, do whatever you do, but don't file any stories. Okay. And when I came back to Gotham, no one ever said a damn thing."

Dorothy was sensitive to the problem. She complained to Sann that editors sometimes vetoed reporters' requests to cover an out-of-town story by saying it would be too expensive. Expense should never be the basis of a journalistic decision, she reminded him. The Post should always be willing to send a reporter anywhere around the globe if the story under consideration was of major interest to the paper's readers, but only if there was no adequate coverage available from wire services or other sources.

Dorothy's argument was not wrong, but the problem was more pervasive than the occasional big-ticket trip to cover a breaking story.* Sann periodically asked for more staff. In the summer of 1967, in response to a question from Dorothy about why the paper was being scooped on New York stories by The Wall Street Journal, he pointed out that the Journal had 125 general assignment reporters. The Post had forty in New York and one in Washington. He suggested expanding those numbers, beginning in DC. Dorothy nixed his request, saying that Post readers wanted more local, not national, news. But she did not approve of any staff additions in New York, either.

Dorothy knew the Post was going slack. She wrote Sann in 1968 that the paper was not doing as good a job as it had in former years uncovering local corruption by investigating collusion between city officials and local businessmen. Despite rising profits, however, she was unwilling to reinvest real money.

---

*For big stories of interest to New York readers, Dolly was, in fact, willing to send a Post reporter. For example, Helen Dudar went to California for the trial of Sirhan Sirhan, and Carl Pelleck covered the New Orleans trial of Clay Shaw, a reputed accomplice in the assassination of Jack Kennedy. Pete Hamill was sent to Vietnam and then to Florida for the trial of Cathy Mossler, a woman accused of plotting with her nephew-lover to murder her older, wealthy husband.

To add four pages to the news hole every day, Greenberg explains, would have cost hundreds of thousands of dollars per year in newsprint costs, salaries for more reporters and editors, and advertising sales personnel whose job it would have been to recoup some of the costs through greater ad linage.

Instead of committing herself to such an investment, Dorothy filled the paper with an ever-shifting array of columns by political commentators. At an average syndication fee of $30 to $50 per column per week, this approach was much less expensive than adding to the reportorial staff. The potted commentary of many of these columns gave the *Post* its growing reputation as a static conventional organ rather than the vibrant voice it had once been.

Such everyday parsimony was self-defeating. Dorothy's insistence on trimming costs to the bone was bad for morale. It jeopardized the journalistic excellence she claimed to demand by forcing talented journalists to leave because she would not pay them what they needed to stay.

"New journalism" was on the rise. Writers became the stars of their own work. They could become rich and famous. Potential income from big book contracts and movie sales began to distort their expectations. Disputes over money were at the root of the paper's intermittent difficulties with its most admired columnists, Murray Kempton and Pete Hamill.

In 1960, Hamill had been thrilled to get a job at the *Post*. Within a few years, he was established as one of New York's best young journalists. He wanted to stay at the paper but could not afford to turn down more lucrative offers. Dolly, who liked Hamill and recognized his value to the paper, was forced to loosen her purse strings. By 1966, the *Post* was paying him $225 a week for three columns, which gave him time to take freelance magazine assignments, but he still had trouble making ends meet. Threatening to resign, Pete wrote to Sann, "The economics of the newspaper business make it impossible for me to continue. . . . I have to measure the interests of my family against personal pleasure I get from writing the column. I can't feed them with tearsheets."

Because Hamill owed money to the Internal Revenue Service, his accountant suggested that he live outside the country for the next year. Dolly tried to help. She gave him $5,000—from personal funds—toward his debts and tried to introduce him to her tax lawyers. He was determined to go to Europe, and Dolly agreed to pay him $200 a week for two columns from wherever his travels took him.

From her point of view, she was being quite generous and permissive, but Pete wanted more. He filed his columns for several months, while working on a novel, and then returned to the States to work for *Newsday* for what he said was double the money plus benefits.

He lasted at *Newsday* less than six months. In January 1968, he wrote Dolly from Ireland to say that he had quit because the editors wanted too much control over his column. "I must say," he said, "that my brief experience working for them showed me again how classy the *Post* was to me." Back in the States, Hamill began a regular column in *The Village Voice* and contributed longer articles to major magazines. He wrote a best-selling thriller and hoped for a movie deal. But he could always use a weekly paycheck, and the *Post* remained a possible source. During the next year, Paul and Dolly had several conversations with Pete about returning. Despite their worries that it probably wouldn't last, they re-signed him to write four columns a week, at $100 each, plus benefits, in July 1969.

Kempton also had a turbulent employment history. Throughout the fifties, Dolly and Sann adjusted his pay and his benefits to keep him happy. He was earning $200 a week for four columns in 1958 when he received permission to leave New York and file his pieces from Rome. He was prickly about having his increasingly ornate copy tampered with. At one point in the spring of 1959, Kempton swore he'd quit because the city editor had cut several paragraphs without getting approval. Afraid he would carry out his threat, Dolly proposed that Sann, Kempton's favorite editor, write an apologetic letter. She knew that Paul would find this unpalatable but said that Murray was the type of genius who responded best to rewards rather than censure.

Her insight seemed correct for the time being. But soon after Kempton returned to the States in late 1959, he began to make new demands. He wanted a guarantee no one would edit copy without his approval. He also wanted more money. Dolly approved a raise to $300 a week, but she cautioned Sann to "tell him that he must stop resigning, it's a management nuisance."

Murray's next resignation was not a ploy. In December 1962, on what would turn out to be the eve of the big strike, he left to become editor of *The New Republic.* Unsatisfied there, he moved to the *World-Telegram,* and then, in the wake of the Widget merger, came home again to the *Post* to write four columns a week for $100 each.

He seems to have been miserable almost immediately. He told Dorothy in October 1966 that returning had been a mistake. He found the *Post* less congenial than it had been when he left. He believed the paper was becoming part of the establishment. Kempton admitted that the *Post*'s editorials shared his critical view of President Johnson's Vietnam policies, but he complained that his pieces were questioned by the editors as being too harsh. Dorothy believed Murray was envious of Pete Hamill, who was now the paper's star and got along with everyone.

More and more committed to driving President Johnson from office, Kempton asked for a six-month leave of absence in March 1968 to work for Eugene McCarthy and to write a book. In order to keep his union benefits intact, he finally agreed to take a modified leave, which required that he provide the paper with one column a week. Murray's disappointment at the failure of McCarthy's campaign, plus his legal troubles after his arrest at the Chicago convention, left him demoralized. A segment of the *Post*'s readership was similarly disenchanted with him after his outright support for the Ocean Hill–Brownsville school board during the strike later that year.

In early 1969, he made good on his periodic threat to walk away. In March 1969, the *Post* announced a shake-up within its pages. Kempton was resigning immediately to work on longer magazine pieces. Jules Feiffer's weekly cartoon strip was being dropped at the same time. Jimmy Breslin, who had come to the paper fairly recently, left, he said, to write a book. He soon declared his candidacy for president of New York's City Council.

Dorothy was unapologetic. She cited a "lack of reader interest" for the Feiffer decision, pointing out that his cartoon ran also in *The Village Voice*. She barely registered Breslin's presence or his absence. As for Kempton, she told Sann that they had made a mistake when they brought him back. He had poor-mouthed the *Post* when he worked at the *Telegram*. Murray had become too cynical and set in his ways, she said, and the *Post* would be better off starting afresh with bright, enthusiastic younger reporters.

In 1967—the year the *Post* began making big money—Paul Sann pleaded with Byron Greenberg, who established the annual payroll with Dorothy, to give substantial raises to his subordinates. Sann pointed out that some of the editors were earning less than reporters they supervised, because the reporters received Guild-mandated raises while the editors were dependent on management's judgment. His plea was partially heeded; the men in question received modest raises and substantial annual bonuses.*

---

*The bonus system, which had been in place for some years, enabled management to reward individuals without establishing a general hike in pay levels, but bonuses could never be counted on and were not included in the calculations regarding eventual pensions.

In 1967, James Wechsler asked for $40,000, which he claimed was on a par with what his counterpart at the *Times* received, in combined recompense for his columns and his services as editorial page editor and writer. He also asked for five weeks of paid vacation. Four years passed before Jimmy received a raise to $40,000 and was permitted to take a fifth week of vacation in the form of occasional Fridays. The pot was sweetened by annual bonuses of $5,000.

Sann's annual salary also advanced haltingly from $33,000 in 1961 to $37,600 in 1967. This latter raise was evidently not what he had hoped for, as evidenced by a bitter memo he sent Dorothy at the time. He claimed that he had not asked for a raise since 1955 nor had he challenged the size of the increases that were granted to him since then because the whole process was too humiliating. He barely ever requested reimbursement for expenses and routinely paid for the business phone calls he made from home. Perhaps Dorothy was abashed. The next year she jumped Sann's income to $46,500 including his bonus, and in 1970 increased the total to $50,000.

Soon after the 1962 strike/lockout that shut down all seven New York newspapers, Victor Navasky, the publisher of *Monocle,* a humor magazine, assembled a group of talented young journalists and would-be journalists to create parody issues of the major papers. "Our aim," says Navasky, "was to publish, simultaneously, parodies of four papers—the *News,* the *Post,* the *Times,* and the *Tribune*—all with the same headline and see how the different papers would have treated it. We came up with this great headline for the *Post:* 'Cold Snap Hits Our Town. Jews, Negroes Suffer Most.' But there was no story. And no way to use it for the other papers. So we went with something about the strike. We did a parody of the *News* and the *Post*—called the *New York Pest*—and a modified version of the *Trib.* We never did the *Times* at all. And we made a mistake—we should have used that headline for the *Post* because it was perfect, and it's what we all remember talking about."

Despite the failed opportunity, the *Post* parody was the liveliest Navasky and friends produced. At least in part because it was a labor of love.

Navasky says, "I thought of the *Post* as my paper. And Max Lerner, I'm embarrassed to say, was my model. That's what I wanted to be when I grew up—I wanted to write a column, and write books, and teach. And he did it all. But he was pretty pontifical, even in those days. Dan Wakefield did his

parody of Lerner's column called 'Wags and the West,' about the death of a
little dog named Wags that belonged to a girl in the Bronx. The dog became
a metaphor for the East-West struggle and the fate of America as a civilization."

Nora Ephron, fresh out of Wellesley College and working at *Newsweek,*
contributed a riff on Leonard Lyons's column that got the name-dropping
and the pointless anecdotes just right. Sidney Zion, an assistant district attorney, took on Murray Kempton. Pitch-perfect versions by other pals of
Navasky's mocking Rose Franzblau's column, Wechsler's editorial style, and
Pete Hamill's aspirations to write like Ernest Hemingway filled out the eight-
page paper.

Ephron says, "The story was that the editors of the *Post* were in a rage.
Paul Sann and Al Davis wanted to sue. And Dolly said, 'Don't be idiots. If
they can parody us, they can write for us. Hire them!' "

Davis invited Navasky down to his office. Navasky says, "He asked, 'Who
wrote this?' And 'Who wrote this?' And he ended up hiring Sidney Zion and
Nora Ephron."

"Writing the Kempton piece changed my life," Zion says. "I was on my
honeymoon in Mexico, and I came back to find this pile of messages from Al
Davis on my desk. I thought maybe I had libeled Dolly Schiff, because I was
making fun of the thing." Worried, Sidney called Navasky, who said the *Post*
wanted to hire him as soon as the strike was over.

Dolly could afford to be amused. The implied criticism of the predictable
tics of the *Post*'s stars produced by Navasky and friends was affectionate, and
the idea that the *Post* had a place for some of those who produced it showed
the paper to good advantage.

As the sixties wore on, however, criticism of the *Post* began to bite. In
1964, Nat Hentoff complained in the *Voice* that the *Post* had lost its distinctive dedication to investigative journalism. Kempton had left for the first
time, and many other top reporters and columnists were gone as well.
Though the *Post*'s editorial point of view was still better than that of any
other local paper, Hentoff wrote, it was increasingly hidebound. "How about
a hard-hitting look at the Liberal Party?" he asked. "Or at the local labor
movement, which is quite corrupt also?"

The *Daily Mirror* had shut down a few months earlier. Hentoff figured the
Post was next. He hoped that a more aggressive publisher would buy the paper before it was too late. "The way it is now," he wrote, "if the *Post* should

eventually go under, it may be a day or two before anybody notices it has disappeared."

Hentoff kept up his criticism from time to time. It always stung. Dolly was particularly incensed by his comment that, after the collapse of the Widget, New York was basically left with only two papers—the *Times* and the *News*—because "if you don't read the *Post,* you miss little hard news." Wechsler tried to soothe her by saying that Hentoff seemed to have it in for her and that his record on accuracy was not good.

Hentoff's argument was expanded in the September 1969 issue of *Harper's* by Jack Newfield, a young writer who'd had a brief tryout at the *Post* several years earlier. Newfield said he was a disillusioned *Post* reader who'd revered the paper during its glory days. "From about 1954 to 1961 the *Post* was probably the most exciting daily tabloid in the country," Newfield believed, but those days ended when Dolly replaced Jimmy Wechsler with Paul Sann. Now there was no crusading spirit, no reportorial zeal. By 1967, "Commercial and entertainment values became enshrined in the city room, at the expense of literacy and political values. And the editorials had gone from chicken broth to oatmeal mush."

What had gone wrong? Newfield isolated three problems. The first he called "the Candy Store Syndrome," because the paper had become "schlock—unprofessional and cheap." Dolly refused to pay top dollar to keep talented staffers. Because the paper was understaffed, night editors did not generate stories, they simply copied them from the *Times,* the *News,* or the wire services. Because Dolly refused to pay travel expenses, *Post* reporters could not cover important stories out of town.

Newfield's second complaint was that the senior editors, chosen by Paul Sann and reflective of his training and values, were uneducated and anti-intellectual. They stifled good writing—another reason why talented writers moved on. He cited Pete Hamill's explanation of why he left the paper. In 1963, Pete went to Sing Sing to cover the last execution in the upstate prison. "And I came back and wrote a piece telling exactly how it was, with the urine running down the guy's pants' leg as the electricity shot through his body," Hamill told Newfield. "But Bob Friedman [the night city editor] made me rewrite the whole thing. He just wanted a nice, straight news lead. Who died, what time, how many minutes. That's when I decided to quit the first time."

Finally, Newfield laid the blame for the *Post's* decline directly at Dolly's feet because she was "capricious" and "impersonal," forcing the editors to spend too much time trying to figure her out or second-guess her. She was "preoccupied, often quite imaginatively, with trivia and gossip. Thus, she pays almost no attention to the essentials of the paper."

Blair Clark told Newfield that Dolly was an amateur in a job that should be filled by a professional. He said that her management style was formed during the years when the paper barely hung on, and she couldn't adapt to relative prosperity. "She has no idea of expanding now that the *Post* is a monopoly," said Clark, "because she made the paper a success by cutting corners."

The paper had never been more prosperous, Newfield noted, or more irrelevant. People bought it to read on the train home—mostly for the stock tables and the sports coverage. It had no good columnists, no critic of pop culture, no Puerto Rican reporters, and no bureaus outside the city. It was suffering "a slow, internal death of its moral authority." People turned to *The Village Voice* or *The New York Review of Books* for insight into what was happening in the city. They got their hard news from the *Times* and television. "The Jewish Mother of us all is gone," Newfield concluded, repeating Jerry Tallmer's metaphor, "and there are few mourners around to say a proper Kaddish."

Dolly had been on edge since Newfield called Wechsler months before publication to ask a few questions. At that point, she had to be dissuaded from trying to get her friend John Cowles, the owner-publisher of the Minneapolis *Star Tribune,* who also owned *Harper's,* to intervene.

Newfield had had an equivocal history with the *Post*. After making a name for himself with some pieces in the *Voice,* he came to the paper in 1964 for a tryout, which was not successful. However, the editors were unwilling to give up on him, and a year later he, Sann, and Dolly discussed whether or not he might become a columnist. No one seemed in much of a hurry to get a deal done, and eventually Newfield decided he was happier at the *Voice,* where he took potshots at the *Post* from time to time.

When Newfield's piece appeared in *Harper's,* Dolly marked up a copy and sent it to her top editors for comments and rebuttals. Determined to sue Newfield and the magazine, she compiled a fourteen-page letter in which she cited errors and opinions that she considered "malicious." Newfield's reporting was undoubtedly sloppy. He could easily have avoided some errors by checking his facts: he criticized the *Post* for not sending a reporter on the press plane from Washington to Dallas to cover the Kennedy assassination, not knowing that a writer was dispatched direct from New York; he asserted that the paper maintained no out-of-town bureaus, ignoring the understaffed but long-standing office in Washington; he garbled Dolly's role in the 1962–1963 strike. He said that Wechsler was "dumped" or "demoted" in 1961, which may have been what actually happened but was not technically correct.

There were a slew of minor errors. Newfield slightly misstated the facts of his own employment. He told a story about Dolly not recognizing Pete Hamill at a party that Hamill had already denied elsewhere. He got some details wrong about the paper's compensation policy. But all in all, the damage done by the piece was largely to Dolly's ego.

Her lawyer Arthur Liman counseled that although the article was negative in tone and inaccurate in places, she should content herself with asking for an apology for the inaccuracies in a future edition of *Harper's*. After some months of stalling, the editors complied.*

In her concentration on the sloppiness of Newfield's article, Dolly blinded herself to the substantial criticisms that he and other commentators were making. The *Post* was often dull; it had lost its muckraking zeal; its columnists were often boring. Because she set so much of the paper's policy, and because Sann and his associates frequently invoked her name when they needed to justify themselves, issues such as these that were routinely blamed on midlevel managers at other papers were charged directly to Dolly's influence.

Many of the problems at the *Post* could be traced to the owner's parsimonious ways. In the late 1960s, the *Post* was a $35-million-a-year operation, but Newfield's metaphor of the paper as a neighborhood candy store was all too apt. It was, in fact, a comparison made by her top associates. Byron Greenberg says, "Absolutely. We always used to talk about it, she was running this place like a corner candy store. That's what we always said. And when we became the only afternoon paper, she was so into this mode of operating on a shoestring, she couldn't change. She couldn't think big. She missed the moment. Absolutely."

---

*In 1971, Newfield reprinted the article in a collection of his journalism published by Dutton. He excised one or two of the most glaring errors that Dolly had complained about in the original piece, but all his other criticisms, including some misstatements of fact, were intact. Once again, Dolly had to be talked out of suing.

Of course, Newfield and other critics of the *Post* were not primarily interested in the bottom line. Underlying their attack was their dissatisfaction with the paper's political posture. Sick of the status quo, they aligned themselves with student rebels who challenged the organization of American universities and with antiwar activists who sought to shake up the mainstream political parties. They believed that the *Post,* formerly an underdog paper championing underdog causes, had become another insensitive agency of the establishment.

TWENTY-THREE

The Young Turks

From the time Dorothy Schiff acquired the *Post* through all the vicissitudes of the forties, fifties, and sixties, most reporters, although they groused about the substandard working environment and the personal foibles of the lady upstairs, were basically tolerant of the circumstances under which they worked. The paper's reputation as an advocate for society's less fortunate reinforced their pride in their vocation. For some, the scruffy surroundings and less-than-optimum pay even added to the glamour of the job.

But in the late sixties, despite the fact that working conditions were dramatically improved by the move to South Street, a sense of alienation began to pervade the newsroom. Many reporters no longer confined their complaints to the usual half-serious gripes. Influenced by the campus revolts, the antiwar protests, the civil rights movement, and demands for women's equality, younger members of the staff began to assert themselves against the prevailing culture of the paper. The publisher and her top editors found themselves accused of insensitivity to the needs of minority groups in their own employ.

Ted Poston continued to be the most prominent black reporter on a mainstream publication in the city, perhaps in the nation. Poston began to criticize the *Post*'s coverage of events in Harlem and other Northern ghettos. He believed that the paper no longer deserved its reputation as a champion of black causes. "Lately," he wrote Sann, "I hear that the *Post* has lost interest in the Brother." The *Herald Tribune,* he thought, was doing a better job than the *Post* in covering Harlem, and both the *Trib* and the *Times* had better distribution there.

Poston stepped up his complaints after the 1962–1963 strike, and the editors didn't want to admit that he was probably correct. There were other problems. Ted was drinking heavily, and the copy he submitted was sloppy. Wechsler and Sann proposed to Dorothy Schiff that Ted be taken out of the general assignment pool and offered a weekly column. He refused, and they relented. He was still an icon for the paper; everyone respected him for the work he had done earlier. And his contacts were superb. But the situation deteriorated.

In 1968, although Poston went to Memphis when Martin Luther King Jr. was assassinated, he got drunk and failed to file a story. He was seldom productive. Most reporters and editors were deferential. One rewrite man says that when he worked on a Poston story, there were likely to be errors, and all the information needed to be checked. Another man says, "The general word in the city room was that you had to cover his ass. But that was only fair; he'd put his life on the line for them."

Just after Poston retired in 1972, already showing signs of the dementia that would kill him two years later, Sann said he would never have forced him out. "The *Post* owed Ted enough of a debt to carry him forever."

According to Ted's obituary in the *Post,* his last contribution to the paper had been to encourage the employment of more minority reporters. The reality was more complex. In the late sixties, every newspaper, every television station, every wire service in the city was scrambling to hire people of color, but the results were meager. From the beginning of 1968 through the spring of 1970, the *Post* took on nine probationary minority reporters, of whom two were hired. That brought to five the number of black reporters on the staff, but two were promptly hired away.

In June 1970, William Artis, a twenty-eight-year-old who'd already worked at the *Buffalo Evening News,* came to the *Post* as a probationary reporter. George Trow, an assistant managing editor, was in charge of such newcomers, but his supervision was cursory. Al Ellenberg later took over Trow's job. "There wasn't time or money to bring anybody along slowly," says Ellenberg. "Maybe the *Times* could afford to do that, but we couldn't. If you wanted to catch on, you had to push yourself forward, and more than that, you had to be fast, you had to catch on fast."

Whatever skills Artis brought to the *Post* were not deemed sufficient, and he was let go after six weeks. He promptly filed a complaint with the New York State Division of Human Rights, stating that he was not judged on his merits but because of his color. The *Post* had an unwritten quota of three black reporters, Artis claimed, and he would have made four. He also claimed that the source of his information was Ted Poston, who had written an angry memo earlier in the year concluding that a quota existed because three was the maximum number of black reporters at any time.

Dorothy was enraged. She told Sann that Poston's memo had not mentioned a quota and that he had merely urged more minority hires. She pointed out that the reporters who left had moved to better jobs, and that probationers like Artis had been brought in specifically to add to the *Post*'s roster, not just to keep the numbers constant. The *Post* had a higher percentage of minority reporters than the *Times* or the *News,* and, although Poston had been asked repeatedly to recommend specific black candidates to the editors, Dorothy maintained he had never done so.

The human rights commissioner who heard the case ruled against the *Post*. He said that Artis's complaint about prejudice seemed justified, that the *Post* was at fault for not allowing the probationary period to run the full three months, and that the paper erred in not giving Artis more editorial assistance. He did not comment on the examples of Artis's work that the *Post* submitted as evidence of the reporter's lack of skill, and he ordered that Artis be reinstated.

The *Post* took Artis back, gave him special training, and then let him go again just before his second three-month trial was up. It's hard to believe that the editors weren't vindictive this time around. The paper protested the commissioner's ruling, and eventually it was exonerated. In August 1971, the Human Rights Appeal Board cleared the *Post* of any wrongdoing, declaring the paper had demonstrated that Artis failed to meet its standards and there was nothing in the record to show a pattern of racism. Artis pursued his case all the way to the Appellate Division of the State Supreme Court, which ruled against him in 1973.*

More members of minorities joined the staff. In November 1972, the four

---

*Years later, Trow praised Dolly's tenacity in a letter to Sann: "You and I spent many dreary hours at those dreary hearings. Dolly and you backed me up all the way. It would have been much easier—and cheaper—to give in."

black reporters then at the paper suggested to Dolly that—since they were constrained by journalistic ethics from editorializing in their copy—the *Post* find a black columnist who would comment on events more freely. They admitted that there were no black columnists at any other New York paper (*The Washington Post* had a black columnist and a black editor), but they rehashed the familiar argument that the *Post* as a liberal paper should take the lead.

Dorothy reminded them that the paper was currently running a syndicated column by Roy Wilkins, the president of the NAACP. Although Wilkins had been a journalist before joining the organization, his was hardly the voice of the new generation of black writers. The four men proposed writing a column themselves on a rotating basis. Dolly and her editors endorsed the idea, but nothing came of it.

During the early seventies, the *Post* had more black general assignment reporters on its tiny staff than the *Times* and the *News* had jointly in their vastly larger newsrooms. But some of the blacks felt they were there on sufferance, and some old-timers resented the change.

Gerry Passarella stepped down as head of the *Post*'s Newspaper Guild chapter in 1971. Miss Gerry, as everyone called her, says, "I nominated a Negro girl, Evangeline Foster-Waldron, to replace me. She was an absolute doll and understood labor relations better than I did, which I used to admit. But they didn't vote for her. And it was then that I realized that half the goddamn *Post* was so bigoted. It was okay to criticize others from the liberal standpoint, but they didn't look at themselves in the same light."

To her credit, Dolly did not share in the bigotry. At one point Paul Sann sent her a memo about a routine scheduling matter: "I know it makes some of the other colored folks unhappy, but this interview with Mr. [Bayard] Rustin would be more timely this weekend than the one on the Summer Jobs." Dolly reminded him that one of her secretaries was a black woman. Even if that were not so, she said, she deplored racist remarks and requested that he never use them again. Sann apologized.

Such semiconscious condescension, as Sann's memo revealed, was not uncommon in American society at the time. At the *Post* specifically, the tension over minority hiring left blacks and whites alike uneasy, adding to a sense of malaise.

———

The question of women's rights at the paper began innocuously enough with a dispute over an off-the-sports-pages aspect of the *Post*'s coverage of the New York Mets. In 1969, the Mets, whose hapless entry into the National League eight seasons earlier had endeared them to many New Yorkers, suddenly emerged as winners. On the eve of their clinching the pennant, a young reporter named Lindsy Van Gelder was assigned to write a profile of Nancy Seaver, the wife of the Mets' star pitcher. She was unhappy with the assignment.

Van Gelder says, " 'The Woman in the News' feature was a great idea, but there weren't enough women in the news in those days, so often it would be a wife. I actually liked what I wrote about Nancy Seaver, but as a protest I said that I didn't want my byline on it. And Sann completely flipped."

Van Gelder had been hired at the *Post* as a reporter in the summer of 1968. She was already conscious of women's rights. After graduating from Sarah Lawrence two years earlier, she had worked for the United Press and interviewed for a job at the *Daily News*. "It was a really successful interview," Lindsy says. She was on the verge of being hired when her prospective boss found out she was married. "The guy said, 'I'm not going to hire you, because you're married, and a cute little thing like you ought to be home having a baby every year.' "

She filed charges with the State Human Rights Commission and eventually won her case, but by that time she'd found a more congenial employer. "The *New York Post,* aside from being the most liberal place in town, even if it didn't always live up to its principles, was the only place where there was a significant female presence in the newsroom," Van Gelder says. "It was not weird to be a woman at the *Post*."

But it was unusual for a woman to assert her concerns about how other women were portrayed in the paper's pages. When Van Gelder squawked about putting her name on the Nancy Seaver piece, the editors were dumbfounded. She was within her rights; a long-standing clause in the Newspaper Guild contract allowed reporters to pull their bylines if they were unhappy about an article. But the clause was rarely invoked and usually in circumstances in which the editors altered the piece substantially from that which the reporter had filed.

Sann and Van Gelder worked out what she thought was a compromise. She agreed to keep her byline on the profile, as long as the editors understood the nature of her objection to the assignment and didn't place her in a similar situation again. But Sann couldn't let it rest. "Almost immediately he called me in and said, 'Okay, now we want you to do Mrs. Gil Hodges—the wife of the Mets' manager.' And I said, 'Okay I'll do Mrs. Gil Hodges, but you know that my byline will not be on it this time.' And he said, 'No. That's insubordination.' So it was like, you can pull your byline for any reason except if it seems that you're questioning my judgment."

Sann made it clear that he would find grounds to fire her if she didn't give in. Stunned, she walked out of his office and told a few colleagues what had happened. At which point, another young reporter, Bryna Taubman, told Sann she wanted to remove her byline from a story she'd submitted to the next day's paper. "That really changed things," says Van Gelder. "I'm very grateful to her because that meant that I wasn't isolated."

Sann reported his version of the events in several sarcastic memos to Dorothy. He referred to Van Gelder and Taubman as "Les Girls" and the Lucy Stoners, referring to a leading nineteenth-century American suffragist. He admitted that neither of the women had refused an assignment and both had said they would not do so, but they maintained their right to withhold their names. Sann argued that that was the equivalent of refusing an assignment. Therefore, he fired both women for insubordination.

Half the paper's fifty-four general assignment reporters and copy editors requested that their bylines be omitted from any stories they filed. Two financial writers, one sportswriter, and two assistant city editors added their support. Miss Gerry threatened to pull all the Guild members off the job, and the printers' local agreed to back them up.

Sann had no defense. The women were reinstated. Miss Gerry asked the frustrated editor not to assign them immediately to stories that would revive the dispute.

Resentfully, Sann agreed. Dorothy Schiff, more mystified than resentful, invited Van Gelder and Taubman to her office a few days later. Lindsy says, "She was curious about us. Yes, we had been a personnel problem. But I think anybody who took on Sann had to be of interest to her. So she invited Bryna and me up for tea.

"It was the first time I met Mrs. Schiff. I think she could be very superficial, but she was very curious. At one point, she asked us how we felt during the time we were fired. Bryna said it had shaken her up, not the loss of her paycheck or being called a troublemaker, but we had to turn in our press cards, and she said she really felt naked without her press card, and how much of her identity was tied up with this job. And Dolly says to us, 'I can relate to that, girls, because during the newspaper strike I was without my mouthpiece. In my own way, working for a newspaper is a big part of my identity.'

"I then said, 'You know, I don't really feel that way. I love my job. I like being a reporter, but I guess I don't feel the way you two do about it.' And she turned to me and said, 'You must have had a very happy childhood!'

"We had a big discussion about feminism, and she told us about various things in her life, with her husbands, about the various kinds of disrespect she had gotten as a woman in the business. And we kind of bonded. Because, I mean, she knew things about feminism at her own level, when we were still in diapers.

"And I remember coming downstairs afterwards and telling someone, 'Hey, you know the publisher's kind of a groovy chick.'"

Dolly liked women to speak up for themselves. When Sann hired Helene Eisenberg to replace his longtime male secretary, Pete Skiko, one of the reporters told Eisenberg that she would never be able to take Skiko's place. "I was taken aback by that," she says. "But I answered, 'Well, I expect I have my own style.' Dolly happened to be standing nearby, and she loved that. She said, 'Oh, way to go, Helene!'"

Dolly got along well with Gerry Passarella, the head of the Guild local. "She used to say we were the two most powerful women at the *Post*," says Miss Gerry. "Except for one thing, I used to tell her—she makes more money than me. So I was a little fresh with her. And she liked that, because not many other people spoke to her that way.

"Once she had me up there in the penthouse, and she asked what my family background was. She had a way of asking these questions. I said, 'The same as yours, Mrs. Schiff.' And she said, 'How can you say that?' In other words, I'm a millionaire, more than that.

"So I said, 'Well, your grandfather came from the Lower East Side. And I came from the Lower East Side too, but your grandfather stole more than my grandfather did.' Well, she went bananas. I said, 'You know, he maneuvered more than my grandfather did. My grandfather had a pushcart, and your grandfather had money.' And she roared then, and she told it all the time."

As one of the most prominent businesswomen in the country, Dorothy had developed a limited kind of feminist agenda that was consistent with— perhaps even a bit ahead of—her class and her generation. Nan Rosenthal, who worked at the paper in the late fifties and early sixties, says, "My general recollection is that Dolly took a particular interest in the women on the paper. I don't mean that she was some kind of proto-feminist. She wasn't. But she regarded women as human."

After American women got the vote in 1920, the feminist movement divided over the question of whether women were different from men and therefore in need of special protection, or whether they were basically equal and could therefore compete effectively in the marketplace and the workforce. Dorothy seemed to want it both ways.

On the one hand, she argued that women and men should be treated equally. In an early column, she wrote of her dismay on learning that the list of New York delegates to the 1952 Democratic National Convention, which had been prepared by the party bosses, consisted of seven men and one woman. Given that a large number of party volunteers in New York were women, Dorothy believed that women should "be given equal representation on this primarily honorary delegation. Although I think women should be judged by their qualifications as people, and not as a separate group, it seems to me that this sort of recognition would encourage more of us to enter politics."

Conversely, when it suited her needs to play the coquette or the helpless woman to get what she wanted, she was perfectly willing to do so. She flirted with advertisers, politicians, and labor leaders if she thought it would help her cause. Many men report that at some point during a meeting, she would carefully shift her posture so that her legs, of which she was very proud, were particularly visible. She was more interested in being thought of as feminine than in being a feminist. And she was not above seeing women in stereotypical ways.

Nan Rosenthal says, "I'm almost certain that it was her idea to send Beverly Gary—who was a good reporter—to Cuba to interview Castro, because Beverly was extremely pretty and I don't know what fantasy Mrs. Schiff had. It was rumored that she wanted to know what Castro was like in bed. And that Beverly would be the most suitable person to send to find this out—not because Beverly slept around, which she didn't, but because she was so attractive!"

Dorothy was fascinated by *Sex and the Single Girl,* Helen Gurley Brown's

1962 best seller, and she invited the author to write a column for the paper. Although their working relationship was brief, the two women became friends. Brown says, "At that time, if you were a hard-hitting business-woman, you were supposed to have lost all your feminine wiles, and that's something that I've argued about with some feminists. I've said, 'You can wear lipstick, and you can wear pretty clothes, and you can be very successful at your work. You don't have to give up being a woman just in order to be successful.' And they said I was leading women astray.

"But Dorothy was actually the epitome of what we're talking about. She was not on a soapbox, but she was showing that you could be feminine, and be crazy about men, and get on with your work."

Dorothy was sensitive to women's second-class status. She never lost sight of her childhood resentment at being an undervalued girl, and she under-stood that social prejudice led to injustice. In a January 1957 column, she ex-pressed anger that Princess Caroline, the newly born daughter of Princess Grace and Prince Rainier of Monaco, was automatically barred from inherit-ing the throne of the principality, even though it would lose its independence if there were no male heirs. "But have we a right to make fun of the Mone-gasques?" she asked rhetorically. "Are we so advanced that we no longer dis-criminate against women?"

Her answer was, of course, no. She noted how frequently married women were criticized for choosing to work rather than to stay home. "I agree that jobs don't necessarily spell happiness for women," she wrote. "But insuffi-cient employment for either sex is a design for misery. A bored wife and mother depresses the entire household. A busy one is stimulating, a challenge to husband and children. Maybe that's why there's so much resistance."

Dorothy returned to the subject in a series of columns the following year. She was particularly interested in the problems faced by women who chose to work, essentially overlooking those who were forced to because they were the sole support of themselves and/or their families. Once again she argued that a woman who was "naturally aggressive is better off having an outlet for her energy so she doesn't drive her husband and children crazy."

She foresaw a better future. Already women made up more than one-third of the American workforce, and half of all working women were mar-ried. "More and more women are entering business and the professions. As ancient prejudices break down, ability and not sex will become the yardstick for promotion. The number of women in elective office will increase, too. This is an ideal field for women, who for centuries have understood how to influence men. Women have learned to be expert managers of people and money through their administration of home finance and handling of complex human relations with relatives and tradesmen."

Some years later, Dorothy told an interviewer that she did not consider herself a feminist but that she was always dismayed when women were treated like second-class citizens. She repeated several personal gripes: "At the Gridiron Club dinner, women were not invited as guests. When Charles de Gaulle was here with his wife, and the mayor gave a dinner for de Gaulle, I wasn't invited; all the male publishers were. I had lunch with Madame de Gaulle instead. And the Inner Circle, an organization of City Hall reporters, gave a dinner every year with skits spoofing the mayor and other public officials. Male publishers sat downstairs, while the women, including the only female publisher, had to sit in the balcony,* as in an Orthodox Synagogue."

If these were the most stinging examples of gender discrimination she could cite, Dolly's life had been privileged indeed. She seldom acknowledged the roles that her inherited wealth and social connections had in making her success possible. Not only had money opened the door for her, it also made it easier for her to divide her attentions between her family and her job. She was not particularly alert to the problems of working mothers with fewer financial resources, nor was she willing to make special arrangements that might help such women on the job.

Until 1964, there was no legal requirement that any employer to do so. Companies could refuse to hire married women or mothers of small children. They could fire women as soon as they became pregnant and did not have to guarantee that they could return to the job after they gave birth.

Although the *Post* had had many women reporters during Dolly's tenure, the first to raise the question of how to balance work and motherhood was probably Roberta Brandes Gratz, who came to the paper in 1963. She had her first daughter in 1967 and her second two years later. At each birth, she took the full three-month leave of absence provided for in the union contract.

---

*The practice was finally changed in 1972.

"Nonetheless, it was tricky," says Gratz. "Even though the paper was owned and operated by a woman, it was not exactly women-friendly. Certainly we had more women there, but they were women who could be treated as if they were one of the boys. None of them had children."

Both times Roberta returned from maternity leave, she had to fight for important assignments. "For a while, I would be happy to get feature stories which gave me more time at home with my kids. But as the girls got older, I had to push for more challenging work even if it meant working late."

A few years later, Lindsy Van Gelder had her first child. She and Roberta asked to work part-time, in effect sharing one job. At first the Newspaper Guild was hostile to their demand, although it eventually relented. Their employer adamantly refused.

"Dolly wouldn't have it," says Gratz. "She just didn't approve of part-time for mothers. She just didn't get it." Several other reporters joined Gratz and Van Gelder to discuss the issue with Dolly. Roberta says, "She had the nerve to tell us, 'I raised three children and worked full-time.' And I almost went through the floor. I wanted to say, 'Well, sure. Give me your chauffeur, your cook, and your nursemaid, and maybe I wouldn't have such a problem.' It was a staggering revelation of how removed from the real world she was."

But the real world intruded. By the mid-1960s, more women were members of the workforce—not just black and single women, as always, but also growing numbers of white middle-class women with children. These were the women who were the leading advocates of Title VII of the 1964 Civil Rights Act, which banned sex discrimination in the workplace, and other traditional feminist reforms like legal abortion and subsidized child care. Betty Friedan's *The Feminine Mystique,* published in 1963, was their bible.

Many young women who had been active in the civil rights or antiwar protest movements had become sensitive to the rampant sexism of their male cohorts. In response, they developed their own agenda. They saw sexism in every aspect of American society. Some of the most outraged among them resorted to civil disobedience or turned to ideological lesbianism to make their points, but even the more moderate majority demanded a change in the status quo.

Women began challenging the use of stereotypes and unequal job opportunities. In March 1970, the women on the professional staff of *Newsweek*,* incensed that the magazine—which had only one female writer on staff—was forced to hire a freelancer, the star *New York Post* writer Helen Dudar, to write a cover story on the women's movement, filed a sex-discrimination charge with the federal government's Equal Employment Opportunity Commission. Female staffers at *Ladies' Home Journal,* Time Inc., CBS, NBC, and other national media enterprises raised similar concerns.

The byline crisis was the beginning of an across-the-board challenge of management practices at the *Post.* "A number of things were happening around the same time," says Van Gelder. "I was part of a conscious-raising women's group, and there were other people who were against the war and other things. What we had in common was wanting to carve out new ways to be reporters within mainstream media." Members of these groups, together with other reporters and editors whose concerns had mostly to do with structural problems at the *Post,* had been meeting sporadically for months, grousing about their discontents. Galvanized by the byline crisis, they put together a plan and a strategy for achieving change.

They drafted a list of complaints—"What is Wrong with the *New York Post*": the lack of a proper training program for reporters, arbitrary editing without consultation between reporters and editors, not enough minority reporters or enough coverage of minority communities in the city, not enough coverage by *Post* reporters of major stories outside the city, not enough coverage of science or the arts, a lack of contact with the publisher.

They prepared a manifesto calling for changes in the paper's governance: "New York Post News Staff Charter—Preamble. Working Draft. Open to

---

*Newsweek, not coincidentally, was owned by the Washington Post Corporation, whose president and principal stockholder, Katharine Graham, was at the time far less enlightened about women's issues than Dolly Schiff. In 1966, Graham told an interviewer from Women's Wear Daily that she deferred to the men who worked for her and thought it was appropriate to do so. Thirty years later, in her memoir, Graham reflected on the mind-set that produced such a statement:

> *I adopted the assumption of many of my generation that women were intellectually inferior to men, that we were not capable of governing, leading, managing anything but our homes and our children. . . . Pretty soon this kind of thinking took its toll: most of us became somehow inferior. . . .*
>
> *Women traditionally also have suffered—and many still do—from an exaggerated desire to please, a syndrome so instilled in women of my generation that it inhibited my behavior for many years, and in ways it still does.*

Amendment and Change." Claiming to represent "the reporters and writers whose daily contact with the public and whose work produces the written part of the paper," the group demanded an "institutionalized consultative voice in the policies which guide the final product," which they believed would "lead to a significantly improved newspaper."

They proposed to establish an executive committee representing the whole group that would consult regularly with the publisher and the editors regarding news coverage policy, including "which stories are covered and printed; the way stories are covered; staff hiring; [and] editorial budget." The group acknowledged that their demands might seem impractical, but they believed that management should not have the sole right to decide which stories are covered without consultation with the staff.

About half the reporters and copy editors who were eligible to sign, signed, even though some recognized that the actions proposed would have been unwieldy in operation. Alan Whitney, a night editor at the time, says, "What they wanted was completely absurd. Lindsy told us that what she was ready to propose to Mrs. Schiff—what she wanted Mrs. Schiff to agree to— was that they would form a committee, and if the committee wanted something done, then it had to be done, whether Mrs. Schiff wanted it or not. We told her she was crazy. Pete Hamill was there, and he couldn't believe it."

Pete tried to be sympathetic to the rebels, even if he thought their remedies were unworkable. He says, "Looking back now, I think feminism was the force behind it all. Feminism was the part of the sixties that was the real cultural shift. The antiwar movement ended when the draft ended. It was made up of a lot of college boys who didn't want to get shot at for no good reason. And even though I had two daughters, I wasn't a big feminist. But you could feel how powerful it was. And I was trying desperately to understand all this. It was really more my own curiosity. What is this about? What's seething around here?"

Even if the group's demands had been totally workable, Sann and his closest buddies were not about to change their style to please young upstarts. Pete Hamill says, "Part of it's generational, of course. These were guys a generation older than I was. It was even harder for them. And you put that together with the kind of cynicism that grows, I don't mean skepticism, but real cynicism that comes from working on a daily paper—you see life at its most appalling. It was probably more, not right-wing feeling exactly, but you know, 'we're not going to be gulled by this latest fad.' I don't think it was 'give me the good old days when men were men and women were carpets.' I don't think it was that bad. But it was a kind of much more dark skepticism than contempt. Certainly on the part of Sann. And I did talk to him about it. It had to come up."

Dolly was startled that some of her favorites among the younger people at the paper had joined the dissidents. William "Woody" Woodward III, the scion of a wealthy New York family and grandson of one of Dolly's old friends, was a twenty-five-year-old reporter whom she had personally hired even though he had no previous journalistic experience.* Woodward soon emerged as one of the leaders of the rebellion.

Tony Mancini, who was also among the ringleaders, says, "Woody was sheltered. He came in not knowing much about how to do these things, and he wasn't a great writer. But he came from a position of some social power, and he had a lot of ambition in that direction. I think he was a decent guy, and he wanted very much to be one of the boys. And he couldn't be one of the boys—he came into the city room to a bunch of people from working-class backgrounds who made it somehow in the newspaper world, who could never accept him as a bosom buddy or as a social equal. In a way it was kind of a reverse discrimination."

Mancini thinks Woodward was looking for a cause, especially one that would ingratiate him with his fellow reporters. "He took charge naturally. And we working-class types let him because we recognized that he knew how to talk to Dolly. We would benefit from that because he knew her, she had hired him. It was to our advantage."

An item in *New York* magazine about a similar attempt by some reporters at *The New York Times* pointed out that the *Post* was ahead of the *Times* in this respect. "The publisher, Mrs. Dorothy Schiff, has been meeting over the last few months with small groups of Post writers and reporters to hear their case for more specialists, for a top editor who is black or Puerto Rican, for more money for travel, for more coverage of non-white news. Fortunately for the movement at the Post, there is a reporter who is both *engagé* and very social; Mrs. Schiff consented to talk to the Post group if he was the spokesman. ('The very rich *are* different,' says a Post writer.)" Dolly immediately called

---

*Wealth had not shielded the Woodward family from tragedy. On October 30, 1955, when Woody was eleven, his mother, thinking she heard an intruder, grabbed a shotgun, blasted away at a shadow near her door, and killed her husband. The police cleared her of any wrongdoing, but gossips and society writers revisited the case repeatedly.

her friend, *New York*'s founding editor Clay Felker, to complain that Woody had been chosen not by her but by his peers. She didn't discuss their motives.

For a time, Dolly met weekly with Woodward and his fellows. She was attentive, polite. She took notes, challenged the editors who were present to explain themselves, and often asked Jean Gillette to bring in back issues of the paper to clarify a point. One disgruntled young reporter wrote later, "We should have known that something was wrong. The meetings were held in her fancy penthouse, she served drinks, and cookies. . . . To her it had been just another cocktail party all along." After two months, Dolly canceled the meetings. Lindsy Van Gelder says, "Dorothy Schiff met with us at her pleasure. And she stopped when it stopped being amusing."

No more was heard of the News Staff Charter or of management by committee. Sann remained ostensibly indifferent to the new mood in the city room, although he eventually replaced a few old-time editors with young men like Bob Spitzler, Al Ellenberg, Larry Nathanson, and Warren Hoge, who were more attuned to the point of view of the dissident reporters.

Most reporters, including the leaders of the rebellion, were more concerned with their daily assignments than with ideological disputes. Most young reporters continued to go about their jobs with enthusiasm, proud of their contribution to what most still thought of as the best-written paper in the city. Most considered the city room, though inevitably home to personal and generational rivalries, a congenial place to work.

When the Newspaper Guild contract with the *Post* came up for renewal in 1970, the negotiations bogged down over the most predictable issue— money. After a two-week strike in October, Guild members accepted the same package of raises that had already been agreed upon by members of other unions, plus some adjustments to the retirement benefits formula. Participatory democracy was not among the items on the table.

Woodward was on the negotiating committee, and Dolly told Paul Sann she thought his choosing to join the picket line was "treasonable." He was joined in his insurgency by another well-placed young reporter, Pamela Howard, the daughter of Scripps-Howard president Jack Howard. Bob Friedman, a night rewrite man who had been a member of the Communist party and an editor of the Marxist magazine, *New Masses,* was contemptuous of them. Years later he wrote Sann, "William Woodward and Pamela Howard very briefly flirted with what they thought was revolutionary fervor by ardently backing a totally unnecessary strike at the Post. Drunk with the heady wine of militancy, at an impromptu staff gathering in the corridor the day before the strike date set, Woodward said something like 'I don't care who else is there, I'm hitting the bricks in the morning.'

"This greatly amused me," Friedman continued, "especially since when I had called his home sometime previously to send him on an early assignment, his manservant answered the phone with 'Mr. Woodward's residence.' Both the young scions, whom I dubbed 'the millionaire Maoists,' seemed gravely disappointed in me, considering my heroic reputation, because I noted that people whose children depended for their food and shelter on a weekly pay check were not inclined to strike except when it was inevitably necessary."

Dolly was more indulgent. She checked with Ted Kheel, who was mediating the dispute, about the behavior of Woodward and Howard. Kheel reassured her that "the two rich kids behaved properly during the meetings."

If Dolly thought class ties were tighter than generational bonds, she was mistaken. Within months, Woody asked for a leave of absence to become publisher of [MORE], a new journal dedicated to critiquing the New York press. In one of [MORE]'s first issues, a long article by Dick Pollak, a former editor at Newsweek, criticized the Post for its behavior in the Artis case, despite the fact that the Human Rights Appeal Board had exonerated the paper two months before the article appeared.

What stung was Pollak's conclusion. "In fairness to the Post," he wrote, "it should probably be noted that few able reporters—black or white—want to work for a newspaper so dedicated to 1930s journalism. . . . Mrs. Schiff complains that good journalists depart her city room because the Post is 'raided' by the Times. Yet she does almost nothing to make her newspaper a place where a reporter might want to remain."

Dolly complained directly to Woody, who was polite but noncommittal. She also prepared a lengthy rebuttal, citing minute errors of fact, which she finally decided not to send, and contented herself with a brief note pointing out that Ted Poston's name was misspelled "Posten" throughout the piece.

In April 1972, [MORE] sponsored a convention to counter the American Newspaper Publishers Association meetings across town. One panel, composed of Murray Kempton, Blair Clark, Nora Ephron, and others, asked the question, "What kind of P.M. Paper Should New York Have?" Woody led off by saying that the Post, as a monopoly, was lazily resting on its former reputation. Joel Dreyfuss, a black reporter at the paper, offered something of a defense by pointing out that the two morning papers were much bigger operations, with a wider financial base. Ephron poked fun at Dolly personally. Kempton, in trying to defend her, succeeded only in making her seem irrelevant. The meeting ended inconclusively, but the tone was very critical.

A few years later, Ephron renewed her attack in the media column of *Esquire*. She called the *Post* "a terrible newspaper" and blamed that state of affairs on Dolly Schiff, who showed contempt for her staff by permitting them to work in dreadful surroundings. Ephron recounted her first day at the paper in 1963: "The hallway leading to the city room was black. Absolutely black. The smell of urine came wafting out of the men's room. . . . The glass door to the city room was filmed with dust, and written on it, with a finger, was the word 'Philthy.' The door was cleaned four years later, but the word remained; it had managed to erode itself onto the glass."

Because Dolly's daughter Adele was a friend and neighbor of Ephron's parents in Los Angeles, Nora believed the publisher "felt safe with me, thought I was of her class." This presumed connection led Dolly to drop her guard during a meeting soon after Nora arrived at the paper. She told Nora she was lucky to be working. "When I was your age, I never did anything but go to lunch," she said. When Ephron raised the question of the filthy bathrooms, she said that Dorothy replied that her employees weren't the kind of people who would keep the facilities clean.

However unpleasant the working conditions were, it wouldn't have mattered if the product were better. Ephron said that Dolly was interested only in ephemera, that she assigned reporters to do her personal bidding, and that she personalized all her political decisions. Dolly had kept the paper going during lean years by paring expenditures to the minimum, but, isolated in her executive office and protected by her intimidated editors, she had no idea of the realities of the newspaper business or much else.

It was a devastating portrait, and Dolly was stunned. She found Nora's article as painful in its way as Woodward's apostasy. Dorothy annotated a photocopy of the piece in pencil. "Not true!" she wrote about several anecdotes that were indeed exaggerated. "Not true!" beside a perfectly reasonable account by Blair Clark about her managerial style. "Not true!" about yet another retelling of her serving guests a sandwich for lunch.

She might have remarked that Ephron spent half the article complaining about the conditions at West Street when in fact the city room at South Street, where the *Post* moved after Nora left the paper, was adequately equipped and maintained. She might have pointed out that the article failed to acknowledge that the *Post* was still one of the few papers that gave women like Ephron a chance to shine. Better yet, she might have taken to heart the truth hidden beneath Nora's rather overheated account that many of the young reporters at the *Post* considered their boss to be irrelevant, obsolete, or both. Instead, in what was becoming a dismal ritual, she had to be dissuaded by her lawyer from pursuing a libel suit.*

In considering whether her mother was too thin-skinned, Adele Sweet says, "She had a thing about accuracy. It made her crazy when someone said something that wasn't true. She'd take it if she thought she deserved it. But being wronged, having something said that was wrong, that made her crazy." Unfortunately, she vented all her rage on the tiny errors and ignored the more salient points in the criticism of Ephron and others. She'd have been better served if she could have seen the bigger picture.

On the other hand, the tone of much of the criticism aimed at Dolly and the *Post* at the time was more mean-spirited than constructive. "By then it was very PC to piss on Dolly," says Bob Spitzler, who became managing editor of the paper in 1972 after a decade rising through the ranks. "Her eccentricities were more visible. Nora zeroed in on that. But what was important to the [MORE] crowd or the *Voice* guys was that they wanted the paper to return to its more politicized days. Maybe not the specific politics of the Wechsler days, but to the fact that there was a political cast to the news reporting."

A reporter says, "They said they wanted us to be 'objective'—an old communistic term, by the way—but what they really wanted was for the paper to represent their political point of view. You had to be antiestablishment, and they didn't mean the old WASP establishment. They meant males, whites, liberals. Remember when the kids said, 'Don't trust anybody over thirty'? Well, lots of them, Newfield and Hentoff, and Mailer and Breslin, for that matter, were white men in their thirties or forties, but they wanted to line up with the kids. They wanted to say, 'Fuck you,' to the likes of us who were just trying to do our jobs."

Much of the criticism of Dolly and the *Post* was based on generational politics, and many of the critics were unable or unwilling to balance their complaints with an acknowledgment of things she did right.

---

*She had to be dissuaded again in 1978 when Ephron included the article in a book of her collected essays about the media.

Jerry Tallmer says, "Dolly had many, many blind spots about many things. But she was also really smart and insightful. She could think up wonderful features, and more often than not she was on to something. She came up with this wonderful series I worked on. She gave one full page to every member of the staff to write about where they were born and raised in the city. And then they would go back and see what it was like." Tallmer grew up on Park Avenue and wrote about what had happened to his neighborhood and his building. "It was a great idea and a great series."

Lindsy Van Gelder remembers the egg story: "This memo came down to the city desk from the publisher saying, 'My hard-boiled eggs are not what they once were, and I want to know why. They don't crack properly, and the yokes are mushy. And I remember the old days when a hard-boiled egg was a hard-boiled egg.'

"Well, of course they tried to put her off, but she was having none of it. So I was basically assigned for a whole week to do an investigative report on hard-boiled eggs! I was a pretty good reporter in those days, and I got into it. I ended up interviewing all of the professors of agronomy, egg and chicken boards, and so on. And it turned out that there really had been a change. In Dolly Schiff's youth, eggs were more likely to be stored at room temperature, and that did something to the way oxygen inside the shell separated, I don't even remember exactly. But there was something to her perception. So I ended up writing a full-page monster Saturday feature on what was happening in the egg world."

Schiff was not a journalist, but she was unfailingly curious, and she believed from her first days at the paper until her last that if she was interested in something, her readers would be too. She was often correct. But the political interests and instincts that had guided her so well during the early years and had helped give the *Post* the gravitas to balance its tabloid side were less tuned to the public mood of the late sixties and early seventies. The *Post* seemed increasingly rudderless as its owner/publisher's tenure moved into a fourth decade.

TWENTY-FOUR

The Worst of Times

Toward the end of 1970, Dorothy Schiff, Paul Sann, and Stan Opotowsky had lunch together to generate some ideas for improving the paper in the coming year. Opotowsky summarized their thoughts in a brief memo: as an afternoon paper, whose last edition was timed to include the 3:40 . Wall Street closing, the *Post* could never hope to match the *Times* and the *News* in full coverage of world or even local news. It should continue to do what it did best—provide its readers with entertaining features and well-written analyses of the events they'd first read about in the morning paper.

"There's a difference in what people want later in the day," he wrote. "They're tired, they're on their way home. Yes, they want any new headlines, but they don't want to be depressed. They want some entertainment." Readers wanted good feature stories, good sports coverage, and good continuing series—particularly about New York. "In summary," Opotowsky wrote, "I would say the newspaper today is, by nature of the news, too much of a village scold. I would like to try to change the paper into a cheerful friend."

Dolly agreed, adding only that the editors must be sure that the paper appealed not only to men who picked it up on the way home from the office but to their wives and to working women as well. The *Post* was the only New York paper that had more female than male readers. Since women did most of the shopping in the family, engaged female readers were attractive to advertisers.

Tweaking the women's pages or turning the *Post* into "a cheerful friend" were not forceful initiatives in a period when the economy and the public morale of the city were worsening steadily and poised to decline even further. The racial and generational conflicts that had dominated both the front page and the city room of the *Post* during the late sixties had taken their toll on morale at the paper and in the city it served.

The public rifts became manifest during the 1969 election of citywide officers. Both the primary and the election served as an extended referendum on what voters thought about the administration of the city under Mayor John Lindsay, who'd been such a fresh and welcome face in 1965.

Once in office, Lindsay was confronted with four years of urban turmoil: racially tinged violence; crises in the schools; increases in drug traffic and related crimes; the contraction of the city's job market, particularly for low-income workers; and the deterioration and abandonment of whole neighborhoods, especially in Brooklyn and the Bronx. While some New Yorkers credited the mayor with policies that enabled the city to avoid the kind of widespread destruction that ravaged many other American communities, others said the price was too high.

Sensing Lindsay's vulnerability, an unusually large number of candidates put themselves forward in the 1969 primaries. Seven challengers, including former Mayor Robert Wagner Jr. and Norman Mailer, sought the Democratic nomination, which was won by City Comptroller Mario Procaccino, a party hack. John Marchi, a state senator from Staten Island, who was also endorsed by the Conservative party, defeated Lindsay in the Republican primary. Alex Rose offered Lindsay the Liberal party nomination, and Victor Gotbaum, head of the influential union of city employees, endorsed Lindsay with the expectation that the mayor would approve a generous contract for his members.

The dominant issue in the election was race. White working- and middle-class New Yorkers felt that blacks were taking away their access to good schools, union memberships, jobs, and decent housing. Procaccino coined the phrase "limousine liberals" to describe those Manhattan Democrats, like

Dorothy Schiff and James Wechsler, who supported Lindsay because they were protected from the results of his perceived pro-black policies. There were just enough of such liberals, whose votes combined with a big black turnout to give Lindsay a meager plurality. His opponents split the backlash vote. Together they attracted 58 percent of the total—Procaccino got 35 percent and Marchi got just over 20 percent. But Lindsay's 42 percent carried the day.

Dorothy was thrilled. She wrote Wechsler that John Lindsay was the brightest rising star in American politics. She speculated that President Nixon would be smart to replace Vice President Agnew with the mayor on his 1972 ticket, which would put Lindsay in the lead for the presidential nomination in 1976.

Things played out differently. During Lindsay's second term, it became clear that the mayor's policies had contributed to the continued decline of New York's financial affairs. Even Lindsay's staunchest supporters began to turn against him. The tone of the *Post*'s editorials grew more exasperated. In November 1970, on the eve of yet another round of negotiations over municipal workers' contracts, Paul Sann and Dorothy exchanged a round of memos criticizing the mayor and his administration for being out of touch with reality. "None of us have respect for anyone around the man," wrote Sann.

In July 1971, Sann recapped Lindsay's flaws in a memo to Dorothy: the school system was in disarray; the property tax rate was extremely high; housing was terribly costly, and nothing new was being built; the streets were filthy and the air was foul; street crime was so prevalent that many homeowners' associations were hiring private security guards; and because the mayor had caved in to municipal unions, the city was forced to borrow money at the highest interest rate in its history just to stay afloat. Sann wanted to know which of these transgressions the *Post* should go after. There is no evidence that Dorothy replied. Nothing in the paper suggests a focused campaign against public policies such as the *Post* might have mounted in the days when Joe Kahn, Bill Haddad, and others were digging around.

One problem was that the flaws in Lindsay's policies were easy to spot, whereas viable solutions were hard to come by. Liberals knew that something had gone very, very wrong. They just had no idea how to fix it. Their New

Deal–based philosophy that government must intervene to provide for the needs of society's least fortunate citizens was proving to be naïve vis-à-vis the social realities of the sixties and seventies. The city government was throwing billions of dollars at poverty without solving the difficulties it caused. Race added more complications.

Lindsay joined the Democratic party in 1971 and campaigned unsuccessfully for its presidential nomination in the spring of 1972. When he asked Dorothy to contribute to his presidential race, she turned him down. He did not run for reelection in the mayoral race the following year. The Democratic candidate Abe Beame, as Lindsay's city comptroller, had been deeply involved in the financial shenanigans that were pushing the city toward fiscal calamity. Reluctantly, the *Post* backed Beame, the eventual winner over John Marchi, who ran with Republican and Conservative support.

The economy of the entire country was in trouble during the early seventies. A worldwide recession was exacerbated by the Arab oil embargo in late 1973. To show their approval of the attack by Egypt and Syria on Israel in the Yom Kippur War in October, Arab members of OPEC cut off shipments of crude oil to those nations that had supported Israel. This led to significant fuel shortages as well as higher prices and price controls in the United States. The embargo ended in March 1974, but not before the stock market nearly collapsed and the country was left to struggle with a lethal combination of inflation and recession for the rest of the decade.

The financial implications for New York were terrible. The city had stopped growing by the mid-1960s. In the years that followed, sixteen major corporations, including Pepsico and Shell Oil, relocated their headquarters from Manhattan. Thousands of smaller enterprises moved or went under. The city lost more than half a million jobs. Welfare rolls and Medicaid enrollments swelled, just as the Nixon administration began cutting funds for these federally mandated programs, leaving the city to finance them by a combination of higher taxes, deficit spending, and creative accounting to cover the facts. There was no money left over for schools, crime prevention, or the regular maintenance of the city's deteriorating infrastructure.

By 1975, after nearly a decade of duplicity on the part of elected officials and Wall Street bankers, the city was on the verge of bankruptcy. A failed appeal to the president for help prompted the famous October 30 headline in the *Daily News:* "Ford to City: Drop Dead."* Catastrophe was averted when New York Governor Hugh Carey turned over effective control of the city's finances to a hastily created Municipal Assistance Corporation (MAC). Under the leadership of civic-minded Wall Street financier Felix Rohatyn, MAC slowly brought the city back from the edge of collapse.

Josh Friedman, the *Post's* man in Albany, had already begun looking into the scandals surrounding the Urban Development Corporation (UDC), a state housing agency that had flourished during the Rockefeller years despite shaky—even shady—fiscal policies. Soon after Carey became governor, the UDC was forced to declare bankruptcy in February 1975, the first public agency to default on its obligations since the Depression. Friedman's reportorial skills led him to scoop the other papers on this story, even if, as he is the first to admit, he didn't understand all the implications at the time. Later in the year, Friedman in Albany and George Artz at City Hall provided sustained and insightful coverage as the city teetered on the edge of its own crash, only to be saved at the last minute by MAC.

Post reporters Judy Michaelson, Joyce Purnick, Clyde Haberman, Arzt, and Friedman covered local and state politics effectively. Joe Kahn still produced articles about corruption in the city's rent control program, but his information seems to have been based more on revelations at watchdog hearings than facts he'd dug up by himself. Mary Connelly reported on scandals that were almost clichés of the category: slowdowns in pothole repair, cops on the take from local merchants, municipal workers sleeping on the job.

The *Post* continued to attract ambitious aspiring journalists. Peter Freiberg began his career in journalism at UPI in 1967. In 1971, he had a choice between joining the *Post* or the *Daily News.* "I didn't think the *Post* was a great paper," he says. "I knew it had a lot of good reporters, although the paper did not reflect that to the extent it should have. But as far as what I wanted to do—which was cover local communities—the *Post* would be better for me. And it was."

Not everyone at the paper appreciated what Freiberg was up to. "Wechsler had great difficulty understanding the neighborhoods and neighborhood activists: people who wanted neighborhood schools, who didn't want public

---

*The *Post,* which as an afternoon paper had the story of Ford's speech on October 29 (the day he delivered it), ran with "Ford: Let City Go Broke."

housing crammed down their throats, and stuff like that. He thought these people were just being ornery, he had no understanding." Dolly was a bit more sympathetic. "Listen, this was a wealthy woman who didn't get up to the Bronx a hell of a lot, except maybe to Riverdale once in a while. But she did have a sense of the city. She realized that there was that vast, other city out there. Even if it wasn't the city she knew firsthand."

Freiberg remembers writing a series on the Bronx. "It was called 'The Forgotten Borough.' I worked very hard on it for maybe two months. The editors asked for a few changes, and then they sent it up to Mrs. Schiff, because that was one of her babies. She knew the Bronx was important, she had a lot of readers there." The editors were nervous. "Remember that old TV ad for coffee with the farmers around El Exigente, who sniffed the beans and then smiled, and then music played, and everyone began to dance around," Freiberg says. "Well, she loved the series, and, as it were, everyone began dancing around."

Steve Lawrence was hired fresh out of Columbia journalism school in 1970. Although he'd worked at CBS, the *Post* was his first newspaper job. "It was the intelligent tabloid in town. It had that old civil liberties, Jewish liberal tradition. I felt that I had joined a company of colleagues, people who believed in what I believed journalism should be. It was a fabulous newsroom with wonderful people."

The *Daily News* and the *Times* also had full-time environmental reporters, with whom Lawrence competed. "That was one of the wonderful things about the *Post*'s newsroom—they really let you have your head. And they relied on me as the expert. It was a great start to my career."

Joyce Purnick had been trying to get a job on a New York paper since her Barnard graduation in 1967. Joyce wrote a letter to Dorothy Schiff after reading an article in *The New Yorker* that said that Dolly answered all her mail. She was called in for an interview and hired in February 1970. After some months as a clerk in the features department, Purnick became a reporter. She says, "Maybe the *Post* wasn't what it could have been by the time I got there, but I didn't know that. I had a great job. I was learning my craft and having a great time. On a daily newspaper, there's not much reflective conversation. You're concerned with getting the paper out. And after work, there was a lot of socializing. A lot of parties. It was a very friendly environment."

The air of friendliness did not, on the whole, emanate from the publisher's office. Although veterans like Fern Marja Eckman, Sylvia Porter, and

Helen Dudar were still at the paper, the days were gone when they went out for a casual lunch with the boss. Now lunches in her office were scheduled if a reporter who already had established some comfort level with Dolly had business to discuss.

Steve Lawrence gives Dorothy Schiff little credit for supporting him or his young colleagues. "There were never any performance bonuses, she never sent a note, she barely ever came down into the newsroom. And she had this group of people who worked their asses off. We loved working our asses off. But it wasn't for her; it was for each other, or for the editors—Bob Spitzler and Warren Hoge, you know—and we were having a ball."

Some young staffers, like Bill Woodward and Pam Howard, had special privileges, but they did not stay at the paper long. Warren Hoge was a different matter. Hoge joined the *Post*'s Washington bureau in 1967. In the summer of 1970, Dolly invited him to New York to fill in for vacationing editorial writers James Wechsler and Richard Montague. He was asked to stay on and soon became night city editor, a heady assignment for the ambitious Hoge. He says, "At twenty-seven, to be the night city editor of a downtown tabloid in New York City! It doesn't get any better than that."

Despite the memos that continued to descend from the publisher's office to the city room, Warren believes that by the mid-seventies, Dolly was not much involved in the daily decision-making process either on news coverage or editorial policy. "Sometimes she made direct suggestions about someone, making them the subject of one of those 'People in the News' features. Maybe to do a favor, or it could be someone she was genuinely interested in. Otherwise she had Paul Sann putting out the gutsy tabloid on our floor and Jimmy Wechsler putting out the high-minded editorial columns on his floor. And she was pretty happy with that."

Although Dolly had not met Warren before he was hired, she knew of his father, a prominent New York lawyer. Warren's older brother, Jim, had married into Chicago's Albright-Patterson clan and became editor of the *Chicago Sun-Times* in 1968. Warren was yet another of Dolly's handsome, well-connected, WASP favorites. Soon after he arrived in New York, she made him something of a confidant. He was frequently invited to the publisher's office; he went to dinner at her apartment and saw her during the summer in the Hamptons. "All in all," Hoge says, "I was quite aware of the fact that I enjoyed some access to her that others did not have. It certainly opened the door. I was aware of it, and I was constantly ragged about it at the time. Sann ragged me about it to my face, and it was probably worse behind my back."

Most reporters glimpsed Dolly only when she arrived in the morning, as she and her Yorkshire terrier, Susie Q, were swept into an elevator cleared of other passengers by Everette Lawson, the chauffeur. On the rare occasions when Dolly came downstairs to see Sann or Wechsler, few engaged her in casual chat.

Some remember contact with the owner as strained and artificial. Joyce Purnick says, "At one point, she began inviting reporters to her aerie for lunch. It was billed as 'she wants to reach out to the staff and get to know them.' I don't know. All I can remember is that it was unusually formal. Awkward. It was during the Watergate hearings, because the television was on. And she was talking about Bob Woodward, about how cute he was, and about if he were single and she was a reporter, she would reach out to him, or something like that.

"This flirtatious, girly thing made all of us uncomfortable," says Joyce. "She was too old for that. She had that marbleized grey hair. I didn't know what to make of any of it, and I was eager to get out of there."

In March 1974, Dolly turned seventy-one. As of June 1, she had owned the paper for thirty-five years. She did not celebrate the anniversary, but it could not be ignored. Would she be around for the fortieth? Would Paul Sann? Dolly and Paul knew each other's strengths and weaknesses, for which they alternated tolerance and contempt. In the past, their intermittent quarrels and reconciliations had energized them both, but now the game seemed to leave them tired.

Often they fought about things that did not seem serious. A typical fuss was generated in November 1970, when Paul complained that Byron Greenberg and Dolly had made some personnel changes without consulting him. Paul stormed into Dolly's office and announced that he was leaving. Dolly accepted his resignation, which was not the response he expected.

She told Byron she would be satisfied if that was the way it ended. She said that Paul was no longer happy in his job and that his negative attitude was poisoning the atmosphere in the city room. That evening, Byron spoke to Paul, who was willing to leave but didn't want to do anything that would jeopardize his severance package. Byron reassured Paul that he would get his full payout even if he left before he reached official retirement age.

After stewing for several days, Sann, on Greenberg's advice, went to see Dolly at her apartment. He was in a conciliatory mood. They discussed staffing issues and Sann's hours. Eventually he said that he would be back to work as usual on Monday morning. From his point of view, the crisis was over, though nothing particular had been resolved. Dolly was skeptical, but she was willing to drop the discussion. Just before he left, Paul told her he guessed that their love affair would go on forever. She did not answer. When he left, he kissed her good-bye.

Sann carefully surrounded himself with editors who, though usually competent, posed no threat to his own tenure. He had come to believe that his biggest potential rival was Pete Hamill. Pete was a star; his byline appeared in national papers and magazines. Although he exasperated Dorothy at times, he could usually charm her when necessary. No wonder Sann was suspicious. At one point, discussing Hamill in another context, he told Dorothy, "I believe it is very dangerous to talk to Pete. He is more than a columnist now. He is a Fifth Column."

In fact, Hamill loved the *Post* and often gave Dorothy unsolicited suggestions on how to make it better. In January 1970, he offered some ideas about improving the weekend paper. He proposed a redesign to make it more distinctive. The weekly perennial, "Man [or Woman] in the News," should be scrapped. Reporters hated writing the pieces, and readers thought they were a cliché. Dorothy, who took a special interest in the series, wrote, "It's our most popular feature," in the margin of her copy of the memo.

Hamill suggested allowing reporters to take on an occasional longer piece than the daily paper could handle, and he advocated offering a similar opportunity to young freelancers, "the kind of people now making their name in *The Village Voice*." (Dorothy wrote in the margin, "Who wants them?") He proposed adding a column in Spanish or one of interest to Spanish readers. She thanked him for his ideas and did nothing about them.

But Paul was right to be wary of Dorothy's fondness for Pete. In September 1971, Paul asked for permission to go to Los Angeles to tape a television program honoring Earl Wilson. He ducked Dorothy's question about whether or not the days he would be gone were important ones, when, in fact, one was the day of a primary election in New York. He also neglected to tell her that Bob Spitzler, the managing editor, was planning to be out of the office at the same time.

During the time Sann was away, a riot broke out at Attica prison, which put a terrible burden on the reduced staff. Dorothy and Byron Greenberg were eventually pressed into emergency service in the city room. When Byron spoke to Paul the following morning, Sann knew he was in trouble. He said he wanted to quit and collect his full severance pay. He also told Byron that he'd heard rumors that Hamill was being groomed to succeed him anyhow. Dorothy told Byron that Paul's fears were unjustified. He relayed her comments to Paul, who seemed relieved.

Dorothy was being disingenuous. There was truth to the Hamill rumor. As Dorothy herself later admitted, she and Pete had been drinking with friends at Elaine's the night before. During the course of the evening, she suddenly asked him if he'd like to become the editor of the paper. He said yes, and she told him to start the following week. When Pete called her next morning to find out if she had been serious, she equivocated.

In any event, Hamill was reluctant to take on the assignment immediately. He needed to finish some freelance assignments, and he was uneasy about displacing Sann, to whom he was always loyal. Hamill said that he might like to keep his column and that he had some ideas about changing the design as well as the content of the paper, which he would put in a memo. Dorothy reminded Pete that design interested her much less than content. But she recognized that Pete was very intelligent and brought fresh ideas to the table.

Within a few weeks, Pete produced the memo, then promptly left for London. Both he and Dorothy were getting cold feet about her somewhat flippant offer. When a *Newsweek* reporter called to check out the gossip that Pete would soon take over as executive editor, Dorothy denied it vehemently.

Although Pete was not really interested in running the *Post,* his memo had some thoughtful things to say about the paper's current weaknesses. He began by saying that the *Post* was "now in a condition something like stasis: it is largely dull, unresponsive to the changing city, not respected by the best people in the city, and not really admired by the rest. The result has been falling circulation." (Dorothy wrote in the margin of her copy, "Not true.") He worried that escalating costs and diminished readership could lead to the death of the paper.

Hamill felt that most of the writers currently on staff were competent, if they could be infused with renewed energy. The paper should get rid of some deadwood—he cited Max Lerner and Rose Franzblau. Their day was past; now they were a joke and an embarrassment. Similarly, it should replace its theater and movie critics with younger people.

The women's pages should reflect the interests of young women and single mothers. The paper should look into day care; it should create a regular feature on things to do with kids. The business section should be expanded. The sports section was fine. The paper should beef up its coverage of the arts in general, as well as the business of the arts—New York's movie and television production industries, for example.

Pete implored Dolly to hire a top graphic designer to change the style of the front page, the daily magazine, the editorial pages, and anything else that could be improved. Whatever you do, he wrote in conclusion, "make it bold. Pick a target date. Don't go gradual. Announce the new *New York Post* for, say March 1. Go all out."

By the time Dolly received the memo, her enthusiasm for change was spent. She thanked him for his thoughts, some of which she said were terrific, and some unfeasible. "Let's discuss when you get back [from London]," she wrote him. They never did.

In the meantime, Hamill evidently decided he'd better cover himself with his immediate boss. From England, he wrote Sann that he'd had a tentative conversation with Dolly in which he'd told her he didn't even know if he would be interested *if* the job were available. He remembered that Paul had once told him there are questions of "whether or not anyone can do that job while Dolly is alive. . . . I did make it clear to Dolly that I didn't even want to *talk* about it if it involved some sort of palace coup of which you would be the victim, that I could never do the job without a long couple of months of transition at your elbow, and that I would have to think about it."

Paul accepted this at face value. He and Dolly continued to spar and make up. Jean Gillette says, "You didn't want to be around when they got going. Then they'd work it out. It's as if each of them knew just exactly how far to push the other one and exactly when to back off." Sann grew increasingly bitter. Some of the problems were his health and his age—Sann was only fifty-seven, but he had been at the *Post* for a taxing forty years—and he was worn down by events.

Al Ellenberg, the assistant managing editor at the time, says, "I think that he'd run out of patience with her. He'd been, for a long time, very protective of her. Almost a kind of a courtier, in the sense that he had a kind of fealty to her. It was more than just the fact that she owned the candy store; I think he felt that there was some legitimacy to her. I think he even admired her toughness, because she was actually tougher than a lot of people ever realized. But as she got older, and as the economics of the paper became more difficult, she became cranky and more idiosyncratic, more unpredictable. He, I think, found it more and more difficult to deal with that unpredictability. More exhausting."

In a way, they were like a long-married couple, which Dolly acknowledged at one point in 1974. Thanking Sann for some kindness, she wrote that their relationship had become the "most enduring" of her life.

Perhaps Sann always knew his job was safe. When he had a heart attack in the fall of 1975 and was forced to take several months' leave, Bob Spitzler, the managing editor, and Warren Hoge, the city editor, ran the paper in his absence. But Dolly never considered Bob an adequate permanent replacement. Although Warren would have seemed a plausible candidate, she did nothing to formalize his possible ascendancy, and within a few months he left for *The New York Times.*

At this point Dorothy's pattern was to jump at possible solutions to the *Post*'s problems and just as suddenly to back off. Her indecision in the matter of the paper's editorial leadership was paralleled by her sporadic efforts to find someone she could groom to take her place at the top. Her experiments with Sally Kramarsky, Blair Clark, and Tim Seldes had been just that— experiments, dictated by desire, not necessity. In a similar vein, she subsequently approached but ultimately did not hire Bill Moyers, who instead became the publisher of *Newsday,* and Emmet Hughes, who signed on as Nelson Rockefeller's chief speechwriter.

As Dorothy entered her seventies, she needed to think seriously about a successor. She had always told her family that she had acquired the paper on a whim, possibly to keep George Backer busy. She had kept it because it suited her to, but she believed the idea of a dynastic responsibility to maintain it would have been more of a burden than a benefit. Adele Sweet says, "Mother always said she was highly opposed to nepotism. She called us in to work for her when she needed us, but there was never a sense that it was to be permanent."

Dorothy encouraged her children and grandchildren to take a strong interest in politics but not in journalism. In fact, she discouraged them from journalistic careers. After graduating from Radcliffe, granddaughter Wendy

Gray lived with Dorothy in New York while trying to figure out what career to pursue. "I was invited to stay for dinner one evening," Wendy says. "There was this man there from the paper. I didn't know who he was. He offered me a job." It was James Wechsler, who asked her to work with him on the Letters to the Editor column. Wendy stayed at the *Post* for a year and then, convinced that she had no aptitude for reporting, applied to graduate school in public policy. Just before she left, she became friendly with a young woman who worked in management. "Accounting, maybe," Wendy says. "And I thought afterward that that would have been interesting. To work on the business side. But Goggi (as Dolly's grandchildren called her) never mentioned it. She didn't appear to take much interest in the fact that I was at the paper, in any case."

The most obvious heir, should Dorothy have wanted one, was her son, Morti Hall. Morti, his wife, Diana, and their children had moved to New York from California in 1967. They settled on East Sixty-fourth Street, just down the block from Dolly's apartment, and Morti joined the *Post* as director of advertising. He was also appointed treasurer of the Post Corporation, which gave him a role in strategic planning, such as it was, and made it possible for him to sign checks in his mother's absence.

Morti says that his tenure was always meant to be temporary and that he had no intention of grooming himself, or being groomed, as his mother's eventual replacement. Nevertheless, Morti, who had had wider management experience than many of the people on the financial side of the paper, began to make his mark. He reviewed the paper's reciprocal advertising contracts with local radio stations, which provided for the paper to run ads for radio programming in exchange for the stations' broadcasting ads for articles in the *Post*. He discovered that the *Post* provided more advertising linage to the stations than it recouped in airtime. Although this was not a cash loss, it was unproductive, and he promptly canceled the deals.

When the *Post* moved to South Street, Morti believed that the new six-column format and added color capability would make the paper more attractive to national advertisers. He encouraged his mother to meet with executives of McCann-Erickson to talk about the possibility of the agency pitching the paper to such accounts. After one or two exploratory meetings, Dolly canceled the talks on the grounds that the costs incurred would be too high and the benefits were not clear.

Morti did not build on his early success. Most people in the city room regarded him as a negligible presence. Joe Rab says, "For a while Morti would come by every day and visit the different departments to see what was going on, and then he seemed to lose interest."

Miss Gerry, the Guild leader, says, "Morti got into a lot of trouble. People in advertising and accounting hated dealing with him. He had a terrible temper. But then again, his mother wouldn't let him do too much. She handled everything. There was no question, he couldn't go against her."

Matters came to a head during the Guild strike late in 1970. Perhaps Morti, who was going to leave the paper at the end of the year, although this decision had not been announced, didn't feel the need to preserve even the pretense of civility any longer. According to Miss Gerry and others, he prowled around the picket line, excoriating the striking reporters. He berated one young man for not doing any work and having long hair. Then he lost his temper completely and charged the line, going specifically for Al Ellenberg, against whom he presumably had no personal grudge.

That evening, Ellenberg received a phone call from Stan Opotowsky. "He apologized on behalf of the publisher and told me that Morti Hall would never be let back into the building. And I never saw him there again."

Morti brushes aside accounts of the incident. He reiterates that he always assumed his job was temporary and that he never intended it to be otherwise. Early in 1969, Dorothy talked with Otis Chandler of the *Los Angeles Times* about the possibility of his buying the *Post*. Otis, who'd known Morti in California, asked her what her ambitions for her son were. She said she had no expectations for him, that Morti could make up his own mind about what he wanted to do. Otis said he had the impression that Morti enjoyed working at the *Post* but wasn't sure he wanted to be there permanently.

Some months later, Dorothy was chatting with Robert Morgenthau, an old friend, who had recently lost a gubernatorial election to Nelson Rockefeller and was presumably looking for a job. Morgenthau asked which of her children might eventually take control of the *Post*. He assumed that Morti would be willing to step in. Dorothy replied that she thought Morti's wife, Diana, was more focused on having him become publisher than Morti was.

Jean Gillette says, "I don't remember that Mrs. Schiff made any attempt to groom him, to bring him along. She consulted him from time to time, but not in a way to make any of the rest of us think that she particularly valued him. It's hard to know if she would even have liked it if he had shown more of a lasting interest. She was so independent. She didn't even think that way."

Jean's opinion is seconded by Byron Greenberg. "I liked Morti. He was tough, he had guts," says Byron. "But it just didn't work. And I don't think she ever indicated to any of us that we should see him as the heir apparent."

Family members recall that Dolly was often dismissive of Morti. Several say that she always described him as a charming man who was attractive to women. Others recall her praising his sense of humor. Noticeably missing are any recollections that she ever praised his business acumen. Lisa Schiff says, "Dolly thought that Morti was one of the funniest people she'd ever known, but she didn't take him seriously. And it was very hurtful." The trouble with having a parent who doubts a child's ability to perform is that often the parent's lack of confidence becomes a self-fullfilling prophecy. Morti appeared to be intimidated by his mother—not a mind-set conducive to making good business decisions, or any decisions, for that matter.

With Morti out of the management picture, although he continued to serve as treasurer of the corporation, Dorothy resumed her fitful search for a white knight who could protect her and her interest in the paper. After Bill Moyers left *Newsday* in 1970, several advisers suggested she talk to him again about joining the *Post,* but she knew he would not be interested. Dorothy told a colleague that Moyers had frequently said that in the future he wanted to be "Number One and not Number Two," and, Dorothy said, no one would hire him under those conditions. The statement was revealing. She was still more comfortable thinking about a number two—an assistant—rather than contemplating a formal process that would end in her relinquishing command.

She toyed with the idea of filling the slot with Morris Abram, who'd been representing her at Paul, Weiss for several years. She first mentioned it to him in the spring of 1971, without making a firm offer. A year later she told Byron Greenberg that if she were suddenly incapacitated without having a proper successor in place, he was to ask the law firm to give Abram a leave of absence to take over the paper, at least until it could be sold. Abram was flattered, but he had few subsequent conversations with Dolly about issues of daily management or corporate policy. She may have dealt with the problem formally, but her actions proved that it was a hollow solution.

In 1973, Dolly startled her editors by announcing that William Woodward would sit in for her during her annual vacation. This would be Woody's trial run as assistant publisher. Despite how badly he had treated her in the pages of *[MORE],* he was a known quantity and one who now had some publishing experience.

Bob Friedman, who was scornful of Woody as a reporter, was pleasantly surprised by his new incarnation. "Woodward," Friedman told Sann, "despite or maybe because of his Ivy League education, couldn't write a decent sentence to save his life and couldn't stitch two coherent thoughts together. I rewrote everything of his that came my way. Later, when he was briefly DS's executive assistant to the publisher, he sat down with me to talk about the *Post,* and he spoke lucidly and perceptively about *Post* finances and money generally."

Woody was unpopular with most of the news staff, who remembered him as a poor reporter and resented his promotion, which they rightly ascribed to class. Warren Hoge told Dolly that he and his colleagues were afraid Woody would become publisher if she died. She said that wouldn't happen; at her death, the paper would have to be sold so that her heirs could pay the inheritance taxes. She then asked Warren if he was angling for Woodward's job. Shocked, he said he had no interest in being part of management. The experiment with Woody was brief, in any case. Soon after the summer passed, he was gone.

Dolly's next candidate was her daughter Adele. Adele had moved back to New York and married lawyer and civic leader Robert Sweet, who had served as deputy mayor under his college classmate John Lindsay. Labor lawyer Sidney Orenstein says, "Late in 1975, Dolly was beginning to think about the future again, and she may have had an idea that Adele would succeed her. So she invited Adele to sit in on some negotiations with the mailers' union. That was a way to get started."

In February 1976, Dolly appointed all three of her children to the board of the New York Post Corporation. Adele was elected vice president of the board and named assistant publisher of the paper, but her duties were not spelled out. Dolly told a friend that Adele's leadership role in the California Democratic party proved that she was good at administration. She said that as she got older, she needed someone in place who could sign checks and official documents in an emergency. This was not exactly an executive training program.

Adele says, "I came in for the union negotiations. Automation was going to be a major issue. And I loved politics, and 1976 was a political year." She soon found herself immersed in many aspects of management. She monitored the union negotiations that dragged on until April. She consulted with Paul Sann over changes in staffing. She joined her mother during a brief courtship of Warren Hoge's older brother, Jim, as a possible candidate to take over the job she had so recently stepped into.

In spring 1976, Marshall Field V and his brother Ted were quarreling over how to manage their Chicago newspaper and broadcasting empire. There were rumors that they might get rid of Jim Hoge, the editor of the *Sun-Times*. Dolly and Adele, who knew Jim socially, invited him to a meeting with Byron Greenberg in April. They discussed the *Post*'s ongoing union negotiations and how to spruce up the paper. According to Dolly's notes, Jim said that he saw the future of the *Post* following one of two scenarios. It could focus on a small, sophisticated readership, which would attract upscale advertisers, or it could broaden its appeal in an attempt to regain outer borough readers. Dolly told him she was always more interested in the masses than the classes. Jim gave the impression that he would consider an offer but made it clear that his first loyalty was to the *Sun-Times*.

In July, Adele invited Hoge to meet her and her mother at Dolly's apartment. After a brief discussion of the *Post*'s prospects—which Hoge had doubts about—the women got right to the point: would he consider coming to the *Post* as assistant publisher for $75,000 a year plus the possibility of buying a share of ownership?

Politely, Jim turned them down. "I was sitting on a good job on a major paper that was doing reasonably well, not great, but reasonably well, and was advancing in its market," he says. "So it just wouldn't make sense to go from that to an unlikely rescue operation. And then the last thing was that, true to Dolly, the financial part of the offer was far off the mark. Because I liked her, and she was such an elegant lady, I walked right by without pointing out that she could probably get an accountant for that, but she wasn't going to get a publisher."

Neither Dolly nor Adele had any real sense of the market for top executives, nor did Dolly consult her lawyers or businesspeople before she made her offer. Hoge says, "Well, she knew me a little bit, and she knew I had a good reputation professionally. But you would have to say that there was no due diligence process in the search. I'm trying to remember if we even talked about what I would do with the paper if I came in, and I don't remember much, because she moved right to the endgame. Which is another reason not to have taken her offer very seriously."

The end of discussions with Jim Hoge left Adele in place but with no clear plan for a managed succession. Adele assumed she would stay on to assist her mother for several years and the future would resolve itself. That it did so within a matter of months was not something she, or anyone else, would have foreseen.

VI

RESOLUTION

TWENTY-FIVE

The Man from Oz

National trends within the newspaper industry underscored the *Post*'s woes. In the mid-seventies, there were about 1,750 daily papers in America. That number had held fairly constant for some years, but total readership was down and dropping. More and more Americans got their news from television and radio. Executives of *The New York Times* estimated that only half their target audience in the metropolitan area regularly bought the paper.

Papers like the *Times, The Washington Post,* and the *Los Angeles Times* had become units within publicly held, diversified media conglomerates that continued to expand. Corporate ownership of broadcasting stations and newspapers in the same city allowed them to offer attractive deals to local advertisers, and their control over properties in several cities gave them an edge with national advertisers as well.

In general, morning papers were more successful than those published in the afternoon. Morning papers had many subscribers, which lessened the need to rely on expensive promotions to build or retain circulation. Morning papers could be delivered at dawn while afternoon deliveries had to battle traffic during working hours. Afternoon papers' deadlines often hit right in the middle of a developing story. Their primary audience—office workers on their way home—no longer relied on public transportation; outside of New York and a few other major cities, most people commuted to work by car, which was not compatible with reading anything. Even in the New York area, more and more bus and train riders waited until they got home to check out the news on television, leading businesses to limit their advertising dollars to the morning papers and the evening local newscasts. These factors, when added to plant and personnel costs, had deterred the *Times* and the *Daily News* from launching afternoon editions after the collapse of the Widget in 1967.

Despite its afternoon monopoly, the *Post* was increasingly the also-ran among New York papers. The *Times* was the *Times,* and the *Daily News* was much improved. From the mid-sixties on, editor Mike O'Neill steadily purged the *News* of its former know-nothing, racist editorial slant. He expanded coverage of local affairs, beefed up an already strong sports section, and, without alienating its traditional base of conservative Irish and Italian readers, made the *News* attractive to blacks and those members of the growing Hispanic community who chose an English-language paper.

The economic and civic malaise that gripped the city and the country exacerbated the *Post*'s problem. White middle-class families continued to leave New York City, often centering their lives around employment and shopping hubs in Westchester County, northern New Jersey, southern Connecticut, or Long Island. Suburban papers like *Newsday* and the *Bergen* (NJ) *Record* became enormously successful. Many of the Jews and Italians who had been the *Post*'s core readers left the Northeast altogether and resettled in the South, especially Florida.

The financial pressures on all independently owned newspapers were onerous. The difficulty of raising capital needed for expansion and mechanization, and tax laws that made it almost impossible for families with closely held corporations to retain control over generations, led the owners of many of these enterprises to fold, merge with competitors, or sell to the growing chains.

Dorothy Schiff was a wealthy woman by any measure, but much of her wealth was tied up in the paper. Her additional resources were more than adequate to maintain a life of comfort and privilege, but they were not enough to underwrite a faltering corporation. The alternatives—acquiring significant corporate debt or selling common stock to outside shareholders—held no appeal. Dorothy couldn't have tolerated the scrutiny of market analysts or stockholders looking over her shoulder. Lacking offsetting investments, and being unwilling to increase her dependence on the banks, Dorothy had to ask herself whether or not she could—or should—maintain her ownership of the paper.

Ever since she was approached by Phil Graham and others in the early sixties, Dorothy had listened to offers but ultimately rejected potential buyers. Most recently, she had entertained an overture by Otis Chandler, publisher of the *Los Angeles Times* and vice chairman of its parent Times Mirror Company, which his family controlled. Otis had known Morti Hall slightly in California and used that as an opening to invite Dorothy to lunch in October 1968. He came right to the point: he might be interested in acquiring the *Post* in exchange for stock in Times Mirror and a five- or ten-year management contract for Dorothy Schiff.

Impressed by Otis's good looks and by his proposal, Dorothy contacted her lawyer Simon Rifkind for advice. Rifkind made some attempts to widen the conversation—and perhaps stimulate a bidding war—by contacting representatives of *Newsday* and the Washington Post Corporation, but nothing came of his efforts.

Early in 1969, Dorothy deputized Morti to meet with Chandler and Henry Necarsulmer of Kuhn, Loeb to determine a price. Necarsulmer outlined the costs of the South Street project; he estimated that the Post Corporation's gross revenue for 1968 would be about $30 million and net profit would be about 10 percent of that.* Dorothy's team agreed that the sale price should be between $70 million and $100 million, based on a projection that the paper's revenues would grow by approximately 15 percent each year over the next decade.† The question was if she really wanted to sell even if she got her price.

At the end of February, Necarsulmer and Morti pressed her to make a decision so they could enter into serious negotiations. After brooding overnight, she decided she could probably do better by waiting until the paper was installed at South Street and could demonstrate real earnings rather than projected ones. Morti and Adele concurred. They agreed to tell Chan-

---

*Necarsulmer, perhaps on the advice of Byron Greenberg and Morti, was being optimistic. The figure for gross revenue was roughly correct; the estimated profit was more than twice what it turned out to be.

†This estimate also turned out to be optimistic. Retained earnings leaped an astonishing 45 percent in 1969 compared to the previous year, but they fell in 1970 and 1971, remained static in 1972 through 1974, and then dropped precipitously.

dler that they were not interested at the time, but should they reconsider in the future, he would be given first consideration.

Dorothy seems to have believed that a deal was available if she wanted it. But no one on the Times Mirror management team—neither Chandler nor his leading corporate officers—remembers Chandler's effort as much more than a fishing expedition. Times Mirror was indeed in a buying mode. In September 1969, the company bought the *Dallas Times Herald* and its television station KRLD-TV. They were also looking to acquire an East Coast property, but the *Post* was not the most attractive option. *Newsday,* with a much bigger circulation, much greater advertising linage, and enormous growth potential, was. "That paper was a gold mine. Harry Guggenheim probably gave Alicia about $50,000 to get started, and he never had to put up another dime," says Morti Hall. "Frankly, it was a much more attractive property than the *Post.*" In October 1970, Times Mirror completed a deal to buy the paper from Harry Guggenheim and Alicia Patterson's heirs for approximately $100 million. The figure was further evidence that Dorothy's wished-for price was wildly off the mark.

The *Post*'s average circulation was slipping slowly but relentlessly from a high of more than 700,000 in the late sixties to about 625,000 in the early seventies, and then, in what looked like a permanent trend, to fewer than 600,000 in 1974. Even more ominous was the parallel slide in advertising. In comparable quarters of 1968 and 1973, billed advertising linage fell from 3,954,200 to 3,534,067; by 1976 it had sunk to 2,616,771. During the early seventies, advertising revenues held their own because of rate hikes, but by 1975, total revenue was dropping absolutely.

With the decline in advertising, the paper shrank from an average of just over ninety-one pages in 1968 to seventy-eight in 1971 to just over sixty-seven pages in 1976. Editorial linage rose a bit because there were empty pages to fill. Dolly and Sann had a recurrent discussion about how to cut back on copy, perhaps by eliminating some of the syndicated columns that cluttered the paper, but those columns were cheap at the price. Cutting back on homegrown writers might have been more cost-effective, but it would also have forced Dolly and Paul to make some tough decisions.

Pete Hamill was the one *Post*-based columnist who continued to write with vitality and relevance, but most of the discourse between Hamill and Sann and/or Schiff after 1971 had to do with Pete's restlessness at the paper. In May 1972, he resigned in a dispute over the placement of his column. Two months later, when he ran into Dolly at a party in East Hampton, he asked to return, which he did in September. A year later, he left again. He came back once more in the spring of 1974, only to leave for good a few months after that. Pete's growing love for the high life meant that he needed more money than the *Post* could pay.

Dr. Rose Franzblau had long since become a caricature of a Freudian busybody. At one point, Sann suggested dropping her altogether, but Dolly demurred, reminding Paul that her column was extremely popular, even if many people read it for laughs, and it was inexpensive. Because Franzblau had always been too timid to ask for a raise, she was still being paid the same $150 a week she had started at nearly thirty years earlier. Earl Wilson also cost the *Post* little; his income came largely from syndication.

Leonard Lyons was another matter. Dolly and Paul were unhappy with his work. The editors and rewrite men found him arrogant and self-important. Lyons hardly ever wrote his own material. Increasingly the column was compiled from press agents' handouts and clips from old files by his secretary, Anita Summer. In 1972, Sann and Schiff learned that Lyons was ill with a degenerative brain disease, and that his wife, Sylvia, was hiding the fact to keep the column going and the weekly paycheck of $678.50 plus syndication fees coming in. For a time, their son, Jeffrey Lyons, tried to take over, but Dolly was unsatisfied with his efforts. After some legal skirmishing over union-mandated severance payments, "The Lyons Den" ran for the last time on May 21, 1974, forty years to the day of its first appearance. The *Times* noted that "Leonard Lyons dropped his last 151 names in the *New York Post* yesterday" and reported that his space in the paper would be filled by the returning Pete Hamill.

Lyons was an iconic contributor to the paper, but his role was never as central as that of Max Lerner. Lerner had been an ally of Schiff and Wechsler in the late forties and early fifties when they were hammering out the *Post*'s liberal editorial position, and he frequently pinch-hit for Jimmy on the editorial page. By the mid-seventies, Lerner was moving increasingly to the right politically, and he was making something of a public spectacle of himself by hanging out with Hugh Hefner at the Playboy Mansion.

By the early 1970s, Dolly and Sann were convinced that Max was over-the-hill and overpaid. He earned $75 a week for his column plus an annual consultant's fee of $10,000, which Dolly, in a rare burst of corporate generosity, had justified for some years because, as she told Byron Greenberg, Max was aging, he had no Guild pension, and he was unlikely to increase his income in the years to come. But the *Post*'s own perilous finances suggested that even this small stipend come to an end. After calculating that Lerner earned about $30,000 a year from syndication fees and an undetermined amount from teaching, speeches, and other writing, Greenberg broke the news that they were dropping the consultant fee, while continuing to run his column.

No one was immune. As the paper's profits diminished, Dolly tightened up on executive salaries. Paul Sann received $57,000 in 1974 and 1975. But in December 1975, when the time came to discuss year-end bonuses with Byron Greenberg, Dolly insisted that Sann be penalized because he had been out sick for two months on full pay. They agreed on a mingy $500 increase in his 1975 bonus and no raise in salary for 1976.

Such economies on the editorial side did little to stem the financial trends affecting the *Post*'s bottom line. Costly settlements with the unions strained the budget even more. After protracted negotiations in 1973, the three New York papers settled on a package with the Guild and others that would raise base pay by $13.85 per week in each of the next two years.

For members of craft unions like Local 6, wages were almost irrelevant; they were fighting automation and the resulting death of their trade. Around the country, most papers had long since outmaneuvered the unions and had automated their pressrooms, but Bert Powers had managed to stave off the inevitable in New York. Now, his position was no longer tenable; the papers made it clear that they needed automation to survive, even if, in the short run, they paid a premium to achieve it.

The settlement that Powers and the publishers worked out in July 1974 provided for automation in the pressroom in exchange for guaranteed jobs for all the full-time members of the union then employed by the three papers. Only through attrition and retirement would the printers lose their salaries, after their retirement they could count on guaranteed pensions, and when the active status of all the current employees was ended, the unions would effectively cease to exist. It was estimated that by the time the contract was due to run out in 1984, perhaps two-thirds of all the printers would have departed, not to be replaced.

In essence, the papers achieved their goal of automation by agreeing to postpone the full financial benefits of the change. Management expected that full savings would finally kick in by the end of the ten-year contract. It was still a deal worth making. Eventually the owners put almost $1 million into the union's special pension fund in exchange for the freedom to automate. The price of the settlement was not inconsistent with what a standard wage increase package would have been, but any increase in personnel costs, however small, was burdensome to the *Post*'s fragile balance sheet.

The paper's profit margin was even more at risk in the fall of 1975 when the *Times* and the *News* negotiated a three-year contract with the Newspaper Guild that would provide a basic weekly wage increase of $25 for the first year, plus weekly increases of $20 in each of the two subsequent years. Pleading poverty, Dolly refused to accept the deal and even agreed to open her books to union inspection. She also demanded the right to make staff reductions and to change some other work rules in exchange for wage hikes, but the Guild claimed that there was not much to give because, unlike the craft unions, its work rules did not condone featherbedding.

Negotiations dragged on for almost six months, despite the intervention of mediator Ted Kheel. In May 1976, the union threatened to strike, and Dolly replied that if it did, she would close the paper for good. Finally the antagonists arrived at a deal that committed the *Post* to pay an increase of $25 per week the first year, $20 more for the second and omitted a commitment for the third year. Dolly said she would have to make further staff cuts through attrition.

In the middle of these negotiations, a minicrisis involving Guild members roiled the *Post* city room and revealed how vulnerable Dolly had become to the needs of her remaining advertisers. Steve Lawrence, who had expanded his environmental beat to include consumer issues, had been working for some months on a series of thirteen articles about New York supermarkets. The first piece was published on January 13, 1976, and others appeared once or twice a week thereafter. Lawrence says, "They were about how a supermarket works, things people think they know about and they don't: shelving, aisles, sanitation issues, short-weighting, supermarkets violating city ordinances, pricing, shelf fees. It was very good." He worked closely with editors Al Ellenberg and Bob Spitzler, who routinely sent the articles up through channels to Sann and Schiff for approval.

After the sixth piece—a critical look at weekly specials and supposed discounts offered through newspaper coupons—appeared on January 27, Sloan's, a local chain that was one of the *Post*'s major advertisers, pulled its ads. Lawrence says, "The chairman of the firm was actually a fairly good guy, but they complained to the publisher, and I remember exactly what Spitzler said to me. He called me into his office, and he said, 'There's blood on the moon. The series is dead. We ran the last one today. Dolly killed it.'"

The mood in the city room was mutinous. Lawrence and several of his most outspoken colleagues, including Lindsy Van Gelder, met several times with Dolly, who, they claim, told them that she could not afford to offend advertisers. The *Post* had been averaging eight full pages of supermarket ads every Wednesday—a significant item in a period of diminishing linage.

Lawrence says, "We were all outraged. This was my first experience with advertiser pressure making a difference in our coverage. No one had said I'd made any errors. There was no challenge to the facts. They just didn't want that material published in the paper. And she complied."

The Guild members demanded that their bylines be pulled. When the *Times* got wind of the incident, a spokesperson from Sloan's, fearful of being accused of interfering with a free press, said that the chain had never intended to end its relationship with the *Post*. They had been planning, he said, to transfer advertising temporarily to Spanish-language dailies to test its effectiveness with Hispanic customers, and it was only coincidental that the test had coincided with the supermarket series.

On some level, Dolly knew that the whole flap was ridiculous. Al Ellenberg remembers being in her office during the crisis. "While I was up there, another supermarket owner called and said he was going to drop his advertising. And she was very blasé. She said, 'He'll be back. Where's he going to go? He needs us.'"

Publicly, Dolly offered no comment at all. Privately, she told a reporter who tried to mediate between the publisher and her aggrieved staff that she had never been in favor of squelching a series because of pressure, but she had not seen any of the articles in advance. Her editors had worked on it behind her back, she said, and she felt as if she had been blindsided by the fuss. In 1977, she offered a different explanation, arguing that she had never killed the series—just the one article about specials and coupons—although she did not explain why the series was never resumed thereafter.

The byline strike, which lasted for ten days and then petered out, was very damaging to morale. Steve Lawrence left soon afterward for the *Daily News*. Today Ellenberg says that he believes some of the complaints were justified. "I came to have grave doubts about the journalism of it as time went on. I started to have doubts about the material. Some of the stuff that [Lawrence] was basing his reporting on was two or three years old. The complaints that were coming from the supermarkets were that many of these things had been corrected. Don't forget, that story is always a quagmire. Every ten years or so, somebody revives it. And they all bump into the same problem—which is that this stuff is based on old documentation. The owners can complain that they've cleaned it up. And you can't get them."

Dolly's behavior, however, was not motivated by such considerations. Her caving in to an advertiser indicated a flagging of her professional courage. Ducking responsibility by blaming the problem on her editors or misrepresenting what happened was worse. She no longer exhibited the firmness of purpose that had characterized her leadership in the glory days when she encouraged her reporters to go after corporate and civic bad guys no matter what pressures might be brought on her and her paper.

Yet she was still capable of shrewd leadership in matters both serious and small. Al Ellenberg says, "You could still sell her a story if it was a good one. Absolutely." In early 1974, Dorothy turned down his suggestion that the *Post* run a series on Secretary of State Henry Kissinger on the grounds that he was of interest only to national policy buffs and that such a series belonged properly in *The Washington Post*. Ellenberg persisted, supplying Sann and Schiff with notes on secret meetings Kissinger had held with New York Jewish leaders about his efforts to broker a deal for peace between Israel and Syria as part of the Nixon administration's policy plans for the Middle East. Persuaded that Ellenberg was on to something, Dorothy insisted that the paper immediately devote a considerable amount of its resources to a series on the secretary.

Dorothy had first met Kissinger, then Nixon's national security adviser, at a gala for the New York City Ballet in 1969. They talked about Bismarck. She asked Kissinger about international negotiations, which she assumed were not dissimilar to labor negotiations, in that you had to know what your opponent's needs were. She found him very intelligent but humorless and rigid. Kissinger admitted to her that he knew little about Asia, which left her "appalled," in view of his responsibilities for negotiating an end to the war in Vietnam.

Curious, she asked Paul Sann to find out more about Kissinger's private life. He put Warren Hoge, then still at the Washington bureau, on the case.

Warren sent back word that Kissinger was divorced, and that, although his name had been linked with various actresses and socialites, he had been seeing Nancy Maginnes seriously for a long time. The scuttlebutt was that they were not yet married because her mother objected to the fact that Henry was Jewish—just the sort of gossip that Dorothy loved.

Several years later, Dorothy asked Nelson and Happy Rockefeller to give a small dinner party at which she could meet Kissinger and Maginnes, who were married by then. She compared what he had to say about dealing with the Russians or the Chinese to her experiences negotiating with labor leaders. Once again, she found him wanting in insight and ruthless in manner.

The twelve-part Kissinger series ran in June 1974. It was written by Ralph Blumenfeld with the help of eleven other reporters and Ellenberg. Although admiring of the secretary's intelligence and implicitly proud that a Jewish immigrant had risen to the top of the Republican hierarchy, the series was not a puff piece. One article covered Kissinger's less than stellar career as a faculty member at Harvard. Another noted his ability to find powerful mentors like Rockefeller and Nixon, and his sometime servile behavior toward them. The series raised questions about the secretary's morality in continuing to serve a discredited president, and it ended by suggesting that he had frequently compromised his principles in the past when given the opportunity to wield power.

The Kissinger profile earned a lot of attention and praise, and brought the paper about $42,000 in domestic and overseas syndication sales. A further $52,000 from the sales of a paperback original commissioned by New American Library, written by Blumenfeld and based on the series, was divided among the paper, the principal author, and the reporters who had worked on the project.

Dorothy still had her self-described "common touch" for smaller stories, too. Alan Whitney, one of the night editors, remembers a suggestion she made in the summer of 1976. "We would go up to her office for a meeting," says Whitney. "It was mostly fooling around and drinking her gin. But she was a major television fan. She liked Redd Foxx, and *Mary Hartman, Mary Hartmann,* which was a very hip takeoff on soap operas. She and I both liked that. At one of these meetings, she got the idea that I should write every day for the paper a summary of what had happened the night before. Which I did. And that became a very popular feature."

Such bursts of Dorothy's old editorial flair became less and less frequent.

She was preoccupied with the paper's financial condition, which was steadily worsening. From 1968 through 1973, the *Post*'s net retained earnings hovered around $1,250,000 annually. In 1974, the combination of higher labor costs plus dwindling advertising and circulation revenues cut earnings to just over $900,000; in 1975, that dropped to $485,000; in 1976, the paper was projected to lose money for the first time since the strike year of 1962, and Dolly's equity was also poised to fall for the first time in more than a decade.

Jim Hoge was aware of Dolly's concern during their meetings in early 1974. "It was quite clear that she was aware that she was on a downward cycle," says Hoge, "and that she didn't have the answers internally. She was looking around on an urgent basis for some new path to go down and probably some new people. The part that was missing—and I wasn't in a position to talk to her much about it—was that she just didn't have the resources."

In addition to lacking adequate financial reserves, Dolly did not always receive outstanding financial advice.* Byron Greenberg knew the newspaper business, but he was not a sharp fiscal officer. Pete Hamill says, "I liked Byron Greenberg a lot, but he was essentially a guy who could go down and talk to the deliverers and say, 'Look, you can steal five thousand, but you can't steal ten.' Like a guy running a bar who says to the bartender, 'You can steal fifty dollars a night, but you can't steal a hundred.' In that sense it was management on the fly—with no vision of the future. That was one of the problems, that Greenberg didn't say, 'Where are we going? What's going to happen? Where's the potential audience in the future?'" Greenberg was not a strategic thinker, and Dolly never asked him—or anyone else—to be one.

Morti Hall agrees. "She was a very smart businesswoman. And that paper was her life—she wanted to keep it going. But Kay Graham had Warren Buffett; Mother didn't."

Dorothy had threatened the Newspaper Guild that she would close the paper rather than accede to higher wage demands. She'd already ascertained that it would cost her almost $8 million in severance payments to shut down operations and that the real estate at South Street was probably worth $2 mil-

*By contrast, Kay Graham not only surrounded herself with astute financial officers, but in 1973 she welcomed a new shareholder in the Washington Post Corporation, Warren Buffett, who would soon play a vital role in guiding the company's fortunes.

lion at best. But closing the paper was really an idle threat—after all she had done to revive it, how could she possibly be the person to kill off the property she had nurtured for so long?

It was not clear what she could do to ensure its future, or if she could tolerate going back to the old days of red ink. Adele Sweet says, "She saw that the future wasn't going to be kind. She saw the end for privately owned newspapers."

Many *Post* employees believe that Dorothy could have revived the paper by investing more in order to gain a higher return. The argument goes that she should have shaken up the editorial staff, perhaps pensioned off Sann, who had little rapport with many of the younger reporters, and hired more staffers to restore the editorial élan of the good old days. In short, follow many of the suggestions of Pete Hamill and others to revitalize the news and opinion pages. No one in the city room was asking how she could have attracted more advertisers or built circulation. Afternoon papers with corporate backing were going out of business all over the country. A private owner faced having to subsidize the *Post* indefinitely.

Dorothy's best bet to salvage the paper was to find a buyer, although the conditions that made the *Post* a poor fit for the Times Mirror interests had only worsened in the years since that deal disappeared. Any potential purchaser had to understand that Dorothy had postponed going into the red only by the most stringent economies. Any potential purchaser had to be prepared to spend money with only a remote chance of getting it back.

Word of just such a purchaser began to make its way to Dorothy's South Street aerie. In April 1972, John Schiff told his sister that Henry Necarsulmer had been approached casually on behalf of a young Australian newspaper owner named Rupert Murdoch to find out if the *Post* was for sale. She and John agreed to send word back that it could be purchased only at some "unspecified astronomical price." Subsequently Dorothy and Rupert met socially a few times, but nothing more was heard of the matter.

Murdoch had inherited his first paper, the *Adelaide News,* in 1952, from his father, influential Melbourne publisher Sir Keith Murdoch, who died at a low moment in his own corporate fortunes. Rupert, who was just twenty-one when he began his career, put together a chain of acquisitions across the country over the next few years. *The Australian,* an upmarket broadsheet that he founded in 1964, was the country's first national newspaper and was a lone respectable counterweight to the sleazier journals that were the basis of his growing reputation.

In 1969, Murdoch bought the London *Sun,* a failing daily tabloid that he turned into a huge success by combining operations with the Sunday *News of the World,* which he acquired at the same time. Next Murdoch turned to America; he looked into a number of properties including the *Post* before buying the *San Antonio Express* (morning) and the affiliated *News* (afternoon) in 1973 for $19 million. He immediately began cutting costs and lowering editorial standards.

At Dorothy's request, her editors analyzed Murdoch's results at the *Express.* Sann summarized, "It's basically a tear-off-the-wire kind of paper. No local reporting. No investigative reporting. No sign of where it's based. . . . In a word, if we wanted to put out a newspaper like Mr. Murdoch's Texas product, the staff here could come down appreciably. It would be easy, but it just wouldn't be the *New York Post* that survived the jungle warfare in this city."

Murdoch's ambitions were made clearer in 1974 when he started the *National Star,* a weekly tabloid, with which he hoped to challenge the supermarket gossip sheet the *National Enquirer.* The *Star* failed in that chase, but Murdoch was undaunted. In the spring of 1976, with an international empire that now included more than eighty newspapers and magazines as well as television stations in Australia and England, he once again put out feelers about buying the *Post.*

Byron Greenberg recalls that he would run into Murdoch from time to time and make small talk about the New York newspaper business. "Then one day I was having lunch with Dorothy Schiff. And she mentioned that her attorney, Judge Rifkind, I think, had advised her that there was about to be a change in the inheritance tax situation and if she wanted to leave any kind of an estate, she should consider selling the paper now. And she said to me— you know that line from *Oliver,* 'Who will buy?', and I said I know somebody who would be interested. I said I had met Rupert on occasion, and I thought he was acquisition minded."

"So she said, 'Invite him in for lunch.' "

They met on September 14. Murdoch later told a reporter, "I went down and had a bite of lunch with her, and we got talking about business and politics, and she said she was very tired. She knew what was necessary to turn the paper around and get it done right, but she felt she just didn't have the energy left. She really made the opening, though she didn't really mean to, I think.

"I said, 'If you want to get rid of it, let me know. I'm here.' She said, 'Oh, you'd be interested, would you? Everyone tells me you were, but you've never said it.'"

Murdoch mentioned that he thought the paper was worth between $10 million and $15 million. Dolly said nothing but had her sights set on nearly three times that amount. She told Murdoch that the Post Corporation had $20 million in its physical plant alone. He was dismayed but not driven away. They agreed that Greenberg should meet with Ray Dittrich, Murdoch's money guy, to discuss financial details.

The *Post* balance sheet showed net fixed assets (real estate and equipment) of just over $15—not $20—million. The paper had no substantial debt. Payroll obligations totaled just over $12 million, exclusive of severance commitments. In 1974 and 1975, despite annual revenues that remained steady at about $40 million, the paper's net profit had dropped from just under $1 million to less than $500,000, and it was poised to show a net operating loss in 1976.

Price was not Murdoch's primary concern. "I was very enthusiastic about getting a newspaper in New York," he says, "and she was enthusiastic about selling." He and his associates looked cursorily over the *Post*'s financial papers. They knew the paper was not in great shape. Murdoch says, "We did want to see that there weren't any worse things than it appeared."

During a follow-up meeting at Dolly's apartment, they talked price. Dittrich had told Greenberg that Murdoch would probably offer between $25 million and $30 million. Dolly said the paper was worth $50 million, a figure suggested by John Schiff. Murdoch responded by offering $20 million in cash, which she rejected. He said that was close to his limit.

Things moved fast thereafter. Byron Greenberg met with his counterparts in Murdoch's organization; Henry Necarsulmer of Kuhn, Loeb conferred with Murdoch's investment banker from Allen & Co; lawyers from Paul, Weiss dickered with Murdoch's attorneys; and within two months of that first lunch, the deal was roughed out.

On November 17, Rupert called Dorothy at her office to congratulate and thank her. She claimed not to know why. He explained that a purchase price had been agreed to and only details remained to be negotiated.

The formal deal memo, dated November 19, stated that the purchase price for the paper, the building on South Street with all its furnishings, and all financial obligations including payroll would be $31 million to be delivered in cash* at the closing, which took place on November 25. Dorothy would stay on as consultant for five years at a fee of $100,000 annually, which could not be canceled even if she did not perform. The *Post* was to provide office space on the premises for her and for Jean Gillette and pay customary secretarial and office fees.

Buyer and seller sat down together in Dorothy's South Street office just after noon on November 19. They issued a joint statement announcing the sale pending final negotiations and details. Dorothy said, "Rupert Murdoch is a man with a strong commitment to the spirit of independent, progressive journalism. I am confident he will carry on vigorously in the tradition I value so deeply." Murdoch said he hoped to add pages and more good writers. He stressed that the *Post* would continue to be a "serious newspaper."

Morti Hall was very surprised by the news. "The paper was her first love," he says. "It seemed to be her whole life. I thought she would dry up and die without it. But she was a very smart woman, and she knew how to make smart judgments."

Bob Spitzler revealed the news to a stunned newsroom. Jerry Tallmer says, "It was a blinding shock to me to come to work and learn that the paper had been sold. I had been telling everybody—everybody was telling everybody—that this was her life, she was only seventy-three, she's in the prime of her life, and she'll never let it go."

The *Times* quoted reporter Carl Pelleck as saying, "There was undoubtedly some confusion because this comes without a leak—a very well-kept secret. But it was not a wake. It was a rebirth. The *Post* is an orphan that has been adopted." Most of the reporters quoted thought the sale was a positive development because Murdoch would spend money to make money.

Several weeks later, *New York* magazine reported, "Many of the *Post*'s 100 or so reporters and deskmen profess to be glad about the change. Said one *Post* newsman: 'Dolly [Schiff] hadn't hired anyone down here for a year and a half, and the circulation was dropping. People were leaving a sinking ship.' " Characteristically, Dolly wrote "libel" on the clipping before she filed it in her scrapbook.

---

*Murdoch borrowed much of the money from banks in the United States, Australia, and Great Britain.

The evening after the deal was announced, the principals convened in Dolly's apartment. Byron Greenberg says, "There we were: Mrs. Schiff, myself, Rupert Murdoch, and some of his people. Maybe eight of us. Maybe Morti, maybe Adele. We had a drink or two. And on the surface it was very pleasant. But I found it slightly heartbreaking. It was the end of an era.

"The Murdoch people asked me to join them—they were going out to celebrate. And I declined. It was a changing of the guard. But I must say the negotiations went extremely well. And it was what needed to be done at that point."

The next day Murdoch told a reporter from the *Times* that "the political policies [of the *Post*] will stay unchanged." He added, somewhat confusingly, that to the degree that he would change the paper at all it would probably be less political. "Over the years we've been hostile to politicians of all parties."

Dolly told the *Times* that she admired Rupert's journalistic skills. "I've always been a mass-circulation person myself," she said. "Although I've never achieved it really. I do not feel the way most people do about mass circulation, what we call human interest. I have very common tastes anyway. I look at the *Enquirer* and the *Star* every week, and I get ideas from them—about tests, self-improvement, the best husband personality profile for you."

She said she had a good feeling about the sale. Among other things, she and Rupert shared a March 11 birthday. "Neither of us believes in astrology—but I love coincidences." She said that she had cried when everyone left her apartment but then bounced back. "I'm very resilient." She was looking forward to her new role as consultant and hoped to be useful if called upon, but she would turn over control of the paper to Murdoch as soon as possible. "I feel like Ford—a lame duck President—the sooner you get out the better." The actual transfer of power would take place at the end of the year.

Roberta Brandes Gratz remembers that Dolly didn't want anything to happen that might foul up the deal. "The only time that Dolly ever interfered with a story of mine came at the end," Roberta says. "I was covering the nursing home scandal, and I had a story which would have been essentially the little black box, a payoff thing with a judge. The sale to Murdoch had been announced, but it hadn't gone through. And Paul Sann put a kibosh on my story, because Dolly didn't want anything that might lead to a lawsuit, even if it wasn't legitimate, that could hinder the sale. So the story never saw the light of day."

On the eve of the closing, Mordechai Rochlin, a tax specialist at Paul, Weiss, explained the financial details and its tax implications to Dolly. She would turn over to the purchaser* her 3,829 shares of stock, plus the 131 shares held by the Post Foundation. In return, she would be paid $29,674,750, and the foundation (which Dolly promptly renamed the Pisces Foundation) would receive $1,325,250. Her personal capital gains tax would be about $12,100,000, leaving her with net proceeds of about $17,575,000. Another lawyer's letter explained that as her present assets—exclusive of the *Post*—were about $6,500,000, after the sale of the paper and the payment of the gains tax as well as estimated expenses of a million dollars, her taxable estate would be just under $25,000,000.

What motivated her to sell the paper, Dolly maintained at the time, was the change in the federal tax code due to kick in at the beginning of 1977. She said her lawyers had explained that—assuming she had made up her mind to divest herself of the paper—the tax implications to her heirs would be "prohibitive" if she did not sell by year's end.

Several weeks later, *The Wall Street Journal* speculated about her reasoning. "Several estate lawyers doubt that tax considerations alone persuaded Mrs. Schiff to sell the *Post*. But the lawyers say that once she had made the decision to sell, it might very well benefit her heirs to sell before the end of the year." Assuming that Dolly acquired the *Post* for $2 million in 1939 and sold it to Murdoch for $30 million, her gain would be a tidy $28 million, before capital gains taxes. At her death, her estate of approximately $24.4 million would be taxed about $16 million, leaving a net inheritance of about $8 million to be shared among her heirs.

If the paper had not been sold before 1977, and it were not to increase in value by the time of her death, it would pass into her estate at a value of $30 million, on which the estate tax would be about 66 percent, or $20 million. Under the old law, if her heirs were to sell at some time after her death for that same $30 million, they would not be liable for an additional capital gains tax. The old law would consider the transaction a wash: they acquired it at the same value for which they sold it. But under the new law, a capital gains tax could be charged to the sellers. If, for example, Dolly were to die in 1981,

*The paper was formally acquired on a fifty-fifty basis by two wholly owned companies of Murdoch's: News Limited, which was incorporated in Australia, and News International Limited, which was based in Great Britain.

and her heirs were to sell it that year for $30 million, in addition to that $20 million estate tax bill, they would be hit with a capital gains tax bill calculated by the *Journal* as an additional $1.3 million.

Even if her children wanted to keep the paper, which was not likely, they presumably did not have the assets to pay the inheritance tax and maintain ownership after her death—a common problem for family-owned businesses. That they would have sold the paper to raise cash was probably inevitable. By selling before the end of 1976, she saved them that additional $1.3 million.

Adele Sweet says that her mother was also motivated to sell by her growing sense of sadness about basic changes in the business. "She was very discouraged about automation," Adele says. "She didn't really quite get it. And I think it was frustrating, because she was dogged in her determination to find out about everything. But it was baffling to her."

Adele thinks her mother was moved by what was happening to the men in the composing room. "Here were these old guys, these behemoths who had run the linotype machines, still wearing their green visors and trying to learn on this very small keyboard. She hated what it was doing to these people, even though they would continue to be paid forever. And there had already been a lot of attrition. It caused her pain to see the frustration, that they were being put out to pasture, that they were no longer needed. She was the least sentimental person imaginable, but that kind of personal thing affected her a great deal."

Wynn Kramarsky agrees. "I think she really, really felt empathy. And it wasn't condescending. It was real empathy. Also," he adds, "she didn't want to be hated." Which she would have been had she had to cut more jobs through attrition or been forced to shut down the paper altogether.

In the long run, an afternoon paper was doomed to lose money. In the short run, Dolly must have been looking for excuses. "Have you ever met Rupert Murdoch?" Adele Sweet asks. "He's one of the most interesting people I've ever met in my life. I think she was fascinated by him. He suggested to her, or she wanted to believe, that he would carry the paper on as she wanted. Murdoch sold her a bill of goods, really, in terms of the direction the paper would take. I think that, more than any tax change or anything else, she thought, this is the guy."

Murdoch had an excellent track record of restoring circulation to failing papers. A few days before he was scheduled to take over the *Post,* the *Times* quoted one of his associates as saying, "Rupert has turned around some papers that were nonexistent. For once he's getting a healthy paper, and it's going to be exciting to see what he will do with it."

Critics of Murdoch, the *Times* said, were convinced he would transform the *Post* into "a sex-and-scandal sheet similar to some of the Murdoch papers in Sydney, London, and San Antonio. But Mr. Murdoch says he will not. He says that the formula will not work in New York where he is aiming at 'the big evening readership' and where he presumably cannot afford to offend readers with too much sensationalism."

Murdoch announced that he would be serving as both editor and publisher. People who worked with him cited his "enthusiasm and his intense personal interest in any new property he acquires." He told the *Times* that the *Post* needed to be crisper and to feature more crime reporting. That, according to Murdoch, would drive circulation, which in turn would bring back advertisers. But he was not contemplating major changes.

Judy Michaelson remembers the moment the new regime took over. "It was the day of the funeral of Alex Rose, the old Liberal party boss. Murdoch spoke in the newsroom, and when I came in after covering the funeral, people were playing a tape of what he'd said. 'I will not do this, I will not do that.' And when people say 'not,' you know damn well that's exactly what they're going to do."

The very first change Murdoch made was to isolate the former publisher. Joe Rab says, "A day or two after Murdoch took over, Mrs. Schiff called me with a suggestion for a feature of some sort. Later in the day Murdoch and I were in Sann's office talking, and I mentioned that 'the consultant' had suggested such and such. There was a big laugh all around, and that was that."

The meeting was followed by a confidential memo from Rupert to Paul Sann, James Wechsler, Byron Greenberg, and Ray Dittrich: "You all know that part of my deal with Mrs. Schiff was to give her an office and a consultancy for five years. While I know and respect your affection for Mrs. Schiff and expect you to pay her every courtesy, I want to make it clear that I am the only person this consultancy affects."

A second, more general, change soon followed. On January 9, 1977, Murdoch appointed Edwin Bolwell, an Australian who had worked on newspapers in Canada, and most recently for *Time* magazine, to be the paper's editor. Sann and Spitzler would now report to Bolwell. The new editor said he wanted to stir things up a bit. "I hope to make the Post lively but not irresponsible," he told the *Times*. "We want to entertain and inform at the same time, make it the most readable paper in New York. I think it's an exciting challenge to give people something they want to read—not a paper you have to read as a duty." One way Bolwell intended to make the paper sprightlier was by importing more Murdoch hands from Australia.

Reporter Tony Mancini says, "We were all skeptical about Murdoch. Right after he took over and had a city room conference and said, 'Relax, nothing's going to change,' he started to bring in the Aussies.

"One of them, Steve Dunleavy, appeared on a television program and bad-mouthed us and called us the old guard and said that we objected to their methods, because we were lazy and set in our ways. He said we didn't know how to go out there and enterprise a story, which was a lot of crap, because we were all very good journalists. Better than these guys. Because we cared about a story, whether it was balanced or not, and we cared about the city. They would refer to Yanks in their headlines, which to us meant the New York Yankees, and they meant the Americans. They had really tin ears."

Roberta Brandes Gratz says, "It was clear when the Murdoch people came in, suddenly they were talking about lifts instead of elevators and queues instead of lines, and they didn't know East Side from West Side. It was bizarre. They didn't know New York, and they didn't care."

To rebuild circulation, Murdoch concentrated first on his tested formula of skin and scandal. Soon after taking over, he told an interviewer from *The Village Voice* that there was "something gray, something dull about the paper. . . . It's badly written and the headlines are terrible." He believed that most readers bought the paper for the sports section, which was excellent.

He pointed the way to the future in vaguer terms: to broaden the appeal of the paper, he planned to go after the ethnic readers, "the Irish and the Italians and whoever else," meaning a more conservative population. Slowly he recast the editorial page, and then the news coverage, to reflect his own politics. Disruptions in circulation were less than might have been expected. Murdoch claims today that even for many Jewish readers, liberal politics were not as important as they had been a decade earlier. "The paper had its Upper West Side audience. And pockets in Brooklyn and the Village as well," Murdoch says. "When we took the paper off its liberal course, I thought that we'd lose a lot of them. But we didn't, really, which led to the conclusion that maybe there weren't that many of them there in the first place. Or that they, too, were mainly buying it for the sports."

Judy Michaelson says it was almost too pat that Murdoch took over the paper on the day of Alex Rose's funeral, which was emblematic of the death of New York's ruling liberal coalition. "It was the end of that era, the end of liberalism as we knew it," she says. "Even within the paper itself, you had people making fun of the slum stories. To use a newspaper expression, not everyone was on the same page anymore."

Some younger staffers welcomed the change. Steve Cuozzo, who started at the *Post* in 1972, wrote a memoir-history of the paper in 1996. Cuozzo represented the handful of reporters and editors whose politics, like those of many of the *Post*'s readers, had moved to the right during the late 1960s and early '70s. He claimed that in the final years of the Schiff-Sann regime, the paper was increasingly out of touch with what was happening in the city. The paper was not responsive to the political ideals of readers in the outer boroughs, and it had not tuned its antennae to what might have been its new constituency in the black and Hispanic ghettos or in the fledgling counterculture of the East Village. Cuozzo was happy with Murdoch's reemphasis on traditional tabloid coverage of crime and gossip and his gradual introduction of neoconservative editorial politics.

Most of the paper's reporters and editors had stayed loyal to the old regime precisely because of its liberal politics, no matter how out-of-date, and they were restive in the new environment. Paul Sann was one of the first to get out. A tiny paragraph in the January 31, 1977, *Post* announced that Sann had quit. Andrew Porte, who'd been an assistant managing editor, was named acting executive editor, and managing editor Bob Spitzler was shunted aside to run the Saturday magazine.

Alan Whitney says that Sann was old-fashioned, in the best sense. "I remember one of the Murdoch guys once said to me, 'We can't be prisoners of the day's events,'" Whitney says. "In other words, if you don't have something exciting to say on page 1, you gotta make something up, or change something around to make it look exciting. And Dolly and Paul were very much against that. They wanted to be straight, like in the old days when people still got their hard news from the newspaper. Which they don't anymore."

Paul went to see Dolly the day he quit. He didn't mind Murdoch, he said. He thought Rupert was exhilarating, and even approved of his editorial changes. He just couldn't stand Edwin Bolwell, the new chief editor. Paul said he had been contemplating retirement in any case, even if she had not sold the paper. Just before saying good-bye—after having worked closely with her for nearly fifty years—he kissed her on the forehead, and she started to cry. Paul was more upbeat. He thought he might move to Hollywood with his son Howard and write screenplays.

Many people followed Sann out the door. Warren Hoge had already left. "Early in 1976," Warren says, "Dolly mentioned to me that she had always promised her brother that she would sell the paper if it ever lost money. It was primed to lose money in 1976. And she mentioned she'd heard about this wonderful potential savior.

"I was having the time of my life at the *Post*. Getting a paper out on a shoestring, with a gloriously eccentric boss, and with this wonderful editor, Paul Sann, who interpreted her for me. But I knew it was over when I heard her mention Murdoch's name." Warren had recently spent a vacation in Australia and knew firsthand Murdoch's salacious papers there. "I called Abe Rosenthal immediately and moved to the *Times* in April."

Helen Dudar left within months. Fern Marja Eckman stayed for almost a year and then reluctantly retired. "I never regretted leaving the *Post*, but I certainly missed working," she said later. Roberta Brandes Gratz took a fortuitous leave of absence in mid-1977 to do research for a book and had ample time to observe the changes in her old workplace. "It was clear there wasn't going to be any place for me to write about the things I wanted to write about," Roberta says. She resigned. Tony Mancini, Peter Freiberg, Joyce Purnick, Al Ellenberg, Josh Friedman, Lindsy Van Gelder, and many others decamped as well.

Some chafed under the new regime but had little choice. One man says, "I had two daughters in college and a house I was still paying off, and there weren't a whole lot of jobs out there. It was difficult. There were times when I asked to have my byline taken off stories. But that was about as much leeway as I had." He stayed on until 1993 when the Guild struck the paper. At the end of the strike, Murdoch fired all the reporters and rehired only those willing to leave the union.

James Wechsler seemed to many to be a particularly sad case. He continued writing editorials almost without pause. He also wrote speeches for

Murdoch, including, some said, the speech the publisher delivered in the newsroom the day he took over the paper. Helen Dudar later told Sann, "The day I left the *New York Post* I went in to see Jimmy. . . . I said, 'I came to say goodbye, Jimmy. I'm leaving.' And he said, 'Why?' I think I got a little short of breath, and I'm sure my mouth fell open. He clearly felt we all had a big future there. I saw little point in disillusioning him. I mumbled a few dopey-sounding reasons and left, feeling sadder than I ever had about him."*

Dorothy went to her office on South Street regularly during the five years it was contractually allotted to her. She and Murdoch saw each other socially from time to time. In March 1977, she organized a party at her apartment to celebrate their mutual birthday. Among the guests were Nelson and Happy Rockefeller, Jackie Onassis, Kurt Waldheim, Franklin Roosevelt Jr., William Paley, Kitty Carlisle Hart, Adele and Bob Sweet, Sally and Wynn Kramarsky, John and Fifi Schiff, and Bill Woodward. Dorothy had Jean Gillette ask her accountant if she could deduct the costs as a business expense on her taxes, "since she is the consultant to the *New York Post* and the dinner was to introduce Mr. Murdoch to various VIPs."

Jean Gillette believes that Dorothy was more surprised than angry when she discovered she had no continuing role in the new regime. Dorothy's friend Myra Appleton thinks there was more to it than that. "She was always very politically correct in public about her view of his paper, but privately I think she was furious. She thought Murdoch was an ass not to take advantage of her years of experience, at the very least."

Rupert himself says, "I remember her mainly as being very nice. Some of what we did must have horrified her, and we never heard a peep out of her."

Perhaps Murdoch bought the *Post* believing that he could turn it into a moneymaker. If so, he was soon disillusioned. The News Corporation has never published operating figures for the *Post,* but Martin Fischbein, a young friend of Dorothy's who worked for Rupert, told her that although circulation was up, the paper lost $8 million in Murdoch's first year and was running more than $20 million in the red annually in the early 1980s. Murdoch's critics

*Wechsler was in charge of the *Post* editorial page until 1980 and continued to write his column until the spring of 1983, when he was forced to resign because of illness. At the memorial service following his death that September, Dorothy was not among the speakers. But she arranged for her personal foundation to endow three prize scholarships at the Columbia journalism school in his name.

said from the beginning that his reasons for keeping the paper going had little to do with its balance sheet and everything to do with the fact that he could manipulate the editorial pages to influence local politicians and businessmen into advancing his larger corporate interests.*

Whatever Murdoch's motives, his *New York Post* was not a paper that many people who had worked there during the Dorothy Schiff years recognized or respected. As time passed and Murdoch's politics became more apparent, the attitude of many of the *Post*'s ex-employees hardened against their former boss.

Conspiracy theories bloomed. Al Ellenberg saw that Dolly's day was done, and the change in the tax laws encouraged her to grab the best deal available to her at the time. But, he says, "I kind of buy the idea that she sold it as a kind of revenge. . . . I'm sure she didn't mind leaving Rupert as a time bomb to hit the people she left behind." He believes she was always somewhat contemptuous of the hired help. "I think she enjoyed the idea that he would wreak havoc."

Roberta Brandes Gratz reports the scuttlebutt that Dolly had previously turned down bids from reputable buyers; she mentions Kay Graham (who never came close to considering an offer for the Post) and Alicia Patterson (who was long dead and who had no money of her own in any case). "The conjecture was that she sold the paper to Murdoch to make herself look good," Gratz says. "Dolly was always criticized for the content and quality of the *Post,* and she is remembered appropriately better because of how Murdoch changed everything."

The myth about alternative buyers took hold in the mind of Paul Sann as well. Embittered by the politics of the seventies, unable to sell a memoir that he hoped would solidify his dream to be considered the leading tabloid journalist of his time, and increasingly convinced that Dolly should have given him a chunk of the money she netted from the sale of the paper, Sann began to believe his own fantasies. In 1985, he wrote an angry letter to Pete Hamill

*Following the purchase of WNEW-TV by the News Corporation in 1988, Murdoch was required to sell the *Post* to satisfy new FCC regulations prohibiting joint ownership of a major paper and a television outlet in the same city. The purchaser, Peter Kalikow, a real estate developer, then suffered a series of financial reverses that led him to declare personal bankruptcy in 1993 and forced him to sell the paper. Following an embarrassing period when the paper was held briefly by Steven Hohenberg and then Abe Hirschfeld, two self-promoters with more nerve than money, Murdoch received an FCC waiver allowing him to reacquire the *Post*. Once again, he brought it back from the grave.

in which he maintained that Dolly had turned down a bid from Otis Chandler earlier in 1976 for more money than Murdoch eventually paid that November. There was no truth to this account.

It's unlikely that Dolly heard any of these alternative scenarios, or would have given them much thought if she had. Fern Marja Eckman told Sann, "At some point after Dolly sold the paper to that bastard, I met her daughter, and I asked her, 'How could she have done that?' and she said, 'She doesn't regret it.' Which surprised and infuriated me."

Wynn Kramarsky says, "She certainly didn't have any regrets. She knew she had done what she had to. She made that decision pretty much on her own, and pretty much on the basis of, I want to be shed of this. I don't know what the hell to do, and I want to be shed of this. And now I am."

From Dorothy's point of view, she had made a sound business decision that also satisfied her sense of responsibility: she cashed out of a money-losing situation, ensuring a generous estate for her heirs, and she had preserved "the oldest continuously published daily newspaper in America."

TWENTY-SIX

Thereafter

Selling the paper was not the only event in Dorothy's life in 1976 that brought her public attention. In May—just about the time of her first lunch with Rupert Murdoch—a biography titled *Men, Money & Magic: The Story of Dorothy Schiff* by Jeffrey Potter hit the nation's bookstores.

Potter and Dorothy met for the first time at the home of Tim Seldes at Water Mill on Long Island in the summer of 1972. Seldes, who had known Potter casually for a few years, says, "Jeffrey was good-looking, delightful. He was certainly very well connected with the art world, and he'd written an interesting book about oil tankers." Fifty-four-year-old Potter was a socially prominent WASP of the sort that always attracted Dorothy's attention. He was a grandnephew of Jacob Schiff's friend Bishop Henry Potter; his father was a schoolmate of Franklin Roosevelt's at Groton, which Jeffrey also attended.

Potter remembers the evening at Tim Seldes's house. "It was a black-tie dinner presumably in Dorothy's honor. I brought my girlfriend, who spent the evening by the pond in the backyard. I went out from time to time to check on her. Finally Dorothy said, 'Either you have a weak bladder or terrible manners!'"

Potter was charmed. So, evidently, was Dolly. They chatted some more, and as the party was breaking up, she suggested that he drive her to the beach where they would look at the stars and discuss the book about her that he was going to write.

The idea of having her life chronicled may have been planted in Dolly's head after Geoffrey Hellman's profile appeared in *The New Yorker* in August 1968. Several publishers asked Hellman if he was interested in expanding the article into a book. He was not, but Dolly resurrected the idea when she met Jeffrey Potter.

Tim Seldes says, "My vague memory is that this was a way that Dolly thought she could engage his attention. And of course from Jeffrey's point of view, the same value would be attached to it. My guess is that they met, and they were sitting around drinking, and they said, 'Here's a good idea.' And they both thought it was."

The book was authorized by Dolly but not commissioned by her, although Potter says that she was in charge from the beginning. They drew up a simple contract that gave her the right to look over the manuscript and insist on the correction of any factual errors. She could give editorial advice, but he was not obliged to accept it. If any serious disputes developed between them, Sally Kramarsky would be called upon to arbitrate.

Dolly introduced Jeffrey to Julian Bach, a respected New York literary agent, who shipped the proposal to a number of publishers. Potter stated that the book grew out of a conversation between author and subject about the "emotional poverty material wealth brings to women." It would be based on interviews with more than sixty of Dolly's friends, family members, and colleagues, many of her famous memos, and more than thirty hours of interviews with Dolly herself. Bach negotiated a contract with Coward, McCann & Geohegan. Potter would own the copyright and be paid a small advance against royalties.

He and Dolly went to work almost immediately. They taped their interviews in Long Island or at her apartment on Sixty-fourth Street. Sometimes Jeffrey stayed at the apartment, because he didn't have a place of his own in the city. He thinks that's what led people to assume that they were sleeping together, which, he says, they weren't.

"She was very comfortable with Jeffrey," Sally Kramarsky says, "and she talked with him extremely freely about everything. If they were lovers, I didn't know it. They certainly weren't sleeping together in my house. I know he spent time with her in her apartment, but I wasn't living there, and I don't know what their arrangement was. It's not something that we talked about. They had a lot of good chemistry together, that I can tell you. She had fun with him. He knew how to make her relax and talk about a lot of things. So sure, he got a lot out of it. He gave her a lot too, I think it was a good relationship."

Potter was frequently at Dolly's side during the next three years. An old friend of both says their relationship was a source of amused speculation. "We all laughed about it. We said the book was Jeffrey's excuse to see her. We thought it was part of the game, he wanted to be with her, and it was entertaining for her to talk about herself. To have this very handsome man, and charming, and just enough younger to be a challenge. So it was a nice two-way street."

Jeffrey sat in on many meetings at the *Post*. For several months, he worked in the unused boardroom at South Street, while Jean Gillette transcribed the interviews he had taped. "I don't know how much of a romance it was," Jean says. "But a flirtation, yes." She remembers that one day when she'd been working with Jeffrey, he asked her to join him for lunch. "Then he came to me later and said, 'I don't think it's a very good idea.' I assumed that was uneasy for him."

Dolly dictated a number of memos about significant incidents in her life—political and business decisions as well as personal events. Some of these memos are straightforward amplifications of the record. Others seem more like special pleading. Typical are some amendments and additions she made in 1973 to memos originally written in 1967 about various meetings with Bobby Kennedy, the net effect of which is to underline her antiwar, anti-Johnson stance and to make it appear that she was influential in Bobby's decision to enter the Democratic presidential primary.

Bob Spitzler says that Dorothy wrote many of the memos with the intent of justifying herself to posterity. "To beat the rap. She started that sort of thing when she was very young," says Spitzler. "There are millions and millions of words saying, 'This is the way it happened. Don't blame me.'"

Jean Gillette concurs. "If she thought about something long enough, she would figure out a story that would be completely true—in her mind. She would convince herself that that's the way it was. And then she came to believe it. She was always eager to set the record straight. I do remember that!"

As the book took shape, Dorothy read each draft and suggested numerous editorial changes. She seemed satisfied with the final version, which Potter handed in to Coward, McCann in the fall of 1975. After the manuscript was accepted, he left for Paris with a new girlfriend. Just before publication the following spring, he was dismayed to learn that editor Jack Geohegan had made significant cuts in the text. Jeffrey's protests were ignored. He believes Geohegan took out anything that was mildly critical of Dorothy, and he feels the book was weakened as a result.

Sally Kramarsky says the book is true to what Potter and Schiff intended it to be. "It is a record of what she achieved and what she wanted said about her family. She got sidetracked by various things that interested Jeffrey. So it's only one side of Mother. It didn't give you the complete person, but what's in it was, from her point of view, accurate."

Men, Money & Magic would probably have made Dorothy quite happy had the publisher not prepared a press release that made it appear that she claimed in the book to have had an affair with FDR. *The New York Times* picked up on this tidbit, which it featured in a front-page story on May 27, 1976. Under the headline, "Dorothy Schiff Tells of Affair with Roosevelt," reporter Nan Robertson wrote, "Dorothy Schiff, editor-in-chief and publisher of the New York Post says in a new biography that she had a romance with President Franklin Delano Roosevelt that lasted from 1936 to 1943."

In fact, the book was inconclusive on the subject, which was probably Dolly's intent. Potter implied there was an affair but never said so. The book makes it clear that whatever was going on was over by 1941 at the latest. Dorothy refused to comment and immediately deputized her lawyer Morris Abram to say that "she did not ever have and has never claimed to have had a romance or an affair with the late President Franklin Delano Roosevelt."

Chastened by the implied threat of a lawsuit, *Times* editors changed the word "affair" to "relationship" and "romance" to "personal relationship" in the second edition of the paper and added a statement by Joe Lash averring that while Dorothy had certainly been part of FDR's circle, and that the president certainly liked to flirt, he, Lash, never heard anything about an affair. In a follow-up article the next day, Robertson quoted Jeffrey Potter as saying that he had not asked Dorothy directly if she'd slept with FDR and added that the only people who could say for sure were "FDR, who is dead and can't, and Dorothy Schiff, who won't." He said later that she used her "I was at the edge of the ledge" line with him several times.

The brouhaha gave Dolly's friends and her critics something to gossip about. Pauline Phillips, aka Abigail Van Buren, whose syndicated "Dear Abby" column ran in the *Post,* wrote Paul Sann, "What's this about your boss lady Dorothy and F.D.R.? Was she in the sack with him or wasn't she? And if she was, what kind of husband did she have that he would be 'proud' of it? And where did the author get such a quote? And who really cares, except maybe Ms. Schiff?"

Columnist Liz Smith, who'd left the *Post* several years earlier, wrote in the *Daily News* a few days later, "Let's just add a little to this story. Jeffrey Potter, the book's author, was once upon a time around constantly as an escort of the glamorous publisher. For at least three years the 50-ish writer was so omnipresent but self-effacing that Dolly's intimates seldom referred to him by name, preferring to call him merely 'The Biographer.' Potter was so close that there was said to be some concern by Mrs. Schiff's children that she might be thinking of marrying him.

"Question: wrote Smith. How could a biographer working with the collaboration of his subject get things so wrong? Or did he?"

Dolly convinced herself that Nan Robertson, having misinterpreted the book, was responsible for the whole mess. She refused to admit that her own coyness and Jeffrey Potter's unwillingness to pin her down had created the problem.

Another public reminder of Dorothy's persona was more benign. In the fall of 1977, CBS premiered the *Lou Grant* television series. The title character was spun off from *The Mary Tyler Moore Show* and given a new job as executive editor of a newspaper called the *Los Angeles Tribune.* The strong-willed owner of the *Tribune,* Margaret Pynchon, played by Nancy Marchand, was based on a composite of Kay Graham, Dorothy Chandler, and Dorothy Schiff. Ted Thackrey Jr., a rewrite man for the *Los Angeles Times,* was a friend of James Brooks, one of the creators of the series. Thackrey was among the many newspaper people the producers consulted for authenticity. He told a reporter he had met Dorothy Schiff years before and that he knew she carried her Yorkshire terrier to the office and used a cigarette holder, which became leitmotifs for the character of Mrs. Pynchon.

Many of Dolly's former employees watched the series regularly; it made them nostalgic for the old days, and even for the boss whom they had been all too eager to disparage. Judy Michaelson says, "Those of us who had been there for a while watched that show with a real sense of sadness, because that was a real newspaper—even if it was actually a fake one!—and it was *not* the one the *Post* had turned into—which many of us were still going to every day."

Dolly was still going to her office at the *Post* every day, but she had little to do there. Worse yet, the outside world, though still respectful of her social position and her former achievement, began to focus its attention elsewhere. Tim Seldes says, "Not being publisher meant that she couldn't pick up the phone and just assume that people would necessarily take her call."

Myra Appleton, a magazine editor, and her husband, John, a book editor, were close to Dolly at the time. Myra says, "She so loved to be at the center of things." Myra remembers discussing a political dinner Dolly had recently attended, and Dolly remarked that was the last time she would ever do anything like that. "Then the phone rang," says Appleton. "It was Nelson Rockefeller, asking her if she would sit at his table at some event. She said she'd be delighted. When she hung up, I said, 'Dolly, you just said that was the last thing you ever wanted to do,' and she said, 'If there's anything I can teach you in this life, it's never say no to number one!' "

Seeking a way back to the center of things, Dolly began a search for something purposeful to do. At seventy-three, she may have felt too old to wrestle with all the problems of running the *Post,* but she was young enough to devote her energy to a less strenuous project. Since publishing was the world she knew best, and the world in which her lifetime of personal contacts would be most valuable, she looked into several publishing projects that came her way.

The venture that she found most intriguing involved *The Nation.* The weekly magazine had been around since the mid-nineteenth century, but it had been losing money for years. By 1976, James Storrow, the wealthy Bostonian who had been supporting it for some time, was ill and searching for a successor who would continue to underwrite its persistent losses. The sale was being handled by Morris Abram, who brought it to Dolly's attention and, coincidentally, also represented two other possible buyers. Since Storrow's primary concern was not to make a profit but to ensure the future of the magazine, it made sense for Abram to see if he could put the potential purchasers together into one consortium.

Dolly, on the other hand, had no desire to work with partners. She'd run the *Post* without having to consult anyone else; why would she take on *The Nation* under different terms? She was also unhappy to learn that Blair Clark, who had agreed to help his old college friend Storrow by editing the magazine on an interim basis, was now hinting that he wanted to stay on, or at least have some say in whatever new management emerged.

Storrow was most attracted to a proposal from Victor Navasky, who would replace Clark as editor, and Hamilton Fish III, who would raise money for the venture. Navasky had written and published several books while running *Monocle* magazine. He had also worked for several years as an editor at *The New York Times Sunday Magazine*. Fish, the grandson of an ultraconservative congressman from upstate New York, had organized a get-out-the-student-vote campaign while an undergraduate at Harvard. The two met in 1976 when they ran Ramsey Clark's unsuccessful campaign for the U.S. Senate from New York.

Navasky and Fish had the right politics—that is to say, left politics—and the extensive publishing, political, and social connections to ensure that *The Nation* would continue to be lively and influential beyond the size of its circulation. What they lacked was money. They began a campaign to raise the cash—estimated at about $1,500,000—they would need to acquire the magazine and keep it going. Dolly was one of their primary targets. She needed little convincing to buy in but a lot of convincing to take a limited role.

Ham and Victor had met Dolly during the Ramsey Clark campaign but knew her more by reputation than protracted acquaintance. They went to her apartment to make their pitch. Navasky says, "She was as charming as can be. Displaying her attractive legs. She was enamored of Hamilton, this bright, attractive young man.

"Ham's way of raising money, especially with attractive women in their sixties or seventies, was not to ask for it. What he did was, he described what a great institution *The Nation* was, and then he described our plans for it. When he said, 'We want you to know what we're trying to do,' she said, 'Oh, well, thank you. And why don't you come to dinner, young man, and meet my granddaughter?'

"So Hamilton was invited back to have dinner with the family. And again he didn't ask for anything, just told her, 'We want to keep you apprised of what is going on here.' My memory is that we went back to meet with her two or three more times. And finally I said to her, 'What Ham really wants, Mrs. Schiff, is for you to join the partnership, and our goal is to have about ten partners at about $100,000 each or whatever.'" Which was just what Dolly didn't want.

The affair dragged on through 1977. Ham and Victor visited Dolly from time to time to ensure her continuing interest. "She was flirtatious in a flattering way," Ham says.

> I mean this is a seventy-plus-year-old woman, who was clearly aware of the impact she had, this power she had. Even with that sort of severe fashion—that rigid hairstyle, the high forehead. Clearly such a striking person. You could always pick her out in a crowd. She was rail thin. Very chic. The shoes and the hose and the skirt—everything was absolutely right. And it wasn't as if it was the product of four or five maids-in-waiting behind a screen; she just took care of herself. She made a great presentation.
>
> It was infectious. I had one jacket and beat-up shoes. And Victor's not exactly a fashion plate. And we always had a fastidious moment before we showed up, just out of respect for her.

Dolly pressed Victor for his opinions about key issues of the day: What was his stand on capital punishment? Did he believe the United States should turn over custody of the Panama Canal to Panama? What did he think about homosexual teachers? Eventually they would settle into a theoretical discussion of how those topics might be covered in *The Nation* when Navasky took over the editorship.

"There would be a kind of staccato interrogation," says Ham,

> in which she would fire off questions about how we would handle this, what we would do about that. I don't think she ever expressed anything more than a small interest in the business operation. This was about content. She was interested in the ideas.
>
> But she didn't have a patient interest in the ideas. Either she had decided on her take on the idea, or it didn't actually interest her, or your answer didn't interest her. There were a number of possibilities. But they all led to the same outcome, which was that, in midanswer, she would fire another question at you, frequently on another topic altogether.

"In the end," says Navasky, "she reluctantly agreed to become a partner who put up more money than all but one of the others in the group.* But she kept saying that she didn't believe in taxation without representation. So we struck a deal with her. She would be a consultant, and I would meet with her every week and get the benefit of her ideas."

The group of limited partners assembled by Navasky and Fish received Storrow's approval, and the deal was done early in 1978. Ernest Rubenstein of Paul, Weiss, who advised Dolly in this transaction, wrote her a lawyerly letter protecting himself: "You made it clear to me that you were not relying upon me for business or financial advice. Nevertheless, based on my limited study of the recent financial history of the magazine, and my general familiarity with the magazine industry, I have the rather firm conviction that you are almost certain to lose your entire investment." Rubenstein recommended that Dorothy form a corporation to be called Independent Communications, chartered in Delaware, of which she would be president and sole shareholder, Jean Gillette would be secretary, and Adele Sweet, assistant secretary. Independent Communications invested $150,000 in *The Nation* in the form of a loan that it had no intention of calling.

The Navasky-Fish regime began in February 1978. Dolly took her duties as consultant seriously, Victor Navasky says.

I have to believe she thought that my meeting with her on a weekly basis would be like Jimmy Wechsler meeting with her on a weekly basis, where she would tell him what to do and he would go do it. And I thought, she's a limited partner, I'm happy to talk to her.

She was a delightful woman, by the way. Over the years I'd heard all these stories from all these friends about this difficult person. And she wasn't difficult at all. The only difficulty with her was her attention span. It was very limited. She would start with one subject, then she'd move on to another, and then to another. But she was full of gossip and charm and fun

---

*The partner who made the largest contribution was Alan Sagner, a New Jersey businessman who pledged $250,000 and intended to be the publisher of the magazine. However, Sagner was at the time serving as treasurer of the reelection campaign of Brendan Byrne, the incumbent Democratic governor of the state. When Byrne, the underdog, won, he rewarded Sagner by naming him head of the Port Authority. So while Sagner honored his financial pledge, he never became active as publisher, which led to Ham Fish's filling the job.

to be with. And I looked forward to meeting with her. On the one hand. Other the other hand. I had no illusion that she would be setting policy or anything.

Dolly, however, expected the weekly meetings to be substantive. After her first terrifying encounter with a rickety elevator in the building where *The Nation* had its offices, she arranged for her driver to pick up Victor and bring him to her office at the *Post*. He says, "This lasted about three swiss cheese on rye sandwich lunches, at which point it became clear to both of us that it was not quite working out."

Victor says, "I think we went to lunch one day at Number One Fifth Avenue with Hamilton, and she made it clear she had lost her enthusiasm, because she wasn't running the show. And we knew by that time that we were going to have to refinance, bring in some more money. So we spoke to her about that, but she had no interest."

Rather than invest more, Dolly walked away. Rather than ask for her money back, she made a gift to the magazine of her investment. She took the whole thing as a tax loss. "There was never any bitterness, any acrimony," says Navasky. She allowed *The Nation* management to use her apartment for occasional fund-raising events. She remained a close reader of the magazine, pestering Victor for information about various contributors and occasionally sending him a letter commenting on his editorial positions.

At about the same time, Dorothy made a generous contribution to a publication that she had no particular interest in. *Ms.* magazine had been founded by Gloria Steinem and a group of like-minded feminists in 1972. Although monthly circulation reached nearly half a million copies, the project was underfunded from the start. By 1978, *Ms.* was deep in debt. Warner Communications, which had initially invested $1 million for a 25 percent share of ownership, was unwilling to increase its commitment. Kay Graham had given Steinem and her colleagues $20,000 in seed money, but she turned down a request for another charitable contribution. Kay offered to have the Washington Post Corporation buy *Ms.* from Warner, while simultaneously warning that it would end the magazine's independence.

Steinem and Pat Carbine, the publisher, planned to turn the magazine into a nonprofit entity to be published by the Ms. Foundation for Education and Communication. The Ford Foundation promised them a sizable grant if they could attract matching funds.

Steinem decided to make a cold call on Dorothy Schiff. "Aside from Kay Graham, she was the only woman I could think of who had publishing experience and power," Steinem says. "I do remember that people were very discouraging about her. The idea was that she would be antifeminist, not profeminist, which was not the case at all. I suspect that she supported the freedom and the idea that women should be taken seriously."

Dolly needed little coaxing. Through her Pisces Foundation, she arranged a grant of $200,000, which fulfilled the Ford Foundation's conditions. Steinem and Carbine were very grateful for what they called her "life-saving decision."

Gloria says, "She and I became friends. I went to lunch or tea a few times. We would have welcomed more involvement on her part, but she was content to be a benefactor." Dolly read the magazine and discussed current politics with Steinem but did not debate feminist issues as such.

"What I remember more are her audacious stories which came out of personal discussions," Steinem says. "For instance, we were talking about marriage, and I said that it was hard for me to imagine getting married, because it would mean moving into the same apartment, and putting all your books and records together, and . . . And I remember her saying something like, 'Well, my dear, that's the difference between you and me. I have a large apartment. They move in, and they move out!'"

Gloria believes that Dorothy's level of feminist awareness was reasonable for her generation.* "She was supportive of women as individuals," Gloria says, "and she wanted to see women do well. But she had made her way by identifying with men because that's who exercised power. But she was not a queen bee. She did not have a pervasive hostility to other women. She was very supportive."

The financial expression of that support was an annual contribution to the Ms. Foundation from Pisces, although never on the scale of the original grant. In 1984, when Dorothy refused a request from Gloria to guarantee a note for $400,000, there were no hard feelings.

---

*In this attitude, Steinem echoes the opinion of another of Dolly's admirers, Helen Gurley Brown.

Other propositions came Dorothy's way. Would she like to buy *The Village Voice*? How about *The Atlantic Monthly*? Might she start a weekly paper aimed at New York's Upper East Side? Would she underwrite a new quarterly about foreign affairs? A television series on the history of relations between the United States and the Soviet Union? Some of these projects would have required an investment on her part; others a grant from Pisces. Some were pipe dreams; others were viable but not of interest to her. Some she investigated thoroughly; others she dismissed because she didn't like the other participants.

Even for nonpublishing projects that Dorothy supported, her decision-making process was not systematic. Tim Seldes helped her out at the Pisces Foundation for a few years. They met monthly, usually with Jean Gillette. "We would look at these applications," Seldes says. "We would discuss them, and once in a while she would say, 'You ought to go and see these people.' It was sort of done in the same way she did the paper, very impulsively. But usually her instincts were right. The things the money was given to were good things."

Ham Fish says, "Dorothy Schiff was right up among the mature men and women who had zest for life and active intelligence and an openness to something that was probably pretty far from the locus of their social and professional lives. For example, there were people who would not help *The Nation*, though they might have wanted to, for fear that it might affect their status. They might meet someone at a cocktail or dinner party who might frown on this association. I never had that feeling with her. And there was certainly no Park Avenue grande dame other than her who was interested in this operation."

Lisa Schiff agrees. "Dolly was interested in world events; she was interested in people who did things. She was a dynamic, curious woman. She could be coy. She could be girly. She could be clever. She could be ridiculous. But she was a very honest woman. And she was gutsy, just totally gutsy. So she didn't care—at a certain level—what people thought."

Inevitably, however, the outside world began to recede. More and more of Dolly's time was taken up with reading, needlepoint, and television viewing.

When Peter Kovler, a young Washington-based political insider, called her at home to enlist her support for a project, she told him she couldn't talk while her favorite soap opera, *The Edge of Night,* was being aired. Kovler was astonished. He told Dolly he had never met anyone who watched it.

The writer Steven M. L. Aronson, who became a close friend to Dolly in the mid-seventies, says, "She was curious about everything. She had this enormous range of interest. She read widely. She loved politics. And yet she would call me—I'm not kidding—three times a week to discuss what developed on *The Edge of Night,* which she had got me hooked on." Steven agrees that for Dolly the soap opera was a form of gossip—it just happened to be about people who didn't exist.

Jean Gillette also recalls Dolly's devotion to her favorite entertainment. "One day she was going out, so she'd miss watching, and I was supposed to watch it for her. This was before many people had tape machines. And I forgot. I thought, well, one day to the next, it doesn't change much. But then she found out I forgot. And all hell broke loose. 'You forgot?' So she went out and bought a tape machine. And then she bought one for me, too."

As Dolly's closest associate for three decades, Jean was often under fire. "When you did something wrong, you knew about it," Jean says. "When she got mad at you for some reason, there was a reason. You'd get on the phone with her, and she'd start inquiring about this, and you'd say, 'Yes I did it, and I'm sorry I did it.' And you'd get in this long, long conversation, where she'd go on and on, till you ended up saying, 'Well, shoot me.' 'Cause you couldn't win to begin with. But thank God, she'd forget about it. She didn't hold a grudge."

Despite her occasional short temper, Dolly was devoted to Jean. She was solicitous and understanding about Jean's intermittent drinking problem. There were few recriminations when too much alcohol over the weekend would keep Jean from the office on Monday morning. Dolly, who believed that an exercise of willpower should help overcome most human failings, never gave up on Jean even though self-discipline did not work in her case. Finally Jean went to a hospital for treatment. "Mrs. Schiff [Jean never called her by any other name] said she wasn't surprised when I went into rehab. And she was marvelous. She called me every day to see how I was doing. And she would gossip about people we knew."

Gillette was privy to all Dolly's personal affairs. "Eventually she confided in me many things." Jean was cosignatory to Dolly's corporate and personal financial accounts at Kuhn, Loeb and her commercial bank, and she handled all her personal correspondence. Despite Dolly's deserved reputation for being tight with payroll, she was very generous to Jean. Every year she marked Jean's birthday with a gift in cash. She gave her a substantial bonus when the paper was sold to Murdoch, arranged for her to remain on salary after the sale, and continued to pay her an additional monthly wage on top of that.

Of all Dolly's colleagues at the *Post*, including Wechsler and Sann, Jean was the only one with whom she had a continuing relationship after she sold the paper. Even when the consultancy came to an end and Dolly moved her office into her apartment, Jean showed up for work every day. Dolly's dictatorial style had long since mellowed; she was more dependent on Jean than Jean was on her. "On the whole," says Jean, "I had a wonderful job. You felt important. And after all those years I knew what she was like, and I could deal with it better. I got to meet fabulous people. John Lindsay. Adlai Stevenson. He was a wonderful man. I loved him. All in all, I was lucky."

So were Everette and Aery Lawson, Dorothy's longtime chauffeur and cook. Although there was a period in the late seventies when the Lawsons commuted from Teaneck, New Jersey, to East Sixty-fourth Street rather than live in, they were generally at Dolly's side whenever she wished them to be. In addition to annual gifts to the Lawson family and other benefits, Dorothy made generous contributions on the Lawsons' behalf to the Lions and Lioness clubs of Teaneck, which enabled Everette to become president of the Lions chapter in 1981. By the mid-eighties, she budgeted $20,000 a year for gifts to the extended Lawson family. Some years earlier, when Everette Jr., stationed at the time in Japan, was about to have a baby, she paid for his parents to visit him and purchased a complete layette for them to take along. Everette Jr. wrote to thank her: "You know I often reminisce about all that you have done for my family and myself, and wonder if there will ever come a day when I'll be able to do something for you. . . . Some day when I am in the position to do something extra nice for you, I'll have satisfied my conscience. Conscience may not seem appropriate, but I feel that it's just right."

Dolly's relationship with the Lawsons was shaped by the comfort level she'd experienced since childhood with household help, and there was an element of noblesse oblige in her style, but she was genuinely fond of the whole family. For many years, Aery in particular was one of her closest confidantes about personal matters.

———

By the late seventies, all three of Dorothy's children were living in the East. She saw Morti less often after he moved out of the city in 1972, but she had lunch with Sally every Saturday and saw Adele frequently. Their children only slowly developed their own relationships with their grandmother. Dorothy was not the kind of grandparent who had much patience for sitting around on the floor playing children's games. She was not the kind of grandparent who happily took her grandchildren to the circus or a Disney film.

Matthew Hall remembers Sunday dinners at his grandmother's apartment. "We played with these Lego sets that she had for us," he says, "and the grown-ups would talk about politics. It seems to me that Goggi could never stop talking about politics." His sister Mary adds, "We children would be served fried chicken and chocolate milk in the kitchen, and she always had these amazing Lego sets to occupy us, so I remember it always as being a wonderful time, but it was really not 'Now Mary, tell me what you're doing . . .' So, no. I didn't really get to know my grandmother until I was a teenager."

Wendy Gray, Adele's daughter, recalls being intimidated when she was finally considered old enough to join the grown-ups at her grandmother's table. "There were finger bowls. I remember once trying to eat peas with my knife and fork. Goggi said, 'No! You have to chase them with your fork!' "

Later, when Wendy had graduated from Harvard and was teaching at a New York private school, she lived with her grandmother for a year. One summer, she spent a month with Dorothy in East Hampton, as her companion and designated driver. Wendy remembers that much of the time they talked politics. Her grandmother would reminisce about politicians she'd known and chat about the other guests at the parties Wendy drove her to. "Goggi liked to talk about people, but not gossip about them. Well, it depends what you mean by gossip. Some of the people around that summer would say just devastating things about people. She wasn't like that. She wanted to know what people were like, what they were doing, maybe even who they were sleeping with, but she wasn't mean. She wasn't vicious. She was just curious."

Wendy's other job was shopping. Her grandmother gave very explicit instructions. "She wanted a certain kind of mayonnaise, a certain kind of cheese. If I tried to expand her choices, or slip in new things, she didn't appreciate it."

Dolly's choices were partly a matter of taste and partly based on price. She liked bargains. "She was certainly tight," says Wendy. "And I think she passed that on. We all are."

"She was like that at home too with Aery and Everette," says Wendy's mother, Adele. "If Aery was sent to buy something at the five-and-ten-cent store and it turned out to be defective, Mother would send Aery back with this fifty-cent item. It was not cost-effective, but she didn't see that. It was wrong, and that had to be righted. And the intensity was just the same if it was fifty cents or quite a large sum." Dorothy regularly looked over the sales slips and charges that Aery incurred at the grocery store. She once sent her back to complain because Dorothy felt that she'd been overcharged for an order of green beans. Unlike employees of the *Post,* Aery apparently never complained about Dorothy's frugality.

Petty finances were upstaged by an important family matter that dominated Dorothy's life starting in the fall of 1978, when Mary Hall, the third child and second daughter of Morti and his third wife, Diana Lynn, was going through a crisis. Diana had died suddenly of a stroke in 1971, when Mary was nine. Morti soon married Penelope Wilson, and the family moved from Manhattan to Millbrook, New York, about two hours north of the city.

In the spring of 1978, Mary left her boarding school before the end of sophomore year and took her final exams at home. "I was having a horrible time at Ethel Walker," Mary says. "Very unhappy. My second year towards the end started to bore me a lot. Not academically; I was a star student as always. But just, something happened, I don't know exactly what. I became very, very unhappy." When she returned to begin her junior year, things were no better. She was depressed and not eating. "It was clear to everyone that I couldn't stay there."

No secondary school in Millbrook was considered suitable, and Morti had no clear idea of how to proceed. Many family members agree that all of Morti's children were at risk in some way or other. Morti seldom saw his first son, who lived in California with his mother. The others were devastated by the death of Diana, who was by all accounts a loving and attentive mother, even though their stepmother tried very hard to make up for their loss. Although Mary says no particular event caused her to break down, the accumulated upheavals of the previous few years could have overwhelmed her.

Mary's cousin Laura Kramarsky says, "Morti never understood kids. He never wanted kids. Diana wanted kids. She had kids, and then she died. And he didn't know what to do. He barely relates to us now that we're adults. I don't think he had a clue about what to do with children." Lisa Schiff speculates, "I've often wondered if at some level Dolly didn't want to show Morti that she could be an outstanding mother. That she could save a life. Especially one of his children. Showing Morti who she was. But I never asked her that."

Mary had spent several pleasant weekends visiting her grandmother during the onset of the crisis. Dolly raised the possibility with Morti and Penelope of inviting Mary to live with her. The year Wendy Gray had lived with her had gone well, and Wendy's sister Kathy had spent part of a year on East Sixty-fourth Street also. But Kathy and Wendy were older at the time—each had graduated from college—and had not imposed on Dorothy anything like the responsibility that looking after Mary would entail.

Lisa Schiff says, "Dolly and I had a lot of long talks about this, and I said to her, 'This is a huge commitment. It's not enough to have a doctor to send her to, you've got to change the environment for the child, totally. Do you wish to do this at this time in your life? This can't be something you're going to get bored with, because the child could die, given all that's happened.' And she had to think about it, hard."

Mary says, "It was presented to me, 'Would you like to go and live with Goggi and go to school in New York City?' I said, 'Yes.' And so I did." Mary was enrolled at the Hewitt School and put in the care of a doctor who specialized in eating disorders. And grandmother and granddaughter settled into a domestic routine.

"This was 1978," Mary says. "Goggi was at that point a consultant to the *Post*. She was going in usually three days a week. I was in school till four. On the days she was in the office, we got home at roughly the same time. We would chat briefly. I would do my homework, and she had homework. We would always meet up for the last half of the *McNeil-Lehrer News Hour*. Then we would talk till about eight. We did not have dinner together. We tried that at first, and it just seemed silly. Sometimes we would sit on the terrace, just the two of us and Susie Q, her Yorkie.

"Aery and Everette were no longer living in, which she loved. As did I." Holiday weekends without the Lawsons were especially intimate. "Aery would leave us things. And then Goggi loved to—in those days there was a little, I guess you'd call it a deli, at the corner, and she loved to order from them. She would take the dog in there and pick up a few things. Those were our favorite weekends."

Lisa Schiff says, "Dolly became that child's mother." Mary agrees. "She kind of rescued me. I shouldn't say 'kind of.' She absolutely did rescue me. She was not smothering. I had someone who really cared about me. I don't think that would have been her choice. But boy, she took it on, and one thing she always said to me was, 'Don't take anything on unless you're going to see it through.' And she did."

Dorothy took an interest in Mary's schoolwork and her social life. She told her about her own childhood. She talked casually about her marriages and romanticized her affairs. "She would talk to me about Max Beaverbrook, Serge Obolensky," Mary says. "She would talk about them night, after night, after night. She would reminisce, and she would extract wisdom. At the time, she had gone over Max's letters, and she said, 'I can't believe at the time I didn't realize how much he loved me.' And reading these letters, and she would read me a bit, it was like she was a young woman."

Dolly was seldom overtly affectionate, but Mary came to realize how much she cared. "One time there was somewhat of a crisis. I was badly burned in the kitchen. It was my habit that after talking to her, at about eight-thirty, I'd go make tea and then take it downstairs and finish my studies and go to bed. She had this wonderful old gas-burning kitchen stove, and I was as usual in my flannel nightgown, and she had a little TV in front of the stove, and I was watching. And like an idiot I leaned against the stove, my nightgown caught on fire, everything went up in flames, I rolled around and screamed bloody murder. And she came up the stairs—it was all kind of a blank to me. She thought I had the volume up too high on the TV and it was the television show that screamed.

"Anyhow, to make a long story short, she takes me downstairs, she puts ointment on my back, she calls my psychiatrist, and my doctor, they come, they take me away. Two weeks, maybe three weeks in the hospital—she came every single day. Every single day."

Mary was released from the hospital in the care of a full-time nurse, who made the mistake of complaining to Aery about some request Dolly made to her. Mary says, "Aery of course can't wait to tell my grandmother. My grandmother tells me. I burst into tears and say to her, 'I feel like I've ruined your life. I feel like you hate me.' And she opens her arms, and grabs me and hugs me, and says, 'I don't hate you. I love you.'" Mary knew it was true.

After two years, Mary went off to Vanderbilt. She wrote her grandmother a long letter every week and followed it up with a phone call. "My letters were always not about who was dating whom but about what I learned in, say, American history. I remember she was fascinated by the revisionist theories. Because heretofore you just learned American history the usual way. So I would write her about that, because I knew she'd have something to say. And then I'd maybe say it in class if I felt it was appropriate.

"She would often send me back letters with my spelling mistakes marked. Because I am a lousy speller. She would say, 'I don't want this to stop you from writing letters. I won't correct them if it'll stop you from writing letters.' And I'd say, 'No, no, no.'"

One summer Dorothy got Mary a job at a private library on the Upper East Side. It was not Mary's favorite assignment; much of her time was spent collecting books to be sent off to members at their vacation homes. "Goggi said she would have loved being a librarian. She could have told people to 'Shush.' She would have loved being around the filing, putting everything in its place. Having a complete system. It would have appealed to the anal side of her nature!"

During school breaks, Mary returned to her grandmother's apartment. "That was my home," she says. "I would come home every single vacation." It caused some tension with her parents. "But really I wanted to be with her anyway, so we worked it out. We would always say, 'Well, I need to be with Goggi for the holidays because Aery and Everette are away. That was always my excuse to my parents. And certainly Daddy was grateful."

Morti says, "Well, it was awfully nice of Mother to do that. It was very good for Mary." He says he never thought to ask himself what it must have done for Dolly.

After college, Mary sublet an apartment in the city for a few months until her grandmother invited her to return home. "She was like, 'Come back.' And I was, 'Thank you.' I stayed there until 1985—a year before I got married."

When Mary announced her engagement to Post Howland, Dolly called his mother, who later told Mary that Dolly had been in tears. "I feel as if my daughter is being married," Dolly said.

For Mary, her grandmother's devotion was lifesaving. It was for Dolly as well. Many family members believe that caring for Mary not only gave Dolly the satisfaction of having rescued the young woman she came to love, it enabled her to feel better about her nurturing skills in general. Dorothy often told people that she had been neglectful of Morti and Adele when they were young—too willing to leave them in the care of others.

Mary says, "Goggi felt she was, in hindsight, too young to have Daddy and Adele. I think she had a lot of guilt about her parenting of them. I suspect that she was a much better mother to Adele and Daddy than she thought she was. I think Goggi was very, very hard on herself, about many things."

Sally, everyone concurs, had gotten more of her mother's attention. Dorothy told Mary as much. "I think Aunt Sally she focused on, and adored, and enjoyed. That's the word, enjoyed," says Mary. Laura Kramarsky says that her mother benefited from Dolly's having decided after raising her first two children to do some things differently. And, adds Laura, "If you think about Mary as her last child, she became a better parent through practice, each time."

As Dorothy's professional life receded, family in general took up more and more of her time and her attention. On Saturdays when Sally came to Sixty-fourth Street for lunch, she occasionally brought her children. Late Sunday afternoons, Adele and some of her children and grandchildren might stop by. Goggi's Lego sets occupied the younger generation while the adults sipped white wine and talked politics. Granddaughter Kathy Gray remembers that Dorothy was usually the center of attention. "She loved to tell stories about her own life and about others. It wasn't exactly gossip. There was usually a point. Goggi was a fabulous raconteur. She loved to tell quote-dirty-unquote stories."

From 1963 on, Dorothy had spent her summer vacations and occasional weekends throughout the year in East Hampton, either renting a house or staying with the Kramarskys. Travel never held any appeal as a retirement diversion. In 1975, she arranged to have a pool installed on the Kramarsky's property and a modest apartment built for herself above their garage.

The interactions between generations were not always easy. Anna Kramarsky says, "She was present in so many ways, so much a part of the fabric of our lives. Augusts were intense. So much of the house ran around her. She and my mother made menus. There were events; there were parties; there was a lot of, how do we manage Goggi and keep her happy?

"We dressed for dinner every night. She dressed for dinner. And when she swam, she had her swimsuit and her bathing cap. It was a whole event. She kind of made a procession to the pool. I think it was about controlling anxiety, her anxiety. And really a kind of sense that things had to be a certain way, and moving outside of that was very dangerous. And she also brought a lot of light into the household. That's who she was."

Laura Kramarsky says too, "Goggi was very much a part of our lives." But she was not a confidante. "Oh, my goodness, no. You wanted to confide in her, but you only wanted to tell her the things that would make her proud. You didn't want to tell her any of the worries or the concerns. She could be very judgmental. About things that are major, but about small things, too.

"I bite my nails," Laura says, "and that was not something that young women should do. And in a funny way, the reasons for it were not necessarily what some people might think. They might think that it's socially unacceptable or something like that, but her thing was, 'You'll never find a man!' I know that sounds unenlightened. But she wanted you to be happy, and she didn't see any way that that might come about if you did these things. She wasn't ill spirited, it just came out wrong."

Anna also attracted unwanted criticism from Dorothy. "We had a difficult time when I was a young teenager. I wasn't hugely overweight, but I wasn't skinny. She gave me a hard time about it. And she gave my mother a hard time about it. She would say to me things like, 'You're so fat, no one will ever love you.' And I really feared that.

"I think she thought, you will be happier. It wasn't meant to be malicious. It was more like the world is like this, and you need to fit in. And it's funny, because there are a lot of ways that she didn't fit in the world she moved in, but this one way was exactly important to her, in terms of physical presentation."

Anna broke through to her grandmother's good graces when she helped Dorothy take care of her beloved animals. Dorothy was always devoted to her dogs. Sally Kramarsky remembers, "When I was younger, we had a dachshund named Froly. When Froly got to be about fifteen, he finally had to be put to sleep, and Mother was totally devastated. She just cried and cried and cried."

In the 1980s, Dorothy's ménage included a stray cat she took in whom she named David. Anna says, "Goggi wouldn't go to bed unless David was in the house. And she was not about to prowl around in the yard in the dark looking for him. I would have to find him, so she could get to sleep."

Anna won total acceptance when she volunteered to take an ailing Susie Q to the vet several times a week for dialysis. Sally Kramarsky says, "Anna said to me, 'I don't believe I'm doing this, Mom. Her kidney's got to be the

size of a pea.' But anyway she did it, and Susie got three more years of life."
Anna says, "After that, I was quite prized."

Anna, like all of Dorothy's grandchildren, also earned approval as she developed intellectual interests she could share with her grandmother. Echoing Mary Hall, Anna says, "She wasn't interested in the process of my education per se. But I wrote a paper on FDR, for example, and I remember talking to her about that. When I showed curiosity about things that she was interested in, she would give me books to read."

Laura concurs. "She would bring up things, and she wanted to know what you thought about them. She wanted to know that you had an opinion about social issues. She wanted to know that you knew what was going on in the world, as opposed to you got good grades."

Dorothy also needed information that their generation had which she lacked. Laura remembers, "She always wanted to be in the know. She didn't want to embarrass herself." Dorothy told a story about being at a party where she was offered a cigarette that tasted "nasty," so she stubbed it out. The other guests laughed because it was marijuana, and she was embarrassed. She asked Laura and her brother Daniel, who, she knew, had some experience in the matter, how people used cocaine. "Because if she was ever offered it," Laura says, "she wanted to be on her guard. So she wasn't a confidante exactly, but neither was she unapproachable."

As she did with her older granddaughters, Dorothy enjoyed regaling the Kramarsky girls with stories about her romantic life. Laura says, "She was happy to tell you about it. She didn't think there was anything wrong with that. And that is so novel for someone of her age." Anna agrees. "She was very blunt. She'd say, 'I had four marriages and five prominent affairs,' or whatever. And it was sort of amazing, as a child, to hear that. Not your average grandmother."

Dorothy's bluntness carried over in the pointed advice she gave the girls about choosing a spouse. Laura says, "She was a firm believer in 'try before you buy.' She also would say that she loved my grandfather George Backer but that he was weak, and she couldn't stand a weak man. I think that may be the only thing anybody said to me when I was growing up about what one is supposed to look for."

The family has chosen to portray Dorothy's bluntness as a habit that indicates her strength of character; sometimes, however, the anecdotes they tell sound insensitive at best.

Anna Kramarsky says, "There were a lot of these extraordinary family tales of how she treated people. Once she and George Backer were visiting somebody in the hospital, long after they were divorced and George was re-married. As they were leaving, Grandpa George said to her, 'Do you have a car?' She said, 'Yes,' and gave him a ride. A few days later they were in the hospital again, and he asked for another ride. Goggie said, 'Well, no. What would people think?' And didn't give him the ride.

"The way the story is told is about, 'Isn't it funny that she did this?' And it is funny, and it's dramatic. But it's also about not being close to people. Plus, I think it was always hard for her that he remarried and was happy. That someone else could live with George was not so good for her. So there was this kind of dramatic, but also isolating, experience with her."

Perhaps these stories are consistent with a persistent coldness in Dorothy's character all her life. They also reveal her need to control small events when her capacity to have an impact on the larger world was dimin-ishing. It seems, too, that her need to settle some lifelong resentments never flagged.

Soon after Dorothy sold the *Post,* an institution that had been identified with her family for more than a century also passed into the hands of out-siders. For some years, Kuhn, Loeb had been slipping badly in prestige and importance among the city's investment banks. An international financier who had an insider's view says, "John Schiff was a great gentleman with su-perb ethics. He was excellent at customer contacts among the old school clients, but he was caught in a time warp. His was not a lively mind, nor was he willing to take risks. John—and therefore the firm—was standing still in a rapidly changing world.*

Morti Hall says that his mother tried to encourage John to give a free hand to a distant cousin, Siegmund Warburg, who tried for a time to merge his own thriving firm with Kuhn, Loeb. Morti says, "Mother saw that Sieg-mund Warburg was very smart. He could have saved the firm. She begged John to work with him, but he just couldn't."

By 1977, although John was still chairman of the board of Kuhn, Loeb and still went to the office—by subway—every day, he was no longer active in

---

*John's cousin and partner Freddie Warburg was clear-eyed about the laid-back character of the firm. Once asked how many people worked at Kuhn, Loeb, Freddie is said to have answered, "About half."

daily management. His son David was vice chairman but had not succeeded his father as the most active partner. The firm itself, though in trouble, still had a respected name and a distinguished client list. In November 1977, Kuhn, Loeb and Lehman Brothers announced a merger. In fact, Kuhn, Loeb with assets of about $18 million (about one-third of which were presumed to be held by John and David Schiff) was being swallowed by the larger firm, which had nearly $60 million in assets at the time. John was named honorary chairman of the new entity, which was itself bought by American Express in 1984, at which time the venerable name of Kuhn, Loeb disappeared from Wall Street.

Dorothy and John differed in almost every imaginable way: she was a liberal Democrat, while he remained an ardent Republican; she loathed sports, while he played golf and had a passion for horse racing; she shunned public commitments that distracted her from her work, while he sat on half a dozen prestigious and time-consuming boards; she loved controversy and gossip, which made him very uncomfortable. Despite these fundamental differences, their shared childhood memories and their mutual affection kept them close.

They lunched or dined together frequently. Once, when asked by a reporter how he and Dolly reconciled their political differences, John answered, typically and graciously, "That's what makes this a great country. We both want the same things for our country. Any differences are merely over the matter of how we should go about getting them."

They exchanged notes or clippings on subjects of mutual interest. Dorothy sent John a genealogy of the Schiff family taken from a book on the Jews of Frankfurt. She found the information in it fascinating, she wrote, because among other things, "No girls [are] mentioned, except when good marriages were made."

He sent her a picture he'd found of the two of them that was taken in August 1905. "I think that I have changed considerably," he wrote in the accompanying note. "Frankly I think at that point you already had the look of a publisher, and a very attractive one too."

In 1981, several years after Kuhn, Loeb was taken over by Lehman Brothers, John sent Dorothy an article about Guy de Rothschild, who was leaving France after the expropriation of private banks by the new Socialist government. The demoralized French banker was quoted as saying, "Of the house of Rothschild, nothing remains but a few scraps. Perhaps not even that. A

Jew under Pétain [an outsider under Mitterrand] for me it is enough. To re-build from the ruins twice in one lifetime is too much."

Dorothy thanked John for the clipping, in the margin of which she wrote, "I wonder if John identifies?" She couldn't help but notice how different her brother's life trajectory had been from her own. The undervalued girl child had had the final victory.

Bill David, a stockbroker who managed the private accounts of some of the principals at Lehman Brothers, took on the same role for members of the Schiff family when Kuhn, Loeb was acquired by his firm. Dorothy became his client, and, after reviewing her holdings, he made an appointment to meet at her South Street office. "With some trepidation," David says. "She had a reputation of being a difficult woman. I was told that she did not entertain fools lightly.

"I was ushered into her office, and the first thing I did was trip. She had one of these terrible little dogs that looked like a mouse with a bow on it, and I tripped over the dog!"

Dorothy's portfolio was conservatively invested in municipal bonds and blue-chip stocks. David had only a few suggestions to make. "I thought she might trade off some bonds where she had a loss and take that loss against some gains. Things like that . . . So I went through my spiel with her, and she didn't say much. Maybe a few questions. Then as I was leaving, I said to her, 'So with respect to these portfolio changes, would you like me to review this with your brother?' "

She said, " 'Mr. David, when I bought the *Post,* we didn't have much profit. Some years we'd make a little profit, some years a great deal, and some years there were substantial losses. John was always on my case about how I was di-minishing the family fortune by this venture, and it was very liberal, and that in itself was quite offensive. And,' she said, 'just over a year ago, I sold the *Post* to Rupert Murdoch for something on the order of $25 million or more, and just this year my brother, who'd taken Kuhn, Loeb down the tubes, had to sell out to Lehman Brothers.

" 'So if you ever discuss my portfolio—or my affairs—with my brother, I shall remove you from the management of it!' " Bill David was enchanted, and they worked together for several years until he moved to another job within the firm.

Whatever Dorothy thought of John's financial acumen, she remained devoted to him. She was devastated when he began to show signs of dementia in the early 1980s. Mary Hall Howland remembers a lunch at John's apartment when Dorothy told the story of an incident from their childhood of which he now had no memory. "It clearly frustrated her," Mary says. "And probably hurt her because you could see her brother . . . Oh, and he screamed at the help, and that upset her a lot."

When John died in May 1987, Dorothy, looking shaken and frail, attended his funeral at Temple Emanu-El on the arm of Tim Seldes. Her world had shrunk considerably, and so had she. Steven Aronson says, "She closed down after about age eighty. She ran out of steam. She was still in perfectly good health. She looked good. She just took the gearshift down a few levels."

In the spring of 1989, she told a few people close to her that she was not feeling well. "She said she was very, very tired," says Mary Hall Howland. "And the doctor suggested a blood transfusion. So we did that. But afterwards Goggi said to me, 'You know, he told me that I would feel like dancing on the tabletops after the blood transfusion, and I just don't.' And I said, 'Well, maybe you need some more time.'

"So, after a week or a couple of days, she called and said, 'Have you heard?' And I said, 'Have I heard what?' She said, 'I have cancer. But I'm okay, and I'm not going to do anything about it. I'm just very, very tired. I'm ready.' She was completely matter-of-fact."

Lisa Schiff says, "She was very firm. She said, 'I don't want any pain. I have no regrets. I'm making this decision. And I hope you'll support me.' I was very upset, and I tried to talk her out of it, but she had made up her mind. I don't think she ever mentioned her mother. She just said, 'I don't want to go through operations, the pain of operations. I just want to be sure that I won't have pain.' And we agreed that it would be helpful if you can stay home."

Perhaps because Dorothy had seen her own mother's protracted suffering, perhaps because she had a feeling that her life was complete—whatever the reason, she refused all treatment. The cancer, which originated in her colon, spread rapidly. Within weeks, she was home, confined to bed, and turning away all visitors. No one was allowed in except Adele and Sally. Not even Mary.

"I just couldn't believe it," Mary says. "She wanted me to see her a couple of times, and then she said, 'You can't come anymore.' It was painful, but she was a very vain person, and I could understand this. My best friend said, 'You have to go storm the place. You have to go.' And I said, 'You know, I can't do it. She doesn't want me to see her.' But I would call as always, every Wednesday. And towards the end, I just got the nurse."

Anna Kramarsky says, "You know, she had millions of people in her life, and yet she felt none of them could accept this, her being in bed, her being sick. She didn't want to be remembered that way. And I get that. I get it, but it's sad."

Dorothy died on August 30, 1989. She was eighty-six. Because she had made it very clear that she wanted no religious service, her children, their spouses, fifteen grandchildren, nine great-grandchildren, and a few friends gathered at Sixty-fourth Street several days after her death for a brief remembrance. She had left instructions that she was to be cremated and that, subject to the wishes of her family, her ashes either be placed in the family mausoleum at Salem Fields in Brooklyn or be scattered over a cow pasture.

As Dorothy once explained to Jeffrey Potter, she had long since renounced her right to be interred near her parents in Cold Spring Harbor. She said she had no interest in the place. "I have never been back since the day [my mother] was buried, which was a year after my father. I think John goes and does all the anniversaries. I mean, if it's the anniversary of their death, he'll send flowers or . . . I'm afraid I don't do anything. I never did like it."

Morti, Adele, and Sally opted for Salem Fields rather than the cow pasture. A small group of family members placed Dorothy's ashes in the mausoleum that held the remains of, among others, Jacob and Therese Schiff, as well as Therese's father, Solomon Loeb.

Under the terms of Dorothy's will, which she wrote in 1987, her grandchildren and great-grandchildren received $10,000 each, the final installment in a series of annual gifts she had given them for some time. Mary Hall Howland was singled out for a larger bequest, because, as the will stated, she had lived with Dorothy for several years and "had therefore become more like a daughter than a granddaughter to me." Jean Gillette, Tim Seldes, his sister Marian, and Dorothy's two sons-in-law received substantial gifts. Morti's wife, Penelope, received a painting by Jane Freilicher. A trust was established for the benefit of Aery and Everette Lawson.

Dorothy's personal property was to be divided among her daughters and Morti's daughters. Her papers were entrusted to Adele and Sally, with the suggestion that they be given to the Schlesinger Library at Radcliffe.* Sally Kramarsky, Mary Hall Howland, and Tess Leopold, Adele's youngest daughter and a lawyer like Mary, were named executors of Dorothy's will and trustees of her estate.

At probate, it was established that Dorothy's estate, including her apartment and personal items, was worth a bit more than $32 million. After taxes, there would have been approximately $10 million available to divide among her heirs. Her children soon changed the name of the Pisces Foundation to the Dorothy Schiff Foundation. Over the years they honored her name by providing support to programs, many having to do with education, of which she would have approved.

As important as the cash Dorothy left her family was the legacy of public responsibility she bequeathed them. Many of the grandchildren speak of an enduring interest in politics engendered by conversations with Dorothy; many have chosen careers of public service or in the service professions. Several talk about Dorothy's belief that people have it within themselves to change their circumstances through the exercise of intelligence and willpower. Laura Kramarsky, who stopped using cocaine on her own, says, "If I hadn't been living in the Bible Belt but was in a more rational and less religious community, if I'd had access to a twelve-step program where you could have turned to whatever higher power was important to you, my grandmother would have been my higher power. The person, or whatever it is, that you need to think about to stop you from doing it. And that's what she was."

Anna Kramarsky says, "I think Goggi would have been surprised by the impact she had on people, because that sense never entirely left her of being a shy, insecure woman. But I think she knew that family mattered, and she left money for college tuition and things that were important to her. So maybe she would not have been surprised by how much we internalized her. I don't know that she would have felt she could do that. But she knew she was trying to do something. And it mattered to her."

At the memorial service, Murray Kempton was one of the few people asked to speak. He said that when Mrs. Schiff, as he always called her, acquired the *Post,* she was "heiress to a substantial property and presumably

*They were eventually given to the New York Public Library because, as Adele explains, "Mother was such a quintessential New Yorker."

susceptible to being agreeable to its consumption by a great cause. If she had been no more than that, she would of course have been too soon bored; and the *Post* would have been long gone and almost as long forgotten.

"But she was of the solid will that survives; and it is only to her that we who played—I shan't say soldiered—on her battleground owe the wonderfully-protracted salad years when we served the illusions of the young that the world is black and white and that right will rise and wrong go under the day after tomorrow.

"I still run into younger reporters who say that the *Post* of thirty-five years ago made them what they are today. . . . And that is my debt to your grandmother. For while the rest of us rioted with her substance, she fought the war to save it and keep us in our fields of play."

In the early seventies, when Dorothy still ran the *Post,* she asked Jerry Tallmer to prepare her obituary for the paper. She told him, "Most people don't get to read their obituaries. I'm going to read mine." They had one long interview and planned several others, but three days later she canceled the project. At her death, the editors of the paper—which was then owned by Peter Kalikow—asked Tallmer to resurrect his notes for the paper's farewell editorial. After affectionately retelling some familiar stories about his old boss, Tallmer quoted Ted Kheel who said, "She was the only publisher in New York with balls."

Notes

The Dorothy Schiff Collection in the Manuscript and Archives Division of the New York Public Library was a primary resource for this book. Dorothy, with the aid of her remarkable administrative assistant, Jean Gillette, kept legal and business correspondence, interoffice memos, and other business files, in addition to some letters, scrapbooks, and other personal memorabilia. In the chapter notes that follow, I have cited all material drawn from the collection as NYPL/DS, followed by the specific box number.

Material from the James A. Wechsler papers at the Wisconsin Historical Society in Madison is cited as WHS/JAW. Similarly, the Paul Sann papers at the Howard Gotlieb Archival Research Center at Boston University are identified in the notes as BU/PS, to distinguish them from documents retained by Howard Sann, which I identify as HS/PS.

I interviewed more than one hundred people in the course of research. In the notes that follow, I have given the name of each interviewee and the date of our interview at the first citation of his or her words. Throughout the text, I used a verb in the present tense—"says," "recalls," "remembers"—to indicate that the material is from an interview. I give the name of an interviewee in the notes only the first time an interview is cited, unless the person's name is not given in the text.

I have honored the request of those few interviewees who asked not to be identified. When necessary, I cross-checked their statements with other sources, and I am comfortable using their comments despite the lack of attribution.

Verbs in the past tense indicate material drawn from secondary sources, which are always cited.

Introduction

ix *Over the years, Dolly told a story* Geoffrey Hellman, "Profiles: Publisher," *New Yorker,* August 10, 1968, p. 65. Also Gail Sheehy, "The Life of the Most Powerful Woman in New York," *New York,* December 10, 1973, p. 54.

xi *"I like to make money"* Hellman, "Publisher," p. 53.

1. "The Background"

For information concerning Jacob Schiff, I drew primarily on Cyrus Adler's two-volume study, *Jacob H. Schiff: His Life and Letters* (Grosse Pointe, MI: Scholarly Press, 1968), as well as Naomi W. Cohen's *Jacob H. Schiff: A Study in American Jewish Leadership* (Hanover, NH: University Press of New England, 1999). For insights into the character of Morti Schiff, Frieda Warburg's *Reminiscences of a Long Life* (privately printed, 1956) was immensely helpful. For Dorothy's childhood, the main sources are the Hellman interview and Jeffrey Potter, *Men, Money & Magic: The Story of Dorothy Schiff* (New York: Coward, McCann & Geohegan, 1976).

3 *"These German-Jewish families"* Stephen Birmingham, *"Our Crowd": The Great Jewish Families of New York* (New York: Harper, 1967), p. ix.

4–5 (footnote) *In the early 1890s, Schiff acquired* NYPL/DS, Box 243; Susan E. Tifft and Alex S. Jones, *The Trust: The Private and Powerful Family Behind* The New York Times, (Boston: Little, Brown, 1999), p. 37.

7 *"As a youngster" . . . "'I can't sit down'"* Warburg, *Reminiscences,* pp. 74–75.

8 *"I rather encouraged"* Ibid., p. 85.

8 *"It's wonderful to be the master"* Ibid., p. 78.

8 (footnote) *"I probably must follow"* John Kobler, *Otto the Magnificent: The Life of Otto Kahn* (New York: Scribner, 1988), p. 21.

9 *Dorothy's earliest memory* Potter, *Men, Money & Magic,* pp. 25–26.

9 *several people who knew her well . . . "very special in a boy"* Dorothy Schiff interview with Robert Conway, New York *Daily News,* December 18, 1950.

9 *"He followed the ancient custom"* Warburg, *Reminiscences,* p. 53.

10–11 *"Not counting ocean liners" . . . if she had been adopted* Hellman, "Publisher," pp. 57–58.

11 *"She gave us what we called 'Bible Lessons'"* Dorothy Schiff, "Dear Reader," *New York Post,* January 24, 1954.

11 *Far different was Dolly's relationship* NYPL/DS, Boxes 243, 244.

12   *"the graveyard of my childhood"*   Hellman, "Publisher," p. 54.

12   *"I think she thought I was rather hopeless"* . . . *"he was afraid of her"*   Potter, *Men, Money & Magic,* pp. 43–44.

13   *Dorothy came to be somewhat forgiving* . . . *"other interests" as well*   Ibid., pp. 110, 46–47.

13   *"I suppose while there"*   Dorothy Schiff, "Dear Reader," *New York Post,* June 15, 1952.

14   *"Goggi would tell me"*   Author interview with Mary Hall Howland, January 23, 2003.

15   *During labor negotiations*   Author interview with Sidney Orenstein, December 7, 2002.

17   *In 1917, he wrote to a rabbi*   Adler, *Jacob H. Schiff,* 1: 211.

17   *"I wish you joy to your happiness"*   Ron Chernow, *The Warburgs* (New York: Random House, 1993), p. 185.

19   *A certain ambivalent attitude*   Birmingham, *"Our Crowd,"* p. 342.

19–20   *Lewis Strauss recalled*   Lewis L. Strauss, interview with George Herman, William E. Wiener Oral History Library of the American Jewish Committee, 1972–73, New York Public Library, Humanities—Jewish Division.

20   *"Dolly's parents"*   Author interview with Phyllis Farley, May 28, 2003.

20   *Over the years, Dorothy told different stories*   See Potter, *Men, Money & Magic,* p. 35; Conway, Dorothy Schiff interview; author interview with Sally Kramarsky, January 16, 2003.

2. Society Girl

The main sources for information about Dorothy's young adulthood and her relationship with Franklin Roosevelt are, once again, Hellman, "Publisher," and Potter, *Men, Money & Magic,* as well as interviews with her daughters, Adele Hall Sweet and Sally Backer Kramarsky. Judy Backer Grunberg and Sally Backer Kramarsky amplified my understanding of George Backer's family background.

22   *"I was ambitious"*   Hellman, "Publisher," p. 38.

22   *The society columnist*   *New York Times,* November 10, 1921, p. 74.

23   *Adele insisted that her daughter* . . . only one of the three Junior Assemblies. Dorothy Schiff to James Wechsler, January 7, 1959, NYPL/DS, Box 70.

24   *"He was the best-looking man"*   Potter, *Men, Money & Magic,* p. 52.

24   *"Dick was very handsome"*   Author interview with Timothy Seldes, October 2, 2002.

25   *Years later, Dorothy told a friend*   Author interview with Steven M. L. Aronson, June 14, 2003.

25   *"We did what most young couples did"*   Conway, Dorothy Schiff interview.

25   *"Having litter like a bitch"* Potter, *Men, Money & Magic,* p. 63.

26   *Morti remembered . . . when they were youngsters*   Potter, *Men, Money & Magic,* p.94.

27   Details of Dorothy's romance and friendship with Serge Obolensky   NYPL/ DS, Box 291.

29–31 For the character and career of Max Beaverbrook, I relied on Anne Chisholm and Michael Davie, *Lord Beaverbrook: A Life* (New York: Knopf, 1993).

32   *"The peacock spreading his tail feathers"*   Max Beaverbrook to Dorothy Schiff, September (n.d.), 1931, NYPL/DS, Box 1.

32   *Years later, Dorothy told her daughter*   Author interview with Adele Sweet, November 7, 2002.

32   *"I was so green"*   Hellman, "Publisher," p. 51.

32   *Nevertheless, a barrage of telegrams*   Max Beaverbrook to Dorothy Schiff, NYPL/DS, Box 1.

38–39 Details about Dorothy's investments in the theater can be found in NYPL/ DS, Box 291. Also Emma Bugbee interview with Dorothy Schiff Backer, *New York Herald Tribune,* July 3, 1939.

40   *"I never thought much"*   Emma Bugbee interview.

40–41 (footnote) *"As a volunteer"*   "Dear Reader," *New York Post,* March 8, 1953.

41   *"I was asked if I would like to go" . . . "a long stream of petty complaints"*   "Dear Reader," *New York Post,* January 27, 1952.

42   *"There was a class thing too"*   Potter, *Men, Money & Magic,* p. 136.

42   *"The President loved to tease and joke"*   "Dear Reader," *New York Post,* March 8, 1953.

43   *One day a guest*   Potter, *Men, Money & Magic,* p. 171.

44   *"George saw it all"*   Ibid., p. 146.

44   *A man who met her in her later years*   Author interview with Steven Aronson.

44   *James Roosevelt, who was his father's aide*   James Roosevelt, *My Parents: A Differing View* (Chicago: Playboy Press, 1976), p. 104.

44   *In the early 1980s*   Ted Morgan, *FDR: A Biography* (New York: Simon & Schuster, 1985), pp. 256, 453.

46   *A niece of George's*   Author interview with Judy Backer Grunberg, June 29, 2002.

47   *When Dorothy was asked later*   Potter, *Men, Money & Magic,* pp. 148–49; also Conway, Dorothy Schiff interview.

47   *Dolly wrote in her diary . . . primary topic at their dinner parties*   Dorothy began keeping a diary when she returned to New York in the fall of 1931 after her affair with Beaverbrook, and she apparently continued for about a decade. At some point in the last years of her life, as she went through her papers with an eye toward posterity, she appears to have destroyed the diaries or arranged to have them destroyed at her death. One volume, which covers the second half of 1939, was evidently mistakenly included among some family photographs and papers belonging to Rudolf Sonneborn, and therefore survives.

3. Acquiring the *Post*

Most of the information concerning the history of the *Post* comes from the paper's celebratory 200th Anniversary Issue, November 16, 2001; J. David Stern's autobiography, *Memoirs of a Maverick Publisher* (New York: Simon & Schuster, 1962); and the Dorothy Schiff papers at the New York Public Library. The details of Dorothy's acquisition of the *Post* and the financial travails of the paper during the early years of her ownership can be found in NYPL/DS, Boxes 147, 184, 208, 228.

51   *"Then began the hardest"*   Stern, *Memoirs,* p. 247.

53   *In conversations with Stern, Backer got the impression*   Interview with Dorothy Schiff, *News Workshop,* June 1956, NYPL/DS, Box 220; see also Hellman, "Publisher," p. 46.

53   *"We think you need" . . . "few ways to lose money faster"*   Edward Greenbaum to George Backer, April 16, 1939, NYPL/DS, Box 208.

53–54   *Dorothy's brother, John . . . the Backers could not resist*   Stern, *Memoirs,* pp. 253–54.

54   *"The truth is I didn't really buy the* Post*"*   *News Workshop;* see also Hellman, "Publisher," p. 46.

54   (footnote) *she speculated that Dorothy bought the paper*   Sheehy, "Life of the Most Powerful Woman," p. 62.

54   (footnote) *Supporting this view is a letter*   Dorothy Schiff to Max Beaverbrook, NYPL/DS, Box 1.

54–55   *George soon told* Editor & Publisher   July 8, 1939.

55   *Most of her days*   See above note (page [47]) about Dorothy's diary for the second half of 1939.

55   *"I knew she was very picky"*   Author interview with Kitty Carlisle Hart, February 14, 2003.

56   *During a visit Dorothy made to Hyde Park*   Diary entry, August 12, 1939.

57   *Last spring you took over . . . not a good option*   Edward Greenbaum to George Backer, December 21, 1939, NYPL/DS, Box 182.

58   *The Backers turned to a group . . . such groups were usually a waste of time*   NYPL/DS, Box 16.

58–59   *In April, Thackrey offered . . . "is economic suicide"*   Ibid.

62–63   *"This is a tremendous change for me" . . . liberal Democratic course*   New York Times, April 5, 1942, p. 39.

63   *"a girl gets a job on a paper"*   New York Times, April 21, 1942, p. 15.

63   *On the eve of their daughter, Sarah-Ann's, marriage . . . "She was the one who got things done"*   Author interview with Sarah-Ann Kramarsky, January 16, 2003.

64   *Arthur Schlesinger Jr. says*   Author interview with Arthur M. Schlesinger Jr., July 1, 2002.

64   *Julius C. C. Edelstein, a longtime New York*   Author interview with Julius C. C. Edelstein, July 2, 2002.

65   *Ted, unlike George, was not amused*   Potter, *Men, Money & Magic,* pp. 184–85.

4. Media Adventures

Invaluable for this chapter was a publication consecutively titled *Broadcasting, Broadcasting/Telecasting,* and *Telecasting* (Washington, DC: Broadcasting Publications), selected volumes of which are available at the New York Public Library for the Performing Arts at Lincoln Center. Access to a complete set is available upon request at the reference desk at Butler Library, Columbia University.

68   *Morti had worked*   Author interview with Mortimer Hall, November 4, 2005.

68   *Dorothy had told a reporter*   New York Times, April 5, 1942, p. 39.

69–70   *In February 1944, Ernst told the Thackreys*   Morris Ernst to Dorothy Schiff Thackrey, February 7, 1944, NYPL/DS, Box 203, which is the repository for all the information about the purchase of WLIB. Information about the station's initial expenses and operational losses is in Boxes 199, 200, 201.

70–71 Information about the Thackreys' attempt to purchase the *Chicago Daily News* NYPL/DS, Box 178.

70–71 *Adlai Stevenson . . . figure of national potential* J. B. Martin, *Adlai Stevenson of Illinois* (New York: Doubleday, 1976), pp. 220–22.

71 Information about the Thackreys' attempt to purchase the *San Francisco Chronicle* NYPL/DS, Box 195.

71–72 *Bartley Crum did not let up . . . he was drinking heavily* Patricia Bosworth, *Anything Your Little Heart Desires* (New York: Simon & Schuster, 1997), pp. 37–80.

72 Information about the Conference Edition of the *New York Post* NYPL/DS, Box 47.

72 *proposed that the Thackreys buy the* Berkeley Gazette NYPL/DS, Box 10.

72–73 Information about the purchase of KYA and KMTR NYPL/DS, Boxes 194, 208; also *Broadcasting,* 1946, 1947 passim.

73 *"It is because of my passionate belief"* NYPL/DS, Box 192.

74–77 Information about the *Paris Post* and the *Post* news service NYPL/DS, Box 48.

77 Information about Dorothy's total investment in various media properties NYPL/DS, Boxes 228, 247; also Boxes 81, 199, 203.

77 *WLIB required a particular suspension* NYPL/DS, Box 199.

77–78 *"All of this is certainly"* Leo Rosen to Ted Thackrey, April 10, 1946, NYPL/DS, Box 201.

79–80 Information on the sale of KYA and KMTR to Warner Bros. *Broadcasting,* May 19, 1948; also NYPL/DS, Box 192.

5. Ted's Tenure

For background information on the history of Communists and anticommunism in America, I relied primarily on Thomas C. Reeves, *The Life and Times of Joe McCarthy* (New York: Stein & Day, 1982), and Ted Morgan, *Reds* (New York: Random House, 2003).

81 *In 1945, Dolly told an interviewer* Current Biography, July 1945; NYPL/DS, Box 283.

82 Information on various Theodoro transactions NYPL/DS, Boxes 252, 196.

82   *"Based on the assumption"*   Leo Rosen to Dorothy Schiff Thackrey, March 15, 1945, NYPL/DS, Box 196.

83   Information about the purchase of the *Bronx Home News*   NYPL/DS, Box 178.

83–84 Information about the purchase and sale of Jessup & Moore   New York Post Corporation financial statements for 1946 and 1948, Sonneborn papers.

84   *By 1948, the investments Dorothy had made*   New York Post Corporation financial statements, 1939–1948, Sonneborn papers; also NYPL/DS, Box 228.

85   *Just before the end of World War II*   An English-language version by Margaret Jacobson of her interview with Dorothy Schiff, which appeared in *Aufbau,* April 1944, can be found in NYPL/DS, Box 283a.

86   *The views of Irgun supporters . . . making it their homeland*   Correspondence between Ted Thackrey and Bruce Bliven, editor of *The New Republic,* July–August 1944, NYPL/DS, Box 80.

86   *Harry Truman didn't come close*   See, for example, Arthur M. Schlesinger Jr., *A Life in the 20th Century: Innocent Beginnings, 1917–1950* (Boston: Houghton Mifflin, 2000), pp. 346, 406.

89   *Other liberals who had toyed*   See, for example, James Wechsler, *The Age of Suspicion* (New York: Random House, 1953), p. 210.

90   *Max Lerner, writing in* PM   Schlesinger, *A Life,* p. 410.

91   *"Nowhere was the battling over Communism"*   Joshua B. Freeman, *Working-Class New York: Life and Labor Since World War II* (New York: New Press, 2000), p. 72.

94–95 *They told. . . . we run a newspaper Editor & Publisher,* September 18, 1948.

95   *"He never traded up to fancier clothes"*   Author interview with Milton Rich, March 13, 2003.

96–97 Details about Dorothy's trip to Europe can be found in NYPL/DS, Box 249. Also Robert F. Keeler, *Newsday: A Candid History of the Respectable Tabloid* (New York: Arbor House, 1990), pp. 110–11.

98–99 *On March 10, 1949, Lash sent a letter . . . "grave dangers from the right"* WHS/JAW, Box 5.

99   *The Paper, she said*   New York Times, April 7, 1949, p. 27.

99–100 *The newsweeklies implied . . . "I resigned"*   "Family Trouble," *Time,* April 18, 1949, p. 42; "Where Dolly Came In," *Newsweek,* April 18, 1949, pp. 64–65.

100 *"A technically perfect newspaperman"* . . . *other men in the newsroom* Conway, Dorothy Schiff interview.

100–101 *The subject came up again* Sheehy, "Life of the Most Powerful Woman," p. 67. Ted's rebuttal appears in "Letters," *New York*, January 14, 1974, p. 5. Dorothy's notes on the article as well as subsequent correspondence between her and the editors of the magazine are collected in NYPL/DS, Box 254.

101 *"Bart simply could not convince me"* Bosworth, *Anything Your Little Heart Desires,* p. 270.

102 *Dolly was not inclined to help* Dorothy Schiff to Richard Manson, August 11, 1949, NYPL/DS, Box 249.

6. Transition Time

106–107 *Sann wrote a memo* Paul Sann to Maureen McKernan, April 17, 1949, NYPL/DS, Box 66.

107 Details of the sale of WLIB NYPL/DS, Box 203.

107–108 *Disputing a bill* Dorothy Schiff to Edward Greenbaum, September 7, 1949, NYPL/DS, Box 201.

108–109 details of the negotiations with Warner Bros. and the subsequent sales of the California properties NYPL/DS, Boxes 192–94; also *Broadcasting* (and successor publications), 1948–1957 passim.

7. Finding Her Way

111 Correspondence between Dorothy Schiff and Richard Manson NYPL/DS, Box 249.

113 *She consulted Mrs. Ogden Reid* Potter, *Men, Money & Magic,* p. 217.

113–114 *She said later that she was influenced* Ibid., p. 210.

115–116 Details of the Henry Moscow dispute NYPL/DS, Box 212.

118 *"I wanted to be Hildy Johnson"* . . . *"the Christians did"* Paul Sann, "How I Became a Newspaperman," n.d., HS/PS.

118 (footnote) details of the scandal in the sports department NYPL/DS, Box 178; also WHS/JAW, Box 8.

121–123 Details of Ted Poston's life and career Kathleen A. Hauke, *Ted Poston: Pioneer American Journalist* (Athens: University of Georgia Press, 1998).

124 *"You had to retire"* Alice Davidson to Paul Sann, August 25, 1983, PS/BU, Box 3.

124   (footnote) *"A lot of us"*   Author interview with Judy Michaelson, January 29, 2003.

125   *Fern Marja . . . "I happened to be involved in"*   Author interview with Fern Marja Eckman, October 30, 2002.

126   *"My mother's whole relationship with Dolly" . . . "'She was with Dolly Schiff!'"* Author interview with Jane Isay, May 9, 2003.

126   *Thinking back on their first meeting*   "Dear Reader," *New York Post,* July 5, 1953.

127   Anecdotes about Earl Wilson   Paul Sann, "That's Earl Wilson, Brother!" *Saga,* July 1951, PS/HS.

128–129   *"Lyons didn't make a fortune" . . . did not endear her to Summer*   Author interview with Anita Summer, January 28, 2003.

130   *"Dolly was a marvelously elegant lady"*   Author interview with Ben Schiff, October 13, 2002.

131   *"I had at least one editorial conference there"*   Author interview with Ed Koch, February 27, 2003.

131–132   *"Her office called me in, like, February"*   Author interview with Joan Davidson, January 15, 2003.

132   *"He came to lunch" . . . "Which isn't even Irish"*   Author interview with Pete Hamill, June 2, 2003.

132–134   Freeman's *Working-Class New York* is an excellent source for the demographics and sociology of the city in the fifties.

136   *In the summer of 1961*   Jerry Tallmer, "The Mama of Us All," *Dissent,* Summer 1961, pp. 309–403.

8. The Fabulous Fifties

141–143   Information about Dorothy Schiff's involvement with the Lexington Democratic Club   NYPL/DS, Box 230.

141–142   *"We were having a tough time" . . . "absolutely charmed by the idea"*   Author interview with Russell Hemenway, February 13, 2003.

142   *Several years later she told Adlai Stevenson*   Dorothy Schiff, memo to files, January 29, 1960, NYPL/DS, Box 256.

142   *"About twice as many people"*   "Publisher's Notebook," *New York Post,* April 27, 1952.

143   *She subsequently discovered*   "Dear Reader," *New York Post,* May 26, 1955.

143–144   *"it has been interesting to watch him"*   "Publisher's Notebook," *New York Post,* April 17, 1952.

144   *"Because of my confidence"*   "Publisher's Notebook," *New York Post,* June 1, 1952.

144–145   *Stevenson had grown up with Dolly's friend . . . Mrs. Luce leave in a rage*   Keeler, pp. 148–53.

145   *"She wanted him to win"*   Author interview with Elizabeth Shannon, January 7, 2003.

145   *"With Adlai, sex is not urgent" . . . a passionate appeal*   Keeler, *Newsday,* p. 154; Potter, *Men, Money & Magic,* p. 251.

145   *"He was not a particularly sexy character"*   Author interview with Marian Schlesinger, February 21, 2003.

146   *The paper's editors had been working . . . "his economic needs"*   "Facts of Life for Newspaper Readers," *New York Post,* September 22, 1952.

147–148   *Dolly barely mentioned the fuss . . . "said I, conceitedly"*   "Dear Reader," *New York Post,* September 6, 1952.

148   *Dolly accompanied members . . . "Stevenson, of course"*   "Dear Reader," *New York Post,* October 26, 1952.

149–150   *Well, Election Day has come*   "Dear Reader," *New York Post,* November 9, 1952.

9. Charges and Countercharges

Once again, for the history of Communists and anticommunism in America, I relied primarily on Thomas Reeves's *The Life and Times of Joe McCathy* and *Reds* by Ted Morgan. For Wechsler's account of his experiences with McCarthy and Winchell, see James A. Wechsler, *The Age of Suspicion* (New York: Random House, 1953). Neil Gabler's *Winchell: Gossip, Power and the Culture of Celebrity* (New York: Knopf, 1995) is an indispensable biography.

155   *"Pilat and Shannon revealed considerable research"*   Reeves, *Life and Times of Joe McCarthy,* p. 383.

157   *Dolly accompanied him to Washington*   Victor Navasky, *Naming Names* (New York: Viking, 1980), p. 62.

157   *Symington and fellow Democrat . . . editorial policy of the Post*   Hearing before the Permanent Subcommittee on Investigations of the Committee on Government Operations, U.S. Senate, 83rd Cong. 1st sess., April 24, 1953, part 4. Also WHS/JAW, Box 15.

157   *After his appearance, Wechsler was offered*   Navasky, *Naming Names,* pp. 60–61.

157   *Before this second session . . . no doubts about her support*   Author interview with Irwin Ross, March 6, 2003.

158   *Eugene S. Pulliam*   *New York Times,* August 13, 1953, p. 23.

158   *Authur Krock*   *New York Times,* May 19, 1953, p. 28; also May 22, 1953, p. 26.

158   *Dear Mrs. Schiff*   William Tobey to Dorothy Schiff, May 2, 1953, WHS/JAW, Box 15.

158   Wechsler's notes on his dispute with Lillian Hellman   WHS/JAW, Box 4.

158–159   *In December 1979 . . . to go after McCarthy*   Dorothy Schiff, memo to files, December 4, 1979, NYPL/DS, Box 87. See also Navasky, *Naming Names,* pp. 60–68.

160   *"Winchell was incensed"*   Gabler, *Winchell,* p. 409.

160   *"the air and the newspapers" . . . J. Edgar Hoover and the FBI*   "Footnote to Winchell," *New York Post,* January 7, 1952. The series ran from January 7 to 26 and resumed from April 7 to 12.

160   (footnote) *Leonard Lyons was not among them*   Gabler, *Winchell,* p. 446.

161   *Midway through the run . . . look closely into his record*   "Dear Reader," *New York Post,* January 13, 1952.

161   *"The* Post *series put an almost imperceptible crack"*   Gabler, *Winchell,* p. 429.

162   *"We believe in the old journalist principle"*   *New York Post,* January 28, 1952.

162   *"But he was still beleaguered"*   Gabler, *Winchell,* pp. 432–33.

162   *"Ordure au Lait"*   *New York Post,* March 9, 1952.

162–163   A complete account of the Lait-Mortimer suit and Grand Union's behavior can be found in Wechsler, *Age of Suspicion,* pp. 250–56. Also WHS/JAW, Boxes 1, 5; NYPL/DS, Box 85.

163   Winchell citations   *Daily Mirror,* September 5–October 25, 1952 passim; also NYPL/DS, Box 284.

164   *The* Post *and Wechsler filed libel suits*   Gabler, *Winchell,* p. 256.

164   *The* Post *team was eager to learn*   Marvin Berger to James Wechsler, "Tentative Outline and Content of Winchell Examination," May 12, 1953, WHS/JAW, Box 1.

164   *Rifkind offered . . . mostly unfavorable*   Gabler, *Winchell,* p. 265.

164–165 *Winchell's decline was more protracted . . . Schiff, Wechsler, and the paper*
Ibid., pp. 476–82. See also *Time,* March 21, 1955, p. 56, and *Editor & Publisher,* March 19, 1953, p. 34.

165 *"This was not a personal argument"* *New York Post,* March 28, 1953.

10. "I Got Married"

Information about Rudolf Sonneborn's family background is available in Charles B. Sonneborn, *Sonneborn: A Celebration of Generations* (Bethesda, MD, 1994). Mary Barasch and Deborah Hermann shared with me further details about their uncle's life. Sonneborn's involvement with the founding of the State of Israel is described in Leonard Slater, *The Pledge* (New York: Simon & Schuster, 1970), and Charles E. Shulman, "The Sonneborn Story—An Untold Epic of American Zionism," *American Zionist,* May 1966.

166–168 Dorothy's approach to the cardinal and her visit to his residence are described in Dorothy Schiff, memos to files, cc. to James Wechsler, January 25 and February 12, 1952, NYPL/DS, Box 76.

168 *John Cooney, Spellman's biographer* John Cooney, *The American Pope: The Life and Times of Francis Cardinal Spellman* (New York: Times Books, 1984), pp. 204–08.

168 *The paper's overall financial situation* New York Post Corporation financial statements for 1951, 1952, 1953, Rudolf Sonneborn papers.

168–169 *"The* Post *probably was"* Author interview with Marvin Smilon, January 14, 2003.

169 *At a dinner party* Potter, *Men, Money & Magic,* p. 223.

171 *Dorothy and Rudolf sailed for Europe* Ibid., p. 225.

171–172 Details of Dorothy's trip to Israel can be found in the correspondence between Dorothy Schiff and Richard Manson, July–August 1951, NYPL/DS, Box 249.

173 *At their hotel* Adele Sweet interview.

173–174 *In my last letter* "Dear Reader," *New York Post,* September 13, 1953.

174–175 *One of my hobbies is cooking* "Dear Reader," *New York Post,* January 10, 1954.

175 *Some of our more serious-minded readers* Ibid.

176 Correspondence between Rudolf Sonneborn and John Schiff October 1954, NYPL/DS, Box 243; income tax information, Box 247.

176–177 *Dick was* "Dear Reader," *New York Post,* September 19, 1954.

177   *"She wasn't very nice"*   Author interview with Jean Gillette, October 25, 2002.

177   *"I think I understand"*   Murray Kempton to James Wechsler, September 10, 1954, WHS/JAW, Box 5.

177   *Dolly grieved for Dick . . . hastened his death*   WHS/JAW, Box 6.

11. Party Politics

For background on the careers of the contestants in the New York 1958 gubernatorial election, I relied on Rudy Abramson, *Spanning the Century: The Life of W. Averell Harriman* (New York: William Morrow, 1992), and Cary Reich, *The Life of Nelson A. Rockefeller: Worlds to Conquer, 1908–58* (New York: Doubleday, 1996).

182   *"The Liberal Party" . . . "I don't know for sure"*   Author interview with Gus Tyler, December 22, 2002.

182   *"Dolly aspired"*   Author interview with Jesse Simons, December 17, 2002.

182–183   *Last week I read*   "Dear Reader," *New York Post,* February 15, 1953.

183   *"by far the most intelligent"*   "Dear Reader," *New York Post,* June 24, 1956.

183   *"bubblehead"*   James Wechsler to Dorothy Schiff, October (n.d.) 1953, NYPL/DS, Box 85.

183–184   *"a man of integrity"*   "Dear Reader," *New York Post,* September 26, 1954.

185   *She told Jimmy Wechsler that her daughter Sarah-Ann*   Dorothy Schiff to James Wechsler, June 22, 1955, NYPL/DS, Box 86.

185   *In an October column*   "Dear Reader," *New York Post,* October 28, 1956.

187–188   *"a new star" . . . "they often called him by that name"*   "Dear Reader," *New York Post,* October 31, 1958.

188   *At a routine upstate . . . "has been the oil interests"*   Abramson, *Spanning the Century,* pp. 567–68; Reich, *Life of Nelson A. Rockefeller,* pp. 758–59.

188   *During a weekend . . . with the text she'd written*   Reich, *Life of Nelson A. Rockefeller,* p. 760.

188–189   *To Post Readers*   *New York Post,* November 3, 1958.

189   *"Now she has divorced"*   *Time,* November 17, 1958.

189   *"my forceful, outspoken grandfather"*   "Dear Reader," *New York Post,* November 7, 1958.

189 *While sticking to her guns* Michael Kramer and Sam Roberts, *"I Never Wanted to be Vice-President of Anything!": An Investigative Biography of Nelson Rockefeller* (New York: Basic Books, 1976), pp. 207–208; also Abramson, *Spanning the Century,* p. 571.

190 *"My guess is that Nelson"* Author interview with Louis Harris, June 25, 2004.

190 *Harriman's biography believes* Abramson, *Spanning the Century,* p. 578.

190–191 Dorothy Schiff–Charles Abrams correspondence, March–October 1958, is in NYPL/DS, Box 1.

191 *Jimmy Wechsler sent her a memo* James Wechsler to Dorothy Schiff, November 4, 1958, WHS/JAW, Box 11.

12. Protecting the Little Guy

For information on the career of Robert Moses, I relied on Robert Caro, *The Power Broker: Robert Moses and the Fall of New York* (New York: Alfred A. Knopf, 1974).

194 *"Then as now there were no"* *New York Post,* December 20, 1956.

194 *In 1955, Lerner convinced Dolly* James Wechsler–Dorothy Schiff exchange of memos, November, December 1954, WHS/JHS, Box 5.

195 Details of Murray Kempton's remuneration Correspondence among James Wechsler, Dorothy Schiff, Richard Manson, and Murray Kempton, October 1953–December 1954, NYPL/DS, Box 28.

196 *"It was a writer's paper"* Author interview with Joe Rabinovich (Joe Rab), October 22, 2002.

196 *"The great thing about working"* Author interview with Bernard Bard, December 16, 2002.

196 *Bernard Lefkowitz . . . "'take care of management'"* Bernard Lefkowitz, "Good-bye to Dolly's *Post,*" *Present Tense,* August 1977, p. 56.

197 *Levitas, who was known as Mike . . . "they never interfered or imposed"* Author interview with Mitchel Levitas, September 23, 2004.

197–198 *Haddad was a Florida-born product* Author interview with William Haddad, April 10, 2003.

199 *Kahn's investigation . . . management fees* *New York Post,* May 23–25, 1956.

199–200 *"Between 1946 and 1953"* Caro, *Power Broker,* p. 7.

200–201 Details of the Tavern on the Green fuss Ibid., pp. 986–91.

201   *Irwin Ross, with the help of Ed Katcher*   New York Post, June 26–July 2, 1956.

201   *In fact, a Wechsler editorial*   New York Post, April 25, 1956.

201   *Other reporters picked up the scent*   Caro, Power Broker, p. 1005.

202   *In May 1959, Haddad and Kahn*   Ibid., pp. 1042–44.

203   *Thanking a friend*   Dorothy Schiff to Charles Abrams, n.d. (presumably 1958), NYPL/DS, Box 1.

203   *Haddad told Robert Caro*   Caro, Power Broker, p. 1048.

204   *Praising a series by Ted Poston*   Dorothy Schiff to James Wechsler, February 18, 1960, NYPL/DS, Box 70.

204   *"Bleeding-heart journalism"*   Author interview with Lenore Kahn, December 3, 2002.

205   *"When I got a job"*   Author interview with Arthur Pomerantz, November 25, 2002.

205   *"During the fifties and early sixties"*   Author interview with Alan Whitney, April 11, 2003.

13. Civil Rights and Wrongs
For the history of the civil rights movement, I relied on Volume 1 of Taylor Branch's magisterial three-volume study, *Parting the Waters: America in the King Years, 1954–63* (New York: Simon & Schuster, 1988). For details about Ted Poston's career, I consulted Kathleen Hauke's *Ted Poston: Pioneer American Journalist*.

209   *Typically, in November 1954, Dolly wrote*   Dorothy Schiff to James Wechsler, November 23, 1954, NYPL/DS, Box 86.

209–210   *Poston's series run in the* Post   April 16–29, 1956.

210   *Although Grover Hall had originally said*   Hauke, Ted Poston, pp. 132–40.

211   *Powell responded to her opposition by letter*   Adam Clayton Powell Jr., to Dorothy Schiff, May 5, 1952, NYPL/DS, Box 57.

211–212   Memos and clippings about Powell, Sally Backer, and Dorothy Schiff are in NYPL/DS, Box 57.

212   *A week later*   NYPL/DS, Box 285.

213   Dorothy's response to the Harlem series, the controversy about the series, and subsequent internal memos   NYPL/DS, Box 73.

213–214   *Battle of Harlem*   New York Post, August 4–12, 1958.

214 *Charles Stone, who was Powell's press secretary* Author interview with Charles Stone, August 20, 2002.

214–215 Details of the Hulan Jack–Sidney Ungar case *New York Post,* December 15–21, 1959.

14. Bringing Down the Titans

Warren Moscow, *The Last of the Big-Time Bosses: The Life and Times of Carmine De Sapio and the Rise and Fall of Tammany Hall* (New York: Stein and Day, 1971), is the best source for the details of the defeat of De Sapio and Tammany by the reform Democrats. Robert Caro's *The Power Broker* is the source for information about Robert Moses.

217 *"Almost immediately"* Dorothy Schiff, "My Secret Life with J. Edgar Hoover," *New York Post,* October 5, 1959.

218 *Hoover's friends in Washington . . . did not deter the director's supporters* WHS/JAS, Box 3.

218–219 *"The business world" . . . prevailed upon her not to sue* NAM News, February 20, 1959; Dorothy Schiff to Stanley C. Hope, March 5, 1959, Stanley C. Hope to Dorothy Schiff, March 10, 1959, NYPL/DS, Box 40.

219 *In April 1959, Dolly received a call . . . but he kept trying* Memos between Dorothy Schiff and Jean Gillette, NYPL/DS, Box 73. Also Schiff, "My Secret Life with J. Edgar Hoover."

219–220 *In May she sent Wechsler* Dorothy Schiff to James Wechsler, c.c. Marvin Berger, May 19, 1959, WHS/JAW, Box 1.

220 *Finally, in October* "J. Edgar Hoover," *New York Post,* October 5–17, 1959.

220 *"without a shred of evidence"* Time, October 19, 1959, p. 92.

222 *"I was never assigned" . . . without competitive bidding* Caro, *Power Broker,* pp. 1098–1100.

222–224 The continuing discussion between Dorothy and her editors and executives about World's Fair coverage is in NYPL/DS, Box 43.

224 *In January 1965, he made some allegations* Mary Perot Nichols, "The Press: Suffocation in the Establishment Bosom," *Village Voice,* January 28, 1965, pp. 1, 14–18; Sidney Zion, *Read All About It!: The Collected Adventures of a Maverick Reporter* (New York: Summit Books, 1982); author interview with Sidney Zion, February 6, 2003.

224 *When the* Voice *article appeared* Correspondence among Dorothy Schiff, Paul Sann, Al Davis, and Jean Gillette, NYPL/DS, Box 43.

226   *Years later, Bob Friedman*   Bob Friedman to Paul Sann, n.d., (probably August 1983), PS/HS, Box 7.

15. Ethnic Journalism

Cardinal Spellman's career is judiciously assayed in John Cooney, *The American Pope.*

228   *The articles by Irwin Ross*   *New York Post,* September 25–October 3, 1957.

229   *a series of articles by Joe Kahn and others*   *New York Post,* May 22–July 24, 1958.

229   *an admiring profile of Dr. Morris A. Jacobs*   *New York Post,* March 17, 1957.

229–230   Data on Jews in New York at midcentury can be found in Nathan Glazer and Daniel P. Moynihan, *Beyond the Melting Pot: The Negroes, Puerto Ricans, Jews, Italians, and Irish of New York City,* 2d ed. (Cambridge, MA: M.I.T. Press, 1970), pp. 143–71.

231   *"There is a huge gap"*   Author interview with Werner (Wynn) Kramarsky, May 25, 2004.

232   *"You worried if Jewish issues"*   Author interview with June Bingham, October 23, 2002.

232   *Typically, in April 1954, she reprimanded*   Dorothy Schiff to James Wechsler, cc. Paul Sann and James Graham, April 21, 1954, WHS/JAW, Box 11.

232   *Dolly was clueless*   Hadassah questionnaire, July 1980, NYPL/DS, Box 80.

233–234   The Schiff-Einstein contretemps is documented in NYPL/DS, Box 15. The article by Isaiah Berlin appeared in the November 18, 1979, issue of *The New York Review of Books.*

234   *"I was required to submit"*   Author interview with Jerry Tallmer, October 12, 2002.

235   Series on Great Neck   "Suburbia, L.I.," *New York Post,* October 12–18, 1956.

235   *Dorothy Schiff loved the series*   Dorothy Schiff to James Wechsler, November 11, 1956, NYPL/DS, Box 86.

236   The genesis and history of what would become the Melting Pot project is documented in NYPL/DS, Box 33.

236   *"Dan approached me"*   Author interview with Nathan Glazer, June 3, 2004.

16. Alone Again

241   *The financial statements were reassuring*   New York Post Corporation financial statements for 1954, 1955, 1956, Rudolf Sonneborn papers.

241   *Because Dorothy was the sole owner*   Leon Cook to Dorothy Schiff, February 4, 1954, NYPL/DS, Box 115; see also financial memos, Box 292.

242 *Dolly pored over reports* Leon Cook to All Department Heads, November 12, 1954; Dorothy Schiff to Leon Cook, July (n.d.) 1954, NYPL/DS, Box 115.

242–243 *Dolly's attention to the fine print ... ran a few weeks after that* The memos cited, like those below on p. 244, are in NYPL/DS, Box 86.

245–246 Details and mementos of the Sonneborns' travels are in Rudolf's scrapbooks, Sonneborn papers.

245 *"The Ile de France is noted"* "Dear Reader," *New York Post,* September 19, 1954.

245 *"My recollection is of a beautiful"* "Dear Reader," *New York Post,* September 24, 1955.

246 *In June 1956, Dolly told an interviewer* *News Workshop* interview.

246 *Rudolf's niece Deborah Hermann* Author interview with Deborah Hermann, February 20, 2003.

247 *"I couldn't"* Potter, *Men, Money & Magic,* p. 248.

247 *Rudolf was given the guest bedroom* Dorothy Schiff to Jean Gillette, July 15, 1960, NYPL/DS, Box 249.

248 *"The Sonneborn thing ended so poorly"* Author interview with Lisa Schiff, January 31, 2003.

248 *Several years later* Sheehy, "Life of the Most Powerful Woman," p. 68.

248–249 *After Rudolf left, Dorothy hired ... Madison Avenue galleries* NYPL/DS, Box 218.

249 *The butler who'd been so attentive* NYPL/DS, Box 226.

249–250 Details of the employment of Aery and Everette Lawson and their relations with Dorothy Schiff Author interview with Everette and Aery Lawson, January 29, 2003. See also NYPL/DS, Box 229.

250 *Dolly told Max Lerner* Dorothy Schiff to Max Lerner, October 27, 1959, NYPL/DS, Box 33.

251–252 Correspondence and other documents pertaining to the friendship between Dorothy Schiff and Jenny Baerwald NYPL/DS, Box 220.

252 *In her will, she left Dolly* Dorothy Schiff to John Schiff, February 11, 1966, NYPL/DS, Box 243.

17. Changing the Guard

253–254 Circulation figures for the *Post* and other New York papers, some with Dorothy's annotations and comments NYPL/DS, Boxes 179–183. Information about the Learn-A-Language promotion is in Box 183.

254 Correspondence about advertising between Dorothy Schiff and James Wechsler February–March 1961, NYPL/DS, Box 12.

255 *"Mrs. Schiff suggests"* Jean Gillette to James Wechsler, February 9, 1960, NYPL/DS, Box 70.

255 *Paul Sann, the executive editor, was enthusiastic* Paul Sann to Dorothy Schiff, cc. James Wechsler, August 27, 1959, WHS/JAW, Box 8.

255 *"I have no principled objection"* James Wechsler to Joe Rauh, June 6, 1961, WHS/JAW Box 5.

256 *"You said that our Page One"* James Wechsler to Dorothy Schiff, June 1, 1961, NYPL/DS, Box 85.

256 *She read it carefully* Dorothy Schiff to James Wechsler, December (n.d.) 1959, NYPL/DS, Box 86.

256 *She told Humphrey's chief fund-raiser ... looking for someone else to back* Dorothy Schiff to Marvin Rosenberg, April 20, 1960; James Wechsler to Dorothy Schiff, April 26, 1960, both in NYPL/DS, Box 25.

256–257 *"I have just read a provocative book"* "Dear Reader," *New York Post,* April 15, 1956.

257 *In October, he came to West Street* Dorothy Schiff, memo to files, October 13, 1960, NYPL/DS, Box 30.

257 *Joe Kennedy took Dolly to dinner* NYPL/DS, Box 31; also Potter, *Men, Money & Magic,* p. 263.

259 *"When Sann and Wechsler began their feud"* Author interview with Carl Pelleck, December 13, 2002.

259 Circulation figures are in NYPL/DS, Box 39.

259 *Dolly called each man* Potter, *Men, Money & Magic,* p. 267.

259 *"Jimmy tried all kinds of stuff"* Author interview with Edward Kosner, June 19, 2003.

260 *"I told him that you"* James Wechsler to Dorothy Schiff, September 7, 1961, WHS/JAW, Box 11.

261 Newsweek *was more direct* *Newsweek,* September 25, 1961, p. 64, in Dorothy Schiff's scrapbook, NYPL/DS, Box 285.

261   *"Jimmy wasn't thrilled"*   Author interview with Nancy Frankel Wechsler, June 5, 2002.

262   *A week after the changes went into effect*   Dorothy Schiff to James Wechsler, September 18, 1961, WHS/JAW, Box 11.

263   *"The people who made their way"*   Author interview with Nora Ephron, May 14, 2003.

263   *in May 1961, he asked Wechsler*   Bill Haddad to James Wechsler, May 31, 1961, NYPL/DS, Box 21.

263–264   *Dolly told Jimmy that she felt . . . belittled Haddad's presumptuous tone*   Dorothy Schiff to James Wechsler, June 5, 1961; Paul Sann to Dorothy Schiff, September (n.d.) 1961, both in WHS/JAW, Box 13.

264–265   Details of Hamill's life are from Pete Hamill, *A Drinking Life: A Memoir* (Boston: Little, Brown, 1994), and Hamill interview. All direct quotes are from the interview.

265   *It is 6 in the morning*   Pete Hamill, "The Legacy of Paul Sann, Newspaperman," *New York Post,* September 6, 1986.

266   Dorothy's attempts to solicit financial advertising   NYPL/DS, Box 245.

267   *She explained to Jimmy*   Dorothy Schiff to James Wechsler, May 14, 1962, WHS/JAW, Box 11.

268   *"When I was young"*   Author interview with Howard Sann, March 28, 2003.

268   *she was always slightly testy about them*   NYPL/DS, Box 66.

268   *Dolly dutifully made a note to herself*   Dorothy Schiff, memo to files, June 24, 1965, NYPL/DS, Box 66.

268–269   *she wrote him a note on her letterhead*   September 20, 1965, BU/PS, Box 3.

269   *At one point, he got huffy . . . call and ask what she thought*   Paul Sann to Dorothy Schiff, October 30, 1967; Dorothy Schiff to Paul Sann, November 1, 1967, both NYPL/DS, Box 66.

270   *"The* Post *gave me basic training"*   George Carpozi to Paul Sann, n.d. (presumably summer 1983), BU/PS, Box 3.

18. "The Only Survivor"

For chronology and details about the 1962–1963 strike, I relied on the reportage of A. H. Raskin, the labor specialist of the *Times,* especially his extensive article, "The Newspaper Strike: A Step-By-Step Account of How and Why It Happened," *New York Times,* April 1, 1963, pp. 1, 22–24. I was also helped by the account of the same

events in Chapter 4 of Tom Shachtman's unpublished manuscript about Theodore
Kheel, which the author graciously made available to me.

273–274   *The Post was terribly hurt*   "Dear Reader," *New York Post,* December 27,
          1953.

276   *During the 1958 strike, many New Yorkers*   Penn Kimball, "People Without
      Papers," *Public Opinion Quarterly,* Spring 1959, pp. 389–98.

277   *"Different unions had different issues"*   Author interview with Bertram Powers,
      May 29, 2002.

277   *"He's serious, sincere, dedicated—and wrong"*   Raskin, "Newspaper Strike."

278   *Despite the bleak prospects*   Author interview with Theodore Kheel, May 23,
      2002.

279   *Walter Thayer told Dorothy . . . and announced she was leaving*   Raskin,
      "Newspaper Strike."

279   *Dorothy later admitted*   Hellman, "Publisher," p. 43. See also Potter, *Men,
      Money, & Magic,* pp. 270–01.

280   *"Bert told me to hold a press conference"*   Hellman, "Publisher," p. 44.

281   *"Dolly was a traitor"*   Author interview with Marian Sulzberger Heiskell, April
      3, 2003.

281   *"We made our bones"*   Author interview with Byron Greenberg, November 20,
      2002.

282   *In a survey that had alarming implications*   Penn Kimball, "New York Readers
      in a Newspaper Shutdown," *Columbia Journalism Review,* Fall 1963, pp. 47–56.

282   *By the middle of April*   Byron Greenberg to Dorothy Schiff, April 18, 1963,
      NYPL/DS, Box 179.

284   *When the time came to renew the contracts . . . until several disputed items were
      resolved*   A. H. Raskin, "The Great Manhattan Newspaper Duel," *Saturday
      Review,* May 8, 1965, pp. 58–72.

284   Details of the automation experiment at the *Post*   NYPL/DS, Box 174.

285   *"Mrs. Schiff, as an apostate"*   *World Telegram and Sun,* June 24, 1965.

285   Details of the *Post's* financial position   New York Post Corporation balance
      sheets, NYPL/DS, Box 178.

285–286   *Several ad agency executives*   *Wall Street Journal,* September 13, 1966.

286   Details of the *Post* response to the Widgit   NYPL/DS, Boxes 91, 179.

286 *Dolly began thinking immediately of moving* "Alone in the Afternoon," *Newsweek,* May 22, 1967, p. 68.

287 *Dorothy later told a reporter* Potter, *Men, Money & Magic,* p. 278.

287 *James Wechsler said* Ibid., p. 228.

287 *"By every rule of newspaper economics"* Max Lerner, *New York Post,* May 14, 1967.

287 *"Much of the warmth"* "Alone in the Afternoon."

287 *"if only the unpredictable lady"* *Editor & Publisher,* May 6, 1967.

287 *She said later that she had terrible* Potter, *Men, Money & Magic,* p. 277.

288 *"I have great respect"* Interview with Dorothy Schiff, *Women's Wear Daily,* June 5, 1967.

288 *Some years later, Dorothy* Sheehy, "Life of the Most Powerful Woman," p. 58.

19. Planning for the Future

289–290 Information about the New York Times Corporation at midcentury Tifft and Jones, *The Trust,* pp. 320–22.

290 Information about the *Washington Post*'s financial history Katharine Graham, *Personal History* (New York: Knopf, 1997), pp. 177–92. Also Carol Felsenthal, *Power, Privilege and the Post: The Katharine Graham Story* (New York: Putnam, 1993), p. 110.

290 *She was at a meeting* Felsenthal, *Power, Privilege and the Post,* p. 228.

291 *In 1961, Phil Graham had introduced Dorothy . . . make a deal* James Wechsler memos to files, April 7 and 10, 1961, WHS/JAW, Box 16. Also Felsenthal, *Power, Privilege and the Post,* p. 198.

291 *According to one participant* Author interview with Richard Sachs, March 5, 2005.

292 *The following year, Sylvia Porter* Dorothy Schiff to James Wechsler, October 19, 1978, NYPL/DS, Box 87.

292 *"I like running a newspaper"* *Editor & Publisher,* January 25, 1964.

293–294 Details of Robert Gray's career before and during his time at the *Post* NYPL/DS, Box 117.

295–297 Details of Blair Clark's employment history at the *Post* are in NYPL/DS, Box 9.

296–298 Blair Clark's account of his experience at the *Post* and his relationship with Dorothy Schiff is taken from in an unpublished memoir by Clark, a copy of which was graciously given to me by his widow, Joanna Clark.

297   *In a note Dolly wrote some years later*   Dorothy Schiff to James Wechsler, September 20, 1972, WHS/JAW, Box 12.

299–302   Details of the purchase of the South Street property are in NYPL/DS, Boxes 153–55.

302   *"We will still have our problems"*   Byron Greenberg to Dorothy Schiff, October 29, 1969, NYPL/DS, Box 153.

20. The Rise of the New Left

306   *Bobby reminded her of Jack*   Dorothy Schiff to files, September 9, 1964, NYPL/DS, Boxes 255, 31.

307   *Jimmy rebutted Bobby Kennedy*   New York Post, October 10, 1965.

307   *"A Beame victory"*   New York Post, November 1, 1965.

308   *The meeting with Jack*   Dorothy Schiff memo to files, n.d., NYPL/DS, Box 256.

308–309   An account of Dorothy's meetings with Jackie Kennedy is in Potter, *Men, Money & Magic,* pp. 290–98. Also NYPL/DS, Boxes 45, 255.

309   *Johnson greeted her warmly . . . before he rang off*   Potter, *Men, Money & Magic,* pp. 284–85.

310   *"Apparently they are very famous" . . . "not considered* comme il faut." Ibid., pp. 287–88.

312   *"For them the government" . . . "seemed much too dangerous"*   Todd Gitlin, *The Sixties: Years of Hope, Days of Rage* (New York: Bantam Books, 1987), pp. 58–60.

313   *"The unstated background murmur"*   Ibid., p. 247.

313–314   *In January 1966, Schiff and Wechsler*   James Wechsler, memo to files, January 15, 1966, NYPL/DS, Box 26.

314   *Later in the year, Dolly invited*   James Wechsler, memo to files, September 26, 1966, NYPL/DS, Box 2.

315   *Murray Kempton sympathized*   New York Post, May 3, 1968.

316   *Max Lerner disagreed . . . Mark was a good boy*   New York Post, May 3, 1968.

316   *He did interview the current editors*   James Wechsler, New York Post, May 10, 1968.

316   *"were motivated by honest convictions"*   New York Post, August 23, 1968.

317   *"Not since Stevenson"*   James Wechsler, New York Post, May 8, 1968.

317 *Dolly was more wary*   NYPL/DS, Box 31.

317 *Bobby had come . . . everyone seemed very friendly*   Dorothy Schiff, memo to files, January 29, 1968 (with additional notes added on January 25, 1972); also memo to files, April 1, 1968, both NYPL/DS, Box 255.

318 *Wechsler feared that McCarthy*   James Wechsler, *New York Post,* April 2, 1968.

319 *profile of Chicago's Mayor Richard Daley*   *New York Post,* August 24, 1968.

320 *Several days later, Humphrey tried to explain*   CBS transcript (August 21, 1968) with Dorothy Schiff's notes, NYPL/DS, Box 25.

321 *she drafted Max Lerner*   Dorothy Schiff, memo to files, September 3, 1968, NYPL/DS, Box 87.

321 Account of Dorothy Schiff, James Wechsler, and Hubert Humphrey meeting   Dorothy Schiff, memo to files, October 21, 1968, NYPL/DS, Box 25.

21. Blacks vs. Jews

For excellent coverage of the wider sociopolitical implications of the material in this chapter, I relied on Jonathan Rieder, *Canarsie: The Jews and Italians of Brooklyn Against Liberalism* (Cambridge, MA: Harvard University Press, 1985), as well as, once again, Freeman's *Working-Class New York.* For the history of urban disorder and the crisis in the New York public schools, I relied on the coverage in *The New York Times* (which published a particularly useful chronology of the 1968 teachers' strike on November 4, 1968). I also consulted two differing but equally thoughtful scholarly accounts of the turmoil in the schools: Diane Ravitch, *The Great School Wars: New York City, 1805–1973* (New York: Basic Books, 1974), pp. 233–378, and Jane Anna Gordon, *Why They Couldn't Wait: A Critique of the Black-Jewish Conflict over Community Control in Ocean Hill–Brownsville, 1967–1971* (New York: RoutledgeFalmer, 2001).

325 *The commission's findings*   Report of the National Advisory Commission on Civil Disorders (Washington, DC: Government Printing Office, February 29, 1968).

325 *Dorothy Schiff had serious reservations*   Dorothy Schiff to James Wechsler, March 6, 1968, NYPL/DS, Box 87.

328 *Wechsler editorialized that although the UFT*   "Neither Side Was Harmless," *New York Post,* September 29, 1967.

328 *The so-called Bundy Report*   *Reconnection for Learning, A Community School System for New York City: A Report of the Mayor's Advisory Panel on Decentralization of New York City Schools,* McGeorge Bundy, chairman (New York: The Panel, 1967).

331   *Even before the trouble broke out*   James Wechsler to Dorothy Schiff, June 6, 1967, NYPL/DS, Box 87.

331   *Bernie Bard, the* Post*'s education columnist*   "The Blackboard," *New York Post,* September 16, 1967.

331   *Bard continued to favor*   "The Blackboard," *New York Post,* September 21, 1968.

331   *"I got an invitation"*   Bernard Bard interview.

332   *Weeks into the strike, Jimmy sent a memo*   James Wechsler to Dorothy Schiff, October 23, 1968, NYPL/DS, Box 78.

332   *"It would be hard to draw a sharper contrast"*   *New York Post,* October 31, 1968.

332   *"I don't know anyone who has seen"*   *New York Post,* October 9, 1968.

332–333   *Dear Mrs. Schiff*   Allen Green to Dorothy Schiff, n.d., NYPL/DS, Box 79.

333   *Dear Dorothy Schiff*   Esther Soretsky to Dorothy Schiff, January 24, 1969, NYPL/DS, Box 70.

333   *We have received your communication*   Jean Gillette, NYPL/DS, Box 79.

334–335   For a good overview of the mainstream American Jewish community, see Samuel C. Heilman, *Portrait of American Jews: The Last Half of the 20th Century* (Seattle: University of Washington Press, 1995), and Marshall Sklare, *Observing America's Jews* (Hanover, NH: University of New England Press, 1993).

335   *Commentary,*   March 1969, pp.33–42.

335   *Dolly told Sann she thought*   Correspondence between Dorothy Schiff and Paul Sann, April 3–4, 1969, NYPL/DS, Box 66.

335–336   *Commentary,*   April 1969, pp.92–98.

336   *Glazer's conclusions that anti-Semitism*   Dorothy Schiff to Paul Sann, April 10, 1969, NYPL/DS, Box 66.

22. The Candy Store

338   Circulation figures are in NYPL/DS, Box 182; Post Corporation financial records are in Boxes 185, 190.

339   *"On certain issues, they anticipated Dolly"*   Author interview with Roberta Brandes Gratz, November 7, 2002.

339   *Overtime was a big deal*   See typical correspondence between Paul Sann and Dorothy Schiff, April 1–2, 1964, NYPL/DS, Box 78.

340   *She complained to Sann that editors*   Dorothy Schiff to Paul Sann, October 7, 1968, NYPL/DS, Box 13.

340   *In the summer of 1967*   Correspondence between Paul Sann and Dorothy Schiff, October 4, 1967, NYPL/DS, Box 19.

340   *Dolly knew the* Post *was going slack*   Dorothy Schiff to Paul Sann, October 7, 1968, NYPL/DS, Box 13.

341–342   Details of Pete Hamill's career and remuneration   NYPL/DS, Boxes 22, 23, and BU/PS, Box 6.

342   Details of Murray Kempton's career and remuneration   NYPL/DS, Box 28.

343   *Paul Sann pleaded with Byron*   Paul Sann to Byron Greenberg October 29, 1967, BU/PS, Box 6.

344   Details of Wechsler's compensation   NYPL/DS, Box 87.

344   Details of Sann's compensation   BU/PS, Box 3.

344   *"Our aim," says Navasky*   Author interview with Victor Navasky, October 1, 2002.

345   *In 1964, Nat Hentoff complained*   "Goodbye, Dolly," *Village Voice,* June 25, 1964.

346   *Dolly was particularly incensed*   Correspondence between Dorothy Schiff and James Wechsler, May 6–7, 1968, NYPL/DS, Box 87.

346   Jack Newfield, "Good–bye Dolly!" *Harper's,* September 1969, pp. 92–98.

347   *Dolly had been on edge*   Correspondence between Dorothy Schiff and James Wechsler, May (n.d.) 1969, NYPL/DS, Box 43.

347   Details of Newfield's employment history at the *Post*   NYPL/DS, Box 43.

347–348   Dorothy's response to the Newfield article and subsequent book   NYPL/DS, Box 210.

348   *The editors complied*   *Harper's,* July 1970.

23. The Young Turks

350–351   *Ted Poston continued to be*   Ted Poston to James Wechsler, September 9, 1958; Ted Poston to Paul Sann, July 17, 1962, both WHS/JAW, Box 7.

351   *Wechsler and Sann proposed to Dorothy Schiff . . . seldom productive*   Hauke, *Ted Poston,* pp. 184, 178.

351   *One rewrite man says*   Robert Friedman to Paul Sann, n.d. (presumably summer 1983), HS/PS.

351   *Just after Poston retired*   Hauke, *Ted Poston,* p. 188.

351   *According to Ted's obituary*   *New York Post,* January 11, 1974.

351–352   Details of the Artis case   BU/PS, Box 4, and NYPL/DS, Box 38. See also Hauke, *Ted Poston,* pp. 180–82.

351   *"There wasn't time or money"*   Author interview with Al Ellenberg, April 21, 2003.

352   (footnote) *Years later, Trow praised*   George Trow to Paul Sann, June 20, 1983, BU/PS, Box 3.

352–353   *In November 1972, the four black reporters . . . but nothing came of it*   Dorothy Schiff memos to files, November 1972, NYPL/DS, Box 5.

353   *"I nominated a Negro girl"*   Author interview with Gerry Passarella, March 31, 2003.

353   *"I know it makes some of the other colored folks" . . . Sann apologized*   Memos between Paul Sann and Dorothy Schiff, May 14–15, 1969, BU/PS, Box 6.

354–356   *" 'The Woman in the News' feature" . . . " 'kind of a groovy chick' "*   Author interview with Lindsy Van Gelder, March 22, 2003. Also assorted memos, NYPL/DS, Box 8.

355   *Sann reported his version*   Paul Sann to Dorothy Schiff, October 8–10, 1969, NYPL/DS, Box 8.

356   *"I was taken aback by that"*   Author interview with Helene Eisenberg, April 10, 2003.

357   *"My general recollection is that Dolly"*   Author interview with Nan Rosenthal: January 29, 2003.

357   *women should "be given equal representation"*   "Dear Reader," *New York Post,* May 11, 1952.

358   *"At that time, if you were a hard-hitting businesswoman"*   Author interview with Helen Gurley Brown, April 15, 2003.

358   *"But have we a right"*   "Dear Reader," *New York Post,* January 27, 1957.

358–359   *a woman who was "naturally aggressive". . . . "relations with relatives and tradesmen"*   "Dear Reader," *New York Post,* March 17 and 21, 1958.

359   *"At the Gridiron Club dinner"*   "Dorothy Schiff," *Contemporary Authors,* 1986. It was a persistent complaint; see also "Dear Reader," *New York Post,*

March 15, 1953, and Dorothy Schiff interview with Philip Schuyler, n.d., NYPL/DS, Box 220.

361 (footnote) *"I adopted the assumption"* Graham, *Personal History,* pp. 416–47.

361–362 I am grateful to Lindsy Van Gelder for supplying me with the texts of "What is Wrong with the *New York Post*" and the "New York Post News Staff Charter."

363 *"Woody was sheltered"* Author interviews with Tony Mancini, December 6, 2002, and May 23, 2004.

363 *"The publisher, Mrs. Dorothy Schiff"* Edwin Diamond, "The Cabal at the 'New York Times': Which Way to the Revolution?" *New York,* May 18, 1970, p. 45.

363 *Dolly immediately called her friend* Dorothy Schiff, memo to files, May 18, 1970, NYPL/DS, Box 40.

364 *"We should have known something was wrong"* Perry Deane Young, "Oh, Miss Dolly, can't you see de light?" *Chicago Journalism Review,* June 1972, p. 14.

364 *"treasonable"* Dorothy Schiff, memo to files, October 27, 1970, NYPL/DS, Box 25.

364–365 *"William Woodward and Pamela Howard"* Friedman letter, HS/PS.

365 *She checked with Ted Kheel* Dorothy Schiff, memo to files, October 27, 1970, NYPL/DS, Box 25.

365 *a long article by Dick Pollak* "An Intra-Family Sort of Thing," *[MORE],* October 1971, pp. 3, 14–15.

365 *Dolly complained directly to Woody* Dorothy Schiff memo to Paul Sann and James Wechsler, October 5, 1971, NYPL/DS, Box 38.

365 A report about the April 1972 *[More]* convention is in NYPL/DS, Box 38.

366 *"a terrible newspaper"* . . . *the newspaper business or much else* Nora Ephron, "Media," *Esquire,* April 1973, pp. 8, 60, 63.

366 Dorothy's reaction to the Ephron piece and its subsequent republication NYPL/DS, Box 15.

367 *"By then it was very PC"* Author interview with Robert Spitzler, October 17, 2002.

24. The Worst of Times

For the details of New York politics in the late 1960s and early '70s, I relied on *The New York Times.* For the implications of those events, Freeman, *Working-Class New York,* and Rieder, *Canarsie,* were extremely helpful.

369–370   *Opotowsky summarized their thoughts ... attractive to advertisers* Memos between Stan Opotowsky and Dorothy Schiff, December 22, 1970, NYPL/DS, Boxes 4, 12.

371   *Dorothy was thrilled* Dorothy Schiff to James Wechsler, November 8, 1969, NYPL/DS, Box 34.

371   *"None of us have respect"* Paul Sann to Dorothy Schiff, November 10, 1970, NYPL/DS, Box 34.

371   *Sann recapped Lindsay's flaws* Paul Sann to Dorothy Schiff, July 9, 1971, NYPL/DS, Box 66.

373   *Josh Friedman, the* Post's *man in Albany* Author interview with Joshua Friedman, June 22, 2005.

373   *"I didn't think the* Post *was a great paper"* Author interview with Peter Freiberg, April 3, 2003.

374   *"It was the intelligent tabloid"* Author interview with Steve Lawrence, April 9, 2003.

374   *Joyce wrote a letter* Joyce Purnick to Paul Sann, August 18, 1983, BU/PS, Box 3.

374   *"Maybe the* Post *wasn't what it could have been"* Author interview with Joyce Purnick, May 19, 2005.

375   *"At twenty-seven, to be the night city editor" ... "probably worse behind my back"* Author interview with Warren Hoge, July 27, 2002.

376   *A typical fuss was generated* The confrontation between Schiff and Sann is recorded in a series of memos to files written by Dorothy Schiff between November 19 and 23, 1970, NYPL/DS, Box 66.

377   *In January 1970, he offered some ideas* Pete Hamill to Dorothy Schiff, January 16, 1970, NYPL/DS, Box 22.

377   *In September 1971, Paul asked ... who seemed relieved* Dorothy Schiff, memo to files, September 16, 1971, NYPL/DS, Box 66.

378–379   Schiff's equivocal offer of Sann's job to Pete Hamill is recorded in several memos to files by Dorothy Schiff, September 9 and 30, 1971; Hamill's correspondence with Schiff about possible improvements in the *Post* and her response are in an exchange of memos on September 30, 1971, all in NYPL/DS, Box 22.

379   *From England, he wrote Sann* Pete Hamill to Paul Sann, September 28, 1971, BU/PS, Box 6.

380   *Thanking Sann for some kindness*   Dorothy Schiff to Paul Sann, May 24, 1974, NYPL/DS, Box 66.

380   Memos suggesting Dorothy's interest in hiring Bill Moyers and Emmet Hughes are in NYPL/DS, Box 25.

381   *"I was invited to stay for dinner"*   Author interview with Wendy Gray, June 18, 2005.

381   Memos between Dorothy Schiff and Mortimer Hall concerning advertising by the *Post* are in NYPL/DS, Box 192.

382   *Matters came to a head . . . "I never saw him there again"*   Details about Morti's behavior during the strike are in NYPL/DS, Box 131. Also Ellenberg interview.

383   Conversation with Otis Chandler   Dorothy Schiff, memo to files, February 11, 1969, NYPL/DS, Box 189.

383   Conversation with Robert Morgenthau   Dorothy Schiff, memo to files, June 3, 1970, NYPL/DS, Box 38.

383   *After Bill Moyers left* Newsday   Dorothy Schiff, memo to files, May 6, 1970. NYPL/DS, Box 25.

383   Dorothy's consideration of Morris Abram as a possible successor   Dorothy Schiff, memos to files, April 7, 1971, October 16, 1972, both NYPL/DS, Box 1.

383   *In 1973, Dorothy startled her editors*   Dorothy Schiff to Paul Sann and James Wechsler, June 28, 1973, BU/PS, Box 3.

384   *"Woodward," Friedman told Sann*   Bob Friedman to Paul Sann, n.d. (probably August 1983), PS/HS, Box 7.

384   *Warren Hoge told Dolly*   Dorothy Schiff, memo to files, June 7, 1974, NYPL/DS, Box 25.

384   *Dorothy told a friend*   Dorothy Schiff, memo to files, April 19, 1976, ibid.

385   *According to Dolly's notes, Jim said*   Dorothy Schiff, memo to files, May 3, 1976, ibid.

385   *In July, Adele invited Hoge . . . "another reason not to have taken her offer very seriously"*   Author interview with James Hoge, September 25, 2003.

25. The Man from Oz

389–390   Information about the American newspaper industry in the 1970s can be found in Peter Benjaminson, *Death in the Afternoon: America's Newspaper Giants Struggle for Survival* (Kansas City: Andrews, McMeel & Parker, 1984). Also author interview with Michael O'Neill, February 12, 2002.

391–392   Information about the conversations among Dorothy Schiff, Mortimer Hall, and Otis Chandler, as well as Dorothy's advice from her banker, Henry Necarsulmer   NYPL/DS, Box 189. Also author interviews with Otis Chandler, October 23, 2002; Dennis Stanfill, November 1, 2002; and Henry Necarsulmer, October 15, 2002.

391   (footnote) Earnings and other financial data   NYPL/DS, Boxes 185, 190.

392   Circulation figures   NYPL/DS, Box 182; additional circulation information as well as advertising linage and revenues is in Box 185.

392–393   The history of Pete Hamill's sporadic employment at the Post in the 1970s is based on memos in NYPL/DS, Box 23, and BU/PS, Box 6.

393   Communications between Dorothy Schiff and Paul Sann regarding Rose Franzblau   Dorothy Schiff to Paul Sann, December 12, 1968, NYPL/DS, Box 8.

393   Details of Leonard Lyons's last years at the *Post*   NYPL/DS, Box 35.

393–394   Details of Max Lerner's financial arrangements with the *Post*   NYPL/DS, Box 33.

394   Details of Paul Sann's earnings   Dorothy Schiff, memo to files, January 3, 1976, NYPL/DS, Box 117.

394–395   For the details of the intermittent struggles between the newspaper unions and the publishers in the 1970s, I relied on *The New York Times*, 1973–1976 passim. Also Bertram Powers interview; A. H. Raskin, "Bert Powers at War With Himself," *[MORE]*, May 1972; and A. H. Raskin, "The Once and Future Newspaper Guild," *Columbia Journalism Review*, September/October 1982, pp. 20–27. There is some additional information about the 1970 strike in NYPL/DS, Box 131.

395   *Pleading poverty, Dolly refused*   New York Times, December 12–14, 1975.

395   *Dolly replied that if it did*   New York Times, May 21, 1976.

395   *"They were about how a supermarket works"*   Lawrence interview. Also *New York Times*, February 12, 1976.

396   *Privately, she told a reporter*   Dorothy Schiff to Barbara Yuncker, February 19, 1976, NYPL/DS, Box 91.

397   *Dorothy had first met Kissinger . . . ruthless in manner*   Dorothy Schiff, memo to files, n.d. (probably November or December 1969); Warren Hoge to Paul Sann, December 29, 1969; Dorothy Schiff to files, April 14, 1973; Dorothy Schiff interview with Jeffrey Potter, April 29, 1973, all NYPL/DS, Box 32.

398   *The Kissinger profile earned a lot of attention*   NYPL/DS, Box 73.

399   *From 1968 through 1973*   Financial figures from NYPL/DS, Box 190.

399   Severance obligations   Frank Daniels to Dorothy Schiff, Byron Greenberg, April 28, 1976; real estate value   Paul Sann to Dorothy Schiff, n.d. 1972, both NYPL/DS, Box 153.

400   *In April 1972, John Schiff*   Dorothy Schiff, memo to files, April 20, 1972, NYPL/DS, Box 243.

400–401   Details of Rupert Murdoch's early career can be found in Neil Chenoweth, *Rupert Murdoch: The Untold Story of the World's Greatest Media Wizard* (New York: Crown, 2001).

401   *"It's basically a tear-off-the-wire kind of paper"*   Paul Sann to Dorothy Schiff, April 19, 1974, BU/PS, Box 3.

401–402   *Murdoch later told a reporter, "I went down"*   Alexander Cockburn, "The Man Who Bought the New York Post Tells All," *Village Voice*, November 29, 1976.

402   *Murdoch mentioned that he thought*   Dorothy Schiff to Henry Necarsulmer, October 29, 1976, NYPL/DS, Box 195.

402   *Post* financial details   NYPL/DS, Boxes 185, 190, 195.

402   *"I was very enthusiastic"*   Author interview with Rupert Murdoch, March 29, 2004.

402   *During a follow-up meeting . . . deal was roughed out*   Dorothy Schiff to Henry Necarsulmer, October 29, 1976, NYPL/DS, Box 195.

402   *On November 17, Rupert called Dorothy*   Dorothy Schiff, memo to files, November 17, 1976, NYPL/DS, Box 187. The formal deal memo is in, Box 195.

403   *"Rupert Murdoch is a man" . . . "serious newspaper"*   *New York Times,* November 20, 1976.

403   *"There was undoubtedly some confusion"*   Ibid.

403   *Several weeks later,* New York   "New York Intelligencer," *New York,* December 20, 1976, p. 74.

404   *The next day Murdoch told a reporter . . . take place at the end of the year*   The interview with Rupert Murdoch is in *The New York Times,* November 21, 1976, p. 38; the interview with Dorothy Schiff is on p. 39.

405   The financial details and its tax implications   Mordechai Rochlin to Dorothy Schiff, November 24, 1976; Ernest Rubenstein to Dorothy Schiff, November 23, 1976, both NYPL/DS, Box 195.

405   *Dolly maintained at the time*   New York Times, November 21, 1976.

405–406   *Several weeks later* The Wall Street Journal . . . *she saved them that additional $1.3 million*   Wall Street Journal, November 29, 1976.

407   *"Rupert has turned around some papers" . . . not contemplating major changes*   New York Times, December 29, 1976.

407   *"You all know that part of my deal"*   Rupert Murdoch to Paul Sann et al., December 31, 1976, WHS/JAW, Box 5.

408   *"I hope to make the Post lively"*   New York Times, January 9, 1977.

408   *Soon after taking over, he told an interviewer*   Cockburn, "Man Who Bought the New York Post."

409   Steven Cuozzo, *It's Alive: How America's Oldest Newspaper Cheated Death and Why It Matters* (New York: Times Books, 1996), pp. 19–36.

410   *Paul went to see Dolly the day he quit*   Dorothy Schiff, memo to files, February 3, 1977, NYPL/DS, Box 66.

411   *"The day I left the NY Post"*   Helen Dudar to Paul Sann, January 11, 1984, HS/PS.

411   *Dorothy had Jean Gillette ask*   Jean Gillette to Edward Morris, March 14, 1977, NYPL/DS, Box 291.

411   *"She was always very politically correct"*   Author interview with Myra Appleton, April 21, 2003.

411   *Martin Fischbein, a young friend of Dorothy's*   Dorothy Schiff, memo to files, March 24, 1978, NYPL/DS, Box 18.

412   *Sann began to believe his own fantasies*   Paul Sann to Pete Hamill, June 5, 1985, BU/PS, Box 6.

26. Thereafter

414   *"It was a black-tie dinner"*   Author interview with Jeffrey Potter, June 25, 2003.

415   *Several publishers asked Hellman*   Dorothy Schiff to Geoffrey Hellman, n.d. (presumably September 1968), NYPL/DS, Box 254.

415   *Potter stated that the book grew*   Proposal for what was then called "Off the Record with DS: Her New York Post, Men, Money & Magic," NYPL/DS, Box 259.

416   *"We all laughed about it"*   Author interview with Liz Fondaras, April 25, 2003.

416   Revised memos about Bobby Kennedy, typical of a larger selection, are in NYPL/DS, Box 255.

417 The original story alleging a Schiff-Roosevelt romance appeared in *The New York Times* on p. 73 of the first edition of the May 27, 1976, paper. In the revised second edition, the story appeared on p. 1 and included Dorothy's "no comment," Morris Abrams's denial, and Joe Lash's comments. The *Times* acknowledged the editorial changes in a follow-up article the next day (also on p. 1), which quoted Jeffrey Potter as well.

418 *"What's this about your boss lady"* Pauline Phillips to Paul Sann, May 27, 1976, BU/PS, Box 6.

418 *"Let's just add a little to this story"* New York *Daily News,* May 31, 1976.

418 *He told a reporter* Los Angeles *Times,* October 25, 1977.

419–423 Sources for Dorothy's involvement with *The Nation* and its eventual publisher and editor are in NYPL/DS, Boxes 39, 213; author interview with Hamilton Fish III, October 17, 2002; and the Navasky interview.

423–424 Sources for Dorothy's involvement with *Ms.* are in NYPL/DS, Box 231; and author interview with Gloria Steinem, June 1, 2004.

426 *When Peter Kovler* Dorothy Schiff, memo to files, October 14, 1982, NYPL/DS, Box 228.

427 Details of Dorothy Schiff's generosity to Jean Gillette are in NYPL/DS, Box 290; also the Gillette interview.

427 Details of Dorothy Schiff's generosity to the Lawsons are in NYPL/DS, Box 229; also the Lawsons' interview.

428–436 Author interviews with Dorothy Schiff's grandchildren: Matthew Hall, January 29, 2003; Mary Hall Howland; Wendy Gray; Laura Kramarsky, June 2, 2004; Kathleen Gray, September 18, 2005; Anna Kramarsky, June 4, 2004; also Adele Sweet, Lisa Schiff, Morti Hall, and Sally Kramarsky interviews.

436 (footnote) *John's cousin and partner* Chernow, *The Warburgs,* p. 618.

437 *"That's what makes this a great country"* Morning Telegraph, October 29, 1956; *Dorothy sent John a genealogy* April 1953; *He sent her a picture he'd found* September 7, 1995; *John sent Dorothy an article* New York Times, November 1, 1981, all in NYPL/DS, Box 243.

438 *"With some trepidation"* . . . *until he moved to another job within the firm.* Author interview with Bill David, March 11, 2003.

440 *As Dorothy once explained* Jeffrey Potter interview with Dorothy Schiff, NYPL/DS, Box 258. Also a document from 1951, in which Dorothy appears to have given up the right to a burial plot at Cold Spring Harbor, Box 292.

440–441   Dorothy's will, prepared by Bernard Finkelstein at Paul, Weiss, is dated June 30, 1987, with a First Codicil dated July 15, 1987. The probate copy can be found in the Office of the Surrogate's Court, County of New York, State of New York, File No. 4178/59, date of death August 30, 1989.

441–442   *"heiress to a substantial property"* "Remarks of Murray Kempton," *Dorothy Schiff 1903–1989*, privately printed.

442   *she asked Jerry Tallmer to prepare her obituary* New York Post, August 31, 1989.

Bibliography

Manuscript and Archival Collections

Rose Franzblau Papers, Rare Book and Manuscript Library, Manuscript Collection, Columbia University.

Max Lerner Papers, Manuscripts and Correspondence, Manuscripts and Archives, Yale University Library.

Oral History Research Office, Columbia University.

Paul Sann Collection, Howard Gotlieb Archival Research Center, Boston University.

Dorothy Schiff Papers, Manuscripts and Archives Division, Humanities and Social Sciences Library, New York Public Library.

James A. Wechsler Papers, Archives, Wisconsin Historical Society.

Private Collections

Paul Sann papers, Collection of Howard Sann.

Rudolf Sonneborn papers, Collection of Mary Barasch and Dorothy Hermann.

Books

Abramson, Rudy. *Spanning the Century: The Life of W. Averell Harriman*. New York: William Morrow, 1992.

Adler, Cyrus, *Jacob H. Schiff: His Life and Letters*. 2 vols. Grosse Pointe, MI: Scholarly Press, 1968.

Aldrich, Nelson, Jr. *Old Money: The Mythology of America's Upper Class*. New York: Knopf, 1988.

Auletta, Ken. *The Streets Were Paved with Gold*. New York: Random House, 1979.

Baragwanath, John. *A Good Time Was Had*. New York: Appleton, 1962.

Benjaminson, Peter. *Death in the Afternoon: America's Newspaper Giants Struggle for Survival*. Kansas City: Andrews, McMeel & Parker, 1984.

Biale, David, ed. *Cultures of the Jews: A New History*. New York: Schocken Books, 2002.

Birmingham, Stephen. *"Our Crowd": The Great Jewish Families of New York*. New York: Harper, 1967

Bosworth, Patricia. *Anything Your Little Heart Desires*. New York: Simon & Schuster, 1997.

Branch, Taylor. *Parting the Waters: America in the King Years, 1954–63*. New York: Simon & Schuster, 1988.

———. *Pillar of Fire: America in the King Years, 1963–65*. New York: Simon & Schuster, 1999.

Brands, H. W. *The Strange Death of American Liberalism*. New Haven: Yale University Press, 2001.

Caro, Robert. *The Power Broker: Robert Moses and the Fall of New York*. New York: Knopf, 1974.

Chisholm, Anne, and Michael Davie. *Lord Beaverbrook: A Life*. New York: Knopf, 1993.

Chenoweth, Neil. *Rupert Murdoch: The Untold Story of the World's Greatest Media Wizard*. New York: Crown, 2001.

Chernow, Ron, *The Warburgs*. New York: Random House, 1993.

Cohen, Naomi W. *Jacob H. Schiff: A Study in American Jewish Leadership*. Hanover, NH: University Press of New England, 1999.

Cook, Blanche Wiesen. *Eleanor Roosevelt. Volume 2: The Defining Years, 1933–1938*. New York: Viking, 1999.

Cooney, John. *The American Pope: The Life and Times of Francis Cardinal Spellman*. New York: Times Books, 1984.

Cottrell, Robert C. *Izzy: A Biography of I. F. Stone*. New Brunswick, NJ: Rutgers University Press, 1992.

Cuozzo, Steven. *It's Alive: How America's Oldest Newspaper Cheated Death and Why It Matters*. New York: Times Books, 1996.

Daly, Charles U., ed. *The Media and the Cities*. Chicago: University of Chicago Press, 1968.

Davis, Flora. *Moving the Mountain: The Women's Movement in America Since 1960*. New York: Simon & Schuster, 1991.

Davis, Kenneth S. *The Politics of Honor: A Biography of Adlai E. Stevenson*. New York: Putnam, 1967.

Ehrlich, Judith Ramsey, and Barry J. Rehfeld. *The New Crowd: The Changing of the Jewish Guard on Wall Street*. Boston: Little, Brown, 1989.

Felsenthal, Carol. *Power, Privilege and the Post: The Katharine Graham Story*. New York: Putnam, 1993.

Freeman, Joshua B. *Working-Class New York: Life and Labor Since World War II.* New York: New Press, 2000.

Fried, Richard M. *Men Against McCarthy.* New York: Columbia University Press, 1976.

Frommer, Myrna Katz, and Harvey Frommer. *It Happened in Brooklyn.* New York: Harcourt, 1993.

Gabler, Neal. *Winchell: Gossip, Power and the Culture of Celebrity.* New York: Knopf, 1995.

Gitlin, Todd. *The Sixties: Years of Hope, Days of Rage.* New York: Bantam Books, 1987.

Glazer, Nathan, and Daniel P. Moynihan. *Beyond the Melting Pot: The Negroes, Puerto Ricans, Jews, Italians, and Irish of New York City.* 2d ed. Cambridge, MA: M.I.T. Press, 1970.

Goldstein, Judith S. *Crossing Lines: Histories of Jews and Gentiles in Three Communities.* New York: William Morrow, 1992.

Gordon, Jane Anna. *Why They Couldn't Wait: A Critique of the Black-Jewish Conflict over Community Control in Ocean Hill–Brownsville, 1967–1971.* New York: RoutledgeFalmer, 2001.

Graham, Katharine. *Personal History.* New York: Knopf, 1997.

Hamill, Pete. *A Drinking Life: A Memoir.* Boston: Little, Brown, 1994.

Harris, Louis. *Black-Jewish Relations in New York City.* New York: Praeger, 1970.

Jackson, Kenneth T., and David S. Dunbar, eds. *Empire City: New York Through the Centuries.* New York: Columbia University Press, 2002.

Hauke, Kathleen A. *Ted Poston: Pioneer American Journalist.* Athens: University of Georgia Press, 1998.

Heilman, Samuel C. *Portrait of American Jews: The Last Half of the 20th Century.* Seattle: University of Washington Press, 1995.

Hohenberg, John. *The News Media: A Journalist Looks at His Profession.* New York: Holt, 1968.

Kahn, E. J., Jr. *The World of Swope.* New York: Simon & Schuster, 1965.

Keeler, Robert F. *Newsday: A Candid History of the Respectable Tabloid.* New York: William Morrow, 1990.

Kempton, Murray. *America Comes of Middle Age: Columns 1950–1962.* Boston: Little, Brown, 1963.

———. *Rebellions, Perversities, and Main Events.* New York: Times Books, 1994.

Kobler, John. *Otto the Magnificent: The Life of Otto Kahn.* New York: Scribner, 1988.

Kramer, Michael, and Sam Roberts. *"I Never Wanted to Be Vice-President of Anything!" An Investigative Biography of Nelson Rockefeller.* New York: Basic Books, 1976.

Lakoff, Sanford. *Max Lerner: Pilgrim in the Promised Land.* Chicago: University of Chicago Press, 1998.

Lamont, Edward M. *The Ambassador from Wall Street: The Story of Thomas W. Lamont* Lanham, MD: Madison Books, 1994.

Lash, Joseph. *Eleanor and Franklin.* New York: Norton, 1971.

Liebman, Arthur. *Jews and the Left.* New York: John Wiley, 1979.

Madsen, Axel. *The Marshall Fields*. New York: John Wiley, 2002.

Martin, John Barlow. *Adlai Stevenson and the World: The Life of Adlai E. Stevenson*. Garden City, NY: Doubleday, 1977.

———. *Adlai Stevenson of Illinois*. Garden City, NY: Doubleday, 1976.

Milkman, Paul. *PM: A New Deal in Journalism, 1940–1948*. New Brunswick, NJ: Rutgers University Press, 1997.

Morgan, Ted. *FDR: A Biography*. New York: Simon & Schuster, 1985.

———. *Reds*. New York: Random House, 2003.

Morris, Joe Alex. *Nelson Rockefeller: A Biography*. New York: Harper, 1960.

Moscow, Warren. *The Last of the Big-Time Bosses: The Life and Times of Carmine De Sapio and the Rise and Fall of Tammany Hall*. New York: Stein and Day, 1971.

Navasky, Victor. *Naming Names*. New York: Viking, 1980.

Newfield, Jack. *Bread and Roses Too*. New York: Dutton, 1971.

Potter, Jeffrey. *Men, Money & Magic: The Story of Dorothy Schiff*. New York: Coward, McCann & Geohegan, 1976.

Powell, Adam Clayton, Jr. *Adam by Adam: The Autobiography of Adam Clayton Powell, Jr*. New York: Dial Press, 1971.

Putnam, Robert D. *Bowling Alone: The Collapse and Revival of American Community*. New York: Simon & Schuster, 2000.

Ravitch, Diane. *The Great School Wars: New York City, 1805–1973*. New York: Basic Books, 1974.

Reeves, Thomas C. *The Life and Times of Joe McCarthy*. New York: Stein & Day, 1982.

Reich, Cary. *The Life of Nelson A. Rockefeller: Worlds to Conquer, 1908–1958*. New York: Doubleday, 1996.

Rieder, Jonathan. *Canarsie: The Jews and Italians of Brooklyn Against Liberalism*. Cambridge, MA: Harvard University Press, 1985.

Roosevelt, James. *My Parents: A Differing View*. Chicago: Playboy Press, 1976.

Schlesinger, Arthur M., Jr. *A Life in the 20th Century: Innocent Beginnings 1917–1950*. New York: Houghton Mifflin, 2000.

Sklare, Marshall. *Observing America's Jews*. Hanover, NH: University Press of New England, 1993.

Slater, Leonard. *The Pledge*. New York: Simon & Schuster, 1970.

Sonneborn, Charles B. *Sonneborn: A Celebration of Generations*. Bethesda, MD: 1994.

Stern, J. David. *Memoirs of a Maverick Publisher*. New York: Simon & Schuster, 1962.

Strauss, Lewis L. *Men and Decisions*. Garden City, NY: Doubleday, 1962.

Strouse, Jean. *Morgan: American Financier*. New York: Random House, 1999.

Tifft, Susan E., and Alex S. Jones. *The Trust: The Private and Powerful Family Behind The New York Times*. Boston: Little, Brown, 1999.

Warburg, Frieda Schiff. *Reminiscences of a Long Life*. New York: privately printed, 1956.

Wechsler, James A. *The Age of Suspicion*. New York: Random House, 1953.

———. *Reflections of an Angry Middle-Aged Editor*. New York: Random House, 1960.

Winchell, Walter. *Winchell Exclusive*. Englewood Cliffs, NJ: Prentice Hall, 1975.

Zion, Sidney. *Read All About It! The Collected Adventures of a Maverick Reporter*. New York: Summit Books, 1982.

Periodicals

Broadcasting, Broadcasting/Telecasting, Telecasting, Broadcasting Yearbook, Broadcasting/Telecasting Yearbook, Telecasting Yearbook 1943–1963.

Ephron, Nora. "Media." *Esquire*, April 1975.

Glazer, Nathan. "Blacks, Jews & the Intellectuals." *Commentary*, May 1969.

Hamill, Pete, et al. "Goodbye Dolly: Remembrances of Posts Past." *[MORE]*, January 1977.

Hellman, Geoffrey T. "Profiles: Publisher." *New Yorker*, August 10, 1968.

Hentoff, Nat. "Goodbye, Dolly." *Village Voice*, June 25, 1964.

Himmelfarb, Milton. "Is American Jewry in Crisis?" *Commentary*, April 1969.

Kimball, Penn. "New York Readers in a Newspaper Shutdown." *Columbia Journalism Review*, Fall 1963.

———. "People Without Papers." *Public Opinion Quarterly*, Fall 1959.

Lefkowitz, Bernard. "Good-bye to Dolly's *New York Post*." *Present Tense*, August 1977.

Liebling, A. J. "The Wayward Press: Back." *New Yorker*, March 16, 1963.

Newfield, Jack. "Good-bye, Dolly!" *Harper's*, September 1969.

New York Post, 1935–1977.

New York Times, 1910–1989.

Pollak, Dick. "An Intra-Family Sort of Thing." *[MORE]*, October 1971.

Raskin, A. H. "Automation's Armageddon." *Saturday Review*, July 11, 1970.

———. "Bert Powers at War With Himself." *[MORE]*, May 1972.

———. "The Great Manhattan Newspaper Duel." *Saturday Review*, May 8, 1965.

———. "The Once and Future Newspaper Guild." *Columbia Journalism Review*, September/October 1982.

Shulman, Charles E. "The Sonneborn Story—An Untold Epic of American Zionism." *American Zionist*, May 1966.

Sklare, Marshall. "Jews, Ethnics, and the American City." *Commentary*, April 1972.

Tallmer, Jerry. "The Mama of Us All." *Dissent*, Summer 1961.

Town and Country, January–April 1922.

Young, Perry Deane. "Oh, Miss Dolly, can't you see de light?" *Chicago Journalism Review*, June 1972.

Unpublished Manuscripts

Clark, Blair. Untitled memoir, courtesy of Joanna Clark.

Shactman, Tom. Untitled biography of Ted Kheel, courtesy of Tom Shactman.

Acknowledgments

This project would not have been possible without the help of Adele Hall Sweet and Sarah-Ann Backer Kramarsky, who facilitated my access to their mother's papers at the New York Public Library; Mary Barasch and Deborah Hermann, who loaned me invaluable financial records of the *New York Post,* photographs, and other memorabilia that they inherited from their uncle, Rudolf Sonneborn; Howard Sann, who gave me permission to quote from his father's papers at Boston University and afforded me access to papers and other materials of which he has retained personal possession; and Nancy Wechsler, who permitted me to quote from her husband's papers at the Wisconsin Historical Society.

I am grateful for the assistance of Daniel Bell, Ellen Blair, Patty Bosworth, Charles Bullock, Lisel Eisenheimer, Beth Elon, Barbara Epstein, Pat Falk, Nathan Glazer, Alan Goldberg, Dalma Heyn, Daniel Kevles, Sarah-Ann Kramarsky, Zane Kotker, Christopher Lehmann-Haupt, Millard Midonick, Ted Morgan, Joan Nathan, Victor Navasky, Letty Pogrebin, Diane Ravitch, Joseph Ravitch, Richard Ravitch, Natalie Robins, Elisabeth Scharlatt, Elizabeth Shannon, Joan Sudolnik, Kathy Sulzberger, Adele Hall Sweet, Lindsy Van Gelder, and Bonnie Hirsch and Sarina Roffe of America ORT, all of whom helped me locate interviewees or other important resources. Judd Kahn and Irwin Kramer helped me make sense of balance sheets and other financial information.

Rupert Murdoch generously made many resources of the *New York Post* available to me. His administrative assistant, Marilyn Strakey, located photographs and information in the corporate archives, and David Boyle, the Photo Editor, and Stacy

Grossman of the Newscorp legal staff were also very helpful. Tim Seldes advocated for me in crucial instances, and his sister Marian Seldes showed me family photos. Joanna Clark sent me the relevant pages from the unpublished memoirs of her late husband, Blair Clark. Tom Shachtman shared sections of his unpublished book about Ted Kheel.

I am indebted to the following people (as well as a few others who prefer not to be identified) for talking with me about Dorothy Schiff's life and her career, or other aspects of New York politics and culture during her lifetime: Myra Appleton, Steven M. L. Aronson, Ken Auletta, Bernard Bard, Mary Barasch, June Bingham, Helen Gurley Brown, Pat Buckley, William Buckley, Otis Chandler, William David, Joan Davidson, Fern Marja Eckman, Julius C. C. Edelstein, Helene Eisenberg, Garth Eliassen, Al Ellenberg, Nora Ephron, Pat Falk, Phyllis Farley, Clay Felker, Hamilton Fish, Liz Fondaras, Joshua B. Freeman, Peter Freiberg, Joshua Friedman, Jean Gillette, Nathan Glazer, Roberta Brandes Gratz, Kathleen Gray, Wendy Gray, Byron Greenberg, Ruth Gruber, Judith Grunberg, Clyde Haberman, William Haddad, Matthew Hall, Mortimer Hall, Mary Hall Howland, Louis Harris, Pete Hamill, Kitty Carlisle Hart, Marian Heiskell, Russell Hemenway, Deborah Hermann, James Hoge, Warren Hoge, Jane Isay, Yves-Andre Istel, Alex Jones, Lenore Kahn, Johanna Kaplan, Mina Kempton, Ted Kheel, Ed Koch, Edward Kosner, Anna Kramarsky, Laura Kramarsky, Sarah-Ann Kramarsky, Werner Kramarsky, Steve Lawrence, Aery Lawson, Everette Lawson, Mitchel Levitas, Anthony Mancini, Aileen Mehle, Judy Michaelson, Rupert Murdoch, Victor Navasky, Henry Necarsulmer, Helen Neuborn, Michael O'Neill, Sidney Orenstein, Gerry Passarella, Carl Pelleck, Art Pomerantz, Jeffrey Potter, Bertram Powers, Joyce Purnick, Joe Rabinovich, Milton Rich, Mordechai Rochlin, Nan Rosenthal, Irwin Ross, Richard Sachs, Ben Schiff, David Schiff, Lisa Schiff, Arthur Schlesinger Jr., Marian Schlesinger, Timothy Seldes, Elizabeth Shannon, Jesse Simons, Marvin Smilon, Eugene Smith, Robert Spitzler, Gloria Steinem, Charles Stone, Anita Summer, Adele Sweet, Jerry Tallmer, Gus Tyler, Lindsy Van Gelder, Nancy Wechsler, Joseph Wershba, Alan Whitney, Perry Deane Young, and Sidney Zion.

I wish to thank William Stingone, Charles J. Liebman Curator of Manuscripts, and the entire staff of the Rare Books and Manuscripts Division of the New York Public Library; archivist Harold L. Miller and his staff at the Wisconsin Historical Society; Sean Noel and the archivists at the Howard Gotlieb Archival Research Center at Boston University for their various courtesies; and Ingrid Richter of the New York Society Library, who helped me access Proquest online.

Linda Gottlieb, Susan Jonas, Bettyann Holtzmann Kevles, Christopher Lehmann-Haupt, Natalie Robins, Kate Nissenson Scott, and Amy Kovner White read the manuscript at various stages and offered me invaluable criticism, advice, and support. My agent, Wendy Weil, was encouraging throughout the gestation and completion of my work; lawyers Neil Rossini and Henry Kaufman provided reassuring counsel at stressful moments. My editor, Diane Reverand, was ever clear-eyed about what was essential and what was irrelevant, and she and her colleagues, editor Phil Revzin, assistant editor Regina Scarpa, copy editor Cynthia Merman, designer Maggie Goodman, and publicist John Karle, guided me and the book through the publication process with a minimum of fuss and a maximum of professional skill. I am grateful to them all.

Without the wisdom, forebearance, and encouragement of Hugh Nissenson, this book would not have been possible. My gratitude is boundless.

Index